Understanding and Managing Children's Classroom Behavior

Understanding and Managing Children's Classroom Behavior

Creating Sustainable, Resilient Classrooms

Second Edition

Sam Goldstein, PhD

Robert B. Brooks, PhD

John Wiley & Sons, Inc.

Copyright © 2007 by John Wiley & Sons, Inc. All rights reserved.

Published by John Wiley & Sons, Inc., Hoboken, New Jersey.
Published simultaneously in Canada.

Wiley Bicentennial Logo: Richard J. Pacifico

For general information on our other products and services please contact our Customer Care Department within the United States at (800) 762-2974, outside the United States at (317) 572-3993 or fax (317) 572-4002.

Wiley also publishes its books in a variety of electronic formats. Some content that appears in print may not be available in electronic books. For more information about Wiley products, visit our web site at www.wiley.com.

Library of Congress Cataloging-in-Publication Data:

Goldstein, Sam, 1952–
  Understanding and managing children's classroom behavior : creating
sustainable, resilient classrooms / edited by Sam Goldstein, Robert B. Brooks—
2nd ed.
    p.   cm.—(Wiley series on personality processes)
    Includes bibliographical references.
    ISBN-13: 978-0-471-74212-8 (cloth)
    ISBN-10: 0-471-74212-0 (cloth)
  1. Classroom management. 2. Behavior modification. I. Brooks, Robert B.
II. Title. III. Series.
  LB3013.G63   2007
  371.102′1—dc22
                                                    2006025194
Printed in the United States of America.

10 9 8 7 6 5 4 3 2 1

Only in quiet waters do things mirror themselves undistorted. Only in a quiet mind is adequate perception of the world.

—Hans Margolius

When dealing with people, let us remember we are not dealing with creatures of logic, we are dealing with creatures of emotion, creatures bustling with prejudices and motivated by pride and vanity.

—Dale Carnegie

Science is nothing but developed perception, interpreted intent, common sense rounded out and minutely articulated.

—George Santayana

Contents

CONTENTS

Contents

Foreword

LAWRENCE LEWANDOWSKI, PHD

This book, authored and guided by Goldstein and Brooks, has been revised to include the most up-to-date research on the understanding and management of challenging behavior in children. It is unique in that it has both breadth—covering nearly every element of classroom environments a teacher might encounter—and depth—providing detailed analysis and advice on each element. It is organized and written in a way that sophisticated concepts and research can be understood easily and incorporated into the classroom. I hope every teacher in training is required to read it in the context of dealing with students with special needs and/or challenging behaviors. This book does such a thorough job of explaining the characteristics of various disabilities, behavioral disorders, and emotional states that any professional in the field would be wise to keep it as a desk reference.

Changes in our society and educational system have created classrooms of diverse learners with wide-ranging differences and complex needs. Coupled with mandates to improve learning outcomes, leave no child behind, and strict educator accountabilities, teachers' responsibilities have never been greater. Both classroom teachers and support staff can rely on this book to help them meet those responsibilities. It is a comprehensive, instructive, and practical guide that will help any teacher do a better job of meeting the academic, cognitive, social, developmental, and emotional needs of students.

It is encouraging to see a book that focuses on students' strengths and abilities rather than on their clinical symptoms and shortcomings. *Understanding and Managing Children's Classroom Behavior* also emphasizes effective strategies that can help children learn and grow in competence and confidence. If teachers apply the techniques and strategies outlined in this book, they will surely help educate a generation of competent, resilient, and emotionally healthy individuals and prepare them to handle the complex challenges of tomorrow.

I would put this book in a class by itself. It would be ideal as the core text for educators in training and continuing education classes. Every teacher needs to become better acquainted with the knowledge in this book, and no other source presents this information in such a readable and useable way. My daughter is studying to become an elementary school teacher; I will give her a copy of this book as soon as it is published. Thanks to Sam, Bob, and an all-star cast of experts for this outstanding resource.

Professor of Psychology
Meredith Professor for Teaching Excellence
Syracuse University

Foreword

ROBERT H. PASTERNACK, PhD

In 1980, I began more than a decade of work at a state institution for incarcerated juvenile delinquents. While much discussion occurred bemoaning the purportedly high recidivism rate among juvenile delinquents, it soon became apparent that the empirical evidence supported the identification of two distinct subgroups: those that were able to successfully return to the school and community; and those that were unsuccessful and entered the adult criminal justice system. I was able to conduct a research project on the variables that discriminated between these two subgroups, and learned that resilience and a sense of optimism were critically important to those young people who were able to benefit from their incarceration and return to school, community, and family.

Sam Goldstein and Bob Brooks have written eloquently about these issues in this book, and contribute to the body of literature providing educators and consultants with the information they need to become knowledgeable about the concepts of resiliency, and learned optimism. While I studied the seminal work of Emmy Werner and others, I found that many teachers were unaware of the concept of resiliency, and the key role that they and members of the learning community can play in fostering resiliency in all students, including students with disabilities.

During my tenure as the Assistant Secretary for the Office of Special Education and Rehabilitative Services at the U.S. Department of Education (2001–2004), I had the privilege of serving on a number of

Presidential Commissions, including the President's New Freedom Commission on Mental Health. This Commission noted the lack of mental health services in our schools, and the sad reality that the majority of students who need mental health services in schools don't receive them. This book helps teachers and other members of the learning community become aware of the biopsychosocial factors related to student success, and the need to nurture these skills in America's classrooms. Although No Child Left Behind places needed emphasis on accountability, outcomes, results, and the development of proficiency in academic skills, many students continue to struggle to become proficient due to behavioral and emotional problems. Teachers must learn the science of teaching reading and math to address struggling students, however, this book provides the critically needed information required to meet the behavioral and emotional needs of today's students.

Special educators are cognizant of the fact that students in the category of "Emotionally Disturbed" exhibit the worst results of any disaggregated category among the 13 categories of students with disabilities eligible to receive special education and related services. While a paucity of data exist to suggest the reasons for these unacceptable and chronically poor results, teachers who understand the biopsychosocial factors underlying the behaviors exhibited by their students have a dramatically higher probability of effectively educating their students and helping them become proficient in the areas of reading and math. This book helps teachers acquire these skills and improve their ability to serve all students, particularly those who exhibit behavioral and emotional problems requiring intervention.

Former Assistant Secretary for the
Office of Special Education and Rehabilitative Services
U.S. Department of Education

Preface

In 1647, a law known as the "Old Deluder Law" was enacted in Massa-chusetts to promote education among the commoners. The first sentence of the act revealed that its real purpose was to forestall Satan, the old deluder, from gaining souls by providing the masses knowledge of the scriptures. In knowledge, a reservoir of strength to guide behavior could be found. By the close of the American Revolution, numerous social, economic, democratic, and political forces came into play, making education vital for a new nation. Formal education helped citizens attain material wealth and power. As the United States grew, schooling became increasingly necessary for successful industrialization, scientific achievement, and government. By the early 1800s, state boards of education were enacted. On July 3, 1839, three young women reported for the first teacher training program. Today, there are hundreds of colleges and programs with over 100,000 students preparing for the public service of teaching. The new millennium has led to an increased effort to, as President George Bush advocates, leave "no child behind." There has been an increasing emphasis on effective methods and strategies coupled with new insight and understanding that success is based not just on the acquisition of knowledge but on building strengths and abilities as well as developing the mindset of the effective learner.

As the United States assimilated millions of immigrants in the twentieth century, education achieved a paramount role in creating the American melting pot. Although Horace Mann wrote in the 1850s of children whose school behavior was less than acceptable, only in the past

35 years has students' behavior toward each other and toward their teachers become of prominent concern to educators. In this text, we define behavior broadly to include academic performance, communication, and socialization as well as relationships. As noted in the first edition of this book and still true today, it is an unfortunate statement of our times that in some school systems ensuring the safety of teachers from their students and managing student misbehavior to the point of severe violence has become a higher priority than the job of preparing children to become functional adults.

The first edition of this book was not written only in response to this epidemic of misbehavior, violence, and indignity in the schools. Rather, its purpose was to contribute to the movement to bring education in an effective way into the twenty-first century. Methods of education, the design of curricula, the management of student behavior, and the development of emotionally healthy individuals are increasingly less based on philosophical or hypothetical ideas but find their tenets in scientific research blended with practical experience. Our focus is to mesh the curricula and methods of education with the fast-paced technological drive of our society. The age of the isolated one-room schoolhouse or, for that matter, the larger but disconnected school in which children are mere numbers is changing. In this rapid communication age, every school must create connected citizens, to each other, to their teachers, to their families, and to their communities.

The first edition of this book was structured on a clinical model of children's classroom behavior and functioning. Chapters were divided based on clinical conditions (e.g., Attention Deficit Hyperactivity Disorder, depression, anxiety, learning disabilities). This completely rewritten second edition reflects a shift away from categorical models of understanding assessment and intervention, to dimensional models that speak to qualities of thinking, feeling, and behaving that either facilitate development and behavior or cause risk and adversity.

In addition to a significant change in focus, this second edition contains 11 new chapters, 3 extensively rewritten chapters, and 4 chapters that have been modified and updated from the original edition. Additionally, there is a new appendix addressing language milestones in school-age children and two new Forewords. There are also 16 new contributors to this book in addition to the return of three contributors from the original volume. As such, this second edition serves more as a companion to, rather than a replacement for, the first edition.

As with the first edition, Parts I and II provide essential background information and offer a thorough overview of current knowledge about children's behavior, emotions, development, learning, and, most importantly, resilience or protective factors. Classroom consultants will find an extensive, research-based presentation of these phenomena, their definitions, causes, and interventions as they relate to the educational setting. There are also a number of new chapters in this second edition.

Part III strongly reflects the significant shift toward creating sustainable classrooms by focusing on the mindsets of effective teachers and students. We take a protective approach consistent with our work in resilience. We move away from a deficit model and instead focus on identifying and harnessing strengths as a means of coping with adversity. We move away from a model that suggests that symptom relief equates with changing long-term outcome. We have come to appreciate that the qualities of resilience, the qualities we describe and define in this book, provide a critical foundation to foster and facilitate school success. We move away from a "fix it" approach to a model that begins by appreciating the differences within each child and teacher, identifying strengths and assets, and building on those.

We are very pleased that so many of our colleagues have agreed to contribute to this book, lending their knowledge and expertise. Mark Steege and colleagues provide a working model to complete functional behavioral assessments in the classroom. Jack Naglieri and colleagues provide a cogent overview of the relationship between thinking, learning, and behavior in the classroom. Lauren Braswell provides an update of her chapter in the first edition, focusing on cognitive behavioral approaches in the classroom. Educator Sandra Rief provides practical strategies for teachers to improve self-regulation. Janay Sander and colleagues focus on helping consultants assist teachers in creating climates in the classroom to promote emotional health and assist in working with children experiencing internalizing problems related to depression and anxiety. Emily Warnes and colleagues provide an extended contribution from the first edition focusing on facilitating social skills in the classroom. Myrna Shure focuses her thinking model on bullies and victims in the classroom, offering a problem-solving approach to treatment and prevention. Larry Diller contributes to a chapter providing an overview of medications and their relationship to behavior in the classroom.

This text cannot stand alone. It will not replace caring, conscientious, well-trained teachers nor will it serve as a substitute for a curriculum that engages children, making them active participants in their education, holding their interest, bringing a love for education, and most importantly, preparing them to be world citizens in the twenty-first century. We believe the first edition of this book accomplished its goal by contributing to a humanistic approach to understanding human behavior and education. It is our hope and intent that this second edition continues and fosters this important work.

SAM GOLDSTEIN, PhD
ROBERT BROOKS, PhD

Acknowledgments

We wish to thank Kathleen Gardner, as always, for her superb editorial support and assistance. A large volume such as this one could not be efficiently compiled nor prepared for publication without such support.

Thanks also to our editor, Patricia Rossi at Wiley, for seeking out and supporting the second edition of this book.

S. G.
R. B.

Contributors

Lauren Braswell, PhD
University of St. Thomas
St. Paul, Minnesota

Robert Brooks, PhD
Harvard Medical School
Cambridge, Massachusetts

Rachel Brown-Chidsey, PhD, NCSP
University of Southern Maine
Gorham, Maine

Cara Conway
School Psychology Training
  Program
George Mason University
Farifax, Virginia

Lawrence Diller, MD
University of California—San
  Francisco
San Francisco, California

S. Andrew Garbacz, MA
University of Nebraska—Lincoln
Lincoln, Nebraska

Janet Goldstein, MS, CCC-SLP
University of Utah
Salt Lake City, Utah

Sam Goldstein, PhD
University of Utah School of
  Medicine
Salt Lake City, Utah

Jennifer A. Herren, BA
University of Texas—Austin
Austin, Texas

Lawrence Lewandowski, PhD
Syracuse University
Syracuse, New York

F. Charles "Bud" Mace
University of Southern Maine
Gorham, Maine

Jack A. Naglieri, PhD
Department of Psychology
George Mason University
Centerville, Virginia

Robert H. Pasternack, PhD
Senior Vice President for Special
  Education
Voyager Expanded Learning
Alexandria, Virginia

Sandra Rief, PhD
Educational Resource Specialist
San Diego, California

Dawn S. Reinemann, PhD
Cardinal Stritch University
Milwakee, Wisconsin

Richard Rider, PsyD
Neurology, Learning, and
    Behavior Center
Salt Lake City, Utah

Janay B. Sander, PhD
University of Texas—Austin
Austin, Texas

Susan M. Sheridan, PhD
Department of Educational
    Psychology
University of Nebraska—Lincoln
Lincoln, Nebraska

Myrna B. Shure, PhD
Department of Clinical and
    Health Psychology
Drexel University
Philadelphia, Pennsylvania

Mark W. Steege, PhD
School of Psychology
University of Southern Maine
Gorham, Maine

Emily D. Warnes, PhD
University of Nebraska Medical
    Center
Crete, Nebraska

PART

I

Background

CHAPTER

1

Introduction

SAM GOLDSTEIN AND ROBERT BROOKS

It has been more than 10 years since the publication of the first edition of this book. During that time, there has been an increased emphasis on assessing the effectiveness of schools to teach basic skills, especially in the areas of mathematics, reading, and language. Terms such as *high stakes testing, accountability,* and *merit pay* have become a major part of the educational landscape. Some educators have lamented a focus on what they perceive to be "teaching to the test," while others believe holding schools accountable for student success is long overdue.

At the same time that educators are feeling the pressure of high stakes testing, there is a renewed awareness that the social/emotional dimension of a student's life must not be neglected (J. Cohen, 1999). This awareness has been prompted, in part, by events such as the Columbine High School shootings, as well as the impact that the attack on the World Trade Center in New York City on September 11, 2001, has had on our nation's psyche. Unfortunately, rather than embracing the need to educate the "whole" child, a dichotomy has emerged prompting some educators to perceive that nurturing a student's emotional and social health is mutually exclusive from the task of teaching academic skills (Brooks, 2004). However, it is our position that strengthening a student's sense of self-esteem and emotional well-being is not an "extra" curriculum; if anything, a student's sense of belonging, security, and self-confidence provides the scaffolding that supports the foundation for enhanced learning, motivation, and self-discipline. Required is an educational atmosphere

3

capable of instilling what we have called a *resilient mindset* in students. The schools must now provide social, emotional intervention hand-in-hand with academic education (Merrell, 2002; Weist, 2003). In fact, a sustainable school environment must be capable of meeting the social, emotional, and academic needs of all students (Elias, Zins, Graczyk, & Weissberg, 2003).

This second edition reflects our shift away from efforts to just manage classroom behavior toward the creation of a framework to develop sustainable classroom environments by shaping the mindsets of educators, students, and consultants. In this book, we examine the components of effective educators. Such educators are capable of appreciating the forces that truly motivate students, even those with behavioral and developmental challenges. These educators are capable of recognizing that their activities in the classroom day in and day out contribute not just to students' self-esteem and resilience, but it also provides an essential foundation for successful transition into adult life.

Our hope for the future lies in our children; children instilled with the skills necessary to create a sensible world. The more effective teachers are in developing and implementing strategies for fostering learning and a sense of competence and optimism in their students, the better chance students have for success. The more effectively consultants can articulate the components of effective mindsets for teachers and students, the more they make these frameworks conscious guides for educators. When students are actively involved in the learning process, when they feel connected and make contributions, discipline as author E. B. White once wrote, "Will take care of itself."

This second edition is built on our work over the past 10 years to bring a resilience model into the schools. The basic feature of resilient children is that their self-esteem and sense of competence are intact or if damaged, capable of repair. Resilient children possess feelings of hope and optimism, of ownership and personal control. They are nurtured by charismatic educators capable of providing experiences to reinforce their strengths and enhance their feelings of self-worth. In such an environment, all children, even those with challenging behavior can flourish. We acknowledge the goal for all students is to develop self-esteem, self-respect, and compassion first and foremost. The school environment, as the late Dr. Julius Segal noted and Dr. James Comer reminds us, is a prime location for resilience to be nurtured. The mindset of effective educators and productive consultants provides a framework for understanding the life-long impact adults can have on their students based on day-in and day-out classroom activities. Unlike our previous book that focused on behaviors to be defined, changed, or modified, this book focuses first on the understanding, appreciation, and building of assets and strengths and second on the management of weaknesses and liabilities.

We set out to achieve this goal through a consultation model. Behavioral consultation is a model in which a consultant assists the teacher in changing student behavior (Bergan & Kratochwill, 1990). The degree to which the consultee accurately and consistently implements treatment or intervention has been referred to as *treatment/intervention integrity*. Interventions may fail because the treatment itself is ineffective or has not been properly implemented (Watson, 2000). Failure of effective methods often reflects failure to ensure generalization and implementation. The model promoted in this book is based on a framework for consultants to effectively utilize methods and means by which effective interventions are recommended, discussed, and set into motion with teachers. Such means include direct training, availability by the consultant in the classroom, and strategies to facilitate generalization (Sterling-Turner, Watson, Wildmon, Watkins, & Little, 2001; Watson & Kramer, 1995).

Four themes impact educator's effectiveness in the classroom. All must be considered by effective consultants. These are:

1. Impact of causal attributions on beliefs about student behavior and required interventions by teachers.
2. The manner in which direct and indirect services are combined.
3. The impact of causative beliefs and academic standards on teachers' perceptions of intervention effectiveness.
4. Opportunity for ongoing support within the consultant relationship.

School psychologists and other classroom consultants, the primary group charged with implementing the model in this book, often focus on factors outside of the child, such as home and school influences, in explaining behavior (Athanasiou, Geil, Hazel, & Copeland, 2002). In contrast, teachers tend to believe that family factors play a part but largely tend not to address these contributions to the child's problems. Teachers generally blame student failure or behavior problems on internal characteristics of the student or home (Soodak & Podell, 1994). In general, teachers have been found to believe that children's problems are due to something within the child. They place more emphasis than consultants on treatments aimed directly at the student, often suggesting the student needs to take ownership for the problem and solution. Athanasiou and coworkers (2002) note that the internal attributional style of teachers is reflected in their beliefs about needed classroom treatment and that problems are caused by something wrong within the child. Teachers tend to attribute lack of progress to students while crediting either themselves or students when progress is made. Yet, teachers high in efficacy tend to de-emphasize home variables in students' success and failure, pointing instead to the instructional program and the teachers' role (B. W. Hall, Hines, Bacon, & Koulianos, 1992). Consultants often view lack of progress as related to teacher behavior toward students and general issues related to stress. Teachers' stress and its impact on withdrawal from the teaching profession has been increasingly recognized (V. L. Anderson, Levinsohn, Barker, & Kiewra, 1999). In educator surveys, teachers uniformly complain of large classrooms, discipline problems, low salaries, unsupportive parents, and the demands of a national educational curriculum. Effective consultants recognize this issue and set out to provide support without indicting teachers. Contrary to past theories of consultation as exclusively an indirect service, effective consultants not only consult but also when needed engage in direct service. In fact, even when teachers choose consultation as an intervention method, they typically want direct services provided by the consultant to the student (K. M. Jones, Wickstrom, & Friman, 1997). However, when consultants provide exclusively direct service, consultation is often unsuccessful in facilitating long-term change in classroom behavior.

In 1997, Alderman and Gimpel reported that teachers in general did not find consultation to be their preferred method of service. They further reported consultation to be only moderately effective in changing students' behavior. Yet, direct consultee training led to higher treatment integrity. Treatments implemented with high integrity are more likely to lead to successful outcomes (Sterling-Turner, Watson, & Moore, 2002). As noted, a number of mitigating factors are likely responsible for this lukewarm response. In fact, years of teaching experience has been found to be inversely proportional to the desired participation in consultation by teachers (Stenger, Tollefson, & Fine, 1992). Teachers with good problem-solving skills are more likely to seek out consultation. Severity of the child's behavior problems is also an issue. Further, teachers tend to value academic progress (e.g., work completion) over behavioral progress (e.g., stay seated and don't speak out of turn). Studies of teacher-child relationships have examined children's adjustment in classrooms in terms of how the relationship develops during typical classroom interactions such as instructions, socialization, and management of activities and time (Pianta, 1999). Classroom interactions have social and affective components for both child and teacher. The degree to which it is a good fit for a child reflects the child's needs and strengths.

A Crisis in Discipline

Annual Gallup education polls continue to find discipline as the public's primary educational concern (Gallup, 2005). Problems with discipline have been rated as second only to problems with drug use. Teachers have been reported to view lack of school discipline as a serious problem, often blaming the problem first on lack of discipline at home; second on lack of educational resources. As noted, this attributional style may interfere with the potential for effective interventions to be applied successfully (Lloyd, Kauffman, & Kupersmidt, 1990). Though teachers today as a group are likely more effective educators and behavior managers than teachers years ago, many perceive that they are fighting a losing battle. Focusing exclusively on "bad behavior" does not appear to stem the tide of childhood problems. In 1971, a thousand teachers in Erie, Pennsylvania, went on strike in part because of their principals' failure to provide support for discipline problems in the classroom. Nearly 20 years ago, teachers reported believing they spent too much time on behavioral problems (Wheldall & Merrett, 1988). Boys are often described as more problematic and complained about three times more frequently than girls.

Psychiatric terms are increasingly used as explanations for children's school problems, yet in reality they simply provide a convenient label for a cluster of behavioral, educational, and/or emotional differences. Thus, it is not surprising that as educators report more problems in the classroom across all domains, the rates of psychiatric diagnoses have increased. Providing data that there are more children meeting psychiatric diagnoses does not necessarily provide an explanation for the phenomena nor clear paths for solutions. Yet, it is important to note that rates of psychiatric problems in children have risen from approximately 17% to 22% in studies in the mid- to late-1980s (Costello, 1989) to nearly 30% based on recent surveys (U.S. Census Bureau, 2005). Further, the risk factors that appear to increase children's vulnerability for problems and ultimately receive diagnoses have increased as well over the past 10 years (Commission on Children at Risk, 2003). The lifetime prevalence of psychiatric disorders is much greater than rates of diagnosis and treatment (Kessler, Berglund, Demler, Jin, & Walters, 2005). Further, the problems observed epidemiologically in the general population are not necessarily reflected in the classroom where incidence of problems varies greatly depending on classroom demands, educator methods, and ultimately methods of data collection.

When researchers ask a single question related to a label (e.g., behavior problem) but not a specific, operationally defined behavior, respondents usually identify a significant minority of children. Nonetheless, regardless of how the data are collected, teachers report frequent behavioral problems in the classroom and have done so for nearly a century. Wickman (1928, as cited in D. P. Morgan & Jenson, 1988) reported an incidence of 42%. Reported incidence rates since have not been as high but have continued to represent a significant group of children. Rates of 10% with behavior problems (Bower, 1969); 20% with behavior problems, including 12% as mild, 5.5% moderate and 2% severe (T. J. Kelly, Bullock, & Dykes, 1977); 20% to 30% (Riebin & Balow, 1978); 6% to 10% requiring special education services as behavior disordered (Kauffman, 1985); and 33% (Cullinan & Epstein, 1986) provide a representative sample of statistics over the past 60 years. Typically of these children, only a small group are ultimately served in the school setting under a defined disability criteria related to the Individuals with Disabilities Education Improvement Act (2004). Although a number of other students with behavioral or related problems may be served by school counselors or psychologists, classroom teachers are on their own when educating the majority of children with mild to moderate limitations and impairments in the classroom.

In a 7-year longitudinal study still relevant today, Riebin and Balow (1978) found that 60% of children identified as having behavioral problems were rated in at least 3 different years by three different teachers as demonstrating such problems. Of the problem-identified children, 7.5% were nominated by every teacher throughout the study. A significant group of children identified early on in their educational careers as problematic persist and appear treatment resistant. These researchers concluded that the tolerance limits of teachers may be as much a function of which children are labeled problematic as the children themselves. Eventually, almost every child's behavior will test some teachers. Further, child attributes such as age, ethnicity, and gender are often identified as correlates of teacher ratings of children's classroom adjustment (Pianta & McCoy, 1997). Teacher-child communication patterns and teacher expectations vary by ethnicity of the student (Brady, Tucker, Harris, & Tribble, 1992). First grade teachers responded differently to African American and Caucasian children displaying the same behavior, indicating different ways of interpreting child behavior based on child ethnicity (Alexander & Entwisle, 1988). Further, the teacher's own ethnicity has also been shown to relate to their perceptions of children's behavior independent of the child's ethnicity (Zimmerman, Khoury, Vega, Gil, & Warheit, 1995). Child gender may be a predictor of teacher ratings for both conduct problems and academic achievement (C. J. Patterson, Kupersmidt, & Vaden, 1990). Males are more often referred for remedial educational services and have higher levels of conflicts with female teachers in preschool (J. Brophy, 1985), whereas females are less likely to be criticized by teachers overall (Eccles & Blumenfeld, 1985). Females tend to receive less teacher attention than males (V. Morgan & Dunn, 1988). Teachers' perceptions of relationships in kindergarten were found to predict eighth grade outcomes differently from males than females (Hamre & Pianta, 1999). When teachers experience more conflict with kindergarten males, these males had more disciplinary problems over time. Further, dependency on a kindergarten teacher was a stable predictor of poor long-term academic outcome for males but not females. Teacher perceptions of the negative and positive qualities of their relationships with students contributed for up to 27% of the variance in teachers' perceptions, most notably with predictions higher for aspects of relationships that teachers experience as negative such as conflict and dependency. The quality of teacher-child relationships is related concurrently and predictively to children's scholastic and behavioral competence in the early school years (Hamre & Pianta, 1999; Pianta, Steinberg, & Rollins, 1995).

It should also be noted that measurement of teacher-child relationships has generally relied on teacher perceptions. Students are rarely queried (Birch & Ladd, 1997; Pianta, 1999). Yet, school dropouts retrospectively rated perceived school climates significantly lower than graduates. Graduates rated the importance of attending college significantly higher than dropouts. Dropouts and graduates who left school did not report differences on the risk factors measured nor do they differ on perceived school climate or the importance of attending college (Worrell & Hale, 2001). However, hope in the future significantly predicted dropout versus graduate status for these participants, particularly the perception participants had about relationships with teachers. Perceived social support has also been found to relate to clinical conditions such as anxiety (K. S. White, Bruce, Farrell, & Kliewer, 1998) and depression (Cheng, 1997, 1998). A statistically significant relationship has been found among perceptions of social support and academic indices including grades, teacher ratings, and standardized test scores (Levitt, Guacci-Franco, & Levitt, 1994). Students with low perceived support particularly from teachers obtain significantly higher scores on problem behavior indicators and lower scores on positive behavior indicators (Demaray & Malecki, 2002).

Yet teachers alone, as we have noted, do not primarily define the optimal educational experience. Over the past 30 years, researchers and educators alike have recognized that student and classroom variables also play determining roles in the day-in and day-out functioning of the classroom and individual students. Student variables such as home experience, learning disability, temperament, language skills, social, and interpersonal abilities exert a significant impact on the classroom. A student capable of following teacher directions and rules, completing classroom work, and responding appropriately to conventional management techniques is going to experience far more success and positive feedback from teachers than a student who will not use or has not mastered these skills. Further, the structure of the classroom, including the number of students, range of student abilities and achievement, size of the room, and the manner in which work is presented also contributes to successful educational experiences. The educational climate is contributed to by all of these factors and nurtured by educators competent in behavioral and educational strategies but first and foremost concerned with creating a safe, accepting climate. Thus, teacher, student, and classroom variables at any given moment interact and contribute in varying degrees to the manner in which the classroom operates.

In 1928, Wickman suggested that the primary concern of most educators was aggressive-disruptive students rather than those who appeared depressed, anxious, or withdrawn. Over the past century, the primary educational mindset has been achievement oriented rather than person based. It has not typically been of concern to teachers how children feel but rather that they perform. Thus, it is not surprising that teachers and mental health workers report that shy, anxious, quiet children are easier to work with and respond better in the classroom than those who are disruptive (Cowen, Gesten, & Destefano, 1977). Further, when a disruptive child also experiences achievement difficulties secondary to a specific learning disability, fitting into the classroom is even more difficult. These authors reported that teachers felt that this group of children was "hopeless."

In 1964, Cremin described the American School System as being founded on an authoritarian model and supported on that basis. The basis of an authoritarian model is corporal punishment. The National Association of School Psychologists (NASP) defines corporal punishment as an intentional infliction of physical pain, physical restraint, and/or discomfort on a student as a disciplinary technique (NASP, 1986). Though corporal punishment has been increasingly on the decline in schools, it is still banned in only 27 U.S. states (Center for Effective Discipline, 2005). Every industrialized country in the world prohibits school corporal punishment except the United States, Canada, and one state in Australia. In the 1999/2000 school year, 9% of children in Arkansas and Mississippi were reported to have been struck by educators (Center for Effective Discipline, 2005). Yet, the preponderance of the data generated suggests that when teachers focus on academics and effective teaching strategies, provide work that students are capable of understanding, provide an emotionally safe and supportive atmosphere, and respond in a democratic way to behavioral problems, disciplinary difficulties in the classroom are at a minimum. As H. H. Marshall noted in 1972, successful classroom environments are conducive to learning and positive discipline and are constructive and preventive as well as remedial and ameliorative. For this model to be effective, a holistic approach must be taken. Applying various behavioral strategies in a band-aid fashion is not likely to be successful. The preponderance of the research data suggests that efficient teachers establish relationships of mutual respect and trust with their students, plan programming in the classroom carefully to meet students' needs, set appropriate rules and limits, but most importantly focus on helping students feel connected and competent in the classroom.

In the early 1800s, a Quaker named Joseph Lancaster described pinching the young where they are most tender as a philosophy of behavior management and education (Emblem, 1979). Lancaster's theory was that discipline worked when it hurt or embarrassed youngsters. His principles included making certain that punishments were novel and varied. According to Lancaster, punishments must create displeasure, be repeatable, not interfere with regular work, and be self-administered. Interestingly enough, the teacher was advised to administer the punishment to him or herself before employing it with children (Lancaster, 1803/1808). Lancaster also wrote that he believed school disciplinary procedures would be ineffective in managing behavior problems caused by poor home environments. Schools, as he noted, could not fix family problems. Punishable offenses in Lancaster's day included tardiness, hyperactivity, short attention span, profanity, and immorality. Leg shackles and pillories were routine devices used for misbehavior.

Horace Mann (1855) described schools of his day as following the model of punishment and pain. Among the more severe forms of punishment was to place offending students in a sack or basket and suspend them from the ceiling of the school for all to see. Among the more unusual interventions was one for inattention and restlessness. A cord was slipped over the head of a student attached to a six-pound log that had to be balanced on the student's shoulders. The slightest motion one way or the other and the log would fall, putting weight around the neck. This intervention was described as effective because it did not completely hinder movement nor interrupt class work.

Disruptive problems of inattention, over-activity, and noncompliance are still the most common complaints of teachers. Corporal punishment slowly has given away to the application of behavioral principles, problem solving, and token economies. Yet as A. C. Sabatino (1983) noted the model of authority, force, fear, and pain was still likely practiced covertly if not overtly in many schools. Countless cases are reported in which students are inappropriately disciplined even today with excessive punishment, teacher name calling, or excessive time out. In 1980, Unks described an incident in which a child developed hyperactivity after recovering from encephalitis. This child's increased activity level was labeled as disobedience even though it was caused by incompetence rather than noncompliance or purposeful misbehavior. As a punishment, the child was repeatedly restricted from participating with others with the intent that this punishment would change the child's neurologically based behavior. Keep in mind that even as of the mid-1970s, half of teachers and principals in the United States reported using corporal punishment as a primary means of discipline (Hyman & Wise, 1979). Though much has changed in the past 30 years, there are still many places in the United States and certainly other countries as well where corporal punishment is used to deal with childhood misbehavior and related problems. In 1968, only the state of New Jersey forbade corporal punishment. Even today, many states continue to permit its use. Yet, corporal punishment teaches children to rule by aggression and bullying because teachers model the very behavior they are trying to eliminate (Fishbach & Fishbach, 1973). The risks and the use of corporal punishment outweigh the benefits. Students become angry. Teachers are likely more stressed than helped. The intervention suppresses but does not change behavior. Finally, it creates a climate that does not foster resilience. Thirty years ago, the National Institute of Education concluded that corporal punishment is an inefficient way to maintain order, tends to lead to more frequent rather than less frequent punishments, and has undesirable effects on students. This outcome has been reported across all settings as well (Gershoff, 2002).

A New Direction

Parts I and II of this book set the foundation of a model to create resilient, sustainable environments in our schools. Such a model fosters effective behavior management in the classroom by thoroughly exploring teacher, student, setting, and consultant variables. Part III of this book focuses on interventions based on a foundation of cognitive/behavioral theory. Teacher and student behavior can be impacted in general ways such as reinforcement or token economies (H. M. Walker & Buckley, 1974), active feedback (Drabman & Lahey, 1974), group consequences (Greenwood, Hops, Delquadari, & Guild, 1974), social approval (Becker, Madsen, Arnold, & Thomas, 1967), motivation and attribution (Brooks, 1991), building educational opportunity (Elias, Parker, & Rosenblatt, 2005) and violence prevention (Taub & Pearrow, 2005). These strategies are equally appropriate for children and adolescents with disruptive, nondisruptive, or developmental problems. Further, an emphasis on preventive discipline through sound instructional strategies undoubtedly leads to the most efficient classroom management. Nearly 40 years ago, Kounin (1970) suggested that teachers in both well- and poorly managed classrooms respond similarly to student behavior. However, teachers of well-managed classrooms were much more efficient in monitoring student attention and performance, structuring beginning of the year activities and implementing classroom rules and procedures (Emmer, Evertson, & Anderson, 1980; Gettinger, 1988). Note that the majority of these efforts are prophylactic or preventive rather than reactionary in punishing.

Kazdin (1975a) describes five classes of techniques available to teachers to effectively manage their behavior:

1. Knowledge of the power of various stimuli in triggering certain good or negative behaviors increases the likelihood of successful student behavior.
2. Teachers can monitor their own behavior and make changes accordingly.
3. Teachers may reinforce or punish themselves contingent on their own behavior.
4. Teachers can learn to guide and instruct themselves more efficiently through self-monitoring.
5. Teachers can learn alternative responses or new ways of responding to problem behavior.

Teachers possess basic techniques to manage student behavior, including positive reinforcement, extinction, punishment modeling, and desensitization (Clarizio, 1976). When used appropriately, all of these techniques can be quite effective across all student ages. These strategies are based on the premise that the consultant and teacher will first observe, define, and target problem behaviors for intervention (Ulrich, Stachnik, & Mabry, 1966). The consultant must then effectively communicate these five basic behavioral techniques to teachers.

A basic principle for teachers is that consequences determine behavior. A negative consequence decreases the likelihood that a behavior will reoccur; a positive consequence has just the opposite effect. If the behavior results in what we desire, we will repeat it. If following the rules results in praise that a student values, he or she will respect those rules. If being disruptive results in sought after attention, the student will repeat the objectionable action. All behaviors regardless of what they are lead to some kind of payoff. They attract attention, gain power, express hostility, or achieve isolation (Dreikurs, Grunwald, & Pepper, 1971). There is no doubt, however, that the offering of primary and secondary reinforcers constitutes a teacher's most valuable tool. Yet teachers frequently misuse reinforcement by committing sins of either commission (rewarding unwanted behavior) or omission (ignoring positive behavior). For example, in 1970, Madsen and Madsen evaluated students' responses to teachers' commands to sit down. When teachers were directed to give this command every time a student stood up, the incidence of standing behavior, not surprisingly, increased. This is basic premise of negative reinforcement. Yet, teachers did not expect this outcome. The command appeared to serve as a reinforcer for the behavior. When teachers were trained to ignore the inappropriate behavior and reinforce more appropriate behavior by paying attention to students when they were sitting down, sitting down behavior increased.

Why do teachers commit sins that reinforce omission? Despite their best intentions teachers, frequently miss opportunities to strengthen desirable behaviors because of personal bias, motivation, expectation, and likely their past history. Many teachers develop misconceptions about difficult students and come to focus on misbehavior, overlooking occasions to reward positive behavior. Due to these biases, teachers often fail to reward a problem child, even when he or she is behaving appropriately. When such children are not behaving in bothersome ways, teachers like parents appear to have a tendency to leave them alone so as not to "rock the boat." Finally, teachers expect all students much beyond kindergarten age to behave. Therefore, they often find it difficult to consistently reward appropriate behavior in the students who may need such reinforcement most. Data consistently suggests that the quickest way to gain teacher attention in the classroom is to misbehave.

Successful classroom management includes the use of group contingencies to keep the group on task and functioning smoothly without disrup-

14

tion as well as management techniques to keep individual students involved in productive work (Grossman, 1990). Management techniques must include strategies for dealing with disruptive and nondisruptive behavior as well as peer-directed behaviors (Heward & Orlansky, 1990). However, management must also be placed within a framework of an appreciation for each student's developmental capabilities and level of achievement. The message is clear. With understanding and preventive planning techniques, anticipatory responses and systematic interventions, teachers can avoid behavioral problems by motivating students to want to behave in desirable ways (Linn & Herr, 1992). Preventive planning techniques, because they are proactive rather than reactive, represent a key component in creating a resilient classroom and sustainable school.

To assure positive classroom behavior, teachers must possess a basic system to identify and deal with problems. They must be able to target specific behavioral problems and define them in a predictable, consistent, and measurable fashion. They also must be able to define an acceptable end point behavior. They must prioritize problems that require intervention first based on their impact on the child's academic or social adjustment and the ease with which they can be measured, reinforced across a variety of settings and eliminated by focusing on a more appropriate substitute. Once the behavior has been identified, teachers must carefully evaluate the antecedents and consequences. This stage requires finding answers to questions about the problem—when, where, how, and by whom—as well as gauging its impact on others. Third, teachers must select a strategy that either develops a new behavior or eliminates the aversive behavior. Finally, they must develop a system for tracking progress and measuring success.

It is critical that educators learn to state problems in ways that lead directly to intervention. The problem statement must allow them to focus on a specific situation, develop practical strategies, monitor the target behavior, and consistently provide consequences or alter interventions if necessary. Using this model, Schoen (1983) focuses on how students learn compliance:

- Students must understand the relationship between the teacher's request and the appropriate response.
- They must have the opportunity for consistent practice of that response with reinforcement.
- The behavior must be generalized to other settings.

In the initial phase, compliant responses must be reinforced quickly and consistently every time with noncompliant responses resulting in consistent consequences every time. The next phase relies on two basic sets of management strategies. The first set uses positive approaches such as different attention, token economy, and the PREMACK principle (using a frequently occurring behavior to reinforce a low frequency behavior). The second set of interventions is reductionist and involves interventions such as response cost, reprimand, time out, and in the extreme, physical manipulation. In the last stage, teachers must make an effort to generalize appropriate behavior across settings, class situations, and with a variety of activities.

In the next chapter, we describe the basic model to create sustainable school environments. Effective teachers are a key component of this environment. The consensual description of the effective teacher is based on a wide variety of classrooms educating many different students. To truly understand an effective teacher and to help all educators be effective requires an appreciation of attitudes, beliefs, teacher behaviors, and instructional strategies. Though some believe these characteristics are generic to good teaching (Kauffman & Wong, 1991), others suggest that generic skills may serve the general population but not be as effective for students with specific problems (R. H. Zabel, 1987). Yet, as was noted by Hobbs in 1966 and is still consistent today, within the special education field, little is known about the requirement for effective teaching of behaviorally impaired students.

Four classes of behavior appear to disturb teachers most. These are: social immaturity, disobedience, motor and physical activity, and outright disruptive behavior (Curran & Algozzine, 1980). Among classroom teachers, outright student defiance toward authority is found consistently to be the most disturbing classroom problem. Aggression and poor peer cooperative are also rated as quite aversive to teachers (Safran & Safran, 1984, 1985, 1987). In contrast, teachers find anxiety and learning difficulties the least disturbing and most tolerable.

Although most teachers perceive disruptive behavior and those behaviors that threaten their authority as unacceptable, educators effective in dealing with these problems are more demanding, set standards, and stick with them. There appears to be positive correlation between teachers' effective instructional practices and their demands for appropriate behavior, lack of tolerance for misbehavior, and general tolerance for behavioral problems (Gersten, Walker, & Darch, 1988; H. M. Walker & Rankin, 1983). Teacher variables include those problems owned by the teacher that present difficulties because student behavior interferes with the teacher's satisfaction or causes the educator to feel frustrated, irritated, or angry (T. Gordon, 1974). Some teachers react aggressively when their need for authority and control is threatened. In contrast, student-owned problems, such as feeling inadequate or experiencing anxiety, come primarily from within the student. Finally, some problems are shared by students and teachers. Teachers perceive situations involving teacher-owned problems more negatively than those involving student owned problems (J. E. Brophy & Rohrkemper, 1981). Most teachers, as noted, view children as responsible for intentionally causing a teacher-owned problem and capable of exercising self-control. This is a critical issue for consultants. The assumptions of these educators is that the child was purposely non-compliant rather than lacking in skill to meet the teacher's expectations or reacting to past reinforcement for that pattern of behavior. Teachers confronted with teacher-owned problems are more pessimistic about their ability to achieve positive outcome and change student behavior. In the J. E. Brophy and Rohrkemper (1981) study, these teachers were less committed to helping such students. In contrast, when dealing with student-owned problems, teachers seem to perceive these students as victims of incompetence rather than as perpetrators of deliberate noncompliance. In these situations, teachers appeared to be more positive, committed, and willing to attempt classroom interventions. Thus, student-owned problems do not represent as great a threat as teacher-owned problems, especially those related to student defiance, aggression, or disruption.

Effective Teachers

Since teachers form the lynch pin in the model proposed in this book, we briefly review effective teacher variables in this introduction. Regardless of interventions used, consultants must always keep these issues in mind. An appreciation of the mindset of effective educators forms a critical foundation in the consultation model. For example, elementary teachers frequently utilize strategies using threat or punishment (e.g., loss of privilege or suspension) to pressure aggressive students into controlling their behavior (J. Brophy et al., 1986). However, teachers found to be more effective based on direct classroom observation use instructive positive interventions much more successfully to deal with aggressive noncompliant students than these reductionist interventions. In 1985, Larrivee reported 15 basic teacher behaviors that were found to have a positive correlation with improved behavior and performance in children exhibiting behavioral problems in the classroom. These 15 behaviors form the foundation for this book:

17

1. Providing positive feedback to students
2. Offering sustained feedback to students
3. Responding supportively to students in general
4. Responding even more supportively to low-ability students
5. Responding supportively to students with behavioral problems
6. Asking questions that students are able to answer correctly
7. Presenting learning tasks for which students have a high probability of success
8. Using time efficiently
9. Intervening in misbehavior at a low rate
10. Maintaining a low ratio of punitive to positive interventions
11. Being punitive at a low rate
12. Using criticism at a low rate
13. Keeping the need for disciplinary interventions low through positive classroom interventions
14. Wasting little time on student transitions
15. Keeping off task time to a minimum

When standards and tolerance of educators is measured accurately, a good fit between teacher and misbehaving students could be made by using one or more of the following strategies as described by Kauffman and Wong (1991):

- Modifying the student's behavior to match the teacher's standard and tolerance.
- Placing the student with a teacher whose standards and limits the teacher can meet.
- Modifying the teacher's standards and tolerance to match the student's.

These three strategies constitute the basic alternatives available to the classroom consultant. By evaluating student, teacher, and setting variables, the consultant must initially determine which options stand the best chance for success. In general, effective teachers for misbehaving students—likely those who can quickly bring about change for the better in behavior—may be less demanding and more tolerant as well as willing to modify their behavior in dealing with problem students.

Effective educators also include higher demands for students' academic performance and conduct, carefully design activities to maintain high rates of corrective responding and low rates of off-task behavior, frequently praise students for appropriate behavior, minimally utilize criticism or punishment, and are generally confident in their ability to help students learn and behave appropriately (Kauffman & Wong, 1991). As noted by these authors 25 years ago and still of concern: "Researchers need to establish effective teaching strategies for students with different types of behavioral disorders (e.g., internalizing versus externalizing behavior) and to distinguish effective teaching of students with behavioral disorders from effective teaching of those with other disabilities" (pp. 233–234).

Summary

This book as with its predecessor, begins with the premise that classrooms are vibrant, dynamic, complex settings in which teacher, student, and setting variables contribute to varying degrees in determining students' educational experiences, behavior, and the development of a resilient mindset. The complex bi-directional relationship of these areas is increasingly recognized (Downer & Pianta, 2006; Ray & Elliott, 2006). Because variables in each of these key areas play a critical role, they must be understood in and of their own as well as in their interactions. This text is written for classroom consultants, including school psychologists, special educators, social workers, counselors, principals, or master teachers. The titles after an individual's name and his or her degrees take a back seat to interest in the subject and ability to combine scientific knowledge with practical interventions facilitating the development of an effective, sustainable educational setting. This text provides a comprehensive, research-based exploration of the classroom, a model to understand and assess behavior as well as well-defined guidelines for consultation and intervention. The regular education (mainstreaming) initiative has gathered steam over the past 10 years culminating in significant changes in the current version of the Individuals for Disabilities Education Improvement Act (2004). Within this model in which response to intervention and problem solving are emphasized, consultants assume an increasingly important position. Effective consultants provide many invaluable services: They develop a consistent and practical referral system; they empower teachers to identify and begin evaluating behavioral problems in a comprehensive, scientific fashion; they are readily available, knowledgeable, and capable of offering a variety of interventions. This scenario represents a biopsychosocial model at its best. At any given moment, teacher, student, and setting variables interact and in turn are affected by learning history, biology, temperament, development, and cognition. The effective and efficient consultant must understand all of these issues, how they interact and, most importantly, how they impact the school environment.

Classroom consultation has become an increasingly popular means of providing cost-effective assistance to teachers. Research in this area has steadily increased over the past 10 years. Recent trends in education to deal with problems as they occur rather than through a special education maze place an even greater emphasis on the consultant's role. When teachers are presented with a rationale for intervention that matches their perspectives, greater intervention acceptability incurs (C. W. Conoley, Conoley, Ivey, & Scheel, 1991). When consultants join consultees by framing interventions in a way that is in line with the consultee's causal notions and classroom system, effective change occurs (Wickstrom & Witt, 1993). Classroom consultation has become an increasingly prevalent and effective means of offering service to a broad group of children (Lepage, Kratochwill, & Elliott, 2004). Consultation reflects an indirect service model in which the consultant helps teachers solve classroom problems as well as increase their ability to prevent or deal with similar problems effectively in the future (Gutkin & Curtis, 1990). We have come to realize that consultation involves more than simply providing intervention. Intervention does not guarantee significant success (Kratochwill, Bergan, Sheridan, & Elliott, 1998; Noell, Gansle, & Allison, 1999). Implementation becomes unstable or exhibits a downward trend in effectiveness in the absence of follow-up. Consultation is an ongoing process. Brief meetings that review the intervention are essential. Performance feedback results in more stable implementation. As Noell, Duhon, Gatti, and Connell (2002) note, "Despite its fundamental importance to the practice of school psychology and the broad advocacy for its expanded use, the empirical basis for consultation remains a work in progress" (p. 217). These authors also note that "although consultation interactions typically focus on the students or clients' behavior, supporting behavior change on the part of the consultee is frequently the initial challenge confronting consultants." As Foxx (1996) noted, it has been argued that insuring plan implementation is frequently more challenging than developing an appropriate intervention. Thus, the model proposed in this book places an initial emphasis on understanding and examining teachers' mindsets. Although relatively little research has documented the preventive or long-lasting benefits of classroom consultation (Aldrich & Martens, 1993) indirect evidence supports this intervention to suggest that the data simply await collection (Ponti, Zins, & Graden, 1988).

There is an increased need to examine better ways to create and deliver mental health services for all children within our schools (Bierman, 2003). Sustainable school environments must include attention to children's mental health. Effective and sustainable implementation of mental health services in the schools needs to consider the use of local data to guide ongoing decision making, invest in team-based implementation, develop local training capacity, establish ongoing coaching support, give priority to evidence based practice, establish district level support systems, and have a long-term plan in mind (Sugai, 2003). Consultation in the classroom must today and into the future provide a balanced focus on behavior for those in need as well as stress hardiness and the development of a resilient mindset for all students. Twenty-five years ago, it was reported that classroom conduct was deteriorating at a rate equivalent to the escalation of felonies committed by underage youth (Stoops, Rafferty, & Johnson, 1981). Discipline problems are rated by most adults as a primary example of ineffectiveness in the American Educational System. This is equally true today as children's medical, mental health, and general adjustment continues to be eroded away, making it increasingly more difficult for children to negotiate every day life successfully. The enormity of the task defined by Lloyd et al. in 1990 has continued to grow. Yet, inroads have and continue to be made. As Seligman has pointed out (1998a, 1998b), attending to those issues that are preventative and that create a resilient mindset and wellness will require a significant paradigm shift in mental health professionals and the educational community. Seligman has suggested that the shift will not be easy to make. It is the intent of this book to introduce and advocate for the implementation of a model of effective prevention and positive social science.

CHAPTER

2

Creating Sustainable Classroom Environments: The Mindsets of Effective Teachers, Successful Students, and Productive Consultants

SAM GOLDSTEIN AND ROBERT BROOKS

What defines a behavioral problem in the classroom? On the surface, children's varying behavioral problems can be hypothesized to reflect inadequate or inconsistent performance relative to expectation. The term noncompliance is often used to describe these phenomena. It has been suggested that noncompliance is a marker for maladaptive behavior patterns in children, including aggression, antisocial activities, social maladjustment and general disobedience (Schoen, 1983). Noncompliance or failure to comply with an instruction has several interchangeable components, such as not responding, delaying responding more than a prescribed time, or offering some other nonrequested behavior. Noncompliance is a prevalent problem for educators and parents. Other terms for noncompliance are disobedience (Zeilberger, Sampan, & Sloane, 1968), negative behavior (Wahler, 1969), oppositional behavior (Scarboro & Forehand, 1975) and uncooperative behavior (O'Leary, Kaufman, Kass, & Drabman, 1970).

There appear to be two distinct etiologies responsible for noncompliance. Some children are noncompliant because they choose to be disobedient, while others with emotional and developmental disabilities may fail to respond because they lack the competence to do so (S. Goldstein & Goldstein, 1998). This child's behavior may not meet teacher expectations for reasons other than outright disobedience.

Labeling a student with one diagnosis or another is not the purpose of this book nor does our interest lie in simply providing strategies to create a problem-free classroom. Our interest lies in developing operational, consistent, and understandable methods to identify children with behavioral differences in the classroom; a system to define and measure those differences consistently; and a means to understand the forces that shape and maintain those differences. Our focus in this second edition is strength-based. Further, our interest is in helping consultants provide teachers with a set of systematic interventions that not only respond to the behavioral needs of students but also foster a resilient, sustainable classroom thereby insulating students from present and future problems.

Traditionally in educational systems, children who repeatedly do not comply with teacher requests and expectations in the classroom are considered to have a behavior disorder. Yet, there are many ways of defining such a disorder. The condition could be defined statistically as the difference between one child and another, or administratively as a set of criteria used to decide whether a child's behavior qualifies for a particular special program. Statistical definitions of behavioral problems in the classroom provide a standard by which the majority of the group functions and then allows a specific child to be compared with that standard. Thus, the average amount of time spent on task or the average number of aggressive incidents exhibited by all students might be used as standards against which to compare a particular child's behavior. It is more likely, however, that in day-to-day interactions, qualitative as opposed to quantitative data influences most teachers' opinions of children with problems. As a marker of a child's disability and/or justification for intervention an educator may use particular child idiosyncrasies, styles of interacting, or patterns of responding. Qualitative definitions are helpful. Yet, to thoroughly understand, define, prevent, and successfully intervene when classroom behavioral problems present, quantitative definitions are essential. Such definitions also allow for the development of research protocols to test models of identification, assessment, prevention, and intervention.

Concerns about student misbehavior extend beyond the disruptive nature of these behaviors to the impairment of academic performance and ultimately achievement. Misbehaving students rarely perform well academically. The actions of children with behavior problems deviate from classroom standards or teacher expectations and impair student functioning across all academic activities. These behaviors are often uncharacteristic of the child's age or gender. Their frequency, intensity, and persistence are extreme, often presenting over a substantial period.

In a position paper written for the Council of Children with Behavior Disorders, Huntze (1985) suggests that the term *behaviorally disordered* is far preferred to other terms such as *emotionally disturbed*. The former is hypothesized to lead directly to assessment and intervention and to be less stigmatizing. It is also easier for educators to accept that they can affect behavior rather than impact emotional disturbance or psychiatric problems. This is among the many reasons the focus of this second edition book has moved away from symptom-driven categories toward an appreciation, understanding, measurement, and modification of functional behavior. Classroom teachers can be and are important change agents.

In 1979, F. H. Wood provided four key issues for defining behavioral problems in the classroom: (1) recognizing what or who is the focus of the problem, (2) defining the problem, (3) understanding how the environment around the student contributes to the problem, and (4) understanding how the problem impacts the environment. Thus a set of variables involving the teacher, child, and environment must be carefully understood, evaluated, and managed if positive change is to take place.

Within the classroom, it is frequently timing rather than excesses of a child's behavior that causes problems. Developmental pediatrician, Dr. Mel Levine, in his lectures for teachers has noted that children with problems related to self-discipline "know how to do everything but just don't know when to do anything in the classroom." Thus, a significant percentage of classroom problems reflect poor timing in addition to behavioral excesses. Some children may exhibit either not enough or too much of a given behavior and may also exhibit such behaviors at the wrong times. It is important to recognize that children's behavior is labeled as problematic when it disturbs or disrupts individuals in the environment, typically the teacher. Thus, the observer often defines the problem rather than the exhibitor of the problem. Expectations for classroom behavior and standards vary widely from educator to educator. Standards, and in fact educators' personalities, differ and likely play a significant role in determining whether a teacher identifies behavior as problematic and manages it appropriately, structures a classroom in a way to prevent the occurrence of such behavior, or takes the misbehavior personally and inadvertently reinforces the undesired behavior.

Researchers and practitioners alike agree that compliance is a learned behavior. Students must first develop an understanding of the relationship between the teacher's request and the appropriate response. Second, students must be afforded the opportunity for consistent practice of that response with reinforcement. Finally, the behavior must be generalized to other settings. For this model to be effective, compliant responses in the first phase must be reinforced quickly and consistently every time with noncompliant responses causing consistent consequences every time. In the second phase, positive approaches such as differential attention or a token economy must be combined with interventions that reduce the noncompliant behaviors such as response cost, reprimand, or time out. Finally, efforts must be made to generalize improved behavior across settings, class situations, and with a variety of adults. Even within the resilience framework offered in this book, the acceptance of this basic behavioral model is essential. Teachers and consultants must accept that children's behavior can be shaped, modified, and developed when the behavioral, cognitive, and emotional variables affecting that behavior are understood.

This chapter begins with an overview of teacher variables that impact student's behavior. What do we know and what do we think we know about the mindsets and behaviors of effective educators? It continues with an overview of similar child variables and then reviews environmental variables as they impact classroom behavior. Finally, an overview of the productive role of the classroom consultant is offered.

Effective Teachers

Educators, similar to all individuals, possess different mindsets or assumptions about themselves and others (Brooks, 2001a, 2001b; Brooks & Goldstein, 2001, 2003, 2004). These assumptions play a significant role in determining one's expectations and behavior. Even seemingly hidden assumptions have a way of being expressed to others. People often begin to behave in accord with the expectations that are held of them and when they do, others are apt to interpret this as a sign that their expectations are accurate. Expectations subtly and sometimes not so subtly shape the behavior of others.

An examination of the school environment reveals that educators possess many different assumptions about their students and the process of education. Given these differences, the question can be posed: "What is the mindset of the effective educator?" or worded somewhat differently, "What are the assumptions and behaviors of an educator more likely to touch the mind and heart of students and in doing so, reinforce cooperation and motivation while decreasing noncompliant behavior?"

The following list of the key characteristics of the mindset of effective educators is elaborated on in Chapter 9:

- They understand their lifelong impact on students, including instilling a sense of hope and resilience (Brooks, 1991; Brooks & Goldstein, 2001; Segal, 1988). Each word a teacher utters and each action a teacher takes may make the difference whether students become cooperative and optimistic or feel alienated and then resort to noncompliant behaviors.

- They believe that the learning that occurs in the classroom and the behavior exhibited by students has as much, if not more, to do with the influence of teachers than what students might bring into the situation. This should not be interpreted as blaming teachers for the misbehavior of students but rather as empowering them to identify the sources of student difficulties and to develop new interventions for addressing these problems. A hallmark of effective individuals is that they focus their time and energy on what they can do differently when faced with challenging situations rather than asking what others should do first (Brooks & Goldstein, 2004; Covey, 1989).

- They believe that all students wish to be successful and if a student is not learning, educators must ask how they can adapt their teaching style and instructional material to meet student needs. Effective educators understand that students have different learning styles and temperaments and that these differences must be respected and accommodations must be made lest the student fail and misbehave (Keogh, 2003; Levine, 2002, 2003; Rief, 2005).

- They believe that attending to the social-emotional life of students is not an "extra-curriculum" that draws time from teaching academic subjects (J. Cohen, 1999). Effective teachers appreciate that a student's sense of belonging, security, and self-confidence in a classroom provides the scaffolding that supports the foundation for enhanced learning, motivation, self-discipline, responsibility, and the ability to deal more effectively with obstacles and mistakes (Brooks, 1991, 1999). This belief applies to all students but has special relevance for youngsters struggling with learning. These students are vulnerable to feelings of frustration, low self-worth, and helplessness and in response are likely to resort to coping strategies that represent noncompliant behaviors such as avoidance of the task and disruptive behavior (Canino, 1981; Deci, Hodges, Pierson, & Tomassone, 1992; Licht, 1983).

- They recognize that if teachers are to relate effectively to students, they must be empathic, always attempting to see the world through the eyes of the student. Empathy is not the same as sympathy, which means to feel sorry for another person, nor does it mean we must agree with another person. Rather, the concept of empathy implies that we assume the perspective of the other person so as to respond most effectively to their needs. Goleman (1995) highlights empathy as a major component of emotional intelligence.

- They appreciate that the foundation for successful learning and a safe and secure classroom climate is the relationship teachers forge with students (Brooks, 1991; Dwyer, Osher, & Warger, 1998; R. Fried, 1995; Palmer, 1998). Effective educators respect the adage, "Students don't care what you know until they first know you care" and they are constantly searching for ways to connect in a genuine fashion with students.

- They recognize that students will be more motivated to learn when they feel a sense of ownership for their own education (Deci & Flaste, 1995; Glasser, 1969; McCombs & Pope, 1994). Nurturing a sense of ownership includes demystifying the concept of learning styles, involving students in discussions about educational practices in the classroom, reinforcing problem-solving skills by requesting their input into classroom decisions, providing opportunities for students to make choices, and encouraging critical thinking in students even if it means disagreeing with the teacher's point of view (Adelman & Taylor, 1983; Brooks, 1991; Levine, 2002; McCombs & Pope, 1994; Shure, 1994).

- They understand that one of the main functions of an educator is to be a disciplinarian in the true sense of the word, namely, to perceive discipline as a teaching process rather than as a process of intimidation and humiliation. Effective educators can identify and actualize two of the main goals of discipline, namely, to have clear-cut guidelines, rules, limits, and consequences in order to ensure a safe, secure environment, and to nurture self-discipline and self-control. The latter relates to point 7 since it implies a sense of ownership and responsibility for the rules of the classroom. Students are more likely to adhere to rules when they have been involved within reason in the creation of the rules and consequences (Brooks, 1991; Charney, 1991; Curwin & Mendler, 1988; M. Marshall & Weisner, 2004; Mendler, 1992; Rademacher, Callahan, & Pederson-Seelye, 1998).

- They realize that one of the greatest obstacles to learning is the fear of making mistakes and feeling embarrassed or humiliated. Effective teachers know that students will often rely on noncompliant behaviors to avoid this fear. Thus, such educators are proactive in taking steps to minimize this fear and to ensure that students are willing to take risks and not be preoccupied with anxieties about being humiliated (Brooks, 1991, 1999).

- They subscribe to a strength-based model, which includes identifying each student's strengths or "islands of competence" (Brooks, 1991; Brooks & Goldstein, 2001). Successful educators recognize that students will be more receptive to learning when they believe their teachers appreciate and reinforce their talents. As Gardner (1983) has emphasized, we all possess "multiple intelligences," but many schools and educational tests focus only on two, mathematical-logical skills and verbal-linguistic skills. Students who are not proficient in these two intelligences are likely to feel at a disadvantage in a classroom if their teacher does not notice and reinforce those intelligences at which they excel.

- They recognize that constructive relationships with parents facilitate the learning process for students (Brooks, 1991; Brooks & Goldstein, 2001; Chapman, 1991; Davies, 1991; J. Epstein, 1987; Warner, 1991). Increasing evidence indicates that parent-teacher cooperation and parental involvement are influential forces in creating effective schools. Effective teachers view parents as allies rather than adversaries and actively strive to create positive interactions with and a welcoming attitude toward parents.

- They develop and maintain positive, respectful relationships with colleagues. Teaching can be an isolating experience and thus, it is vital that educators support and share information and talent with each other. Many teachers leave the field of education after just 1 or 2 years. They are less likely to drop out when they have mentors to whom they can turn for information and encouragement. Experienced educators are more likely to maintain their enthusiasm when they are placed in the mentoring role and when they have opportunities to share their wisdom with others.

Successful Students

Just as effective educators possess a mindset filled with assumptions upon which their success is based, so too do successful students possess a mindset that contributes to their accomplishments in school. It is essential that educators appreciate and understand how to reinforce a resilient mindset in their teaching practices. It is difficult for students to develop a positive mindset for learning if teachers do not apply a positive mindset to the creation of a positive, energizing learning environment in which students believe they are active participants. As is evident from the following list, elaborated on in Chapter 10, the mindset of successful students is intimately tied to the mindset and practices of their teachers:

- They believe that whether they learn or not is based in great part on their own motivation, perseverance, and effort (Brooks, 1991; Canino, 1981; Raskind, Goldberg, Higgins, & Herman, 2003; Seligman, 1995; Weiner, 1974). If students do not view themselves as active participants in the learning process but rather as passive recipients of what is being taught, their interest and enthusiasm for learning will be greatly diminished.
- They recognize that making mistakes and not immediately understanding certain concepts or material are part of the learning process. When confronted with challenging learning tasks, successful students recall past experiences in which difficult material became more comprehensible with time. They appreciate that learning takes time and effort.
- They perceive the teacher as a supportive adult. When confronted with difficulty with an academic task or with nonacademic issues, the successful student feels comfortable in taking the initiative and asking the teacher for assistance. They should not perceive requesting help as reinforcing dependence, especially when educators skillfully offer their assistance, but in the process teach students strategies for solving problems.
- They understand their learning style, learning strengths, and learning vulnerabilities. As Mel Levine (2002) has so eloquently advocated, it is essential that one's learning style be "demystified" for students. The more that students gain an understanding of their learning profile, the more they can develop strategies for learning actively and successfully. When students don't comprehend why they are struggling with learning, when they believe they are dumb or stupid or lazy, they are more likely to resort to self-defeating ways of coping represented by noncompliant behaviors.
- They treat classmates with respect and avoid teasing or bullying, recognizing that such behaviors work against a positive school climate and adversely affect the learning of all students (Davis, 2003; Olweus, 1993). Students must realize that a caring, respectful

classroom and school are the responsibility of each member of that classroom and school.

Sustainable Environments

As is evident from our description of the mindset of effective educators and successful students, the classroom environment reflects a unique interaction of the style and personality of the teacher, students, curriculum, and physical placement. Like people, no two classrooms are identical. The classroom is a microcosm of the school environment, broader community, and culture. It is a place in which children are expected to learn the academic, social, emotional, and behavioral skills necessary to transition successfully into adult life. The optimal classroom environment is not necessarily the environment in which grades are highest or behavior best, but rather a miniature community in which values, ideas, and curriculum are sustainable. A sustainable classroom environment is one in which students are equal stakeholders; in which there is an appreciation and respect not just for members of the classroom and school community but for the surrounding community and culture as well.

Unfortunately in such a setting in which the ideal focus should be on creating a cooperative, sustainable, nurturing environment, problems with discipline and misbehavior have become paramount. Discipline and behavior management issues in many schools have become a greater focus for educators than the curriculum. Over the past 40 years problems with discipline have been rated second only to problems with drug use year after year in educational polls. In 1984, Gallup reported that teachers viewed lack of school discipline as a serious problem. A number of well-respected authors have concluded that despite years of behavioral research and applied practice, efforts to train teachers to create environments that are sustainable, efficient, and well managed have met with only mixed success (Lepage et al., 2004; Lloyd et al., 1990). Over the past 15 years, authors have suggested that the task of significantly reforming the teaching and behavior management skills of the majority of teachers was unlikely to be accomplished in the near future. We now recognize that to accomplish this task doesn't require more rules or stringent punishments but rather a shift in mindset (Truscott, Cosgrove, Meyers, & Eidle-Barkman, 2000). This shift recognizes that the path to create motivated learners—learners actively involved in their education—requires not stronger walls and bigger locks but rather the application of a positive psychology. Such a psychology focuses on strengths rather than liabilities, on creating a sustainable environment in which all students feel connected, productive, and accepted (Brooks, 1991).

However, it is still the reality that on a daily basis many kindergarten through high school teachers deal with disruptive behavioral problems. Some are minor such as murmuring, talking, or lack of attention. Others are more significant, such as aggression, resistance, and defiance. In some classrooms, students openly do not conform to accepted classroom rules, while in others students behave within acceptable limits when the educator is present but become unruly or aggressive quickly when adult supervision is absent. Such students often exhibit problems in out-of-classroom settings such as hallways, lunchroom, or playground. Other students may be indifferent to completing tasks, apathetic, simply disconnected. Optimal, sustainable classroom environments begin with effective teachers and successful students. In 1978, R. M. Smith, Neisworth, and Greer described five key teacher characteristics contributing to an optimal learning environment. These are as true today as they were nearly 30 years ago. These characteristics are flexibility, consistency, understanding, a positive attitude, and a planned instructional approach.

Physical qualities of the classroom, however, also play a role in creating an optimal, sustainable environment. When teachers have too many students needing extra attention due to developmental, temperamental, emotional, or behavioral problems, classrooms have been found to not function optimally (L. V. Johnson & Bany, 1970). An escalation of problems often occurs in such settings. Effective classrooms are likely those in which teachers pay careful attention to how they present material and allow students enough time to respond to and interact with the material.

The physical size and layout of the classroom is also a critical variable. Sometimes a simple intervention such as relocating desks may solve disruptive behavioral problems. The rate of on task behavior has been found to double as conditions change from desk clusters to rows in the classroom (Wheldall & Lam, 1987). The rate of disruptions was three times higher in the desk-cluster seating arrangement in an elementary school setting. Teachers also need to actively structure their classroom to induce compliance and prevent noncompliance, improve teacher-student relationships to a maximum point and manage difficult teacher-student interaction successfully (H. M. Walker & Walker, 1991).

In 1983, Paine, Radicchi, Rosellini, Deutchman, and Darch, reported their research-based classroom model describing 11 key components necessary to manage and structure a classroom for success. This research-based model was designed to not just manage but prevent problems as well. The model offers an approach to the entire classroom that can be used across grades in a comprehensive, standardized fashion. Many aspects of this classroom success model are incorporated into this book. These authors noted the following key components:

- Organizing classroom space efficiently
- Using volunteers and aides effectively in the classroom
- Using teacher attention to manage student behavior
- Establishing and teaching classroom rules in an active manner
- Structuring and managing classroom time
- Managing the flow of materials in the classroom
- Handling student requests for assistance in a timely fashion
- Correcting students' work and keeping track of their performance
- Dealing with minor behavior problems
- Developing good work habits in students
- Phasing out the need for special procedures once students are well adjusted in the classroom

Productive Consultants

Consultation involves a voluntary, professional relationship between individuals of different fields to assist the effective functioning of one of the individuals (J. C. Conoley & Conoley, 1992; Sheridan et al., 2004). In a school setting, the consultant, by spending time with the teacher, provides indirect services that may aid more than a single child (Wickstrom, Jones, LaFleur, & Witt, 1998). Intuitively, this model offers both efficiency and effectiveness. There is a limited database predicting which type of consultant behaviors, models, or programs lead to the greatest success in meeting teachers' needs for assistance with student behavior management. A number of writers have offered definitions of the consultant's role with classroom teachers (Athanasiou et al., 2002; Erchul et al., 1999; D. S. Graham, 1998; Schill, Kratochwill, & Elliott, 1998). According to Idol-Maestas (1983), effective consultants establish a consistent and practical referral system that allows teachers to request assistance. Such a system can help teachers independently identify, define, and prioritize problem behaviors. With this approach, teachers have at their disposal a workable model to collect data based on their concerns before seeking pro-learning, developmental, emotional, and behavioral skills and be readily available for initial meetings with consultants as well as for follow-up and modification. A repertoire of appropriate interventions that can be easily and quickly demonstrated and implemented is essential to the system's success.

The school principal must actively support the effective classroom consultant as a resource for teachers as well as a provider of general in-service training concerning behavior management when necessary. Evaluation of teachers should not be part of the consultant's role. Consultants must offer help that they can in fact deliver, act as a team member, and emphasize that with assistance teachers can solve their own problems. Further, consultants must accept teachers' observations and opinions, be prepared to offer a menu of continuum of suggestions tailored to a specific teacher's program, and make certain that teachers are valued and reinforced for their effort (Deno & Mirkin, 1977).

Due to the mainstreaming initiative, classroom consultation, especially for school psychologists, has become a high priority (Kratochwill, Elliott, & Rotto, 1990; D. Smith, 1984). Authors note unique features associated with what has been defined as *behavioral consultation* (K. M. Jones et al., 1997). These include indirect service delivery, a problem-solving focus, and the development of a collegial relationship between consultant and teacher. The concept of indirect service is not new but may offer the greatest potential for change in the classroom (Bergan & Kratochwill, 1990). The consultant delivers service to the teacher, who then provides service to the student. This efficient method of service delivery allows the consultant to access many more students and to establish a collaborative relationship with the teacher. Therefore, the consultant's interpersonal skills, even gender and race, can be paramount in making this collegial relationship work (J. C. Conoley & Conoley, 1982; Erchul, Raven, & Wilson, 2004; Rogers, 1998). The consultant's interpersonal skills repertoire must include the ability to accept the teacher, to make nonjudgmental statements, and to be open, nondefensive, and flexible. The effective consultant identifies problems efficiently, analyzes them, and plans implementation and evaluation (Bergan, 1977).

The behavioral consultation model embraces two important goals. First, the consultant must provide methods to change a child's behavior and second, to improve a teacher's skills and repertoire of interventions so that he or she can respond independently and successfully to similar problems in the future (Kratochwill et al., 1990). Studies spanning 20 years suggest that this model has worked effectively (Gresham & Kendell, 1987; Matheson & Shriver, 2005; Noell, et al., 2005).

Limited research has been available concerning guidelines for selecting treatments when consultants deal with classroom behavioral problems (S. N. Elliott, 1988; Witt, 1986), though recent studies are helpful (Sheridan, Meegan, & Eagle, 2002). Many variables may affect intervention choice and outcome. For example, teachers' knowledge of, opinion toward, and belief about various interventions likely exert a significant impact on how well they respond to and follow through on those interventions. The effective consultant must be aware of such variables.

Witt and Elliott (1985) first offered a model to understand the variables that contribute to a teacher's acceptance of interventions. This model includes careful assessment of issues related to intervention acceptability by the teacher, intervention use, integrity, and effectiveness. All four of these areas likely interact. These authors believe that the relationship among these four elements is sequential and reciprocal. Reimers, Wacker, and Koeppel (1987) expanded this model and developed a more complex set of variables suggesting that the teacher must understand an intervention before he or she will accept it (see Figure 2.1). Issues related to the effectiveness of an intervention include the teacher's willingness to comply with the recommendation, as well as a willingness and ability to maintain the recommended intervention after

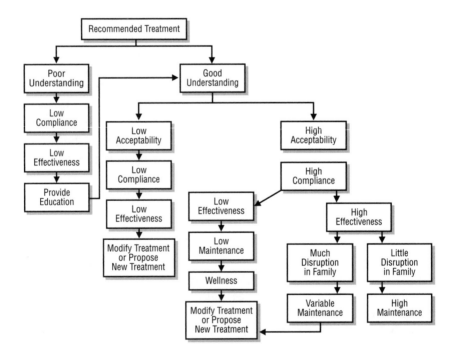

Figure 2.1 Treatment acceptability

Source: "Acceptability of Behavioral Treatments: A Review of the Literature," by T. M. Relmers, D. P. Wacker and G. Koeppel, 1987, *School Psychology Review, 16,* 212–227. Reprinted with permission of Guilford Press.

initiation. Follow-up studies strongly support the impact of these multiple variables (Gilman & Gabriel, 2004).

To predict the potential effectiveness of a particular intervention, consultant, teacher, setting, and child variables must all be carefully evaluated (S. N. Elliott, 1988). The language the consultant uses to present the intervention, that professional's regular involvement with the teacher, and the rationale he or she presents for the intervention all affect intervention outcome (see Table 2.1). For example, teachers who watched a videotape providing basic examples of behavior modification in the classroom were more positive about the personal qualities and effectiveness of the teacher whom they viewed when the methods they were observing were labeled as humanistic education rather than behavior modification (Wolfolk, Wolfolk, & Wilson, 1977). Further, when interventions are suggested to teachers in pragmatic terms (e.g., staying in at recess is a logical consequence), teachers tend to rate the intervention as more acceptable than when it is described in either humanistic (e.g., staying in at recess helps children understand and express their feelings by reading a book about feelings or talking with teacher) or behavioral terms (e.g., staying in at recess is a punishment to control children's inappropriate

Table 2.1   Variables within a consultant framework that can influence teachers' evaluations of treatment acceptability

Consultant (Psychologist)	Consultee (Teacher)	Treatment	Client (Child)
Jargon	Years of experience	Time required	Severity of problem
Involvement	Knowledge of behavior principals	Type of treatment	Type of problem
Rationales for treatment	Type of training	Reported effectiveness	
	Class management techniques used		

Note: The variables in this table have been investigated empirically. Many more variables such as the race and sex of the consultant, consultee, and client could be investigated. Most analogue research to date has been with female teachers and hypothetical male problem children because this is most representative of reality. The headings from left to right are in the order of information flow.

Source: "Acceptability of Behavioral Treatments: Review of Variables that Influence Treatment Selection," by S. N. Elliott, 1988, *Professional Psychology Research and Practice,* 19, 68–80. Copyright © 1988 by the American Psychological Association. Reprinted with permission.

behavior; Witt, Moe, Gutkin, & Andrews, 1984). Consultants should also recognize that teachers who do not refer as often for special education and are more receptive to consultation, likely provide a greater diversity of materials in the classroom, a wide range of activities, and a more interesting system for instruction.

Teachers are more accepting of reinforcing than punishing interventions (Hyatt & Tingstrom, 1993). However, when time-out in this study was described in behavioral jargon rather than nontechnical terminology, it was rated as potentially more acceptable (e.g., jargon: operant conditioning to correct behavior by implementing a time-out punishment procedure; nonjargon: teach children to sit correctly by using punishment). Hyatt, Tingstrom, and Edwards (1991) and Rhoades and Kratochwill (1992) also suggest that jargon appears to exert a positive influence on teachers' perceptions of classroom interventions. Teachers are more likely to view the jargon-presented intervention as acceptable. As Hyatt and Tingstrom (1993) found, however, jargon may facilitate teacher acceptability of punishment-based interventions, but teachers are more likely to favor reinforcement-based interventions over punishing interventions irrespective of the terminology used.

Researchers suggest that addressing the instructional environment as well as students' behavioral problems can enhance the preventive effects of consultation (Beavers, Kratochwill, & Braden, 2004; Gettinger, 1988; McKee & Witt, 1990). Variables such as teacher planning and evaluation activities, instructional style, and opportunities for interactive teaching and feedback all affect classroom behavior (Christenson & Ysseldyke, 1989). Modification of classroom instruction appears to serve a proactive function by focusing on antecedent consequences (Martens & Kelly, 1993). The importance of attending to antecedent consequences is discussed in later chapters. This model starts with what the teacher is doing, thus building on strength rather than attempting to teach a brand-new skill. Such a model increases the likelihood of effective consultation (Witt & Martens, 1988).

S. N. Elliott, Turco, and Gresham (1987) have demonstrated that the more severe a child's problem is, the more acceptable teachers find any given intervention. Among positive interventions, the least complex intervention (praise) is often rated as the more acceptable intervention for the least severe teacher-described problems (daydreaming). In general, teacher acceptability for treatments appears higher overall for positive rather than negative procedures (Kazdin, 1980, 1981).

Teachers prefer interventions that they themselves can implement. Further, these interventions are rated more favorably when problems are rated as more severe (Algozzine, Ysseldyke, Christenson, & Thurlow, 1983; Martens, Witt, Elliott, & Darveaux, 1985). However, Kazdin (1982) reported that time is also a significant variable when teachers evaluate a behavior change procedure before using it. Thus, time is an important factor in teacher's pretreatment acceptability ratings for various interventions. Witt, Martens, and Elliott (1984) found that time to implement a procedure as a variable interacts significantly with both problem severity and treatment type. With all other things being equal, teachers prefer treatments that are more time efficient. When confronted with a severe problem, however, they are willing to increase their acceptance of a complex, successful intervention and consequently the time they will have to invest in making that treatment work efficiently. Thus, it is fair to conclude that teachers are time conscious but not time obsessed (S. N. Elliott, 1988).

E. E. Jones and Nisbett (1971) found that individuals tend to make different attributions or their own versus other people's behavior. They tend to attribute the behavior of others as internal but provide external attributions (excuses) for similar behaviors in themselves. Thus, teachers' tendency to do this with students is not surprising. Burger, Cooper, and Good (1982) found that expected outcome (teacher expects inappropriate behavior to occur and it does) is more often attributed by teachers to stable factors, whereas unexpected outcome (appropriate behavior occurs when unexpected) is more often attributed to unstable factors. Once teachers' attributions are associated with stable factors, beliefs about the child's behavior may be very resistant to change. These negative attitudes toward disruptive students persist even when the students' behavior improves (Lewin, Nelson, & Tollefson, 1983). Consultants must recognize this phenomenon as a variable impacting teacher effectiveness.

Von Brock and Elliott (1987) reported that teachers might also be more responsive to interventions before a problem becomes too severe. Because of the nature of our educational system, teachers often see themselves as ineffective in handling students with severe problems and perceive their primary option as referring such students for special services. Teachers also appear to possess preconceived options about various interventions. They often feel there are more options for handling mild problems and are therefore likely to be more willing to experiment. Von Brock and Elliott reported that when teachers view an intervention as less acceptable, they also rate it as less effective. Teachers' views and opinions concerning acceptability will influence their views on treatment effectiveness and likely influence the effort they invest in initiating the treatment.

When teachers find a treatment unacceptable, they may be quick to judge it as ineffective (S. N. Elliott, 1988).

Teachers with information that increases their sense of control over the child's problems express a greater desire for consultation and willingness to attempt various interventions (Gutkin & Hickman, 1988). When teachers perceive a child's behavior as stable, originating within the child and caused by life problems beyond their control, they are less willing to consider consultation. In such situations, they are also less willing to modify classroom variables and more likely to try and move the child out of the classroom setting.

Three other issues must be briefly mentioned. McMahon, Forehand, and Griest (1981) reported that more positive attitudes by teachers toward behavioral techniques follow increases in knowledge of such techniques. Thus, the effective consultant can facilitate teachers' willingness to accept and utilize interventions by increasing their knowledge and understanding of the basic principles and rationale for those interventions. Second, there appears to be an inverse relationship between years of teaching experience and intervention acceptability (Witt & Robbins, 1985). Teachers with greater experience in the educational field appear to find new interventions less acceptable. Thus, veteran teachers may begin to adhere rigidly to a fixed set of interventions and become less willing to try new ones. The consultant must consider this factor when entering a classroom. Finally, teachers may not always do what they say or believe they are doing leading to inconsistent intervention integrity (K. M. Jones et al., 1997). This necessitates building an observation/feedback component into consultation.

S. N. Elliott, Witt, Galvin, and Moe (1986) evaluated children's responses to a variety of classroom interventions. Among a group of sixth graders, interventions that emphasized individual teacher-student interaction, group reinforcement, or negative actions for misbehaving were rated as most acceptable. Public reprimands and negative contingencies for the entire group because of one child's misbehavior were rated as least acceptable. A consultant must be aware of these child issues as well. S. N. Elliott (1986) further suggests that children differentially evaluate the acceptability of interventions by age. Younger children prefer positive interventions, whereas older children appear to prefer more adverse interventions. Some data also suggest that sex and racial or ethnic background may also affect intervention acceptability in ways that are not well defined. The severity of the problem does not in the child's eyes appear very important for younger children, but it does influence adolescent acceptability ratings. The effective consultant must remember that not only the teacher's willingness to accept the treatment but the students' as well will play a key role in effective behavior change.

Salmon (1993) points out that consultants must rely heavily upon information about the child when planning actions. This is especially true for beginning consultants. Thus as with classroom educators, consultants are likely to miss or underestimate the role teacher and setting variables play in regards to children's behavior, as well as the opportunity to intervene in those areas. Salmon's findings with trainee school psychology consultants suggest that beginning consultants may approach their role assuming the consultant behaves as an expert, believing consultants have all the answers and must tell teachers what to do. However, effective consultants do not initially offer solutions but gather information (Salmon & Fenning, 1993).

Rosenfield (1985) suggests that the consultant's recommendations alone may not provide sufficient motivation for the teacher to utilize as intervention. Instead, the consultant must actively market the procedure by educating the teacher as to its potential benefits and advantages versus those of techniques already in place.

Finally, teachers have reported that they would be more likely to maintain a student exhibiting behavioral problems in the classroom if they received greater support and assistance to deal with that student (Myles & Simpson, 1989). Further, teachers' perception of their ability to deal with such problems successfully can improve when a consultant not only offers behavior management procedures but also suggests efficient instructional strategies and assists in obtaining smaller class size or additional classroom staff (Gerber & Semmel, 1984).

PART

II

Understanding
and Evaluating
Classroom Behavior

CHAPTER

3

Functional Behavioral Assessment of Classroom Behavior

Mark W. Steege, F. Charles "Bud" Mace, and
Rachel Brown-Chidsey

Functional Behavioral Assessment (FBA) is one of the most significant developments to affect school psychology practice (Mace, 1994). In the 1970s, classroom consultants began to emphasize behavioral approaches to improve children's social and academic performance (e.g., Bergan, 1977). However, behavioral technologies at that time were limited to a collection of procedures known as *behavior modification* that included token economies, time out, and various interventions based on punishment and positive and negative reinforcement (Kazdin, 1975a; Sulzer-Azaroff & Mayer, 1977). Although numerous research studies demonstrated that behavior modification was effective for reducing interfering behaviors and improving academic performance, the technology was widely seen to have significant limitations. First, critics of behavior modification claimed the interventions simply suppressed interfering behavior through the use of artificial and conspicuous tangible rewards (e.g., candy, games) and unnecessarily punitive measures (e.g., time out, response cost, overcorrection). As a result, the acceptability of behavior modification diminished among educational professionals and parents (Witt & Elliott, 1982). A second concern was that behavior

43

modification generally gives little consideration to why a student may be engaging in interfering behavior or failing to perform well academically. The conditions that compete with or interfere with pro-social behavior are not identified and taken into consideration when designing interventions. As a result, behavior modification was criticized for emphasizing the needs of care providers to have compliant children, rather than identifying the needs being met by interfering behavior in order to teach pro-social alternatives to meet those needs (Winett & Winkler, 1972).

Functional Behavioral Assessment leads to a very different approach to behavioral intervention. The goal of FBA is to identify the reasons why a student engages in interfering behavior or is doing poor academically. Using a variety of assessment methods, classroom consultants assess the presence or absence of motivating variables, triggering events, and reinforcing consequences for both interfering and pro-social behavior. By identifying events that motivate, trigger, and reinforce interfering behavior, the classroom consultant is able to design interventions for the individual student that alter these variables to promote pro-social behavior and concurrently reduce interfering behavior (Watson & Steege, 2003).

In this chapter, we suggest a multistage process for conducting an FBA and implementing FBA-based interventions, provide an overview of assessments methods available to conduct an FBA, and illustrate the application of FBA methods with two children—one with interfering behaviors associated with an emotional disability and the other whose disruptive behavior was related to academic difficulties. We begin with a brief review of the historical origins of FBA illustrating its strong linkage to behavioral psychology and applied behavior analysis.

The Origins of Functional Behavioral Assessment

FBA has its roots in the behavioral psychology of B. F. Skinner. After 3 decades of laboratory research with animals, Skinner and his colleagues had delineated many of the basic principles that influence the behavior of most mammals, including humans. The first extensions of these principles beyond the laboratory were interpretive. Extrapolations were made from laboratory-derived principles to human behavior in various social contexts (F. S. Keller & Schonfeld, 1950; Skinner, 1948, 1953). Behavioral accounts of human behavior were offered that emphasized the role of contingencies of reinforcement in shaping and maintaining a wide range of behaviors including psychopathology, educational practices, and self-control.

Early applications of behavioral principles to mental health problems reflected this functional account of behavior. For example, Ayllon and Michael (1959) successfully treated a psychiatric inpatient who compulsively hoarded towels. On the assumption that towels were reinforcing, Ayllon and Michael provided the patient with an unlimited amount of towels invoking the principle of satiation to reduce towel hoarding. Similarly, D. R. Thomas, Becker, and Armstrong (1968) hypothesized that a student's disruptive behavior was related to teacher attention. By alternately supplying teacher attention for disruptive behavior and then extinguishing disruption by withholding attention, the researchers demonstrated that the student's interfering behavior was positively reinforced by attention.

Bijou, Peterson, and Ault (1968) developed the first systematic assessment methodology to identify environmental influences on behavior. They devised a data collection system to record observations of events antecedent and subsequent to child behaviors and demonstrated that the frequency of targeted behaviors covaried with specific environmental situations (e.g., instructions, physical proximity). This methodology was the first *descriptive* approach to FBA and it has been refined and applied across a wide range of populations, target behaviors and settings (Lalli, Browder, Mace, & Brown, 1993; Mace & Lalli, 1991; Sasso et al., 1992). Touchette, MacDonald, and Langer (1985) developed a descriptive assessment methodology for low-frequency interfering behaviors called the *scatterplot*. Counts of behavior, activities, and staffing patterns are recorded in blocks of time throughout the day in order to identify times and events that are correlated with more and less interfering behavior. Several authors have developed *functional assessment interviews* aimed at obtaining similar information from teachers and parents (Bergan, 1977; Iwata, Dorsey, Slifer, & Bauman, 1982; R. O'Neill, Horner, Albin, Storey, & Sprague, 1997; see Indirect FBA methods in the following section and Watson & Steege, 2003).

Other researchers directly manipulated environmental variables hypothesized to motivate, trigger, or reinforce interfering behavior. To simulate natural conditions, environmental events are systematically presented to the individual being assessed and the frequency of target behaviors is recorded. These data are compared to a control condition in which the environmental events in question are not present. This hypothesis testing approach was first developed by Carr in the assessment of self-injurious behavior (Carr, Newsome, & Binkoff, 1976) and aggression (Carr, Newsome, & Binkoff, 1980) in persons with developmental disabilities. Expanding Carr's single variable test, Iwata et al.

(1982) developed a comprehensive FBA methodology that allowed testing of three or more hypotheses at the same time. The individual is exposed to different test conditions and a control condition that are alternated in multielement single case design. This methodology is known as *functional analysis* and it allows for the assessment of the effects of attention, tangible reinforcement, escape/avoidance of demands, and sensory reinforcement on one or more target behaviors. The Iwata et al. (1982) methodology has been widely applied to a wide range of social and academic behaviors in school-age children (see McComas & Mace, 2000).

In the following section, we provide an overview of FBA procedures and suggest a process that can lead to valid identification of behavioral function, yet is efficient for use in daily practice. Each FBA methodology is described and its potential applications and limitations are identified.

Functional Behavioral Assessment Procedures

Functional Behavioral Assessment is a process for understanding why interfering behaviors occur. Functional Behavioral Assessment is both (a) a theoretical framework for understanding human behavior and (b) a set of assessment procedures (Steege & Brown-Chidsey, 2005). From a best-practices perspective, a FBA involves the use of a multi-method, multi-source, multi-setting assessment process (Knoff, 2002). Within this model, information is gathered using several assessment procedures (e.g., interviews, direct observation) across informants (e.g., teachers, parents) and environments (e.g., classrooms, home, school, community).

FBA Process

There are five key components included in a comprehensive and defensible FBA:

1. Identify and describe behaviors that interfere with a student's acquisition and/or display of skills and social behaviors.
2. Identify and describe controlling variables:
   - Antecedents (events that motivate and trigger interfering behaviors).
   - Individual (e.g., language skills, social skills, medical variables).
   - Consequences (e.g., social attention, withdrawal of task).
3. Determine the magnitude of the behavior (e.g., frequency, duration, intensity).

4. Develop hypotheses regarding the function(s) of behavior.
5. Design FBA-based interventions.

Identification and Description of Interfering Behavior

Perhaps the easiest part of the FBA process is the identification of interfering behaviors. Parents, teachers, and staff are unusually quite adept at identifying behaviors that are problematic. The description of behaviors is a critical step because the accuracy of the FBA is dependent on precise definitions of behavior. Behaviors need to be described such that the definition is understandable to all members of the team. As a general rule, a description of behavior should be objective, clear and complete (Kazdin, 1975b). To be objective, the description should refer to observable features and not to internal characteristics or intentions. To be clear, the definition should be unambiguous so that it can be accurately repeated by others. To be complete, the definition must delineate all observable characteristics of the behavior (Watson & Steege, 2003).

Identification and Description of Controlling Variables

The identification and description of interfering behaviors includes use of at least one of the following behavioral assessment methodologies: (a) Indirect FBA, (b) Direct-Descriptive FBA, and (c) Functional Analysis.

Indirect Functional Behavioral Assessment

Indirect FBA methods are characterized by the assessment of behavior based on information provided by teachers, parents, staff, and in some cases, the referred person (Steege & Brown-Chidsey, 2005). Examples of indirect FBA procedures include record review, unstructured interviews, semistructured interviews, behavior rating scales, adaptive behavior scales, and social skills assessments, among others. Table 3.1 includes

Table 3.1   Indirect FBA methods

Method	Source
Functional assessment interview	O'Neill et al. (1997)
Functional behavioral assessment screening form	Watson & Steege (2003)
Behavioral stream interview	Watson & Steege (2003)
Antecedent variables assessment form	Watson & Steege (2003)
Individual variables assessment form	Watson & Steege (2003)
Consequence variables assessment form	Watson & Steege (2003)
Functional assessment informant record for teachers	Edwards (2002)

examples of several interview procedures. One example of an Indirect FBA procedure that is especially relevant to school settings is the Functional Assessment Informant Record for Teachers (FAIR-T; Edwards, 2002). The FAIR-T is a teacher-completed record form that allows educators to identify interfering behaviors and to report and describe information about setting events, antecedents, consequences, and previously implemented interventions.

Due to their relative efficiency and cost-effectiveness, conducting an FBA using only Indirect FBA procedures has some appeal. However, interviews are subject to reporting errors and biased accounts of behaviors and related controlling variables. These errors will likely result in inaccurate information, faulty hypotheses and ineffective interventions (Watson & Steege, 2003). In many cases, the Indirect FBA is the first step in conducting a comprehensive FBA. If the results of the Indirect FBA are consistent across informants and the practitioner is able to form solid hypotheses regarding behavioral function, then additional assessments may not be indicated. In these cases, the validity of the FBA will be determined by the effectiveness of the intervention (Watson & Steege, 2003). If, on the other hand, the practitioner is not confident about the results of assessment and hypotheses are tentative at best, then additional assessments are indicated. In these cases, the next phase of the FBA process typically involves the use of direct observations and recordings of behavior (Steege & Brown-Chidsey, 2005).

Direct Descriptive Functional Behavioral Assessment Procedures

Direct Descriptive FBA procedures include observation and recording of interfering behaviors and associated antecedents and consequences. Unlike indirect assessment methods where information is based on informant-report, direct assessment includes observations of the individual within natural settings (e.g., classrooms, cafeteria, playground, home). Direct types of recording procedures include anecdotal recording methods (i.e., observing and writing a narrative description of behaviors and relevant variables) and behavior recording procedures (e.g., frequency, duration, intensity of behaviors). Observations may be conducted directly by the evaluator (e.g., school psychology practitioner) or by a trained observer (e.g., classroom teacher, educational technician, parent). Table 3.2 includes examples of several Direct Descriptive FBA procedures.

Two Direct Descriptive FBA procedures that we have found to be particularly useful are the Functional Behavioral Assessment Observation Form (FBAOF; Watson & Steege, 2003) and the Interval Recording Procedure (IRP; Watson & Steege, 2003). The FBAOF is an extension

Table 3.2   Direct descriptive FBA methods

Method	Source
Antecedent-Behavior-Consequence (ABC)	O'Neill et al. (1997)
Conditional probability record	Watson & Steege (2003)
Functional behavioral assessment observation form	Watson & Steege (2003)
Functional assessment observation form	O'Neill et al. (1997)
Interval recording procedure	Watson & Steege (2003)
Task difficulty antecedent analysis form	Watson & Steege (2003)

of the standard ABC (antecedent-behavior-consequence) assessment model and involves direct observation and recording of interfering behaviors and associated contextual variables (e.g., time of day, setting events, antecedents, consequences) for each behavioral incident. The FBAOF may be used directly by the evaluator or by teachers/staff/parents to record behavioral incidents on an ongoing basis. The FBAOF is particularly useful in recording low frequency behavioral episodes (e.g., behaviors that occur a few times per day or per week).

The IRP (Watson & Steege, 2003) involves a process of: (a) identifying and describing interfering and appropriate behaviors, (b) designing recording procedures that are matched to the dimensions of each interfering behavior, (c) identifying predetermined intervals to record behavior (e.g., 5, 10, 15, 30 min), (d) designing a behavior recording form, and (e) recording behaviors and related contextual variables (e.g., setting events, immediate antecedents, relevant staff persons) at specified intervals throughout the school day. The IRP allows for an examination of the relationship of interfering variables with factors such as time of day, setting events (activities, assignments, etc.), other interfering behaviors, appropriate behaviors, and teaching staff. In addition, the IRP serves as a running record of the rate of occurrence of each target behavior and as such is used to determine baseline levels of interfering behaviors and as a procedure for progress monitoring in determining the effectiveness of interventions.

Thus, Direct Descriptive FBA procedures may be used to: (a) document the occurrence of interfering behaviors and associated triggers, antecedents and consequence, and (b) measure the magnitude (e.g., frequency, duration, intensity) of interfering behaviors over time. While Indirect and Direct Descriptive FBA procedures are valuable in identifying associated (or spurious) contextual variables, a true functional relationship between these variables and interfering behaviors has not been demonstrated. To validate hypotheses regarding functional relationships between the interfering behavior and contextual variables, you need to conduct a *functional analysis* (Brown-Chidsey & Steege, 2005).

Functional analysis refers to an assessment model in which environmental events are systematically manipulated and examined within single case experimental designs (McComas & Mace, 2000). Functional analysis procedures involve an experimental analysis of the cause-effect relationships between interfering behavior and specific predetermined antecedents and consequences. Functional analysis involves a structural and a consequence analysis, used either singularly or in combination. A structural analysis is a process for testing hypotheses about variables that appear to trigger interfering behaviors and involves arranging antecedent conditions and recording subsequent interfering behaviors (O'Neil et al., 1997). A consequence analysis is conducted to confirm hypotheses about variables that appear to reinforce interfering behaviors and involves arranging situations and providing specific consequences contingent on the occurrence of interfering behaviors (e.g., O'Neil et al., 1997; Steege, Wacker, Berg, Cigrand, & Cooper, 1989; Steege et al., 1990). Both brief (Steege & Northup, 1998) and extended (e.g., Iwata et al., 1982) models for conducting functional behavior analyses have been described. Both procedures involve the observation of behavior and the direct manipulation of antecedent and/or consequence variables for the purpose of empirically identifying behavioral function(s). The brief functional analysis model incorporates the same general procedures as the extended analysis, except the number and duration of assessment sessions is limited (Watson & Steege, 2003).

While a functional analysis is the "gold standard" for assessing interfering behaviors, there are many situations that preclude its use. For example, functional analysis methods may be contraindicated in cases in which: (a) the interfering behavior is dangerous to the individual (e.g., severe self-injury) or to others (e.g., aggression), (b) the interfering behavior is of such a low rate that observation is unlikely (e.g., high intensity but low rate property destruction), (c) direct observation causes the individual to change his/her behavior (i.e., reactivity), (d) the situation is at a point of crisis and immediate intervention is required, and/or (e) staff trained to complete either a brief or extended functional analysis are not readily available. Furthermore, although a functional analysis may be highly accurate at the time of assessment, changes in antecedent and consequence variables may result in a "morphing" of behavioral function over time (Steege & Brown-Chidsey, 2005).

Measuring the Magnitude of Behavior. Measuring the magnitude of behavior is an objective way of determining its severity. For example, is the frequency of self-injurious hand biting once per day or 355 times per day? Is the cumulative duration of tantrum behavior 2 minutes per school day or 124 minutes per school day? As stated previously, Direct Descriptive procedures are particularly useful for documenting behavior magnitude. There are several methods for recording various dimensions of behavior (e.g., frequency, duration, interval, intensity, performance-based). The selection of the recording procedure is determined by each of the following considerations: (a) the dimensions of the behavior (i.e., topography, frequency, duration), (b) the goals of the intervention, and (c) pragmatic considerations such as time, resources, and competency of observers (Watson & Steege, 2003).

Determining Functions of Behavior

A functional relationship refers to a cause-effect relationship between an independent variable and a dependent variable (Skinner, 1953). Consider the case of the high school student who displays inappropriate verbal comments during a social studies class. The inappropriate verbal comments (the dependent variable) is predictably followed by laughter from classmates (the independent variable). The frequency and duration of inappropriate verbal comments increased over time, thereby showing a cause-and-effect, or functional relationship.

When conducting an FBA, the *function* of a specific interfering behavior refers to the variables that are reinforcing the behavior. There are three possible functions of behavior: (1) positive reinforcement (e.g., social attention, access to tangibles and activities), (2) negative reinforcement (e.g., escape for or avoidance of unpleasant stimuli or situations), and (3) automatic reinforcement (e.g., sensory consequences). Analysis of the relationships among the observed antecedents, individual variables and consequences of behavior results in the identification of the function of behavior. It is important to recognize that a single behavior may have multiple function(s). For example, aggressive behaviors exhibited by a high school student may be reinforced by attention from classmates and by the removal (e.g., being sent to the principal's office) from difficult classes. In this case, the functions of aggressive behavior are positive reinforcement (i.e., attention from classmates) and negative reinforcement (i.e., termination of participation in aversive classroom situations).

Designing FBA-Based Interventions

During its formative years, FBA was often referred to as a prescriptive process in which the results of assessment directly lead to the identification of specific interventions (e.g., Steege et al., 1989). More recently, the selection of interventions has included a problem-solving process that incorporates an "exploring solutions" stage in which relevant antecedents, individual variables, and the functions of behavior are considered (Steege & Brown-Chidsey, 2005). Identification of antecedents allows for the design of antecedent modification strategies to reduce the probability of the occurrence of interfering behaviors. Analysis of individual variables allows for the selection of logical replacement behaviors; these are behaviors that when increased may concomitantly result in a decrease or elimination of interfering behaviors. In most cases, this involves teaching behaviors that are either motorically incompatible with the interfering behavior or that are functionally-equivalent to the interfering behavior. An understanding of the function(s) of the interfering behavior informs interventions in the following ways: (a) the intervention includes procedures for making sure that the reinforcing contingencies are not delivered (e.g., extinction procedures), (b) stimuli and events that reinforce interfering behavior may be used to reinforce appropriate behaviors, (c) knowing the *schedule of reinforcement* that maintains interfering behavior is important because the intervention may then be tailored to provide a more dense schedule of reinforcement for appropriate behavior (Steege et al., 1990; Wacker et al., 1990).

FBA of Disruptive Behavior Related to a Student's Emotional Disability

Although the majority published research on FBA has been with individuals with developmental disabilities, the methodology has clear potential for use with other populations (e.g., Mace & West, 1986; Northup, Brousard, Jones, George, Vollmer, & Herring, 1995). The following example, illustrates application of FBA to identify environmental influences on the severely disruptive behavior of a student with an emotional disability.

Lucy

Lucy is a 12-year-old girl placed in a self-contained classroom for children with emotional disabilities and other health impairments. She has a history of emotional and physical abuse that resulted in her separation from her birth family at the age of 8. Since that time Lucy has lived in three different therapeutic foster homes. Each home placement has been strained by Lucy's oppositional and disruptive behavior. The foster parents in Lucy's first two foster homes withdrew the placement because they believed they could not manage Lucy's behavior; both families characterized Lucy as "out of control." Lucy's current foster placement is also at risk for termination and residential placement is being considered.

At school, Lucy engages in numerous behaviors that disrupt classroom instruction and other activities. Her disruption takes the form of speaking loudly at inappropriate times, screaming, offensive profanity, throwing objects across the room and in the direction of others, knocking over furniture, and minor property destruction (damaging papers, books, and various school supplies). On three occasions, Lucy's disruptive behavior escalated to the level in which she became physically aggressive toward other students, necessitating physical restraint on one occasion to maintain a safe environment for Lucy and others in her classroom.

Lucy is a very capable student in many respects. Her scores on tests of cognitive ability place in her in the above average range, with special strengths in the areas of language and abstract reasoning. However, Lucy's academic performance in class is highly variable, tending to cycle from above average/excellent to poor. Her teacher reports that these cycles in academic performance covary inversely with bouts of disruptive and oppositional behavior.

This suggests that resolution of Lucy's interfering behavior may have beneficial effects on her school work.

Functional Behavioral Assessment Activities

Following a referral for behavioral services, the classroom consultant conducted a joint FBA interview with Lucy's special education teacher and the educational technician who normally works with Lucy. Lucy's long history of disruptive classroom behavior and her placement in a special education classroom obviated the need for standardized measures of child behavior to establish that Lucy's behavior was clinically significant. The FBA interview was useful for identifying the behaviors of primary concern and obtaining their operational definitions (Iwata et al., 1982; R. O'Neill et al., 1997; Watson & Steege, 2003). However, both respondents reported that Lucy had good days and bad days and that, when Lucy engaged in disruptive behavior, it occurred throughout the school day and did not appear to occur more in one situation than another. For this reason, the classroom consultant chose to conduct a Direct Descriptive FBA during different classroom activities in an attempt to identify events that may be influencing Lucy's disruptive behavior.

The Descriptive FBA employed the methods described by Bijou et al. (1986) and Mace and Lalli (1991), in two phases. The first phase assessed the influence of a broad range of antecedent events on Lucy's disruption. The second phase focused on the situation associated with the most disruptive behavior in order to identify the elements of that situation that evoked disruption. All events in both phases were recorded during continuous 10-s intervals using a partial-interval recording procedure for antecedent and subsequent events, and a count within interval procedure for disruptive behavior. The antecedent events recorded in the first phase included academic activities, periods of transition from one activity to another, leisure/recreational activities, and unstructured activities (with few performance demands, and low levels of adult attention and activity stimulation). Two categories of Lucy's disruptive behavior were recorded: verbal disruptions (loud comments, screaming, profanity) and motor disruptions (inappropriate use of materials and furniture as described earlier). Events occurring subsequent to disruptive behavior that have the potential to reinforce it were recorded including task avoidance, adult/peer attention, and activity changes.

The results of the first phase of the Descriptive FBA are presented in Figure 3.1. Lucy's disruptive behavior occurred most often during academic activities. Fifty-four percent of the intervals scored as academic activities were followed by disruption within 20 seconds. Less evocative were unstructured activities and transition periods. Disruptive behavior following these situations occurred 28% and 17% of the time, respectively. By contrast, during preferred leisure and recreational activities, Lucy displayed infrequent disruption (3% of the intervals observed). Events occurring subsequent to disruptive behavior during academic activities varied. Forty-five percent of disruptive behaviors were followed

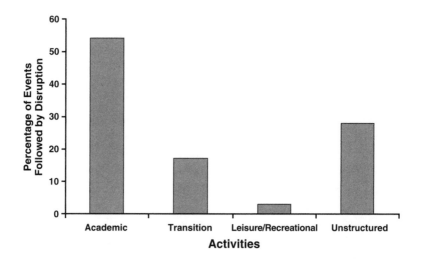

Figure 3.1 Effects of antecedent events on disruption: Classroom activities

by task avoidance, 60% were followed by attention, and 12% led to activity changes.

In an attempt to clarify which aspects of academic activities were more likely to evoke disruptive behavior, a second phase of Descriptive FBA was conducted. Academic activities were classified as individual seat work (math, spelling), group lecture (math, grammar, social studies, science), group reading, individual instruction (math), and group table activities (science, art). In addition to data on verbal and motor disruptions, appropriate questions and comments were also recorded. Results of the second phase of FBA are presented in Figures 3.2 and 3.3. Lucy engaged in disruptive behavior at similar levels in all forms of academic activity except individual instruction. Disruptive behavior followed individual seat work 47% of the time, group lecture 56% of the time, group reading 41% of the time, and group table activities 50% of the time (see Figure 3.1). By contrast, Lucy engaged in much less disruptive behavior during individual instruction (11%). One variable that differentiated individual instruction from the other academic activities was the availability of adult attention. Figure 3.3 shows the likelihood that Lucy's appropriate questions or comments would result in adult attention compared to her disruptive behaviors. During all types of academic activities except individual instruction, adult attention followed Lucy's disruptive behavior 82% of the time compared to only 13% of the time

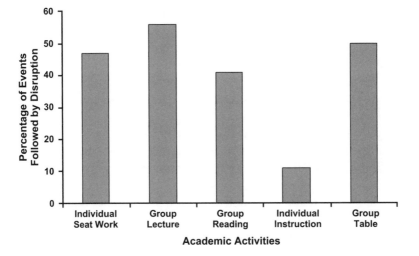

Figure 3.2 Effects of antecedent events on disruption: Academic instructional activities

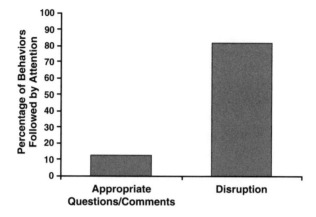

Figure 3.3 Effectiveness of appropriate questions/comments
versus disruption

for her appropriate behavior. Findings from both phases of the FBA
findings suggest that Lucy is more likely to engage in disruptive behavior
when she is involved in academic activities that afford comparatively little adult attention. And although Lucy does ask appropriate questions
and make appropriate comments during these academic activities, they
infrequently meet with adult attention. Her disruptive behavior is far
more likely to result in attention in these situations. Thus, the hypothesized function of Lucy's disruption was positively reinforced by adult attention when her appropriate comments were not attended to.

Intervention and Progress Monitoring

Based on the FBA results, a simple intervention recommended by the
classroom consultant was implemented during a 4-week period. The
goals of the intervention were to (a) increase the percentage of Lucy's
appropriate questions/comments that were responded to, and (b) minimize adult attention for disruptive behavior. The classroom consultant
met with Lucy's teacher and the educational technician to discuss the
FBA findings and the recommended intervention. Both school staff
were unaware that they did not respond to many of Lucy's appropriate
comments. The team generated a list of appropriate questions/com-
ments that Lucy had made to increase awareness of the kinds of verbalizations the staff would aim to respond to. The educational technician
offered to be primarily responsible for observing and responding to
Lucy's questions/comments, or prompting another member of staff to do
so if she was unavailable at that time. The classroom consultant also

made recommendations for methods of redirecting Lucy when she became disruptive that would re-engage her in the assigned activity and minimize attention for the disruptive behavior. Because Lucy's disruptive behavior occurred too frequently for staff to keep records of the behavior during the entire school day, the classroom consultant took observational data for 1-hour periods, once per week during the intervention period. Lucy's pre-intervention rates of disruption were 87 per hour. During the 4 weeks of intervention, these rates dropped to 58/hr, 45/hr, 14/hr, and 6/hr, respectively.

Functional Behavioral Assessment Showing Problem Behavior Related to Academic Difficulties

Functional Behavioral Assessment methods can be used to evaluate many types of school behaviors, including externalizing problem behaviors as well as academic behaviors such as reading and math skill acquisition and performance. The following example shows how FBA methods can be used to identify the function of a student's off-task problem behaviors. In this example, the student's out-of-seat and off-task behaviors were related to reading and math skill deficits, thus the FBA provided a way to identify and address both academic and behavioral difficulties.

Casey

Casey is a 9-year-old third grader. Casey lives with her father who is a sergeant in the Marine Corps. Casey's parents are divorced and she sees her mother during specific holidays. Casey has moved five times in her lifetime, having spent 2 years living with her grandparents during one of her dad's deployments. Casey's school records indicate that she has had mixed success in school. In Kindergarten, Casey was described as a "bubbly sweet girl" who "enjoys everything about school." Her first-grade teacher reported that Casey "was more interested in social activities than learning." Casey's family moved in November of her second-grade year; the end of year report for second-grade indicated that Casey was not on grade level in reading and math.

In October of Casey's third-grade year, her teacher contacted the student assistance team (SAT) at her school to request help for Casey. The teacher reported that Casey was loveable, but demanded too much attention. She indicated that Casey was out of her seat "all the time" and rarely finished any assignments. The teacher indicated that she had tried a "behavior plan" with Casey that included earning stickers for every assignment she completed. The teacher stated with frustration, "it's just not working."

Funcrtional Behavioral Assessment Activities

The FBA of Casey's behavior began with a review of records. The cumulative folder was reviewed to learn the details about Casey's school history. Next, Casey's teacher and father were interviewed to learn more details about her school performance. Casey's father reported that Casey does like school, but finds it very difficult. He said that getting Casey to do her homework is very difficult and she often breaks into tears and hides in her room. He said he has tried to help Casey with homework but that Casey "lacks discipline." He has used "time-out" procedures at home when she refuses to do her homework and most nights the homework does not get done.

Casey's teacher reported that Casey started the year with enthusiasm and energy. The teacher said that she had to move Casey's desk in late September due to her frequent talking with other girls seated near her. The teacher reported that Casey can do the work expected of her but she is off task all the time. When asked during which subjects Casey is more or less off-task, the teacher reported that Casey is most attentive during morning meeting, social studies, and at dismissal, but often out of her seat and not paying attention during reading, math, and science. The teacher noted that Casey's favorite class is physical education.

Next, a set of structured observations was conducted in Casey's classroom and during her physical education class. These occurred over a period of 3 days so that Casey could be observed across a variety of instructional settings. Each observation lasted for 30 minutes and included recordings of Casey's behavior at 6-second intervals. At the end of each 6-second interval, Casey's behavior was coded and recorded according to three behavior types: (1) on-task, (2) off-task verbal, (3) off-task motor. On-task behavior was defined as any behavior that included looking at, touching, or talking about the assigned activity. Off-task verbal was defined as any verbalizations made by Casey that were not related to the assigned activity. For example, when Casey spoke with another student about what to play at recess, it was coded as off-task verbal. Off-task motor was defined as any motor activity made by Casey that was not related to the assignment. For example, when Casey got out of her seat and went to another student's desk and showed off a new bracelet, that was coded off-task motor. Observations were conducted during reading, math, social studies, and physical education instruction sessions. In addition to the recordings of Casey's behavior, a randomly selected same-sex classroom peer was observed to learn whether Casey's behaviors were different from others in her classroom. A summary of the observation data is found in Table 3.3.

During the math lesson, the teacher demonstrated how to add fractions with common denominators. She used an overhead projector to show the students the steps and then distributed a worksheet with 20 fraction problems for the students to complete. During the reading lesson, the teacher began by asking the students to get their reading journals and to write for 10 minutes. Next, the teacher told the students to get with a "reading buddy" and to read from chapter 3 of the reading book. During the social studies lesson, the teacher posted a map of Africa and showed students the location of specific countries. Then, the students were given outline maps of Africa and told to locate and label the countries on a corresponding list. During the physical education class, the students practiced soccer drills and then played a short soccer game for 15 minutes.

The observational data revealed that Casey was off-task much more often than the observed peer during math and reading; however, Casey was on-task at a rate similar to her peer during social studies and physical education. In addition to the observational data, additional classroom data were considered. The worksheets that Casey was expected to have completed during the academic subjects were reviewed. A review of Casey's journal showed that she wrote part of one sentence and then

Table 3.3   Observations of Casey's behavior using momentary
6-second time sample recording

Subject (Day/Time)	On-Task (%)		Off-Task Verbal (%)		Off-Task Motor (%)	
	Casey	Peer	Casey	Peer	Casey	Peer
Reading (10/11, 9:40–10:10)	57	96	21	4	22	0
Math (10/12, 1:45–2:15)	62	93	20	3	18	4
Social studies (10/12, 11:00–11:30)	98	97	2	3	0	0
Physical education (10/11, 1:10–1:40)	96	95	2	3	2	2

Table 3.4   Casey's curriculum-based measurement scores on reading and math

Grade Level	Reading		Math	
	Casey	Target	Casey	Target
Grade 3	4	49–103	2	13–24
Grade 2	9	27–79	4	8–20
Grade 1	12	2–22	6	5–15

stopped. Her teacher reported that the students are expected to write at least five sentences in a journal entry at this point in the year. On the math worksheet, Casey filled in the denominator on all the problem answers, but only two of the numerators were completed; both of these were 1 + 1. Casey's map of Africa was very detailed and included both the countries listed on the handout as well as others. Of note, Casey was observed to say during the map activity that her dad had been posted to three different places in Africa.

The data collected so far suggest that Casey has the skills necessary to fill in a map of Africa and play soccer, but something was interfering with her completion of assigned work in reading and math. In order to evaluate Casey's general reading and math skills, curriculum-based measurement probes were administered (see Table 3.4). First, third-grade reading and math skill probes were given to Casey. Casey scored well below the expected level for third graders on these probes so second-grade probes were given next. On the second-grade probes, Casey's scores showed that she was still below second-grade expectations. First-grade CBM probes were given next. Casey's scored in the range of scores set as a target for students in the fall of first grade. The CBM data revealed that Casey appears to have significant skill deficits in reading and math. Together with the other assessment data, a tentative hypothesis about Casey's classroom behavior is that Casey engages in off-task verbal and motor behaviors in order to escape and avoid reading and math assignments that she does not (yet) have the skills to complete (see Table 3.5).

Intervention and Progress Monitoring

Based on the FBA data, an intervention for Casey was developed that focused on improving her reading and math skills. Casey was placed in

Table 3.5   Hypothesized functions of Casey's classroom behavior

Interfering behavior	Off-task.
Description	Verbal, visual, and motor behaviors not related to assigned activities.
Recording procedure	6-second momentary time sample.
Antecedent variables	Assigned activity requires skills that Casey does not yet have.
Individual (organism) variables	Different rates of participation during preferred versus nonpreferred activities.
Consequences	Task avoidance.
Magnitude	57–62% off task during nonpreferred activities.
Hypothesized function(s)	By engaging in off-task behavior Casey avoids working on assignments that are difficult for her.

reading and math groups in her classroom that worked on the skills she needed to develop. For reading, her teacher worked with Casey for 30 minutes per day in a small group of four students learning sound-symbol matching and word attack skills. Casey's progress in reading was monitored using weekly 1-minute second-grade oral reading fluency passages. For math, Casey's teacher worked with her in a small group of three students that performed addition and subtraction of single digits up to 10 for 20 minutes each day. Casey's progress in math was monitored using weekly 2-minute second-grade math fluency probes. Second-grade items were selected for progress monitoring because Casey's baseline skills were so far below the third-grade level that they might not detect growth in her skills. In addition to monitoring Casey's progress in reading and math, her on-task behavior was monitored weekly. The classroom consultant observed Casey each Friday for 10 minutes each of reading and math instruction to determine whether the interventions also produced more on-task behavior. Casey's progress after 3 weeks of intervention is summarized in Figure 3.4.

Casey made gains in both reading and math during the 3 weeks of initial intervention. She also showed an increase in on-task behavior as compared with the baseline observations. Although still below the level expected of third-grade students, Casey's gains suggest that the selected

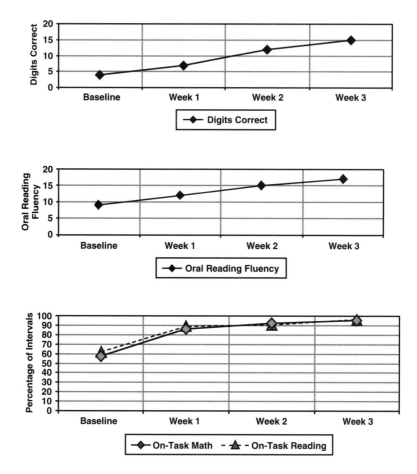

Figure 3.4 Results of Casey's intervention

interventions have improved her skills in the target areas. These results appear to confirm the hypothesis that Casey's off-task behavior had served the function of escaping and avoiding reading and math tasks that she did not know how to do. When given instruction matched to her current needs and skills, Casey was considerably more on-task during class.

Summary

Functional Behavioral Assessment refers to the broad range of assessment procedures available to identify environmental influences on behavior. Functional Behavioral Assessment procedures can be used for both academic and behavioral problems. Indirect and Direct Descriptive FBA procedures are used to: (a) identify interfering behaviors, (b) describe behaviors in behavioral terms, (c) identify environmental antecedents and consequences, (d) identify related individual variables, (e) measure the magnitude of behavior, and (e) identify hypotheses regarding the function(s) of behaviors. Functional analysis procedures are used to test experimentally these hypotheses and objectively determine which variables are controlling the occurrence of interfering behaviors. The results of the FBA are used as the basis for designing individually tailored intervention strategies.

CHAPTER 4

Cognition, Learning, and Behavior: The Role of Intellectual Processes in Classroom Behavior

JACK A. NAGLIERI, CARA CONWAY, AND SAM GOLDSTEIN

Billy enters the room with his usual flair and high level of energy. He yells I'm here! only to be told by the teacher that he needs to put his belongings away and be seated without disrupting the class. Billy begins to unload his backpack, until he sees his friend reading a new comic book across the room. As the teacher begins to take attendance, she notices that Billy's backpack is on the floor with crumpled papers spilling out, and Billy is out of his seat reading a comic book across the room. Once the teacher reminds Billy again that he is not following the morning routine, he quickly tries to organize his belongings and get to his seat. Only a few minutes later, Billy talks out of turn in the middle of the teacher's morning announcements to let the entire class know about the new puppy his dad brought home the previous day. Even though Billy is enthusiastic about being a part of the class, he has a difficult time controlling that energy. But why does Billy act this way? Why is it that, despite how much Billy wants to, it is so difficult for him to follow the classroom rules? How could an understanding of Billy's cognitive strengths and weakness help us understand Billy.

It has been well documented that intellectual processes impact children's achievement (see Naglieri, 2003, for a review). But do they play as powerful a role in shaping children's behavior and adjustment in the classroom? Could Billy's behavior be symptomatic of intellectual strengths and weaknesses? Could an understanding of those strengths and weaknesses help to change Billy's behavior? In this chapter, we offer a theory of intelligence based on the work of A. R. Luria accompanied by emerging research suggesting that intellectual processes play as powerful a role in affecting children's classroom behavior and adjustment as they do in achievement. The theory proposed was termed PASS, for Planning, Attention, Simultaneous, Successive cognitive processes, by Naglieri and Das (1997b) and operationalized with a test called the Cognitive Assessment System (CAS; Naglieri & Das, 1997a). The PASS theory provides a view of intelligence from the perspective of basic psychological processes that are associated with different brain regions.

A Modern Redefinition of Intelligence and Its Relationship to Behavior

To understand the cognitive components of Billy's behavior, it is best to move from a traditional approach of intelligence based on the concept of general intelligence to a multidimensional theory. The PASS theory is one view of intelligence that aims to define four basic abilities, termed basic psychological processes, which underlie performance in social as well as academic areas. The theory is rooted in A. R. Luria's research (1966, 1973b, 1980) about how the brain works (Das, Naglieri, & Kirby, 1994). Das and Naglieri and their colleagues used Luria's work as a blueprint for defining the important components of human intelligence. Their efforts represent an important effort to use neuropsychological theory to reconceptualize the concept of human intelligence.

Luria theorized that the four PASS processes could be conceptualized within a framework of three separate but related functional units. The three brain systems are referred to as functional units because the neuropsychological mechanisms each contribute unique abilities but they work in concert to achieve a specific goal. Luria (1973b) stated that "each form of conscious activity is always a complex functional system and takes place through the combined working of all three brain units, each of which makes its own contribution" (p. 99). This means that the four processes produced by the functional units form a "working constellation" (Luria, 1966, p. 70) of cognitive activity.

Brain Function, PASS, and Behavior

Each of the four PASS processes fall within one of the three functional units that can be associated with specific regions of the brain. The first functional unit (Attention) provides regulation of cortical arousal and attention; the second analyzes information using Simultaneous and Successive processes; and the third (Planning) provides for strategy development, strategy use, self-monitoring, and control of cognitive activities.

The first of the three functional units of the brain, the Attention-Arousal system, is located primarily in the brainstem. This unit provides the brain with the appropriate level of alertness, directive, and selective attention (Luria, 1973b). When a multidimensional stimulus array is presented to a person who is then required to pay attention to only one dimension, the inhibition of responding to other (often more salient) stimuli, and the allocation of attention to the central dimension, depends on the resources of the first functional unit. Luria stated that optimal conditions of arousal are needed before the more complex forms of attention involving "selective recognition of a particular stimulus and inhibition of responses to irrelevant stimuli" (Luria, 1973b, p. 271) can occur. Moreover, only when individuals are sufficiently aroused and their attention is adequately focused can they utilize processes in the second and third functional units. This ability to track cues, sustain attention, choose among potential responses, and self-monitor once a commitment is made to a particular behavior is critical for functioning effectively academically and behaviorally in the classroom. This construct was conceptualized and operationalized similarly to the attention work of Schneider, Dumais, and Shiffrin (1984) and Posner and Boies (1971) particularly the selectivity aspect of attention that relates to intentional discrimination between stimuli (Figure 4.1).

The second functional unit is associated with the occipital, parietal, and temporal lobes. This unit is responsible for receiving, processing, and retaining information a person obtains from the external world using Simultaneous and Successive processes. Simultaneous processing is a mental process that requires the child to integrate separate stimuli into a whole (Figure 4.2). It involves integrating stimuli into groups such that the interrelationships among the components can be understood. An essential feature of Simultaneous processing is the organization of interrelated parts into a cohesive whole. Simultaneous processing tests have strong spatial aspects for this reason. Simultaneous processing can be used to solve tasks with both nonverbal and verbal content as long as the cognitive demand of the task requires integration of information. Simultaneous processing underlies use and comprehension of grammatical

Strength		Weakness
Can multitask without loosing focus on overall objective	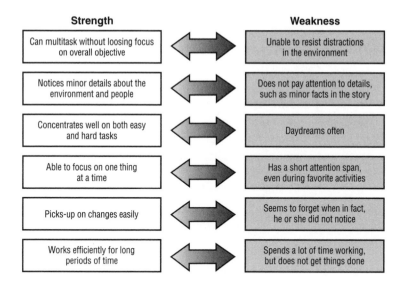	Unable to resist distractions in the environment
Notices minor details about the environment and people		Does not pay attention to details, such as minor facts in the story
Concentrates well on both easy and hard tasks		Daydreams often
Able to focus on one thing at a time		Has a short attention span, even during favorite activities
Picks-up on changes easily		Seems to forget when in fact, he or she did not notice
Works efficiently for long periods of time		Spends a lot of time working, but does not get things done

Figure 4.1 Behaviors associated with Attention

statements because they demand comprehension of word relationships, prepositions, and inflections so the person can obtain meaning based on the whole idea. For example, the use of Simultaneous processing is necessary in order to follow the direction: Put your book on the top shelf to the left of the door. This direction requires an understanding of the relationships among the different physical locations, the integration of the different parts of the direction into a single task, and the comprehension of logical and grammatical relationships. This construct of simultaneous processing is conceptually related to the examination of visual-spatial reasoning particularly found in progressive matrices tests such as those originally developed by Penrose and Raven (1936) and now included in nonverbal scales of intelligence tests such as the Wechsler Nonverbal Scale of Ability (Wechsler & Naglieri, 2006) and the Stanford-Binet Fifth Edition (Roid, 2003) as well as the simultaneous processing scale of the Kaufman Assessment Battery for Children, Second Edition (Kaufman & Kaufman, 2004).

Successive processing involves information that is linearly organized and integrated into a chainlike progression (Figure 4.3). This process is required when a child must arrange things in a strictly defined order where each element is only related to those that precede it, and these stimuli are not interrelated. For example, successive processing is involved in the decoding of unfamiliar words, production of syntagmatic aspects of

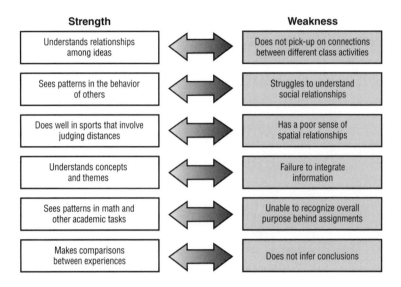

Figure 4.2 Behaviors associated with Simultaneous processing

language, and speech articulation. Following a sequence such as, Billy, put your coat on the hanger, then put your book in your cubby, and then go sit in your seat demands that the tasks and their order be remembered, which demands successive processing. Whenever information must be remembered or completed in a specific order, successive processing will be involved. This process, therefore, is involved in the perception of stimuli in sequence as well as the formation of sounds and movements in order. For this reason, successive processing is integral to activities such as phonological decoding and the syntax of language. Importantly, however, the information must not be able to be organized into a recognizable pattern (like the number 993311 organized into 99-33-11), but instead each element can only be related to those that precede it (like the number 958371). Successive processing is usually involved with the serial organization of sounds and movements in order and, therefore, it is integral to working with sounds in sequence and early reading. Successive processing has been conceptually and experimentally related to the concept of phonological analysis (Das, Naglieri, et al., 1994). The concept of successive processing is similar to the concept of sequential processing included in the K-ABCII (Kaufman & Kaufman, 2004), and tests that require recall of serial information such as Digit Span Forward.

The third functional unit is associated with the prefrontal areas of the frontal lobes of the brain (Luria, 1980), and provides what Naglieri and

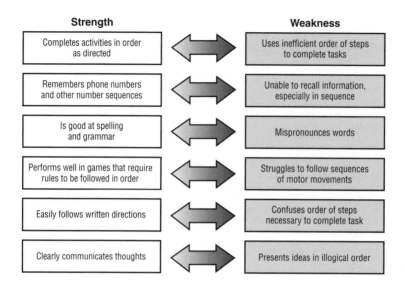

Strength		Weakness
Completes activities in order as directed		Uses inefficient order of steps to complete tasks
Remembers phone numbers and other number sequences		Unable to recall information, especially in sequence
Is good at spelling and grammar		Mispronounces words
Performs well in games that require rules to be followed in order		Struggles to follow sequences of motor movements
Easily follows written directions		Confuses order of steps necessary to complete task
Clearly communicates thoughts		Presents ideas in illogical order

Figure 4.3 Behaviors associated with successive processing

Das (1997b) call Planning processing. The prefrontal cortex plays a central role in forming goals and objectives and then in devising plans of action required to attain these goals. It selects the cognitive processes required to implement the plans, coordinates them, and applies them in a correct order. Finally, Planning processing is responsible for evaluating our actions as success or failure relative to our intentions (Goldberg, 2001, p. 24) and is one of the abilities that distinguishes humans from other primates. Planning, therefore, helps us achieve through the use of plans or strategies, and is critical to all activities where the child or adult has to determine how to solve a problem. This includes generation, evaluation, and execution of a plan as well as self-monitoring and impulse control. Thus, Planning allows for the solution of problems, control of attention, simultaneous, and successive processes, as well as selective utilization of knowledge and skills (Das, Kar, & Parrila, 1996) to provide for the most complex aspects of human behavior, including personality and consciousness (Das, 1980).

The essence of the construct of Planning and tests to measure it is that they provide a novel problem-solving situation for which children do not have a previously acquired strategy (Figure 4.4). This is the hallmark of the concept of executive function (Hayes, Gifford, & Ruckstuhl, 1996) and a view that is closely aligned with the definition of Planning provided by Goldberg (2001) particularly in that it includes

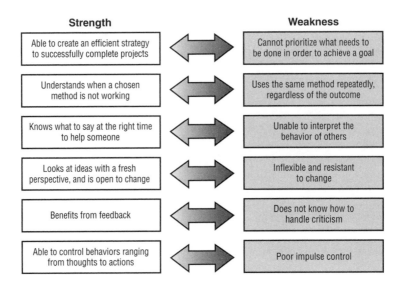

Strength		Weakness
Able to create an efficient strategy to successfully complete projects		Cannot prioritize what needs to be done in order to achieve a goal
Understands when a chosen method is not working		Uses the same method repeatedly, regardless of the outcome
Knows what to say at the right time to help someone		Unable to interpret the behavior of others
Looks at ideas with a fresh perspective, and is open to change		Inflexible and resistant to change
Benefits from feedback		Does not know how to handle criticism
Able to control behaviors ranging from thoughts to actions		Poor impulse control

Figure 4.4 Behaviors associated with planning processing

self-regulation, skillful and flexible use of strategies, allocation of attention and memory, response inhibition, goal setting, self-monitoring, and self-correction (Eslinger, 1996). Consider Billy's behavior; it is defined by impulsivity, disorganization, and problems with control of his behavior all of which can be attributed to a cognitive weakness in Planning.

How PASS Processes Are Assessed

The four PASS processes are assessed using the Cognitive Assessment System (CAS; Naglieri & Das, 1997a) which was specifically built according to the PASS theory. There is a strong empirical base to support both the theory and its operationalization in the CAS (see Das, Kirby, & Jarman, 1979; Das, Naglieri, et al., 1994; Naglieri, 1999, 2003, 2005; Naglieri & Das, 1997b, 2005b). The CAS measures the four basic psychological processes using 12 subtests (three for each of the four scales) and was standardized on a sample of 2,200 children aged 5 through 17 years who were representative of the U.S. population on a number of important demographic variables (see Naglieri & Das, 1997b, for more details). The CAS Full Scale has a high internal reliability ranging from .95 to .97 for the different age groups. The average reliability coefficients for the scales are .88 (Planning), .88 (Attention), .93 (Simultaneous processing), and .93 (Successive processing).

There is considerable evidence that the CAS can be used to gain an understanding of how well the child thinks and learns (Naglieri & Rojahn, 2004); to discover strengths and needs of children that can then be used for effective differential diagnosis (Naglieri, 2003, 2005); is particularly appropriate for assessment of minority children (Naglieri, Otero, DeLauder, & Matto, in press; Naglieri, Rojahn, & Matto, in press; Naglieri, Rojahn, Matto, & Aquilino, 2005) and to select or design appropriate interventions (Naglieri, 2003, 2005; Naglieri & Pickering, 2003).

While the CAS requires administration by a trained professional (e.g., a school psychologist), the four processes can be informally evaluated using a PASS rating scale included in Naglieri and Pickering's (2003) book *Helping Children Learn*. The teacher can complete this rating scale. The four processes can be informally evaluated using a PASS Rating Scale (Naglieri & Pickering, 2003). This scale can be reproduced for personal use.

PASS in Perspective

The field of intelligence has been dominated by measures of general ability since the early 1900s. General ability has been measured using subtests that differed in content along a verbal and nonverbal dichotomy. More recently, other factors such as working memory and speed have been introduced but they have been subsumed under the umbrella of general intelligence. The composition of traditional tests reflects the recognition of the value of general ability measured using tests that vary in content and specific requirements. There is a long and strong research base that supports the use of tests of general ability. However, measures of general ability are not good predictors of children's classroom behavior, nor do these types of data provide guidance to understand, define, and most importantly improve classroom behavior. The PASS theory is an alternative to intelligence theories that have traditionally included verbal, nonverbal, and quantitative tests. Not only does this theory expand the view of what abilities should be measured, but it also puts emphasis on basic psychological processes and precludes verbal achievement-like tests such as vocabulary. Additionally, the PASS theory conceptualizes the functions of the brain as the building blocks of ability within a cognitive processing framework. While the theory may have its roots in neuropsychology, "its branches are spread over developmental and educational psychology" (Varnhagen & Das, 1986, p. 130). Thus, the PASS theory of cognitive processing, with its links to development and neuropsychology, provides an advantage in explanatory power. That is, we can use PASS to help us better understand children's behavior and better predict their behavior in the classroom. Each of the PASS processes can be assessed using the individually administered test CAS (Naglieri & Das, 1997b). The administration and interpretation of the CAS must be done by a specially trained professional, such as a school psychologist (see Naglieri, 1999, for more details). The CAS gives four scores, one for each PASS process, that are set at a mean of 100 ($SD = 15$) and can be used to describe a child's cognitive strengths and weaknesses. This interpretation of these scores can be used as a guide to create classroom interventions based on the child's PASS scores. Initially, careful observation of a child's classroom behavior will quickly reveal valuable information about strengths and weaknesses in PASS processes.

How Do PASS Abilities Relate to Behavior?

Several researchers have examined the profiles of PASS scores obtained for populations of children with problems beyond achievement, such as attention-deficit/hyperactivity disorder (ADHD) and mental retardation. The important finding among the various studies has been that differences between groups have emerged in predictable ways. Children with mental retardation earned low and similar PASS scores, children with reading disabilities received mostly average scores but low successive scores, and those with ADHD Hyperactive/Impulsive type earned average scores except in Planning (Naglieri, 1999). The studies of ADHD have found that children earn low scores on Planning, a seemingly contradictory result because ADHD is thought to be a failure of *attention* but instead, as Barkley (1997) and others have suggested, it is a failure of control related to frontal functioning intimately involved in regulating and self-monitoring performance that fits squarely with the Planning part of the PASS theory.

Paolitto (1999) was the first to study matched samples of ADHD and normal children. He found that the children with ADHD earned significantly lower scores on the Planning Scale. Similarly, Dehn (2000) and Naglieri, Goldstein, Iseman, and Schwebach (2003) found that groups of children who met diagnostic criteria for ADHD earned significantly lower mean scores on the Planning Scale of the CAS. More important, Naglieri et al. (2003) also found that children with ADHD had a different PASS profile than those with anxiety disorders. These results support the view of Barkley (1997, 1998) that ADHD involves problems with behavioral inhibition and self-control, which is associated with poor executive control (Planning). These findings are in contrast to those reported by Naglieri and Das (1997b) for children with reading disabilities who earned low scores on the CAS Successive Scale, and Naglieri and Rojahn (2001) who found children with mental retardation to have similar PASS scores.

The various studies involving special populations lead to the conclusions that children with mental retardation evidence minimal variation among the four PASS scales. In contrast, the LD and ADHD children's profiles are quite disparate. The children with reading decoding problems evidence a successive weakness whereas the children with ADHD evidenced a Planning deficit. These findings are consistent with Das view (see Das, Naglieri, et al., 1994) of reading failure as a deficit in sequencing of information (Successive) as well as Barkley's view (1997) of ADHD as a failure in control (Planning) (also see Naglieri & Goldstein, 2006). As a group, these findings suggest that the PASS processing scores have utility for differential diagnosis, intervention, as well as response to intervention (Naglieri, 2003, 2005).

PASS Case Studies

The PASS theory has substantial implications for helping classroom teachers understand the bases of children's behavior, emotions, and response to instruction. The process theory focuses on dimensions of behavior rather than categories. Such a theory provides a functional appreciation of problems rather than simply a description of behavior. Finally, such a theory well lends itself to intervention in a much more practical way than suggesting emotionally or behaviorally impaired children require treatment.

Case 1: Nate's Problem with Planning

Nate is a friendly fourth-grade student who wants to please his teachers. If Nate thinks a teacher is unhappy with him, he becomes noticeably anxious because he does not know how to make the situation better. Despite his desire to do well in school, Nate does not participate in class discussions, and rarely turns assignments in on time. He needs constant reminders to perform daily tasks such as putting his books away, or throwing away his trash at lunch. Nate turns his work in late because he does not understand the assignments, but rarely asks for help. When his teacher offers help, Nate does not even understand what he needs help with. He grapples most when starting assignments because he does not know where to begin. Yet when his teacher directs him through the process of the assignment, Nate does very well. Unfortunately, as soon as his teacher leaves him to work on his own again, Nate becomes confused about what to do next.

Fridays are Nate's least favorite day of the week because of the weekly math quiz. These quizzes make Nate extremely nervous, especially when he has to do word problems. Nate almost always has stomachaches on Fridays and has a hard time eating at school. On several occasions, he came late to school because his parents reported that he could not sleep the night before. In the middle of one word-problem quiz, Nate went to the nurse's office because he said his chest was pounding like a loud drum. Once he felt better, his teacher tried to do the quiz with him, and found that Nate had trouble keeping track of the different steps he needed to follow to complete the word problems. Nate only did worse on the next quiz and turned his work in without completing it. When asked why he did not use the available time to finish, Nate said that he did not want to be the last one to turn in the quiz because he was afraid of what the other kids might think.

Math is not the only area in school where Nate struggles. It seems difficult for him to figure out how to solve any kind of problem, both inside and outside of the classroom. This leaves Nate in a constant state of anxiety, because he feels like he does not know how to handle daily tasks. His social relationships have started to suffer because of this as well. Recently, Nate's friends stopped including him in their daily game of ball. When the teacher confronted them about excluding Nate, they said that Nate only plays ball his way, and acts like a baby if they want to play the game differently. According to Nate, he does not understand how to play the game differently. More importantly, he does not know how to convince his friends to play with him again.

Nate's parents are concerned with his overall performance at school, yet they are particularly worried about his level of anxiety. Thursday nights are devoted to helping Nate deal with his anxiety about his Friday math quizzes. They try to help him study, and work on relaxation techniques, yet nothing ever seems to completely calm his nerves. By bedtime, Nate is often in tears. Now due to his recent problems with his friends, Nate is always upset about school, and wishes he did not have to go.

It is a challenge for Nate's parents to get him to finish his homework and his chores. Compared to his two brothers, Nate is the most eager to please, however, he is also the one who is the least likely to finish his school and house work, even with constant reminders. When his parents structure the tasks for Nate, he does an excellent job. They realize that he needs his tasks organized for him, but they feel that he should be able to do this on his own by now. On one occasion, Nate's parents asked him to help clean the dining room instead of his usual chore of helping out with the family room. Even though the new chore consisted of the same, overall task of tidying-up, Nate seemed rattled by the change. He was unsure of where to start and wanted his parents to direct his actions. After an hour of arguing with him, they gave in and told him exactly what to do. Nate's parents are worried that he will never learn how to do things for himself, because he does not seem to have the ability to figure things out on his own.

Nate's teachers met with each other and his parents on multiple occasions to try to think of ways to help him. A few of his teachers tried to give him simplified directions throughout the day. One teacher even had him plan out his daily assignments in a journal. Most of Nate's entries in this journal were either incomplete or directly copied from the original entry the teacher wrote with him. In retrospect, the teacher realized this was not the best solution for the problem since Nate found it difficult to complete essays or other tasks involving writing. Other methods to help Nate also had limited success, so his teachers requested that the school psychologist conduct an assessment on Nate's levels of achievement and ability.

The results (shown in Figure 4.5) indicate that not all of Nate's scores on measurements of cognitive ability fell within the average range. Test results from the Cognitive Assessment System (CAS) showed that Nate has a cognitive weakness in Planning processing. This finding goes along with Nate's scores on measures of achievement. He also earned scores in the 70s and low 80s on tests of math calculation, math word problems, written language, and math fluency; all of which demand Planning processing. Whenever Planning processes played a substantial part in an achievement task, either on a formal test or in the classroom or at home, Nate experienced considerable problems because he cannot manage the demands of the task. Nate's problem with Planning processing is a vital piece of insight into why he has so much trouble completing projects, and figuring out how to work through multistep problems, including resolving conflicts with his friends.

Nate has problems whenever the task requires that he manage his own behavior and, figure out *how* to solve a problem on his own; these things demand Planning ability. Planning is a cognitive process that provides children with the intellectual tools needed to manage their behavior in social as well as academic environments. Fortunately, children can be taught to better utilize Planning processes (Naglieri, 2005; Naglieri & Das, 2005b). In the past 15 years, there has been a series of

CAS Results	Standard Scores	Difference from Mean	or Weakness
Planning	78.0	−16.5	Weakness
Attention	91.0	−3.5	
Simultaneous	107.0	12.5	Strength
Successive	102.0	7.5	
Mean	94.5		

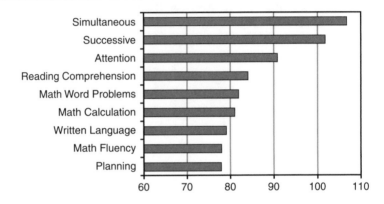

Figure 4.5 Nate's PASS and selected achievement scores

research studies that have consistently shown that children can be taught to better utilize plans and strategies when doing lots of different things. The cognitive strategy instruction that teaches children to be more playful has been shown to improve academic performance. The initial work of Cormier, Carlson, and Das (1990) and Kar, Dash, Das, and Carlson (1992) taught children to discover the value of strategy use without being specifically instructed to do so. The children were encouraged to examine the demands of the task in a strategic and organized manner. These authors demonstrated that children who performed poorly on measures of Planning demonstrated significantly greater gains than those with higher Planning scores. Similarly, Naglieri and Gottling (1995, 1997) conducted two studies, and showed that cognitive strategy instruction in Planning improved children's performance in math calculation.

Naglieri and Gottling (1995, 1997) designed a method to indirectly teach children to be more strategic and use Planning in 1 on 1 tutoring sessions (Naglieri & Gottling, 1995) or in the classroom by the teacher (Naglieri & Gottling, 1997) about two to three times per week in half hour blocks of time. The intervention format was as follows: The students were given a 10-minute period for completing a mathematics page, then a 10-minute period was used for encouraging the use of strategies and then another 10-minute period for mathematics. Students were encouraged to recognize the need to plan and use strategies when completing mathematic problems. The teachers provided probes that facilitated discussion and encouraged the children to consider various ways to be more successful. When a student provided a response, this often became the beginning point for discussion and further development of the strategy. This method is more fully described by Naglieri and Pickering (2003) and shown in Figure 4.6. Additional information about teaching children to be more strategic is also provided by Ashman (1982), Ashman and Conway (1993, 1997), Pressley and Woloshyn (1995), and Scheid (1993).

Naglieri and Johnson (2000) further studied the relationship between Planning Facilitation and PASS profiles for a class of children with learning disabilities and mild mental impairments. They showed that children with a different cognitive weakness (an individual PASS score significantly lower than the child's mean and below 85) in Planning or Attention or Simultaneous, or Successive processing responded differently to the same intervention. Children with a cognitive weakness in Planning improved considerably over baseline rates, while those with no cognitive weakness improved only marginally, and those with a cognitive weakness in Simultaneous, Successive, or Attention showed substantially lower rates of improvement. This study showed that the different groups of children responded very differently to the same intervention. Thus, PASS processing scores were predictive of the children's response to this math intervention. Planning strategy instruction has also been successfully used with reading by Haddad et al. (2003) who found that PASS profiles were predictive of response to instruction.

Most recently, Iseman (2005) compared regular instruction to Planning facilitation for two groups of students with ADHD and found that those who received the Planning strategy instruction method consistently outperformed the regular instruction group on classroom math worksheets (Effect sizes = 0.6 versus 2.4 for regular and Planning instruction groups, respectively) as well as standardized tests of Math Fluency (0.1 versus 1.3) and Numerical Operations tests (−0.2 versus 0.4). This study in particular, suggests that children with ADHD should receive instruction that takes into consideration their particular cognitive processing need. Taken as a whole, this series of studies suggests that children who are poor in Planning improved considerably when provided an intervention that helped them be less impulsive, more thoughtful, and reflective when completing academic work.

Planning Facilitation for Math Calculation

Math calculation is a complex activity that involves recalling basic math facts, following procedures, working carefully, and checking one's work. Math calculation requires a careful (i.e., planful) approach to follow all of the necessary steps. Children who are good at math calculation can move on to more difficult math concepts and problem solving with greater ease than those who are having problems in this area. For children who have trouble with math calculation, a technique that helps them approach the task planfully is likely to be useful. Planning facilitation is such a technique.

Planning facilitation helps students develop useful strategies to carefully complete math problems through discussion and shared discovery. It encourages students to think about how they solve problems, rather than just think about whether their answer is correct. This helps them develop careful ways of doing math.

How to Teach Planning Facilitation

Planning facilitation is provided in three 10-minute time periods: 1) 10 minutes of math, 2) 10 minutes of discussion, and 3) 10 more minutes of math. These steps can be described in more detail:

Step 1: The teacher should provide math worksheets for the students to complete in the first 10-minute session. This gives the children exposure to the problems and ways to solve them. The teacher gives each child a worksheet and says, "Here is a math worksheet for you to do. Please try to get as many of the problems correct as you can. You will have 10 minutes." Slight variations on this instruction is okay, but do not give any additional information.

Step 2: The teacher facilitates a discussion that asks the children about how they completed the worksheet and how they will go about completing the problems in the future. Teachers should not attempt to reinforce the children. For example, if a child says, "I used xyz strategy," the teacher should not say "good, and be sure to do that next time." Instead, the teacher may probe using a statement designed to encourage the child to consider the effectiveness of the strategy ("Did that work for you?"). Discussion works best in groups in which students can learn from one another. The general goals are to encourage the children to describe how they did the worksheet. The teacher's role is to encourage the children to verbalize ideas (which facilitates planning), explain why some methods work better than others, encourage them to be self-reflective, and get them to think about what they will do the next time they do this type of work. Here are a list of suggested probes:

- "How did you do the page?"
- "Tell me how you did these problems."
- "What do you notice about how this page was completed?"
- "What is a good way to do these pages, and what did this teach you?"
- "Why did you do it that way? What did you expect to happen?"

Figure 4.6 Procedures for teaching children to
better utilize planning processing

Source: Helping Children Learn: Instructional Handouts for Use in School and at Home, by
J. A. Naglieri and E. Pickering, 2003, Baltimore: Brookes. Reprinted with permission.

- "How are you going to complete the page next time so you get more correct answers?"
- "What seemed to work well for you before, and what will you do next time?
- "What are some reasons why people make mistakes on problems like these?"
- "You say these are hard. Can you think of any ways to make them easier?"
- "There are many problems here. Can you figure out a way to do more?"
- "Do think you will do anything differently next time?"

Step 3: The teacher gives each child a math worksheet and says, "Here is another math worksheet for you to do. Please try to get as many of the problems correct as you can. You have 10 minutes."

Aids to Facilitate Discussion

- Make an overhead of a blank worksheet so the children can see it during discussion.
- Make an overhead of a completed worksheet (with the name omitted).
- Have the children do a blank worksheet as a group on the overhead projector.

It is important for teachers not to say things like, "Watch me. This is how to do it," "That's right. Good, now you're getting it!" "You made a mistake. Fix it now," or "Remember to use your favorite strategy." This discourages discussion among the students and does not help to meet the goals of the strategy.

Who Should Learn Planning Facilitation?

This instruction is likely to benefit students who are poor at mathematics calculation. Because planning facilitation helps students focus on their approach to solving problems, it helps them be more careful or planful. Children who score low in planning are likely to improve the most from this instruction.

Resources

Good starting points for mathematics intervention can be found at www.mathgoodies.com/, www.sitesforteachers.com/, and www.mathprojects.com/.

Kirby, J., & Williams, N. (1991). *Learning problems: A cognitive approach.* Toronto: Kagan & Woo Limited.
Naglieri, J.A. (1999). *Essentials of CAS assessment.* New York: John Wiley & Sons.
Naglieri, J.A., & Johnson, D. (2000). Effectiveness of a cognitive strategy intervention to improve math calculation based on the PASS theory. *Journal of Learning Disabilities, 33,* 591–597.
Naglieri, J.A., & Gottling, S.H. (1997). Mathematics instruction and PASS cognitive processes: An intervention study. *Journal of Learning Disabilities, 30,* 513–520.
Pressley, M., & Woloshyn, V. (1995). *Cognitive strategy instruction that really improves children's academic performance.* Cambridge, MA: Brookline Books.

Figure 4.6 (*Continued*)

Behavioral Signs of Planning

What signs might give insights into a student's proficiency with Planning? Look to see how well the student can control his or her behavior in all domains. Students who have good Planning processing are well controlled and appear organized and efficient, but those who have Planning problems are not. They seem unable to solve problems using any kind of foresight or strategy and appear rigid and inflexible. Importantly, they don't evaluate the success of their actions and will often insist on solving the same problem the same way even when it does not work! Students who are good in Planning come up with many solutions to one problem, choose wisely about which one to use, and alter their selection when the first strategy proves ineffective. Those who are really good in Planning may choose a good strategy but modify it to make it even better. In contrast, students who struggle with Planning often do not even recognize that there is a need to be strategic. The evaluation component of Planning is also integral to good social interactions and can lead to interpersonal problems. Those who are able to evaluate the behavior of others and interpret it adequately will better understand interpersonal relationships and social contexts. Examples of behaviors strengths and weaknesses associated with Planning are seen in Figure 4.4.

Case 2: Emily's Weakness in Attention Processing

Emily is an outgoing second grader who has more friends than she can count. Her upbeat personality rubs off on everyone she is around, and sometimes she is characterized as being a class clown. Emily also has a reputation for being easily distracted. It is a challenge for both adults and her classmates to keep Emily engaged for any substantial amount of time. At the beginning of the year, Emily sat by the window, which proved to be a huge disaster due to the many distractions outside. Her teacher quickly moved her to the front of the classroom, and surrounded her with students that are known for staying focused. Unfortunately, Emily proved capable of finding a distraction in any place, at anytime. Whether it was the tapping sound her chair made against the floor or a daydream passing through her mind, keeping Emily's attention became an upward battle.

Even when Emily is doing her favorite activities, she cannot stay focused on one thing. Emily loves anything art related, however she rarely finishes any of her art projects because she does not stay focused. She might start off working on her own piece of art, but it is not long before she is distracting her classmates with a song and a dance. When the class is working on long-term art projects, Emily often mistakes a classmate's artwork for her own, even if there are distinct differences in the details, including the other child's name. These features go unnoticed by Emily, and on multiple occasions, she has ruined other children's work.

Baseball is one of Emily's all-time favorite games, yet the only time she actually seems focused is when she is hitting the ball. If she is on the field, she most likely is doing cartwheels, or talking to her teammates. Although most of the children are amused by her behavior, she has missed opportunities to catch the ball because she was preoccupied by something else. One time a classmate told her that he never wanted her on his team again because he could not count on her to be a good player.

Although Emily is very popular with classmates, she has unintentionally hurt people's feelings because she did not pay attention to their needs. For example, one of her best friends brought a model airplane to class for show and tell. The girl worked on it for weeks with her father, and was really excited to show it off. Even though she told everyone numerous times not to touch the wings, Emily broke the left wing by the end of the day. Her friend was furious, Emily felt horrible, and they were both in tears. Emily knew it was her fault, but she just wished her friend had told her not to touch the airplane's wings. When the teacher told Emily that her friend had warned the class several times about the wings, Emily insisted that she never heard those instructions. Most likely, Emily never did.

Emily's parents are aware of her attention problems. They have changed the family's routines to accommodate her difficulties, yet they are frustrated because they do not know how to get her to focus. After one too many incidents of Emily bringing home the wrong backpack or lunchbox, her parents covered all of Emily's school supplies with unusual markings and her name. Her parents wish Emily could remember to do simple things, like checking her cubby at the end of each day. Currently, one of Emily's parents has to physically come into the classroom once a week to make sure Emily emptied out all of the important papers from her cubby. Emily insists that it is not that she forgets to check her cubby, it is that she never notices when there is stuff in it.

When things change at home, Emily hardly ever realizes it. Whether it is a new tree planted in the backyard or the rearrangement of furniture in the family room, changes need to be pointed out to Emily. On one occasion, Emily's dad secretly switched her old, beat-up bike with a new one. Emily's dad really wanted her to notice the surprise on her own, but after several days of Emily walking by the new bike without noticing, her dad finally had to point out the surprise.

Both Emily's parents and teachers agreed that meeting with the school psychologist could only benefit Emily. The school psychologist conducted a thorough assessment, and found that Emily's scores were very consistent with the behavioral concerns. Emily's scores on the CAS showed that she had a significant weakness in attention processing (see Figure 4.7). Although this finding was not a surprise, the school psychologist was confident that an intervention focusing on Emily's weakness in Attention processing would be extremely beneficial and effective. Behaviors associated with Attention processing are shown in Figure 4.1.

Emily's poor performance on tests of Attention illustrate how a student with otherwise good abilities can have a solitary cognitive processing weakness that has considerable impact on behavior. Emily needs to understand the nature of her attention problem and how to overcome it (see Figure 4.8). Naglieri and Pickering (2003) give other suggestions for improving attention (p. 63). The methods described in the handout begins with helping Emily, as well as her teachers and parents, understand the challenges this attention-processing weakness presents and give her options for overcoming these extraordinary demands. This step is very important, because it will help Emily realize that she can be successful despite his cognitive weaknesses and that she can be successful. To im-

CAS Results	Standard Scores	Difference from Mean	or Weakness
Planning	92.0	−0.9	
Attention	75.0	−17.9	Weakness
Simultaneous	106.0	13.1	Strength
Successive	98.5	5.6	
Mean	92.9		

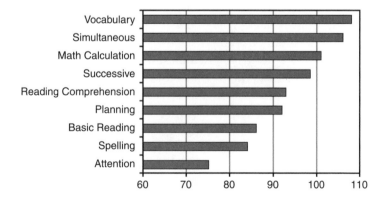

Figure 4.7 Emily's PASS and selected achievement scores

Overcoming
Problems with Inattention

Attention is the process a person uses to focus thinking on a particular stimulus while ignoring others. Throughout a school day, a student must pay attention to the teacher, the instructions being given, what must be done, and what specific materials are needed, while ignoring other students talking, the students playing outside the window, and the cart rolling by in the hall. Attention processes allow a child to selectively focus on things heard or seen and resist being distracted by irrelevant sights and sounds. *Focused attention* is direct concentration on something, such as a specific math problem. *Selective attention* involves the resistance to distraction such as listening to the teacher and not the cart in the hall. *Sustained attention* is continued focus over time.

Some children have difficulty with focused thinking and resisting distractions. These children fit the description of attention-deficit/hyperactivity disorder (ADHD), predominantly inattentive type (American Psychiatric Association, 2000). Children with the inattentive type of ADHD are different from those with ADHD, predominantly hyperactive-impulsive type, described by Barkley (1994) as a delay in the development of inhibition, disturbed self-regulation, and poor organization over time. Children with ADHD, hyperactive-impulsive type cannot control their behavior and have inattention problems that are related to a failure in the process of planning on the CAS.

How to Help a Child
Overcome Problems with Inattention

The first step is to help the child understand the nature of their attention problems, including

1. Concepts such as attention, resistance to distraction, and control of attention
2. Recognition of how attention affects daily functioning
3. Recognition that the deficit can be overcome
4. Basic elements of the control program

Second, teachers and parents can help the child improve his or her motivation and persistence:

1. Promote success via small steps
2. Ensure success at school and at home
   - Allow for oral responses to tests
   - Circumvent reading whenever possible
3. Teach rules for approaching tasks
   - Help the child to define tasks accurately
   - Assess the child's knowledge of problems
   - Encourage the child to consider all possible solutions

(continued)

Figure 4.8 Procedures for teaching children to manage
an attention problem

Source: Helping Children Learn: Instructional Handouts for Use in School and at Home, by
J. A. Naglieri and E. Pickering, 2003, Baltimore: Brookes. Reprinted with permission.

- Teach the child to use a correct test strategy (Pressley & Woloshyn, 1995, p. 140)

4. Discourage passivity and encourage independence
   - Provide only as much assistance as is needed
   - Reduce the use of teacher solutions only
   - Require the child to take responsibility for correcting his or her own work
   - Help the child to become more self-reliant

5. Encourage the child to avoid
   - Excessive talking
   - Working fast with little accuracy
   - Giving up too easily
   - Turning in sloppy disorganized papers

Third, teachers and parents should give the child specific problem-solving strategies:

1. Model and teach strategies that improve attention and concentration.
2. Help the child to recognize when he or she is under- or overattentive.

Who Should Receive Help with Overcoming Problems with Inattention?

This instruction benefits students who have problems maintaining attention and/or who are overactive. These strategies may be particularly helpful for children who demonstrate low scores in attention and children who show weaknesses in attention along with problems with planning. Because a student that has a planning weakness may have a particularly difficult time monitoring and controlling his or her actions, these strategies may be useful to provide structure and help the student follow specific plans to increase his or her self-control and focus of attention.

Resources

Sources for information on attention problems and other educational problems can be found at www.hood.edu/seri/serihome.html/, www.chadd.com/, and www.iss.stthomas.edu/studyguides/adhd.htm/.

American Psychiatric Association. (1994). *Diagnostic and statistical manual of mental disorders* (4th ed., text rev.) Washington, DC: Author.

Barkley, R.A., & Murphy, K.R. (1998). *Attention deficit hyperactivity disorder: A clinical workbook* (2nd ed.) New York: The Guilford Press.

Naglieri, J.A. (1999). *Essentials of CAS assessment.* New York: John Wiley & Sons.

Pressley, M., & Woloshyn, V. (1995). *Cognitive strategy instruction that really improves children's academic performance* (2nd ed.). Cambridge, MA: Brookline Books.

Welton, E. (1999). How to help inattentive students find success in school: Getting the homework back from the dog. *Teaching Exceptional Children, 31,* 12–18.

Figure 4.8 (*Continued*)

prove her chances for success, Emily's teachers and parents should also help her use strategies for controlling her thoughts so she can better attend and concentrate. Emily must also come to recognize when she is not attending and to use strategies to improve her concentration. Finally, Emily should receive emotional support from her teachers so that she can be resilient to the adversities placed upon her due her attention problem.

Case 3: Victor's Problems with Simultaneous Processing

Victor is a quiet fifth grader who loves to help his teachers with small tasks, such as passing out papers and collecting homework. Despite his helpful nature, Victor is shy and behaves awkwardly with his classmates. He hardly ever raises his hand to answer questions, and even avoids eye contact with the teacher during class discussions. However, what troubles Victor's teachers even more is that he often gets lost when walking between classrooms. Victor has been going to the same school for the past 2 years, but still he gets confused in the hallways. The result is not only a seemingly unnecessary record of tardiness that Victor cannot explain, but also constant teasing from his classmates because of this odd problem.

Even though Victor does not participate during lessons, he works diligently during the school day. He remains focused for long periods of time without letting the activities of the classroom distract him from the task at hand. Yet, it is what he concentrates on that is the problem. If it is a straightforward assignment such as filling in the blanks, Victor does well. However, he finds the more complex tasks that require integration of information from multiple sources almost impossible because he does not know how to pick out the important details. For example, each child had to create a poster that represented his or her interests in and outside the classroom. At first, Victor was really excited about the assignment because he has so many different interests in movies, animals, and airplanes. However when Victor finished the poster, it did not reflect his broad spectrum of interests. Instead, the poster only had pictures of his golden retriever. When asked why he did not include any of his other interests, Victor said that he did not know how to put all those ideas on the page, and he was confused.

Victor is a timid child who has always had difficulty making friends. When he does try to interact with his classmates, they often complain that he is annoying, and he does not know when to leave them alone. When he first started going to school, Victor tried very hard to become friends with two of the boys in his class. Victor followed them around, and tried to imitate their behaviors. After a few weeks, the boys became tired of Victor, and tried to make it clear that they did not want him around. At first, they demonstrated their feelings through actions, such as hiding from him at recess. Victor never picked-up on the boys' feelings toward him, so finally they bluntly told Victor that they did not want to be his friend. Victor does not understand why he bothers his classmates so much, so he has learned to leave them alone altogether. He does not see the common pattern in his behaviors that irritates his classmates. His teachers feel that Victor's main problems are his failure to understand the social dynamics behind friendships.

Victor's family loves watching movies together, but Victor finds it difficult to follow the plot. He cannot anticipate what will happen next in the most basic of storylines. His older sister refuses to watch movies with Victor anymore because he gets confused and constantly asks questions. When his family talks about themes in the movie, Victor is clueless. All he remembers about movies are random details about scenes that often have little to do with the plot.

Lately, Victor has become frustrated with his poor grades. In his first few years of elementary school, his hard work resulted in good grades. Now he feels that he is working even harder and cannot understand why he is not doing well. He seldom understands the purpose behind his assignments, and lately does not know why he should continue to work so hard. Both his parents and his teachers are concerned that eventually Victor will stop trying. Due to both his academic and social problems, Victor's teachers asked the school psychologist to meet with him.

Victor's school psychologist conducted a thorough assessment that produced test scores consistent with his difficulties in the classroom. Victor's scores on the CAS showed a significant weakness in Simultaneous processing (see Figure 4.9). This weakness helps to explain the poor scores he earned on tests in reading comprehension, writing, and math reasoning. Victor's CAS scores are also very consistent with the problems Victor is having in school. Simultaneous processing is used to recognize patterns, relate separate pieces into a whole, and understand relationships. Victor's academic and interpersonal problems are directly linked to his weakness in Simultaneous processing. Due to this weakness, it is very difficult for Victor to understand social dynamics, pick-up on themes, figure out spatial relationships, and recognize the overall purpose behind assignments.

Victor's weakness in Simultaneous processing should be managed by helping him see the relationships among, for example, behaviors exhibited by his peers. This could be achieved through diagrammatic representations like Story Maps (see Naglieri & Pickering, 2003, pp. 97–98) used in academic areas. Reading comprehension would likely be enhanced through the use of graphic organizers (see Naglieri & Pickering,

CAS Results	Standard Scores	Difference from Mean	Strength or Weakness
Planning	95.5	−1.6	
Attention	109.5	12.4	Strength
Simultaneous	81.0	−16.1	Weakness
Successive	102.5	5.4	
Mean	97.1		

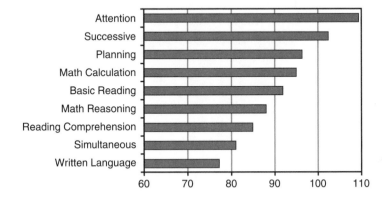

Figure 4.9 Victor's PASS and selected achievement scores

2003, pp. 51–52). These methods would help him see how things are interrelated. The behaviors that could provide insights into other student proficiency with Simultaneous processing will be any of those that require the child get the big picture. Look for confusion about the goal of the classroom activity, the purpose of the project, or reasons why something does or does not make sense. Students who are good in Simultaneous processing have a good understanding of social relationships because they can easily see patterns in behavior. They are able to understand and relate the verbal and nonverbal forms of communication into a whole and extract the meaning, sometimes hidden meaning, behind interactions among people. They are sometimes described as people who are good with visual-spatial tasks which, of course, demand that relating many parts into a coherent whole. Those who are poor in Simultaneous seem to miss the point of discussions, get lost easily, and have problems working in complex environments. These and other behaviors associated with Simultaneous processing are shown in Figure 4.2.

Case 4: April's Weakness in Successive Processing

April is a social third grader who loves spending time with her friends at school. She tries to do well in everything she does, but she has trouble getting things done correctly. Although she turns her assignments in on time, she often hands in work that is only partially complete, or obviously done out of order. One example of this was when April's teacher began to teach the class how to write a letter to a friend. April was taught the sequence of steps to follow in order to write a proper letter, and given enough time to practice before being required to turn in a letter that showed she understood letter writing. April's letter was disorganized because she did not write the letter in the required, linear order. The first paragraph was crammed at the top of the page, and the date was squeezed into the middle of the right side of the page, between two paragraphs. When the teacher asked to look at several of April's letters a pattern emerged. None of her letters followed a logical sequence of steps as instructed. When asked why she did not use the order taught to the class, April said she forgot the right order, and started with the part that she remembered.

April has problems with many tasks that have to be completed in a specific order. For example, one of the major themes this year in April's class is learning about the cultures of different countries. When the class studied Japan, they spent an art period doing origami. This proved to be impossible for April. No matter how hard she tried, she could not follow the folds the teacher demonstrated for the class. The teacher gave her a copy of the written instructions, but this only helped minimally. April was very frustrated by the end of class. Her friends had neat looking shapes, but all she had were oddly folded pieces of paper, and some crumpled piles that indicated her frustration. Before she left art, she tore up all of her origami papers, and then had to stay after class to clean up her mess.

Communication is also a problem for April. When she speaks in class, she rarely finishes her thoughts, and often expresses them in an illogical order. It is not uncommon for April to use the incorrect tense in basic sentences, or to mispronounce words. Her classmates have even said that she is hard to understand. In her written work, she struggles with spelling, and frequently leaves words out of sentences. Even when April is reminded to proof read all her work, she hardly ever catches her errors. When her teacher points out the errors to April, it is unclear whether she understands her mistakes.

April's difficulty with sequencing limits the fun she can have. For example, in the talent show this year, two of her friends wanted to perform a magic trick. April loved the idea, and begged to be part of the act. When they said she had to audition by learning two tricks, she immediately began to practice. Her mother even bought her a few, basic magic tricks. The tricks were too difficult for April because each trick required her to follow a linear order of steps. Even when there were only three steps involved, April became confused. After an hour of practicing, she became insecure about her ability to do any of the tricks, and gave up. April told her friends the next day that she did not want to be in the talent show. Her friends tried to get her to do one trick with them, but she refused and became angry. April later apologized for getting mad, but told her friends not to talk to her about the talent show because she did not have any talents that anyone would want to see. When the school had an assembly to watch the talent show, April asked to go to the nurse's office due to a headache. She later told her mother she never had a headache. The truth was watching other people's talents just reminded her that she did not have any of her own.

April's mother first noticed her sequencing problems when she tried to teach April how to tie her shoes in Kindergarten. It took April an unusually long time to master this skill. Even now April prefers buckles to shoelaces. April also struggled much more than her siblings to memorize her personal information, such as her phone number and address, and with reading decoding. On her own, she performed daily routines such as getting ready for bed in an illogical order. Her mother finally made charts for April that listed the steps of her daily routines. Originally, April's mother thought she would only need to leave the charts up for a month until April got a hang of the tasks. That was a year ago, and April still uses the charts as a reference throughout the week.

The school psychologist suspected that April had a Successive processing problem by examining her school work and listening to her mother describe her behavior at home. April's problem with sequencing is apparent in the slowness with which she learned to pronounce words, tie her shoes, read words, and spell. The correspondence of sounds and letters in sequence has been a consistent problem. April also has had a hard time with following directions, according to her teacher. She often does not perform tasks as instructed and has considerable difficulty remembering information like phone numbers and the combination for her bicycle lock. After the school psychologist evaluated April using the CAS, the findings clearly revealed that she had a significant weakness in Successive processing (see Figure 4.10). Knowing this, April's mother, teacher, and school psychologist worked on a number of methods to use with April to help her with this weakness.

April can better manage her difficulty with tasks that demand sequencing by learning to recognize when she is experiencing a problem, and using strategies to better solve tasks that demand this process. Techniques such as chunking or other methods of grouping information (see Naglieri & Pickering, 2003) into segments should be utilized to help

CAS Results	Standard Scores	Difference from Mean	or Weakness
Planning	108.0	12.3	Strength
Attention	100.5	4.8	
Simultaneous	95.5	−0.3	
Successive	79.0	−16.8	Weakness
Mean	95.8		

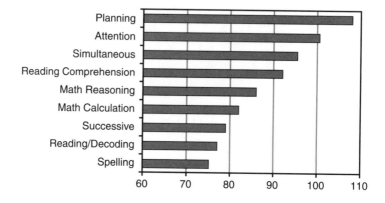

Figure 4.10 April's PASS and selected achievement scores

April better cope with the demands of tasks that require Successive processing. Reading problems could be addressed using a cognitive approach described by J. Carlson and Das (1997). Children like April will demonstrate Successive processing problem by failures in remembering information that is linearly arranged and when performing tasks that demand a specific sequential act. Signs of Successive problems will include academic and basic life skills that rely on actions or procedures that must follow a specific sequence. Examples of behaviors associated to Successive processing are shown in Figure 4.3.

Summary

Classroom consultants can provide valuable insight to classroom educators by utilizing PASS theory of basic cognitive processes to understand and modify children's classroom behavioral as well as academic problems. In a classroom atmosphere increasingly driven by the emphasis to improve classroom performance, the PASS theory can facilitate the efficient selection and implementation of effective strategies to not just modify classroom behavior but to provide students with essential life skills.

5

Disruptive Behaviors

SAM GOLDSTEIN AND RICHARD RIDER

Regardless of the labels applied to disruptive children and their problems, these youngsters present the most difficult challenges faced by classroom teachers. Impulsivity, hyperactivity, verbal and physical aggression, tantrums, destruction of property, stealing, lying, and noncompliance create problems between student and teacher that often radiate and impact other students as well. Disruptive students can be defiant toward authority figures and classroom rules. They may also be inattentive and hyperactive. Many struggle academically either because they experience a co-existing learning disability or they slowly fall behind in subjects requiring practice and proficiency. Twenty years ago, Kazdin (1985, 1987) suggested prophetically that such disruptive problems are likely to contribute to long-term risk for school failure and serious adult maladjustment. When these patterns of behavior present in a specific combination causing functional impairment, clinical thresholds for specific disruptive behavior disorders are also met. This chapter provides an overview of the three disruptive behavior disorders of childhood, discuss the risks posed as children grow when these disorders are present, and as they transition into adulthood. We also offer brief guidelines to enhance resilience with these youth in the classroom. Later chapters provide specific behavioral, cognitive, and related educational strategies to reduce the adverse impact these students have in the classroom and ultimately to improve their behavior and achievement adjustment.

The disruptive behavior disorders (DBDs) of childhood are comprised of attention-deficit/hyperactivity disorder (ADHD), oppositional defiant disorder (ODD), and conduct disorder (CD) (American Psychiatric Association, 2000). These conditions are among the most commonly treated in mental health settings with epidemiological studies suggesting that between 3% and 16% of all youth meet the diagnostic criteria for at least one, if not two or more, of these conditions (Eiraldi, Power, & Nezu, 1997; Loeber, Burke, Lahey, Winters, & Zera, 2000; see Barkley, 2006; S. Goldstein & Goldstein, 1998; for a review). The majority of students served in Special Education programs within the public schools manifest at least one DBD (Déry, Toupin, Pauzé, & Verlaan, 2004). These conditions have traditionally been referred to as externalizing disorders as opposed to internalizing disorders such as anxiety, depression, or learning disability. The former disrupt and disturb the classroom environment and are easily visible. Symptoms and impairments of the latter are not as often observed nor are classrooms disrupted by affected children and adolescents.

Given that the behavior of children with DBDs are rarely viewed as benign by teachers, it is not surprising that these conditions are comprised of patterns of impulsive, hyperactive, aggressive, and defiant behaviors. These pose as significant, adverse risk factors for a host of adverse outcome variables into the late adolescent and young adult years. In fact, even a single DBD compromises the probability of positive life adjustment into young adulthood. A combination of DBDs (e.g., ADHD and CD, ODD and CD) speak to significant adverse outcome in major life domains, including school, family, health, vocation and even activities such as driving (Barkley & Gordon, 2002; S. Goldstein, 2002). The DBDs may also act catalytically reducing a child's opportunity for normal life adjustment by precipitating a cascade of adverse outcomes into adulthood.

A small percentage of children with ADHD and CD and an even greater percentage of children with ODD alone manage to transition and adjust reasonably well into young adulthood (Teeter-Ellison, 2002). Thus, if a specific risk such as chronically demonstrating a DBD significantly contributes to adverse outcome, and current treatment efforts for DBD demonstrate that symptoms can be managed but symptom relief in the long term doesn't appear to significantly alter the adult outcome of these conditions, then researchers and educators must identify and understand those variables within the child, immediate family and school that predict better outcome. Thus, there has been an interest in studying resilience processes in children with DBDs. If a group of children suffering from one or more DBDs can be identified who demonstrate the ability to function well in school and transition successfully into the late adolescent and young adulthood years, then the lessons learned from studying these youth can generate a treatment protocol of those thoughts, feelings, behaviors, experiences, attitudes, and opportunities enhance resilience in a group of children whose adult outcome have been demonstrated to be significantly more risk filled than those of others. Particularly for youth with DBDs, an increasing body of literature operating from a developmental pathways model has demonstrated that a number of childhood variables can be used to predict risk of adult problems as well as identifying insulating or protective factors that reduce risk and increase the chances of a satisfactory transition into adult life (see Katz, 1997, for a review). As a field, researchers in the DBDs are slowly beginning to examine these protective factors. Though much is known about the risk factors, for the time being, there is only limited data available about protective factors. It is quite likely, however, that those factors that insulate and protect children from other psychiatric conditions affect those with DBDs as well. Thus, living in an intact household, above the poverty level, with parents free of serious psychiatric problems, consistent in their parenting style and available to their children when needed, appear to be among the most powerful family factors predicting resilience in all children as well as those with DBDs (see S. Goldstein & Brooks, 2005, for a review).

In long-term follow-up studies, at least 70% to 80% of adolescents with a childhood diagnosis of ADHD or another DBD continue to meet the diagnostic criteria for at least one DBD with at least 60% reporting impairing symptoms but fewer meeting the diagnostic criteria during the adult years (see Ingram, Hechtman, & Morgenstern, 1999, for a review). These authors suggest that the decrease in prevalence is in part due to the developmental nature of the diagnostic protocols for DBDs. Prognosis for individuals with ADHD in adulthood for example appears to be influenced by the severity of their symptoms, comorbid conditions, level of intellectual functioning, family situations such as parental pathology, family adversity, socioeconomic status, and treatment history (see Barkley, 2006; S. Goldstein, 2002; for a review). These variables are likely predictive for the other DBDs as well.

There is a broader literature available concerning the absence of certain negative phenomena in predicting outcome. For example, Herrero,

Hechtman, and Weiss (1994) demonstrated that females may experience less risk of adverse outcome with a DBD simply due to their gender. Subtype differences in ADHD, specifically children with the inattentive type, may also reduce risk. The absence of impulsive behavior appears to predict to better outcome. In fact, it has been hypothesized that problems with self-control characteristic of all three of the DBDs may be the best predictors of future adult outcome into young adulthood when evaluating young children (see Barkley, 1997, for a review).

Not surprisingly, aggressive behavior in general, a diagnostic characteristic of ODD and CD as well as a common consequence of ADHD, has been found to predict outcome into adulthood (Loney, Whaley-Klahn, & Kosier, 1983). Emotional lability has also been highly correlated with aggression (Hechtman, Weiss, & Perlman, 1984). It is also likely that within the symptom listing for the DBDs some may hold stronger positive or negative predictive power. Algorhythmic research with these conditions has slowly begun to identify the presence or absence of certain symptoms as not only predictive of condition presence but also speak to outcome (Mota & Schachar, 2000).

Overview

Over the past quarter century, multiple longitudinal and retrospective studies have demonstrated that youth exhibit two broad dimensions of disruptive behaviors. The first dimension present for many children at a young age, are characterized by a trinity of inattentive, hyperactive, and impulsive behaviors. Over the past 100 years, this trinity first described by George Still (1902) as a disorder of defective moral control, has been described by various labels attesting to hypothesized cause (minimal brain dysfunction), or key symptom (hyperactivity or inattention) but is increasingly recognized as not so much a behavioral disorder but one of faulty cognitive functioning (Barkley, 1997). The second dimension of disruptive behavior falls in two distinct groups. The first, a group of overt oppositional and aggressive behaviors, has consistently been found to be distinct from a second group of covert behaviors (Fergusson, Horwood, & Lynskey, 1994; Frick, Lahey, & Loeber, 1993; Quay, 1979). Overt behaviors include, but are not limited to, fighting, disobedience, tantrums, destruction, bullying, and attention seeking. The second group of covert behaviors include, but are not limited to, theft without confrontation of the victim, choice of bad companions, school truancy, running away, lying, and loyalty to delinquent friends (Achenbach, Conners, Quay, Verlhulst, & Howell, 1989; Loeber & Schmaling, 1985). These problems impact classrooms in different ways. Both dimensions have traditionally been thought to be strongly influenced by experience but likely also find their roots in genetic vulnerability. Further, overt behaviors can be divided into those that are nondestructive such as simply resisting adult authority and those that are aggressive toward others and destructive of property. Covert behaviors can be further divided into those, again that do not confront victims, such as vandalism and those that are nondestructive such as truancy or running away from home (Lahey, Frick, et al., 1990).

Within the DBDs, ADHD has consistently been found as distinct from ODD and CD (see Barkley, 2006; S. Goldstein & Goldstein, 1998; Hinshaw, 1987; for a review). The DBDs can also be clearly distinguished from the internalizing disorders of depression and anxiety (Bussing et al., 2003; E. Taylor, Schachar, Thorley, & Wieselberg, 1986). Oppositional defiant disorder and CD appear to be distinct, although the two disorders may well overlap in a number of behaviors such as mild aggression and lying. The onset of ODD in comparison to CD appears to be earlier. Children manifesting CD before age 10 appear to have a much worse prognosis than those demonstrating symptoms after that time (Moffitt, 1990; G. R. Patterson, DeBaryshe, & Ramsey, 1989). Although some children demonstrate the onset of CD and ODD simultaneously, the most serious symptoms of CD, including vandalism, repeatedly running away, truancy, shoplifting, breaking and entering, rape, assault, and homicide, generally emerge at a later age than symptoms of ODD.

It can be easily argued that the DBDs fall on a continuum from mild to severe beginning with ADHD then progressing through ODD and CD. A growing body of research has documented the contribution of limitations in attentional and behavioral regulation as well as negative emotionality in early childhood as contributing to risk for development of a DBD (N. Eisenberg et al., 2000). Though not all children with ADHD develop ODD and CD, a significant percentage of youth with CD have histories of ADHD. The younger a child progresses to CD, the more adverse their outcome (Biederman, Faraone, Milberger, Jetton, et al., 1996; Campbell, 1991). Further, boys experiencing CD in comparison to those with only ODD, scored lower on tests of intelligence, came from families of lower socioeconomic status and had a history of greater conflict with school and judicial systems (Robins, 1991). Boys with CD demonstrated the strongest family history of antisocial personality, a problem that could reflect a combination of family, environment, and shared family genetics.

Diagnostic Overview

Attention-Deficit/Hyperactivity Disorder

Due to the complex effects problems of self-discipline and impulsivity characteristic of ADHD, Chapter 7 discusses these issues in depth. This chapter briefly reviews ADHD to set a foundation to understand the DBDs. Attention-deficit/hyperactivity disorder is described as a "persistent pattern of inattention and/or hyperactivity" more frequent in severity than is typical of children in a similar level of development (American Psychiatric Association, 2000). Some symptoms are apparent before the age of 7 years, although many children are diagnosed at later ages after symptoms have been observed for several years. Impairment must be present in at least two settings and interfere with developmentally appropriate functioning in social, academic, or work setting. Assessment of impairment has been an increasing focus in making the diagnosis of ADHD (M. Gordon et al., 2006). Attention-deficit/hyperactivity disorder appears more common in males than females, a problem that may or may not be a function of the DSM field studies and/or differences in prevalence and presentation (S. Goldstein & Gordon, 2003). Attention-deficit/hyperactivity disorder is characterized by developmentally inappropriate, often limited attention span and/or hyperactivity and impulsivity. Six of nine inattentive symptoms must be present to confirm the inattentive aspect of the disorder. DSM-IV-TR (2000) did not delineate these symptoms by importance. As noted, algorhythmic research finds some symptoms may in fact demonstrate better negative or positive predictive power than others (Mota & Schachar, 2000). The nine inattentive symptoms are failing to give close attention to details, problems with sustained attention, not listening when spoken to directly, failing to complete tasks, difficulty with organization, avoiding or reluctant to engage in tasks requiring sustained mental effort, losing things, being easily distracted, and forgetful in daily activities.

Six of nine hyperactive-impulsive symptoms must be met to confirm the hyperactive-impulsive aspect of the disorder. The six hyperactive symptoms include fidgeting, having trouble remaining seated, demonstrating inappropriate activity, difficulty engaging in leisure activities quietly, acting as if driven by a motor, and talking excessively. The two impulsive symptoms include blurting out answers before questions have been completed, difficulty waiting for turns and interrupting others. If in fact ADHD represents failure to develop effective self-discipline as evidenced by impulsive behavior, then only three of 18 symptoms reflecting this phenomena may well be a problem (Barkley, 1997). Diagnosis is made by confirming six or more symptoms in the inattention domain, hyperactivity-impulsive domain, or both. An individual may qualify for ADHD Inattentive Type, Hyperactive-Impulsive Type, or Combined Type. It is important to note that the diagnosis requires that there must be "clear evidence of clinically significant impairment in social, academic, or occupational functioning."

Oppositional Defiant Disorder/Conduct Disorder

Oppositional defiant disorder is described in the *DSM-IV-TR* as a recurrent pattern of negativistic, defiant, disobedient, and hostile behavior toward authority figures. This pattern of behavior must have lasted for at least 6 months and be characterized by frequent occurrence of at least four of the following: loss of temper, arguments with adults, defiance or refusal to comply with adults' request or rules, deliberately doing things that annoy people, blaming others for personal failings, touchiness, anger, resentment, spite, or vindictiveness. Conduct disorder is described in the *DSM-IV-TR* as a "repetitive and persistent pattern of behavior in which the basic rights of others or major age appropriate societal norms or rules are violated" (p. 83). Oppositional defiant disorder reflects an enduring pattern of negativistic, hostile, and defiant behaviors in the absence of serious violation of societal norms and the rights of others. Thus, children with ODD argue with adults, lose their temper, and are quick to anger. They frequently defy reasonable requests or rules and deliberately annoy others. They tend to blame others for their mistakes.

Conduct disorder appears to reflect an enduring set of behaviors that evolve over time. Conduct disorder is characterized most often by significant aggression and violation of the rights of others. The average age of CD is younger in boys than in girls. Boys may met the diagnostic criteria for CD if it is going to develop by 12 years of age, whereas girls often reach 14 to 16 before the diagnosis is made. Three or more of the following behaviors must occur within a 12-month period with at least one present in the past 6 months for youth to qualify for a diagnosis of CD: bullying, threatening, or intimidating others; initiating physical fights; using a weapon that causes serious harm; stealing with confrontation of the victim; physically cruel to others; physically cruel to animals; forcible sexual activity with others; lying to avoid obligation; staying out overnight without permission; stealing items of nontrivial value; deliberately engaging in fire setting with the intention of causing harm; deliberately destroying others' property; running away from home overnight, at least twice; truant from school; and burglary. The diagnostic protocol for CD includes two different types, Child-Onset and Adolescent-Onset. These are largely based on the classification system identified by Moffitt (1993). Moffitt utilized a developmental approach to distinguish between individuals who engage in temporary versus persistent antisocial behavior. Life-course-persistent individuals were thought to demonstrate risk factors such as neuropsychological abnormalities and poor home environments contributing to their difficulty. Individuals classified as adolescent-limited did not demonstrate these risk factors and had no prior engagement in antisocial behavior. Bullying also presents at a higher rate in the ODD/CD population (Kokkinos & Panayiotou, 2004).

The life-course-persistent pattern might well equate with the juvenile court characterization of delinquency. To test her dual trajectory theory, Moffitt examined a birth cohort of over 1,000 children in New Zealand for trends in parent, teacher, and self-reported antisocial behavior biennially aged 3 to 15 years. Five percent of the sample accounted for nearly 70% of the stability of crime across time. Despite these efforts at delineation, there continues to be little consensus as to the distinction between CD as a clinical diagnosis and delinquency as a legal/societal description.

Disruptive Behavior Disorders and Delinquency

The lack of consensus in defining delinquency as a condition distinct from CD is not surprising. In fact, most professionals and laypersons use the terms CD, delinquency and even antisocial behavior interchangeably. However, in a legal sense, a delinquent is defined as someone who breaks the law, those that apply to youth as well as adults. Tremblay (2003) suggests the term *delinquent* should be used to describe youth in studies that specifically focus on legal issues. He suggests three classes of delinquent behavior from a legal perspective:

1. Vandalism and theft with or without confrontation of a victim;
2. Physical, verbal or indirect aggression, predatory or defensive; and
3. Status offenses of underage youth (e.g., consuming alcohol prior to age 21).

Aggression alone has not always been found to predict delinquency (T. Anderson, Bergman, & Magnusson, 1989). These authors suggest that delinquency is best predicted when aggression is accompanied by peer rejection and other problems, many of which are present in most youth with ADHD. In young children, a combination of aggression and social problems appear to be predictive of later drug abuse and duress

(Farmer, Bierman, and Conduct Problems Prevention Research Group, 2002; Kellam, Simon, & Ensminger, 1983). Rose, Rose, and Feldman (1989) suggested that early antisocial behavior predicts more than the single well-established developmental path that ends in delinquency. Early signs of DBD among a preschool population, including tantrums, defiance, and overactivity predicted the diagnosis of a DBD by midchildhood in 67% and later delinquency (Campbell & Ewing, 1990).

In 2001, Moffitt and Caspi attempted to identify the childhood risk factors of life-course-persistent delinquence. Their results with the same 1,000 individuals found that males and females classified as life-course-persistent delinquents were highly similar on most risk factors and had significantly higher levels of risk factors in their adolescence-limited peers. With regard to childhood risk factors, life-course-persistent individuals demonstrated significantly greater risk on 21 of the 26 factors measured. In contrast, the risk factors reported by adolescence-limited individuals were similar to their comparison peers with no history of juvenile court involvement on all but one of the factors measured. Thus, youth who exhibit rule violations that are limited to their adolescent years tended to have fewer pathological histories, personality problems, reading problems, inadequate parenting, and broken attachments and relationships than life-course persistent delinquents. Although Moffitt and others (Moffitt, Caspi, Harrington, & Milne, 2002; H. R. White, Bates, & Buyske, 2001) refer to both adolescence-limited and life-course-persistent youth problems as delinquency, it would appear that the latter group certainly provide a better working definition of the community's perception of the chronic, recurrent antisocial behaviors exhibited by delinquents. White et al. (2001) extension of Moffitt's work demonstrated that delinquents manifested higher disinhibition, impulsivity, and parental hostility and lower harm avoidance and less intact family structure than nondelinquents.

Perhaps a distinction between CD and delinquency should also focus on persistence. Conduct disorder, based on *DSM-IV* field studies tends to have an average duration of 3 years. That is, most youth meeting the CD criteria recover within that period of time. Conduct disorder may thus equate with Moffitt's conceptualization of adolescence-limited delinquency. It should be noted, however, that receiving a diagnosis of CD is not a benign phenomena over time. Associations between parent and teacher reports of conduct problems at age 8 and psychosocial outcomes at 18 report elevated rates of educational underachievement, juvenile offending, substance abuse/dependence, and mental health problems at 18 even after adjusting for social disadvantage, attention problems, and IQ

(Fergusson & Lynskey, 1998). Further, maternal communication/problem-solving skills and family variables (e.g., marital status, maternal depressed mood, and interparental conflict) during early adolescence, both independently and interactively, predict severe delinquent behaviors during early adulthood (K. Klein & Forehand, 1997).

Developmental Course

The greatest comorbidity for the DBDs may be with each other rather than other psychiatric conditions (Cunningham & Boyle, 2002; De-Wolfe, Byrne, & Bawden, 2000; DuPaul, McGoey, Eckert, & Van Brakle, 2001). Comorbidity may in fact reflect the differentiation in what begins as unitary pattern of disruptive symptoms. For example, Bauermeister (1992) generated factor analytic data suggesting that at 4 to 5 years of age disruptive symptoms appear to fall on a single dimension.

Attention-Deficit/Hyperactivity Disorder

Attention-deficit/hyperactivity disorder appears to develop relatively early in childhood before the other DBDs present and is a risk factor for later antisocial disorder (Mannuzza, Klein, Abikoff, & Moulton, 2004). At least a dozen controlled studies have demonstrated these symptoms present and are identified in preschool children (Connor, 2002). However, the majority of children with ADHD are identified within their 1st year of school. Nonetheless, symptom patterns may shift as children mature making subtype diagnoses of ADHD unstable (Lahey, Pelham, Loney, Lee, & Willcutt, 2005). These authors suggest that patterns of hyperactive-impulsive behavior may be the best way of identifying and understanding this population of children over time. Early signs of inattention, hyperactivity, and impulsivity in children quickly cause impairment in multiple settings leading to problems with social relations, self-esteem, and underachievement (Barkley, Fischer, Edelbrock, & Smallish, 1990; Graetz, Sawyer, Hazell, Arney, & Baghurst, 2001). Interpersonal difficulties with peers, adults, and family members often result in rejection and subsequent social neglect due to the inappropriate pattern of behavior resulting from an impulsive manner of dealing with thoughts, feelings, and others (R. Milich & Landau, 1981; R. Milich, Landau, Kilby, & Whitten, 1982). Problems with language impairment may further contribute to poor interpersonal relations, school achievement, and developing self-regulatory patterns of behavior (Cantwell & Baker, 1977, 1989; Cantwell, Baker, & Mattison, 1981). In a vicious cycle, isolation from peers due to the combined effect of ADHD and its impact on the normal course of development as well in combination with other adversities leads to reduced opportunity to develop appropriate social interaction, self-esteem, coping skills, academic progress, and likely resilience processes (Brooks, 1998).

The academic performance and achievement problems in youth with ADHD have been reported to be well over 50% (Fischer, Barkley, Fletcher, & Smallish, 1990; Semrud-Clikeman et al., 1992). Poor persistence and limited motivation (Milich, 1994), organizational deficits (Zentall, Harper, & Stormont-Spurgin, 1993), careless mistakes (Teeter, 1998), and noncompliant behavior (Weiss & Hechtman, 1993) have all been implicated as contributing to the pervasive scholastic problems experienced by youth with ADHD. Problems with independent seat work; school performance; deficient study skills; poor test taking; disorganized notebooks, desks, and reports; as well as lack of attention to lectures and group discussions are consistent themes for youth with ADHD (DuPaul & Stoner, 2003). This pattern of impairment results in a variety of negative consequences in the social arena (Antschel & Remer, 2003; Coie, Dodge, & Coppotelli, 1982), poor test performance (Nelson & Ellenberg, 1979), impaired working memory (Douglas & Benezra, 1990), and poor overall success in school (DuPaul & Stoner, 2003). As Teeter-Ellison (2002) notes, an inability to persist and be vigilant interferes with classroom behavior, especially when tasks are repetitive or boring. These difficulties, unfortunately, present early and in particular when classroom expectations require sustained attention, effort, and goal directedness. Many children with ADHD are "exquisitely attuned to the fact that they are not performing up to their peer group, that they are not meeting the expectations of important adults in their lives and that they are not well liked by their peers" (p. 10). This cycle, described by others (Barkley, Fischer, Smallish, & Fletcher, 2004; S. Goldstein & Goldstein, 1990) creates increased vulnerability limiting opportunities for youth with ADHD to develop resilient qualities. Self-doubt and lack of confidence, combined with academic, social, and avocational (e.g., sporting activities) failure, impedes self-esteem, increasing vulnerability for conditions such as depression and anxiety. By late elementary, many youth with ADHD may disengage from the learning environment as a means of avoiding failure, choosing instead patterns of inappropriate behavior, preferring to be labeled misbehaving rather than "dumb" (Brooks, 1991). Because elementary experience provides the basis foundational skills necessary to learn, including basic achievement, study, test taking, and organizational skills, many youth with ADHD enter the middle school years ill-prepared for the increasing demands of autonomy required by the upper grades. This then fuels their problems leading to a cycle of increased risk for drop out, school failure, academic underachievement, and significant risk in transitioning successfully into adulthood (Barkley et al., 1990; Barkley & Gordon, 2002).

The preponderance of these data argue strongly that symptoms of ADHD, in particular failure to develop self-discipline, dramatically reduces positive outcome by decreasing opportunities to demonstrate resilience in the face of these adversities. Unfortunately, this pattern continues and intensifies in the adolescent years. What is most disturbing about the increasing body of research about ADHD in the adolescent years is the growing evidence of the wide spread effects of ADHD on all aspects of academic, interpersonal, behavioral, emotional, and daily living activities. Up to 80% of youth carrying a diagnosis of ADHD continued to demonstrate clinically significant symptoms into their adolescent years (Barkley et al., 1990; Biederman, Faraone, Millberger, Guite, et al., 1996; Weiss & Hechtman, 1993). Even early studies examining outcome found only a significant minority (between 20% to 30%) of children with ADHD followed into their adolescent years demonstrating limited differences from controls. Seventy percent of a cohort followed over 20 years demonstrated significant academic, social, and emotional difficulties relative to their ADHD (Hechtman, 1999). The emerging literature suggests that adolescents with ADHD demonstrate significantly greater than expected presentation of comorbid disorders that during the adolescent years also appear to influence the development of adverse personality styles (e.g., antisocial or borderline personality disorder). Further, adolescents with ADHD demonstrate signs of social disability and appear at significantly greater risk for mood, anxiety, disruptive, and substance abuse disorders than comparison boys without social disability (Greene, Biederman, Faraone, Sienna, & Garcia-Jones, 1997). In this 4-year longitudinal study of boys with ADHD, the presence of social disability predicted poor social and psychiatric outcome including substance abuse and conduct disorder. The authors concluded that assessing social function in adolescents with ADHD is critical to their treatment. Once again, ADHD is demonstrated to strip away or limit the potential to develop critical, resilient phenomena. These include the ability to connect and maintain satisfying reciprocal relationships with others, achieve in school and maintain mental health facilitate resilience (Brooks & Goldstein, 2001).

Oppositional Defiant Disorder/Conduct Disorder

Not surprisingly, with ODD and CD, less serious symptoms tend to precede moderate symptoms that precede the presentation of more serious symptoms. Preschoolers demonstrate a single disruptive pattern of behavior often composed of oppositionality and mild aggression (Achenbach, Edelbrock, & Howell, 1987). These findings are consistent with the developmental view that ODD usually precedes the onset of CD. The risk of onset of CD was found to be four times higher in children with ODD than in those without (P. Cohen & Flory, 1998). Multiple authors have investigated developmental pathways of these patterns of behavior, identifying three often parallel pathways as (1) overt, (2) covert, and (3) authority conflict (B. T. Kelly, Loeber, Keenan, & DeLamatre, 1997; Loeber et al., 1988; Loeber, Keenan, & Zhang, 1997). On the overt pathway, minor aggression leads to physical fighting and finally violence. On the covert pathway, minor covert behaviors such as stealing from home often lead to property damage (e.g., fire setting) and then to moderate to serious forms of recurrent status and criminal behavior. On the authority conflict pathway, problems progress from stubborn behavior to defiance and authority avoidance (e.g., truancy and running away). Youth often start down this pathway well before age 12, though it is not well understood whether aggression in preschoolers in and of itself significantly increases risk to precede down one of these pathways (Nagin & Tremblay, 1999).

Prevalence

When *DSM* symptoms are used epidemiologically, an incidence rate of up to 15% is found for ADHD. In a study of nearly 500 children evaluated on an outpatient basis at a children's hospital, 15% received a diagnosis of ADHD based on a comprehensive assessment (McDowell & Rappaport, 1992). Field studies for the *DSM-IV* identified nearly 9% of the population as meeting at least one of the diagnostic subtypes for ADHD (Applegate et al., 1997). When a careful analysis is conducted, the rate of ADHD most likely falls between 3% and 7% (see Barkley, 2006, for a review). A higher incidence of ADHD as well as other DBDs occurs in lower socioeconomic families. A variety of additional life variables appear to affect the prevalence of ADHD as well as the other DBDs. For example, among adopted or foster families the incidence of ADHD has been found to be twice as high as among other children (Molina, 1990).

Few studies have generated consistent prevalence data for ODD or CD as a function of age. Epidemiological studies estimating the occurrence of CD in the general population vary from just over 3% of 10-year-olds (Rutter, Tizard, & Whitmore, 1970) to almost 7% of 7-year-olds (McGee,

Silva, & Williams, 1984). Based on a review of the existing literature, Kazdin (1987) suggested a range of 4% to 10% for CD. The rate of ODD in the general population has been reported as equally high (J. C. Anderson, Williams, McGee, & Silva, 1987). Oppositional, negativistic, behavior may be developmentally normal in early childhood. However, epidemiological studies of negativistic traits in nonclinical populations found such behavior in between 16% to 22% of school-age children (Loeber, Lahey, & Thomas, 1991). Although ODD may begin as early as 3 years of age, it typically does not begin until 8 years of age and usually not later than adolescence. In boys aged 5 through 8 years, fighting, temper tantrums, disobedience, negativism, irritability, and quickness to anger appear to decrease with increasing age (Werry & Quay, 1971). MacFarlane, Allen, and Honzik (1962) found similar decreases with age for both sexes in the prevalence of lying, destructiveness, negative behavior, and temper tantrums. The greatest decline in these problems appeared to take place during the elementary years. Tremblay (1990) reported a decline in oppositional behavior in boys, particularly between the first and second grades. J. C. Anderson and coworkers (1987) report that mothers' ratings of aggressive behavior decreased between the ages of 5 and 11 years in children without a reported history of psychiatric problems. In contrast, teacher rated aggression scores for this same group increased for children with histories of psychiatric problems. Certain covert disruptive behaviors such as alcohol and drug use, as well as various forms of theft appear to increase from late childhood to adolescence equally for males and females (Loeber, 1985; McCabe, Rodgers, Yeh, & Hough, 2004). Lying, interestingly enough, appears to present at all age levels (Achenbach & Edelbrock, 1981). Further, there is little doubt that prevalence varies as diagnostic criteria change. For example, when comparing the revised third edition of the DSM with the original third edition ADHD criteria, the revised criteria were found to identify 14% more children than the original criteria identified (Lahey, Loeber, et al., 1990). Lahey, Loeber, et al. (1990) concluded that boys are more likely to meet criteria for DSM definitions of CD than their female counterparts.

Comorbidity

Attention-deficit/hyperactivity disorder co-occurs with other DBDs as well as multiple other developmental and psychiatric disorders in children to such an extent that authors have suggested subtypes of ADHD to include combinations of ADHD with other DBD (e.g., ADHD and CD) as well as with internalizing disorders (e.g., ADHD and Anxiety; Jensen, Martin, & Cantwell, 1997). Attention-deficit/hyperactivity disorder co-exists with other disorders at a rate well beyond chance (Seidman, Benedict, Biederman, & Bernstein, 1995). As described, impulsiveness likely acts as a catalyst, increasing risk for development of other problems, especially in the face of additional risk factors (e.g., family, developmental, educational).

S. Goldstein and Goldstein (1998) posit that certain events instigate or increase the probability that ADHD will be diagnosed. These include individual characteristics such a intellectual functioning, biological predisposition, and the physical and psychosocial environment. Events in the school or home then either strengthen or decrease the behavioral symptoms of ADHD. Once ADHD is diagnosed, the risk of depression is increased as the result of social problems, school failure, and possibly the side effects of medication. The risk for CD is increased by school and social problems as well as the presentation of antisocial role models that have been demonstrated to be critical risk factors.

In a review of empirical studies, Biederman, Newcorn, and Sprich (1991) attempted to define the comorbidity of ADHD with other disorders. The authors suggested that the literature supports considerable comorbidity of ADHD with CD, ODD, mood disorders, anxiety disorders, learning disabilities and other disorders such as mental retardation, Tourette's disorder, and borderline personality disorder. The qualities of ADHD may act as a catalyst: Leave them alone and they may not be terribly aversive; mix them with negative life events or risk factors and they appear to catalytically worsen those events and the impact they have on children's current and future functioning (S. Goldstein & Goldstein, 1998).

In a community sample of over 15,000 14- to 18-year-old adolescents, Lewinsohn, Rhode, and Seeley (1994) compared six clinical outcome measures with four major psychiatric disorders (depression, anxiety, substance abuse, and disruptive behaviors). The impact of comorbidity was strongest for academic problems, mental health treatment utilization, and past suicide attempts; intermediate on measures of role, function and conflict with parents, and nonsignificant and physical symptoms. The greatest incremental impact of comorbidity was on anxiety disorders; the least was on substance abuse. Substance use and disruptive behavior were more common in males, depression and anxiety in females. The effect of comorbidity was not due to psychopathology. The authors conclude as others have that there is a high rate of comorbidity in adolescence referred in clinical practice.

In clinic referred populations, the comorbidity between ADHD and CD has been reported as high as 50% with an incidence of 30% to 50% reported in epidemiological or comorbidity samples (Szatmari, Boyle, & Offord, 1989). Children with ADHD and comorbid ODD and CD exhibit greater frequencies of anti-social behavior such as lying, stealing, and fighting than those with ADHD who do not develop the second disruptive comorbid disorder (Barkley, 1998). It has also been suggested that this combined group is at greater risk for peer rejection. These children may be neglected due to their lack of social skills and rejected due to their aggressive behavior. Common sense dictates that the comorbid group is going to require more intensive and continuous service delivery. The comorbid group also holds the greatest risk for later life problems. In fact, it is likely the co-occurrence of CD with ADHD that speaks to the significant adult problems a subgroup of those with ADHD appear to develop. As Edelbrock (1989) noted, more predictive of outcome than severity of ADHD symptoms is the development in children with ADHD of oppositional and aggressive behaviors. Environmental consequences, including parent psychopathology, marital discord, ineffective parenting, parent aggressiveness, and antisocial parent behavior are better predictors of life outcome for children with ADHD than the ADHD diagnosis per se. In fact, these factors become highly stable over time and are resistant to change. Data also suggests that the comorbid conditions presenting before age 10 have a much worse prognosis than if the second behavior disorder develops after age 10 (McGee & Share, 1988).

After careful review of the literature, Loeber et al. (1991) suggest that CD and ODD are strongly and developmentally related but clearly different. Factor analyses indicate that distinct covarying groups of ODD and CD can be identified but that certain symptoms relate to both disorders, particularly mild aggression and lying. Nearly all youth with CD have a history of ODD but not all ODD cases progress to CD. In some studies, children with ODD demonstrate the same forms of parental psychopathology and family adversity but to a lesser degree than for CD. Clearly, the age of onset of some CD symptoms, specifically fighting, bullying, lying, and vandalism suggest that some youth with CD show nearly simultaneous onset of ODD and CD. However, the more serious symptoms of CD such as vandalism, running away, truancy, shoplifting, breaking and entering, rape, and assault appear to emerge at a much later age than ODD symptoms. Biederman, Faraone, Milberger, Jetton, and coworkers (1996) generated data suggesting two types of ODD which appear to have different correlates, course, and outcome. One type appeared prodromal for CD the other subsyndromal to CD and not likely to progress into CD in later years. Not surprisingly, the higher risk form of ODD was characterized by a stronger profile of negative, provocative, spiteful behavior.

There is a growing body of literature suggesting that DBDs and anxiety disorders are often comorbid. Loeber and Keenan (1994) found that CD and anxiety disorders are comorbid substantially higher than chance during childhood and adolescence.

Epidemiologically the overlap between ADHD and depression occurs at a beyond chance level with some studies suggesting nearly 30% (McClellan, Rubert, Reichler, & Sylvester, 1990). While Capaldi (1992) found that CD is likely a precursor to depression in some children, Biederman, Faraone, Mick, and Lelon (1995) questioned the psychiatric comorbidity among referred juveniles with major depression. In a sample of 424 children and adolescents consecutively referred to a psychiatric facility, nearly 40% were identified with a depressive disorder. They had a history of chronic course and severe psychosocial dysfunction. They also demonstrated a high rate of CD, anxiety disorder, and ADHD. Seventy-four percent with severe major depression and 77% with mild major depression received a diagnosis of ADHD compared to 74% of the psychiatric controls and none of the normal controls. The authors hypothesized that major depression was more likely the outcome rather than the cause of co-occurring disorders based on an analysis of age of symptom onset. These patterns of comorbidity persist into adulthood. In a retrospective study of over 9,000 individuals with childhood history of ADHD lifetime, 45% experienced any mood disorders; 59% any anxiety disorder; 36% any substance disorder; 88% had at least an additional psychiatric condition beyond ADHD life time, representing a six-fold increase from the general population (Kessler et al., 2005). Appendix A contains an overview of language milestones by grade. Given the high rate of language impairments in children with disruptive behaviors as well as patterns of disruptive behaviors exhibited by language impaired children absent severe disruptive disorders, it is important for classroom consultants to be well-versed in language milestones. These milestones should be reviewed and considered when children are assessed for disruptive behavior in the classroom.

Risk for Acquisition and Exacerbation

Biological, psychological, and psychosocial factors are all posited to be risk factors for the development of a DBD. J. D. Burke, Loeber, and Birmaher (2002) considered genetics, intergenerational transmission, neuroanatomy, neurotransmitters, preautonomic nervous system, pre- and perinatal problems, and neurotoxins as biological risk factors for the development of a DBD. Approximately 75% of the variance in determining ADHD appears genetic (Fisher et al., 2002). While the evidence is not as conclusive, several studies suggest a moderate genetic influence on ODD and CD. Eaves et al. (2000) concluded that there is a high genetic correlation across gender in the liability for ODD and CD.

Several researchers (e.g., Lahey et al., 1998) have found that a history of parental antisocial behavior disorders is associated with preadolescent onset of CD. Loeber, Green, Keenan, and Lahey (1995) concluded that parental substance abuse, low socioeconomic status, and oppositional behavior are key factors in boys' progression to CD, as are parenting styles (Glasgow, Dornbush, Troyer, Steinberg, & Ritter, 1997).

Biological

Frontal lobe dysfunction has been associated with the increased risk of violent behavior (Pliszka, 1999). Impairments in the functioning of the amygdala are associated with deficits in the reading of social cues and the connection between the amygdala and prefrontal cortical regions serves to aid in the suppression of negative emotion (Davidson, Putnam, & Larson, 2000).

Low levels of serotonin in cerebral spinal fluid have been linked to aggression (Kruesi et al., 1990). Moffitt, Brammer, and Caspi (1998) found that in men metabolites of serotonin in a general population sample of 21-year-olds was related to past year self-reported and lifetime court-recorded violence. J. D. Burke et al. (2002) concluded that the link between serotonin and aggression reflects a complex relationship between neuroanatomical and neurochemical interconnectivity, executive brain function, and behavioral dysregulation.

Pliszka (1999) reported that individuals with DBD experienced general physiological underarousal. Lower heart rates have been reported to be associated with adolescent antisocial behavior (Mezzacappa, Tremblay, & Kindlon, 1997) and predictive of later criminality (Raine, Venables, & Williams, 1990).

Evidence exists of the contributions of genetic factors to DBD as well as the contributions of prenatal and early developmental exposure to toxins, other perinatal problems and physical damage to brain structures (J. D. Burke et al., 2002). Maternal smoking during pregnancy has been found to predict CD in boys (Wakschlag et al., 1997). Pregnancy and birth complications have also been shown to be associated with the development of behavior problems in offspring (Raine et al., 1990). Environmental toxins such as lead have also been implicated in the development of DBDs. Elevated levels of lead in bones of children at age eleven are associated with greater parent and teacher ratings of aggressiveness, higher delinquency scores, and greater somatic complaints (Needleman, Riess, Tobin, Biesecker, & Greenhouse, 1996).

The psychological substrates of temperament, attachment, neuropsychological functioning, intelligence, academic performance, and social cognition have all been found to influence an individual's propensity to develop a DBD. Sanson and Prior (1999) concluded that early temperament (specifically negative emotionality, intense and reactive responding, and inflexibility) is predictive of externalizing behavior problems by late childhood.

Low intelligence is often considered a precursor to a DBD. However, as Loeber et al. (1991) point out, the issue of the association between CD, ADHD, and IQ is not well understood. Additionally, IQ appears to be related to low achievement and school failure that are also related to later antisocial behavior (Farrington, 1995). Moreover, high intelligence does not preclude conduct problems. Boys with psychopathic characteristics, parental antisocial personality disorder, and conduct problems were found to have IQs equivalent to those of controls and higher than those with boys with conduct problems but without psychopathology and parental APD (Christian, Frick, Hill, Tyler, & Frazer, 1997).

Psychological and Psychosocial Factors

Several aspects of child rearing practices such as degree of involvement, parent-child conflict management, monitoring, and harsh and inconsistent discipline have been correlated with children's disruptive or delinquent behavior (Frick, 1994; Wasserman, Miller, Pinner, & Jaramilo, 1996). Coercive parenting behaviors appear to lead to aggressive behaviors in younger girls as well as boys (Eddy, Leve, & Fagot, 2001).

Fergusson, Lynskey, and Horwood (1996) reported that a harsh or abusive parenting style including sexual or physical abuse, significantly increased the risk of CD. Childhood victimization of boys and girls, including abuse and neglect is predictive of later antisocial personality disorder (Luntz & Widom, 1994). Peer effects also appear to be importantly related to potential development and maintenance of DBD symptoms. The stability of peer rejection in children identified as having conduct problems is significant (Coie & Dodge, 1998; Coie & Lenox, 1994) and related to aggressive responding (Dodge, Price, Bachorowski, & Newman, 1990). Association with deviant peers appears to lead to the initiation of delinquent behavior in boys (D. S. Elliott & Menard, 1996).

Exposure to delinquent peers may enhance preexisting delinquency (Coie & Miller-Johnson, 2001).

Disruptive behaviors among children are particularly associated with poor and disadvantaged neighborhoods (Loeber et al., 1995). Wickström and Loeber (2000) found that the effects of living in public housing countered the impact of any individual protective factors that were present. Specific social and economic risk factors such as unemployment (Fergusson, Lynskey, & Horwood, 1997), neighborhood violence (Guerra, Huesmann, Tolan, Van Acker, & Eron, 1995), family poverty and children's aggression (Guerra et al., 1995), low SES and duration and poverty (McLloyd, 1998) are associated with antisocial behavior. Finally, exposure to daily stressors may add to the risk for DBD in children and as noted can be exacerbated by life circumstances caused having a DBD.

Are Some Youth with DBD More Resilient Than Others?

The biological bases of resilience have yet to be carefully studied, but likely will be found to play a role in predicting outcome. Traditionally, within the DBDs the study of positive outcome has focused on reduction of symptom severity over time and the reduction of exposure to significant adverse family, educational, and environmental phenomena. Yet, there is increasing interest in studying individuals who suffered from DBDs, in particular CD and managed to transition successfully into adult life despite struggling through adolescence and at times young adulthood. Stories collected by the Office of Juvenile Justice and Delinquency Prevention (Office of Juvenile Justice and Delinquency Prevention, 2000) exemplify that efforts focusing on rehabilitation, providing mentors, and individual attention and, most importantly, providing youth with a second chance, can and have been demonstrated to be part of the formula that leads to resilience.

Enhancing Resilience in Youth with DBD: Guidelines for Classroom Consultation

What are the factors that help some youth and adults bounce back while others become overwhelmed with feelings of helplessness and hopelessness. Some attain success that could have never been predicted by early life circumstances, finding the inner strength to overcome obstacles in their paths. Those who find success are viewed as resilient. Their positive outcome in the face of adversity precisely reflects the scientific studies that have demonstrated positive outcome in the face of variety of youthful problems, including those related to DBDs. A number of later chapters in this book are devoted to developing and applying resilience processes in the classroom along with behavioral and cognitive strategies. The remainder of this chapter provides a very brief overview of 9 proposed guidelines for educators.

1. Develop strategies with these youth to help them learn to rewrite negative scripts. Negative scripts are those words or behaviors that are followed day after day with predictable negative results.
2. Provide youth having a DBD opportunities to develop stress management skills.
3. Take the time to nurture and develop the capacity for empathy in youth with DBDs.
4. Teach effective communication through modeling and instruction. Effective communication includes an appreciation for both understanding as well as seeking to be understood.
5. Help youth with a DBD accept themselves without feeling inadequate or as second-class citizens.
6. Facilitate connections to others in the classroom, including providing opportunities for youth with a DBD to help and serve as teachers for others.
7. Help youth with DBDs view mistakes as challenges to appreciate and overcome rather than signs of inadequacy.
8. Help every youth with a DBD experience success and develop an island of competence in school; an area of strength in which success is experienced and appreciated by others.
9. Patiently help youth with a DBD develop self-discipline and self-control.

Summary

Disruptive behaviors of students are a challenge for educators. In isolation, a disruptive behavior is often manageable. However, when these behaviors cluster together, they are best understood and managed by beginning with an appreciation of the DBDs. The DBDs encompass the most common and disruptive childhood symptom composites. They affect a wide percentage of children, often present in combination and are catalytic in fueling a variety of adverse outcomes. The DBDs act to reduce protective influences, decreasing the opportunity for school success and the opportunity to develop a resilient mindset and a resilient outcome into adulthood. An increasing body of research is providing an understanding of those protective factors that may mitigate and insulate youth with DBDs. Efforts at applying the qualities of resilience strategies in the classroom to enhance a resilient mindset, offer the promise of helping youth with DBDs overcome adverse odds as they progress through their education.

CHAPTER

6

Problems of Self-Discipline

Sam Goldstein and Robert Brooks

Although ADHD was briefly reviewed and discussed as part of the previous chapter dealing with disruptive behavior disorders (DBDs), problems with self-discipline arising secondary to inattention, impulsivity, and hyperactivity are complex, easily misunderstood, and difficult to work with in the classroom. For this reason, problems related to self-discipline and self-regulation are expanded on in this chapter. As with many behavioral excesses, problems of self-discipline are common for all children. However, when these problems occur chronically and pervasively, cause significant impairment and associated risk, they cross the diagnostic threshold of attention-deficit/hyperactivity disorder (ADHD).

Most self-regulatory or self-discipline functions are well on their way to development by elementary school age. These skills, however, continue to develop into early adulthood (Barkley, 1997). By 7 years of age, there is a noticeable improvement in self-regulatory ability (Berkowitz, 1982). Most developmental theories acknowledge this improved shift in mental functioning (Erickson, 1963; Piaget, 1973). During these formative years children become responsible for and consciously aware of their actions and thoughts. During this period of time, self-directed, internalized speech develops (B. Berk, 1994). The environment plays a major role in the development of self-regulatory abilities in children. In particular, schools have a major impact (see Bronson, 2000, for a review). Children and adolescents can be taught strategies learning processes and problem

113

solving to assist in control of behavior. Further, children's growing awareness of self makes them psychologically vulnerable to environmental challenges. Those who develop a resilient mindset learn to deal effectively with mistakes and challenges. Their perceived successes and failures are internalized and affect their motivation. When they believe they are competent and able to control important aspects of their lives, motivation to exercise self-control increases (Deci & Chandler, 1986). When children believe they can control the outcome of school tasks they are more interested in those activities and persistent in pursuing them. As Prawat (1998) has noted, motivation and self-regulation are so closely tied that in everyday life they are often inseparable. The ability to control actions and thoughts is separate from the wish to do so but when voluntary self-regulation occurs in the natural environment, motivation must be involved (Bronson, 2000). Children are innately rewarded by competence and control and they require self-regulated control to reach their goals. Educators have become increasingly interested in self-regulated learning, behavior management, and motivation to help children succeed in the classroom (Biemiller & Meichenbaum, 1998). Finally, social development is also inextricably linked to the development of self-regulation.

The childhood cognitive and behavioral problems categorized over the past 50 years have presented a challenge for educators. The symptom constellation referred to as ADHD (American Psychiatric Association, 2000) has become one of the most widely researched areas in childhood and adolescence with an increasing interest throughout the adult life span. Problems arising from this constellation of symptoms have constituted the most chronic childhood behavior disorder (Wender, 1975) and the largest single source of referrals to mental health centers (Barkley, 1990; Gadow, Sprafkin, & Nolan, 2001). In clinic-referred settings, males out number females 6 to 1. In epidemiological studies of community-based settings, the ratio is 3 to 1 (see Barkley, 2006, for a review). The incidence of diagnosis continues to increase with a 70% increase in the diagnosis of children and nearly a 100% increase in the diagnosis of adults between 2000 and 2003 (Center for Disease Control [CDC], 2005). It is now estimated that between 4% to 8% of the population has received a diagnosis of ADHD (CDC, 2005; Cuffe, Moore, & McKeown, 2005). Females are the fastest growing group (Medco Health Solutions, 2005). Broad-based definitions of ADHD used in epidemiolic studies report an incidence rate of nearly 16% in adults while more narrow definitions report an incidence of 3% to 4% (Faraone & Biederman, 2005). Additionally, incidence has been reported to be higher in populations of individuals with mental health problems and even those with other nonpsychiatric impairments such as obesity (Altfas, 2002). Further, given the dimensional nature of these problems, it is likely that an additional 10% to 15% of children in all classrooms though not meeting full syndrome criteria for a diagnosis of ADHD nonetheless demonstrate some impairments secondary to ineffective self-discipline.

Increasing data has been generated to suggest that for the majority of affected children impulsivity and impaired executive functions represent core deficits (see Barkley, 2006; S. Goldstein & Schwebach, 2005; for a review). Children with ADHD typically experience difficulty in all aspects and situations of their lives. Their behavior is often uneven, unpredictable, and inconsistent. Neuropsychologists evaluating ADHD today must not only be concerned with the core symptoms of this disorder and their impact on childhood, but with the significant secondary impact these problems have on children's current and future lives as well as the lives of their family members. An increasing body of research is demonstrating increased vulnerability adults with ADHD face for psychiatric, emotional, cognitive, academic, vocational, substance, and anti-social problems (Barkley et al., 2004; Barkley & Gordon, 2002; Murphy, Barkley, & Bush, 2002).

In part, the controversy and at times confusion concerning various aspects of ADHD may in part be the result of a tradition to view this disorder as a unitary phenomenon with a single cause. Voeller (1991) suggests that rather than viewing ADHD as a single behavioral abnormality with associated comorbidities it may be better to conceptualize ADHD as a "cluster of different behavioral deficits, each with a specific neuro-substraight of varying severity occurring in variable constellations and sharing a common response to psychostimulants" (p. S4). There is no doubt, however, that the cluster of symptomatic problems that comprise the diagnosis of ADHD represents a distinct disorder from others of childhood and adulthood (Accardo, Blondis, & Whitman, 1990; Biederman, Faraone, Mick, et al., 1996). A significant percentage of affected youth continue to demonstrate the condition into adulthood, often underreporting their symptoms and impairment relative to observers (Barkley et al., 2002). The consensus among researchers and clinicians is that the core symptoms of ADHD effect a significant minority of our population. For affected individuals, however, ADHD represents a poor fit between societal expectations and these individuals abilities to meet those expectations. This phenomenon is distinct from other disorders of child and adulthood and can be reliably evaluated and effectively treated.

Toward a Working Definition of
Attention-Deficit/Hyperactivity Disorder

Sustained mental effort, self-regulation, planning, execution, and maintenance are considered measures of executive functioning (Daigneault, Braun, & Whitaker, 1992). Mirskey, Anthony, Duncan, Ahearn, and Kellam (1991) developed a neuropsychological model of attention defining four basic concepts involving the ability to focus, execute, sustain or code, and shift. Eight traditional assessment measures of attention were used in a factor analytic study to arrive at this model.

Increasingly, there is a consensus that ADHD represents a problem of faulty performance rather than faulty input. It is not so much that this population of individuals does not know what to do but they do not do what they know consistently. It is a problem of inconsistency rather than inability (S. Goldstein & Goldstein, 1998). Even in their adaptive skills, this pattern of difference between possessing a skill and using it efficiently has been well defined for individuals with ADHD (Stein, 1997).

The traditional disease model is not relevant to the definition of ADHD (A. W. Ellis, 1985). Attention-deficit/hyperactivity disorder is more like obesity or intelligence. Individuals differ not in having or not having the traits but in the degree of manifestation. Attention-deficit/hyperactivity disorder symptoms are multi-dimensional rather than unitary (Guevremont, DuPaul, & Barkley, 1993). However, there continues to be discussion as to which dimensions represent the most distinguishing deficits of the disorder. The frequency and severity of symptoms fluctuate across settings, activities, and caregivers (Tarver-Behring, Barkley, & Karlsson, 1985; Zentall, 1984). Neuropsychological profiles have also been demonstrated to differ between subtypes (Chabildas, Pennington, & Willicutt, 2001). However, these differences have not lent themselves to a differential diagnosis. There is a general consensus, however, that symptoms of ADHD fall into two broad factors defined by those related to the behavioral manifestation of faulty attention and those related to hyperactivity and impulsivity (Crystal, Ostrander, Chen, & August, 2001; Faraone, Biederman, & Friedman, 2000). Symptoms of hyperactivity and impulsivity appear to co-occur at such a high frequency that it is difficult on a factor analytic basis to separate them. However, research has demonstrated subtype differences in neuropsychological profiles and patterns of comborbidity (Eiraldi et al., 1997). It is also important for consultants to recognize that at times the lines blur between the symptoms and consequences or impairments of ADHD. Thus, a diagnostic strategy for ADHD should include identifying symptoms as well as a list of skills and classroom impairments hypothesized to be directly impacted by symptoms (M. Gordon et al., 2006). Having the symptoms but not having a negative impact would, in fact, preclude the diagnosis of ADHD according to current *DSM-IV-TR* criteria.

The *DSM-IV* diagnostic criteria published in 1994 made an effort to move forward and correct the mistaken course that ADHD represents a unipolar disorder. The field studies for the ADHD diagnosis were more comprehensive and better structured than previous efforts. The *DSM-IV-TR* (American Psychiatric Association, 2000) criteria appear in Table 6.1. They are identical to the *DSM-IV* criteria (American Psychiatric Association, 1995). Since *DSM-III*, each succeeding diagnostic protocol has focused increasingly on the issue of impairment. Impairment has and will continue to be critical in making the diagnosis of ADHD but is not well explained by symptom severity (M. Gordon et al., 2006). Further, the measurement of neuropsychological processes has been advocated to be considered as part of the *DSM-V* criteria for ADHD (Naglieri & Das, 2005a).

Of the 276 children diagnosed with ADHD in the *DSM-IV* field studies 55% had the Combined Type, 27% the Inattentive Type, and 18% the Hyperactive-Inattentive Type (Lahey et al., 1994). Less than half of the ADHD Hyperactive Type (44%) received that diagnosis when *DSM-III* criteria for ADD with Hyperactivity were used. These two diagnoses, therefore, only partially overlapped. The hyperactive-impulsive group had fewer symptoms of inattention in comparison to children with the combined type. They also had fewer symptoms of hyperactive-impulsive problems suggesting that this represents a less severe variant of the disorder. The hyperactive-impulsive group contained 20% females, the combined group 12%, and the inattentive group 27%. This latter number represents that long held perception that females more often demonstrate the inattentive type of ADHD (Biederman et al., 2002). This overrepresentation has not been well explained by any theoretical model (Silverthorn, Frick, Kuper, & Ott, 1996) nor has it been understood why preliminary research suggests that females with ADHD may be less likely to demonstrate executive function deficits than males (Seidman et al., 1997). The hyperactive-impulsive population was also younger in the field studies. Additionally, they had fewer disruptive symptoms of oppositional defiance or conduct disorder than the combined type of ADHD.

A number of researchers have demonstrated the validity of the current *DSM-IV-TR* diagnostic conceptualization for ADHD utilizing a variety of clinical and laboratory measures. Such research has included a full battery of neuropsychological tests (Brand, Das-Smaal, & DeJonge,

Table 6.1 *DSM IV-TR* Criteria for
Attention-Deficit/Hyperactivity Disorder

The guidelines for a diagnosis of ADHD outlined in the Diagnostic and Statistical Manual of Mental Disorders (fourth edition, text revision, 2001) are as follows:

A. Either (1) or (2):

(1) Six or more of the following symptoms of *inattention* have persisted for at least 6 months to a degree that is maladaptive and inconsistent with developmental level:

Inattention
a. Often fails to give close attention to details or makes careless mistakes in schoolwork, work, or other activities
b. Often has difficulty sustaining attention in tasks or play activities
c. Often does not seem to listen when spoken to directly
d. Often does not follow through on instructions and fails to finish schoolwork, chores, or duties in the workplace (not due to oppositional behavior or failure to understand instructions)
e. Often has difficulties organizing tasks and activities
f. Often avoids, dislikes, or is reluctant to engage in tasks that require sustained mental effort (such as schoolwork or homework)
g. Often loses things necessary for tasks or activities (e.g., toys, school assignments, pencils, books or tools)
h. Is often easily distracted by extraneous stimuli
i. Is often forgetful in daily activities

(2) Six (or more) of the following symptoms of *hyperactivity-impulsivity* have persisted for at least 6 months to a degree that is maladaptive and inconsistent with developmental level:

Hyperactivity
a. Often fidgets with hands or feet or squirms in seat
b. Often leaves seat in classroom or in other situations in which remaining seated is expected
c. Often runs about or climbs excessively in situations in which it is inappropriate (in adolescents or adults, may be limited to subjective feelings of restlessness)
d. Often has difficulty playing or engaging in leisure activities quietly
e. Is often "on the go" or often acts as if "driven by a motor"
f. Often talks excessively

118

Table 6.1   (Continued)

Impulsivity
    g. Often blurts out answers before questions have been completed
    h. Often has difficulty awaiting turn
    i. Often interrupts or intrudes on others (e.g., butts into conversations or games)

B. Some hyperactive-impulsive or inattentive symptoms that caused impairment were present before age 7 years.
C. Some impairment from the symptoms is present in two or more settings (e.g., at school [or work] and at home).
D. There must be clear evidence of clinically significant impairment in social, academic, or occupational functioning.
E. The symptoms do not occur exclusively during the course of a Pervasive Developmental Disorder, Schizophrenia, or other Psychotic Disorder and are not better accounted for by another mental disorder (e.g., Mood Disorder, Anxiety Disorder, Dissociative Disorder, or a Personality Disorder).

Types

Attention-Deficit/Hyperactivity Disorder, Combined Types: if both Criteria A1 and A2 are met for the past 6 months

Attention-Deficit/Hyperactivity Disorder, Predominantly Inattentive Type: if Criterion A1 is met but Criterion A2 is not met for the past 6 months

Attention Deficit/Hyperactivity Disorder, Predominantly Hyperactive-Impulsive Type: if Criterion A2 is met but Criterion A1 is not met for the past 6 months.

Coding note: For individuals (especially adolescents and adults) who currently have symptoms that no longer meet full criteria, "In Partial Remission" should be specified.

Attention-Deficit/Hyperactivity Disorder Not Otherwise Specified
This category is for disorders with prominent symptoms of inattention or hyperactivity-impulsivity that do not meet criteria for Attention-Deficit/Hyperactivity Disorder.

Source: Diagnostic and Statistical Manual of Mental Disorders, fourth edition, text revision, by American Psychiatric Association, 2000, Washington, DC: Author. Reprinted with permission.

1996; Halperin et al., 1993; Harrier & DeOrnellas, 2005) reversal and memory tasks (M. E. O'Neill & Douglas, 1996); executive function tasks (C. Clark, Prior, & Kinsella, 2000; Geurts, Verte, Oosterlaan, Royers, & Sergeant, 2005; C. C. Hart & Harter, 2001) and neurological evaluation (Luk, Leung, & Yuen, 1991). The general consistency of symptom, co-morbid, and related findings among large, well-controlled clinic and epidemiologic studies suggest that the conceptualization of ADHD in *DSM-IV-TR* has become increasingly more refined. Nonetheless, these criteria continue to focus excessively on inattention as the primary problem for the disorder, limiting the scope and focus on the impact of impulsivity as the core deficit. This perpetuates a number of major misconceptions, including that the inattentive type of ADHD represents a subtype of the combined disorder (Anastopoulos, Barkley, & Shelton, 1994). Increasing research suggests that it does not. More likely, the inattentive type represents a distinct disorder, primarily reflecting difficulty attending to repetitive, effortful tasks, and problems with organization. C. L. Carlson and Mann (2002) described children with the Inattentive Type ADHD as distinct from the Combined Type as possessing hypoactivity, lethargy, and a lack of ability to stay focused. The problems this group experiences may very well be the result of faulty skills as opposed to inconsistent or inadequate use of skills. There is also emerging data that raises questions about the lack of stability of *DSM-IV* ADHD subtypes over time as children mature (Lahey et al., 2005).

The Genetics and Etiology of ADHD

ADHD is among the most common disorders of childhood. It is estimated that it affects between 5% and 8% of the population throughout life. Estimates vary with the American Psychiatric Association (American Psychiatric Association, 2000) suggesting an incidence of 4% to 6%. Statistics vary depending on populations studied, thresholds, and definitional criteria (Sherman, Iacono, & McGue, 1997). The genetic contribution has been postulated over the past 20 years by a number of authors (Hechtman, 1993; Rutter et al., 1990; Stevenson, 1992; Swanson et al., 2000). The underlying mechanism genetically has recently been suggested to be associated with a single dopamine transporter gene (Cook et al., 1995) as well as with a variation in the DRD4 (LaHoste et al., 1996) and DRD5 (N. Lowe et al., 2004) receptor genes as well as in the DAT1 transporter (Winsberg & Comings, 1999). Further, it has been suggested that the trait locus for reading disability on chromosome

6 identified by Cardon et al. (1994) may also be a locus for ADHD (Warren et al., 1995).

Etiology of ADHD must also be considered from related disorders or teratogen basis. Fragile X, Turner Syndrome, Tourette's, neurofibromatosis, sickle cell anemia, phenylketonuria, Noonan's Syndrome, and Williams' Syndrome are all chromosomal and genetic abnormalities in which attentional problems and ADHD have been reported (Hagerman, 1991; Mautner, Kluwe, Thakker, & Laerk, 2002). Bastain et al. (2002) suggest that expensive laboratory tests for genetic disorders are not indicated unless a genetic disorder is suspect due to family history, clinical signs, or low IQ. Toxins resulting in disorders such as fetal alcohol syndrome, cocaine exposure in utero, lead and vapor abuse, perinatal complications, medical problems such as hypothyroidism, encephalitis, even radiation therapy secondary to leukemia have all been reported as responsible for creating inattentive and impulsive problems (see Barkley, 2006; S. Goldstein & Goldstein, 1998; for a review). Niederhofer and Pittschieler (in press) report an elevated set of ADHD symptoms in untreated patients with Celiac Disease. These symptoms reduce significantly in relation to pain reduction secondary to Celiac treatment. Attention-deficit/hyperactivity disorder and depressive symptoms are also commonly identified after pediatric traumatic brain injury but may pre-date the trauma (Bloom et al., 2001).

The neurobiology of ADHD implicates impairment in brain structure, particularly differences in size of certain structures, interacting with metabolic differences (Zametkin & Rapoport, 1987). Efficient brain metabolism in prefrontal and cingulate regions as well as the right thalamus, caudate, hippocampus, and cerebellum have been reported in adults with ADHD (Zametkin, Nordahl, & Gross, 1990). Regional abnormalities of glucose metabolism demonstrated by PET studies generally demonstrate a fundamental biologic difference between ADHD and normal subjects. Castellanos et al. (1996) suggest that connections between the right prefrontal cortex, caudate, and cerebellum reflect the brain's "braking system," a system that operates inefficiently in individuals with ADHD. Semrud-Clikeman et al. (2000) found reversed caudate asymmetry on MRI scans of 10 males diagnosed with ADHD. They noted the right prefrontal cortex, cerebellum, and basal ganglia appear to be associated with behavioral measures of inattention and inhibition. Children with ADHD have been found unable to activate the caudate nucleus suggesting a core abnormality in this function for ADHD (Vaidya et al., 2005). These authors conclude that children with ADHD experience reduced engagement of a frontal-striatal-temporal-parietal network when engaging in inhibitory tasks.

Developmental Course and Comorbidity

Although the core problems children with ADHD experience are homogeneous reflecting difficulty with impulse control, attention, and hyperactivity, each child's presentation is unique in terms of the manifestation of these problems and associated comorbid factors (S. Goldstein & Goldstein, 1998). As an increasing body of scientific data is generated concerning the developmental course and adult outcome of children with ADHD, it appears that the comorbid problems they develop rather than the diagnosis of ADHD best predicts their life outcome. Attention-deficit/hyperactivity disorder in isolation appears to best predict school struggles, difficulty meeting expectations without the home setting, and possible mild substance abuse as an adult. However, it does not predict the significant negative emotional, behavioral, and personality outcomes that have been reported.

Infants who have been noted to demonstrate difficult temperament do not handle changes in routines well. They exhibit a low frustration threshold and a high intensity of response (W. B. Carey, 1970; Chess & Thomas, 1986; A. Thomas & Chess, 1977). In follow-up studies of such infants, as many as 70% develop school problems (Terestman, 1980). These infants appear at greater risk than others of receiving a diagnosis of ADHD. It is also important to note that these difficult infants exert a significant negative impact on the developing relationship with caregivers—a relationship that is critical in predicting a child's life outcome (Katz, 1997).

Although early symptoms of ADHD may be viewed as transient problems of young children, research data suggests that ignoring these signs results in the loss of valuable treatment time. At least 60% to 70% of children later diagnosed with ADHD could have been identified by their symptoms during the preschool years (N. J. Cohen, Sullivan, Minde, Novack, & Helwig, 1981). Young children manifesting symptoms of ADHD are more likely to present with speech and language problems than are children not suffering from those symptoms (Baker & Cantwell, 1987) and to develop a wide range of behavioral problems (Cantwell et al., 1981; N. J. Cohen, Davine, & Meloche-Kelly, 1989; DuPaul et al., 2001). This research cogently suggests that the comorbidity of speech and language disorders with ADHD merits routine screening of children suspected of ADHD and language disorders, especially during their younger years. Children with concurrent ADHD and language disorders appear to have a much poorer prognosis than those with ADHD alone (Baker & Cantwell, 1992).

Within school settings, children with ADHD appear to be victims of their temperament and of their learning history which often involves beginning but not completing tasks. The negatively reinforcing model utilized by most educators in this circumstance tends to focus on misbehavior rather than on termination of the behavior. This may further disrupt the classroom by having a disinhibitory effect on other students. Although 30 years ago it was suggested that children with ADHD were intellectually less competent than their peers, it appears more likely that weak performance on intellectual tasks results from the impact of impulsivity and inattention on test-taking behavior rather than an innate lack of intelligence (Barkley, 1995). Kaplan, Crawford, Dewey, and Fisher (2000) identified a normal IQ distribution in children diagnosed with ADHD. Children with ADHD often underperform but may not underachieve during the elementary years. However, by high school it has been reported that at least 80% of these children fall behind in a basic academic subject requiring repetition and attention for competence such as basic math knowledge, spelling, or written language (see Barkley, 2006; S. Goldstein & Goldstein, 1998; for a review). Depending on diagnostic criteria, approximately 20% to 30% of children with ADHD also suffer from a concomitant, often language-based, learning disability (see Willcutt & Pennington, 2000, for a review). Although it has been hypothesized that ADHD may prevent a child from achieving his or her academic potential (Stott, 1981), the presence of a learning disability may make a child appear more inattentive than others (Aaron, Joshi, Palmer, Smith, & Kirby, 2002; McGee & Share, 1988).

Sociometric and play study suggests that children with ADHD are not chosen as often by their peers to be best friends or partners in activities (Bagwell, Molina, Pelham, & Hoza, 2001; Pelham & Milich, 1984). They appear to be cognizant of their difficulties, an awareness that likely precipitates lower self-esteem for children with ADHD (Glow & Glow, 1980). Moreover, they appear to experience either high incidence-low impact problems that result in poor social acceptance or low incidence-high impact problems that result in social rejection (Pelham & Milich, 1984). In addition, these children have difficulty adapting their behavior to different situational demands (Whalen, Henker, Collins, McAuliffe, & Vaux, 1979). It has been suggested that the impulsive behavioral patterns of children with ADHD are most responsible for their social difficulty, making those with comorbid hyperactive-impulsive problems of greater severity at even greater risk of developing social difficulties (Hodgens, Cole, & Boldizar, 2000; Pelham & Bender, 1982). Attention-deficit/hyperactivity disorder has been found to be a risk factor heading to a wide variety of ineffective social coping strategies as youth transition into adolescence (Young, Chadwick, Heptinstall, Taylor, & Sonuga-Barke, 2005). It should also be noted that children who are good responders demonstrating symptom and impairment reduction with medication appear to exhibit fewer chronic social impairments (Gallagher et al., 2004).

Some primary symptoms of ADHD may diminish in intensity by adolescence (Weiss & Hechtman, 1979). However, most adolescents with ADHD continue to experience significant problems (R. S. Milich & Loney, 1979; see Barkley, 2006; S. Goldstein & Ellison, 2002; for a review). At least 80% of adolescents with ADHD continue to manifest symptoms consistent with ADHD. Sixty percent develop at least one additional disruptive disorder (Barkley et al., 1990). Between 20% and 60% of adolescents with ADHD are involved in antisocial behavior, with a normal occurrence of 3% to 4% (Satterfield, Hoppe, & Schell, 1982). At least 50% to 70% of these adolescents develop oppositional defiant disorder, often during younger years, with a significant number progressing to conduct disorder (Barkley et al., 1990). However, the high prevalence of antisocial problems in adolescents with ADHD likely reflects the comorbidity of ADHD with other disruptive disorders, principally conduct disorder (Barkley, McMurray, Edelbrock, & Robbins, 1989). As Barkley (1997) succinctly points out, the preponderance of the available data suggests that while ADHD is clearly a risk factor for the development of adolescent antisocial problems, life experience, principally factors within families most powerfully contribute to the onset and maintenance of delinquency, conduct disorder, and subsequent young adult antisocial problems (Dalsgaard, Mortenson, Frydenberg, & Thomsen, 2002).

Evaluation in the Classroom

Due to the pervasive, multisetting nature of problems related to ADHD and the high comorbidity with other childhood disorders, assessment for ADHD must be accompanied by a thorough emotional, developmental, and behavioral evaluation. It should be noted, however, that the diagnosis of ADHD should be firmly based on the accepted standard, in this case the *DSM-IV-TR* diagnostic criteria. Consultants should be aware that efforts to include additional data to prove/disprove the diagnosis run the risk of introducing increasing variance adding error rather than accuracy to the diagnosis (Naglieri, Goldstein, & Schwebach, 2004). A comprehensive evaluation should collect data concerning the child's behavior at home, with friends and at school, academic and intellectual functioning, medical status, and emotional development.

Within the classroom, consultants should utilize a functional behavioral model as described by Steege, Mace, and Brown-Chidsey in Chapter 3. Consultants should also consider use of behavioral rating scales to supplement classroom observation. These scales might include Attention Problem Scale (Achenbach, 1996), the Conners Teacher Rating Scales—Revised (Conners, 1997), the Comprehensive Teacher's Rating Scale (Ullmann, Sleator, & Sprague, 1988), the Childhood Attention Problem Scale (Edelbrock, 1990), the Academic Performance and ADHD Rating Scales (DuPaul, Power, Anastopoulous, & Reid, 1998; DuPaul, Rapport, & Perriello, 1991) or the Behavioral Assessment System for Children-Second Edition (C. R. Reynolds & Kamphaus, 2005). Because this text is not directed at the diagnosis of ADHD but rather the identification and measurement of impairments caused by poor self-discipline in the classroom, further discussion of assessment is not provided. Interested readers are referred to Barkley (2006) for an overview of current assessment strategies.

Treatment

Treatment of ADHD must be multi-disciplinary, multi-modal and maintained over a long period (see S. Goldstein & Ellison, 2002; S. Goldstein & Goldstein, 1998; Teeter, 1998; for a review). By far, the most effective short term interventions for ADHD reflect the combined use of medical, behavioral, and environmental techniques. Medication has demonstrated the ability to reduce the manipulative power of the child's behavior in eliciting certain responses from teachers, peers, and family members.

An extensive literature attests to the benefits of medicine, specifically stimulants in reducing key symptoms of ADHD and thus improving daily functioning (R. G. Klein, 1987; see Barkley, 2006; S. Goldstein & Goldstein, 1998; for a review). Stimulants and other drugs principally impacting dopamine and norepinephrine (Volkow et al., 2001) consistently have been reported to improve academic achievement and productivity as well as accuracy of class work (Douglas, Barr, O'Neill, & Britton, 1986); attention span, reading comprehension, complex problem solving, and to enhance inhibitory processes

(Balthazor, Wagner, & Pelham, 1991; Pelham, 1987). Related problems, including peer interactions, peer status, and even relationships with family members have been reported improved with these drugs as well (Whalen & Henker, 1991). Chapter 19 provides further discussion of medication effects in the classroom.

Behavior management increases the salience of behaving in a way consistent with environmental expectations. The manipulation of the environment (e.g., making tasks more interesting and payoffs more valuable) reduces the risk of problems within the natural setting. Zentall (1995b) suggests that students with ADHD possess an active learning style with a demonstrated need to move, talk, respond, question, choose, debate, and even provoke. Thus, in classroom settings children with ADHD do not fare well in sedentary situations. Managing interventions have included positive and negative contingent teacher attention, token economies, peer-mediated, and group contingencies, time out, home school contingencies, reductive techniques based on reinforcement and cognitive behavioral strategies (Abramowitz & O'Leary, 1991). Environmental and task modifications are also critical for classroom success for the child with ADHD. However, additional research is needed, especially in the area of school based intervention for adolescents with ADHD. A number of chapters in Part III provide an overview of strategies to reduce impairments arising from self-discipline problems in the classroom.

Though popular, the use of cognitive strategies (e.g., teaching a child to stop, look, and listen) as well as other nontraditional treatments (e.g., dietary manipulation, EEG biofeedback) to permanently alter the symptoms of ADHD have not stood the test of scientific research and thus should not be advocated as first line treatments of choice for children with ADHD. However, these strategies are effective when targeted to specific problems and impairments in the classroom for all students, with or without diagnoses. Shure (1994) suggests that the patient application of cognitive training over a long period of time, applied in the real world setting, can even improve the self-regulatory skills of children with ADHD. Chapter 17 in this book applies Dr. Shure's model to treat and prevent bullying in the classroom. Chapter 13 provides an in-depth overview of cognitive behavioral strategies for a wide range of classroom problems.

Regardless of the treatment modality employed, the basic underlying premise in managing problems of poor self-discipline and self-regulation involves increasing the child's capacity to inhibit before acting. This is consistent with the theoretical construct that the core problem for

ADHD reflects an inability to permit sufficient time to think or respond consistently to consequences.

Summary

Problems of self-discipline and self-regulation typically caused by inattention, impulsivity, and hyperactivity are difficult to understand, define, measure, and manage in the classroom. Consultants must be well versed in the science and behavioral technology related to the assessment and intervention of these problems. This chapter provided an overview of self-discipline issues focusing on knowledge generated by the study of children crossing clinical thresholds for impairments leading to a diagnosis of ADHD.

CHAPTER

7

Worry and Helplessness

SAM GOLDSTEIN AND ROBERT BROOKS

Since children spend the better part of their waking hours in the classroom throughout the year, it might be expected that teachers are in an ideal position to spot the warning signs and identify children suffering from worry and helplessness. Unfortunately, although teachers are very competent at identifying children suffering from a disruptive behavior disorder (DBD) they are much less skilled at recognizing those suffering from nondisruptive problems related to worry and helplessness. At the extreme, these patterns of thinking lead to impaired behavior consistent with the clinical diagnoses of anxiety and depression. There are a number of reasons beyond the fact that these adverse feelings are not easy to observe that makes it difficult for classroom educators to accurately identify children struggling from worry and helplessness. Teachers are not in a position to observe symptoms affecting sleep, appetite, nor inner thoughts. The behavior of most worried and/or helpless children does not call attention to themselves because these children do not act up in class nor are the majority of these students likely to share their fears, worries, helplessness, hopelessness, sadness, or at the extreme suicidal thoughts with a teacher no matter how close the teacher-child relationship.

Unlike the DBDs that usually lead teachers to seek consulting advice, problems of worry and helplessness must be routinely screened for their presence in all students by teachers. Consultants should consider providing classroom educators schoolwide with a framework of these problems and a set of behaviors that might indicate red flags and the need for further consultation. These include:

- *Somatic complaints:* If a student often complains of headaches, stomachaches, or other physical aches and pains, teachers should be alert to the possibility of worry or helplessness. Frequent requests to go down to the office for various ailments are clear signals that something is wrong.
- *Poor frustration tolerance:* Students suffering from helplessness and worry possess little in the way of the ability to be resilient or to bounce back from disappointment. Some are perfectionistic and may fall apart in tears or angry outbursts over minor mistakes or challenges.
- *Lethargy or listlessness:* Students who fall asleep in class or appear to lack energy or enthusiasm for school activities may be suffering from depression. In teens these symptoms may signal drug or alcohol abuse. In either case, they are cause for concern and should be further evaluated.
- *Social isolation and/or peer problems:* Helpless and worried children are particularly likely to have difficulty with friendships and peer acceptance. Although some may be well liked and accepted by their peers, most tend to be ignored.
- *Co-existing conditions:* When children are identified as suffering from attention-deficit/hyperactivity disorder (ADHD), learning disability, or medical problem, they are at a higher risk than others to suffer from worry and helplessness.
- *Mid-year slump:* If a student's performance drops off dramatically during the school year, teachers should not simply write this off as postholiday or spring let down.

This chapter provides an overview of internalizing problems related to worry and helplessness which at their extreme fall under the diagnostic categories of anxiety and depression. Factor analytic studies suggest that among the overcontrolled or internalizing problems children experience, a cluster appear to be related to depressive and anxious behaviors (Achenbach, 1975; Achenbach & Edelbrock, 1981). Quay (1979) described this cluster of problems as being related to difficulty with anxiety-withdrawal. Barrios and Hartmann (1988) list the following symptoms for this factor: feelings of inferiority, unhappiness, worthlessness, timidity, social isolation, and hypersensitivity. Some researchers have described a clinical syndrome referred to as "mixed anxiety-depression" due to the significant overlap of these symptoms (Zinbarg et al., 1998). A tripartite model suggests that anxiety and depression or worry and helplessness share a significant but nonspecific component of generalized distress that might be referred to as negative affect (Mineka, Watson, & Clark, 1998). Symptoms of anxious or depressed mood, poor concentration, sleep disturbances, or irritability are examples of negative affective symptoms shared by anxiety and depression. Despite the overlap in depressive and anxious symptoms in children and adolescents, there is a literature and rationale for reviewing and understanding these two phenomena as independent but likely frequently co-occurring.

Worry, Fear, and Anxiety

Worry, fear, and anxiety are terms often used interchangeably. However, these three phenomena appear to best be understood as falling along a continuum with worry reflecting the mildest problems followed by fear and finally anxiety. Worry, fear, and anxiety are clearly different on a scientific basis. Worry reflects the inability to confidently predict a positive outcome for an upcoming event. It results from repeatedly thinking about the possible negative outcome for the prescribed event and being unable to substitute a more optimistic outlook. For some individuals, worry may not be significantly impairing and may not lead to fear. Fear, however, appears to be generated by worry and is best defined in physical terms. When fearful, the body reacts aversively. When fear occurs individuals attempt to escape the fear provoking event. Fear elicits a physiological response involving the sympathetic nervous system, including changes in heart rate, blood pressure, and hormones. A fear reaction may not necessarily be maladaptive. In fact, it is the physiological experience of fear that drives individuals to seek escape. Yet at different ages, based on a child's intellectual development, certain phenomena may invoke a fearful response simply based on lack of knowledge. Most children outgrow these types of developmental fears as they reach different maturational levels. Finally, the combination of worry and fear often leads to maladaptive behavior and ineffective problem solving. When these phenomena present repeatedly across multiple situations causing impairment in every day functioning beyond that which would be expected for most individuals, a diagnosis of anxiety is considered.

Worrisome thoughts and fears, generally referred to as anxiety, appear to be common in childhood. These thoughts and fears change, and diminish in severity and occurrence, as children grow older. Anxiety might be best defined as a sense of apprehension or uneasiness that is often related to the individual's expectation of some kind of threat to his or her physical well-being (Morris & Kratochwill, 1985; see Barlow,

2002; for a review). This sense of apprehension may be focused on an object, situation, or activity. For some individuals, this sense of anxiety is pervasive or free-floating and may not be tied to a specific stimulus.

Epidemiological studies have suggested that anxiety disorders as a group are the most prevalent form of mental illness in adults in the United States (Regier et al., 1988) and are likely one of the most common clusters of problems among children and adolescents (G. A. Bernstein & Borchardt, 1991). Kessler et al. (1994) in the first U.S. national comorbidity survey reported that one out of four individuals experiences at least one type of anxiety disorder during their lifetime. Based on the adult research, it is likely that most children and adolescents find the threat of loss, criticism, or harm most anxiety producing (A. T. Beck & Emery, 1985).

Kendall, Howard, and Epps (1988) reported that childhood anxiety crosses a threshold of adult concern when the severity or duration of the child's problem impinges on functioning at home, school, or with peers. In many ways, the techniques used by children to avoid anxious or worrisome thoughts, such as staying home from school, are based on a negative reinforcement model. The threat of school generates anxiety that hangs over the child's head, and the child tries to avoid this anxiety by avoiding school. School avoidance, through whatever means, negatively reinforces the child.

Last, Phillips, and Statfield (1987) reported that early symptoms of anxiety in childhood may predict later adult problems with anxiety. Their data also suggest that depressive and affective symptoms presenting prior to age 10 are often of strong prognostic significance for continued problems at least through adolescence. It is critical for the classroom consultant to possess a basic understanding of the normal development of children's fears, worries, and feelings as a means of more effectively identifying those children who are typical in their presentation.

Researchers have hypothesized childhood anxiety as manifesting itself across a number of dimensions involving physical, behavioral, and cognitive components (Lang, 1968). Physical or physiological components are generally considered to reflect activity in the autonomic nervous system, which—among its other roles—is responsible for regulation of internal body functions. Thus, as reported by Barrios and Hartmann (1988), symptoms of perspiration, stomach pain, trembling, even enuresis or tics, can be suggestive of anxiety problems. In 1988, Strauss described anxious children as experiencing multiple somatic complaints, including headache, stomachache, and fatigue.

A major focus in anxiety disorders research with children and adults has been the relationship of cognition or thinking to the development, maintenance, and extinction of anxiety problems. Cognitive theories have lent themselves very well to describing and understanding a variety of anxiety disorders. Interested readers are referred to Barlow (2002) for a thorough review of cognitive theories of emotion and anxiety. Kendall et al. (1988) describe *cognitive structures* as the memory and manner in which information is represented, *cognitive content* as the information that is stored in memory, *cognitive processes* as the manner in which we go about understanding and interpreting these thoughts and, finally, *cognitive products* as the conclusions we draw based on interaction of the previous three variables. These authors hypothesize that because child-hood anxiety may be related to problems in any or all of these areas, effective intervention consider all these factors. Kendall (1985) eloquently describes a variety of cognitive problems that may lead to anxious symptoms. Cognitive deficiencies reflect an absence of thinking in situations where it would be beneficial. This may lead to impulsive behavior or unnecessary worries. Cognitive distortions reflect illogical thought processes that lead to erroneous conclusions and fuel anxious responses. Kendall, Stark, and Adam (1990) reported that depressed youngsters for example, view themselves as less capable than nondepressed youngsters. Interestingly, this judgment was not corroborated by their teachers who viewed both groups equally. This research indicates that children with internalizing problems tend to not only distort but underestimate their capabilities as well. Cognition and experience are increasingly recognized as modifiers of genetically driven risk for anxiety disorders (see Barlow, 2002, for a review).

Cognitive deficiency also contributes to anxiety. Some children may be anxious because they lack the cognitive skills to deal with a particular situation and manage anxious responses, either as a consequence of delayed development or their place on the normal developmental continuum.

Because of the tendency of anxious children to internalize or over control, most of them do not come to their teacher's attention (Kendall et al., 1992). The more subtle symptoms of anxiety are not disruptive and these children may not be referred until their anxious symptoms begin to affect schoolwork. Some of these symptoms, such as fidgeting, off-task behavior, or failure to complete work, may be initially interpreted as reflecting disruptive problems of attention deficit or noncompliance. The teachers' misperception of the problem and subsequent attempts at punitive or even reinforcing intervention stand a significant chance of further fueling the anxiety problems.

Separation Anxiety

The essential feature of this childhood problem is excessive anxiety concerning separation, usually from the mother or father. Separation from the mother is most commonly seen (L. Eisenberg, 1958). Separation anxiety is a normal developmental phenomenon from approximately age 7 months to the early preschool years. Gittelman (1984) points out that separation anxiety may appear as panic. The child secondarily may worry about potential dangers that threaten the family when separated. The child may also report feeling homesick even during short separations. These characteristics may occur separately or in combination.

The *DSM-IV-TR* criteria for separation anxiety disorder require the child to experience at least three of eight symptomatic problems that reflect developmentally inappropriate and excessive anxiety concerning separation from home or an attachment figure:

1. Worry about losing or possible harm befalling the attachment figure.
2. Persistent worry that a traumatic event will lead to separation from the major attachment figure.
3. Refusal to attend school due to fear of separation.
4. Reluctance to be alone without the attachment figure.
5. Reluctance to go to sleep without being near the attachment figure or to sleep away from home.
6. Nightmares involving the theme of separation.
7. Complaints of physical symptoms when separation from the attachment figure is anticipated or occurs.
8. Excessive distress when separation from the figure is anticipated or involved.

For all of these symptoms, separation from home may provoke as much anxiety as separation from the attachment figure. These symptoms must occur for at least 4 weeks, be manifested before the child reaches the age of 18, cause distress or impaired functioning in social, academic, or other important areas of life, and not occur primarily as the result of a pervasive developmental disorder, schizophrenia, or psychotic disorder. The criteria also suggest that age of onset be noted, with onset before age 6 specifically indicated in the diagnosis. The *DSM-IV-TR* criteria do not specify the reason for this distinction; a review of the data, however, will shed some light on the age of onset and symptom problems.

There appear to be developmental differences in the way separation anxiety is expressed. Young children (ages 5 through 8) are more likely to refuse to attend school because of concern about unrealistic harm to attachment figures. Children aged 9 through 12 years frequently report distress at the time of separation. Finally, 13- to 16-year-olds most commonly refuse to attend school and develop a variety of somatic complaints. Nightmares concerning separation are commonly described by young children but are rarely reported after age 9 (Francis, Last, & Strauss, 1987).

In contrast to these data, Ollendick, Matson, and Helsel (1985) suggest that symptoms of separation anxiety and overanxious disorder are not commonly reported by children in the general population. In this study, children with separation anxiety disorder most commonly reported fears of getting lost, germs, illness, and bee stings. Children with generalized anxiety disorder most often reported social and performance concerns. Somatic complaints, however, are not specific to children or adolescents with separation anxiety. A large number of somatic symptoms have been reported in children with other disorders, including psychosis and depression (Livingston, Taylor, & Crawford, 1988).

The overlap of symptoms between separation anxiety and overanxious disorder, as well as school phobia may make distinction in diagnosis difficult. The hallmark of separation anxiety is excessive anxiousness in relation to separation from a major attachment figure, whereas overanxious disorder in contrast appears to be characterized by excessive anxiety about performance or future events (Mattison & Bagnato, 1987). In children with school phobia, anxiety appears to be focused specifically on the school environment and is usually not generalized to other settings (Last, 1989). Thus, for the child with separation anxiety, it is not attending school so much as separation from home or the attachment figure, that generates worrisome thoughts.

Generalized Anxiety

Generally, children with generalized anxiety experience a sensation of anxiety or worry that is not unitarily focused on a specific object, stressor, or situation. This population of children might be best described as worrisome. They worry about future events, past behavior, and their own competence. They frequently exhibit somatic complaints, are self-conscious, feel tense, cannot relax, and appear to need frequent reassurance. In a sample of 55 children and adolescents with overanxious disorder, all but 2 endorsed unrealistic worries about the future (Strauss, Lease, Last, & Francis, 1988).

Generalized anxiety appears to be present at an older age than separation anxiety disorder (Last, Strauss, & Francis, 1987). Researchers have generally thought that an equal number of boys and girls experience overanxious symptoms with an over-representation of middle- and upper-class families. Bowen, Oxford, and Boyle (1990), however, reported a female predominance for this disorder and did not find any particular socioeconomic class as overreproductive.

Overanxious children appear more aware of their symptoms than children with separation anxiety. Older children with generalized anxiety appear to worry more about past behavior than younger children with this disorder (Strauss, Lease, et al., 1988). These authors studied a population of overanxious children in which comorbid diagnoses included 35% with attention deficit disorder, 70% with separation anxiety disorder in the younger group, 41% with simple phobia, and 47% with major depressive disorder in the older group. The older group also demonstrated a greater tendency to self-report these problems on questionnaires such as the Revised Children's Manifest Anxiety Scale (C. R. Reynolds & Richmond, 1978) or Children's Depression Inventory (Kovacs, 1983). The younger group did not. Cantwell and Baker (1989) suggest that among anxiety disorders in children, generalized anxiety stands the poorest chance of recovery. It may well represent a temperamental set of qualities that the individual must cope with rather than an environmentally driven disorder from which recovery is possible.

The *DSM-IV-TR* diagnosis must include at least three of six symptoms for adults but only one for children (restless or being on edge, fatigability, difficulty concentrating, irritability, muscle tension, sleep disturbance), with problems controlling worry and excessive anxiety occurring more days than not for at least 6 months, about a number of events or life activities; the worry, anxiety, or physical symptoms must cause clinically significant distress or impairment in major life areas. Additionally, the diagnosis is not made if it is due to a medical condition or substance abuse. These symptoms should not occur exclusively during a mood, psychotic, or pervasive developmental disorder. Finally, the focus of anxiety and worry should not be confined to another specific disorder such as obsessive-compulsive, social phobia, panic, separation anxiety, post traumatic stress or hypochondriasis.

Fears and Simple Phobias

A simple phobia results in the specific, isolated, and persistent fear of a particular stimulus. It is distinguished from fear of separation, strangers, humiliation, or embarrassment in social settings as well as from panic attack. The diagnosis of simple phobia is made only if the avoidant behavior interferes with normal functioning. Due to children's varied cognitive levels and development, it may be difficult to determine whether a child recognizes the irrational nature of his or her phobia (Silverman & Nelles, 1990). Temporary fears and anxieties are common in children. Many are age or time specific. From a developmental perspective, they may originate with startle reactions to certain stimuli during infancy or toddler years and progress to simple phobias and, in some cases, social anxiety during adolescence (Kashani, Dandoy, & Orvaschel, 1991). These authors conclude that mild fears are quite common in children of all ages. Girls report fears more often than boys (Ollendick et al., 1985; Silverman & Nelles, 1990). These latter authors conclude that the influence of age and socioeconomic class on fears and simple phobias is inconclusive. However, not all authors agree (Lapouse & Monk, 1958).

Children's fears appear to change as they mature cognitively and physically, and their experiences with the world increase (Campbell, 1986). Preschoolers are usually fearful of menacing animals and the dark. Difficulty at this age distinguishing reality from fantasy may result in fears of fantasy characters as well. As children mature, these fears systematically decrease (Maurer, 1965). More realistic fears involving social and school issues then develop. By adolescence, anxieties are more internalized and continue to reflect concerns about the individual's competence in school, and with friend and family. The sequence of these changes appears fairly constant for most children, even independent of cultural experience (L. C. Miller, 1983).

Ollendick et al. (1985) describes five distinct factor-generated clusters of children's fears:

1. Fear of failure and criticism from adults
2. Fear of the unknown
3. Fear of injury and small animals
4. Fear of danger and death
5. Medical fears

The 10 most common fears of children have been reported as being hit by a car, not being able to breathe, a bombing attack, getting burned by a fire, falling from a high place, a burglar breaking into the home, earthquake, death, getting poor grades, and snakes (Ollendick, King, & Frary, 1989).

Although mild fears are common in children, phobias appear to be more unusual (Agras, Sylvester, & Oliveau, 1969). In this study among a population of 325 children, these authors found that mild phobias occurred in just over 7%, with severe phobias occurring in less than 1%. Onset may also vary depending on the type of phobia. According to Marks and Gelder (1966), animal phobias often start before children reach age 5, whereas social phobias appear to have their onset after puberty. Specific situational phobias such as heights, or storms have a variable age of onset. During the early preschool years, however, some children definitely begin to anticipate or imagine harmful or frightening events. These include fear of animals or the dark (Graziano, DeGiorann, & Garcia, 1979). School-age children may fear bad dreams, ghosts, or separation. For both populations, these fears tend to decrease with age. In preschool and younger children, realistic fears are infrequent, but they become more common as children grow older (Bauer, 1976).

In a population of 6- to 12-year-olds, over 40% reported numerous fears and worries (Lapouse & Monk, 1958). The authors suggest that children of lower socioeconomic status (SES) appear to demonstrate more fears and worries than children from higher SES families. In this study, 50% of girls demonstrated seven or more fears and worries compared with 36% of boys. As noted in other studies, prevalence rates for these fears and worries decreased with increasing age. In contrast, a prevalence of 4% was reported among a group of 5- to 6-year-olds (Kastrup, 1976). A teacher-reported study by Werry and Quay (1971) found the incidence of fears and worries in a group of 5- to 8-year-olds to be 16.5%. Regardless of the study cited, excessive fears and worries seem to characterize a significant minority of the childhood population starting from a young age. It is also important to note that while specific phobias are common, treatable, and well understood they rarely present for treatment (unpublished data, Anthony, 2000, as cited in Barlow, 2002). Even if the feared stimulus presents during the school day, it is generally unlikely in most situations that teachers will be aware of the child's fear.

The *DSM-IV-TR* includes criteria for specific phobia as a marked and persistent fear that is excessive or unreasonable and precipitated by the presence or anticipation of a specific object or situation. Exposure to the fearful stimulus produces an immediate anxiety response that may be expressed in children by crying, tantrums, freezing, or clinging. The fear is often excessive and unreasonable, and the fear stimulus is avoided. Often the avoidance interferes with the child's normal routine. Specific types of phobias for the *DSM-IV-TR* include animal, natural environment, blood, injection, injury, situation, and generalized-other. The latter type in children includes avoidance of loud sounds or costumed characters.

The prevalence of test anxiety was found to be 41% in a population of African American school children (B. G. Turner, Beidel, Hughes, & Turner, 1993). This finding is consistent with findings in other populations suggesting that at least a third of all students experience some degree of bothersome test anxiety (Barrios, Hartmann, & Shigetomi, 1981). Whether this anxiety actually reflects a phobia related to fear of failure is unclear. Hill and Sarason (1966) found that there was a negative relationship between test anxiety and achievement test scores, however. Thus, whether this reflects a transient state related specifically to tests, an actual phobia related to failure, or a symptom of generalized overanxious disorder, the pattern does disrupt school performance. Further, it has been suggested based on limited data that test anxiety is a chronic condition (Barrios et al., 1981).

Obsessive Compulsive Disorder

The age of onset for obsessive-compulsive disorder (OCD) is usually late adolescence to the early twenties (Rasmussen & Tsuang, 1986). However, symptoms have been reported in children as young as 5 years of age (Jenike, Baer, Minchiello, Schwartz, & Carey, 1986) and to present in males by mid-adolescents (Rasmussen & Eisen, 1990). Obsessions are recurrent, persistent, private thoughts or ideas, often of an unpleasant nature such as violence or sexuality, that seem intrusive and frequently senseless to the individual. Obsessive thoughts related to irrational fears are also common. Compulsions are repetitive, purposeful behaviors or rituals that often accompany obsessions and are utilized to reduce anxiety, avoid a feared event, or lessen feelings of guilt. Common compulsions include repetitive washing, checking, or repeated rituals.

Symptoms of OCD have been described as being practically identical in children and adults (Berg et al., 1989). Approximately one-third to one-half of adults with OCD report the onset of the disorder in childhood or adolescence. Although it was initially reported that males predominated in this disorder (Last & Strauss, 1989a), more recent data suggest that there is an equal presentation in males and females (Riddle et al., 1990). The age of onset of OCD for most children may vary, with symptoms occurring gradually. In some cases, symptoms occur rather dramatically and suddenly. Additionally, Rapoport (1986) has reported this disorder as occurring in children with no premorbid obsessive-compulsive traits or problems. Flament et al. (1988) reported that only 4 of 20 teenagers with OCD had received any psychiatric treatment prior to the onset of severe problems. Three were treated for associated anxiety or depressive symptoms and did not reveal any OCD symptoms at the time of original diagnosis. According to these authors, the most common obsessions among this group were fear of contamination (35%) and thoughts of harm to self and family figures (30%). Most frequent compulsions reported were washing and cleaning rituals (75%), checking behavior (e.g., checking whether a door is locked, 40%) and straightening (35%). The majority of this population experienced both obsessions and compulsions.

A mean age of almost 13 years at evaluation, with a mean age of symptomatic reports beginning just after 10 years of age has been suggested in children (Last & Strauss, 1989a; Riddle et al., 1990). Boys appear to present an earlier onset by self-report than girls. These authors reported that the most common ritual in this population were washing, arranging objects, checking, and counting. Riddle and colleagues (1990) reported that the most common obsessive symptoms in their population were thoughts of contamination for 52%, and violent images, aggression, or physical concerns in 38%. Rituals for this group included repeating things (76%), washing (67%), checking (57%), and arranging and ordering things (62%).

The *DSM-IV-TR* criteria require either obsessions or compulsions for the diagnosis to be made. Obsessions must include recurrent and persistent thoughts, impulses, or images that are intrusive and inappropriate, causing anxiety or distress. These are not the result of excessive worry due to real-life problems. Efforts to ignore or suppress these thoughts are made by attempting to substitute other thoughts or actions, and the individual recognizes that these are the product of his or her own mind and not the result of thought insertion (e.g., paranoia). Compulsions are defined as repetitive behaviors that the individual feels driven to perform in response to an obsession; these acts are directed at preventing or reducing distress. To make the diagnosis, at some point the individual must also recognize that the obsessions or compulsions are excessive and unreasonable, although this is not always necessary for children. These symptoms must cause marked distress and be time consuming, interfering with normal routines. Finally, they should not be the result of substance abuse or a medical condition. This diagnosis includes the designation of poor insight for individuals who may not recognize that these behaviors are excessive or unreasonable.

Panic Disorder

The essential feature of panic disorder is discrete panic attacks. At times, certain events may precipitate these attacks. More often, they occur unexpectedly for unexplained reasons. Panic disorder has been reported as occurring in less than 1% of adults (Von Korff, Eaton, & Keyl, 1985). These authors report a 3% prevalence in the identified population for a panic attack occurring in the previous 6 months. It is important to note that what defines panic attack is idiosyncratic to the individual.

Panic attacks have been reported as occurring in adolescents as well (Black & Robbins, 1990). Last and Strauss (1989b) reported a prevalence of just under 10% for panic disorder in almost 200 consecutive admissions to an outpatient child and adolescent anxiety disorders clinic. Vitiello, Behar, Wolfson, and McLeer (1990) describe six prepubertal children with panic disorder. Their age of diagnosis ranged from 8 to 13 years with an average of 3 years from onset to diagnosis. This group also demonstrated a positive family history of panic disorders.

The *DSM-IV-TR* criteria list panic disorder with and without agoraphobia (*Dorland's Medical Dictionary*, 1980, defines agoraphobia as a morbid dread of open spaces). For a diagnosis of panic disorder, the child or adolescent must experience recurrent, unexpected panic attacks, and at least one of the attacks must be followed by a month or more of concern about additional attacks, worry about implication of the attack or its consequences, and a significant change in behavior related to the attack. It is likely due to these latter three issues that the diagnosis of panic disorder in children may be more difficult to make based on the *DSM-IV* criteria. For a diagnosis of panic attack to be made, the attack should not be directly due to a medication condition or substance, and the diagnostic symptoms should not be better accounted for by other disorders such as posttraumatic stress, separation anxiety, social phobia, or OCD.

Posttraumatic Stress Disorder

It has become increasingly recognized by researchers that posttraumatic stress disorder occurs with greater frequency than first thought in children and adolescents. Nonetheless, this disorder has been best studied among adults exposed to repeated and significant stress (e.g., combat veterans; K. C. Peterson, Prout, & Schwarz, 1991). Symptoms typical of depression including insomnia, poor concentration, and irritability, as well as symptoms related to anxiety, including nightmares, avoidance, and an exaggerated startle response are characteristic of posttraumatic stress disorder.

Children exposed to a single violent event have been reported to develop posttraumatic symptoms (Pynoos et al., 1987). In this study, children in greater proximity to a sniper attack reported more severe symptomatic problems. Studies of child abuse victims suggest they too develop posttraumatic stress. Among a sample of 31 sexually abused children, 48% met the criteria for posttraumatic stress disorder (McLeer, Deblinger, Atkins, Foa, & Ralphe, 1988). Kiser et al. (1988) reported the onset of symptomatic problems, including sexual acting out, the development of childhood fears, and specific trauma-related fears among a group of young children sexually abused at a day care center. In a study of young adults, risk factors for developing posttraumatic stress disorder after exposure to a stressful event included early separation from parents, neuroticism, preexisting anxiety and depression, and a family history of anxiety disorder (Breslau, Davis, Andreski, & Peterson, 1991).

The *DSM-IV-TR* criteria for posttraumatic stress include the child or adolescent experiencing, witnessing, or being confronted with an event or events involving actual or threatened serious injury or death. The individual's response must involve intense fear, helplessness, or horror. In children, this may be expressed instead by disorganized or agitated behavior. The criteria include the event being re-experienced through at least one of the following: intrusive recollections of the event, including images, thoughts, or perceptions; distressing dreams of the event; feeling as if the event is recurring; psychological distress at exposure to internal or external cues that symbolize or resemble the event; and a physiological reaction to those cues. In children, repetitive play may occur in which themes or aspects of the trauma are expressed, as well as frightening dreams without recognizable content. Additionally, at least three symptoms consistent with avoidance of stimuli associated with the trauma must be observed including avoidance of thoughts, feelings, or conversations; efforts to avoid activities, places, or people; an inability to recall important aspects of the event; markedly diminished interest or participation in usually enjoyable activities; feeling of detachment from others; restricted affect; and a sense of foreshortened future. At least two persistent symptoms of increased arousal must be present that were not present before the trauma, including difficulty falling or staying asleep; irritability or outbursts of anger, difficulty concentrating; hypervigilance, or an exaggerated startle response. These symptomatic problems must occur for more than a month and cause impairment in daily activities. In an acute situation, the symptoms will have occurred for less than 3 months. A diagnosis of chronic posttraumatic stress is made only if the symptoms have occurred for 3 or more months. Additionally, a description of delayed onset is made if symptomatic problems did not occur for at least 6 months after the stressful event.

The *DSM-IV-TR* criteria also include an acute stress disorder diagnosis. It is yet to be well determined how this diagnosis is related to posttraumatic stress. It can be perceived as a more severe, stress-related reaction. The individual is exposed to an event out of the ordinary and must experience at least three symptomatic problems, including a sense of numbering, detachment, or absence of emotional response, reduction in the awareness of his or her surroundings, derealization, depersonalization, and dissociative amnesia. These symptoms occur either while experiencing or immediately after experiencing the distressing event. The event may be re-experienced through images, thoughts, dreams, or flashbacks. The individual must avoid stimuli that arouse recollections, as well as experience symptoms of anxiety or increased arousal. The disturbance must cause distress in daily functioning and exist for a minimum of 2 days and a maximum of 4 weeks. Symptoms must occur within 4 weeks of the event.

Prevalence, Cause, and Comorbidity

Though there are differences among researcher studies, significant, though small, groups of children demonstrate a variety of anxious disorders regardless of how the research is conducted. J. C. Anderson et al. (1987) while screening 11-year-olds reported that 3.5% in the epidemiological sample demonstrated separation anxiety disorder; 2.9%, overanxious disorder, 2.4% simple phobia; and 1%, social phobia. There was some overlap among the groups. Among a sample of 7- to 11-year-old pediatric patients, Costello (1989b) found a prevalence rate of almost 9% for at least one anxiety disorder. This included 4% with separation anxiety, 4.6% with overanxious disorder, 3.2% with simple phobia, 1% with social phobia, 1.6% with avoidant disorder, and 1.2% with agoraphobia. Among adolescents, Kashani and Orvaschel (1988) reported a prevalence of 17% experiencing at least one type of anxiety disorder in a group of 150. However, the percentage declined to just under 9% when the criterion "in need of treatment" was added. This population included just over 7% with overanxious disorder, 4.7% with simple phobia, and just under 1% with separation anxiety disorder.

In an epidemiological population of close to 1,000 adolescents, McGee et al. (1990) reported the most prevalent anxiety disorder as overanxious disorder (just under 6%), followed by simple phobia (3.6%). Most common fear expressed included water, airplanes, heights, and presenting in front of others. Interestingly, in this epidemiological population, nonaggressive conduct disorder presented as the second most common problem (5.7%). Kashani and Orvaschel (1988) reported that among a group of 150 adolescents, the majority of those with anxiety disorder had at least one other concurrent nonanxiety disorder. These authors and others (Kashani et al., 1991) provide strong evidence that anxiety disorders correlate highly with each other and with other nonanxiety disorders, especially depression. There does not appear to be a specific theory to explain this high rate of association.

In a sample of over 3,000 children and adolescents, Bowen et al. (1990) reported an occurrence of 3.6% for overanxious disorder and 2.4% occurrence for separation anxiety disorder. Among a population of 8-, 12-, and 17-year-olds, Kashani and Orvaschel (1990) reported anxiety disorders as the most common problem. Younger children had the highest incidence of separation anxiety, with the older group demonstrating a higher prevalence of overanxious disorder.

Separation anxiety appears to be the most frequent diagnosis made among school-age children, and overanxious disorder the second most common (Kovacs, Gatsonis, Paulauskas, & Richards, 1989). According to these authors, in a population of 104 children, 41% demonstrated anxiety disorders in conjunction with depression. For most of these children, anxiety problems appeared to precede the onset of depression two-thirds of the time. Additionally, the anxiety problems often persisted after the depressive disorder had remitted.

A lifetime prevalence rate of just over 11% for panic attacks had been reported among a population of ninth graders (Hayward, Killen, & Taylor, 1989). This group also demonstrated more depressive symptoms than those without panic attacks. Moreau, Weissman, and Warner (1989) reported that panic attacks occur with symptoms similar to those in adults and approximately 3% of children who are at risk for depression. Although children in this group received a diagnosis of panic disorder, they also had other diagnoses including separation anxiety disorder. Last and Strauss (1989a) identified just under 10% of 177 consecutive admissions to an outpatient child and adolescent clinic as experiencing panic disorder. As reported earlier, this appeared to occur twice as often in girls as boys.

J. C. Anderson et al. (1987) reported a prevalence rate of 17% of children with anxiety disorders as suffering from depression as well. Among the population of adolescents with anxiety disorder, 12% met the criteria for major depression (McGee et al., 1990). Kashani and Orvaschel (1988) report an even higher comorbidity rate for these two disorders, indicating that 69% of their sample with anxiety disorder also experienced major depression. Kovacs et al. (1989) reported that greater than 40% of referred children and adolescents with major depressive disorder appear to be experiencing a concurrent anxiety disorder with separation anxiety being the most common. Just under 30% of a population studied by Strauss, Last, Hersen, and Kazdin (1988) with anxiety disorder appeared to be experiencing a concomitant major depressive disorder. Finally, a report by G. A. Bernstein (1991) states that in a school refusal clinic, 47% of those with anxiety disorders were also suffering from major depression.

It has been suggested that children with a primary overanxious disorder are at the greatest risk to experience secondary anxiety disorders, including simple phobia, panic disorder, social phobia, or avoidant disorder (Last, Strauss, et al., 1987). These authors reported that approximately a third of children with a primary diagnosis of separation anxiety also experience a concurrent diagnosis of overanxious disorder.

The comorbidity among anxious children likely stems from the fact that having one type of anxiety disorder increases the risk of others. Though somewhat different, anxiety disorders in general reflect the same underlying basic temperamental risk and many of their symptoms overlap, raising the possibility that these children will meet multiple criteria (Kashani & Orvaschel, 1990).

The consensus among these authors is that children with concurrent anxiety and depressive disorders tend to be older than those with just an anxiety disorder. In addition, the comorbidity of anxiety and depressive disorders in children and adolescents is associated with increased severity for both anxiety and depressive symptoms compared with children who have one or the other disorder.

At one time, researchers suggested that a differential diagnostic issue for anxiety disorders was related to hyperactive symptoms stemming from anxiety or attention deficit, however, now it is recognized that some children exhibit both disorders (Bird et al., 1988). More recently, Pliszka (1992) reports at least one out of four children with ADHD also meet the criteria for anxiety disorder, with at least 15% to 20% of children presenting with separation anxiety or overanxious disorder also qualifying for a diagnosis of ADHD.

It is also suggested that parents with anxiety problems are much more likely to have children with an anxiety disorder (B. G. Turner, Beidel, & Costello, 1987). A significantly higher rate of current and lifetime anxiety disorders has been reported in mothers of anxiety-disordered children compared with controls (Last, Phillips, et al.,

1987). G. A. Bernstein and Garfinkel (1986) reported that among a group of school refusers with depression and anxiety problems, parents and siblings of this group demonstrate higher rates of anxiety and depressive disorders compared with the families of a control group. Interestingly, among a group of children described as behaviorally inhibited to the unfamiliar, those with parents who had histories of panic disorder or agoraphobia appeared at much greater risk to develop anxiety disorders. This occurred at a rate even greater than that predicted simply based on exposure to affected parents (Biederman et al., 1993). It is likely that for this group of children, multiple risk factors contribute to the onset of anxiety disorders. Further, there appears to be a beyond chance relationship between Tourette's syndrome and OCD (Pauls & Leckman, 1986). This may be caused by an underlying genetic factor linking these two disorders (Cumings, 1990).

Researchers have also suggested that children and adolescents with OCD demonstrate subtle impairments of right hemisphere function on neuropsychological tests (Cox, Fedio, & Rapoport, 1989). Denckla (1989) reported abnormalities on the neurological exam, including left hemisyndrome, choreiform movements, and neurodevelopmental differences among anxious children.

Among clinic-referred populations, certain anxiety disorders (separation anxiety disorder) appear more common in young children, whereas others (OCD) are more common in adolescence (Geller, Chestnut, Miller, Price, & Yates, 1985). Further, Costello (1989b) and others (Kashani & Orvaschel, 1990) suggest that there is a low agreement among researchers for prevalence rates of childhood anxiety disorders.

Last, Strauss, et al. (1987) suggest that based on 73 consecutive referrals to an outpatient anxiety disorders clinic for children and adolescents, primary diagnoses include 33% with anxiety disorder, 15% with overanxious disorder, 15% with school phobia, and 15% with major depression. Children with a diagnosis of separation anxiety were most likely to receive a concurrent diagnosis of overanxious disorder. Those with a primary diagnosis of overanxious disorder appeared at greatest risk to additionally receive diagnoses of social anxiety problems, reflecting either social phobia or avoidant disorder. Children with a primary major depressive disorder often exhibited social phobia and overanxious disorder.

Pliszka (1992) further evaluated 107 children meeting the criteria for ADHD. This population was subdivided into those with and without a comorbid anxiety disorder, and the two ADHD groups were compared with each other and with a control group. The ADHD groups were compared with each other and with a control group. The ADHD children exhibiting anxiety problems appeared to be less impulsive and/or hyperactive than those with ADHD alone. However, they continued to be more impaired than the control group on measures of classroom observation and a continuous performance task. There also appeared to be a trend for the ADHD children experiencing anxiety problems to demonstrate fewer symptoms of conduct disorder than the ADHD group alone. A study evaluating psychopathology among children repeatedly abused by a parent found that 35% suffered from separation anxiety disorder. Of this group, three quarters also demonstrated symptoms consistent with ADHD. These authors concluded that the relationship between ADHD and the separation anxiety in this population of children warranted additional studies. They hypothesized that preexisting ADHD somehow predisposes abused children to separation anxiety or that symptoms of distractibility and poor concentration are secondary to the anxiety (Livingston, Lawson, & Jones, 1993).

Over 60% of individuals with panic disorder or agoraphobia with panic attacks have been reported as having a history of depression (Breier, Charney, & Heninger, 1984). In this group, half experienced major depression prior to the onset of anxiety symptoms, a pattern somewhat different from that reported by Kovacs et al. (1989). Puig-Antich and Rabinovich (1986) report that 30% of children with major depression experience a concomitant anxiety disorder, most frequently separation anxiety. A comorbidity of 30% between anxiety disorders and ADHD in both epidemiological and clinic samples has been reported (J. C. Anderson et al., 1987; Last, Strauss, et al., 1987). There also appear to be higher rates of ADHD among high-risk children with parents experiencing anxiety disorders (Sylvester, Hyde, & Reichler, 1987).

Researchers have reported symptoms of aggression in preschoolers with predominant anxiety symptoms (Wolfson, Fields, & Rose, 1987). L. S. Cohen and Biederman (1988) described an unusual pair of identical twins with ADHD. One developed agoraphobia without major depression, the other developed major depression without agoraphobia or other anxiety symptoms.

Kendall and Watson (1989) describe a number of symptoms overlapping in anxiety and depression such as irritability, agitation, restlessness, concentration difficulty, insomnia, and fatigue. As previously reported, the 1991 normal data of the Child Behavior Checklist (Achenbach & Edelbrock, 1991) finds an internalizing factor of anxious and depressed symptoms co-occurring rather than separating out. Therefore, especially in children under the age of 12, symptoms of anxiety, worry, and depression are likely to overlap and frequently present together.

It is also questionable whether parents can objectively evaluate their children's nondisruptive behavior because most parents harbor distorted perceptions or unrealistic expectations (S. L. Harris & Ferrari, 1983). The pattern of children reporting more anxious symptoms than their parents observed has been consistently reported (Strauss, 1988). Parents are better at reporting overt or disruptive symptoms involving aggression, disobedience, and noncompliance (Herjanic & Reich, 1982). Although the majority of childhood checklists are quite good at helping parents objectify disruptive problems, it is likely that parents' expectations and perceptions, as well as a lack of knowledge concerning the child's feelings further impinge on the accuracy of parental report.

Intervention

Sheslow, Bondy, and Nelson (1982) suggest that a "fear thermometer" can help children understand the severity of their fears for different situations and stimuli on a continuum. Finch and Montgomery (1973) describe a model with stick figures containing various facial features that helps children assess their level of anger and suggest this model also could be used to evaluate anxiety.

C. B. Taylor and Arnow (1988) describe behavioral interventions to manage anxiety problems that lead to social phobia. This pattern of treatment has been found effective with adults. Some literature suggests that it may work with children. In a review of behavioral assessment and treatment for overanxious disorder in children and adolescents, Strauss (1988) reports that although research dealing specifically with overanxious disorders is limited, there is a large body of literature dealing with treatment of specific childhood fears. Strauss suggests a multimodal treatment program consisting of relaxation raining, the use of positive self-statements, a behavior management program to reinforce children for practicing the cognitive exercises, and systematic desensitization.

Kane and Kendall (1989) report on the cognitive behavioral treatment of four children with overanxious disorder. Treatment consisted of 16 to 20 one-hour individual sessions held twice weekly. Children were taught to recognize anxious feelings and physical reactions, modify cognitions and misperceptions contributing to feelings of anxiety, and self-reinforce themselves for making change. Additional treatment components included modeling, desensitization, relaxation training, role-playing, and behavior management. Positive results from this study were based on self-report measures. S. Goldstein, Hagar, and Brooks (2002) expanded on this model to create a workbook for parents using these strategies. This work also contains guidelines for educators.

A related model focusing on the relationship between thoughts and behavior was developed by Kanfer, Karoly, and Newman (1975). The model was conceptualized to help the child or adolescent learn to manage behavior by thinking differently. These authors demonstrated the benefits of this model in teaching fearful 5- and 6-year-olds to tolerate the dark.

McDermott, Werry, Petti, Combrinck-Graham, and Char (1989) suggest that, to treat anxiety problems in children, a family model may be most effective. These authors report that the primary goal of family intervention is to assist parents to function on a daily basis as change agents, helping children replace anxiety-producing thoughts and behaviors with more functional responses.

Although researchers have reported that in single case or uncontrolled studies of OCD, behavioral interventions with adults and adolescents using deliberate and prolonged exposure to cues that evoke rituals and obsessions combined with response prevention can be effective, controlled group outcome studies have not consistently supported the benefits of this treatment (G. A. Carlson, Figueroa, & Lahey, 1986). The best protocol for symptoms related to OCD relies on the antidepressants clomipramine and fluoxetine. Because of the high relapse rate when the medicines are discontinued, they are viewed as management or treatment tools rather than cures (Pato, Zohar-Kadouch, Zohar, & Murphy, 1988).

Kearny and Silverman (1990b) reported successful treatment of a single case of OCD in an adolescent using response prevention and cognitive therapy. Response prevention involves blocking the ritualistic behaviors. Cognitive therapy is directed at helping the adolescent recognize and accept the ego-dystonic behavior pattern and working with the individual to increase self-control. Again, although researchers have reported using cognitive interventions to achieve lasting reductions of ritualistic behavior in adolescents with cognitive interventions, this type of treatment has simply not proven to eliminate symptomatic OCD problems (Bolton, Collins, & Steinberg, 1983).

Gittelman and Klein (1984) reported that up to 80% of children refusing to attend school likely manifest separation anxiety. Desensitization and systematic exposure (Wolpe, 1982), as well as classical conditioning treatment (McNamara, 1988), have been successful with this population. G. R. Patterson (1965) utilized operant behavioral techniques with positive results. A combination of cognitive and operant behavioral treatment has been effective with this population with separation anxiety (Mansdorf & Lukens, 1987). Comparisons of different types of treatments, however, have been inconclusive likely because of poorly controlled studies and limited samples. There is no doubt, however, that active treatments are superior to waiting lists as a means of improving school refusal (Blagg & Yule, 1984; L. C. Miller, Barrett, Hampe, & Noble, 1972). Kearny and Silverman (1990a), utilized a repertoire of treatments dependent on symptom presentation, including relaxation, systematic desensitization, modeling, cognitive restructuring, shaping, differential reinforcement, and contingency contracting. These efforts yielded improvements in six of seven separation anxious subjects in an open clinical trial at a 6-month follow-up.

Depression

Despite recent advances, depression continues to be largely unrecognized and misunderstood by professionals and the lay public. Yet depressive symptoms characterized by sadness, listlessness, and a lack of energy persisting over several months have been reported to occur in as many as 10% of children before the age of 12 (Dolgan, 1990). Further, the incidence of childhood depression may be greater for high-risk populations, including children of depressed or divorced parents, siblings or children hospitalized for serious illness, children with anxiety or attention deficit disorder, incarcerated adolescents, the mild mentally retarded, pregnant teenagers, children suffering from chronic illness, and those from lower socioeconomic strata.

Family variables have consistently been found as increasing the risk for childhood depression. Weissman, Leckman, Merikangas, Gammon, and Prusoff (1984) found that depression in parents tripled the risk of either a disruptive or nondisruptive diagnosis in offspring. Major depression was the most common diagnosis in children of depressed parents, occurring at a rate of 13%, whereas none of the control children demonstrated symptoms of this disorder. Diagnoses of ADHD and separation anxiety each accounted for an additional 10% of the impaired childhood population in this study. Modifications of this line of research have repeatedly validated that children of depressed parents are at significant risk for depression as well as other childhood disorders (Cytryn, McKnew, Bartko, Lamour, & Hamovitt, 1982; Kashani, Burk, & Reid, 1985). Further, the risk for childhood impairment appear even greater when a parent experiences bipolar disorder (Decina et al., 1983). In this study,

149

half the children of bipolar parents were found to experience at least one *DSM-III* disorder with more than half the impaired group receiving a diagnosis of depression.

Trad (1987) suggests that parental psychopathology appears to represent one of the most significant risk factors for childhood depression. The risk may be two-fold, reflecting both qualities genetically transmitted as well as certain patterns of behavior and affect that are modeled for the child. A number of studies have suggested genetic contribution varies, the greatest influence appearing with bipolar as opposed to unipolar depression (Cadoret, O'Gorman, Heywood, & Troughton, 1985; Mahmood, Reveley, & Murray, 1983). Some researchers have suggested that temperament may only introduce a genetic risk factor if the child is placed in environment likely to induce depression symptoms (Trad, 1986).

Theories about parent contribution to childhood depression have also included children mirroring parent behavior by sharing parent affect (Seligman et al., 1984), in an empathic reaction to parent behavior (Trad, 1986). Poor parenting skills and style may lead to the reinforcement of certain depressive symptoms and behavior in children (Bromet & Cornely, 1984).

Depression is best thought of as reflecting a continuum of difficulty from severe mood swings and impairment to mild variations in affect (Matson, 1989). Typical symptoms of depression have been consistently found to include sadness, low self-esteem, and loss of interest in activities. Whereas depressive illness is well-accepted in adults, acceptance for children and adolescents has been slower in coming. There has been a consistent line of research arguing against the existence of depression in children (Rehm, Gordon-Leventon, & Ivens, 1987). However, these arguments, based on psychoanalytic theory, have generally been rejected when empirically derived studies of depressive symptoms in children have been generated (Kazdin, Rodgers, & Colbus, 1986; Kovacs, 1983). Second, symptoms of depression occur on a continuum. Everyone appears to evidence some depressive behaviors at one time or another. It is the number and the severity of symptoms that justify diagnosis. This aspect of depression has been a difficult issue with adults and likely even more so with children due to their marked changes developmentally.

Trad (1987) suggests that defining, evaluating, and understanding depression in children is difficult because the cognitive, physical, and self-regulatory stages of infancy, childhood, and adolescence present varying clinical pictures and differing sets of features. Thus, to define depression in childhood requires a developmental perspective. In Trad's view, childhood depression may be expressed as an affect (external representation of the subjective experience of emotion), a mood (subjective emotion), or a syndrome (a cluster of incapacitating symptoms).

Researchers generally agree that a cluster of symptomatic problems is consistently observed in children described as depressed. These include dysphoric mood (irritability, sensitivity, or sadness); negative ideation (feelings of worthlessness, suicidal thoughts); aggressive behavior (disrespect for authority, fighting, anger); sleep disturbance (problems with sleep cycle or restless sleep); inconsistent school performance, diminished socialization; a change in attitude toward family, school, and community, physical complaints; loss of energy; and a change in appetite or weight (Brumback, Dietz-Schmidt, & Weinberg, 1977; Feighner et al., 1972; Weinberg, Rutman, Sullivan, Penick, & Dietz, 1973).

Ten core behavioral symptoms have been most commonly associated with a clinical diagnosis of childhood depression: flat affect and a distinct look of unhappiness most of the time, inability to find pleasurable activities; low self-esteem, feelings of guilt, social isolation, impaired schoolwork, chronic fatigue, low energy level, difficulty with sleep or appetite, and suicidal thoughts (Poznanski, 1982). Depressed children also often complain of somatic symptoms without an organic basis. They may appear irritable, inattentive, angry, or cry excessively.

It is suggested that at least five of the following should be present if a diagnosis of childhood depression is made: an inability to have fun, low self-esteem, impaired schoolwork, sleep difficulty, excessive fatigue, low energy level, social isolation, and suicidal thoughts (Poznanski, 1985). In normally functioning children, loss through separation, death of a family member, or a stressful experience may combine with predisposing factors to trigger the onset of a depressive episode.

Laurent, Landau, and Stark (1993) studied a population of fourth through seventh graders. Four symptoms had high positive predictive power (inclusion) as well as high negative predictive power (exclusion) as criteria for identifying childhood depression: feeling unloved, anhedonia, excessive guilt, and depressed mood. Worrisome behavior was the most efficient, positive predictor for anxiety disorder, especially worries about future events and school competence. However, these authors also found that anxiety symptoms were more efficient predictors of a depressive than an anxiety diagnosis.

School performance has been suggested as a very sensitive indicator of sudden onset depression in children (Tesiny, Lefkowitz, & Gordon, 1980), but consultants must be aware that the school skills of children with affective problems do not appear to differ from those of other children. Variations in intelligence or learning disabilities do not appear more prevalent in groups of children with or without depression (Stark, Livingston, Laurent, & Cardenas, 1993; Weinberg & Rehmet, 1983). Although nonverbal behavior among depressed adults reflects a characteristic pattern, this is not necessarily the case with children or adolescents. However, there do appear to be characteristic nonverbal signs of depression in children such as facial expression, body movements, head and arm gestures used while speaking, head shaking, and tearfulness (Kazdin, Sherick, Esveldt-Dawson, & Rancurello, 1985). These authors found equivalent symptomatic problems in boys and girls although boys demonstrated less eye contact, fewer smiles, and flat intonation in speech.

Depressed, as well as depressed and anxious, children report a significantly more negative view of themselves, the world, and the future than just anxious or control children (Kaslow, Stark, Printz, Livingston, & Tsai, 1993). In a population of fourth to seventh graders, Stark, Humphrey, Crook, and Lewis (1990) found that depressed and anxious children experienced their families as more distressed on a wide range of dimensions. These authors found these youngsters could be classified correctly into depressed and anxious groups based on their family ratings. These findings suggest that there may be some important deficits or excesses in families raising a depressed or anxious child. These children perceived their family environments to be less supportive, possibly because of higher levels of perceived conflicts. These families appeared to be more disengaged with the world around them and more enmeshed. The children reported that they had little involvement in decisions being made about them and the family. This pattern of disturbance was most prominent in families with a depressed and anxious child. Among the more consistent findings in this study was that depressed children perceived their families to be significantly less democratic than did control children or children with other disorders.

Although some authors have suggested that masked depression may be an issue of clinical significance in children (Cytryn & McKnew, 1974), this concept has not found either research or clinical basis for support (G. A. Carlson & Cantwell, 1980a, 1980b). Nevertheless, some symptomatic problems not usually thought to correlate with depression (e.g., aggression) may be quite characteristic of childhood depression. Alternatively, symptoms characteristic of depression may also be indicators of other childhood disorders, including anxiety and disruptive behavior. Kashani et al. (1987) found that among a sample of 150 adolescents age 14 to 16 years, 28 experienced psychiatric impairment and evidenced considerable overlapping of symptoms related to depression, conduct disorder, anxiety, and oppositional disorder. This pattern has been observed by other researchers as well (Jacobson, Lahey, & Strauss, 1983; Norvell & Towle, 1986). The latter authors also found several items on the Children's Depression Inventory (Kovacs, 1983) indicative of disruptive problems. Other items on this inventory, such as depressed mood, negative self-thoughts, and social withdrawal, appeared clearly indicative of internalizing rather than externalizing disabilities. As Matson (1989) concludes, the "data therefore seemed to support the hypothesis that depression is a distinct disorder, although not entirely separate from other conditions" (p. 9).

Although some studies have found depressed children to be less effective social problem solvers (Marx & Schulze, 1991), others have failed to demonstrate social problem-solving deficits in depressed children compared with normals (Joffe, Dobson, Fine, Marriage, & Haley, 1990). Marton, Connolly, Kutcher, and Cornblum (1993) found in a population of 38 depressed adolescent outpatients, a unique deficit in social self-evaluation. This pattern of deficit appeared to contribute to ineffective social behavior and the maintenance of dysphoric affect.

These authors suggest that treatment of social skills should be based on a careful assessment of the depressed adolescent's skills. Social and cognitive characteristics that differentiated depressed teenagers from normals appeared to center on the depressed adolescents' negative self-concept and lack of social self-confidence. Interestingly, the depressed group did not differ in the ability to solve social problems to adopt a social perspective. Therefore, the depressed adolescents could appropriately assess interpersonal problems and appreciate the perspective of others, as well as formulate an adequate plan of action. Their ability to implement the plan, however, was faulty. This group tended to expect outcome to be negative and gave a low appraisal to their own abilities and performance. These social weaknesses of depressed adolescents appear to be best characterized in the areas of inadequate attribution and low self-appraisal.

Four basic theoretical models appear to be related to childhood depression. The first one, the developmental symptomatology model, argues that certain early childhood experiences are necessary for the subsequent development of depression (Freud, 1965). Proponents, however, did not correlate these experiences as reflecting childhood depression but rather as manifestations of trauma during a specific developmental stage. In fact, Lapouse (1966) argued that depressive symptoms in children were widespread and might be indicative of normal developmental stages taken to excess rather than psychiatric disorder.

The second theoretical model, that of depressive equivalents, argues that an equivalent disorder in childhood is similar to adult depression although the overall syndrome is not the same (Cytryn & McKnew, 1974). These authors included behavior such as aggression, hyperactivity, and somatic complaints as symptomatic of depression or, as noted earlier, even masked depression.

The single factor model accepts depression in childhood as a unitary, clinical entity, analogous to depression in adults (Albert & Beck, 1975; Poznanski & Zrull, 1970). These and other authors posit a single factor to explain childhood depression. This line of research was the precursor of the present multifactorial model.

Finally, the adult model approach, the most recent developed, represents a multifactorial explanation, suggesting that childhood depression is similar in many ways to adult depression. By starting with what is known about adults and their depression, more can be learned about childhood depression. As Trad (1987) noted, "Similarities between adult and childhood forms of depression are probably significant. However, the differences may be equally significant" (p. 31). Weinberg et al. (1973) were the first to modify adult diagnostic criteria for depression for use with children. The use of childhood depression was quickly accepted and in 1977, the National Institute of Mental Health Subcommittee on Clinical Criteria for the Diagnosis of Depression in Children suggested a set of criteria based on modifications of what eventually became the third edition of the *Diagnostic and Statistical Manual of Psychiatric Disorders* of the American Psychiatric Association.

Considering the gradual evolution and acceptance of depression in children, it is not surprising that the variant bipolar depressive disorder, which has been slower to be recognized and accepted in adults, has also been slower to be accepted in children. Major mood swings in children are an accepted phenomenon, yet additional research is needed to understand, diagnose, and treat this population. G. A. Carlson (1983) suggests that when distinguishing major depression from bipolar disorder, children with the latter condition often have a family history of depression, cyclothymia, alcoholism, or suicide. In this population, looking depressed or complaining of depression was not often noted. Conversely, related mood was rarely reported with symptoms of irritability, aggression, emotional lability, and even feelings of grandiosity or reported hallucinations frequently present. Earlier studies suggested that individuals with unipolar or major depression did not have a family history of bipolar disorder and that family history is usually positive for bipolar disorder in children diagnosed with it (Perris, 1966). Gammon et al. (1983) found that the diagnosis of the early onset for bipolar disorder was often obscured by antisocial and impulsive behavior, poor academic performance, and social withdrawal. In fact, the authors found that these symptoms persisted even in the intervals when symptoms of bipolar disorder had remitted. Akiskal et al. (1985) found that acute depressive episodes and dysthymic or cyclothymic disorders constituted the most common presenting problems in referred offspring and younger siblings of adults with bipolar disorder. However, the early onset of classic bipolar symptoms in children is rare. At young ages (before 10 years), the small group of children who may progress to bipolar disorder are most likely to receive diagnoses of attention deficit disorder, conduct disorder, and/or major depressive disorder (Tomasson & Kuperman, 1990). In fact, G. A. Carlson (1983) suggests that attention deficit disorder and conduct disorder are part of the differential diagnosis for early onset bipolar disorder. Kovacs, Paulauskas, Gatsonis, and Richards (1988) reported that 21% of children with an initial diagnosis of major depression and conduct symptoms subsequently developed bipolar disorder.

Definition

The *DSM-IV-TR* diagnosis of major depression must include five of nine symptoms present during a 2-week period, representing a change in previous functioning. At least one of the symptomatic problems must be depressed mood or loss of interest or pleasure. Symptoms include a depressed mood most of the day, every day, diminished interest or pleasure in most activities, decrease in appetite, and weight loss or weight gain; insomnia or hypersomnia nearly every day; physical agitation or retardation nearly every day; fatigue or loss of energy nearly every day; feelings of worthlessness or guilt nearly every day; a diminished ability to think or concentrate or indecisiveness every day; and recurrent thoughts of death or suicidal ideation. Major depressive episodes are characterized as mild, moderate, or severe with psychotic or without psychotic features. Major depressive episodes can occur single or in recurrent periods. The *DSM-IV-TR* criteria include a Not Otherwise Specified depressive disorder in which depressive symptoms are present, but the number is insufficient to make a major depressive diagnosis.

Among the affective disorders, the *DSM-IV-TR* criteria for dysthymic disorder are of interest for professionals working with children. This disorder is defined as depressed mood or irritability for most of the day, occurring more days than not, and indicated by subjective account or observations by others for at least a 1-year period for children and adolescents. During depressed periods, at least three of the following symptoms must be reported: low self-esteem or self-confidence; feelings of inadequacy; feelings of pessimism; despair or hopelessness; generalized loss of interest in pleasurable activities; social withdrawal; chronic fatigue; feelings of guilt or brooding; subjective feelings of irritability or anger; decreased activity or productivity; and difficulty with concentration, memory, or indecisiveness. These symptoms should not be accounted for by major depressive episodes, and the child or adolescent should not have had a major depressive period during the year these symptoms have been observed.

Prevalence and Comorbidity

Depressive symptoms appear modestly to moderately related to the negotiation of a number of developmental tasks at entrance to first grade (Edelsohn, Ialongo, Werthamer-Larsson, Crockett, & Kellam, 1992) including academic achievement, peer relations, and attention to classroom activities. Self-report of depressive symptoms in the 1,300 children studied were relatively stable over 2-week and 4-month intervals. The level of stability was particularly high for children with the greatest complaints suggesting that early symptoms of self-reported depression likely predict children's future functioning. These symptoms are usually chronic and should be attended to. This study did not find evidence of sex-based differences. Utilizing the Children's Depression Inventory (Kovacs, 1983) with an arbitrary cutoff score of 19, 28% of the sample was considered depressed. When the cutoff score was adjusted based on the face validity criteria consistent with *DSM-III-R* criteria, the incidence was about 6% in children reporting symptoms consistent with major depression. This study also provided some limited support to the applicability of adult models of depression in children as young as 5 to 6 years of age. The complaints of these children were similar to complaints made by adults about self-worth, hopelessness, and helplessness. It is unclear whether the stress of first grade creates these symptoms or brings them to the forefront in children at risk (Kellam, Werthamer-Larsson, & Dolan, 1991).

As reported earlier, parenting variables appear to be a significant issue in childhood depression. Brody and Forehand (1986) report that parents who are depressed are more likely to have children with conduct and disruptive problems compared with the normal sample. Other authors suggest that depressed parents have children with an even wider range of symptomatic problems, including shyness, withdrawn behavior, greater attention problems, lower academic performance, and symptoms of depression (Panaccione & Wahler, 1986). These authors suggest both genetic and experiential models to explain these data. Seagull and Weinshank (1984) report that in a group of 82 seventh graders identified as experiencing depressive affect, symptoms of task avoidance and lack of social competence were also observed. In this population, parents had less schooling than the normal population and were more likely to discipline their children with corporal punishment at home. Thus, as with other childhood disorders, family variables consistently are found to correlate with depression.

Stark, Schmidt, and Joyner (1993) studied a population of 133 fourth through seventh graders and their parents for a review of self-world, and future (cognitive triad). These authors found:

- Children's view of self, world, and future was related to the severity of their depression.
- The mother's but not the father's perceptions in these areas was related to the children's perception.
- Perceived parental messages to the child about the self, world, and future were predictive of the child's cognitive perception and ratings of depression.
- The relationship between perceived parental messages and depression appeared to be completely mediated by the child's view of self, world, and future.

These authors did not find a relationship between parents' cognitive triad and the messages they communicate to their children about the children themselves, their world, and their future. The authors hypothesize that the message parents communicate to their children may be more highly related to child variables, immediate environmental variables, and other parent variables (or a combination of these factors).

Interestingly, children who are either depressed or both depressed and anxious were distinguished primarily in the cognitive domain by their cognitive triad and automatic thoughts (Stark, Humphrey, Laurent, & Livingston, 1993). In the behavioral area, these children demonstrated an impulsive-recalcitrant style of interacting. In the family area, they were distinguished by the messages they received from their fathers about self, world, and future and by the parents' less democratic style of managing the family. Both subtypes of depressed children were significantly different from the anxious and normal children across all seven measures used by these researchers. It appeared to be more the magnitude of distress experience rather than the type of domain involved that distinguished depressed children from those who are purely anxious. These data suggest that central cognitive, behavioral, and family factors may underlie the range of childhood disorders, especially those involving affective components of depression or anxiety.

Estimates of comorbidity for anxiety and depression in children range from 17% (Strauss, Lease, et al., 1988) to as high as 73% (Mitchell, McCauley, Burke, & Moss, 1988). Anxiety and depressive disorders likely share a nonspecific component reflecting general affective distress (L. A. Clark & Watson, 1991). The comorbidity of ADHD, anxiety, and/or depressive disorders in a group of children with parents experiencing panic, major depression, or no disorders was much greater for the offspring of parents with depressive and panic disorders (McClellan et al., 1990). These data were generated by parent report. Higher rates of ADD (1% versus 13%) occurred when anxiety or depression was present. These authors conclude that in children referred for evaluation of attention deficit, clinicians must consider the possibility that a primary anxiety or depressive disorder, either is causing or co-occurring with the attention deficit symptoms. These authors also found a significant relationship between attention deficit, anxiety, and/or depression based on parent, child, and consensus diagnoses.

A sample of 59 children in grades four through seven were identified with diagnoses of depression, anxiety, or depression and anxiety (Stark, Kaslow, & Laurent, 1993). In self-reports, these three diagnostic groups differed significantly from the nondisturbed controls across all paper-and-pencil measures. However, the three diagnostic groups could not be differentiated solely based on their self-reports to these measures, which included the Children's Depression Inventory, the Revised Children's Manifest Anxiety Scale, the Hopelessness Scale for Children, and the Coopersmith Self-Esteem Inventory. As will be discussed in the evaluation section, the findings of this study and others suggest that while self-report measures are valuable in identifying children with internalizing problems, alone they are unlikely to distinguish between depressed or anxious disorders.

Using life table estimates, Hammen, Burge, Burney, and Adrian (1990), demonstrated the cumulative estimated probability of an episode of major psychiatric disorder in offspring of unipolar depressed mothers as 80% by late adolescence, a rate much higher than for children whose parents have no psychiatric history. Beardslee, Keller, Lavori, Staley, and Sacks (1993) evaluated the effects of parents' affective disorder on off-spring in a nonreferred population 4 years after initial examination. The rates of major depressive disorder were 26% in the children with parents of affective disorder compared with only 10% for those children with parents experiencing no disorder. The number of children receiving multiple diagnoses was also higher for children with parents experiencing an affective disorder. Further, the children of affective disordered parents appeared to be exposed to a number of family risk factors that did not occur at a similar rate for the nonaffective-disordered families. The constellation of several parental risk factors occurring together appear to associate with very poor child outcome. The parental disorder exposed these children both to psychosocial influences and to genetic influences that increase risk for depression. This study of nonreferred families suggests that children are at significant risk even when parents with affective disorders have not been identified or treated. Because of the high rate of impairment among children in these families, classroom consultants should consider screening a child for adequate school performance and behavior if it is known that the child's parent is experiencing a depressive or other major psychiatric disorder.

As with anxiety disorders, the percentage of children identified as depressed varies widely. A review by the National Institute of Mental Health in 1982 suggested that moderate to severe rates of depression among a number of different studies ranged from almost 0% to 33% (Teuting, Koslow, & Hirshfield, 1982). Lefkowitz and Tesiny (1985) reported an incidence rate of just over 5% meeting the authors' criteria for depression in an epidemiological sample of 3,000 elementary school children. Further, Matson (1989) suggests that differences in diagnostic criteria, ages of children studied, socioeconomic status of families, and other social or environmental variables likely contribute to the disparity in incidence rates.

P. Burke (1991) reported that depression may be a common sequela in chronic pediatric illness. Classroom consultants should keep in mind that children with chronic medical illness are extremely vulnerable to depression (P. M. Burke et al., 1989; Kashani, Lahabidi, & Jones, 1982). With this population, all presenting symptoms should be considered in the diagnosis of depression whether or not they are etiologically related to the medical illness as well (Cohen-Cole & Stoudemire, 1987). Depression can fuel or worsen existing medical problems and many lead to the onset of new problems (Strunk, Morazek, Fuhrmann, & Labreque,

1985). The *DSM-IV* criteria include a mood disorder characteristic of depression as the result of a generalized medical condition. A number of authors have suggested that duration or severity of a medical illness may not be correlated in a simple linear fashion to depressive symptoms (P. Burke, 1991; B. Wood et al., 1987). However, Kashani and Hakami (1982) suggest that significant depressive symptoms often do not immediately follow a diagnosis and if so are short lived. It may also be that a poor early reaction to the stress of the illness diagnosis could predict greater vulnerability for later depressive problems.

Depression and disruptive problems, including ADHD, oppositional defiance and conduct disorder consistently have been reported as occurring at a greater-than-predicted chance level (Ben-Amos, 1992). The comorbidity of depression and conduct disorders appears to be prevalent in children and adolescents, occurring in at least one out of five depressed children (Kovacs et al., 1988). G. A. Carlson and Cantwell (1980b) reported a 30% comorbidity rate for these two disorders. Kovacs et al. (1988) suggest that the co-occurrence of conduct and depressive problems may actually constitute a separate diagnostic group requiring different treatment and management than the other two.

Three possible explanations for the relationship between depression and disruptive conduct problems have been hypothesized: (1) one disorder directly affecting the other, (2) an indirect relationship as the result of some third variable (e.g., learning disability or personality disorder), and (3) a model suggesting that these two disorders reflect a common pathway (Ben-Amos, 1992). However, none of these explanations has found complete support in the research literature.

Although some symptomatic complaints may be similar for depressed and conduct-impaired individuals, the relationship of these two disorders is certainly more complex than linear (G. A. Carlson & Cantwell, 1980b). There also may be different types of depression based on onset (Akiskal et al., 1980). In adults, for example, early onset dysthymia demonstrates a different course and pathway from individuals with dysthymia superimposed on major depressive episodes (D. N. Klein, Taylor, Dickstein, & Harding, 1988). Further convincing evidence has never been generated to suggest that early deprivation, learning disability, or personality disorder (or any other variable for that matter) reflects a common cause for both conduct disorder and depression.

The last theoretical explanation offered by Ben-Amos (1992) is part of a larger theory suggesting that eight distinct disorders may share a common pathophysiological abnormality (Hudson & Pope, 1990). These authors hypothesize that bulimia, panic disorder, obsessive-compulsive disorder, attention deficit disorder, cataplexy, migraine, irritable bowel syndrome, and major depression all respond to antidepressants and thus their etiology must somehow be related. These disorders have been hypothesized to reflect an "affective spectrum." However, this theory requires much additional research before firm conclusions can be drawn.

Undiagnosed bipolar disorder has been mistaken for conduct disorder or hyperactivity (Akiskal & Weller, 1989). These authors reported that in a population of 68 children with bipolar disorder, 15% were initially misdiagnosed as having a conduct disorder; 35%, as having an adjustment disorder; and 9%, as being hyperactive. Although mania is difficult to diagnose in children and adolescents, the majority of children demonstrating conduct disorder or ADHD do not experience bipolar disorder. The emotional roller coaster that ADHD children experience because of their excessive sensitivity may lead some observers to hypothesize manic depression in these children (Weinberg & Brumback, 1976).

Akiskal and Weller (1989) reported cases of primary conduct disorder with secondary depression. In this population, treatment of the depression did not appear to affect the conduct disorder. Puig-Antich (1982) suggests that among prepubertal boys with major depression and conduct disorder, the onset of the depression usually precedes the conduct disorder. In those children responding to pharmacological treatment, the depression is alleviated prior to the conduct disorder. Kovacs et al. (1988) reported in their population that conduct-disordered behavior was secondary to mood disorders. These authors found no pattern of association between type of depression and presence of conduct disorder. Age, however, was a variable in this study with conduct disorder being found most likely in the 11- to 14-year-old population of depressed individuals.

Attention-deficit/hyperactivity disorder and mood disorders have been found to co-occur consistently in at least 20% to 30% of samples receiving a primary diagnosis of ADHD (Biederman, Munir, et al., 1986). It has also been suggested that ADHD in children with a major depressive disorder represents a significantly more psychiatrically impaired group with a poorer long-term prognosis (Gittelman, Mannuzza, Shenker, & Bonagura, 1985). Among psychiatrically hospitalized children, the comorbidity for anxiety and depressive disorders has been reported as exceeding 50% (Woolston et al., 1989).

Although prospective follow-up studies are limited, those available suggest that the early onset of depression is associated with increased risk for recurrence. In a series of studies, Kovacs, Feinberg, Crouse-Novak,

Paulauskas, and Finkelstein (1984) reported a 72% risk of recurrence of depression within 5 years in a sample of preadolescents. In this population, risk of recurrence was not affected by gender, age, duration of the initial depressive episode, or comorbidity for anxiety or conduct disorder. Based on a follow-up study of depressed children and adolescents seen as young adults, Harrington, Fudge, Rutter, Pickles, and Hill (1990) report an ongoing pattern of difficulty with depression for a significant group. McCauley et al. (1993) report generally similar results for length, onset, and course of depression in a population of children followed yearly for 3 years. The majority of studies converge and suggest that the initial length of a depressive episode is approximately 30 to 40 weeks. McCauley and coworkers suggest that gender is a clear-cut risk factor with girls demonstrating greater risk of severity of depression and longer initial depressive episodes. These authors also report that over the 3-year study period, a very small number of children developed problems other than depression. Depression appeared to be a consistent theme for this population rather than differentiation into other disorders with maturity. In this population, the recurrence risk for a depressive episode was 54% and many of the children demonstrated periods of good academic success and improved social functioning. Older age of onset for depression was associated with better school outcome. Finally, family environment, as found in other studies of depression, was a significant factor predicting overall psychosocial competence. Increased levels of stress in the family environment were associated with poorer psychosocial outcome. These authors concluded, "in sum data from this study supports the position that child and adolescent depression represents the initial presentation of the disorder that appears similar in its clinical presentation and episodic nature to depression occurring in adult life" (p. 721).

No significant relationship between depression and academic achievement has been found (Stark, Livingston, et al., 1993) although these authors noted moderate, negative relationships between severity of depression and numerical grade average in science, physical education, and social studies. In contrast, anxious children, although they did not function as well in physical education, did not display any other achievement differences from the normal controls.

Eating disorders and substance abuse have also been frequently reported to co-occur with depression (Attie, Brooks-Gunn, & Petersen, 1990). Extreme weight and excessive eating has been reported as covarying with depression beyond a chance level as well (Richards, Boxer, Petersen, & Albrecht, 1990). In girls, poor body image may lead to eating disorders and then to depression (A. C. Peterson et al., 1993).

The majority of depressed suicide victims have been reported as experiencing a primary affective disorder. Well over four fifths of a population studied by Brent et al. (1993) had received a diagnosis of affective disorder, and 31% of this group of suicide victims had been depressed less than 3 months. Previous suicide attempts, as well as suicidal and homicidal ideation, were associated with adolescent suicide; and substance abuse and conduct disorder also appeared to increase the risk of suicide among depressed adolescents. Substance abuse was a more significant risk factor when it occurred comorbidly with an affective illness than when alone. The most significant single risk factor for suicide is major depression. The risk of anxiety disorder as predictive of suicide at this time is unclear.

Cause

Two broad theories are proposed for causing depression in childhood—biological and experiential variables. For a thorough review of these issues, the reader is referred to Matson (1989), Trad (1987), or Gotlib and Hammen (2002). A parsimonious explanation for these theories suggests that genetics may predispose some individuals to depression through biochemical mechanism. Experience then determines whether depressive symptoms develop and the extent of symptom severity. In a reciprocal fashion, experience may also influence physiological markers that indicate depression such as failure to suppress cortisol when given dexamethasone (Peselow, Baxter, Fieve, & Barouche, 1987), and urinary MHPG (3-methoxy-4 hydroxyphenylglycol, a metabolite of norepinephrine) and growth hormone secretion (Matson, 1989). Although failure to suppress dexamethasone has been reported for children and adolescents in inpatient settings, the use of this measure and others such as muscle tension have yet to demonstrate accuracy and reliability in diagnosing childhood depression (Geller, Rogel, & Knitter, 1983; Livingston, Reis, & Ringdahl, 1984).

The search for biological correlates to depression, however, has prompted a wide and varied series of research studies. Puig-Antich (1986) defined biological markers for depression as "characteristics that have been shown to be specifically associated with the disorder in question, during an episode, during the symptom free intervals or both" (p. 342). As Trad (1987) suggests, some biological markers may reflect a "state" associated with the active period of the disorder, whereas others may reflect a lifetime "trait" associated with the individual. The search for biological markers has included a group of endocrine metabolites (norepinephrine, VMA, MHPG; T. L. Lowe &

163

Cohen, 1980), cortisol secretion (Puig-Antich, 1986), sleep EEG (electroencephalogram) abnormalities (Puig-Antich, 1982), abnormalities in the limbic hypothalamo-pituitary-adrenal axis (Carroll, 1983), and atypical secretions of growth hormone (Puig-Antich et al., 1984).

Many biological markers significant in research studies with depressed adults have demonstrated some clinical utility in research studies in the diagnosis of childhood depression (Trad, 1987). However, the direction and specificity of abnormalities may be different in different age groups. Tests for abnormalities in MHPG and cortisol secretion have not yielded consistent findings in children. Sleep EEG studies of depressed children have shown only a few direct correlations with adult studies. Tests evaluating limbic regulation may prove useful in the diagnosis of childhood depression but as yet are inconclusive (Lingjaerde, 1983). Finally, hypersecretion of growth hormone may prove to be a valid trait marker for depression in childhood. However, the response of hypersecretion of growth hormone has been suggested as being reversed in children versus adolescents and adults with depression. Interested readers are referred to Emslie, Weinberg, Kennard, and Kowatch (1994).

Among experiential variables, having a depressed parent is a major risk factor for depression in childhood (Downey & Coyne, 1990; Goodman & Gotlib, 1999; Hammen, 1990). Children of depressed parents are more likely to experience a wide range of school, behavioral, and emotional problems. Among the causative mechanisms suggested by A. C. Peterson et al. (1993) to affect the transmission of depressive disorders from parents to children are experiential variables including poor parenting, unavailability of parents, and marital conflict. Parental divorce has been suggested as amplifying behavioral disturbances and depression in adolescents (Cherlin et al., 1991). Asarmov and Horton (1990) report that marital discord and family economic hardship appeared to increase the risk of depression in adolescents.

Finally, an alternate experiential theory related to learned helplessness has been proposed as a cause of depression (Abramson, Seligman, & Teasdale, 1978). Learned helplessness results from experiential variables and reflects a common pathway leading individuals to perceive events in their lives as uncontrollable and beyond their capabilities. In children, this may result in an external locus of control that likely contributes to increased helplessness behavior and the child's unwillingness to assume responsibility. This then leads to the child's lack of responsiveness to normal teacher interventions in the classroom.

Chapters 12 and 14 review a number of strategies for managing child-hood helplessness and related depression symptoms that can be applied in the classroom. The most popular cognitive treatments include rational emotive therapy (A. Ellis, 1962) and Beck's approach (A. T. Beck, Rush, Shaw, & Emery, 1979). The latter differs from rational emotive therapy in suggesting a less defined group of faulty modes of thinking as being responsible for depression. Both treatments focus on the impact faulty thinking has on emotion and behavior.

Social Learning Problems

SAM GOLDSTEIN AND ROBERT BROOKS

Problems learning, mastering, and efficiently using social skills represent a complex and often difficult to understand set of problems for classroom educators. Long before they enter the classroom, a significant minority of children experience social learning problems. Though we are social beings, mastering the socialization process is difficult for some children. The thoughts, actions, and reactions children routinely use day in and day out with others represent a complex set of behaviors. These behaviors allow children to connect to others and form the basis of behavior in the classroom. The social mindsets children develop consist of thoughts, feelings, actions, and reactions. Some social learning problems are minor and easily guided and modified. At their extreme, social learning problems reflect significant impairments in developing social competence, leading either to an atypical pattern of social skills or a seemingly total lack of social skills. When sufficiently severe, these patterns comprise a pervasive developmental disorder (PDD).

Some children's social problems result from low incidence, high impact behaviors. Conditions such as attention-deficit/hyperactivity disorder (ADHD), oppositional defiance, or conduct disorder often lead to impulsive and aggressive patterns of behavior that disturb others, leading to social rejection. Conditions such as depression, anxiety, learning disabilities, and various forms of PDD result in high incidence, low impact behaviors. Children with the former set of conditions often struggle to exhibit appropriate social skills. Children with the latter set of conditions often know what to do but do not consistently do what they know.

Children with the first set of conditions are skill deficient. At the extreme, children experiencing social problems secondary to either of these two sets of conditions often require professional help. Their teachers are often in need of support and strategies from an experienced classroom consultant. However, consultants can be equally effective in helping teachers when specific social problems, absent more serious conditions, present in the classroom. This chapter provides a brief overview of basic social learning problems. These problems are discussed in much greater depth along with consulting interventions in Chapter 15. The remainder of this chapter is devoted to the social learning problems characteristic of children with PDDs.

It is impossible to list every single interaction, thought, and behavior that might comprise socialization. But a social mindset can be examined. Social thoughts reflect an internal dialogue—a personal, running commentary about the interactions we have with others. These thoughts foster positive or negative feelings. Positive thoughts often precipitate positive behavior. Negative thoughts, such as feeling dumb or incompetent, precipitate negative behavior. There is just a small, attributional step between positive or negative thoughts and feelings to positive or negative behavior. Negative thoughts and feelings lead to erroneous assumptions about the reasons for others' behavior and erroneous attributes of the quality of others' personality. These negative thoughts lead to certain actions. Actions can be verbal or nonverbal. Actions like thoughts and feelings can be positive or negative. Positive actions are often preceded by a positive thought. Finally, reactions reflect the child's response to another student's attempts at social reaction. Reactions can also be positive or negative. Negative social behaviors such as aggression, arguing, teasing, complaining, or bossing sets the stage for social problems in the classroom.

Social skills are discrete, learned behaviors exhibited by a student for the purpose of performing specific tasks (Sheridan, 1998). Social skills are observable, measurable, and concrete behaviors. Sheridan and Walker (1999) present a framework of what they term *social skillfulness* representing a combination of social skills and social competence. The latter reflects the opinions of others as receivers of social overtures. In this model, social skills are "goal directed, learned behaviors allowing an individual to interact and function effectively in a variety of social contexts." To be socially skillful, a child must first learn a range of important social behaviors necessary in a variety of situations and then learn to relate in a way that is acceptable to others in a range of social situations. Children must then possess within their behavioral repertoire skills that can generalize across situations and they must have an appreciation of the impact their behavior has on others. They must be able to understand social situations and know what is an appropriate response in a particular situation. They must be able to discriminate and generalize from one situation to the next. Considering this framework is not very different from considering the basic framework for learning any behavior or, for that matter, academic skill. Thus, the term *social learning problems* appears appropriate to describe children who struggle in this arena.

Of all the tasks a child must master, the ability to establish and maintain meaningful relationships with peers and adults is perhaps the most important. Successful peer relationships feed many important needs and form a cornerstone of a resilient mindset. Successful peer interactions help children feel worthy, competent, and connected. Peer relations also set a stage for perspective taking and mutual understanding. To develop friendships, children must accomplish at least two related tasks. They must learn to relate in a way that is acceptable to peers and they must learn the skills of friendship that will be necessary for relationships in later life. They must have skills within their behavioral repertoire that allow them to discriminate and generalize from one situation to the next. In social situations, some children are neglected (liked by few, disliked by few) while others are rejected (liked by few and disliked by many). However, it is also important to note that while some children are popular (liked by many, disliked by few), there are some who are controversial (liked by many, disliked by many; Coie & Dodge, 1998).

Socially competent children are capable of the following:

- They initiate social interaction successfully.
- They know how to join groups.
- They possess a variety of interpersonal tactics rather than relying on a single similar behavior each time.
- They demonstrate a balance in their social and communicative interactions.
- They engage in alternative turn-taking exchanges with an understanding of timing and roles within interactions.
- They know how to maintain a conversation, listen, and pay attention to others.
- They can share.
- They offer assistance when needed.
- They provide praise and compliments to others.

Children with a competent socialization mindset have a history of engaging in productive social activities and, most importantly, are effective problem solvers in social interactions. They recognize a variety of behavioral alternatives and can select a strategy or behavior at any given time that holds the greatest potential for successful problem resolution.

In contrast, socially unskilled children lack one or many of these competencies. They may additionally be socially withdrawn or aggressive. In both scenarios, these children are unable to act effectively and appropriately within the social environment. Socially withdrawn children are often neglected and isolated from their peer group. This is a pattern that often results for children with more severe social learning problems secondary to PDD. Socially aggressive children are often rejected and behave in aversive ways leading to segregation from peers. Socially withdrawn children tend to be isolated, shy and passive. Often they are not uncomfortable being alone. Some recognize and are bothered by their isolation, which may lead to feelings of inadequacy, incompetence, or helplessness. An acute onset of social withdrawal may also represent one of the most visible markers of the beginnings of a major depressive disorder. Children demonstrating social withdrawal on a chronic basis often possess few strategies available for solving social problems. They frequently develop a helpless approach as their efforts engaging peers eventually builds a long history of failure and frustration. They struggle to elicit positive responses from peers and eventually in a self-fulfilling manner become increasingly more passive, anticipating that future attempts will meet with similar failure as past attempts.

Socially aggressive children, on the other hand, can be verbally and physically assaultive. They may bully, tease, provoke, or quarrel. They tend to ignore and violate the rights of others which, at the extreme, often leads to diagnoses of oppositional defiant and/or conduct disorders. These children often possess appropriate social skills but use them in an inappropriate way. Their tactics may be effective but are frequently inappropriate and disliked by other students. For some children, this pattern of behavior results from poor impulse control absent forethought. For others, particularly those at risk to develop more serious antisocial problems, socially provocative behavior is often planful. These children often exhibit few pro-social behavior such as helping, sharing, or cooperating. They often resort to aggression and threat to gain control of others. Inappropriate thoughts drive this pattern of behavior. These children at the extreme often perceive and attribute their misfortune to the hostile behavior of others. They misinterpret social cues and then respond in a provocative, aggressive way creating a self-fulfilling prophecy and outcome.

All types of social learning problems likely have a biological basis but are best conceptualized as reflecting a biopsychosocial condition. Though biology and genetics may set the stage for certain patterns of problems, experience and ultimately thought and perception determine course and outcome. The biological basis of social learning problems is particularly obvious in children with PDDs. These children do not "read" facial expressions or body language well, misinterpret the use and meaning of vocal pitch and may misunderstand the use of personal space (Caicedo & Williams, 2002). Their ability to initiate conversation, ask questions, show interest in others as well as extend invitations, offer compliments, smile, and laugh are often impaired due to a biological inability to track these social cues, many of which are related to language.

In the normally developing child and adolescent, the socialization process typically follows a predictable course. Though differences are observed in social competence, the course of development is well defined. The term *pervasive developmental disorder* refers to a group of disorders that appear to exert a significant negative impact on children's general development, communication, behavior, but most significantly socialization. These disorders include autism, Rett's disorder, childhood disintegrative disorder, Asperger's disorder, and an atypical pattern of PDD. Despite recent research and clinical advances in distinguishing these PDDs, in clinical practice today as well as in pre-1980 research literature, all these disorders were and continue to be generally referred to under the term *autism*. In classroom settings across grades, it is the failure to exhibit and maintain appropriate social interaction that presents teachers with the greatest challenge in dealing with youth experiencing a PDD. The remainder of this chapter focuses on the social learning problems of children with normal IQ. Autism, Asperger's and atypical PDDs. Readers interested in a broader overview of the PDDs are referred to D. J. Cohen and Volkmar (1997).

Kanner (1943) first described autism as an inborn, innate condition in which children experience a profound disturbance of social functioning. In Kanner's description, autistic children experience (a) an inability to relate in ordinary ways to people; (b) excellent rote memory skills; (c) language difficulties ranging from mutism to spoken language characterized by lack of communicative intent, echolalia, personal pronoun reversal, and literalness; (d) fear of loud noises and moving objects; (e) repetition behaviors and an obsessive desire for the maintenance of sameness in the physical environment and routines; (f) lack of spontaneous activity; and (g) in some individuals, good cognitive potential. Until the 1970s, autism was considered a form of schizophrenia although the behavior of young autistic children was very different from the psychotic problems of later childhood or teenage years. It has been abundantly clear that young autistic children suffer in many other areas of their development (Kolvin, 1971; see D. J. Cohen & Volkmar, 1997; for a review).

Autism is a spectrum disorder in which individuals can present problems ranging from those that cause almost total impairment to others that allow the individual to function but not optimally. Autistic and pervasively impaired children experience a wide variety of developmental difficulties involving communication, socialization, thinking, cognitive skills, interests, activities, and motor skills. Although critics suggest that the diagnosis of PDD is poorly defined and inconsistent because it does not refer to all PDDs (e.g., retardation), the term seems to best define this group of children. Some children undoubtedly experience specific or partial pervasive impairments (C. Gillberg, 1990). Symptomatic problems of this population frequently include perceptual disorders (Ornitz & Ritvo, 1968), language deficits (McCann, 1989), cognitive problems (Rutter, 1983), memory weaknesses (Boucher, 1981), and impairment in social relations (Fein, Pennington, Markowitz, Braverman, & Waterhouse, 1986; Fein, Pennington, & Waterhouse, 1987). Consistent with Kanner's description of autism, social impairments have been found to be the strongest predictors of receiving a diagnosis (Siegel, Vukicevic, Elliott, & Kraemer, 1989). Dimensionally measured variables such as those related to interpersonal relationships, play skills, coping, and communication are consistently impaired areas for youth with a PDD. Relative to cognitive abilities, children with autism exhibit much lower than expected social skills, even compared to a mentally handicapped group (Volkmar et al., 1987). Delays in social skills are strong predictors of receiving a diagnosis of autism, even when compared to delays in communication (Volkmar, Carter, Sparrow, & Cicchetti, 1993). Clearly, impairments in social skills among those receiving diagnoses of any PDD are greater than expected relative to overall development (Loveland & Kelley, 1991).

The consensus, however, is that the PDDs consist of three major problem areas involving social relations, communication, and behavior. Likely, specific cognitive deficits form a fourth component. Since Rutter's (1978) first description of social impairments absent cognitive deficits in youth with autism, diagnostic criteria for these conditions have expanded to include deficits in nonverbal behavior, peer relations, lack of shared enjoyment and pleasure, and problems with social and emotional reciprocity (American Psychiatric Association, 1994; World Health Organization, 1993). Although age of onset was originally specified in the 1980 *DSM-III* as occurring before 30 to 36 months, this age cutoff is no longer included among the essential diagnostic criteria (Wing, 1990). C. Gillberg (1986) reports that autism can have its onset long after 3 years of age.

Because of the unusual combination of behavioral weaknesses and the lack of a physiological and physical model to understand this disorder, autism is a most perplexing condition (Schopler & Mesibov, 1987). Autism is best conceptualized as a biologically determined set of behaviors that occurs with varying presentation and severity, likely as the result of varying cause.

Autistic children often demonstrate a variable and mixed combination of impairments. Many do not meet full autistic criteria. Some of these children may experience what has been referred to as a schizoid disorder of childhood (Wolff & Barlow, 1979). The autistic child with normal intellect may represent a mild case of the disorder or a variant that has been erroneously referred to as Asperger's syndrome (Wing, 1981). The following criteria best define the autistic syndrome: impairment in social interaction, self-absorbed behavior, odd interests and routines, speech and language problems in spite of superficially competent expressive language skills, nonverbal communication problems, and motor clumsiness (C. Gillberg & Gillberg, 1989). Rutter (1979) found that the pattern of cognitive disabilities in autistic children, especially those with Asperger's, is distinctive and different from that found in children with general intellectual handicaps. Most commonly, language and language-related skills involving problems with semantics and pragmatics are present (Rutter, 1983). Hobson (1989) found that higher functioning autistic children are unable to make social or emotional discriminations or read social or emotional cues well. These deficits appear to impact social relations and likely stem from cognitive weaknesses. The inability to read social and emotional cues and understand others' points of view leads to marked interpersonal difficulties (Baron-Cohen, 1989; MacDonald, Rutter, & Howlin, 1989).

The third edition of the *Diagnostic and Statistical Manual of Mental Disorders* (American Psychiatric Association, 1980) first utilized the term pervasive developmental disorder thus establishing a firm opinion that autism was developmental in nature and distinct from mental illness occurring later in life. Autism is now recognized as an organically based neurodevelopmental disorder (Rutter, 1970) that occurs significantly more often in boys (Smalley, Asarnow, & Spence, 1988) and presents across all social classes (C. Gillberg & Schaumann, 1982). It is estimated that one out of four autistic children experiences physical problems, including epilepsy (Rutter, 1970). Up to 80% are generally found to experience intellectual deficiencies. Lotter (1974) suggests that the level of intellectual functioning and the amount of useful language by 5 years of age, are the best predictors of outcome for autistic children. The work of C. Gillberg and Steffenburg (1987) supports this finding.

Definition

The *DSM-IV-TR* (American Psychiatric Association, 2000) criteria include a group of PDDs. The first, *autistic disorder*, has remained fairly consistent in the manual's past three versions. The diagnosis includes three parts with the first part involving three sets of behavioral descriptions. To qualify for the diagnosis, the child must present at least two from the first set of behaviors and one from each of the second and third sets of behaviors. The first set of behaviors features qualitative impairment in social interaction as manifested by impairment of nonverbal behaviors, including eye contact, facial expression, body postures, and gestures of social interaction; failure to develop peer relationships appropriate to developmental level; markedly impaired expression of pleasure in other people's happiness, and lack of social or emotional reciprocity. The second set of behaviors refers to qualitative impairment in communication as manifested by a delay or total lack of the development of spoken language without efforts to compensate through gestures; marked impairment in the ability to initiate or sustain conversation despite adequate speech; repetitive or stereotyped use of language or idiosyncratic language; and lack of varied, spontaneous make-believe play or social imitative play appropriate for the child's developmental level. The third set of behaviors involves repetitive and stereotypic patterns of behavior; restricted interest or activities, including preoccupation in a certain pattern of behavior that is abnormal in intensity or focus; compulsive adherence to specific nonfunctional routines or rituals; repetitive motor mannerisms (self-stimulatory behavior), or persistent preoccupation with parts of objects. The second two sets of criteria include delay prior to the age of 3 in social interaction, language as used in social communication, or symbolic or imaginative play. Finally, the child's clinical description should not be better accounted for by Rett's disorder or childhood disintegrative disorder.

DSM-IV-TR criteria describe Rett's disorder as being manifested by normal development for at least the first 5 months of life, including normal prenatal and perinatal development, apparently normal psychomotor development through the first 5 months, and normal head circumference at birth. Between 5 and 48 months there is an onset in deceleration of head growth, loss of previously acquired purposeful hand movements with the development of stereotypic hand movements (e.g., hand wringing), loss of social engagement, appearance of poorly coordinated gait or trunk movements, and marked delay as well as impairment of expressive and receptive language with severe psychomotor retardation.

Childhood disintegrative disorder in *DSM-IV-TR* is defined as normal development for the first 2 years and then loss of skills in at least two areas including expressive or receptive language; social skills or adaptive behavior; bowel or bladder control; play or motor skills. In addition, the child begins to manifest qualitative impairments in social interaction, including at least two of the following: impaired use of nonverbal behaviors, failure to develop peer relationships, markedly impaired expression of pleasure in other people's happiness, and a lack of social or emotional reciprocity. There are also qualitative impairments in communication as manifested by at least one symptom involving delay or total lack of spoken language, an inability to sustain and initiate conversation despite adequate speech, stereotyped or repetitive use of language or idiosyncratic language, and a lack of varied, spontaneous make-believe play or social, imitative play. The child with childhood disintegrative disorder also demonstrates restrictive, repetitive, and stereotypic patterns of behavior, interests, and activities. The child's behavior should not be accounted for by another specific developmental disorder or by schizophrenia. Thus, childhood disintegrative disorder reflects an autistic diagnosis that occurs after a clear period of normal development.

DSM-IV defined the criteria for a new diagnosis, Asperger's disorder, which has remained unchanged for *DSM-IV-TR*. Included in the diagnostic criteria are deficits in the qualitative impairment in social interaction, including at least two criteria involving: (1) marked impairment in the use of nonverbal behaviors such as body posture; failure to develop appropriate peer relations; (2) a lack of spontaneous seeking to share enjoyment, interests, or achievements and lack of social or emotional reciprocity. A second set of criteria involves restricted repetitive and stereotyped behaviors, interests, or activities, including at least one symptom of the following: Restricted or stereotyped pattern of interest that is abnormal in intensity or focus; inflexible adherence to specific rituals or routines; repetitive motor mannerisms; or persistent preoccupation with parts of objects. This disturbance must cause clinically significant impairment in social, academic, and other areas of functioning. Further, for this diagnosis to be made, the child should not exhibit a delay in early language development or a significant delay in language or cognitive development or in the development of age appropriate self-help skills and adaptive behavior. Although these criteria are a good start, they do not extend far enough nor are they well enough operationalized based on the data reviewed earlier in this chapter.

Epidemiology

Wing and Gould (1979) refer to the triad of social, language, and behavioral impairments with autistic like conditions. This triad has been reported as occurring in approximately 21 out of 10,000 children (C. Gillberg, 1986; Wing & Gould, 1979). Full syndrome autism likely occurs in 6 to 7 out of 10,000 children (Steffenburg & Gillberg, 1986). Other authors suggest an incidence of autism as high as 21 children in every 10,000 with a male to female ration of approximately four to one (Cialdella & Mamelle, 1989). Asperger's syndrome appears to be at least three to five times more common than full syndrome autism, occurring in approximately two to three children per thousand (I. C. Gillberg & Gillberg, 1989; Wing, 1990).

Etiology

Fotheringham (1991) concludes that the core behavioral disorder in autism is "a disturbance of reciprocal social relations which is due to an information processing defect in assigning social-emotional value to stimuli. The constancy of the core behavioral signs of autism suggests a defined neurologic mechanism within the brain that is disrupted" (p. 689). Brain-related causative theories for autistic populations include deficits in the frontal or temporal lobes, the amygdala, septal nuclei, corpus striatum, thalamus, vestibular regions, or gray matter (Reichler & Lee, 1987). Courchesne, Young-Courchesne, Press, Hesselink, and Jernigan (1988) and Courchesne (1989) suggest that cerebellar dysfunction is responsible for autism. Kinsbourne (1987) suggests autism is a cerebral-brain stem disorder. Finally, Fein et al. (1987) suggest that the limbic system is most likely involved in this group of disorders. For a review of these studies, see Table 8.1. It may be that autism does not represent a single disorder but results from a variety of causes and is a series of disorders with overlapping symptoms (Reichler & Lee, 1987).

In rare cases, environmental factors such as infection (Chess, Fernandez, & Korn, 1978), genetics (Rutter, 1988), or perinatal trauma (Deykin & McMahon, 1980) have been implicated. Although early on it was

Table 8.1 Neurobiological studies in autism

Area	Study	Finding	Reference
Structural	Autopsy of 29-year-old man with clear autism versus age- and sex-matched control	Major cellular and structural changes in hippocampus, amygdala, and cerebellum (including Purkinje cell loss)	Baumann & Kemper (1985)
	Autopsy of four patients with autism	Purkinje cell loss in the cerebellum in all four patients	Ritvo et al. (1986)
Imaging	MRI of 18 relatively high-functioning persons with autism versus 12 normal controls	Hypoplasia of cerebellar vermal lobules 6 and 7 in 14 of 18 patients	Courchesne, Young-Courchesne, Press, Hesselink, & Jernigan (1998)
	MRI of 13 relatively high-functioning persons with DSM-III autism versus 35 "medical" age-matched controls	Brain stem (in particular the pons) significantly smaller in autism group. Same group reported widening of fourth ventricle	Gaffney, Kuperman, Tsai, & Minuchin (1988) Gaffney & Tsai (1987)
	CAT scan of 9 men with autism versus 13 men with normal intelligence	Widening of third ventricle and lower caudate radiodensity	Jacobson, LeCouteur, Howlin, & Rutter (1988)
	PET scan of 14 relatively high-functioning men with autism versus 14 healthy controls	Impairment of interactions between frontal/parietal regions and the neostriatum and the thalamus	Horwitz, Rumsey, Grady, & Rapoport (1988)
	PET scan of six high-functioning men with autism versus six age-matched normal volunteer males and eight other normal volunteers	Normal	Jacobson et al. (1988)

Table 8.1   (Continued)

Area	Study	Finding	Reference
Neuropsychological	Event-related brain potentials (ERPs) from 10 high-functioning adolescents with autism and 10 age-matched controls	Small P3 wave	Courchesne, Lincoln, Kilman, & Galambos (1985)
	ERPs from 17 mildly retarded (6) and high-functioning children (11) with DSM-III autism versus 17 age- and sex-matched control	Small wave vertex and left hemisphere, but no difference in right hemisphere	Dawson, Finley, Phillips, & Galpert (1988)
	Oculomotor function in 11 children (five girls) with high-level autism compared with 26	Abnormalities of saccadic eye movements in patients with autism, which are different from those seen	Rosenhall, Johansson, & Gillberg (1988)
Neurochemical	CSF monoamines in 35 children with autism spectrum disorders (22 with DSM-III autism) compared with various groups, including sex- and age-matched "near normals"	Raised HVA and high HAV: HMPG quotients in patients with autism	Gillberg & Svennerholm (1987)
	Plasma, platelets, and urine study of catecholamines in 22 children with autism versus 22 sex- and age-matched controls	High adrenaline and noradrenaline in plasma, and low adrenaline, noradrenaline, and dopamine in platelets in patients with autism	Launay et al. (1987)

(continued)

Table 8.1   (*Continued*)

Area	Study	Finding	Reference
	Urinary catecholamines measured in 8 young children with *DSM-III* autism and 8 sex- and age-matched controls	Raised HVA (low dopamine) and lowered HMPG (high noradrenaline) levels in patients with autism	Barthèlèmy et al. (1988)
	CSF endorphins in 29 young children with *DSM-III* autism versus 8 normal and 4 neurologically deviant children	Raised endorphin fraction II levels in autism correlating to decreased pain sensitivity	Gillberg (1989)
	CSF beta-endorphins in 31 young children with *DSM-III-R* autism compared with large groups of normal adults and 8 Rett syndrome cases	Low beta-endorphins in autism and Rett's syndrome	Gillberg, Terenius, Hagberg, Witt-Engerström, & Eriksson (1990)
Clinical	20 high-functioning children with *DSM-III-R* autism (17) or Asperger's syndrome (3) were extensively neurobiologically examined	Major neurobiological abnormalities (including tuberous sclerosis, fragile X, and infantile spasms) were found in 75% of cases	Gillberg, Steffenburg, & Jakobsson (1987)
	90 cases with tuberous sclerosis extensively examined	50% fulfilled Rutter's criteria for infantile autism	Hunt & Dennis (1987)
	50 cases with Rett's syndrome examined with respect to first diagnosis received by pediatricians	38% had been diagnosed as autism, a further 42% as childhood psychosis or autistic features	Witt-Engerström & Gillberg (1987)
	Survey of fragile X literature	Strong indications that fragile X is associated with autism and vice versa	Hagerman (1990)

Source: "Autism and Pervasive Developmental Disorders," by C. Gillberg, 1990, *Journal of Child Psychology and Psychiatry, 31,* 99–119. Reprinted with permission of the author and publisher.

suspected that this group of disorders was caused by cold and unemotional parents, research over the past 25 years has not confirmed this hypothesis (Cantwell, Baker, & Rutter, 1978; C. Gillberg & Coleman, 1993).

A number of identifiable medical conditions occur at greater than chance with autism (C. Gillberg, 1988). Most commonly, these include fragile X syndrome (Hagerman, 1990), tuberous sclerosis (C. Gillberg & Steffenburg, 1987), neurofibromatosis (Gaffney, Kuperman, Tsai, & Minchin, 1988), rubella embryopathy (Wing, 1990), and Rett's syndrome in girls. Fragile X chromosome studies suggest there may be a linkage to autism, with approximately 5% of autistic individuals carrying the fragile X chromosome (H. K. Bloomquist et al., 1985; Ho & Kalousek, 1989). C. Gillberg and Forsell (1984) found a relationship between neurofibromatosis and autism. Three autistic children out of 51 experienced neurofibromatosis, a rate significantly higher than expected in the population. Neurological and central nervous system problems are reported in at least a third of all autistic individuals (Cialdella & Mamelle, 1989). Epilepsy is reported occurring in at least 5% (Bryson, Clark, & Smith, 1988) to 33% (C. Gillberg & Steffenburg, 1987). Abnormal brain functioning (measured by EEG, visual and auditory evoked potentials, neuroimaging, and neuropsychological testing) has consistently been found in a significant percentage of children and adults with autism (Hooper, Boyd, Hynd, & Rubin, 1993). At a neurostructural level, abnormalities in individuals with autism have been found in the left hemisphere, frontal region, and temporal region of the brain (C. Gillberg & Svendsen, 1983). Nonetheless, other researchers have not found clear localizable pattern of neurological abnormality in this population. Autism, therefore is best conceptualized as a behaviorally defined disorder with a wide array of underlying medical conditions (see Table 8.2). These problems occur in a greater-than-chance fashion with autism and thus likely cause, consequence or some combination of the disorder.

Genetic factors likely play a major role in the risk and extent of problems of autism (Ritvo et al., 1989). The occurrence of autism in siblings of autistic individuals has been rated as just under 3% (MacDonald, Rutter, Rios, & Bolton, 1989; Smalley et al., 1988). This is significantly higher than the occurrence in the general population. Rates of language delay and intellectual problems in first degree relatives of autistic individuals are also much higher than expected (Bartak, Rutter, & Cox, 1975). MacDonald, Rutter, and Howlan (1989) additionally found that 15% of siblings of autistic individuals demonstrated learning disabilities and 12% experienced significant social problems. Social impairments are observed in very young children with autism (Trad, Bernstein, Shapiro, & Hertzig, 1993).

Table 8.2 Neurobiological findings associated with autism

Neurobiological Findings Associated with Autism	Important Reference
Boy:girl ratio	Wing (1981)
Mental retardation	Rutter (1983)
Epilepsy	Olsson, Steffenburg, & Gillberg (1988)
Infantile spasms	Riikonen & Amnell (1981)
Pubertal deterioration	Gillberg & Steffenburg (1987)
Fragile X (q27) chromosome abnormality	Wahlström (1985)
Other sex chromosome abnormalities	Gillberg & Wahlström (1985)
Tuberous sclerosis	Lotter (1974)
Neurofibromatosis	Gillberg & Forsell (1984)
Hypomelanosis of Ito	Gillberg & Åkefeldt (1990)
Phenylketonuria	Friedman (1969); Lowe & Cohen (1980)
Lactic acidosis	Coleman & Blass (1985)
Purine disorder	Coleman, Landgrebe, & Landgrebe (1976)
Intrauterine rubella infection	Chess et al. (1978)
Postnatal herpes infection	DeLong, Beau, & Brown (1981); Gillberg (1986)
Rett syndrome	Witt-Engerström & Gillberg (1987)
Hydrocephalus	Schain & Yannet (1960); Fernell, Gillberg, & von Wendt (1990)
Moebius syndrome	Ornitz, Guthrie, & Farley (1977); Gillberg & Steffenberg (1989)
Reduced optimality in pre- and perinatal periods	Gillberg & Gillberg (1989); Bryson, Smith, & Eastwood (1989)
Concordance monozygotic twins	Folstein & Rutter (1977); Steffenburg et al. (1989)
Duchenne muscular dystrophia	Komoto, Udsui, Otsuki, & Terao (1984)
Williams' syndrome	Reiss, Feinstein, Rosenbaum, Borengasser-Caruso, & Goldsmith (1985)

Source: "Autism and Pervasive Developmental Disorders," by C. Gillberg, 1990. *Journal of Child Psychology and Psychiatry, 31*, 99–119. Reprinted with permission of the author and publisher.

Often delays in speech acquisition and expression represent the initial concerns prompting referral for evaluation, typically from pediatricians to speech/language pathologists. Young autistic children often demonstrate impairments in eye contact, social smile, and showing interest in others. Table 8.3 provides an interesting comparison of socialization items and behavior differentiating autistic children from controls matched for chronological and mental age. Social impairments are strongly associated with autism and likely present from birth. Most referrals occur between 18 and 36 months of age when parents become concerned about atypicalities in the child's language, behavior, and interactions with others. Prospective studies of autism, though rare, report various social behaviors such as isolation, problems in eye contact and gaze, indifference to others, and problems with imitation are observed much more frequently in children

Table 8.3   Vineland socialization items of behavior differentiating autistic children from controls matched for age and mental age

Item of Behavior	Expected Age (Years–Months)	Significance (*p*<)
Shows interest in new objects/people	<0–2	.05
Anticipates being picked up by caregiver	<0–2	.01
Shows affection to familiar persons	0–4	.001
Shows interest in children/peers other than siblings	0–4	.001
Reaches for familiar person	0–5	.001
Plays simple interaction games	0–6	.001
Uses household objects for play	0–7	.05
Shows interest in activities of others	0–8	.01
Imitates simple adult movements	0–7	.01
Laughs/smiles in response to positive statements	0–11	.01
Calls at least two familiar people by name	0–11	.01
Participates in at least one activity/game with others	1–7	.05
Imitates adult phrases heard previously	1–11	.05

Items drawn from the Vineland Adaptive Behavior Scales (Sparrow, Balla, & Cicchetti, 1984); data abstracted from Klin, Volkmar, and Sparrow (1992). Expected age is the median age at which the behavior is presented in the general population; cases were matched on age and mental age and were included in comparison only if mental age of the pair was equal to that typically associated with the behavior in the general population.

subsequently identified with autism (C. Gillberg, Ehlers, et al., 1990). This pattern continues into school with young autistic school-age children being described as different from those with developmental delay in regards to skills, including imitation, eye contact, and social interest (Adrien, 1991, 1992). Typically the impression formed by observers is that children with autism are aloof (Wing & Atwood, 1987). As they enter school, teachers often have difficulty gaining their attention, disrupting their routines, and finding ways for them to participate in group activities. They are often minimally responsive affectively. These children do not necessarily demonstrate a total absence of social interest but are difficult to engage (Shapiro, Sherman, Calamari, & Koch, 1987).

Some researchers have suggested that after age 5, some autistic children show spontaneous improvements in socialization (Rutter & Garmezy, 1983). However, the majority continue to struggle, often appearing passive and odd in social interactions (Wing & Gould, 1979). These children are often content to be left alone and find atypical interests to entertain their time. Of significance is their difficulty taking another's point of view, often referred to as failure to develop theory of mind (Volkmar & Cohen, 1985). Though they may develop some relationships with adults typically through discussions of their idiosyncratic interests, mutual or cooperative play is often absent. As a defined category under the Individuals with Disabilities Education Improvement Act (IDEIA; 2004), children with autism are increasingly identified, recognized, and provided with services in the schools. However, there is an absence of research demonstrating the long-term success of these programs in improving social engagement and successful transition into adult life.

By the adolescent years, some autistic children show an increased interest in socialization but nonetheless, most continue to struggle. They often have difficulty dealing with social views, conventions, and the give and take of adolescent relationships. They struggle to learn and generalize the rules of adult social interchange (Schopler & Mesibov, 1983).

Despite these associations, Rutter (1990) suggests that better assessment through systematic and standardized observations and data collection likely will lead to lower association rates as clinicians become more proficient in accurately diagnosing autism and PDDs. This certainly speaks to the significant importance of providing a full and detailed neurodevelopmental assessment when autism or PDDs are suspected. It is the higher functioning or Asperger's syndrome child who will likely confront and/or confuse the classroom consultant. C. Gillberg and Steffenburg (1987) also report that at least one out of five individuals with autism or PDDs appear to deteriorate in their functioning at puberty.

Thus, the classroom consultant must be aware of the risk, especially for higher functioning autistics, that the later school years may be increasingly, rather than decreasingly, difficult.

Specific Social Deficits Observed in the Classroom

Within classroom settings, autistic children struggle with social orientation, imitation and play, attachment to others, and pragmatic language skills.

Social Orientation

Problems with eye gaze and making eye contact are consistently reported for autistic youth (Volkmar, Cohen, & Paul, 1986). However, eye contact may appear very normal in many autistic children and often varies depending on task and developmental level. In particular, more developmentally advanced children with autism tend to demonstrate much better eye contact (Sigman & Kasari, 1995).

Significant in the classroom is the failure of many autistic children to develop *joint attention*. Joint attention has been defined as a pattern of social communication allowing two or more individuals to share the experience of a third object or event (Schaffer, 1984). In particular, autistic youth struggle to share joint attention with other children and teachers. Such triadic exchanges are consistently reported as limited in children of similar mental age with autism (Mundy, Sigman, & Kasari, 1990). Young children with autism often fail to show or point to objects or to gaze alternatively at the interactive partner and at a desired or interesting object. Deficits in joint attention have been reported to be the most striking and persistent problems in younger children with autism (Lewy & Dawson, 1992; Mundy, Sigman, & Kasari, 1994). Further, some researchers report that even when joint attention is observed, its quality is unusual (Kasari, Sigman, Munday, & Yirmiya, 1990). Consultants must be sensitive to this foundational, interpersonal impairment in children with autism when consulting with classroom teachers. It is critical for teachers to understand this deficit and avoid creating punitive or negatively reinforcing interactions in an effort to shape gaze and joint attention. Such behavioral strategies may lead to apparent short term improvements but are seductive and typically operate in a negatively reinforcing paradigm, decreasing the likelihood the child will begin to spontaneously exhibit improved gaze and joint attentional skills. Behavioral strategies utilizing differential attention, ignoring, and positive reinforcement are much more likely to lead to improvements in these skills.

Imitation and Play

Young children with autism are reported to have difficulty imitating even simple body movements and those that involve objects (Stone, Ousley, & Littleford, 1995). These children rarely spontaneously imitate the actions of parents or others (Meltzoff & Gopnik, 1993). They often show little ability for reciprocal social play when young such as playing peek-a-boo or patty cake, games which integrate imitation and social dialogue (Klin, 1992). Further, lack of symbolic play in autism may emerge from these social difficulties and may represent a more general problem in achieving symbolic thought and language (Volkmar, Carter, Grossman, & Klin, 1997). The play of these children in the classroom often reflects lack of social engagement and can be characterized by repetitive and stereotyped object manipulation and nonfunctional use of objects (Stone, Lemanek, Fishel, Hernandez, & Altemeier, 1990).

These deficits in symbolic play extend even beyond that which would be expected from children with broader cognitive deficits. Becoming a connected, functional member of the classroom is critical for success in school, particularly in the elementary grades. A classroom consultant should carefully question teachers relative to imitation play and attachment issues. In regards to the latter, children with autism typically fail to develop social attachment to their classmates. They may seek out teachers for conversations about idiosyncratic interests but do so simply to have an opportunity to discuss their interests rather than carry on a two-way dialogue in the classroom. These children may not seek physical comfort from teachers, may ignore friendly greetings and show little response to the speech of others, fail to engage in social interaction or cooperative play, make fewer approaches to others and respond far less often when approached (A. Atwood, Frith, & Hermelin, 1988). These children often appear content to be left alone (Volkmar, 1987). Though not necessarily disinterested in all social interaction, even as they mature levels of social interaction continue to remain limited and different (Lord, 1993). Teachers typically report that these children lack insight into the impact their behavior has on others as well as the reasons others form certain ideas and engage in certain behaviors with them. They are typically devoid of pro-social behavior such as giving, sharing, helping, offering comfort, or affection (Lord, 1993; Ohta, Nagai, Hara, & Sasaki, 1987).

Pragmatics

Although it has been reported that approximately 50% of autistic children do not develop expressive language (Paul, 1987), those who do, often demonstrate echolalia, abnormal pitch, tone and rhythm, or difficulty using speech for communication (Volkmar, 1987). However, as the diagnostic criteria for autism shift and the recognition that these impairments fall on a continuum with some children demonstrating problems and impairment, yet still subthreshold for full diagnoses, classroom teachers are increasingly confronted with this population. Universally this group of children fails to use language effectively within a social context (Tager-Flusberg, 1989). This failure of pragmatics leads to limited social interaction and impairment comprehending another person's meaning, thoughts, and intention. This failure of theory of mind, the inability when speaking to take into account what a listener knows and when listening to others to infer their intent is likely the most challenging behavior in the classroom for teachers working with autistic children (Tager-Flusberg, 1993).

An emerging line of research suggests that autistic children will interact with others for strategic but not affiliative reasons. That is, they will interact to meet their needs but not necessarily to relate to others. Thus, it is critical for classroom consultants to help teachers understand this distinction and make an effort to focus on helping autistic children in the classroom develop affiliative skills and behaviors. Strategies to facilitate this process are discussed in Chapter 15.

PART

III

Intervention

Developing the Mindset of Effective Teachers

ROBERT BROOKS AND SAM GOLDSTEIN

In Chapter 2, we outlined the key characteristics of the mindset of effective educators. We noted that the differing mindsets or assumptions that educators possess about themselves and their students play a significant role in determining their expectations, teaching practices, and relationships with students (Brooks, 2001a, 2001b; Brooks & Goldstein, 2001, 2003, 2004).

Even those assumptions about which we may not be aware have a way of being expressed to others. For example, a teacher may be angry with a child without fully realizing that the anger is rooted in the teacher's assumption that the child's constant asking of questions is an intentional ploy to distract the class. In addition, the teacher may not be aware that his anger is not as disguised as he believes, and is being communicated through facial expressions and tone of voice. In contrast, another teacher with the same child may assume that the child's ongoing questions represent an attempt to understand the material being presented. This teacher is less likely to express negative verbal and nonverbal messages and more likely to offer assistance, perceiving the child as feeling vulnerable rather than being oppositional.

The impact that the mindset of educators has in determining their approach to students was apparent in the following example. Parents of a high school student, John, contacted one of the authors (RB) several years ago. They asked that Bob serve as a consultant to John's school program. John had been diagnosed with learning disabilities and was experiencing difficulty academically. Bob met with John's teachers and asked each to describe him. One teacher immediately responded, "John is one of the most defiant, oppositional, unmotivated, lazy, irresponsible students we have at this school."

Another teacher appeared surprised by the harshness of this assessment. In a manner that remained respectful of her colleague's opinion, she said, "I have a different view. I think John is really struggling with learning and we should figure out the best ways to teach him."

In listening to these two descriptions of the same student, Bob could not help but think that the teachers were offering opinions of two very different youngsters.

After this meeting, Bob interviewed John and asked him to describe his teachers, not revealing what they had said about him. In describing the teacher who had portrayed him very negatively, John said with great force, "She hates me, but that's okay because I hate her. And I won't do any work in her class."

John continued, "And don't tell me that I'm only hurting myself by not doing work (he must have heard that advice on numerous occasions). What you don't understand, Dr. Brooks, is that in her eyes I am a failure. Whatever I do in her class is never going to be good enough. She doesn't expect me to pass, so why even try?" He added that from the first day of class he felt "angry vibes" from her.

"She just didn't like me and soon I didn't like her. I could tell she didn't want me in her class just by the way she spoke with me. Right away she seemed so angry with me. I really don't know why she felt that way. So after a while I knew there was no way I could succeed in her class so I just decided that I wouldn't even try. It would just be a waste of time. She told me I was lazy, but if she was honest she would have to admit that she doesn't think I could ever get a good grade in her class."

John's face lit up as he described the teacher who thought that the primary issue that should be addressed was his struggles with learning and his feelings of vulnerability. He said, "I love her. She went out of her way the first week of school to tell me something. She said that she knew I was having trouble with learning, but she thought I was smart and she had to figure out the best way to teach me. She said that one of the reasons she became a teacher was to help all students learn. She's always there to help."

After hearing John's views of these two teachers, one could understand why he was a discipline problem with the first teacher but not the second. His behavior with each of them reflected what he believed were their mindsets and expectations for him. We recognize that it typically takes "two to tango" and most likely at some point John bore responsibility for adding fuel to the "angry vibes," thereby confirming the first teacher's negative perceptions of him. However, it is important for educators to identify and modify those features of their mindset that might alienate students and set up barriers to the creation of effective teacher-student interactions.

The Mindset of Effective Educators

Prior to discussing strategies for reinforcing a positive mindset in educators, it will be helpful to review briefly the characteristics of this mindset as outlined in Chapter 2. Effective educators:

- Understand the lifelong impact they have on students, including instilling a sense of hope and resilience.
- Believe that the learning that occurs in the classroom and the behavior exhibited by students has as much, if not more, to do with the influence of teachers than what students might bring into the situation.
- Believe that all students yearn to be successful and if a student is not learning, educators must ask how they can adapt their teaching style and instructional material to meet student needs.
- Believe that attending to the social-emotional needs of students is not an "extra-curriculum" that draws time away from teaching academic subjects.
- Recognize that if educators are to relate effectively to students, they must be empathic, always attempting to perceive the world through the eyes of the student.
- Appreciate that the foundation for successful learning and a safe and secure classroom climate is the relationship that teachers forge with students.
- Recognize that students will be more motivated to learn when they feel a sense of ownership for their own education.
- Understand that one of the main functions of an educator is to be a disciplinarian in the true sense of the word, namely, to perceive

discipline as a teaching process rather than as a process of intimidation and humiliation.

- Realize that one of the greatest obstacles to learning is the fear of making mistakes and feeling embarrassed or humiliated.
- Subscribe to a strength-based model that includes identifying and reinforcing each student's "island of competence."
- Recognize that constructive relationships with parents facilitate the learning process for students.
- Develop and maintain positive, respectful relationships with colleagues.

Nurturing the Mindset of Effective Educators

Consultants are in a unique position to assist educators to identify the assumptions that govern their teaching practices as well as their relationship with students, parents, and colleagues. This is a significant task since educators who are aware of these assumptions will be better equipped to assess and modify any features of their mindsets that serve as obstacles to creating a positive school climate.

Consultants can accomplish this task via two major formats. These include meeting with school administrators and/or providing direct in-service training or consultation for faculty and staff (with the permission of the administrators). In either option, the first step is to meet with the administrators and share thoughts about the presence and influence of mindsets in the school environment.

In their meetings with administrators, they can outline specific exercises that administrators can introduce at staff meetings to highlight the themes of mindsets and effective teaching. Or, consultants can offer workshops for faculty that focus on these same themes. If the latter, it is advisable for consultants to discuss the content of the workshop in advance with the administrators. It is also beneficial for the administrators to attend the workshop so that all members of the school community hear the same message at the same time; the attendance of the administrators serves to reinforce the importance of the topic being discussed.

The following are the salient points that should be addressed not only at the initial workshops, but at follow-up meetings as well. Where indicated, we offer specific suggestions for exercises to highlight and reinforce these points:

- *The concept of mindset and the ways in which mindset impacts our behavior must be understood.* A definition of mindset can be offered. We have noted, "Mindsets are assumptions and expectations we have for ourselves and others that guide our teaching practices and our interactions with students, parents, and colleagues." The consultant (or administrator) can emphasize that we all have words to describe ourselves and these words will play a major role in our effectiveness as educators. Teachers can be asked to write a paragraph in which they describe themselves as educators. They can be encouraged to reflect upon the ways in which their self-descriptions impact on their actions. Self-efficacy theory predicts that the words that teachers use will play a major role in determining their actual behavior.

As an example, in our workshops we recount the story of one teacher who used the following words to describe herself:

"I do not feel very adequate as a teacher."

"I do not have good behavior management skills in the classroom."

"I am afraid of my students."

When we asked what she taught, she responded, "Third grade."

We visited her classroom several days later and witnessed what might best be characterized as "chaos." As an eraser flew by our heads, she came over and said, "See, I told you."

In contrast, another teacher who was working in a therapeutic day program with aggressive adolescents, joked, "Most of my students are bigger than I am so I wouldn't want to get into a physical hassle with them. But I have always felt confident that if I develop a good relationship with them, if I recognize their strengths, and if I have clear-cut expectations and consequences, they will be less likely to challenge me." A visit to her classroom confirmed her assumptions. An air of respect between teacher and students was readily apparent. The energy of the students was focused on the academic tasks and not on engaging in disruptive behaviors.

As we tell participants at our workshops, "You get what you expect."

The concept of mindset can be extended to include not only our self-perceptions but the ways in which we understand the behavior of students. An obvious example is that of John, the adolescent we discussed earlier in this chapter. One teacher saw him as unmotivated and lazy, while another perceived that he was struggling with learning and feeling very vulnerable in the school setting. These different views prompted markedly contrasting approaches, which led John to view one teacher as judging him to be a failure and the other as believing in him and wishing to help him. Not surprisingly, his mindset about each teacher led to very different behaviors and academic outcomes in the two classrooms.

It is essential for educators to appreciate that the assumptions they hold for themselves and their students, which are often unstated, have profound influence in determining effective teaching practices, the quality of relationships with students, and the positive or negative climate that is created in the classroom and school building.

- *The focus on a student's social/emotional development and well-being is not an extra curriculum that takes time away from teaching academic skills and content.* It is unfortunate that a dichotomy has arisen in many educational quarters prompting some educators to perceive that nurturing a student's emotional and social health is mutually exclusive from the goal of teaching academic material. This dichotomy has been fueled, in part, by the emergence of high stakes testing and an emphasis on accountability. The following refrain is heard in many schools: "We barely have time to get through the assigned curriculum. We really don't have the time to focus on anything else."

We are not opposed to assessment or accountability. We welcome research conducted to define effective teaching practices. However, what we question is relegating a student's emotional life to the background and not appreciating its important role in the process of learning. This attitude was captured at one of our workshops. A high school science teacher challenged our viewpoint by contending:

> I am a science teacher. I know my science and I know how to convey science facts to my students. Why should I have to spend time thinking about a student's emotional or social life? I don't have time to do so and it will distract me from teaching science.

While many teachers and school administrators would take issue with the views expressed by this science teacher, others might not. We believe that strengthening a student's feeling of well-being, self-esteem, and dignity is not an extra curriculum. If anything, a student's sense of belonging, security, and self-confidence in the classroom provides the scaffolding that supports the foundation for enhanced learning, motivation, self-discipline, responsibility, and the ability to deal more effectively with obstacles and mistakes (Brooks, 1991, 2004).

Consultants can highlight this point by requesting educators to reflect on their own teachers and think about those from whom they learned most effectively. It has been our experience that the teachers they select are also those who not only taught academic content but, in addition, supported the emotional well-being of students and were interested in the "whole child." Very importantly, as educators think about their teachers as well as their own teaching practices, they can be asked to consider the following question: "Do you believe that developing a positive relationship with your students enhances or detracts from teaching academic material? Please offer examples."

Examples should be encouraged whether the answer is yes, no, or maybe. It is important for educators to seriously consider this question. In our experience, most educators are able to offer examples of "small gestures" on their part (or on the part of their teachers) that took little, if any, time, but communicated to students a message of respect and caring (Brooks, 1991). If teachers contend they would like to develop more meaningful relationships with students, but are unable to allot the time to do so, other educators who have been able to accomplish this task can offer specific suggestions.

• *Educators have a lifelong impact on students and their resilience.* Closely associated with this point is the belief by teachers that what they say and do each day in their classroom can have a lifelong influence on their students (Brooks, 1991; Brooks & Goldstein, 2001). While most teachers appreciate that they will be influential in the lives of their students for years to come, many are not aware of the extent of their impact.

It is important for consultants and administrators to share with teaching staff research findings from the resilience literature to highlight this impact. Such knowledge adds meaning and purpose to their role as teachers and lessens disillusionment and burnout.

At our workshops, we review that in the past 20 years there has been an increased effort to define those factors that help children and adolescents to deal more effectively with stress, to overcome adversity, and to become resilient (Brooks, 1994; Brooks & Goldstein, 2001, 2003; S. Goldstein & Brooks, 2005; Katz, 1997; Werner & Smith, 1992). We highlight that schools have been spotlighted as environments in which self-esteem, hope, and resilience can be fortified, frequently quoting the late psychologist Julius Segal (1988) who wrote:

> From studies conducted around the world, researchers have distilled a number of factors that enable such children of misfortune to beat the heavy odds against them. One factor turns out to be the presence in their lives of a charismatic adult—a person with whom they can identify and from whom they gather strength. And in a surprising number of cases, that person turns out to be a teacher. (p. 3)

It is important for teachers to recognize that they are in a unique position to be a "charismatic adult" in a student's life and that even seemingly small gestures can have a lifelong impact. A smile, a warm greeting, a note of encouragement, a few minutes taken to meet alone with a student, and an appreciation of and respect for different learning styles are but several of the activities that define a "charismatic teacher" (Brooks, 1991).

An important issue to address as a consultant is that teachers are often unaware that they are or have been "charismatic adults" in the life of a student. To emphasize this issue, consultants or administrators can ask faculty if they have ever received unexpectedly, a note from a former student thanking them for the positive impact they had on the student's life. While many have been fortunate to be the recipient of such a note, others have not although they are equally deserving of such feedback.

We frequently ask participants at our workshops if there are teachers who had a significant influence on their lives whom they have failed to acknowledge via a note or letter. It is not unusual for many teachers to voice regret they have not thanked several such "charismatic adults." Some have written notes to the latter following the workshop.

We use these exercises to suggest that while we may not receive formal confirmation that we have worn the garb of "charismatic adults," if we approach each day with the belief that today may be the day we say or do something that directs a student's life in a more positive path, we will be more optimistic about our role, and our students will be the beneficiaries of more realistic, hopeful expectations.

- *All students wish to learn and to succeed and if they seem unmotivated or unengaged, they may believe they lack the ability to achieve in school.* We often hear teachers refer to students as lazy or unmotivated. As we have noted, once these accusatory labels are used and a negative mindset dominates, educators are more likely to respond to these students with annoyance. The mindset of an effective educator constantly echoes, "I believe that all students come to school desiring to learn. It they are disinterested and feel defeated, we must figure out how best to reach and teach them."

Subscribing to this view has a profound impact on the ways in which we respond to students, especially those who are struggling. When students lose faith in their ability to learn and when feelings of hopelessness pervade their psyche, they are vulnerable to engaging in counterproductive or self-defeating ways of coping. They may quit at tasks, clown around, pick on other students, or expend little time and effort in academic requirements. When a student feels that failure is a foregone conclusion, it is difficult to muster the energy to consider alternative ways of mastering learning demands.

Teachers who observe such counterproductive behaviors may easily reach the conclusion that the student is unmotivated or lazy, or not caring about school. As negative assumptions and mindsets dominate, teachers are less likely to consider more productive strategies for reaching the student. Instead, thoughts turn to punitive actions (e.g., what punishments would finally get through to the student). However, if educators subscribe to the belief that each student wishes to succeed, negative assumptions are less likely to prevail.

A shift in perspective was obvious in a consultation the first author of this chapter (RB) did about Sarah, a problematic high school student. One of her teachers began by asking, "Don't you think it's okay for a 16½-year-old to drop out of school?" The agenda was clear. These teachers, who typically displayed a caring and encouraging attitude, were very frustrated and angry with Sarah to the extent of wishing her to drop out of school.

The teachers elaborated that Sarah was a student who "sabotaged" all of their efforts. "Even if Sarah agrees to do something, she doesn't follow through. It's obvious that she dislikes school and she's disruptive and disrespectful. She couldn't care less about how she does in school."

As we shall see, Sarah cared a great deal about wanting to achieve in school, but entertained little hope for doing so. It was only when her teachers truly accepted that each student desperately wants to succeed that a positive mindset emerged, which permitted them to consider new solutions.

A turning point occurred when Bob empathized with the teachers about their frustration but then asked, "Can anyone tell me how you think Sarah feels each day when she enters the school building?"

After several moments of silence, one teacher responded, "How Sarah feels. I never really thought about that before."

Another teacher followed, "I never really thought about that before either, but as I'm doing so now, only one word comes to mind, defeated. I think everyday when Sarah comes in to the school building she feels defeated."

As this teacher shared her observation, the shift in mindset that permeated the room was palpable, highlighted by one teacher asking Bob, "You've written a lot about helping kids be more confident and resilient in the school setting. So what can we do to help a student who feels defeated begin to feel less defeated?"

A lively, creative discussion ensued, filled with ideas that had not been considered previously, including having Sarah, who relished being helpful, assist in the office. The teachers also shifted their focus from what punitive action to take to a desire to "get to know" Sarah, not via a tense, confrontational meeting but rather by having lunch with her.

This new approach prompted Sarah to be more responsible and a positive cycle was set in motion. The catalyst for this new cycle was when her teachers shifted their mindset, no longer viewing Sarah's behaviors as oppositional, but rather as a reflection of the despair and defeatism she experienced. They adopted the assumption that students wish to succeed, but at times obstacles appear on the road to success—obstacles that teachers working in concert with students could remove.

• *If our strategies are not effective, we must ask, "What is it that I can do differently?" rather than continuing to wait for the student to change first.* A basic underpinning of resilience is the belief of "personal control," namely, that we are the "authors of our own lives" and it makes little sense to continue to do the same thing repeatedly if our actions are not leading to positive results (Brooks & Goldstein, 2004). While many educators and others say they subscribe to this assumption, their actions frequently belie their assertion. For example, it is not unusual to hear the following statements offered by educators at consultations we have conducted:

> "This student is unmotivated to change. She just won't take responsibility for her behavior."

> Or, "We've been using this strategy with this student for 5 months. He's still not responding. He's resistant and oppositional."

We believe in perseverance, but if a staff has been employing the same approach for 5 months without any positive outcome, one can ask, "Who are the resistant ones here?"

As one perceptive teacher emphasized, "Asking what is it that I can do differently should not be interpreted as blaming ourselves but rather as a source of empowerment." She continued, "Isn't it better to focus on what we can do differently rather than continue to wait for someone else to change first? We may have to wait forever and continue to be frustrated and unhappy."

This same teacher summarized her belief with the statement, "If the horse is dead, get off." We have found that there are many dead horses strewn on the grounds of a school.

The assumption of personal control should be addressed directly at workshops and meetings. Consultants must emphasize with teachers that a change in strategy is not the equivalent of "giving in" (this is a belief that often crops up), but rather as a sign that we are seeking a more productive intervention. If change on a teacher's part is experienced as acquiescing to the student, any new strategy will be tainted by feelings of resentment.

A helpful exercise to illustrate the power of personal control and the need to change "negative scripts" that exist in our lives is to ask educators to think about one or two instances when they changed their usual script and to consider what resulted as a consequence of their new script. Many educators, such as those involved with Sarah, are able to describe very positive results. Unfortunately, others report less satisfactory results, often reinforcing the belief that they had gone out of their way for students, but the students did not reciprocate. When the outcome of a change in script is not positive, a problem-solving attitude should be introduced by asking, "With hindsight, is there anything you would do differently today to lessen the probability of an unfavorable result?"

The possibility that a modification of a script may not eventuate in a positive outcome should be addressed. Consultants can recommend that when a new script is implemented, educators should have one or two back-up scripts in mind should the first prove ineffective. This suggestion conveys the positive message that a strategy that sounds promising in our office may not yield the results we wish; however, rather than feeling defeated, we should learn from the experience and be prepared with alternative actions. We must keep in mind that a new script may create the conditions that encourage students to change their behaviors.

• *Empathy is an essential skill for effective teaching and relationships with students as well as parents and colleagues.* Empathic educators are able to place themselves inside the shoes of their students and others and perceive the world through their eyes, just as Sarah's teachers attempted to do, eventually understanding that she felt defeated. Goleman (1995) highlights empathy as a major component of emotional intelligence.

Being empathic invites educators to ask, "Would I want anyone to say or do to me what I have just said or done to this student (or parent or colleague)?" or "Whenever I say or do things with students (parents or colleagues), what is my goal and am I saying or doing these things in a way that my students will be most likely to hear and respond constructively to my message?"

As an example, a teacher may attempt to motivate a student who is not performing adequately by exhorting the student to "try harder." While the teacher may be well-intentioned, the comment is based on the assumption that the student is not willing to expend the time and energy necessary to succeed. Thus, such a remark is frequently experienced as accusatory and judgmental. When students feel accused, they are less prone to be cooperative. Consequently, the teacher's comment is not likely to lead to the desired results, which, in turn, may reinforce the teacher's belief that the student is unmotivated and not interested in "trying."

In contrast, an empathic teacher might wonder, "If I were struggling in my role as a teacher, would I want another teacher or my principal to say to me, 'If you just tried a little harder you wouldn't have this problem'?" When we have offered this question at workshops, many teachers laugh and say they would be very annoyed if they were accused of not trying. The question prompts them to reflect on how their statements are interpreted by their students.

There are several exercises that can be introduced at workshops to reinforce empathy. A favorite is to have teachers think of a teacher they liked and one that they did not like when they were students and then to describe each in several words. Next, they can be reminded, "Just as you have words to describe your teachers, your students have words to describe you." They can then consider the following questions:

"What words would you hope your students used to describe you?"

"What have you done in the past month so they are likely to use these words?"

"What words would they actually use to describe you?"

"How close would the words you hope they use parallel the words they would actually use?" (One teacher jokingly said, "I would love my students to use the word 'calm,' but I don't think they would since I feel I have been raising my voice a great deal the past month or two and not showing much patience.")

Another exercise that educators have found useful in reinforcing empathy revolves around our own memories of school. Teachers can be requested at workshops to share with their colleagues their response to the following questions:

"Of all of the memories you have as a student, what is one of your favorite ones, something that a teacher or school administrator said or did that boosted your motivation and self-dignity?"

"Of all of the memories you have as a student, what is one of your worst ones, something that a teacher or school administrator said or did that lessened your motivation and self-dignity?"

"As you reflected on both your positive and negative memories of school, what did you learn from both and do you use these memories to guide what you are doing with your students today?"

Recounting one's own positive and negative memories of school with one's colleagues often proves very emotional and leads teachers to ask:

"What memories are my students taking from their interactions with me?"

"Are they the memories I would like them to take?"

"If not, what must I change so that the memories they will take will be in accord with the memories I hope they take?"

These exercises to nurture empathy often prompt teachers to consider how best to obtain feedback from students to gain a realistic picture of how they are perceived. We will address this question in the next point.

• *Ongoing feedback and input from students enhances empathy and promotes a sense of responsibility and ownership in students.* Effective teachers not only welcome the input of students, but they appreciate that such input must be incorporated on a regular basis. When students feel their voice is being heard, they are more likely to work cooperatively with teachers and be more motivated to meet academic challenges. Eliciting student opinion reinforces a feeling of personal control and responsibility—essential ingredients of a positive school climate.

Suggestions can be offered to educators for promoting student feedback and input. For instance, teachers can request anonymous feedback from students. One high school teacher asked students to draw him, describe him, list what they liked about his teaching style and the class, and what they would recommend he change. While one of his colleagues scoffed at this practice, contending that such feedback was not important and took valuable time from teaching, the outcome of the exercise proved the colleague wrong. The exercise actually increased achievement scores and cooperation; this was not surprising since the students felt respected.

Another teacher requested that students complete a one-page report card about him whenever he filled out report cards on them. He asked students to rate him on dimensions such as discipline style, response to student questions, teaching style, and fairness toward all students. Recommendations for change were elicited.

As will be reviewed in Chapter 10, responsibility and ownership in students can also be reinforced by engaging students in a discussion about the benefits or drawbacks of educational practices that are typically seen as "givens," including such activities as tests, reports, and homework. In addition, educators can strengthen a feeling of student ownership by incorporating a variety of choices in the classroom, none of which diminish a teacher's authority but rather empowers students to feel a sense of control over their own education.

Choice and ownership can also be applied to disciplinary practices by asking students to consider such questions as:

> "What rules do you think we need in this classroom for all students to feel comfortable and learn best?" (Teachers frequently report that the rules recommended by students often parallel those of the teacher.)

> "Even as your teacher I may forget a rule. If I do, this is how I would like you to remind me. (Teachers can then list one or two ways they would like to be reminded.) Now that I have mentioned how I would like to be reminded, how would you like me to remind you?" (When students inform teachers how they would like to be reminded should they forget a rule, they are less likely to experience the reminder as a form of nagging and more likely to hear what the teacher has to say. It is easier for students to consider ways of being reminded if teachers first serve as models by offering how they would like to be reminded.)

> "What should the consequences be if we forget a rule?" (We have heard teachers report, especially when asking these questions to angry students, that the consequences suggested by the students are more se-vere than any teacher would use.)

These questions related to disciplinary practices encourage a sense of ownership for rules and consequences, thereby promoting responsibility and self-discipline in students.

• *Each student has a different "island of competence" and learning style that must be identified, respected, and reinforced.* This belief is at the core of a strength-based approach to education and overlaps with all of the other points reviewed in this chapter. Effective teachers appreciate that they must move beyond a philosophy that fixates on a student's problems and vulnerabilities and affords equal, if not greater space, to strengths and competencies.

Researchers and clinicians have emphasized the significance of re-cruiting selected areas of strength or "islands of competence" in building self-confidence, motivation, and resilience (Deci & Flaste, 1995; Katz, 1994; Rutter, 1985). Rutter (1985), in describing resilient individuals, observed, "Experiences of success in one arena of life led to enhanced self-esteem and a feeling of self-efficacy, enabling them to cope more successfully with the subsequent life challenges and adaptations" (p. 604). Katz (1994) noted, "Being able to showcase our talents, and to have them valued by important people in our lives, helps us to define our identities around that which we do best" (p. 10).

There are numerous suggestions that consultants can offer teachers for assisting students to feel more confident and competent in school. At the beginning of the school year, teachers can meet with each student for a few minutes and ask, "What are you interested in? What do you like to do? What do you think you do well?" While some students will respond eagerly, others may simply say, "I don't know." In that case, teachers can respond, "That's okay, it often takes time to figure out what you're good at. I'll try to be of help."

A high school teacher noted that given all of the students attending his classes, he did not have the time to meet with each individually at the beginning of the year. Instead, he devised a questionnaire that he sent out to each student a week before school began. He told them that it was not mandatory that they complete the questionnaire, but if they did it would help him to be a more effective teacher. The questionnaire focused on a number of areas, several of which asked students to list what they perceived to be their strengths and weaknesses. In the 7 years in which he had sent out the questionnaire, not one student had failed to return it. This teacher found the information he obtained to be an invaluable resource in connecting with students.

One of the most obvious guideposts for assisting students to feel competent is to teach them in ways in which they can learn best. Educators must appreciate that each student has a different learning style and strength (Gardner, 1983; Levine, 2002). This requires that teachers familiarize themselves with such topics as multiple intelligences and learning styles.

Another strategy to enhance a sense of competence is to provide students with an opportunity to help others. Students experience a more positive attachment to school and are more motivated to learn if they are encouraged to contribute to the school milieu (Brooks, 1991; Rutter, 1980; Werner, 1993). Examples include: older students with learning problems reading to younger children; a hyperactive child being asked to assume the position of "attendance monitor," which involved walking around the halls to take attendance of teachers while the latter were taking attendance of students; and the use of cooperative learning in which students of varying abilities work together as a team bringing their own unique strengths to different projects.

One of the most powerful approaches for reinforcing a feeling of competence in students is to lessen their fear of failure. Many students equate making mistakes with feeling humiliated and consequently, will avoid learning tasks that appear very challenging. There are students who would rather be bullies or quit at tasks or say the work is dumb rather than engage in a learning activity that they feel may result in failure and embarrassment. In a desperate attempt to avoid failure, they journey down a path that takes them further away from possible success.

The fear of making mistakes and failing permeates every classroom and if it is not actively addressed it remains an active force, compromising the joy and enthusiasm that should be part of the learning process. It is the proverbial elephant in the room and in this case, one that may be on a destructive rampage; yet it is not acknowledged.

Effective educators can begin to overcome the fear of failure by identifying this elephant in the room. The fear must be openly addressed with students. One technique for doing so is for teachers to ask their class at the beginning of the school year, "Who feels they are going to make a mistake and not understand something in class this year?" Before any of the students can respond, teachers can raise their hands as a way of initiating a discussion of how the fear of making mistakes affects learning.

It is often helpful for teachers to share some of their own anxieties and experiences about making mistakes when they were students. They can recall when they were called on in class, when they made mistakes or when they failed a test. This openness often invites students to share some of their thoughts and feelings about making mistakes. Teachers can involve the class in problem solving by encouraging them to suggest what they can do as teachers and what the students can do as a class to minimize the fear of failure and appearing foolish. Issues of being called on and not knowing the answer can be discussed.

Effective teachers recognize that when the fear of failure and humiliation is actively addressed in the classroom, students will be more motivated to take realistic risks and to learn.

• *Realize that one must strive to become stress hardy rather than stressed out.* At the end of one of our workshops, a teacher said, "I love your ideas, but I'm too stressed out to use them." While the remark had a humorous tone, it also captured an important consideration.

At first glance, the remark seems paradoxical since numerous educators have informed us that the strategies we advocate do not take time away from teaching, but rather help to create a classroom environment that is more conducive to learning and less stressful. Yet, we can appreciate their frustration that change requires additional time, a commodity that is not readily available. Some are hesitant to leave their "comfort zone" even when this zone is filled with stress and pressure. They would rather continue with a known situation that is less than satisfying than engage in the task of entering a new, unexplored territory that holds promise but also uncertainty.

If educators are to be effective and if they are to apply many of the ideas described in this chapter, they must venture from their "comfort zone" by utilizing techniques for dealing with the stress and pressure that are inherent in their work. Each teacher can discover his or her own ways for managing stress. For instance, some can rely on exercise, others on relaxation or meditation techniques, all of which can be very beneficial. In addition to these approaches there has been research conducted by Kobasa and her colleagues (Holt, Fine, & Tollefson, 1987; Kobasa, Maddi, & Kahn, 1982; Martinez, 1989) under the label of "stress hardiness" that examines the characteristics or mindset of individuals who experience less stress than their colleagues while working in the same environment.

This mindset involves 3 Cs (the first letter of each of the words of the mindset begins with the letter C). The three components are interrelated and when we describe them at our workshops we encourage educators to reflect on how they might apply this information to lessen stress and burnout.

The first C represents "commitment." Stress hardy individuals do not lose sight of why they are doing what they are doing. They maintain a genuine passion or purpose for their work. While we may all have "down" days, it is sad to observe educators who basically say to themselves each morning in a resigned way, "I've got to go to school. I've got to see those kids." Once a feeling of "I've got to" or "being forced to" pervades one's mindset, a sense of commitment and purpose is sacrificed, replaced by feelings of stress and burnout. As an antidote to burnout, a staff meeting might be dedicated to sharing why one became a teacher, a school administrator, a counselor, a nurse, or a psychologist. Such an exercise helps staff to recall and invigorate their dreams and goals.

The second C is for "challenge." Educators who deal more effectively with stress have developed a mindset that views difficult situations as opportunities for learning and growth rather than as stress to avoid. For example, a principal of a school faced a challenging situation. Her school was located in a neighborhood that had changed in a few short years from a middle-class population with much parent involvement to a neighborhood with a lower socioeconomic makeup and less parent involvement. There were several key factors that contributed to the decrease in parent involvement, including less flexibility for many parents to leave work in order to attend a school meeting or conference as well as many parents feeling unwelcome and anxious in school based on their own histories as children in the school environment.

Instead of bemoaning this state of affairs and becoming increasingly upset and stressed, this particular principal and her staff realized that the education of their students would be greatly enhanced if parents became active participants in the educational process; consequently, they viewed the lack of involvement as a challenge to meet rather than as a stress to avoid. Among other strategies, they scheduled several staff meetings in the late afternoon and moved the site of the meetings from the school building to a popular community house a few blocks away. These changes encouraged a number of the parents to attend the meetings since the new time was more accommodating to their schedules and the new location helped them to feel more comfortable since it was held on their "turf." The relationship between parents and teachers was greatly enhanced and the children were the beneficiaries.

The third C is "control" or what we call "personal control" since some individuals may mistakenly view the word control as a form of controlling others. Control, as used in stress hardiness theory, implies that individuals who successfully manage stress and pressure focus their time and energy on factors over which they have influence rather than attempting to change things that are beyond their sphere of control. Although many individuals believe they engage in activities over which they have influence or control, in fact, many do not. We worked with a group of teachers who were feeling burned out. We reviewed the basic tenets of stress hardiness theory and asked if they focused their energies on factors within their domain of control. They replied in the affirmative.

We then asked them to list what would help their jobs to be less stressful. Their answers included, "If the students came from less dysfunctional families, if they came to school better prepared to learn, if they had more discipline at home." After a few moments one of the teachers smiled and said, "We first said that we focus on what we have control over, but everything that we are mentioning to help us feel less stressed are things over which we have little control."

After the teacher said this, the group engaged in a lively discussion focusing on what educators might do to create classroom climates that nurtured learning even if the students came from home environments that were less than supportive of education. One teacher astutely noted, "We are expecting our students to come to school excited about learning and when they do not we get frustrated and annoyed. Instead, what I'm hearing is that we must ask, 'What can we do differently to help motivate students who are not motivated and what can we do to help students who feel hopeless about learning to feel more hopeful.'" As the discussion continued, the teachers recognized that by focusing on what they could do differently to improve the learning environment was empowering and lessened stressful feelings. The mood of pessimism and burnout that had pervaded the room began to change.

Summary

Consultants are in an influential position to serve as a catalyst for transforming educational practices. They can do so by identifying the mindset associated with effective educators and suggesting strategies to nurture this mindset. They can be available as new scripts are initiated and assessed, offering feedback and encouragement to the faculty. The benefits of such input to both teachers and students will be noteworthy.

10

Developing the Mindset of Effective Students

ROBERT BROOKS AND SAM GOLDSTEIN

In Chapter 9, we outlined the key characteristics of the mindset of effective educators. We emphasized that educators possess different mindsets or assumptions about themselves and their students that significantly influence their expectations, teaching practices, and relationships with students (Brooks, 2001a, 2001b; Brooks & Goldstein, 2001, 2003, 2004).

We noted in Chapter 2 that just as effective educators possess a mindset upon which their success is rooted, so too do successful students possess assumptions that contribute to their achievements in school. It is essential that educators understand the mindset of effective learners in order that they may incorporate strategies within their teaching practice to reinforce this mindset in all students. Obviously, the mindsets of effective teachers and effective students intersect and become a dynamic force for nurturing a positive classroom environment.

Similar to our observations about teachers, students typically do not pause to consider those assumptions about learning and motivation that impact on their success in school. For example, a student struggling to learn math concepts may believe that a high test score he received on a math test was based on luck. The belief that luck was the determining factor in producing this accomplishment will preclude confidence for future success since luck is assumed to be beyond our control and is an inconsistent and capricious variable at best. In contrast, another student also struggling with math, may interpret a good test score in that subject as an indication that the tutoring she has received and the extra studying she has done are resulting in her becoming a more proficient math student. Thus, she credits her success to factors within her control such as effort, a belief that reinforces confidence for continued achievement. Each of these students will confront the next math test with a different mindset and expectations that will influence their probable success.

The Mindset of Effective Students

As we did in the previous chapter, prior to describing strategies for nurturing a positive mindset in students, it will be helpful to review briefly the characteristics of this mindset as outlined in Chapter 2. In many ways they parallel the characteristics or goals associated with the mindset of successful educators. Effective students, those who are motivated to actively engage in the learning process:

- Believe that whether they learn or not is based in great part on their own motivation, perseverance, and effort. They feel a sense of ownership for their own education.
- Recognize that making mistakes is part of the learning process and thus, do not view mistakes as sources of humiliation or indications that they are incompetent as learners. Rather mistakes are perceived as opportunities for learning, a belief that will motivate students to persevere with demanding academic tasks.
- Perceive the teacher as a supportive adult. When confronted with academic or nonacademic challenges, they feel comfortable in taking the initiative and seeking assistance from the teacher.
- Understand their unique learning style, learning strengths, and learning vulnerabilities. This understanding permits them to develop with the input of their teacher strategies that will help them to learn more proficiently.
- Interact with their classmates with respect, avoiding teasing and bullying. They recognize that such negative behaviors work against developing and sustaining a positive school climate in which learning thrives.

Two Frameworks to Nurture the Mindset of Effective Students

There are two frameworks that can serve as helpful guides for teachers as they apply interventions for reinforcing a positive mindset in students.

Both frameworks, which are reviewed next, resonate with the concepts of self-esteem, ownership, motivation, and resilience.

Attribution Theory

One framework was originally proposed by psychologist Bernard Weiner and given the name "attribution theory" (Weiner, 1974). This theory highlights that youngsters attribute their accomplishments or failures to different reasons, a dynamic we witnessed earlier in this chapter with the two students who did well on math tests but possessed contrasting assumptions (mindsets) about the reasons for their success.

In terms of success experiences, research indicates that children who are hopeful and resilient and who are guided by a positive mindset about learning, believe that their successes are determined in large measure by their own efforts, resources, and abilities. These youngsters assume realistic credit for their accomplishments and feel a genuine sense of control over events in their lives. They are motivated to face new challenges and more demanding learning tasks (Brooks, 1991; Canino, 1981; Licht, 1983).

In contrast, students with a negative mindset are more likely to interpret their achievements as predicated on luck, chance, or fate, that is, on variables outside of their sphere of control, thus weakening their confidence for future success.

Children also have varying attributions for their mistakes and failure, which are linked to their self-esteem and resilience. As an example, two students in the same third grade class fail a spelling test. One child thinks, "I can do better than this. Maybe I have to study more or ask the teacher for extra help." The mindset of the second child offers a very different explanation, "The teacher stinks. He never told us these words would be on the test. It's his fault I failed."

Or, to take another example, a child who believed he was incapable of learning, resorted to hitting his classmates. In therapy he gained insight into his feelings and behavior and said, "I'd rather hit another kid and be sent to the principal's office than have to be in the classroom where I feel like a dummy."

Students who are motivated to seek additional help and/or work more diligently, do so because they believe that mistakes are experiences from which to learn rather than feel defeated. Such students typically attribute mistakes to factors that are within their power to modify, such as a lack of effort (especially if the task is realistically achievable) or ineffective strategies (e.g., poor study habits). In marked contrast, students who blame or attack others typically subscribe to the painful assumption, "I

am a failure. I cannot change. I am incapable of succeeding in school."
They do not believe that mistakes are the foundation for future learning.
Rather, they believe that mistakes are a consequence of conditions that
cannot easily be modified, such as a lack of ability or low intelligence.

A vicious cycle is set in motion when students believe they cannot
learn from setbacks. Their mindset is dominated by negative thinking.
Feeling hopeless and wishing to avoid further perceived humiliation,
they are apt to quit, offer excuses, cast blame on others, or resort to ineffective ways of coping, such as wearing the garb of a class clown or
class bully. Our attempts to teach them may be met with angry retorts
such as "Leave me alone!" "I don't care!" "It's my life, I'll do what I
want with it!" These students care much more than they acknowledge,
but overwhelmed with a sense of frustration and despair and believing
they cannot change their situation, it is difficult for them to entertain
the notion that things may improve. While the adults in their lives may
perceive these youngsters as quitters or lacking perseverance, what may
be missed is that their actions are rooted in a desperate attempt to avoid
further humiliation (Brooks, 2002; Wexler, 1991). Working with these
students involves helping to modify their negative attributions and
mindsets (N. Bernstein, 1996).

As is apparent, attribution theory offers guideposts for nurturing
the mindset of effective learners. Consultants can draw on this theory
and pose the following questions for school administrators and teachers to consider:

- How do we create a school environment in which students are more
  likely to develop a resilient mindset, an environment that maxi-
  mizes the probability that students will not only succeed, but that
  they will interpret their achievements as predicated in large measure on their own abilities and efforts? Or stated somewhat differently, how do we assist students to assume an increasing sense of
  ownership and responsibility for their learning.
- How do we create a school environment that reinforces the belief
  that mistakes are not only *accepted*, but *expected*? How do we create a
  school milieu that lessens fears of being humiliated or embarrassed?

Edward Deci's Approach

A second framework is based on the work of psychologist Edward Deci
and his colleagues (Deci & Chandler, 1986; Deci & Flaste, 1995; Deci
et al., 1992). His model bears many similarities to Glasser's (1997)
"choice theory" and the work of Brendtro, Brokenleg, and Van Bockern

(1990). Deci suggests that students will be more motivated to engage in and persevere at school tasks when their teachers develop a school environment that satisfies particular needs. Essentially, Deci notes that when these needs are met, students will be more receptive to learn, more optimistic about succeeding in school, and more resilient.

Deci highlights three needs for educators to consider in their interactions with students. They are:

1. *To belong and feel connected:* In Chapter 9 we highlighted the lifelong impact that educators have on the motivation and resilience of students. Earlier in this chapter we noted that a key feature of the mindset of effective students is their belief that there are adults in school who believe in them and are available to help them when indicated. Deci's research supports the importance of the relationship between students and teachers in the learning process. He observes that children and adolescents are more likely to thrive in environments in which they feel they belong and are comfortable, in which they feel they are treated with respect.

Related to this feeling of belonging is the importance of helping each student to feel welcome in school. When the author (RB) asked more than 300 students from kindergarten through 12th grade what a teacher or school administrator could do each day to help them to feel welcome in school, the two most frequent responses were a teacher or school administrator greeting you warmly by name and smiling at you. The adage that "students don't care what you know until they first know you care" is a powerful reminder that students will be more motivated to learn when taught by an educator whom they trust.

The issue of feeling connected to schools has received increased attention in recent years, especially as educators and other professionals grapple with the problems of school bullying and violence. Several studies indicate when students feel adults care about them, they are less likely to engage in disruptive, angry behaviors. A report issued by the U.S. Department of Education (Dwyer et al., 1998) about safe schools noted:

> Research shows that a positive relationship with an adult who is available to provide support when needed is one of the most critical factors in preventing student violence. Students often look to adults in the school community for guidance, support, and direction. Some children need help overcoming feelings of isolation and support in developing connections to others. Effective schools make sure that opportunities exist for adults to spend quality, personal time with children. (pp. 3–4)

Similarly, Mulvey and Cauffman (2001) cite empirical evidence that indicates "promoting healthy relationships and environments is more effective for reducing school misconduct and crime than instituting punitive penalties. . . . Students who are committed to school, feel that they belong, and trust the administration are less likely to commit violent acts than those who are uninvolved, alienated, or distrustful" (p. 800).

We must never underestimate the power of a relationship in determining success in school.

2. *To feel autonomous and possess a sense of self-determination:* At the core of most theories of motivation, including attribution theory, is the concept of ownership and self-determination. In Chapter 9 we emphasized that a salient feature of the mindset of effective educators is their belief that ongoing input from students promotes a sense of responsibility and accountability for their own education. Motivation at all ages is increased when people believe that their voice is being heard and respected, when they believe they have some control over what is occurring in their lives (Brooks & Goldstein, 2004; Dicintio & Gee, 1999). If students feel they are constantly being told what to do and that their lives are being dictated by teachers, they are less likely to be enthused about engaging in learning tasks that they feel are being imposed on them. If anything, their main motivation may be to avoid or oppose the desires of others.

3. *To feel competent:* We all hope to be successful, to possess skills in our lives that help us to feel competent and accomplished, skills that generate satisfaction and pride. In Chapter 9 we noted that a teacher's belief that each student has a different "island of competence" and learning style that requires identification, respect, and reinforcement is a core value of a strength-based approach to education.

Every student requires positive feedback and encouragement from educators. A focus on encouragement should never be confused with giving false praise or inflated grades since students are quite perceptive in knowing when they are receiving undeserved positive evaluations. Positive feedback must be rooted in actual accomplishments. This requires educators to provide opportunities for children to succeed in areas judged important by themselves and others.

In addition, a focus on competencies and positive feedback is not mutually exclusive with offering feedback to correct a child's performance or behavior. However, as we have emphasized, corrective feedback must be undertaken in a nonaccusatory, nonjudgmental manner that does not humiliate or intimidate the student. Instead, in concert with a strength-based approach, corrective feedback is most effective when presented to the student as a problem to be solved.

Strategies to Nurture the Mindset of Effective Students

Attribution theory, Deci's framework, and the characteristics of the mindset of effective educators provide a rich source of information for developing and implementing interventions to nurture the mindset of students who will be effective in the school setting. In the following section we have outlined a selected group of these interventions. However, we would first like to propose the introduction of an "orientation" period at the beginning of the school year, during which both the mindsets of teachers and students can be primed for success and accomplishment (Brooks, 2002). Consultants can outline the features of an orientation period directly with school administrators and/or through workshops they conduct with faculty. They can also note that while the ideal time for an orientation period is at the beginning of the new school year, teachers can discuss and highlight the key points with their students throughout the year.

The Orientation Period

We envision two phases of the orientation. The first is directed primarily at the mindset of educators and typically takes place a few days before the start of the new school year. In this phase, school administrators or consultants can use exercises to promote a positive attitude in faculty and staff. Some of these exercises were noted in Chapter 9, but can specifically be applied at the beginning of the school year. School administrators or consultants can review the concept and power of mindsets, describing the mindset of both effective educators and students. They can encourage faculty to reflect on and share with their colleagues why they became teachers (or other professionals in the school setting) as a way of emphasizing their purpose at work. As we discovered in research related to stress hardiness, a clear sense of purpose or commitment serves to lessen feelings of disillusionment and burnout.

Faculty can also begin a dialogue to consider what factors they believe are most critical in creating a positive school climate and what steps can be taken to achieve this climate. They can be asked to describe teachers they liked and disliked when they were students and then make a list of the words they hope their students will use to describe them during the upcoming year. As these words are listed, faculty can reflect on their behavior with students and design activities to maximize the likelihood that students will describe them in the ways in which they would like to be described.

Another exercise mentioned in Chapter 9 can be offered during the first phase of the orientation. Faculty can share their most positive and negative memories of school from their childhood and ask themselves, "What memories do I hope my students take from my classroom and what am I going to do to increase the likelihood that they will have these memories?"

These and similar activities can evoke a more positive mindset in faculty and staff accompanied with specific, constructive strategies for reinforcing a mindset in students conducive for learning.

The second phase can be implemented during the initial day or two of school, but its activities can be modified and reinforced throughout the year. It is important that teachers not feel bound to introduce academic content during this phase but instead use the time to plant the seeds for a classroom climate in which attitudes of success and responsibility among students will thrive.

Some educators have questioned if downplaying academic work for the first couple of days of school might be a waste of precious classroom teaching time. We believe that devoting the initial days to address the mindset of students is invaluable. Teachers can use the time to develop and enrich their relationship with students so that students will be more motivated to learn, more involved with their own education, more capable of managing frustration and mistakes, more self-disciplined, and more compassionate and caring.

As we outline strategies for nurturing in students a mindset that promotes learning, we offer examples of how several of these strategies can be initiated as an integral part of the second phase of the orientation period.

Develop Realistic Expectations and Goals and Make
Accommodations When Necessary

If students are to perceive a teacher as supportive and if they are to understand their strengths and weaknesses as a learner, it is imperative that teachers become acquainted with the research that highlights that students have different temperaments (Chess & Thomas, 1996; Keogh, 2003), possess different learning styles (Levine, 2002; Rief & Heimburge, 1996), and that there are "multiple intelligences" distributed among children (Gardner, 1983). If lip service is given to accepting children for who they are and we expect the same rate of learning and performance from all students, we are, in essence, prescribing failure for a number of students. They will fail not because they cannot learn but because we teach them in ways that are not in keeping with the ways in which they learn best.

The topic of accommodations often elicits the question of "fairness." It is not unusual to hear, "If I make accommodations for this student, what will the other students feel? Will they feel that I am not being fair?" It is our position that if children learn differently, if they have different learning styles, then the least fair thing we can do is to treat them as if they all learn the same. If we do not teach students in the ways that fit with their learning style, we will continue to have many youngsters who feel ill at ease and discouraged in the school milieu.

We advocate that during the second phase of the orientation period teachers discuss openly with students the question of fairness. To minimize the possibility of students feeling a teacher is not fair because some children may be doing more reading or homework than others, the teacher can discuss with the class how each one of them is different, how some students can read more quickly than others, that some can solve math problems more efficiently, that some can run a certain distance in less time than others. The teacher can say that in light of these differences, there will be different expectations of the amount and kind of work that is done by each student.

Next, the teacher can emphasize, "Since I will treat each of you somewhat differently because you are different, one of my concerns is if you begin to feel I am not being fair. If that occurs it will interfere with how you feel about me and how you learn. So, if at any time during the year you feel I am not being fair, I want you to tell me so that we can discuss it." Feedback we have received indicates that when a teacher initiates a dialogue about fairness before it emerges as an issue, it becomes a non-issue and allows teachers to accommodate to each student's unique style without negative feelings emerging from classmates.

Most accommodations do not require major modifications in a student's program nor do they demand that a teacher have markedly different educational plans for each student in the classroom. Accommodations will be most effective when students, teachers, and parents work together to define learning strengths and weaknesses and appropriate interventions. Accommodations such as a maximum time devoted for homework even if all of the work is not completed, or untimed tests, or having a peer check to ensure that a struggling student has written down the correct homework assignment are but several illustrations of relatively small accommodations with noteworthy outcomes.

When realistic accommodations are offered, it is a sign to students that they can approach teachers and that teachers genuinely care about their success in school. It also nurtures the belief in students that they are active participants in their own learning, a major feature of a positive mindset.

Reinforce Responsibility by Providing Opportunities to Contribute to the Welfare of Others

In Chapter 9 we noted that a significant intervention for assisting students to feel competent is to provide them with opportunities to help others. The act of contributing not only nurtures a sense of competence, but in addition, feelings of compassion, self-esteem, and self-respect, and a more comfortable classroom environment. The experience of making a positive difference in the lives of others serves as a powerful antidote to feelings of defeat, anger, and despair (Brooks, 2002). As Werner (1993) has captured in her longitudinal research about resilience:

> Self-esteem and self-efficacy also grew when youngsters took on a responsible position commensurate with their ability, whether it was part-time paid work, managing the household when a parent was incapacitated, or, most often, caring for younger siblings. At some point in their young lives, usually in middle childhood and adolescence, the youngsters who grew into resilient adults were required to carry out some socially desirable task to prevent others in their family, neighborhood, or community form experiencing distress or discomfort. (p. 511)

Examples in the school setting of what we call "contributory activities" include involvement in a charity drive, tutoring peers who are experiencing academic struggles, reading to younger children, and helping to beautify the school by taking care of plants or painting murals on the walls. We are reminded of the impressive results of the Valued Youth Partnership Program reported by the Carnegie Council on Adolescent Development (Hornbeck, 1989). The program, which was developed to address the large percentage of youth dropping out of school before they reached high school, involved at-risk middle school students tutoring younger students. It was highly successful as the Carnegie reported noted:

> A rise is tutors' self-esteem is the most noticeable effect of the program. . . . As a result, only 2 percent of all tutors have dropped out of school. This is remarkable given that all of these students had been held

back twice or more and were reading at least two grade levels below their current grade placement. Disciplinary problems have become less severe, grades have improved, and attendance of tutors has soared. (p. 47)

We recommend that educators review a list of each student at their school and next to the student's name record the contributory activity in which the student is involved. When youngsters enter the school building with the belief, "Because I am a member of this school, the school is a better place," they are demonstrating features of a mindset associated with effective students. If students are not afforded opportunities to make a positive difference, they are more likely to engage in behaviors in which they are making a negative impact.

Provide Opportunities to Make Choices and Decisions and Solve Problems, Which Reinforces a Sense of Ownership

Earlier in this chapter, in reviewing attribution theory and Deci's model, we emphasized the significance of possessing a feeling of ownership and control of one's life. To develop this feeling, students require experiences to learn the skills necessary to make responsible, careful choices and decisions. They also need opportunities, in keeping with their developmental level and interests, to apply and develop these skills in school (Adelman & Taylor, 1983; Deci & Flaste, 1995; Deci et al., 1992; Glasser, 1997; Kohn, 1993; Shure, 1994). Educators can establish many activities to reinforce problem-solving and decision-making skills in their students.

As noted earlier, the use of choice is a powerful validation of ownership. For example, we met a group of teachers who always gave their students a choice in which homework problems to complete. If they gave eight math problems on a page, the students were informed that they had to look at all eight and then select six to do that they thought would help them to learn best. Interestingly, the teachers reported that when they instituted this practice, they received more homework on a regular basis than prior to offering choice. One teacher surmised, "They feel it's *their* homework now." Similarly, a resource room teacher found that students were more likely to write when he gave them several pens each with a different color ink and asked them which color they would most like to use that day. The selection of the pen initiated a positive attitude fused with a feeling of ownership.

The first author of this chapter (RB) recalls with fondness a teacher he had in high school who was very demanding and who always asked thought-provoking questions. One aspect of his teaching style was his provision of choices. He would say, "Your test is in two weeks. Let's take a vote. It's your choice. Who would like to have the test on Friday and who would like to have it after the weekend on Monday?" Choices were also offered on when to hand in a paper. "Your paper is due at the end of the month. Let's vote on whether you would like an extra weekend to turn it in. It's your choice."

Never once did the teacher offer the option of not taking the test or handing in the paper. Nor did he present individual options for each student, which would have been unmanageable, especially in terms of when a test was administered. As Bob reflects on this practice, he does not think these choices were a gimmick on the part of the teacher. Rather, this teacher seemed genuinely interested in providing some options within well-defined parameters. The presence of these options reinforced a feeling of ownership, while maintaining high expectations and requirements.

Teachers can incorporate some time in the class schedule to obtain the input of students about solving particular problems that exist in the classroom or the school. As Shure (1994) has demonstrated in her "I Can Problem Solve" program, even young children can be enlisted to solve problems. Assisting students to articulate what the problem is, to think of possible solutions, and to consider the likely consequences of each solution, increases the probability of students learning not only the process of solving problems but also how best to follow through on the solutions. For example, when the first author (RB) was principal of a school in a locked door unit of a psychiatric hospital, he helped to establish a Student Council (Brooks, 1991). The opportunity and structure provided for the students to discuss their concerns and criticisms and consider solutions noticeably lessened hostility and anger while increasing more responsible, prosocial behaviors.

In a public elementary school, a question was raised about whether students should be allowed to use their skateboards on school property. Wisely, the administration referred the issue to the Student Council for consideration. The students discussed what information would be necessary in order to make a sound decision, which prompted conversations with lawyers, the police, and the chairperson of the town's Board of Selectmen to review the existing laws and the extent of the school's liability should an accident occur. Given the data gathered by the students, they recommended that skateboards not be permitted on school grounds.

The principal of the school noted, "Some people are afraid we're giving away our power to the kids. Others worry that, if given the chance to vote on school policy, students will abandon order and pass irresponsible rules. In fact, the opposite is true" (Brooks, 1991). The principal, who maintained veto power over the students' recommendations, stated that he has not had to exercise this authority, observing, "So far the kids have been really great. I'm just an advisor willing to offer wisdom whenever it's necessary."

This principal's actions nurtured a resilient mindset in students, a mindset well prepared for learning and challenges.

Student ownership, feelings of competence, and student-teacher relations are enhanced when from an early age students are encouraged to be active participants in parent-teacher conferences (to be more accurate the name should be changed to parent-student-teacher conferences). An article in *Teacher Magazine* (L. Jacobson, 1999) titled, "Three's Company" about parent-teacher conferences reported:

> When Michelle Baker first learned that her son Colin would take part in a parent-teacher conference, she was skeptical. "I thought, this is going to be a fiasco," she recalls. Instead the meeting turned out to be a big success: Colin . . . showed unusual insight into his academic strengths and weaknesses. "He had the opportunity to hear his teacher talk about him with him sitting there," Baker says. "He was able to communicate and understand better what he was being judged on." (p. 23)

It is interesting to note that Colin was only in the first grade.

Some schools have expanded the role of students in parent-student-teacher conferences by having students take responsibility for leading the meetings. This approach provides teachers an opportunity to review with students in advance the kinds of questions and issues that will be raised at the meeting. It allows students to reflect on their learning strengths and weaknesses and interventions that may prove useful. Obviously, the format of student-led conferences will only be successful if students are prepared in advance for their leadership role.

Ownership is also reinforced when teachers engage students in a discussion of the rationale of particular educational practices, including those that are typically seen as "givens." In our experience, the reasons for these "givens," which include such activities as tests, reports, and homework, are rarely, if ever, discussed in classrooms. Some may counter that a teacher should not consume valuable class time to explain to students the purpose of these basic components of education. However, we believe doing so will strengthen your teaching. Such explanation does not suggest abdicating responsibility for your classroom or allowing students to create all of the rules or decide which classroom requirements are acceptable. Rather, it means educating students about the reason for various class activities with the goal of increasing their feeling of owner-ship and motivation.

As an illustration, a middle school teacher reported that a student sur-prised her by inquiring about the purpose of homework. This teacher, rather than becoming defensive, wisely used the question as an opening to discuss her thoughts about the function of homework. She also en-couraged her students to ask other questions they had about her class-room practices and her expectations.

She said, "I was so impressed with their questions that I decided that in the future I would not wait for students to ask me any questions they had about classroom requirements. I realized they might not do so since I had not structured time for such questions. Instead, I decided I would take part of the first day of class at the beginning of each new school year to review my expectations and what I saw as the purpose of homework or tests or reports. It was a good exercise for me since I was forced to think about why I gave homework or why I gave tests in certain formats."

This teacher continued, "I would never have thought of having this kind of discussion if the student had not asked me about the purpose of homework. Yet, now I would not think of not having this kind of discussion."

When students are afforded realistic choices, when they are encour-aged to voice their opinion and they feel that these opinions are acknowl-edged, valued, and validated, they will demonstrate behaviors in concert with the features of a mindset poised to learn and act responsibly.

Establish Self-Discipline by Learning to Discipline Effectively

Many questions posed by educators revolve around the issue of disci-pline. Answers should be guided by an understanding of the function of discipline. Consultants can emphasize two main purposes of discipline. The first, which most educators state immediately, is that it is important to establish rules, guidelines, and consequences in order to ensure that our home and school environments are safe and that both students and staff feel secure. The second is that discipline should promote self-discipline or self-control in students. It is difficult to conceive of stu-dents developing high self-esteem, motivation, and resilience if they lack a comfortable sense of self-discipline, that is, a realistic ability to reflect on their behavior and its impact on others, and then to change the be-havior if necessary. In essence, self-discipline implies ownership for one's own discipline and self-regulation (Brooks, 2002).

It is also important to keep in mind that discipline stems from the word disciple and is best understood as part of a learning process. In assisting children to develop self-discipline, it is essential not to humiliate or intimidate them (Charney, 1991; Curwin & Mendler, 1988; Mendler, 1992). Humiliation and intimidation are more likely to result in an intensification of anger and uncooperativeness, the very feelings and behaviors that educators do not want to see emerge in the classroom. As we noted in Chapter 9, if we want students to assume responsibility for their actions and perceive rules as justified, they must understand the purpose of the rules and participate within reason in the process of creating these rules and the consequences that follow should the rules be broken.

An assistant principal at a middle school recognized that educators must walk a tightrope when discipline is involved, maintaining a delicate balance between rigidity and flexibility, striving to blend warmth, nurturance, acceptance, and humor with realistic expectations, clear-cut guidelines, and logical consequences. Similar to the role of many assistant principals, he served as the disciplinarian in the school. Students were sent to him for detention. As he shared his thoughts about discipline during a consultation at his school, he observed that at the beginning of his career he was a "punisher" rather than a "disciplinarian" or a "teacher." "Students would come in to serve detention and I would tell them to sit silently and think about what they had done wrong. They looked angry and resentful and not in a learning mood. I thought the only thing they were thinking about were ways of getting revenge against me or their teachers. I knew I had to change what I was doing. It just wasn't working. I had to make detention a place where they could really begin to reflect on their feelings and behaviors and start handling situations more effectively."

This assistant principal initiated a new activity in detention. Rather than have students remain silent, they were given the choice of more than 30 topics about which to write. Topics included what they would do if they ran the school, what they could do in the future to avoid detention, what were some of their best and worst experiences in school, what advice they would give a beginning teacher, what dreams they had for the future and how they would reach these dreams. He told them that if they wished he would read their essays and use the information to become a better administrator and help the school become a more comfortable place for students.

He said, "I wasn't certain how students would respond to answering an essay question while in detention. I knew some of them didn't even like to write. Much to my pleasant surprise, they really got into the activity. Their essays were very revealing and they wanted me to read them. I made certain I discussed what they had written. I soon realized that these discussions helped them to feel I cared. One student actually said in a half-kidding way, 'I like talking with you. I think I'll do something bad each day so I can come down to speak with you.' I hadn't anticipated that problem and I told him it would be better just to set up an appointment to see me."

He then proceeded to show us boxes in his office that were filled with student essays. As we reviewed a sample of them, we were very impressed with the ability of the students to reflect on their lives and their behaviors and to consider alternative ways of behaving in the future. This very impressive assistant principal had truly transformed his role from that of a "punisher" to that of a "disciplinarian." In the process the negative mindset of the students was slowly being replaced by a mindset associated with more effective behaviors and more effective learning.

The disciplinary practices we are advocating, including those that encourage the input of students, can be used to address such critical issues as teasing and bullying. No student should ever fear physical or emotional harm in the school setting (or in any setting). When educators treat students with kindness and respect, it can set a powerful tone for students to treat others with the same kindness and respect. Students are more likely to adhere to rules that prohibit teasing and bullying when they do not feel bullied or teased and when they understand the rationale for rules. Educators must keep in mind that discipline is most effective in the context of a supportive, caring relationship, a relationship that seeks the observations of students while teaching them about accountability and holding them responsible for their actions.

Assist Students to Deal More Effectively with Mistakes and Failure

Both attribution theory and Deci's framework accord a prominent role to the impact that making mistakes has on the demeanor of students. In Chapter 9 we noted that effective teachers are proactive in discussing with students feelings and behaviors associated with the fear of failing and feeling humiliated. Far too many students, wishing to avoid the possibility of looking foolish, engage in self-defeating actions such as becoming a class clown or class bully or refusing to answer questions or failing to complete assignments. Lessening the fear of humiliation must be a major goal in every classroom, especially given the pernicious impact it has. If this fear dominates the mindset of students, learning will be compromised.

In Chapter 9, we recommended that during the first day or two of the school year (the orientation period), teachers introduce the theme of mistakes and share some of their own experiences with failure when they were students. Identifying and discussing the fear of making mistakes renders it a less potent force in the classroom.

There are other strategies that consultants can suggest to educators to address the issue of mistakes. They can indicate that students are very aware of how teachers handle their own setbacks in the classroom. If teachers display frustration and anger when challenging situations arise in the classroom, obviously they are not modeling the behaviors they would expect from students. A high school teacher noticed that she often expressed annoyance, especially when students did not appear to be interested in the class or were unable to provide the correct answers to her questions. Yet, she would tell her students that they should not be afraid to take risks or make mistakes:

> I finally realized one day that I was modeling the behaviors I did not want to see in my students. I also realized that I was too uptight and not playful enough. So I decided to take a risk and use a very different approach. I told my classes that I wasn't pleased with how I sometimes responded to setbacks and mistakes and if they ever caught me in a lousy mood they should let me know. I told them that I might even act negatively just to see if they were on their toes. I also said that I would return the favor and let them know when they seemed afraid to answer questions or offer their opinions. Saying this in a playful way worked wonders. I feel better and my students seem to feel less pressured in the classroom.

With a similar intent, an elementary school teacher gave her students rocks and stones at the beginning of the school year. She then pointed to a jar on her desk and said, "Whenever you or I make a mistake in the class, someone can place a rock or stone in the jar. As soon as the jar gets filled, we will have a party to celebrate our mistakes and I will bring in the refreshments. We were informed by a colleague of this teacher that the rocks were rather large and the jar relatively small. Thus, a celebration took place early in the year. This teacher understood the importance of removing the fear of failure in her classroom. She accomplished this task with playfulness and celebration.

Summary

Consultants, during the process of helping teachers to identify the mindset associated with effective educators, can also define the key features of the mindset of effective students. The mindset of educators is openly displayed in their teaching attitudes and practices. These attitudes and practices heavily influence the mindset that will be reinforced in students. As we understand the ways in which our mindsets and the mindsets of our students influence the classroom environment, we will be better equipped to create an atmosphere that supports motivation, learning, cooperation, responsibility, self-discipline, hope, and resilience.

11

Applying Behavior Modification

SAM GOLDSTEIN AND ROBERT BROOKS

The most effective model to manage children's behavior in the classroom incorporates the themes of behavioral psychology. Over the past 25 years, this is one of the predominant educational models taught at universities and colleges throughout the world and followed in the classroom (Kavale & Hirshoren, 1980). The behavioral model espouses that what you do is influenced by what comes after what you do (Sarason, Glaser, & Fargo, 1972). The reinforcement or punishment that follows behavior adheres to the following basic set of principles (T. B. Roberts, 1975):

1. Reinforcement or punishment always follows behavior.
2. Reinforcement or punishment should follow the target behavior as soon as possible.
3. Reinforcement or punishment must fit the target behavior and have meaning to the individual.
4. Multiple reinforcers or punishers are likely more effective than single reinforcers or punishers.

Behavior management assumes that observable and measurable behaviors are good targets for change. All behavior follows a set of consistent

---

Behavioral science has changed little in the past 10 years. Chapter 11 is updated but reproduced with few modifications from the first edition of this text.

rules. The scientific method is effective not only for defining, observing, and measuring a behavior but also for determining effective interventions. These assumptions are summarized in Table 11.1.

All behavior is maintained, changed, or shaped by the consequences of that behavior. Although there are certain limits, such as the temperamental influence on behavior experienced by an impulsive child, even this child functions more effectively under the right set of consequences. Behavior can be strengthened by rewarding it or weakened by no longer rewarding it. The latter may involve withdrawal of reward or presentation of an aversive consequence. The former can be as simple as attention. In classroom situations, teachers often learn to pay attention to misbehavior rather than appropriate behavior, which strengthens rather than weakens the misbehavior. As an initial means of shaping new behavior in many situations, teachers must be forced to attend to problem children when their behavior is appropriate.

Reinforcers are consequences that strengthen behavior. Punishers are consequences that weaken behavior. What many are unaware of,

Table 11.1   Assumptions of behavior management

1. Behaviors that are observable and measurable are the targets for change rather than underlying causes, which are difficult or impossible to measure.
2. Both normal and abnormal behavior follow the laws of nature and are controlled by essentially the same variables.
3. Past learning histories, genetics, and physiological variables set limits on behavior; however, many behaviors that occur within these limits are controlled by the principles of learning and environmental contingencies.
4. The scientific method with empirical data is the only reliable way to establish which interventions effectively change behavior.
5. The interventions that are validated as being effective by the scientific method form a group of procedures or a technology of behavior change.
6. Not all the procedures that form a technology of behavior change are effective in every situation with every child. Rather, each technique must be tested individually until an effective technique is identified.
7. Applications of behavior management techniques require constant monitoring and assessment to ensure their effectiveness.

however, is a third type of consequence that Bushell (1973) refers to as "noise." "Noise" is defined as a consequence that has no effect on the behavior it follows, neither strengthening nor weakening it. The pattern, as Bushell points out, is simple. The teacher is responsible for changing students' behavior. Behaviors are changed by their consequences. Therefore, students' behaviors are managed and changed by the consequences of classroom behavior. To manage behavior through consequences requires the teacher to use a multistep process:

1. The problem is defined by counting something.
2. A favorable situation is created to change the behavior.
3. An effective reinforcer is chosen.
4. The reinforcer is used to shape or change behavior.

Shaping, which will be described at a later point, is the differential reenforcement of successive approximations of the final behavior. For Bushell, shaping is a critical technique in the classroom, used to slowly elicit more appropriate behavior.

Consequences of behavior are directly related to the antecedent or consequent events to which they are temporally related. Table 11.2 presents examples of behavioral outcomes as they relate to various antecedent and consequent events.

This chapter first discusses techniques that increase or reduce childhood behaviors. The chapter then continues with a review of generalized and other specific applications (e.g., contracting, token economy) to use in the classroom. Consultants must help classroom teachers productively employ praise and attention, reward and privileges, differential attention, time-out, and punishment. Teachers who do not understand how to use these interventions effectively can inadvertently contribute to student misbehavior (Kauffman, Pullen, & Akers, 1986). Common mistakes are using behavior management techniques inconsistently, inadvertently reinforcing undesired behavior, harboring unrealistic educational or behavioral expectations for students, presenting inappropriate subject matter, failing to respond to each child's individual needs, and modeling negative behaviors. When teachers do not understand the importance of positive reinforcement, they may react to unwanted behavior in irritable ways, relying on punishment to manage the classroom. They may be unwilling to look at alternatives when standard interventions are ineffective, especially if they perceive the child's problems as stemming from within the child.

Table 11.2   Behavior: Classification, consequence, and probable effect

Classification	Original Behavior Exhibited	Consequence	Probable Future Effect on the Original Behavior
Positive reinforcement	Jane cleans her room	Jane's parents praise her	Jane will continue to clean her room
Positive reinforcement	Shirley brushes her teeth after meals	Shirley receives a nickel each time	Shirley will continue to brush her teeth after meals
Extinction	Jim washes his father's car	Jim's car-washing behavior is ignored	Jim will stop washing his father's car
Positive reinforcement	Alton works quietly at his seat	The teacher praises and rewards Alton	Alton will continue to work quietly at his seat
Punishment	Gwenn sits on the arm of the chair	Gwenn is spanked each time she sits on the arm of the chair	Gwenn will not sit on the arm of the chair
Negative reinforcement	Bob complains that older boys consistently beat him up, and he refuses to attend school	Bob's parents allow him to remain at home because of his complaints	Bob will continue to miss school
Punishment	Elmer puts Elsie's pigtails in the paint pot	The teacher administers the paddle to Elmer's posterior	Elmer will not put Elsie's pigtails in the paint pot
Extinction	Shirley puts glue on Joe's seat	Shirley is ignored	Shirley will stop putting glue on Joe's seat
Negative reinforcement	Jason complains of headaches when it is time to do homework	Jason is allowed to go to bed without doing his homework	Jason will have headaches whenever there is homework to do

Reinforcement

Schedules

Schedules of reinforcement identify the amount of work required or the time that must elapse between reinforcers. These schedules delineate the pattern for presenting the reinforcer in response to the target behavior (Rusch, Rose, & Greenwood, 1988). There are continuous schedules, fixed- or variable-interval schedules (time related), and fixed- or variable-ratio schedules (related to how much work is completed). Fixed schedules result in higher rates of performance than continuous schedules. The drawback, however, is that the child quickly learns that no reinforcement is going to be available until certain contingencies occur. There is less guesswork. Therefore, there is likely to be a dropoff in the child's performance after earning a reward under a fixed-rate schedule. The child works harder when getting closer to earning rewards and slows down after the reward is provided. In the classroom, a variable schedule that keeps the child guessing is likely to be more effective than others.

The quality of satiation makes continuous reinforcement valuable for shaping new behavior but poor for maintaining behavior. When the individual receives too much reinforcement, the resultant satiation causes loss of interest. Clarizio (1976) suggests that as appropriate classroom behaviors are developing they should be rewarded every single time, and the teacher should slowly shift from consistent to inconsistent payoffs. Rewards should be provided after the task is completed with timing carefully attended to.

Fixed-ratio interval schedules, which most often occur in the classroom, are effective because the child knows exactly what is expected and performance requirements are clearly spelled out. Variable schedules are not good for shaping new behaviors but are excellent for maintenance. These are much harder to implement in the classroom without some specific support or mechanical device to cue the teacher when a reinforcer should be forthcoming.

Positive Reinforcement

Based on teacher responses to questionnaires, Martens and Meller (1989) reported that teachers prefer interventions that reinforce appropriate behavior and consider them to be more acceptable in the classroom than those that punish inappropriate behavior. Shea and Bauer (1987) describe the following multistep process to effectively apply positive reinforcement:

1. Select a target behavior to be increased, define the behavior, and choose a reinforcer.
2. Observe the child, closely watching for the behavior.
3. Initially reinforce the target behavior after it is exhibited.
4. Comment in a positive way about the behavior when providing reinforcement.

5. Be enthusiastic and interested.
6. Offer assistance.
7. Vary the reinforcer.

Positive reinforcement should follow immediately after good be-havior. It should be specific and initially continuous, slowly changing to an intermittent schedule. Social reinforcers involve some positive statement or reflection to the child. Material reinforcers involve giving the child something. Social reinforcers are more versatile, always avail-able, and usually critical to maintain behavior change. There are an endless supply of them and they are what we find in the real world. The teacher has to be careful, however, to avoid giving too much or not enough. In either case, problems will occur. Adults usually get in return what they give their child or students (G. R. Patterson, 1975). Students reinforce, shape, and maintain or extinguish the teacher's behavior and vice versa. Teacher positive reinforcement was found to be in-versely related to students' scolding, but directly related to increased productivity and teacher enthusiasm in the classroom (Gross & Eck-strand, 1993).

An important aspect of positive reinforcement is the choice of a target behavior. Should it be one that the child has not exhibited or one that the child already possesses but does not perform at a frequent enough rate? The latter is referred to as maintenance reinforcement, the former as acquisition of new behavior.

It is easier to increase behavior than decrease it (D. P. Morgan & Jen-son, 1988). Thus when choosing a target behavior, it is preferable to focus on behaviors to be increased rather than on those to be decreased. Preparation, expectation, and data collection are critical. Often teachers comment that they have attempted a particular behavior management strategy and it has not been effective. In these cases, more often than not, it is not the strategy that is ineffective but the manner in which it has been applied. Behavioral contingencies work for everyone when the idiosyncratic differences between students and teachers are identified and the program adjusted to fit those differences. As previously re-viewed, however, the teacher's perception as to the locus of the child's problems (within the child or stemming from the environment) will strongly influence the effort teachers are willing to exert to understand and change a student's behavior.

J. E. Walker and Shea (1991) suggest the following basic principles for reinforcement:

- Reinforcement must be dependent on the exhibition of the target behavior.
- The target behavior is to be reinforced immediately after it is exhibited.
- During the initial stage of the behavior change process, the target behavior is reinforced each time it is exhibited.
- When the target behavior reaches a satisfactory frequency level, it is reinforced intermittently.
- Social reinforcers are always applied along with tangible reinforcers.

Rhode and colleagues (Rhode, Jenson, & Revis, 1992) offer the IFEED-AV model for providing reinforcement. This model, which is shown in Table 11.3, provides an excellent summary of reinforcement contingencies for teachers.

When choosing positive reinforcers, teachers should select rewards that are age appropriate, offer natural reinforcers (e.g., having access to school activities, being a class monitor or a leader, helping out others in the school such as the custodian), use rewards that are appropriate to the child's level of functioning, and make certain that parental and administrative support are available for those rewards. Teachers should avoid partial statements ("I am glad you finished your work—finally"); make the most of opportunities to reward; be generally polite, courteous, and interested; and not deprive students of basic rights (e.g., lunch, bathroom use). And then categorize these rights as positive reinforcers.

Identifying Reinforcers

What do children like? Fantuzzo, Rohrbeck, Hightower, and Work (1991) found no clear relationship between teacher use and young children's preferences for edible, tangible, activity, or social rewards. Nonetheless, a number of studies have identified popular reinforcers for children and adolescents. Consultants should encourage teachers to spend time first identifying what is reinforcing before choosing a reinforcer. Tourigny-Dewhurst and Cautela (1980) evaluated the reinforcement choices of children with problems in school settings. They asked children of various ages (5 to 6, 7 to 9, 10 to 12 years) about their preferred foods and nonfoods. For all three groups, food items were rated in the top 10, the most popular reinforcer being french fries. Among edible reinforcers for children under 5, favorites are lollipops, ice cream, soda, and potato chips.

Table 11.3   IFEED-AV rules

Immediately: The "I" stands out for reinforcing the student immediately. The longer the teacher waits to reinforce a student, the less effective the reinforcer will be. This is particularly true of younger students or students with severe disabilities. For example, reinforcer effectiveness will be limited if the student has to wait until the end of the week to receive it.

Frequently: The "F" stands for frequently reinforcing a student. It is especially important to frequently reinforce when a student is learning a new behavior or skill. If reinforcers are not given frequently enough, the student may not produce enough of a new behavior for it to become well established. The standard rule is three or four positive reinforcers for every one negative consequence (including negative verbal comments) the teacher delivers. If, in the beginning, there is a great deal of inappropriate behavior to which the teacher must attend, positive reinforcement and recognition of appropriate behavior must be increased accordingly to maintain the desired three or four positives to each negative. The reinforcer can be a simple social reinforcer such as, "Good job. You finished your math assignment."

Enthusiasm: The first "E" stands for enthusiasm in the delivery of the reinforcer. It is easy to simply hand an edible reinforcer to a student; it takes more effort to pair it with an enthusiastic comment. Modulation in the voice and excitement with a congratulatory air conveys that the student has done something important. For most teachers, this seems artificial at first. However, with practice, enthusiasm makes the difference between a reinforcer delivered in a drab, uninteresting way to one that indicates that something important has taken place in which the teacher is interested.

Eye contact: It is also important for the teacher to look the student in the eyes when giving a reinforcer, even if the student is not looking at him/her. Like enthusiasm, eye contact suggests that a student is special and has the teacher's undivided attention. Over time, eye contact may become reinforcing in and of itself.

Describe the behavior: "D" stands for describing the behavior that is being reinforced. The younger the student or the more severely disabled, the more important it is to describe the appropriate behavior that is being reinforced. Teachers often assume that students know what it is they are doing right that has resulted in the delivery of a reinforcement. However, this is often not the case. The student may not know why reinforcement is being delivered or think that it is being delivered for some behavior other than what the teacher intended to reinforce. Even if the student does know what behavior is being reinforced, describing it is important.

(continued)

233

Table 11.3 *(Continued)*

For one thing, describing the behavior highlights and emphasizes the behavior the teacher wishes to reinforce. Second, if the behavior has several steps, describing it helps to review the specific expectations for the student. An example is, "Wow, you got yourself dressed—look at you! You have your socks on, our shoes are laced, your pants are on with a belt, and your shirt has all the buttons fastened and is tucked in." This is much more effective than saying, "Good dressing."

Anticipation: Building excitement and anticipation for the earning of a reinforcer can motivate students to do their very best. The more "hype" the teacher uses, the more excited students become to earn the reinforcer. Presenting the potential reinforcer in a "mysterious" way will also build anticipation.

Variety: Just like adults, students and particularly Tough Kids, get tired of the same things. A certain reinforcer may be highly desired, but after repeated exposure, it loses its effectiveness. It is easy to get caught up in giving students the same old reinforcers time and time again. However, variety is the spice of life for nondisabled and disabled alike. Generally, when teachers are asked why they do not vary their reinforcers, they indicate that it worked very well once. It is necessary to change reinforcers frequently to make the reinforcers more effective.

Source: The Tough Kid Book: Practical Classroom Management Strategies, by G. Rhode, W. R. Jenson, and H. K. Reavis, 1992, Longmont, CO: Sopris West. Reprinted with permission of the authors and publisher.

Consultants should make certain that teachers understand the Premack principle (Premack, 1959), which states that if two behaviors occur at different rates the child will engage in the less frequent behavior when the reward offered is the opportunity to engage in the more frequent behavior. For example, the child might be required to do a math assignment (low-frequency behavior) before being able to go to recess (high-frequency behavior) or must sit in his or her seat in order to get called to the fist in line. A combination of tangible and social reinforcers likely will work best for most children. Although teachers are well aware of a wide range of tangible reinforcers, they are often unaware of the wide menu of social rewards available including activities with others.

Tangible rewards should not be used for activities that already hold intrinsic interest for a child (Clarizio, 1976). In such cases, the child's attention may shift away from the activity that is already inherently rewarding to the new reinforcer. It is important for teachers to examine the interest level of curriculum materials before trying to reinforce the learning of material that students simply do not like (O'Leary & Drabman, 1971). Behavior modification is not a substitute for good teaching or an interesting curriculum. Activities often make good tangible reinforcers because rather than providing an object that the child may take away and deal with individually, the activity often promotes interaction with teachers and other students. The use of a reinforcement list or menu can facilitate an interview with the child to identify potential reinforcers and explain the need for eliminating or increasing certain classroom behaviors. The interview should include establishing rapport, explaining the purposes of the discussion to the child, explaining the meaning of reinforcers, eliciting suggestions for rewards by directly asking the child what he or she likes, offering a list, having the child rank favorite rewards, and following up in a few days to verify the consistency of the child's responses (Shea & Bauer, 1987). Actively involving a child in the selection of the reinforcement activity has been referred to by D. G. White, Fremont, and Wilson (1987) as *process reinforcement*. The goal is to boost the child's willingness to internalize and take ownership of responses that lead to successful target behaviors through the augmented power of the child-chosen reinforcer. Homme (1969) suggests the following guidelines for using reinforcement menus:

- Reinforcing activities that relate to educational rather than just entertaining objectives should receive priority.
- When choosing reinforcing activities, the availability of an activity at school, the noise level it will generate, and the likely response level of students should be considered.
- If possible, rewards should be provided in a separate reinforcement area.
- A brief amount of time, not less than 3, nor more than 10 minutes, should be used for reinforcement.
- Some type of control of reinforcement, such as a sign-out sheet or the use of peer pressure, should be utilized to maintain order during reinforcement time.

Clarizio (1976) points out that many behaviors carry their own reward. Taking pride in one's achievements, being able to control and delay gratification, doing something novel or new are all intrinsically rewarding. It is quite likely that the most reinforcing activity at school is the development of the child or adolescent's sense of mastery and ability to overcome a problem. This process leads to increased self-esteem, greater school confidence, and motivation toward completing the next task.

Classroom studies have consistently found a low rate of teachers' delivery of positive consequences (Shores et al., 1993). Teachers in self-contained, special education rooms are nearly three times more likely to use positive reinforcers with their students than teachers in regular education. Although the teacher-to-student ratio may contribute to this disparity, many teachers are much too quick to employ punishment or negative reinforcement rather than positive social consequences for controlling children's behavior.

Negative Reinforcement

Negative reinforcement requires the individual to work for the removal of an already-operating, unpleasant consequence. The child's goal is to get rid of something that is unpleasant rather than to earn something that is desirable (Axelrod, 1983). Consultants must make certain that teachers understand that negative reinforcement is not analogous to punishment. Under the negative reinforcement model, instead of working to earn a positive consequence, the child is working to avoid an aversive consequence. Teachers primarily use negative reinforcement in attempting to manage problem behaviors. They pay attention to a child who may not be complying and withdraw their attention contingent on the child's compliance. This strengthens rather than weakens the noncompliant behavior. The next time a similar situation occurs, this child again will not comply until confronted with an aversive consequence (e.g., the teacher's attention). Negative reinforcement is seductive and coercive. It works in the short run but in the long run makes life harder for classroom teachers.

Many of the same variables that affect positive reinforcement—immediacy, frequency, consistency—affect negative reinforcement. Behaviors that in and of themselves may not be negative become negative reinforcers when paired with certain events. For example, a teacher who approaches a child who is not working quickly becomes a negative reinforcer, even though in and of itself the teacher's walking up to the child does not have a negative connotation (Favell, 1977).

Henderson, Jenson, and Erken (1986) offer an excellent example of both positive and negative reinforcement in a classroom of behaviorally handicapped and learning-disabled students. The goal was to improve on-task behavior. This model demonstrates that negative reinforcement in and of itself is not inherently bad. In this program, a tape recorder played soft beeps at random. Students never knew when the beep would sound. If the students were working when the beep sounded, they earned points that could be exchanged for rewards. This was the positive variable, reinforced component. However, if students were not working when the beep sounded, they did not get the points, which represented a negative reinforcement mode. Had they lost points, this program would have included response cost as well, but this was not done. Students avoided the negative reinforcement contingency by staying on task. To avoid not getting points required the children to increase their attending behavior. Students increased on-task behavior from 10% to 20% at baseline to 80% during the reinforcement contingency.

Modeling

Modeling involves learning a new behavior by imitation after observing others (Bandura, 1965, 1969). Modeling can be as simple as having a child watch another child sharpen a pencil or having a child review self-behavior on video (Kehle, Clark, Jenson, & Wampold, 1986). By watching the model, the child can learn a new behavior, learn to inhibit another behavior, or strengthen previously learned behavior (i.e., saying thank you). To use modeling effectively, teachers must determine whether a child has the capacity to follow a model, be careful to provide rewards for modeling, and choose a model that the student admires and is likely to imitate. Student response to modeling is influenced by three factors: the characteristics of the mode, the characteristics of the observer, and the positive or negative consequence associated with the behavior. Students are more likely to respond to the modeling of teachers who are seen as competent, nurturing, supportive, fun, interesting, and valued. The child's perception of the similarity between self and the person modeling the behavior also determines the degree of response to the behavior. Finally, children are more likely to imitate behavior that results in a positive consequence.

Modeling is affected by age and sex. Younger children have been reported as more frequently imitating others than older children. Children consistently will model someone whom they value or look up to. They will also imitate the behavior of a same-sex child more often than that of a different-sex child. They model someone whom they perceive as successful and socially valued regardless of whether the teacher perceives that person as successful and socially valued. Further, if the child observes the model being reinforced for a certain behavior, it increases the likelihood the child will then model that behavior (Thelen & Rennie, 1972). The opposite is also true (Bandura, 1965). Barnwell and Sechrist

(1965) found that first- and third-grade students selected tasks that they observed their classmates receiving praise for and avoided tasks for which other children received disapproval. Students learn and choose both good and aversive behavior by watching others.

As students learn a behavior, it is not just the consequences that determine whether the behavior recurs, but likely the students' attitudes toward those behaviors as well (Mager, 1968). They watch what happens to other students who exhibit those behaviors. When others are successful and receive positive reinforcement, the observers who also posses those behaviors will exhibit them (and vice versa). Teachers exert a strong influence on students' approach or avoidance of certain behaviors: When teachers are cheerful and enthusiastic, these attitudes can be contagious; when they are respectful of students, students respect each other. Teachers who are patient, fair, consistent, and optimistic tend to have a higher incidence of students who exhibit similar traits. Teacher behavior sets the tone for classroom environment (Clarizio, 1976; Good & Brophy, 1973).

Kounin (1970) describes a ripple effect in transactions between teachers and misbehaving students that affects other students viewing these incidents. Teachers who are firm reduce the deviancy of the offender and the witness. When teachers enforce rules, the ripple effect works in their favor. When they fail to follow through with rules, the ripple effect works against them. Although firmness and follow-through are essential, teachers must avoid being too rough, harsh, or rigid. The misbehaving student's social standing in the classroom is also an issue. When teachers successfully manage the behavior of high-status troublemakers, this control tends to benefit the entire classroom. Likewise, the ripple effect when high-status offenders are not managed increases negative behavior among others. What happens to leaders in the classroom has been demonstrated to be important for the overall classroom ecology (Gnagey, 1968). It is critical to develop control techniques that achieve a positive response from high-status, misbehaving students because these peer group leaders will then model compliance for the other students. Bandura (1969) points out that the teacher's management of key members of the class will rapidly affect the entire group.

Modeling can also help focus the teacher's discipline. When managing students, teachers should focus on tasks rather than on approval. In the latter situation, teachers focus on their relationship with students when trying to get them to behave. A strategy that is usually ineffective. In addition, teachers must realize that it is relatively easy for an inhibited student to engage in an appropriate behavior by watching just a few others. To give up an inappropriate behavior by observing a positive example is much more difficult, however. Students will require repeated exposure to desirable behavior if undesirable behaviors are to be managed this way.

Vicarious reinforcement, an issue related to modeling, is defined as the reinforcing effect a reward has on observers as opposed to the target of the reward (Sharpley, 1985). A number of researchers have suggested that students observing others being reinforced also benefit although they are not the direct recipients of contingencies (Martens & Kelly, 1993). However, such benefits have been reported as short lived unless the observer receives direct reinforcement for exhibiting the desired behavior at some point in the process (Ollendick, Dailey, & Shapiro, 1983).

Shaping

Teachers have the option of waiting for the appropriate target behavior to occur or of reinforcing successive approximations. The latter process is referred to as shaping. Shaping is used to establish behaviors that are not routinely exhibited in the individual's behavioral repertoire (J. O. Cooper, Herron, & Heward, 1987). J. E. Walker and Shea (1991) describe the steps to effective shaping as follows:

1. Select a target behavior and define it.
2. Obtain baseline data.
3. Select reinforcers.
4. Decide on close approximations and reinforce successive approximations to the target behavior each time they occur.
5. Reinforce the newly established behavior each time it occurs.
6. Reinforce the old behavior on a variable schedule and begin reinforcing the new behavior on an every time occurrence. The key to successful shaping is to reinforce closer approximations and not reinforce lesser approximations.

A specific desirable behavior may never occur exactly the way a teacher wants it. If the child exhibits some partial aspect of the behavior, the teacher should reinforce it and gradually work toward success of the approximation. Shaping involves reinforcing success of the approximations to a final behavior (Gelfan & Hartmann, 1984). Any behavior that remotely resembles a target is initially rewarded. Prompts are used and then faded. Shaping can be used for everything from teaching a child to shoot a basketball to spelling words correctly. Shaping is not a simple process, however. The steps toward successive approximation must be carefully thought out, otherwise behaviors that are not working toward the desired goal may be reinforced. The classroom consultant must make certain that the teacher defines and understands the set of steps and behaviors to reinforce in the shaping process.

Punishment

Punishment is an act that suppresses undesirable behavior but may not necessarily extinguish it (McDaniel, 1980). Suppression may be of short duration and in the absence of the punisher, may in fact recur. Punishment can involve presentation of an unpleasant consequence or the loss of a pleasurable consequence following the occurrence of the target behavior. These may or may not be at all related to the exhibition of the inappropriate behavior. Punishment reduces the probability that the behavior that precedes it will recur. Some punishers are aversive to most people, although even extreme punishments such as those that cause pain or restraint have been found to be reinforcing to some. Punishment is an efficient way of changing behavior. However, it is seductive because it can be quite reinforcing to teachers and then be overused (Neisworth & Smith, 1983). Punishment usually provides an aversive stimulus (e.g., something the child does not like) each time an undesirable behavior occurs, but it can also involve the loss of a pleasurable stimulus. Both the introduction of an aversive stimulus and loss of a pleasurable stimulus can be effective although in some situations, punishment may suppress but not eliminate behavior. Punishment doesn't provide an appropriate model of acceptable behavior and for many teachers is accompanied by emotional outbursts. Most commonly used punishments by teachers include depriving students of participation in enjoyable activities, loss of a snack, verbal reprimands, and time out (J. E. Walker & Shea, 1991). These authors also report that some teachers continue to use physical punishment and interventions designed to embarrass children into submission (e.g., having the child wear a derogatory sign) even though these interventions bear a high emotional cost. If punishment is to be used effectively in school, the following guidelines should be followed:

- All students are aware of which behaviors will be punished and how they will be punished.
- Appropriate models for acceptable behavior are provided.
- Punishments are offered immediately, consistently, and fairly.
- Punishments are offered impersonally (J. E. Walker & Shea, 1991).

Shea and Bauer (1987) make a very strong case for minimizing the use of punishment in the classroom, especially more severe punishment such as embarrassment or corporal punishment in the classroom setting because these interventions are likely to erode self-esteem and further impair a tenuous teacher-student relationship. Likely, if punishments are to be used, the primary interventions should comprise the loss of a privilege or reprimands.

When losing privileges, students must understand the relationship between the target behavior and the privilege lost (J. E. Walker & Shea, 1991). A natural or logical consequence as a punisher should be used as often as possible. Loss of the privilege during which the inappropriate behavior is exhibited is fair; warning, nagging, and threatening as well as debating should be avoided.

Bandura (1969) notes that punishment can exert a complex effect and therefore should be used with caution. Some authors suggest that punishment at school should be avoided at all costs, whereas others suggest that rewarding what is approved is simply insufficient for helping children learn what is not approved (Ausubel, 1961). It has also long been recognized that in most cases unless punishing interventions are combined with positive reinforcers, they tend to be ineffective. Almost 60 years ago, H. H. Anderson and Brewer (1946) found that teachers using dominating behaviors of force, threat, shame, and blame negatively affected their students' adjustment. Children working in those conditions displayed nonconforming behavior at a rate higher than in classrooms where teachers were more positive and supportive. Thus the lesson is clear: Personal hostility from teachers and punishments in an atmosphere containing minimal positive reinforcement and emotional warmth are not productive. To be effective, the punishment must be related in form to the misbehavior. It should be consistent, fair, just, delivered impersonally, avoid fear, not generate other emotional reactions, and not involve the assignment of extra work that is unrelated to the act for which a student is being punished. Opportunities must be offered for the student to exhibit and receive reinforcement for more appropriate behavior.

Table 11.4 summarizes commonly encountered problems related to using punishment as well as ways of minimizing or preventing these problems.

Reprimands are the most frequent punishments used by teachers. Contacting parents, losing privileges, and detention come next. For punishments to work they must not be abused. Competing behaviors must be rewarded. Punishments should be introduced at a rate that is

241

Table 11.4   Punishment: Problems and solutions

Undesirable Side Effects and Limitations	Ways to Prevent or Minimize
1. Transitory suppressive effects	1. Combine punishment and reward.
2. Does not indicate what is appropriate alternative behavior	2. Provide and reward acceptable behavior.
3. Produces avoidance behaviors	3. Use removal of rewards as a form of punishment: use behavioral contracts.
4. Reduces behavioral flexibility	4. Combine punishment and discrimination learning procedures.
5. Teacher becomes undesirable model	5. Avoid modeling punitive forms of behavior.

Source: Toward Positive Classroom Discipline, second edition, by Harvey F. Clarizio, 1976, New York: Wiley. Copyright © 1976 by John Wiley & Sons. Reprinted with permission.

sufficiently aversive to effectively change behavior with short periods of use. Reprimands should include a statement of appropriate, alternative behavior. Inattentive elementary school children respond better to shorter reprimands (Abramowitz, O'Leary, & Futtersak, 1988). These authors found that shorter reprimands resulted in significantly lower rates of off-task behavior than did longer reprimands when frequencies of praise and reprimands were controlled. A similar trend was found for academic performance. Longer reprimands were often observed to elicit back talk from the students, whereas the shorter ones did not. J. E. Walker and Shea (1991) note that effective reprimands are specific, do not derogate the child, are provided immediately, are given with a firm voice and controlled physical demeanor, are backed up with loss of privilege, include a statement encouraging more appropriate behavior, and are delivered in a calm way that does not embarrass the child in the presence of others.

Response cost is a punishing technique that translates to the equivalent of losing what you possess or have earned. You earn something for good behavior. You place what you have earned in jeopardy of loss for inappropriate behavior. In many situations, response cost in the form of a penalty or fine is combined with positive reinforcement. To be effective, more reinforcers must be earned than lost. Thus with certain populations, such as children with attention-deficit/hyperactivity disorder, either many more opportunities to earn reinforcers or more reinforcers for each appropriate behavior must be provided to counterbalance the risk of bankruptcy. Response cost has been used effectively in classroom settings to reduce off-task behavior and improve compliance (Iwata & Bailey, 1974; Witt & Elliott, 1982).

Response cost can be difficult to implement. Witt and Elliott (1982) initiated a response cost lottery in a regular fourth-grade classroom. The intervention was initiated during a 30-minute work period in which children either engaged in seatwork or participated in group instruction. The intervention was directed at three boys in the class with histories of significant disruptive behavior. The boys were first taught the rules and told that slips of paper with their names on them would be placed on their desks at the beginning of each work period. Each time a boy broke a rule during the 30-minute period, he would lose one slip of paper. Thus, in this modification of a response cost intervention, the child received all the rewards at the start rather than starting with nothing. This model has been proven to be most effective for impulsive children (Rapport, Murphy, & Bailey, 1982). At the end of the work period, the teacher collected all the remaining slips of paper and placed them in a box for a lottery drawing at the end of the week. The child whose name was drawn would then earn a reinforcer. With this model, appropriate behavior increased. Accuracy on assignments also improved.

A response cost system can be as simple as chips in a cup or marks on a chart placed on the student's desk or pinned to the student's shirt. Such a system can also be as complex as the attention training system (Rapport, 1987). The attention training system is a remote-controlled counter that sits on a student's desk. The device provides the student with a digital read-out showing the number of points earned. Points can accrue automatically, or by using a remote-controlled device, the classroom teacher can add or remove a point from anywhere in the classroom contingent on the child's on- or off-task behavior.

D. P. Morgan and Jenson (1988) suggest the following guidelines for using response cost effectively in the classroom:

- Use the procedure for most if not all of the classroom day.
- Make certain the number of students in the program is manageable for the teacher.
- Conduct the lottery at the end of every day in the initial stages of the program.

- Consider an additional grand prize drawing at the end of each week. To qualify for such a drawing, students must have retained a minimum number of slips.
- Incorporate self-monitoring and self-consequential responses for rule violations. Students should be required to surrender a slip of paper on their own.

If not managed effectively and well thought out, response cost can backfire and increase problem behavior (Burchard & Barrera, 1972). Students who quickly become bankrupt, oppositional students who resist turning in reinforcers, and the use of a group contingency (e.g., everyone must earn the reinforcer or no one has access to it) can all place response cost in jeopardy.

Time-Out

Time-out from reinforcement excludes children from the opportunity to participate with others and receive any kind of positive reinforcement (Powell & Powell, 1982). Time-out is by far the best known disciplinary technique. As best known, therefore, it also is most likely to be overused and misused by classroom teachers. Although a brief time-out (a few minutes' duration) can exert a positive influence on classroom behavior when applied appropriately (Kazdin, 1975a), teachers probably use time-out ineffectively as often as effectively (H. M. Walker & Walker, 1991).

Time-out is best considered as a continuum of interventions. The least restrictive forms of time-out consist of the removal of certain reinforcing activities or objects from the misbehaving child for a short period. The next step for time-out is contingent observation (Porterfield, Herbert-Jackson, & Risley, 1976), in which the child remains in the classroom but is seated a few feet away from a work setting and is required to watch everyone else. This intervention is only possible if the child is willing to sit and not disturb others. Time-out in a restricted environment outside the classroom is the most severe form of this discipline. The child cannot see the classroom or interact with others. For children with severe behavioral problems, time-out in a well-lit, ventilated booth or empty room may be necessary.

K. R. Harris (1985) summarizes the five types of time-out: isolation, exclusion, contingent observation, removal of reinforcing stimulus (extinction), and ignoring. Observational time-out is an effective means of having students watch what they are missing. Exclusion times-out students in a quiet part of the room where they do not see others. Finally, seclusion takes students out to another place. The classroom consultant must help teachers develop a basic set of guidelines for exclusionary, seclusionary, and observational time-out.

As an in-classroom technique, Foxx and Shapiro (1978) developed the "time-out ribbon." The target child wears a ribbon or necklace in class. Every time a reinforcement is provided, the teacher pairs the reinforcement with a comment establishing the ribbon or necklace as something the child can wear when behaving appropriately and completing work. After doing this for at least a week, the ribbon or necklace is then removed for up to 5 minutes following misbehavior. The teacher informs the child of the misbehavior, describes the behavior, and removes the ribbon. The child is not allowed to participate in any classroom activities when the ribbon is off. The ribbon is then returned and the child is allowed to return to either work or other classroom activities. This procedure is then followed by differential attention. Immediately following the return of the ribbon, the teacher seeks something to positively reinforce the child for. This is the least restrictive time-out procedure and can be implemented immediately when a problem occurs. Although it neither involves escorting the child out of the classroom nor is significantly disruptive, it provides a clear signal to everyone else in the room that the child is timed-out. A disadvantage, however, is that this intervention can seldom be used effectively beyond second or third grade. Further a child may become increasingly agitated or resistant when the ribbon is removed. However, the ribbon, which must be established as a conditioned reinforcer, can be effective in reducing the negative attention the child receives from peers and the teacher for misbehavior. It provides the teacher with a specific set of guidelines to follow when faced with misbehavior.

Time-out has been used effectively in classroom situations for problems including noncompliance (Bean & Roberts, 1981; M. W. Roberts, 1982), tantrums (Nordquist, 1971), and aggression (LeBlanc, Busby, & Thomson, 1974). It is extremely effective in extinguishing misbehavior. However, consultants must persistently remind teachers to administer punishments, use established guidelines consistently, and pair time-out with positive reinforcement. There is probably more likelihood of abusing time-out than any other behavioral intervention. Before implementing time-out, teachers must define the types of behaviors that will be punished and make certain the child understands these. Time-out should be long enough to make an impact but brief enough to allow the child to return to the offending situation and demonstrate compliance. The child should not be out of the room or away from activities for so long that important classroom information is missed. Suggested time-out usually involves a few minutes for younger children and up to 15 minutes for adolescents (H. B. Clark, Rowbury, Baer, & Baer, 1973; H. M. Walker & Walker, 1991).

Hobbs, Forehand, and Murray (1978) found that length of time-out is critical to its effectiveness. A 4-minute time-out was found to be significantly better than a 10-second or 1-minute time-out among a group of elementary school children. As D. P. Morgan and Jenson (1988) note, long periods of time-out constitute seclusion and lose their punishing value. Contingent release from time-out (e.g., behaving appropriately to get out of time-out) resulted in fewer noncompliant responses to commands than noncontingent release (Hobbs & Forehand, 1975). This latter issue is important for consultants. Teachers must not only define what types of behaviors result in time-out but what types of behaviors the child must exhibit for the time-out to be ended. It is therefore suggested that release from time-out should be contingent on a specific period of time in which a specific behavior or set of behaviors is exhibited (G. R. Patterson & White, 1970).

If a particular activity the child is leaving is nonreinforcing, this child may in fact learn to misbehave as a means of going to time-out to do something more reinforcing. Work should not be missed due to time-out. Time-out must be boring, uninteresting, and something the child places last on the list of chosen school activities. Some children, especially those with internalizing or emotional problems, may learn actively to seek time-out because it allows them to withdraw from others. Such children may withdraw to fantasy, daydreaming, or self-stimulatory behaviors. The majority of time-out procedures should allow children to remain in the classroom. Children who repeatedly must be removed from the room for time-out, likely require placement in classrooms with specially trained teachers. One means of avoiding too much time-out is for teachers to place a limit on the number of time-outs per day. If the number is exceeded during the day, the entire class may lose a privilege for activity. Thus, limiting the number of time-outs becomes a group contingency.

Time-out must be contingent on the exhibition of the target behavior, and the student must perceive a clear difference between the time-in and time-out environments (Cuenin & Harris, 1986). M. K. Zabel (1986) found that 70% of teachers working with behaviorally disordered students used some form of time-out on a regular basis. Teachers of younger children use time-out more frequently than teachers of older children.

The effectiveness of time-out depends on a number of factors—the individual child, the teacher's ability to apply the intervention consistently, the child's understanding of the intervention, the rules governing the intervention, characteristics of the time-out area, duration of time-out, and the ability to evaluate the effectiveness of time-out on a short-term basis (Cuenin & Harris, 1986). Teachers must learn to stop applying time-out when it does not lead to behavioral change. Teachers must also be careful to enforce time-out consistently and make certain the child understands the rules. If the child does not understand what is expected in time-out, then lack of appropriate behavior may be interpreted as purposeful noncompliance.

Scarboro and Forehand (1975) suggest eight parameters for effective time-out:

1. An explanation to the child before time-out is administered.
2. A warning that time-out may come (a one-warning system).
3. Consistent removal and placement in time-out.
4. A specific location for time-out.
5. A specific duration of time-out.
6. A consistent schedule for time-out use.
7. A defined behavior leading to time-out.
8. Contingent versus noncontingent release from time-out.

Time-out is effective in a regular classroom, especially for very disruptive situations, because it restores order by removing the disrupter, reduces the opportunity for peer approval that maintains some disrupters, reduces the opportunity for students to manipulate situations, affords the student the opportunity to gain self-control, and may allow the student to demonstrate appropriate behavior before exiting time-out (D. A. Sabatino, 1983). D. P. Morgan and Jenson (1988) provide an excellent overview of guidelines for effectively using time-out in a classroom situation (see Table 11.5).

Tables 11.6 and 11.7 offer a set of procedures for using seclusionary time-out and in-school suspension (Rhode et al., 1992).

H. M. Walker and Walker (1991) suggest that time-out in the classroom should be from 2 to 5 minutes; only the last 15 seconds needs to be quiet and controlled for the child to exit time-out. If the student is not in control, an additional minute is added. Time-out within the room has been found to be just as effective as out-of-room time-out (Scarboro & Forehand, 1975). Teachers should not force resistant students into time-out but should seek help from the principal. Finally, as soon as possible after time-out is over, something positive in the student's behavior should be reinforced. To increase the likelihood that students will work to avoid time-out, consultants must help teachers:

Table 11.5   The dos and don'ts of time-out

1. Do explain the total procedure to the child before starting time-out.
   Don't start the procedure without explaining time-out to the child first in a calm setting that is not emotionally charged.
2. Do prepare a time-out setting for the child that is clean, well lighted, and ventilated.
   Don't just pick anyplace. Make sure that it isn't dark, too confining, dangerous, or not ventilated.
3. Do pick a place or situation for time-out that is boring or less reinforcing than the classroom activity.
   Don't pick a place that is scary or that could be more reinforcing than the classroom (e.g., sitting in the hall).
4. Do use a set of structured verbal requests with a child, such as the recommended precision request format.
   Don't threaten a child repeatedly with time-out.
5. Do remain calm, and don't talk with a child when he or she is being taken to time-out.
   Don't get into a verbal exchange with a child on the way to time-out or while in time-out.
6. Do place a child in time-out for a set period of time that you control.
   Don't tell a child to come out of time-out when "you are ready to behave."
7. Do require the child to be quiet for 30 seconds at the end of the time-out period, before being let out.
   Don't let a child out of time-out while crying, screaming, yelling, or tantrumming.
8. Do use a short period for time out, such as 5 or 10 minutes.
   Don't use exceedingly long periods.
9. Do require the child to complete the request that led to time-out or missed academic work.
   Don't allow a child to avoid compliance to a request or miss academic work by going to time-out.

Source: *Teaching Behaviorally Disordered Students: Preferred Practices*, by Daniel P. Morgan and William R. Jenson, 1988, New York: Macmillan. Copyright © 1988 by Merrill Publishing Co. Reprinted with the permission of Merrill, an imprint of Macmillan Publishing Co.

- Make certain that classroom activities are more reinforcing than time-out (e.g., do not offer a time-out to the principal's office).
- Give students ample but not excessive opportunities to comply.
- Utilize a reasonable but not excessive period of time-out.
- With very disruptive students, give additional rewards for not having to go to time-out over a given time span.

Table 11.6   Seclusionary time-out procedures

1. Seclusionary time-out should not be used unless all other procedures have been tried and failed. This should be a last effort technique.
2. Seclusionary time-out should never be used without a parent's written consent.
3. Seclusionary time-out should be used only if it is listed as an approved and agreed-on technique in a student's Individualized Education Plan (IEP) by the IEP Team. The student should only be placed in time-out for approved behaviors on the IEP such as aggression, severe noncompliance, or destructive tantrum throwing.
4. Seclusionary time-out is defined as removing a student from a reinforcing classroom setting to a less reinforcing setting. This setting can be another classroom, a chair or desk outside the classroom, or a room specifically approved for time-out. If a room is used for time-out, it should be used only for time-out and no other purpose (e.g., storage, counseling students, or a special academic work area).
5. The time-out setting should be well lighted, well ventilated, non-threatening, and clean. It must also have an observation window or device. The staff member should try the technique on himself/herself before using the room with a student, and the room should be shown to the student's parent(s).
6. The entire time-out procedure should be explained to the student before it is implemented, prior to the occurrence of misbehavior that will result in its use.
7. If misbehavior occurs, identify it. For example, tell the student in a calm, neutral manner, "That's fighting: you need to go to the time-out room." Tell the student to remove his/her jewelry, belt, and shoes. Tell the student to empty his/her pockets (in order to check for such items as pens, pencils, paper clips, knives, etc.). The student's socks should be checked for these types of items also. If the student does not comply with these requests, call for help and then remove the items and check the pockets yourself. No other conversation should ensue.
8. When a student is placed in time-out room, he/she must be constantly monitored by a staff member. The student must never be left alone.
9. When a student is placed in the time-out room, the following information should be placed in a time-out log:
   a. Name of the student.
   b. Date.
   c. Staff member responsible for monitoring student.
   d. Time in and time out.
   e. Target behavior warranting the procedure.
10. The student should be placed in the time-out room for a specific period of time. A recommended formula is one minute per year of age (e.g., 10-year-old student × 1 minute = 10 minutes).
11. If a student is screaming, throwing a tantrum, or yelling, he/she should be quiet (i.e., quiet for 30 consecutives seconds) before being released

(continued)

Table 11.6 (*Continued*)

from the time-out room. This 30 seconds does not begin until the one-minute per year of age time period has elapsed.

12. Communication between the supervising staff member and the student should not take place when the student is in the time-out room (i.e., do not talk with the student, threaten the student, or try to counsel the student at this time).

13. Do remain calm while taking a student to the time-out room. Do not argue with, threaten, or verbally reprimand the student.

14. If a student refuses to go to the time-out room, add on time to the specified time-out duration (e.g., one minute for each refusal, up to 5 minutes).

15. If a student refuses to come out of the time-out room, do not beg or try to remove the student. Simply wait outside, and sooner or later the student will come out on his/her own.

16. If the student makes a mess in the time-out room, require him/her to clean it up before he/she leaves.

17. Once the time-out period has ended, return the student to the ongoing classroom activity, making sure the student is required to complete the task he/she was engaged in prior to the time-out period. This will ensure that students do not purposely avoid unpleasant tasks by gong to the time-out room.

18. All staff members should be trained, and this training documented before time-out procedures are started.

19. To ensure the effectiveness of time-out, the reinforcement rate for appropriate behaviors should decrease shortly after the technique is started. If they do not, check that the procedure is being used correctly and the reinforcement rate for appropriate behaviors in the classroom should meet the recommended rate of three to four positives to each negative (and never below four positives per contact hour).

20. Data should be collected on target behaviors. If time-out is effective, these behaviors should decrease shortly after the technique is started. If they do not, check that the procedures are being used correctly and the reinforcement rate for appropriate behavior in the classroom is high enough; and consider another technique for possible use.

21. The use of time-out should not be threatened ("If you do that again, I will put you in the time-out room."). Rather, the technique should be combined with a precision request, such as, "I need you to stop . . ." If the student persists, the time-out procedure should be used, and when the student comes out of the time-out room, the precision request should be restated ("I need you to . . .").

22. The student should be reinforced for not needing time-out.

Source: The Tough Kid Book: Practical Classroom Management Strategies, by G. Rhode, W. R. Jenson, and H. K. Reavis, 1992, Longmont, CO: Sopris West. Reprinted with permission of the authors and publisher.

Table 11.7   In-school suspension procedures

In-school suspension is an alternative to out-of-school suspension (being sent home). It should be reserved for very difficult target behaviors (e.g., fighting, teacher defiance, arguing, property destruction, and repeated truancy or tardiness).

1. Decide on a physical place for in-school suspension (e.g., another classroom, desk space in an office, or a carrel).
2. In-school suspension should always occur under the direct observation of a staff member. If students cannot be constantly supervised, in-school suspension should not be used.
3. Time lengths for in-school suspension will usually not exceed several hours to a day. In-school suspension lengths of more than one day are not advisable.
4. When students warrant in-school suspension, they should be placed in it immediately. No waiting lists should exist for in-school suspension.
5. In-school suspension should have rules, including:
   a. No talking to other students.
   b. No sleeping.
   c. Stay in your seat.
   d. Work on your school assignments.
6. Students should be given academic assignments to work on during in-school suspension. This work can be actual classroom work or extra assigned work.
7. If a student refuses to go to in-school suspension or shows up late, the time period can be expanded. For example, a student who refuses to go to in-school suspension should have his/her time increased from two hours to half a day, to three quarters of a day, or to a full day. If the student still refuses, the student's parent(s) should be called.
8. Before in-school suspension is started, the student's parent(s) should be informed and consent given whenever possible.

Source: The Tough Kid Book: Practical Classroom Management Strategies, by G. Rhode, W. R. Jenson, and H. K. Reavis, 1992, Longmont, CO: Sopris West. Reprinted with permission of the authors and publisher.

Increased compliance has been strongly associated with the use of time-out contingency in a group of preschool children (M. W. Roberts, Hatzenbuehler, & Bean, 1981). These authors evaluated the impact of attention, time-out, and attention plus time-out or control on noncompliant childhood behaviors. Interestingly, manipulation of attention did not have a measurable effect on behavior. The absence of a time-out contingency was associated with a decrease in compliance ration. Although differential attention was effective, the time-out component of the intervention likely leads to the significant change. Further, praising positive behavior was found to be effective, but in and of itself inadequate to modify the behavior of this group of noncompliant children. These authors suggest that compliance acquisition in children who are noncompliant appears to reflect avoidance learning. Previously ineffective commands are now followed by the child to avoid time-out. These data strongly suggest that training teachers to attend to positive behavior and ignore negative behavior as a primary intervention in children who are repeatedly noncompliant will likely not prove to be very effective intervention.

Gresham (1979) compared response cost and time-out to determine the effectiveness of each in reducing noncompliance in a classroom of intellectually handicapped children. The response cost procedure consisted of removing tokens contingent on noncompliance with teacher commands. Time-out involved placing the noncompliant child outside the group for 1 minute for each offense. Response cost was found to be as effective as the response cost plus time-out contingency. It appeared to be the response cost that reduced the noncompliant behavior. This author suggests that response cost offers an excellent substitute for time-out.

Overcorrection

Technically, overcorrection is considered a punishing technique. It is designed to reduce the likelihood that the behavior that it follows will recur. There are two types of overcorrection. The first type involves restitution. The child must make right what has been disrupted. If something is broken, it must be repaired. If desks are turned over during a tantrum, they must be straightened. Usually the overcorrection procedure requires the child not only to right what has been wronged but to go beyond that and correct other related elements of the environment as well. Thus the desks not only have to be straightened but chairs and remaining furniture in the room must also be straightened and cleaned up. This model of punishment, therefore, contains an instructional component. It not only decreases unwanted behavior but increases the occurrence of desirable behavior.

Positive practice is the second type of overcorrection. In this procedure, which is more widely recognized by teachers, the child must practice the appropriate competing behavior: A child who teases must compliment others; a child who forgets to flush the toilet must practice entering the bathroom, going through the procedure of toileting, and then flushing the toilet a number of times. Repetition helps actions become automatic and more likely to occur in the next, similar situation. In classroom settings, overcorrection has been demonstrated as effective for everything from out-of-seat and talking-out behavior (Azrin & Powers, 1975) to increasing sharing and reducing selfishness in kindergartners (Barton & Osborne, 1978).

Foxx and Azrin (1972) suggest that in effective overcorrection, the practiced behavior is closely related to the misbehavior. The procedure should follow the misbehavior immediately, the child should perceive the repeated behavior as work and not as play. Further, the behavior should be repeated without pause, and distractors in the environment such as peer attention should be kept to a minimum. Thus, the child is also timed-out during the overcorrection procedure.

A positive practice overcorrection procedure was used with a group of 7- to 11-year-old boys with academic and behavioral classroom problems (Azrin & Powers, 1975). Targeted behaviors included those that were most aversive in the summer school setting such as talking out and being out of seat. In this four-phase study, teachers first repeatedly provided warnings, reminders, and reinforcements for appropriate behavior. During the second phase, children lost 10 minutes of recess for getting out of their seats or talking out in class. In the third stage, delayed positive practice was offered, in which after losing recess, the child had to practice asking permission by raising his hand and asking to speak or get out of his seat. If more than one student had to stay in and practice, all had to demonstrate compliance before the entire group was then allowed to go to recess. Finally, during the fourth stage of immediate positive practice, the student was required to practice (one trial) by asking permission immediately after breaking the rule. The delayed positive practice procedure was also maintained during this phase. The warning reminders and reinforcement procedures had little impact on classroom functioning. Once the loss of recess was introduced, out-of-seat and talking-out behavior reduced dramatically but still occurred an average of 10 times per student per day. When the delayed positive practice procedure was implemented, outbursts dropped to 2 or 3 per student per day. When the immediate positive practice procedure was implemented outbursts dropped to zero per student per day. Thus, an immediate, positive practice procedure appears to be a very effective classroom intervention. As with any punishing intervention, however, teachers need to be careful to not overuse or abuse it. Such an intervention must also be paired with as much positive reinforcement as possible. Children must be compliant and willing to follow instructions from an adult for the overcorrection procedure to work. Thus, classroom consultants can feel comfortable suggesting this intervention for most regular education students because of their history of compliance with adult requests.

There are three additional important issues to consider when using punishment in the classroom:

1. *Timing:* The punishing procedure should be initiated as soon as possible after the aversive behavior is exhibited and should be as closely related to the misbehavior as possible (Parke & Walters, 1967).

2. *Intensity:* If punishments are too mild, they will not be effective, and they may slowly habituate the child to tolerate or adapt to more intensive or lengthy punishments. If too intense, punishments are not only abusive but likely create other problems. As D. P. Morgan and Jenson (1988) note, "The size of a fine and response cost, the duration of time-out, or the number of repeated behaviors in overcorrection can be estimated on the basis of what has been published in the literature" (p. 137). Teachers need to be conservative in using punishing techniques. The least restrictive yet effective punishment is the best. The person delivering punishment should be someone with whom the child has a positive attachment. Students will respond better to a person they like than to someone who seems uncaring and unfair (McMillan, Forness, & Trumbul, 1973).

3. *Consistency:* To be effective, punishments must be consistent and predictable. Following punishment, the teacher should return the child to the situation without showing overt guilt or making efforts to reassure or reinforce the child. Such actions only reduce the long-term effectiveness of punishment by teaching the child that one way of gaining support and empathy from adults is to misbehave and be punished (Parke, 1977). A consistent schedule of punishments should also be used. A continuous schedule of punishment for a specific frequently occurring behavior is best (Walters & Grusec, 1977). Teachers must also try to find out what drives the misbehavior and work toward managing the environment to minimize causative factors. This approach will reduce the need for punishment in the future. By identifying the child's goal in misbehavior, teachers can present more appropriate opportunities to reach that goal.

When used appropriately, punishment can make a positive difference. When used inappropriately, it can be abusive, and can lead to withdrawal, anxiety, anger, frustration, and further misbehavior. Appropriate punishment does not appear to hold many negative side effects (H. M. Walker & Walker, 1991). In fact, it can lead to improved social behavior, calmness, affection, social play, and generally improved interaction in a classroom environment (Newsom, Favell, & Rincover, 1983). Thus, as Walters and Grusec (1977) note, responsible and appropriate punishment can teach acceptable behavior.

Alternatives to Punishment

Alternatives to punishment include extinction, satiation, and differential reinforcement. Extinction has been described as the discontinuation or withholding of the reinforcer for behavior that has previously been reinforced (R. V. Hall & Hall, 1980). Extinction involves the removal of a reinforcer that is sustaining or increasing behavior (Alberto & Troutman, 1986). Extinction must be applied consistently, and the student must have opportunities to be reinforced for exhibiting appropriate behaviors. However, teachers need to recognize that most children will exhibit an extinction burst of behavior during which the target behavior will get worse as the teacher attempts to ignore it. Teachers who respond to this burst will only reinforce the target behavior. Extinction can be an effective classroom strategy but it is critical for teachers to recognize that even one response out of many occurrences will reinstate the misbehavior—frequency at a higher level than if extinction had not been attempted (Bandura, 1969).

Madsen, Becker, and Thomas (1968) suggest that extinction, combined with differential reinforcement, can eliminate oppositional tactics such as negative behaviors, irrelevant verbalizations, conversing with others, whistling, coughing, talking out, and getting out of seat. Extinction through ignoring works best when reward of attention is provided for appropriate behavior. Table 11.8 provides cautionary guidelines for use of extinction.

Extinction is most effective when teachers can easily identify and withdraw inappropriate behavioral rewards and alternative competing behaviors are available for the student. Most importantly, the teacher's ability consistently to ignore the extinction burst appears to be central for success.

Differential reinforcement procedures include the following:

- *Differential Reinforcement of Low Rates of Behavior (DRL):* In this procedure, children receive varying amounts of reinforcers

Table 11.8   Cautions and guidelines for extinction procedures

Caution	Guidelines
Not always economical or effective used alone	Combine extinction with other methods, especially the rewarding of incompatible behaviors.
Old habits can recur	Lay problem to rest again through an additional extinction series.
Occasional reward	Be consistent. Make sure you are not the reinforcing agent.
Inability to ignore unwanted behavior	Combine extinction with other methods such as reward of competing responses and punishment.
Peer-rewarded behavior	Enlist support of peer group.
Self-reinforcing behavior	Combine extinction with other methods such as reward of competing responses and punishment.
Intense misbehavior	Some form of punishment may be the method of choice.
Original misbehavior increases	Expect this initial rise. Continue to apply extinction procedures systematically.
New misbehaviors sometimes emerge	Combine extinction procedures with other methods that foster desired behavior (social modeling, reward).

Source: Toward Positive Classroom Discipline, second edition, by Harvey F. Clarizio, 1976, New York: Wiley. Copyright ©1976 by John Wiley & Sons, Inc. Reprinted with permission.

contingent on the appropriateness of their behavior. Thus a full contingent of points may be earned for meeting the target behavior goal, three quarters of the points for having two problems, half of the points for three problems, and so on (Bolstead & Johnson, 1972). This procedure works best with high-rate behaviors that can be reduced gradually.

- *Differential Reinforcement of an Incompatible Behavior (DRI)*: This procedure reinforces behavior that is incompatible with the inappropriate behavior. Thus, students receive reinforcement for sitting in their seats, which makes it incompatible with being out of seats, or for being quiet in line, which is incompatible with being disruptive in line. This reinforcement pattern is quite effective in reducing aggressive behavior and improving in-seat behavior (Madsen et al., 1968; Twardosz & Sajwaj, 1972).

• *Differential Reinforcement of Zero Rates of Behavior (DRO):* In this procedure, the child is reinforced if during a specific interval the aversive or inappropriate behavior does not occur.

Satiation allows students to exhibit the target behavior until they grow tired of it, resulting in reduced interest and occurrence for the behavior. Although this is an effective alternative to punishment in many situations, it is often difficult for teachers to use for most classroom behaviors.

When ignoring is not paired with attention or the exhibition of appropriate behavior, it has not proved to be an effective intervention for children (Scarboro & Forehand, 1975). Forehand and McMahon (1981) provide a set of guidelines for using ignoring at home that can also be applied in the classroom (see Table 11.9).

One of the best ways of avoiding punishing interventions is to make tasks interesting and the payoffs for completing those tasks valuable to every student (Zentall & Dwyer, 1988). Further, having a proactive management plan to deal with classroom problems minimizes the need for punishing interventions (Paine et al., 1983).

Generalization

Generalization is a process for the transfer of learning (Morris, 1985). In this process, a behavior that has been reinforced in the presence of one stimulus or in one situation is exhibited in the presence of another stimulus or situation. Generalization is essential to learning; for example, children learn mathematics in one setting but must demonstrate their competence in other settings. Generalization means using newly acquired behavior in situations other than that in which it was originally taught, reinforced, or implemented. Although generalization often occurs incidentally (Stokes & Baer, 1977), in classroom settings, it usually does not occur automatically (Vaughn, Bos, & Lund, 1986) but instead must be planned and programmed as part of the educational process. Generalization is a two-stage process (H. M. Walker, 1979): In the first stage, the child learns a new behavior; in the second stage, the teacher implements a set of procedures to ensure that the child retains the behavior over a long term and generalizes it to other settings. Some studies have suggested that generalization can occur spontaneously (Bornstein & Quevillon, 1976), but in all likelihood, some degree of structure or monitoring is essential for generalization.

Table 11.9   Guidelines for ignoring

1. *No eye contact or nonverbal cues:* Unfortunately, often when a child is engaging in behaviors the parent would like to eliminate, it is very difficult to ignore the activity. The child may anger the parent, or may even be rather cute. Whatever the reason, parents often reinforce this inappropriate behavior inadvertently by a brief smile, a frown, or even a glance at the child. For this reason, we instruct the parent to turn at least 90 degrees (and preferably 180 degrees) away from the child. The child will then be less likely to notice any inadvertent facial responses that might reinforce inappropriate behavior.

2. *No verbal contact:* The parent is instructed to refrain from any verbal contact with the child while the child is engaging in the inappropriate behavior. This usually presents a problem to the parent in at least two forms. The first has to do with whether the parent should provide a rationale or explanation to the child for ignoring him or her. This is compounded by the frequent occurrence of the child asking the parent why he or she is being ignored. It is imperative that the parent not maintain *any* verbal contact with the child once the ignoring procedure has started. The appropriate time to provide a rationale for ignoring is when the child is behavior appropriately. Verbal contact at any other time is simply reinforcing the child's inappropriate behavior. We usually have the parent explain the ignoring procedure to the child in the session after the therapist has modeled the procedure for the parent and the parent has role-played with the therapist. The sophistication of the explanation varies depending upon the age of the child but generally consists of a verbal statement such as, "Billy, I am going to ignore you when you're bad. That means I am going to turn around and not say anything to you. As soon as you stop being bad, I will stop ignoring you." The parent then demonstrates the ignoring technique to the child.

3. *No physical contact:* The child will often attempt to initiate physical contact with the parent once the parent has started to ignore. The child may tug on the parent, attempt to sit in the parent's lap, or, in rare instances, become aggressive. It is a good idea to have the parent stand when ignoring the child. This prevents the occurrence of lap-sitting, and it also provides a discriminative cue to the child that the parent is ignoring as opposed to simply being engrossed in some other activity. We also tell parents that in more severe cases they may find it necessary to leave the room in order to avoid reinforcing the child's inappropriate behavior. This "TO procedure in reverse" is useful, but it does have a serious shortcoming: the parent may not be aware that the inappropriate behavior has ceased if she or he is in another room. Since it is important that ignoring be terminated concurrently with the cessation of the child's inappropriate behavior, this solution is not the most desirable one.

Source: Helping the Noncompliant Child, by R. L. Forehand and R. J. McMahon, 1981, New York: Guilford Press. Reprinted with permission of the author and Guilford Press.

Rosenbaum and Drabman (1979) suggest that the majority of studies evaluating generalization deal with time generalization, in which behavioral changes occurring in the therapeutic or experimental setting endure in that setting when contingencies have been removed. Setting generalization, however, is usually of greatest concern and interest to the classroom teacher. Setting generalization occurs when changes in target behavior in one setting transfer and are demonstrated in a different setting without additional contingencies. A third type, response generalization—which also needs further investigation—reflects changes in non-target behaviors observed during intervention. When helping teachers to promote generalization, the classroom consultant must keep all three types in mind: time, setting, and response generalization. Because generalization usually will not occur by chance or luck, it must be planned for as part of the behavior change process (J. O. Cooper et al., 1987).

Stokes and Baer (1977) refer to the most common type of generalization used in school settings as the "train-and-hope" approach. A child may be trained in a certain social skill or behavior and then sent back to the classroom with the hope that it will generalize. This method is rarely successful.

To facilitate generalization, it is suggested that teachers use natural contingencies that commonly occur in the environment as a consequence of behavior (Baer, 1981). Including additional examples, reinforcing generalization, and planning effectively for it all increase the likelihood that generalization will occur. Vaughn et al. (1986) recommend the following techniques for consultants attempting to help teachers promote generalization:

- Reinforcers should be varied in their amount, power, and type. They should be faded from tangible to social reinforcers.
- Similar reinforcers should be used in different settings.
- Instructions should be varied to help the child become accustomed to dealing with different adults.
- The medium or medium material used for the task should be varied.
- Response mode of the student can be varied.
- The stimulus materials provided should be varied.
- Instructional settings should be varied from one location to another or from the individual to the small group.

Kazdin (1975b) describes seven specific ways teachers can strengthen new behaviors as they occur. This model can be used to promote generalization as well:

1. Efforts should be made to substitute intrinsic, naturally occurring rewards for the tangible or social rewards initially offered. Thus a naturally occurring reward system in the environment replaces the externally imposed reward system.
2. Other adults interacting with a student should be trained in the system and provide positive reinforcement when appropriate behavior occurs.
3. Rewards should be removed gradually.
4. Conditions for training should be varied, including different settings with different adults.
5. Reinforcement schedules should not be changed too abruptly.
6. A gradual increase in delay between reinforcement and the desired behavior should be introduced.
7. Efforts should be made to increase self-control and reinforce students for self-management.

Involving the entire class can also be helpful in promoting generalization. H. M. Walker and Buckley (1972) encouraged the regular classroom peer group to support a target student's efforts to behave and to ignore disruptive behavior. The target student earned points for appropriate social and academic behavior. The strategy worked effectively in providing an atmosphere for the target student to exhibit appropriate behaviors. Teachers must also be careful to promote generalization with multiple examples. Baer (1981) points out that the most common mistake teachers make is to assume that the child should be able to generalize behavior from a single example. Even with a good example, generalization usually does not occur from a single exposure. To maximize the chances of generalization, teachers must demonstrate the desired behavior in a variety of settings, under a variety of conditions, with a variety of models.

Ayllon, Kuhlman, and Warzak (1983) introduced the "lucky charm" to promote generalization from a resource setting to a regular classroom. In the resource room, students were urged to identify lucky charms (e.g., small family photos or trinkets) that they could take with them into the regular classroom to remind them that their desk is a place to work. Thus, these items became specific discriminative stimuli for each child. When students were instructed to take their lucky charms to class, classroom performance increased dramatically. Transferred academic skills and on-task behavior were enhanced. Perhaps the charms reminded students about the need to work. Also, because teachers were urged to be positive in regular setting about the potential benefits of these charms, there may have been a carryover, placebo effect.

In promoting generalization, teachers need to consider environmental stimuli (class size, desk arrangement, teacher's desk location, windows), instructional materials (workbooks, games, puzzles, paper), instructional procedures (posters, tapes, bulletin boards, chalkboards), teacher behaviors (class rules, routines, reinforcers, schedule of reinforcers, common and shared goals) and instructional format (large group, small group, individual students at desk, students at work activity centers, verbal instructions, visual instructions, multisensory instructions, method to evaluate work, time allowed to complete work, use of cues or prompts). Teachers who are active change agents and believe in what they are doing will promote generalization much more successfully. Finally, if teachers do not carefully plan, monitor, and evaluate their success with generalization, there is an increased risk that behavioral changes will not be maintained over time.

Group Contingency Consequences

Group contingency consequences can be useful when more than one student demonstrates an inappropriate behavior. This procedure eliminated the inappropriate waving of the middle finger in the air by certain students in a classroom (Sulzbacher & Houser, 1968). Ten cards numbered 1 through 10 were placed in the front of the classroom where they were visible to everyone. The students were allowed to earn 10 minutes of additional recess by not exhibiting the inappropriate physical behavior. If the behavior was seen or talked about, the teacher would flip over one of the cards and students would lose 1 minute of the extra recess. Such group procedures work very well to reinforce appropriate target behaviors and make everyone interested in how all members of the class behave. This differential reinforcement of low rates of behavior procedure can be quite effective in promoting generalization as well.

Contingency Contracting

Contingency contracting is based on the Premack Principle. In reviewing school-based contingency contracting studies, Murphy (1988) reported that contingency contracting has been used to increase academic productivity, study skills, attendance, social behavior, and accuracy of work completion. Contracting is a positive method that allows the child to play an active role in the change process. In fact, Salend (1987) reported that contingency contracting works best when students are actively involved in all processes involved with the contract. Students can help by:

- Selecting a target behavior.
- Understanding how their present behavior is to be modified and altered.
- Choosing their own reinforcers.
- Writing and reviewing the contract or contributing to writing the contract.
- Being allowed to evaluate performance. In this situation, the teacher serves as a contract manager rather than a contract enforcer.

R. V. Hall and Hall (1982) suggest that contingency contracting is effective because the learner is allowed to make decisions about personal productivity, critical thinking, and self-control. Contracts in school are usually verbal. Teachers usually do not have time to write contracts with every student. Nonetheless, a written contract, especially for important target behaviors, is recommended. Contracts can reward successive approximations of behavior, utilizing a variety of differential reinforcement schedules. They should fit the effort required, initially provide reinforcement on a fairly short-term basis, and gradually work toward the longer term.

Homme, Casanyi, Gonzales, and Rechs (1979) provide 10 basic rules to help teachers develop effective classroom contracts:

1. Rewards should be immediate.
2. Contracts should initially reinforce approximations of target behavior.
3. Contracts should provide frequent small reinforcers.
4. Contracts should reinforce accomplishment rather than just obedience.
5. Performance should be reinforced immediately after it occurs.
6. The contract should be fair to both student and teacher.
7. All parties must understand the terms of the contract.
8. The contract must be honest.
9. The contract should be worded positively.
10. Contracting should be used as an ongoing part of classroom management rather than a one-time phenomenon or intervention.

J. E. Walker and Shea (1991) suggest the contract should be negotiated freely and agreed on by all parties. Their suggestions appear in Table 11.10.

Table 11.10 Negotiating teacher-student contracts

Negotiation should be systematic and precise. The teacher, as manager, has an obligation to ensure that the session is productive. It is recommended that the new practitioner use the following negotiation procedure (Shea et al., 1974):

1. Teacher establishes and maintains rapport with the child.
2. Teacher explains the purpose of the meeting by saying something such as, "I know you've been working hard on your schoolwork (reading, writing, spelling, arithmetic), and I'd like to help you."
3. Teacher gives a simple definition of a contract, explaining that a contract is an agreement between two people.
   a. Teacher gives an example of a contract such as: "When your mother takes your TV to the repair shop, the clerk gives her a ticket. The ticket is a contract between your mother and the repairman. He will repair and return the TV, and your mother will pay him."
   b. Teacher asks the child to give an example of a contract.
   c. If child cannot respond, the teacher gives another example and repeats 3b.
4. Teacher explains to the child that they are going to write a contract.
5. Teacher and child discuss tasks.
   a. Child suggests tasks for the contract.
   b. Teacher suggests tasks for the contract.
   c. Child and teacher discuss and agree on the specific task.
6. Teacher and child discuss reinforcers.
   a. Teacher asks the child which activities the child enjoys doing and which things he or she likes. The teacher may also suggest reinforcers.
   b. Teacher writes a reinforcer menu of child-suggested reinforcers.
   c. Child selects reinforcers for which he or she would like to work.
7. Teacher and child negotiate the ratio of task to reinforcer.
8. Teacher and child agree on the time to be allotted for the child to perform the task: for example, the child works 10 additional problems in 15 minutes to receive the reinforcer, or the child completes a unit of science and does the laboratory experiments in 2 weeks to receive an A.
9. Teacher and child identify the criteria for achievement; that is, the child will work the 10 addition problems in 15 minutes with at least 80% accuracy.
10. Teacher and child discuss evaluation procedures.
    a. Teacher discusses various types of evaluations with the child.
    b. Teacher and child agree on a method of evaluation.
    c. Teacher asks the child to explain the method of evaluation. If the child appears confused, the teacher clarifies the evaluation procedure.

(continued)

Table 11.10   (Continued)

11. Teacher and child negotiate delivery of the reinforcer.
12. Teacher and child agree on a date for renegotiation of the contract.
13. Teacher or child writes the contract. If feasible, the child should be encouraged to write it. Teacher gives a copy of the contract to the child.
14. Teacher reads the contract to the child as the child follows on his or her own copy.
15. Teacher elicits the child's verbal affirmation to the contract terms and gives affirmation.
16. Child and teacher sign the contract.
17. Teacher congratulates the child for making the contract and wishes the child success.

Source: Behavior Management: A Practical Approach for Educators, fifth edition, by James E. Walker and Thomas M. Shea, 1991, New York: Macmillan. Copyright © 1991 by Macmillan Publishing Company. Reprinted with permission of Macmillan Publishing Co.

Target achievement and production levels should be noted and the contract should include the date for review and renegotiation. Shae, Whiteside, Beetner, and Lindsey (1974) provide an in-depth outline for teachers to use in negotiating contracts with students.

To be effective, contracts must offer rewards that are attractive and not obtainable outside the conditions of the contract (Homme, 1969). In a manager-controlled contract, the manager or teacher determines the reward, establishes the amount of task to be accomplished, presents the contact to the student, and delivers the rewards. In self-contracting, the student determines the amount of the task and reward. Most often in the classroom, cooperative contracting is used in which the student and teacher jointly decide on the amount of reinforcement and the magnitude of the task (Homme, 1969). Clarizio (1976) offers additional guidelines for establishing an effective contract (see Table 11.11). DeRisi and Butz (1975) suggest the following basic components of a behavioral contract:

- Date the program begins, ends, or can be renegotiated
- Behaviors targeted for change and how they are measured
- The amount of reward or reinforcer to be used
- Schedule of delivery reinforcers
- Everyone's signature
- A schedule for review

Table 11.11   Guidelines for contracting

The following suggestions should aid in the writing and negotiation of contracts:

1. How one negotiates the contract is particularly important. Whenever possible, contracts should be introduced on a positive note. Some contacts arise from class discussions in which the group commits itself to a given course of action. Other contracts grow out of formal case conferences in which all interested parties participate. Still other contracts are negotiated on the basis of the student's desire for greater *self-direction* ("There's a way that you can be more than your own man"), *self-improvement* ("I know a way by which you can use your head instead of your temper"), *enjoyment* ("We can probably work out an arrangement so that school is more fun and yet allow you to get your work done"), or *desire to escape from unpleasantries* ("We can probably set up a plan to stay out of trouble so that your teachers and parents don't scream at you or bug you as much"). The author is reminded by one junior high school student who would do just about everything his teacher asked if he did not have to see the assistant principal any more for "counseling sessions." *Appealing to the student's values* is another tactic ("This will give you a chance to be a man"). Whatever tactic is used, it is important that the compromise entail no loss of face for those involved.
2. Timing appears to be a crucial factor in determining the success of contracting. People are better motivated to compromise and to make commitments to problem solutions at times of stress or conflict, that is, when their behavior produces discomfort or pain for them.
3. The contract should make explicit the responsibilities of each party involved and who will record whether the responsibilities are fulfilled. Try to state the responsibilities in a positive way so as to avoid making this a restrictive approach. Also, select, if possible, a mediator (teacher, counselor, classmate) who is in frequent contact with the student, who is looked up to by the student, and who is consistent and dependable (DeRisi & Butz, 1975).
4. The amount and kind of privileges or rewards or to be earned must be specified. Also, state when the rewards will be given.
5. Do no put rewards that were once free on a contingency basis for this is often perceived as a punitive gesture. For example, one teacher who had allowed a smart-aleck student to visit with her in class before the start of the school day now made such visits contingent upon increased respect for the teacher.
6. It is often desirable to have a bonus clause to reinforce outstanding and/or persistent behavior.

(continued)

Table 11.11   (*Continued*)

7. If possible, write in a rule that eliminates reinforcement of the undesired behavior. For example, the teacher might have a rule stating, "we ignore clowning by others."
8. Penalties can also be built into the agreement. If written into the agreement at all, penalties should be kept to a minimum so as to avoid punitive overtones. Also, the total number of penalty points that a student can accumulate and still remain a member of the class should be specified (Williams & Anadam, 1973). Although penalties are necessary on occasion, "It is usually best to assign points for achieved behaviors and to withhold points for behaviors not achieved. Subtracting points is not desirable for it multiplies the punishment" (Hackney, 1974).
9. A provision allowing for renegotiation of the contract should also be included. Homme (1969) cautions that the contract should be revised when one or more of the following occurs:

   a. Incomplete assignments.
   b. Complaining.
   c. Excessive dawdling.
   d. Talking and wasting time.
   e. Excessive clock watching.
   f. Inattention to instructions or details.
   g. Failure to pass more than two progress checks in one subject area.

   Sometimes it is necessary to shorten the contract by deleting certain terms or by simplifying the required tasks. If this strategy fails, the teacher might suspect that the rewards are not sufficiently enticing. At times, it may be necessary to lengthen the contract by increasing the number of tasks or their difficulty. On these occasions, it may also be necessary to increase the amount of reward to make the harder assignments more worthwhile. It is important that the student be made to feel that he has achieved a new status, for example, "Jim, you've improved so much that you're now ready for the advanced material."
10. State the date that the agreement begins, ends, or is to be renegotiated.
11. Have all parties involved sign the agreement.

- Bonuses
- Penalties

Well-made contracts clearly establish what is expected between students and teachers; structure relationship on a regular basis; give students a voice in designing and modifying their behavior, thoughts, or self-direction; allow opportunities for negotiation; and can be used in group situations. DeRisi and Butz (1975) point out the following issues for teachers to trouble shoot if contracts are ineffective:

- Problems related to inadequate targeting of the behavior to be changed
- The failure to provide for small, frequent, and immediate enough reinforcement after initial changes are observed
- Contract terms that are not clear, fair, positive, systematically used, or mutually negotiated
- Penalties that are too punitive
- The student's failure to understand the agreement
- The student's ability to obtain rewards outside the contract
- The misgauging of a reinforcer's effectiveness
- Failure of the teacher to respond consistently to the contract
- Failure of the teacher to understand the contract
- Unavailability of the teacher to dispense the reinforcement when it is needed
- Association of punishment with the behavior being reinforced
- A data collection process for managing the contract that is too cumbersome for the classroom teacher to use effectively

Teachers must learn to troubleshoot contracts making sure that students understand the definition of the target behavior, the selection of reinforcers, and the criteria defining consequences. If students lose motivation, delay of gratification must be questioned. If students appear confused, their understanding of the terms must be questioned. If students appear confused, their understanding of the terms of the contract must be questioned. If they never buy into the contract, they likely did not participate sufficiently in its structure. If they appear to fight the contract actively after negotiation, perhaps penalties should be provided as well (Rhode et al., 1992). The purpose of the contract is to make the student responsible. Contracts once agreed on and implemented should be adjusted if need be and followed through or they are useless as future interventions.

Home Notes

Daily communication between parents and teachers for children with behavioral problems has consistently been found to contribute positively to behavioral change (Kelley, 1990). When parents and teachers work together to improve classroom behavior, children are presented with a consistent set of expectations and cannot manipulate one set of adults against the other. They are unable to triangulate their problem into a conflict between parents and teachers. Kelley and Carper (1988) and Kelley (1990) suggest six benefits of school-home notes:

1. Parents and teachers define and agree on target behaviors and treatment goals jointly.
2. Parents and teachers share responsibility for behavior change.
3. Teachers can emphasize positive rather than negative behavior on a daily basis.
4. Parents can assist teachers by offering consequences at home based on the school note.
5. Teachers need to make minimal changes in their daily routine.
6. Children receive increased praise and attention from their parents.

In a review of literature, Kelley (1990) suggests, "Whether teachers evaluate children according to operationally defined criteria or provide parents with detailed feedback does not appear to be systematically related to treatment outcome" (p. 13). Thus, home notes are effective whether or not they are very specific. It is likely, however, that some level of objectivity and detail is necessary for parents and teachers to communicate effectively.

School-home notes improve classroom conduct and academic performance in students of all ages, including kindergartners (Budd, Liebowitz, Riner, Mindell, & Goldfarb, 1981), elementary school children (Imber, Imber, & Rothstein, 1979), and secondary school students (Schumaker, Hovell, & Sherman, 1977). Although more studies have used this intervention with younger than older children, home notes are effective at all grades. With teenagers, however, the manner of presenting the school-home note program and the teenager's willingness to accept and participate actively in its use are critical in determining whether the intervention is at all effective. When using school-home notes with teenagers, benefits to offer include the opportunity for objective feedback, the potential advantages of the note in achieving the student's goals, and the opportunity to earn rewards for becoming more competent in school functioning, a process that the home note assists (Kelley, 1990). S. Goldstein and Goldstein (1990) emphasize the importance also of setting a time limit and a set of criteria that this adolescent must meet to no longer require the home note. In this scenario, the home note is a negative reinforcer that the student is able to work toward eliminating. Finally, 20 years ago, Ayllon, Garber, and Pisor (1975) found that although school-based reinforcement only modified academic and disruptive behavior in a special classroom on a short-term basis, a daily school-home note fortified with home rewards reduced classroom behavior problems and resulted in longer lasting positive impact.

Tables 11.12 through 11.15 provide sample home notes, student ratings, progress reports, and assignment records offering simple visual feedback for younger children and more complex class-by-class feedback for secondary school students.

Token Economy

The majority of classroom problems do not require a token economy covering every behavior for every student. Nonetheless, classroom consultants sometimes will need to assist teachers in structuring and implementing token economies for an individual student or an entire class. J. E. Walker and Shea (1991) describe eleven important steps in initiating a token economy (see Table 11.16).

When reinforcement or token systems are used, teachers must be careful to avoid extortion (the child saying, I'll do it if you give me . . .), the teacher bribing with tokens (if you just do two more, I'll give you . . .), the teacher hawking tokens (who would like to help me for . . .), or the teacher threatening (if you don't get this done, you will lose your tokens and not earn recess). A token system is a way of providing "tangible evidence of a teacher's approval" (Bushell, 1973). Children under a token system do not have to be coaxed, urged, or cajoled. The tokens become associated with positive events and are accompanied by praise and encouragement. They are not to be associated with unpleasant events, except in the case of a response cost model. In this situation, as noted earlier in this chapter, what is earned can also be lost.

The consultant will more likely be asked to structure a token economy for a single, problem student. Manageable systems that do not significantly tax teachers' time have the best chance of success. A 5- to 10-token system in which students earn tokens for appropriate behavior

Table 11.12   Home notes

Name _____   **Date** _____

Please rate this student in each of the following:

Completed classwork	☺	☺	☹
Followed class rules	☺	☺	☹
Got along well with others	☺	☺	☹
Used class time wisely	☺	☺	☹

Comments _____

Teacher initials _____

Name _____   **Date** _____

Please rate this student in each of the following areas:

Came to class prepared	1	2	3	4	5
Used class time wisely	1	2	3	4	5
Followed class rules	1	2	3	4	5
Respected the rights of classmates	1	2	3	4	5
Completed classwork	1	2	3	4	5
Followed directions	1	2	3	4	5
Displayed a good attitude	1	2	3	4	5
Participated	1	2	3	4	5

Homework _____

Comments _____

Overall today was a   ☐ Great day
☐ Good day
☐ Average day
☐ Mediocre day
☐ Very poor day

Teacher initials _____

Source: User's Manual, *It's Just Attention Disorder* [videotape], by S. Goldstein and M. Goldstein. Copyright 1991, Neurology, Learning, and Behavior Center. Salt Lake City, Utah. Reprinted with permission.

Table 11.13   Daily student rating

Name _____   **Date** _____

Please rate this student in each of the areas listed below as to how he/she performed in school today using ratings of 5 = excellent, 4 = good, 3 = fair, 2 = poor, 1 = did not work.

	Class Periods/Subjects						
	1	2	3	4	5	6	7
Participation							
Class work							
Interaction with peers: Class							
Recess							
Teacher initials							

Homework: _____

_____

_____

_____

_____

Comments: _____

_____

_____

_____

Source: User's Manual, *It's Just Attention Disorder* [videotape], by S. Goldstein and M. Goldstein. Copyright 1991, Neurology, Learning and Behavior Center, Salt Lake City, Utah. Reprinted with permission.

during specific times of the day can be quite effective. Tokens can be earned tangibly (e.g., presented at the end of each review period) or figuratively (e.g., given on a note at the end of the day). As with school-home notes, token economies have greater effect when reinforcers also are offered at home for appropriate behavior at school. Teachers need

Table 11.14　Daily progress report

Student _____　　**Date** _____

1. Subject _____　　Teacher Initials _____
   Was homework turned in? _____　　Why not? _____
   Is class work completed? _____　　Why not? _____
   Was class time used efficiently? _____　　Why not? _____
   Were class rules followed? _____　　Why not? _____

2. Subject _____　　Teacher Initials _____
   Was homework turned in? _____　　Why not? _____
   Is class work completed? _____　　Why not? _____
   Was class time used efficiently? _____　　Why not? _____
   Were class rules followed? _____　　Why not? _____

3. Subject _____　　Teacher Initials _____
   Was homework turned in? _____　　Why not? _____
   Is class work completed? _____　　Why not? _____
   Was class time used efficiently? _____　　Why not? _____
   Were class rules followed? _____　　Why not? _____

4. Subject _____　　Teacher Initials _____
   Was homework turned in? _____　　Why not? _____
   Is class work completed? _____　　Why not? _____
   Was class time used efficiently? _____　　Why not? _____
   Were class rules followed? _____　　Why not? _____

5. Subject _____　　Teacher Initials _____
   Was homework turned in? _____　　Why not? _____
   Is class work completed? _____　　Why not? _____
   Was class time used efficiently? _____　　Why not? _____
   Were class rules followed? _____　　Why not? _____

6. Subject _____　　Teacher Initials _____
   Was homework turned in? _____　　Why not? _____
   Is class work completed? _____　　Why not? _____
   Was class time used efficiently? _____　　Why not? _____
   Were class rules followed? _____　　Why not? _____

7. Subject _____　　Teacher Initials _____
   Was homework turned in? _____　　Why not? _____
   Is class work completed? _____　　Why not? _____
   Was class time used efficiently? _____　　Why not? _____
   Were class rules followed? _____　　Why not? _____

Any additional comments:

_____

_____

_____

Source: User's Manual, *It's Just Attention Disorder* [videotape], by S. Goldstein and M. Goldstein, Copyright 1991, Neurology, Learning and Behavior Center, Salt Lake City, Utah. Reprinted with permission.

Table 11.15   Daily assignment record

Name _____   Date _____

Subject	Assignment	Classwork Complete	Homework	On-Task
Teacher init ____	Good Average Poor	YES NO	NO YES ____ _____	Poor Good 1 2 3 4 5
Teacher init ____	Good Average Poor	YES NO	NO YES ____ _____	Poor Good 1 2 3 4 5
Teacher init ____	Good Average Poor	YES NO	NO YES ____ _____	Poor Good 1 2 3 4 5
Teacher init ____	Good Average Poor	YES NO	NO YES ____ _____	Poor Good 1 2 3 4 5
Teacher init ____	Good Average Poor	YES NO	NO YES ____ _____	Poor Good 1 2 3 4 5
Teacher init ____	Good Average Poor	YES NO	NO YES ____ _____	Poor Good 1 2 3 4 5

Comments _____
_____
_____
_____

Source: User's Manual, *It's Just Attention Disorder* [videotape], by S. Goldstein and M. Gold-stein, Copyright 1991, Neurology, Learning and Behavior Center, Salt Lake City, Utah. Reprinted with permission.

assurance that a token system does not always have to involve students whose pockets are filled with poker chips. Points, check marks, stars, stickers, even play money can serve as tokens. They can be glued, recorded, or fastened in some secure way on a card to minimize the chances of becoming lost or misplaced.

For token programs to be effective, teachers must (a) identify appropriate target behaviors and define them, (b) select backup reinforcers and fines, (c) set the economy for wages and costs of items, and (d) most importantly, design a system to monitor the program. This last issue is

Table 11.16   Rules for establishing a token economy

The following are the basic rules when establishing a token economy system for the classroom:

1. Select a target behavior. [This topic is thoroughly discussed in Chapter 2 of the Alekr and Shea text and does not warrant further elaboration here.]
2. Conceptualize and present the target behavior to the child or group. It is a well-known fact that an emphasis on "what you can do" is more palatable to children than an emphasis on "what you cannot do." Many unsuccessful behavior modification practitioners have determined their own failure by introducing a program by saying, "Now you boys and girls are going to stop that noise and fooling around in here. I have this new . . ." The children are immediately challenged; they prepare to defeat the teacher and defend their personal integrity.
3. Post the rules and review them frequently.
4. Select an appropriate token.
5. Establish reinforcers for which tokens can be exchanged.
6. Develop a reward menu and post it in the classroom. The children should be permitted to thoroughly discuss and consider the items on the menu. They should be encouraged to make their selections from among the items, available. The children should not be permitted to debate the cost (number of tokens) of the various rewards after prices have been established.
7. Implement the token economy. Introduce the token economy on a limited basis initially. A complex sophisticated system as an initial exposure confuses and frustrates the children. *Start small and build on firm understanding.* Explain the system to the children with great clarity and precision. Be patient and answer all the children's questions. It is better to delay implementation than crate confusion and frustration.
8. Provide immediate reinforcement for acceptable behavior. The children will lose interest in the program if the process for obtaining the tokens is more effort than the reward is desirable. Many systems fail because the teacher neglects to dispense tokens at the appropriate time. Rewarding the children immediately reduces frustration and overconcern with the system. When the children are sure they will receive the tokens at the proper time, they can ignore the delivery system and concentrate on their work or behavior.
9. Gradually change from a continuous to a variable schedule of reinforcement. Quick, unpredictable or premature changes in a reinforcement schedule can destroy the program.
10. Provide time for the children to exchange tokens for rewards. If the token economy is a legitimate class program, time during the school day should be made available for the exchange. Time should not be taken from the children's recess, lunch, or free time.
11. Revise the reward menu frequently. Children, like adults, become bored with the same old fare day after day.

Source: Behavior Management: A Practical Approach for Educators, fifth edition, by James E. Walker and Thomas M. Shea, 1991, New York: Macmillan. Copyright © 1991 by Macmillan Publishing Company. Reprinted with permission of Macmillan Publishing Co.

critical. If teachers structure a program that is beyond their capability to manage, it will fail.

Fading Reinforcers

Often, fading a reinforcer while promoting generalization is more a difficult task for teachers than initiating a behavior change program. However, when the behavior change program is carefully thought out before being introduced, fading reinforcement is built into the program. To make the task easier, the program should start with continuous reinforcement pairing tangible reinforcers with social reinforcers. Next, it should shift from a continuous to an intermittent schedule. Gradually the artificial or tangible reinforcers should be removed, leaving the social reinforcers. The social reinforcers will maintain the behavioral change with occasional tangible reinforcers for continued appropriate behavior. To summarize, J. E. Walker and Shea (1991) suggest three steps to effectively fade reinforcers:

1. Always pair social and tangible reinforcers so that the tangible reinforcers can be faded while the social ones remain.
2. Place tangible reinforcers on a variable schedule while maintaining social reinforcers on a fixed schedule.
3. Begin presenting social reinforcers on a variable schedule once tangible reinforcers are faded. Finally, extinguish the social reinforcers to normal level.

Additional Issues

Long and Newman (1980) describe a number of additional techniques that can be helpful in managing minor behavioral problems in the classroom. D. P. Morgan and Jenson (1988) refer to some of the following suggestions as surface management techniques because they do not require in-depth planning or structure:

- *Planned ignoring:* Research suggests that when teachers ignore off-task, nondisruptive behavior and then pay attention when the student returns to something appropriate, behavior improves. On the other hand, if the behavior is disruptive, teachers must attend. Planned ignoring involves the teacher withholding attention and then differentially reinforcing when something appropriate happens. Behaviors that can be ignored in a planned way include whispering during work time, brief periods of off-task behavior, brief periods of out-of-seat behavior, and so on. When students who are off task disrupt others, teachers cannot use planned ignoring.

- *Signal interference:* Effective teachers can use gestures, eye contact, or even facial expressions as cues to stop misbehavior in the early stages.
- *Proximity control:* The teacher can move closer to a student who is misbehaving or off task. However, this method of returning the student to appropriate work represents a negative reinforcement model. If used excessively, students who return to work because of the teacher's presence will stop working again once the teacher moves off.
- *Humor:* Rather than be distressed by a particular student's behavior, the teacher may respond with a humorous comment. This might diffuse the intervention but certainly gives the student a clear message that the behavior needs to be changed.
- *Routine:* Relying on routine for predictability and consistency in the classroom is one of the best ways of managing minor behavioral problems.
- *Direct appeal:* When teachers maintain good relationships with students and misbehavior occurs, a direct appeal for appropriate behavior can often be effective.
- *Minimizing distractions:* When students have difficulty remaining on task or are bored by work, the more attractive distractors there are in the environment, the less likely it is the students will remain on task and the more likely it is they will find something else to do.

The manner in which verbal rewards are offered also appears to impact outcome. Bernhardt and Forehand (1975) found that when mothers used unlabeled verbal rewards, such as *very good,* versus labeled rewards, such as *very good, you put your marble in the hole,* the labeled condition was associated with a much greater increase in appropriate behavior than the unlabeled condition. This suggests a rationale for teachers to not only verbally reinforce but describe the behavior being reinforced as well. Antecedent strategies (strategies that come before behaviors) can set the stage for appropriate behavior by developing motivation in the child (Rhode et al., 1992). Cuing is an example of an antecedent strategy. In reviewing the use of cuing in the classroom, Olson (1989) found it to be an effective intervention to reduce interruptions and provide students with a minimally disruptive means of managing their behavior.

Other authors have suggested that this is a preventive antecedent strategy, is proactive, and is easy to implement (Slade & Callaghan, 1988). Paine et al. (1983) point out that cuing can be a simple signal between a student and a teacher (e.g., a raised finger or special look) or more complex process (e.g., placing a student's name on the blackboard).

Evertson, Emmer, Clements, Sanford, and Worsham (1984) describe the following easy, quick teacher interventions that can avoid the escalation of behavioral problems:

- Redirect attention by calmly and firmly repeating the task at hand to the student who is off task.
- Make eye contact when speaking to the problem student.
- Provide appropriate reminders and prompts but not negative reinforcers.
- Direct the student what to do rather than what not to do.

Carden-Smith and Fowler (1984) found that peers served as powerful sources of reinforcement in increasing or maintaining both positive and negative behaviors of their classmates. A peer-monitored, token system to reduce disruptive behavior and nonparticipation during transition in a kindergarten class for behaviorally impaired children decreased disruption and increased participation. Peer monitors could successfully initiate the token system without adult prompting. Peers in the classroom have been found to affect social skills (Hendrickson, Strain, Tremblay, & Shores, 1982) as well as academic skills (Parsons & Heward, 1979). However, classmates can also reinforce negative behavior including disruption (Solomon & Wahler, 1973) and noncompliance (Christy, 1975). Peers have been consistently found to be effective classroom change agents (Strain, 1981). Greenwood, Sloane, and Baskin (1974) found that peers trained to manage the academic behavior of small groups of classmates learned to give instructions, pair appropriate behaviors, provide corrective feedback, and manage a response cost reward system effectively. Thus peer monitoring can be beneficial for both target students and the children serving as monitors. Children who provide intervention are either peers who are more skilled or older children. In one study, being a peer monitor became the most requested and apparently most powerful reward of all the reinforcers offered in the classroom (Carden-Smith & Fowler, 1984).

Although behavior modification techniques can be very effective in the classroom, the following variables in using the system may cause failures (Morris, 1985):

- Inconsistent application of rewards and punishments
- Poorly defined behaviors
- Inconsistent monitoring
- Too many behaviors overwhelming the child
- Unattractive reinforcers
- Inadequate delivery of reinforcers (e.g., too long a delay or an inappropriate schedule of reinforcers
- Limited or poor generalization program
- Failure to pair social with secondary reinforcers
- Giving up when the program initially does not seem to work rather than troubleshooting problems

It is important for the classroom consultant to keep all these issues in mind and make certain that teachers understand them as well.

CHAPTER

12

Cognitive
Behavioral Strategies

LAUREN BRASWELL

Considering the wide array of activities in which school children are engaged almost every moment in the classroom, it seems a bit ridiculous to carve out a particular set of techniques and label these as cognitive strategies since all human activity above the level of involuntary brain stem functions has some cognitive concomitant. While acknowledging the cognitive aspect of all activities occurring in the classroom, this chapter, however, focuses on a special class of strategies that emphasize the importance of conscious self-evaluation, attention to thoughts, and enactment of conscious problem-solving efforts. These approaches are often referred to as cognitive-behavioral (CB) interventions for, as with traditional behavioral methods, CB interventions value the measurement of discrete events, the arrangement of antecedents and contingencies, and the inclusion of performance-based practice of skills to be acquired. As the name implies, the CB perspective also emphasizes cognitive events (e.g., thoughts, beliefs, expectancies, information processing) and the impact of these events on our emotions and behaviors.

Since the first edition of this book, there has been an exciting array of research on the use of CB strategies with children facing a variety of emotional and behavioral challenges. As detailed in recent volumes devoted to evidence-based treatment (Hibbs & Jensen, 2005; Kazdin & Weisz, 2003;

Kendall, 2005), there is no question that CB approaches can produce positive change and/or symptom reduction in children presenting with anxiety and trauma-related concerns, depression, conduct problems, anger management issues, or selected academic difficulties. The question that this chapter addresses, is how these exciting findings and observations translate into recommendations of any practical value for teachers, counselors, school psychologists, and other consultants working in a school setting. To answer this key question, the major categories of CB approaches, including self-management or self-regulation, cognitive restructuring, and problem-solving training are described along with practical applications of each approach as applied with children experiencing a variety of concerns. Two frequently included treatment subcomponents, relaxation training and cognitive modeling, are also described. In the second half of the chapter, illustrative programmatic approaches targeting specific childhood disorders/difficulties are presented.

The examples of CB approaches used throughout this chapter focus on efforts to remediate difficulties, but it should be noted that there are an increasing number of studies implementing universal prevention programs that also include CB components, such as the Resolving Problems Creatively Program (RPCP; Aber, Brown, & Jones, 2003), the Promoting Alternative Thinking Strategies program (PATHs; Greenberg, Kusche, Cook, & Quammen, 1995) or the Social Decision Making/Social Problem-Solving Program (Elias & Tobias, 1996). The Collaborative for Academic, Social, and Emotional Learning (CASEL) was created with the goal of promoting high quality, evidence-based social and emotional learning that extends from preschool through the high school years. As part of their work, CASEL (2003) identified a core set of teachable skills or competencies believed to provide a strong foundation for positive development. Interestingly, there is tremendous overlap between these five competencies and the approaches to be discussed in this chapter. As presented by Weissberg and O'Brien (2004), these core competencies include:

- *Self-awareness:* Knowing what we are feeling and thinking; having a realistic assessment of our own abilities and a well-grounded sense of self-confidence;
- *Social awareness:* Understanding what others are feeling and thinking; appreciating and interacting positively with diverse groups;
- *Self-management:* Handling our emotions so that they facilitate rather than interfere with task achievement; setting and accomplishing goals; persevering in the face of setbacks and frustrations;

- *Relationship skills:* Establishing and maintaining healthy and rewarding relationships based on clear communication, cooperation, resistance to inappropriate social pressure, negotiating solutions to conflict, and seeking help when needed; and
- *Responsible decision-making:* Making choices based on accurate consideration of all relevant factors and the likely consequences of alternative courses of action, respecting others, and taking responsibility for one's own choices (p. 89).

Weissberg and O'Brien's view of core competencies of value to all children is consistent with the thinking of other authors who have called for students to receive greater exposure to standard CB elements such as problem solving, social skills training, and cognitive restructuring, for enhanced skills in these areas are viewed as beneficial to all (Evans, Velsor, & Schumacher, 2002; Pincus & Friedman, 2004). As noted by Kendall and Braswell (1993), the ultimate goal of most CB approaches is to help children build a new "coping template" that enables them to meet the challenges specific to their lives, whether these involve decreasing symptoms or enhancing competencies. Before reviewing examples of how CB strategies can promote coping, however, an interesting distinction underlying intervention choices is discussed.

Cognitive Distortions versus Cognitive Deficiencies

There is a burgeoning research literature addressing the extent to which specific types of cognitive dysfunction seem to underlie specific emotional or behavioral disorders. Much of this literature has been reviewed in the chapters describing internalizing and externalizing disorders. One particularly relevant construct in this literature, however, bears additional elaboration.

Kendall and Braswell (1985, 1993) proposed a distinction between cognitive distortions and cognitive deficiencies. Cognitive distortions refer to faulty problem-solving processes, skewed perceptual processes, information processing errors, and/or irrational beliefs or expectations. In these circumstances, the individual is actively processing his or her world but the outcomes of this processing are faulty or at least different from what nonimpaired others might conclude based on the same information. Cognitive deficiencies can be thought of as cognitive absences. In this case, there is no evidence of distortion but rather absence or underfunctioning in key cognitive processes.

As summarized by Kendall and MacDonald (1993), findings from a number of different lines of research indicate depressed and anxious youth, like their adult counterparts, give ample evidence of cognitive distortions (i.e., evaluating their own performance and other aspects of their lives in an overly negative manner). Children manifesting reactive aggression also give evidence of cognitive distortions in the form of misinterpreting or misperceiving the intentions of others (Lochman & Dodge, 1994). Children presenting with ADHD-type behavior appear to experience cognitive deficiencies (i.e., failing to be reflective in situations in which it would be adaptive to do so). Hinshaw (2005) observed that the existing treatment outcome literature suggests it is more challenging to supply or develop deficient thinking patterns than it is to modify or restructure distortions in cognition. To add an additional wrinkle, other observations suggest that it may depend on the hypothesized reason for the deficiency or presumed absence of the cognitive process. As Hinshaw notes, in the past, the deficits of children with ADHD were assumed to be those of sustained attention, but more recently, these deficits have been viewed as the result of problems in inhibitory processes or problems in motivation and dysregulation of emotional control. Children with autism spectrum disorders (ASD) have responded positively to social stories interventions that rely heavily on direct instruction and cognitive modeling as a means of remediating deficits in social knowledge (Scattone, Wilczynski, Edwards, & Rabian, 2002; Thiemann & Goldstein, 2001). We could speculate that the social knowledge and social skills deficits of children with ASD represent "true deficiencies" of certain types of information. These children appear to be unable to understand the expectations of others or form their own realistic expectations or beliefs about situations without special interventions that supply needed information (T. Atwood, 2000; Gray, 1995). The behavior of children with ADHD, however, may be best viewed as an "apparent deficiency" that is more the result of motivational concerns that vary from situation to situation. As Barkley (1997) has observed, children with ADHD struggle more with *showing what they know* in a consistent manner, not with *knowing what to do*. This deficiency-distortion distinction has value in the process of treatment planning, for if we view a student as manifesting a cognitive deficiency, we would take steps to train and reinforce his or her use of the "missing pieces" in his or her cognitive repertoire or help strengthen compensatory mechanisms for accomplishing the goal in question. Successful applications of social story interventions that help children learn the behaviors required in certain circumstances seem to fit with the deficiency model (Scattone et al., 2002). If a cognitive distortion is present, other interventions would be selected that promote correction of the distorted cognitive process or event. For example, if an anxious child fails to turn in completed homework because of beliefs that his work is substandard and/or expectations that his teacher will be displeased, then these (potentially) distorted cognitions could be addressed through cognitive restructuring and the promotion of more accurate self-evaluation.

This heuristic distinction should not be pushed too far. Children are complex. Hinshaw (2005) notes that children with ADHD are frequently comorbid for conditions such as anxiety or anger management concerns that do seem to involve cognitive distortions. In addition, the findings of Hoza et al. (2004) confirm past observations suggesting some children with ADHD display a positive illusory perspective on their own performance in various domains. This cognitive distortion, while self-protective in some ways, may also function to impede treatment to the extent that it contributes to a denial or minimization of the difficulties the child is actually experiencing. Thus, while certain patterns of deficiencies or distortions are believed to be associated with particular diagnostic groups, the more knowledge gained about the cognitive underpinnings of each disorder, the more this information underscores the importance of careful assessment of each child to better understand his or her unique pattern of cognitive deficiencies and distortions.

Self-Control/Self-Regulation Approaches

A number of methods suitable for use with different types of children fall into the category of self-control/self-regulation strategies. Strictly speaking, a behaviorist could make an excellent case for why many of these strategies should be considered as exemplars of behavioral rather than cognitive-behavioral intervention. Historically, these methods are a transitional link between traditional behavioral approaches and perspectives that include greater attention to cognitive factors. In addition, the developers of these methods seemed more intent on using behavioral methods with cognitive events than on using cognitive events to alter behavior.

Most self-regulation approaches have a consistent set of discrete components. Kanfer (1970, 1971) was one of the earliest investigators to outline a model of self-regulation, including the components of self-monitoring, self-recording, self-evaluation, and self-reinforcement. The self-monitoring phase refers to the act of noting the occurrence of a specifically defined behavioral or cognitive event (e.g., tracking negative self-statements or on-task behavior). In the self-recording phase, the individual makes some type of record of the observed event. Depending on the behavior being monitored, this recording process might be as simple as putting a mark on a note card or as elaborate as writing a narrative entry in a specialized diary. The self-evaluation phase involves comparing the individual's recorded data against a predetermined standard. For example, was a particular percentage of on-task behavior achieved during a specific period or were a certain number of problems completed correctly? If the predetermined goal has been achieved, then the individual can administer a prearranged self-reinforcement that could include anything from recording points earned on a special chart to selecting a tangible or activity reward. Some systems also include the option for self-punishment of certain undesirable behaviors though applying point loss within a contingency system or more unique consequences.

Unlike some of the other CB strategies to be discussed, the self-regulation approach to encouraging improved behavior has already received extensive attention in the educational literature. Rock (2005) notes that "for more than two decades, educational researchers have successfully used self-monitoring interventions within the context of special and general education settings to increase students' academic engagement and productivity" (p. 4).

Individual and Small Group Applications

In her discussion of self-management, Carter (1993) presents a classic example of a self-management planning form that can serve as a guide for developing self-control interventions for a wide variety of student issues. A completed example from the Carter article is presented in Figure 12.1. Carter's form nicely illustrates the important principle of designing the system in such a way that the child is focusing on the display of the positive alternative to the behavior in question. Thus, if blurting out in class is the behavior to be targeted, it is desirable to ask the child to monitor the number of times she raises her hand and waits to be called on to speak. If social isolation is a concern, the child might be asked to track the number of times he asks or is asked by others to engage in an activity. This focus on increasing the positive alternative to behaviors of concern is consistent with Goldstein's discussion in Chapter 10 indicating attempts to increase behaviors generally meet with greater success than attempts to decrease behaviors.

Simple self-monitoring of activities, particularly pleasant events, and/or mood states, is also an element in CB interventions for children who are depressed (Rohde, Lewinsohn, Clarke, Hops, & Seeley, 2005;

Student _____ Teacher _____

School _____ Date _____

Step 1: Select a Target Behavior
    (a) Identify the target behavior

Geoff talks without raising his hand and does not wait to be recognized by the teacher during structured class time. Geoff talks to himself and to peers in a voice loud enough to be heard by the teacher standing two feet or more away from Geoff.

    (b) Identify replacement behavior.

During structured class time, Geoff will raise his hand without talking and wait to be recognized by the teacher before talking.

Step 2: Define the Target Behavior

Write a clear description of the behavior (include conditions under which it is acceptable and unacceptable).

Given a structured class setting with teacher-directed instructional activity, Geoff will raise his hand and wait to be called on before talking 9 out of 10 times. Geoff may talk without raising during unstructured, noninstructional times and during class discussion.

Step 3: Design the Data Recording Procedures
    (a) Identify the type of data to be recorded.

Geoff will make a plus mark (+) on his data sheet if he raised his hand and waits to be called on before talking during each 5-miniute interval for 9 intervals. If he talks without raising his hand, Geoff will mark a minus (−).

    (b) Identify when the data will be recorded.

Geoff will self-record during his third period English class.

    (c) Describe the data recording form.

Geoff will use a 5 × 7 index card with 5 rows of 9 squares each, one row for each day of the week. At the end of each row will be a box marked "Total" in which Geoff will record the total number of pluses earned that day.

Step 4: Teach the Student to Use the Recording Form

Briefly describe the instruction and practice.

The teacher will review the data recording form with Geoff, showing him where and how to self-record. The teacher will role-play with Geoff the use of a timer and will model examples and nonexamples of appropriate hand raising.

(continued)

Figure 12.1 Self-management planning form

Source: "Self-Management: Education's Ultimate Goal," by J. G. Carter, 1993, *Teaching Exceptional Children, 25*, pp. 28–31.

Step 5: Choose a Strategy for Ensuring Accuracy

Geoff will match his self-recording form with the teacher's record at the end of each English period. Step 6: Establish Goal and Contingencies

(a) Determine how the student will be involved in setting the goal.

Geoff will meet with the teacher and discuss his goal and then will share the goal with his parents.

(b) Determine whether or not the goal will be made public.

No.

(c) Determine the reinforcement for meeting the goal.

Each day Geoff meets his performance goal, the teacher will buy Geoff a soda from the soda machine.

Step 7: Review Goal and Student Performance

(a) Determine how often the student and teacher will review performance.

Geoff and the teacher will meet one time per week before school to review his progress and make new goals.

(b) Identify when and how the plan will be modified if the goal is met or is not met.

If Geoff has not met his performance goal for 3 consecutive days, the teacher will schedule an extra meeting with Geoff. If Geoff meets his goal 3 consecutive days, the teacher and Geoff will modify his goal at their next meeting.

Step 8: Plan for Reducing Self-Recording Procedures

Geoff will match with the teacher's record daily, then 3 days per week, and eventually 1 day per week (picked randomly).

Step 9: Plan for Generalization and Maintenance

Geoff will self-record initially in English only. When he can successfully self-record, accurately match the teacher's record, and has met his performance goal in English for 2 weeks, he will begin self-recording in math and then social studies. When Geoff has met his performance goal for 3 weeks, self-recording will be eliminated and Geoff will earn the reinforcer for maintaining his performance goals.

Figure 12.1 (*Continued*)

Stark & Kendall, 1996a). The data gathered from these self-monitoring efforts is useful in helping the depressed young people combat their tendency to overlook or discount positive events that are occurring in their lives or miss the helpful impact that certain activities may have on their mood.

Self-regulation approaches are generally viewed as most appropriate for use with children in third grade and older, although very simple self-management strategies involving the use of wrist counters have been successfully implemented with kindergarten children (Apple, Billingsley, & Schwartz, 2005). Adolescents are considered excellent candidates for self-regulation approaches because these methods increase their responsibility in the intervention process and decrease the role of external authorities.

While the Carter (1993) example illustrates an application with an individual child, other types of self-regulation training have been applied in small group contexts. In their work with groups of children with ADHD, Hinshaw and colleagues developed the Match Game approach to training self-evaluation (Hinshaw & Erhardt, 1991; Hinshaw, Henker, & Whalen, 1984a). This method was adapted from the work of Turkewitz, O'Leary, and Ironsmith (1975) and involves clarifying a specific behavioral criterion for reinforcement, such as *waiting for others to finish before speaking* or *cooperating*. After several minutes of class or group activity, the leader halts the ongoing activity and shows the group a Match Game sheet that typically states the behavioral criterion and includes a rating system ranging from 1 (not good at all) to 5 (great). The leader then asks the children to think about how well they have executed the behavioral criterion over the designated time and to rate themselves on the 5-point scale. The leader further explains that he or she will also rate each child, and if the child's rating is within one point of the leader's rating, the child earns a bonus point for accurate self-rating. The children then individually announce their rating and the reasons for their rating and the leader does the same, being careful to give a detailed explanation for why a particular rating was selected. The authors of this procedure recommend that initially bonus points for accuracy should be awarded even if the quality of the behavior is low, but over time the behavioral expectations can be raised by requiring that the quality of the behavior be at least acceptable for the bonus point to be awarded. Standards can also be tightened by requiring the child to exactly match rather than just come close to the leader's rating. This procedure may be most appropriate for use in self-contained classes, resource rooms, or other small group settings. It could also be conducted by a paraprofessional working with a small number of special needs children in a mainstream classroom.

In an interesting experimental application of the Match Game, Hinshaw and coworkers (1984a) trained ADHD children to accurately evaluate their own social behavior and compared the effects of such training with the use of psychostimulant treatment and traditional external reinforcement methods. At posttest, the group receiving both self-evaluation training and medication exhibited the most positive social behavior, and the behavior of the self-evaluation alone group was superior to that of the external reinforcement alone condition. These findings are consistent with those of Chase and Clement (1985), who observed that the combination of psychostimulant treatment and self-reinforcement was more effective than either treatment alone in improving the academic performance of ADHD children.

Potential Classroom Applications

Beyond small group applications, self-regulation methods lend themselves particularly well to use with entire classrooms. As presented in Table 12.1, Braswell, Bloomquist, and Pederson (1991) explain the use of self-management procedures to improve on-task attention in a classroom setting. The classroom consultant has the option of simply sharing this information with the teacher or offering to co-teach the introduction to the use of this method.

To briefly summarize, the process involves clearly identifying what is and what is not on-task behavior in the context in which it will be observed. The method of recording on-task ratings is then explained. Typically, this involves marking a symbol indicating on- or off-task behavior in response to an auditory cue that may be given by the teacher (e.g., ringing a small bell) or emitted by an audiotape at random intervals during the rating period. At the end of the rating period, the students compare their rating performance with previously established standards. If the goal has been achieved, the student then self-rewards. The reader is also referred to Braswell et al. (1991) and H. C. Parker (1992) for additional information about forms and procedures for conducting self-monitoring of attention in the classroom. Depending on the teacher's particular goals, it is also important to consider if these goals will be best achieved by having students self-monitor attention or self-monitor certain dimensions of their performance (K. R. Harris, 1986; Rock, 2005).

In setting the self-evaluation standards, it is recommended that target goals be individualized for students with input from the teacher. For example, for students who are already relatively on-task, the teacher may suggest they work on moving from 70% to 80% on-task. With ADHD students or others who are struggling to attend, the goal may be to move from 50% on-task to 60% on-task. Each child can then self-chart his or her own progress toward the goal by using graph paper to record levels of on-task behavior following each rating period. Anecdotal reports from teachers indicated that some classrooms find the act of self-charting sufficiently reinforcing so that additional reinforcements have not been incorporated.

Table 12.1   Steps to follow for self-monitoring of attention-to-task

1. Teacher explains to the class what on- and off-task attention/behavior is and also has class members model what it looks like to be on-task (either when doing seat work, group work, or listening to teacher instruction) and off-task.
2. Teacher gives students a form for recording attention-to-task and models how the form is to be marked.
3. Teacher explains that students are to rate themselves as on- or off-task whenever they hear a tone on the audiotape the teacher will play at special times.
4. Have the students practice rating themselves for 5 to 10 minutes. Verbally reinforce appropriate rating behavior and verbally correct any inappropriate self-rating or behavior.
5. Show students a poster or handout that presents the standards for self-evaluation that the teacher has selected.
6. Have the children practice rating themselves for at least 20 intervals and then have them evaluate their own performance using the presented standards.
7. Explain how the children earn points, tokens, and so on for achieving the self-evaluation standards and explain how you would like them to keep track of those points, and so on.
8. Explain how you will conduct honesty or accuracy checks and that, at first, children will earn bonus points for being accurate about their behavior, whether on- or off-task. Use several children to help you role play an example of how a child can earn points for honestly rating himself on-task or off-task.
9. Conduct a trial run in which students self-monitor for 10 or 20 minutes, depending on their age, and then evaluate and reward their own behavior in which the teacher conducts accuracy checks.
10. After using the system in this way for a period to time, the teacher can slowly begin to raise the standards required, lengthen the period of self-monitoring, introduce point loss for students who rate themselves inaccurately, and so on. It is recommended that each change be made one at a time.

Source: ADHD: A Guide to Understanding and Helping Children with Attention Deficit Disorder in School Settings, by L. Braswell, M. L. Bloomquist, and S. Pedersen, 1991, Minneapolis, MN: University of Minnesota, Department of Professional Development.

For children with extreme off-task behavior, however, it is recommended that additional forms of self-reinforcement be incorporated to maintain the procedure's effectiveness. Support for the use of this type of self-regulation approach derives from research from both psychological and education circles (Barkley, Copeland, & Sivage, 1980; Blick & Test, 1987; C. A. Hughes, Ruhl, & Misra, 1989; Rhodes, Morgan, & Young, 1983;

Varni & Henker, 1979). With the increasing movement toward individualized educational plans for all students, not just for those in special education, self-regulation methods provide a logical approach to helping students strive for particular individualized goals that would relate to either academic or social/behavioral goals.

Applications with Relevant Adults

Self-control methods are useful for application with important adults in the lives of challenging students, as well as with the students themselves. From the perspective of a school consultant, this type of approach may be especially helpful when adults are feeling helpless about a particular student's behavioral challenges. C. L. Keller and Duffy (2005) describe a specific process a classroom teacher can use to audiotape and review his or her own verbal behavior in the classroom. With this process, the teacher selects a target for improvement, which could be verbal behaviors such as use of more specific academic or social praise, academic questioning, or style of reprimands. The teacher then makes a prediction about his or her baseline use of the targeted behavior and gathers several samples in the selected environment. After reviewing the baseline data, the teacher then sets a goal for improvement, if needed, and adds environmental supports, such as signs or other types of visual reminders, to help cue the use of the desired behavior. Behavioral sampling and charting is then repeated. C. L. Keller and Duffy (2005) promote self-monitoring as a way for teachers to become more actively involved in their own professional development.

In summary, there are consistent data to support the use of self-regulation approaches with at least circumscribed manifestations of disruptive behavior and selected symptoms of internalizing disorders. Self-regulation approaches lend themselves to use by entire classrooms, particularly when goals can be tailored to be sensitive to individual differences. In both circumstances, the self-regulation methods function most frequently as a means of increasing desirable alternative behaviors to the behaviors of concern. The study of teacher applications of self-regulation methods to improve their classroom practices appears to be an interesting area for further development.

Cognitive Restructuring

In part, cognitive restructuring approaches derive from the common-sense perspective that feeling good about ourselves and valuing our own efforts is not just a matter of what happens to us but also involves how we perceive and think about the events we experience. These cognitive inter-pretations of our experiences—whether reflected in expectations, attribu-tions, other types of beliefs, or the way we process information—have become the targets of interventions based on the original work of Albert Ellis (1962) and Aaron Beck (1963).

A. Ellis (1962) formalized the relationship between events, thoughts, and emotional or behavioral consequences in his A-B-C model of mal-adaptive arousal. In this model, "A" refers to a real-life event or an-tecedent (e.g., a math test). "B" represents the thoughts that might ensue (e.g., "I'm terrible at math; I never do well on tests; this is awful"). "C" represents the emotional and behavioral consequences (e.g., feeling extremely anxious and possibly having one's performance impaired by anxiety). Ellis notes that what occurs at "C" is strongly dependent on the intervening thoughts, beliefs, and/or expectations invoked at "B." Thus, it is the perception or interpretation of the event rather than the event itself that is problematic.

This strong emphasis on the cognitive activity of the client is also present in Beck's cognitive therapy for depression (A. T. Beck, 1963; A. T. Beck et al., 1979). Beck hypothesized that the thinking of people experiencing depression is characterized by certain types of errors in in-formation processing that make them more likely to develop depressive schemata or generalized ways of thinking about themselves, the world, and the future. The theories of Ellis and Beck and the treatments derived from these theories have had a tremendous impact on psychotherapy with adults. There has been a lesser but steadily increasing impact on therapeutic interventions with children.

Individual and Small Group Applications

As discussed by Kendall, Aschenbrand, and Hudson (2003), when asked what they are thinking, most children are not particularly forth-coming with adults. So, successful approaches often incorporate non-threatening methods to help children begin to explore this topic. For example the *Coping Cat* program developed by Kendall and colleagues (Kendall, 1990; Kendall, Hudson, Choudhury, Webb, & Pimentel, 2005) and intervention approaches for depressed children developed by Kevin Stark and his research group (Stark et al., 2004, 2005) introduce the notion of examining thinking by presenting children with cartoon-type pictures that include empty thought bubbles. Children are then asked to speculate about what the character might be thinking in that particular situation. These authors note adults can also help identify potentially distorted thinking in the child's descriptions of what he or she is experiencing. Sometimes this can take the form of the adult gently repeating what the child has said but then reformulating the original statement as a question. For example, the teacher could gently repeat, "I'll never be able to get this right?" after a discouraged child has just made this remark. The child can then be encouraged to identify these thoughts herself by tuning into her thinking when she is experiencing depressed mood states. These thoughts can be recorded in a list or diary for later review and examination. Teachers and parents can also encourage the child to write down her thoughts, particularly at points when a mood change seems to have occurred. When done in the context of therapy, the clinician would then help the child look for similar themes or issues across different thoughts in an effort to identify and better understand underlying schemata or beliefs.

Once depressogenic thoughts have been identified, the cognitive restructuring process can proceed. Adults can guide the child to challenge their thoughts by asking three key questions (Stark et al., 2005):

1. What is the evidence for the thought?
2. Is there another way to look at the situation?
3. Even if the thought is true, is it as bad as it seems?

These three lines of possible questioning and discussion were originally articulated by A. Ellis (1962) and continue to serve as the core of many cognitive restructuring efforts. Ideally, adults should help the child discover his own responses to these questions or gather relevant evidence to confirm or deny a certain concern, rather than simply argue for the irrationality of the child's thinking.

In his very practical book on helping students with depression and anxiety in school settings, Merrell (2001) describes a specific form of cognitive restructuring known as *attribution retraining* (Dweck, 1975; Seligman, 1981). This approach was developed to challenge and change the causal explanations that people give to account for important outcomes in their lives. This approach was particularly formulated to address attitudes of helplessness. Seligman believed such attitudes characterize some children who are depressed. Licht (1983) has also concluded that many learning-disabled children possess the self-view that their abilities are low and their achievement efforts are not likely to result in success. These negative beliefs seem to translate into low persistence when faced with academic challenge.

Merrell (2001) notes that as it was originally formulated by Seligman (1981), attribution retraining involved a combination of four techniques that were, in concert, designed to help children move away from a more helpless orientation toward events in their lives. These four elements include the very behavioral approach of *environmental enrichment*, which involves changes to the classroom or home environment so that aversive outcomes are less likely and positive outcomes are more likely. Such an approach could take many forms, such as changing the level of academic or behavioral demand placed on the child so the child sees himself meeting expectations a greater percentage of the time. Or, it could involve adding academic or behavioral supports that make it more likely the child will achieve the existing standards. Either way the point is to halt the process of demoralization that is believed to lead to a sense of helplessness. The largely cognitive technique of *personal control training* has the aim of helping the child develop realistic beliefs about his ability to have control over important events or outcomes. As part of this approach, the child is helped to perceive where his actions might result in some changes in the situation and where action might be less fruitful. A third element, *resignation training*, helps the child who may be longing for a particularly unrealistic outcome by expanding the range of possibly acceptable outcomes in a given situation. For example, if a child is yearning for the reunification of divorced parents, she might be helped to acknowledge that while such an outcome would be wonderful, it would also be good to strive for a loving relationship with each parent. Finally, the fourth element is labeled *attribution retraining* and involves helping the child view failures as the result of factors that are external to himself, and/or more unstable or specific, while attributing success to factors that are internal, stable, and global. To illustrate, this strategy uses tasks or dialogue to help children consider that failure on a task might be the result of lack of effort, lack of knowing the right strategy, or the result of some feature of the situation rather than the result of some permanent lack of ability on the child's part. This approach is another example of the view espoused by Brooks (1992) that children need the opportunity to learn their efforts are directly related to their success. The challenge, is to implement such an approach in a way that is also sensitive to the special needs of children for whom academic difficulty or other problems are not just a matter of effort.

As discussed more fully in a later section, many approaches developed for children presenting conduct problems and/or anger management issues also incorporate elements of cognitive restructuring (Larson, 2005; Larson & Lochman, 2002). For the purpose of illustration, the work of Feindler and colleagues (Feindler, 1991; Feindler & Ecton, 1986) provides an example of cognitive structuring with aggressive adolescents.

293

Feindler and Ecton (1986) recommend providing these youth with a rationale for cognitive restructuring that includes the analogy of rebuilding thoughts being comparable to the efforts of a carpenter rebuilding some area of faulty construction. The rationale also emphasizes the importance of learning to tone down extremely negative thinking that could trigger actions that might ultimately lead to a loss of personal power. Some of the faulty beliefs that Feindler (1991) views as needing "rebuilding" include beliefs about the value of retaliation and the legitimacy of aggression, beliefs about immunity from consequences, and the kinds of hostile attribution biases previously discussed. Feindler and Ecton (1986) then go on to train a self-assessment process that involves the following steps: "(1) identify the tension, (2) identify what triggered the tension, (3) identify the negative thought connected to the tension, (4) challenge or dispute the negative thought, and (5) tone down or rebuild the thought or substitute a positive thought in place of a negative one" (p. 103). These authors have also developed a typology of self-statements to be used as positive alternatives at various stages of a provocation or conflict situation.

Potential Classroom Applications

At the classroom level, the consultant can help teachers identify actions they can take to promote healthy beliefs and expectations in their students. For example, as discussed by various authors addressing self-esteem concerns (E. Anderson, Redman, & Rogers, 1991; Brooks, 1992), teachers can help children understand that the classroom is a mistake-making place. Some children may need help grasping the notion that if one is truly challenging one's self academically, then some mistakes are expected as part of learning. Teachers can play a powerful role in modeling the open admission of mistakes and in framing these errors as golden opportunities for learning. Promoting such a viewpoint may have value for both the anxious or depressed child who may catastrophize over even infrequent errors and the impulsive child who may interpret frequent mistakes as signs of stupidity. Helping children learn to develop appropriate standards of comparison can also be promoted by encouraging children to work for their personal best versus judging their accomplishments in relation to each other. Stark (1990) also discusses the importance of helping depression-prone students develop realistic standards of self-evaluation, rather than comparing themselves with an older sibling, adult, or other inappropriate object of comparison. Together, consultants and teachers can help parents set realistically challenging academic expectations for their children and develop a healthy perspective regarding mistakes. In addition, consultants can guide both parents and teachers in learning how to help children set up "experiments" to evaluate the validity of some of their potentially troubling beliefs or erroneous self-views.

In terms of academic issues, self-efficacy beliefs have been a particular target of exploration. As discussed by Schunk (2003), "researchers and practitioners interested in student motivation and learning in academic settings are focused increasingly on the role of students' thoughts and beliefs during learning" (p. 159). Linnenbrink and Pintrich (2003) argue that student self-efficacy beliefs are inherently changeable and readily influenced by contextual features of the classroom. These authors suggest that promoting domain specific self-efficacy beliefs may be a more realistic goal and, ultimately, a more successful strategy than attempts to promote global self-esteem. B. Walker (2003) offers a number of practical suggestions for enhancing students' self-efficacy beliefs regarding reading and writing activities. For example, Walker suggests that self-efficacy can be encouraged by giving students some element of choice through personalized or inquiry-oriented assignments that allow them to be the classroom expert. Having teachers comment on the strategies they see different students in the classroom already using as they engage in reading and writing activities can also be helpful, along with inviting these students to present mini-lessons to others on the use of these strategies. Self-efficacy beliefs may also be enhanced via the use of variations on the self-evaluation strategies discussed in the previous section, and Walker also suggests giving students a reading or writing strategies checklist to be used to evaluate their own engagement in the activity. As a final practical suggestion, Walker recommends shifting the assessment context from one that emphasizes performance to one emphasizing learning through the use of portfolio-based assessments. This type assessment can require students to make reflective statements explaining what the items selected for their portfolios demonstrate about their reading and writing skills.

With young children, statements made by the classroom teacher can have a powerful impact on how children think about themselves and their activities. A fascinating study of activity preference in preschoolers demonstrates the cognitive restructuring that can occur as a direct result of the statements of adults (Barak, Shiloh, & Haushner, 1992). During a playtime that involved engaging in four different appealing activities, children in the cognitive restructuring condition were exposed to an adult who made positive statements about the child's perceived ability to perform one of the activities, expected success at the activity, and anticipated satisfaction from engaging in that activity. The experimentor then had the children repeat these statements to themselves. This group was compared with another condition in which the children received a reinforcer (food reward) for engaging in one of the activities and a no intervention control. Children's activity preferences were assessed at pretest, immediate posttest, and 2-week follow-up. The group receiving cognitive restructuring displayed a significant positive shift in preference for the activity that had been the target of positive statements. Children in the behavioral reward condition displayed a *decrease* in preference for the rewarded activity. Those in the control group displayed no change in rank-ordered preferences. The authors note these findings have implications for the strong role that adult feedback may play in shaping the preferences of young children. In addition, they note the decrease in preference for the external reward activity is consistent with the theory of Deci (1975) that individuals lose interest in externally rewarding activities over time, whereas interest in activities for which they receive positive verbal feedback increases. Barak et al. (1992) are careful not to argue against the use of external reward, but they suggest that to maintain power over time, external rewards must be administered in such a way that they also present information about the individual's perceived ability, success, or satisfaction with the rewarded activity. This observation is consistent with the findings of research summarized in the section on self-regulation approaches that supports the effectiveness of contingencies such as the self-charting of successful task performance.

Applications with Relevant Adults

In trying to serve the needs of children, the classroom consultant may encounter many situations in which it would be helpful to better understand and perhaps change the thinking of important adults in these children's lives. Following a series of difficult interactions with a child, it is all too human for adults to form negative expectations about future interactions and make possibly inaccurate attributions about the cause of the child's troubling behavior. For example, a teacher might inaccurately view an ADHD child's blurting-out behaviors a deliberate attempt to disrupt the class and annoy the teacher. In another circumstance, an instructor might inappropriately blame himself for a depressed child's apparent social discomfort and difficulty requesting assistance. M. L. Bloomquist (2006) presents a list of unhelpful thoughts about their children that parents may sometimes endorse. This list is reprinted in Table 12.2 and while geared for parents, many of these unhelpful thoughts may also occur with teachers working with challenging children. This list has been used as a tool for

Table 12.2   Unhelpful parent thoughts

Listed below are a variety of common thoughts that parents of struggling children may have. Read each thought and indicate how frequently that thought (or a similar thought) typically occurs for you over an average week. There are no right or wrong answers to these questions. Use the 3-point rating scale to help you answer these questions.

	1	2	3
	Rarely	Sometimes	Often

Unhelpful Thoughts about the Child

1. _____ My child is behaving like a brat.
2. _____ My child acts up on purpose.
3. _____ My child is the cause of most of our family problems.
4. _____ My child's future is bleak.
5. _____ My child should behave like other children. I shouldn't have to make allowances for my child.

Unhelpful Thoughts about Self/Others

6. _____ It is my fault that my child has a problem.
7. _____ It is his/her fault (other parent) that my child is this way.
8. _____ I can't make mistakes in parenting my child.
9. _____ I give up. There is nothing more I can do for my child.
10. _____ I have no control over my child. I have tried everything.

Unhelpful Thoughts about Who Needs to Change

11. _____ My child is the one who needs to change. All of us would be better off if my child would change
12. _____ I am the one who needs to change. My family would be better off if I would change.
13. _____ My spouse/partner needs to change. We would all be better off if he/she would change.
14. _____ The teacher needs to change. We would be better off if he/she would change.
15. _____ Medications are the answer. Medications will change my child.

For each thought you rated a 3, ask yourself the following questions:

1. What is unhelpful about this thought?
2. How would this thought influence my behavior toward my child?
3. How would my behavior affect my child?

Source: Skills Training for Children with Behavior Problems: A Parent and Practitioner Guidebook, revised edition, by Michael L. Bloomquist, 2006, New York: Guildford. Reprinted with permission.

generating discussion with parent and teacher groups. Recognizing that others also struggle with troubling thoughts and beliefs seems to make it more acceptable for parents and teachers to share their own potentially unhelpful thinking. It is important to stress that having such thoughts occasionally is very normal, but difficulties may arise if a person's thinking becomes dominated by some of these beliefs or expectations. A list of more helpful alternative thoughts is also presented in Table 12.3. With parent or faculty groups, it is sometimes useful to discuss the long-term impact of harboring unhelpful thoughts versus the more helpful alternatives.

When working with an individual teacher or parents, the consultant can investigate the presence of such "cognitive roadblocks" by asking the teacher to hypothesize the reasons for the child's actions. The consultant can also inquire about the extent to which the teacher views the child's behavior as potentially the product of a child-by-teacher interaction. If unhelpful beliefs are revealed, open discussion and education often can correct specific misinformation. In some cases, however, more intensive efforts to restructure thinking may be necessary. These efforts could take the form of re-labeling or reframing the child's (or teacher's) behavior to reduce blame-oriented beliefs that may be interfering with taking positive action. In this regard, the consultant can be particularly helpful in guiding the relevant adults to move away from global, stable attributions about the child's behavior and move toward more specific, unstable attributions for the child's actions. For example, if a teacher is explaining a child's actions as being destructive and views this as an unchanging feature of the child, the consultant might encourage the following alternative problem conceptualization: "I notice he is most likely to hit other children when the room is very crowded and others encroach on his space." The latter approach offers hints for intervention in the very way the problem is described; whereas continuing to explain the difficulty as the result of the child's destructive nature offers fewer options for intervention. Encouraging specificity also dovetails nicely with behavioral intervention planning. The consultant can emphasize that these problem formulations are not a matter of truth versus falsehood, but rather a matter of which perspective is most likely to promote constructive attempts to cope with the difficulties at hand.

Taken as a whole, the literature on cognitive restructuring has many implications for adults working with children in a school context. Although the targets of restructuring will vary depending on whether the child is manifesting externalizing difficulties, internalizing difficulties, or learning concerns, the classroom teacher and other school personnel

Table 12.3   Helpful parent thoughts

Listed below are "counter" thoughts that parents can think instead of unhelpful thoughts.

Unhelpful Thought #1 corresponds to Helpful Thought #1 and so on. Compare the unhelpful thoughts to the helpful thoughts.

Helpful Thoughts about the Child

1. _____ My child is behaving positively, too.
2. _____ It doesn't matter whose fault it is. What matters are solutions to problems.
3. _____ It is not just my child. I also play a role in the problem.
4. _____ I'm being irrational. I have no proof that my child will continue to have problems. I need to wait for the future.
5. _____ I can't just expect my child to behave. My child needs to be taught how to behave.

Helpful Thoughts about Self/Others

6. _____ It doesn't help to blame myself. I will focus on solutions to the problem.
7. _____ It doesn't matter whose fault it is. I will focus on solutions to the problems.
8. _____ My child is perhaps more challenging to parent than others, and therefore I will make mistakes. I need to accept the fact that I am going to make mistakes.
9. _____ I have to parent my child. I have no choice. I need to think of new ways to parent my child.
10. _____ My belief that I have no control over my child might be contributing to the problem. Many things are in my control. I need to figure out what I can do to parent my child.

Helpful Thoughts abut Who Needs to Change

11. _____ My child is not the only one who needs to change. We all need to change.
12. _____ I am not the only one who needs to change. We all need to change.
13. _____ My spouse/partner is not the only one who needs to change. We all need to change.
14. _____ The teacher is not the only one who needs to change. We all need to work together.
15. _____ Medications may help, but will not solve the problems. We will also need to work hard to cope with the problems.

Ask yourself the following questions about these helpful thoughts:

1. What is helpful about this thought?
2. How would this thought influence my behavior toward my child?
3. How would my behavior affect my child?

Source: Skills Training for Children with Behavior Problems: A Parent and Practitioner Guidebook, revised edition, by Michael L. Bloomquist, 2006, New York: Guilford. Reprinted with permission.

are presented with many daily opportunities to promote in their students an adaptive, coping orientation to the challenges they experience.

Problem-Solving Approaches

Problem-solving training approaches have a long history within both the adult and child treatment literature (D'Zurilla, 1986; Mahoney, 1977; Spivack & Shure, 1974). Different formulations of the problem-solving process have varied somewhat in their articulated stages or steps; however, there is great similarity in the basic content of various problem-solving formats (Kendall & Braswell, 1993). Table 12.4 presents the key steps in most problem-solving systems. Many systems identify an initial stage of problem recognition and definition in which the problem solver is urged to think divergently and consider a variety of possible solutions. Next, most systems propose a stage in which the consequences of each potential solution are considered and evaluated. A decision is then made, and finally the problem solver is encouraged to evaluate the outcome of the selected choice and, if needed, modify the choice as circumstances dictate.

Approaches to problem-solving training have also developed under the label of conflict resolution or peer mediation training. These variations on problem-solving training have been particularly popular over the decades within educational circles (Elias & Tobias, 1996; D. W. Johnson

Table 12.4   Common components of problem-solving formats

1. *Problem recognition:* Recognition that a challenge or dilemma exists with oneself, others, or some other feature of the environment and formulation of this circumstance as a problem that can be understood and addressed.
2. *Solution generation:* Brainstorming or identifying a number of different possible alternative solutions to the problem without prematurely dismissing any option.
3. *Consequential thinking:* Anticipation of the emotional, behavioral, and other consequences for oneself and others that could arise from the implementation of each alternative solution.
4. *Decision making:* Using the information generated at the preceding stages to make a decision about which alternative or combination of alternatives to enact.
5. *Reviewing the outcome:* Analyzing the actual consequences of the selected alternative and determining if the desired outcome was achieved or if another alternative should be enacted.

& Johnson, 1979; T. S. Jones, 2004). Conflict resolution approaches also offer a stepwise approach to problem solving about interpersonal dilemmas but tend to place greater emphasis on the component skills of this process, such as active listening, effective communicating, and perspective-taking capacities. Peer mediation approaches, as the name implies, place great emphasis on training children to be able to mediate conflicts with each other and not necessarily involve an adult in the problem-solving process. See Goldstein's discussion of conflict resolution methods in Chapter 11.

Applications with Individuals or Small Groups

Social cognitive problem-solving training is a key content in most cognitive-behavioral intervention programs designed for children presenting disruptive behavior (Kazdin, 2005; Lochman, Barry, & Pardini, 2003). Such training efforts teach a stepwise problem-solving process such as those just described. A more detailed discussion of Lochman and colleagues school-based Anger Coping Program is presented later in this chapter, but at this point it is relevant to note that this program involves detailed training and extensive rehearsal of social problem solving. With acting-out children, the component of social perspective-taking may receive particular emphasis to increase awareness of a wide range of possible intentions of others in ambiguous social situations and promote greater awareness of the possible feelings of others in an interaction. In addition, children displaying aggression often need specific training in generating alternative strategies for problem resolution that emphasize verbal assertion and compromise over physical aggression. Social problem-solving training has also been a key component in interventions for younger children with conduct problems. Successful adaptations for younger children, such as the Incredible Years: Dinosaur School curriculum of Webster-Stratton and Reid (2003), make extensive use of features designed to hold the attention of younger children, such as videotape examples, child-sized puppets, and problem-solving stories.

In discussing the treatment of depressed children and adolescents, Stark et al. (2005) suggest that problem-solving training can serve many functions, including helping the student develop "an overarching problem-solving philosophy of life in which depressive symptoms, unpleasant situations, interpersonal conflicts, and so forth are viewed as problems to be solved" (p. 249). In addition to the problem-solving steps previously noted, the authors suggest the addition of a step they call "psych up" to help counter the pessimism so characteristic of depressive thinking. These authors note that providing training in the process of generating alternative solutions is important for countering the rigidity in thinking that is sometimes present in depressed children, and the depressed child may also be at risk to prematurely reject potential options. Adults working with the child may need to help him or her refrain from dismissing possible solutions before adequately evaluating them. In addition, problem-solving methods may be helpful in countering feelings of hopelessness that characterize these children when they are unable to think of other options for addressing their dilemmas. The process of engaging in problem solving and then enacting the selected choice can begin to build a greater sense of self-efficacy as the child experiences some degree of mastery over environmental circumstances.

Possible Classroom Applications

It comes as no surprise to any school consultant or teacher that the typical classroom provides numerous daily opportunities for training the use of problem solving/conflict resolution approaches with a variety of life's dilemmas. The challenge is in integrating this training with all the other curriculum demands placed on the classroom teacher.

In selecting a problem-solving process to promote, the consultant may wish to work with the faculty to select a particular curriculum or approach to be adopted by the entire school. The consultant can then work with teachers at each grade level to assure that the content is appropriate for the cognitive developmental level of the children. The consultant can also help the faculty understand that any system will meet with greater acceptance by the students if the teachers model use of the problem-solving methods in addressing their own dilemmas and in making classroom decisions about positive events (e.g., what to do for rewarding activities or what to do to earn extra credit) and avoid using the system only in disciplinary situations. Once students in a particular class have some familiarity with the steps of the particular problem-solving format being used, the class can then use the steps to solve commonly recurring classroom challenges, such as deciding on a system to determine who gets to be line leaders, how to handle cutting in line, and how to help out fellow students who may need to borrow pencils or paper. When the class has worked through a number of examples of problem solving as a group, the teacher may then be able to designate a certain corner of the room as the "problem-solving conference center" or the "peacemaking corner" and ask children experiencing disputes to go to that spot with a neutral third party, use the problem-solving guidelines to come to a decision about what to do, and then inform the teacher what they have decided to do to handle their problem. A teacher using this approach confessed to the author that she had instituted this method to address the needs of some disruptive boys; however, an unexpected benefit was that it also kept her from having to referee the numerous interpersonal dilemmas of the girls in her fifth grade classroom.

The school-based programming of Sarason and Sarason (1981) offers an interesting example of conducting a problem-solving intervention as a class at the high school level. Working with students identified as at-risk for continued delinquent behavior and possible school dropout, Sarason and Sarason (1981) designed an intervention that was presented as a special unit within a required course. The training content emphasized modeling both the overt behaviors and the cognitive antecedents of adaptive problem solving and included many opportunities for classroom behavioral rehearsal. At posttest, the students participating in the intervention class were able to generate more adaptive solutions for addressing problem situations and were able to give better self-presentations in the context of job interviews for summer employment. The students were blind to the fact that their interview behavior was also being assessed in relation to program intervention. More importantly, at 1-year follow-up, treated students had fewer absences, less tardiness, and fewer referrals for misbehavior than controls.

Applications with Relevant Adults

There are as many opportunities for application of a problem-solving approach in adult-to-adult interaction as there are in adult-child or child-to-child conflicts. It has been demonstrated that outcomes with behavioral child management training can be improved when parents receive formal problem-solving training in addition to the traditional training in contingency management, with problem-solving training being applied to practical issues the parent faces as well as to issues related to the child (Griest et al., 1982; Webster-Stratton, 2005).

Classroom consultants have the option of training the use of problem-solving methods among parents and teachers through either formal or informal mechanisms. Formal options could involve providing in-service training for teachers as a means of introducing problem-solving methods on a schoolwide basis. A series of evening meetings could accomplish a similar goal with parents.

In more informal approaches to encouraging the use of problem-solving methods, the school consultant models these methods in meetings with teachers and parents and/or the building principal uses similar methods when problem solving with faculty and parent groups. The consultant could also develop problem-solving guide sheets for various purposes, such as parent-teacher meetings to discuss specific aspects of a child's behavior. An example of a form for use with children presenting with ADHD-related concerns is presented in Figure 12.2. This particular form is a variation on one used in the Minnesota Competence Enhancement Program (August, Bloomquist, & Braswell, 1991). Anecdotal feedback from teachers using this form in parent-teacher meetings has been extremely positive. They report that the form helps keep the discussion focused on the

---

Directions: This form should be completed during a face-to-face meeting of parents and relevant school staff. With students older than 9 years, it is ideal to have them present for the segment of the meeting devoted to constructive action planning.

1. **Check off all concerns that apply to this child:**

   _____ Frequently off-task   _____ Problems completing homework

   _____ Poor organizational skills   _____ Problems completing classwork

   _____ Argues with adults   _____ Blurts out/bugs other students

   _____ Problems following rules   _____ High anger/low frustration tolerance

   _____ Poor social skills   _____ Doesn't think before acting

   _____ Sad or nervous   _____ Low self-esteem

   _____ Other _____   _____Other _____

2. **Decide top two current concerns:**

   Most important concern _____

   Second most important concern _____

3. **Identify any factors in the environment that may be maintaining these concerns:**

   Most important concern _____

   Second most important concern _____

4. **Check all methods that would be appropriate for addressing the two most important concerns:**

   _____ Modify or eliminate factors in the environment that are maintaining the behavior by _____

   _____

   _____ Develop a school-based contingency system to reinforce positive alternatives to the identified problematic behavior. Describe targets: _____

   _____

   _____ Train child to use a homework notebook or alternative system to assist home-school transfer of work _____

Figure 12.2 Parent-school personnel partnership
planning worksheet

_____ Train child to use an organizational checklist to target specific organizational concerns. Use of this checklist will be reinforced by _____

_____ Train child to use self-monitoring of attention to increase on-task behavior during _____ by implementing _____

_____ Train child in use of problem-solving methods to improve adult-child communication in conflicted situations. Training will be accomplished by _____

_____ Train child in specific social skills, such as _____ by implementing _____

_____ Develop home-school communication system to monitor specific behaviors or support any of the identified goals. System will involve _____

_____ Train relaxation skills to assist in anxiety/tension management by implementing _____

_____ Address self-esteem issues through direct discussion/counseling by appropriate school staff to commence _____

_____ Address self-esteem issues through development of other opportunities to share competencies such as _____

5. **Determine roles/responsibilities for accomplishing selected interventions:**

   Student's role _____

   Classroom teacher(s)'s role _____

   Parent's role _____

   Case manager's role _____

   Other relevant school personnel _____

6. **Decide method of plan review:**

   a. How often should plan be reviewed (e.g., daily, weekly, monthly)? _____

   b. How should review be conducted (e.g., phone calls, emails, meetings, combination)? _____

   c. Who is involved in the review process? _____

Signatures of Agreement:

_____

_____

_____

_____

_____

_____

_____

Figure 12.2 (*Continued*)

problem at hand and keeps discussion oriented toward constructive action rather than letting it get bogged down in blaming and other types of defensive communication. Although the content of this particular form reflects the needs and issues of a specific population in a specific context, the general format can serve as an example for those who would like to create a form relevant to their own setting and population of interest.

Clearly, problem-solving methods have many applications with individual students, entire classrooms, and various types of parent-teacher interactions. In a later section, programs making elaborate use of such methods are described.

Common Subcomponents of Cognitive Behavioral Methods

Two additional components that are commonly included in different forms of cognitive-behavioral intervention merit at least brief attention.

Relaxation Training

Relaxation training methods have a long history within traditional behavioral interventions, most notably systematic desensitization (Wople, 1958). As cognitive-behavioral interventions have developed, many of these approaches continue to include relaxation training as part of their armamentarium (Dobson, 2001). From a cognitive-behavioral perspective, however, relaxation training is considered a coping skill to be trained and used with great consciousness on the part of the client rather than as an alternative conditioned response. Relaxation training has been incorporated into many types of cognitive-behavioral programming for children with a variety of emotional and/or behavioral concerns, ranging from highly anxious youngsters to those who manifest major difficulties with acting-out behavior and anger control.

Various forms of relaxation have been used as part of stress inoculation approaches to anger control training. For example, building on the original work of Novaco (1977), Feindler and Ecton (1986) detail a number of different forms of relaxation training used in their work with adolescents experiencing anger control problems. In their program, relaxation is presented as a skill that can help teens maintain self-control and ultimately increase personal power by being able to maintain self-control while others are attempting to "push their buttons." Early in the training program, participants are introduced to brief relaxation techniques that can be used in provocative situations. These methods include instruction in deep breathing, backward counting paired with arousal decrease, and calming visual imagery. The program emphasizes that these methods help teens reduce physiological tension, focus their attention away from the provoking event and to internal control, and provide a few seconds of extra time before making a decision about how to respond to the provocation. Later in training, both progressive muscle relaxation exercises and passive, imagery-oriented methods are introduced as a means of increasing awareness of physiological cues signaling tension. The teens are then trained to enact appropriate relaxation strategies when they experience these signals of tension. The work of Larson and Lochman (2002) and Hinshaw, Henker, and Whalen (1984b) also emphasize training children with anger control difficulties to use physiological cues as signals to enact relaxation or other self-calming methods.

Historically, relaxation training has been a major component in the treatment of internalizing difficulties in children, particularly anxiety-related problems (Barrios & O'Dell, 1989; Morris & Kratochwill, 1983). Ollendick and Cerny (1981) present a widely used modification of deep muscle relaxation training with children. This procedure involves having children learn to tense and then relax various major muscle groups in the body. With practice, the child becomes more adept at perceiving the physiological signs of muscle tension and can then use these sensations as a cue to enact relaxation strategies. After a child has successfully mastered the basic relaxation skills in the training context, then an individualized audiotape of the relaxation procedures can be created for the child to use in practice outside the training session. Usually, children are taught to pair a certain cue word, such as "relax," "calm down," or "chill out" with their relaxed state. Over time, the children can be encouraged to use this cue word to help themselves relax in circumstances in which enacting the entire protocol is not practical. Relaxation training methods have also been successful both alone and in combination with other approaches in the treatment of various anxiety-related difficulties in children, including specific fears such as test anxiety or more generalized anxiety disorders (see reviews in Barrios & O'Dell, 1989; Kendall et al., 1992). A less extensive but encouraging literature also supports the inclusion of relaxation with depressed children, because this population has such a high incidence of anxiety symptoms (Kendall et al., 1992). Currently, these methods are also suggested for children who are depressed and/or comorbid for anxiety and depression (Merrell, 2001). As described by Rohde et al. (2005), the Coping with Depression Course for Adolescents includes training in both a more extensive progressive muscle relaxation procedure and less conspicuous deep-breathing method that is easier to implement in a public context. Interestingly, a study with depressed middle school students, J. S. Kahn, Kehle, Jenson, and Clark (1990) found relaxation training was as effective as cognitive-behavioral treatment involving self-monitoring, cognitive restructuring, and problem solving in decreasing depressive symptomatology and increasing self-esteem.

At the classroom level, consultants could assist teachers in training the class to use simple relaxation methods. For example, the entire group could participate in brief muscle tension-release or calming imagery exercises. As children experience a more relaxed state, the class could be encouraged to select a cue word or some other type of signal that becomes the prompt to use their relaxation skills at designated times. Establishing a prearranged relaxation signal allows the teacher to calm the class and help children settle down without suggesting punitive consequences.

Variations on Modeling Procedures

In Chapter 10, Goldstein and Brooks discussed the powerful role of modeling in producing behavior change. Modeling typically refers to the learner watching the behavior of a model, either in a live action or filmed context. This type of traditional modeling is a common element in many CB group treatment programs that make extensive use of role-playing activities. Some programs, however, have employed additional engaging applications of modeling. For example in the Anger Coping Program of Lochman and colleagues (Larson & Lochman, 2002; Lochman, Nelson, & Sims, 1981) group members create their own problem-solving videotapes. After group members have been introduced to key social cognitive problem-solving skills, they develop a script depicting an anger coping problem situation. They practice portraying the scene they have created and first present the negative consequences of failing to use good problem solving and anger coping skills. The group then videotapes alternative responses that illustrate how use of anger coping skills can lead to more favorable outcomes. These scenarios are repeatedly rehearsed and, when possible, relevant members of the school staff are incorporated to increase the realism and interest value of the videos. If time and the functioning of the group permit, more than one anger coping story video is created. These videos are reviewed for discussion by the group and are shown to parents, teachers, and other relevant adults as part of the celebration at the completion of the Anger Coping Program.

Building on Gray and Garland's (1993) use of social stories to improve the social understanding and responding of children with autism spectrum disorders, Haggerty, Black, and Smith (2005) described a creative application of self-modeling with a 6-year-old exhibiting tantrums and self-injurious behavior in a classroom setting. After careful behavioral assessment of the child's behavior and the school situations most likely to trigger inappropriate behavior, the school staff worked with the child to create *Kirk's Calming Book*. This storybook included pictures of the target child engaged in desirable classroom behavior or using self-calming strategies that had been introduced to help him decrease his inappropriate outbursts. Each picture was accompanied by a narrative using the child's language to describe the desirable behavior and its positive impact on his peers and his teacher. The child also created artwork about each scene that was included in the book. After this product was completed, the teacher read the story to Kirk several times per week, encouraging his involvement in the reading process and encouraging him to act out the self-calming strategies he modeled for himself in the story. The child was also able to read his book at home with his mother. In addition, the school staff also created cardboard figures of Kirk and other people depicted in the story. Kirk was able to use these to act out the situations presented in the book. Careful assessment indicated that this intervention resulted in a dramatic decrease in the frequency, duration, and intensity of inappropriate behavior and great increases in Kirk's in-class learning time. Haggerty et al. (2005) note that such high-intensity self-modeling seems to help children who are having difficulty with social cognition and need key social information presented to them in a manner that is accessible and invites repetition. It is exciting to see the use of intervention such as social stories and comic strip conversations be extended beyond applications with ASD children to assist other types of students struggling with deficits in social understanding (Pierson & Glaeser, 2005).

With less intense behavioral concerns, educators may be able to achieve positive results with covert cognitive modeling. As an example, Hartley (1986) asked children to imagine someone they thought was very clever and then imitate that person when performing the experimental task. This cognitive manipulation resulted in improved task performance. In their treatment for anxious children, Kendall et al. (1992) recommend having a child imagine how a favorite cartoon or movie character might handle a feared situation. This use helps the child generate a cognitive model of someone who could negotiate the situation. The imagined presence of this superhero or admired character may also serve as a comforting, counterconditioning agent, as proposed decades ago by Lazarus and Abramovitz (1962).

At the classroom level, these findings could encourage teachers to ask students to imagine what they would look like if they were engaging in particular desirable academic behaviors and then have the children attempt to imitate their cognitively generated models. As a group, the teacher could lead a mental rehearsal of how the children might improve their performance at walking quietly in the halls, waiting in line appropriately, or behaving acceptably in the lunchroom or playground. Building on the examples previously described, a classroom teacher could also have her students serve as their own positive models by videotaping students when they are engaged in appropriate seatwork or transition behavior and then use this video as a reminder to the class if behavior becomes problematic or as a means to educate parents or new students about the behavioral expectations of the classroom.

Programmatic Examples with Specific Childhood Disorders

Anxiety Disorders and Trauma-Related Intervention

Reversing a history of relative neglect, the past 12 years have included a significant increase in research on CB interventions for children presenting symptoms of various anxiety disorders (Hudson, Flannery-Schroeder, & Kendall, 2004; Kendall, Robin, Hedtke, & Suveg, 2005). Even more to the point of this chapter, a subset of these studies involved school-based interventions for reducing and/or preventing symptoms of anxiety disorders (Barrett & Turner, 2001; Dadds, Holland, Barrett, Laurens, & Spence, 1999; Dadds, Spence, Halland, Barrett, & Laurens, 1997).

Initial school-based efforts by Dadds and colleagues (Dadds et al., 1999, 1997) targeted 7-to 14-year-old children who were showing mild symptoms of anxiety and those meeting diagnostic criteria, albeit at milder levels of severity. Intervention groups were held at school and were led by clinical psychologists with school guidance counselors as co-leaders. The intervention involved the FRIENDS program which was based on the *Coping Koala Prevention Manual* (Barrett, Dadds, & Holland, 1994) which was originally derived from the Kendall (1990) *Coping Cat* program. In this intervention, participants work on identifying their feelings, particularly fear and anxiety, and then using these feelings as cues to enact other coping skills, such as relaxation methods, techniques for examining and challenging anxious thoughts, and problem solving to create action plans for facing challenging situations. The training context emphasizes peer support and peer learning. While contingency management is an important element in the group interven-

310

tion, the group members also provide each other with social reinforcement and children are encouraged to make internal attributions about their achievements. Three parent groups were also conducted to provide parents with child management information and information about what the children were learning and how parents could encourage child skill use. At 6-month and 2-year follow-up, children receiving the intervention reported a significant reduction in anxiety symptomatology and fewer children in the intervention condition "progressed" to meeting full diagnostic criteria relative to children in the monitoring-only control condition (Dadds et al., 1999).

G. A. Bernstein, Layne, Egan, and Tennison (2005) also achieved positive outcomes implementing a school-based cognitive-behavioral group intervention based on the FRIENDS program. This program involved nine weekly 1-hour training sessions that met in classrooms of the child's home school after regular school hours. One group received the child group only, while in a separate condition at least one parent was required to attend a conjoint parent group that met simultaneously with the child group. Both treatment conditions also had booster sessions at 1 and 3 months post intervention. While both treatment groups achieved positive outcomes relative to a no-treatment control group, the group also receiving parent training achieved significant improvement on a larger number of outcome measures.

With the dual goals of eliminating stigma that might be associated with attending a special group and insuring improved attendance of participants, Lowry-Webster, Barrett, and Dadds (2001) evaluated a universal prevention program administered to 594 10-to 12-year-old children in their regular classrooms during regular school hours. The FRIENDS program was conducted during one 75-minute block per week for 10 weeks, with two booster sessions conducted at the end of 1 and 3 months postintervention. Group sessions were led by regular classroom teachers who had participated in a 1-day curriculum training workshop. Teachers also conducted the three parent sessions. At posttest, children in the intervention classrooms showed a reduction in anxiety symptoms, whether or not they were considered high risk participants. Those who were initially scoring in the high anxiety group also displayed reductions in reported levels of depression. At 1-year follow-up, Lowry-Webster, Barrett, and Lock (2003) reported that intervention gains were maintained as assessed by self-reports. In addition, diagnostic interviews were completed with students originally scoring above clinical cut-offs for anxiety and depression. Of this more symptomatic group, 85% did not meet criteria for diagnosis while only 31% of the control group was diagnosis-free. This program also received high acceptability ratings from parents, teachers, and students. Lock and Barrett (2003) implemented the same universal prevention program with two age groups, 9- to 10-year-olds and 14- to 16-year-olds. Both age groups displayed significant decreases in anxiety at posttest and 12-month follow-up, but the younger group displayed greater change, with the 9- to 10-year-old females seeming to be particularly responsive to the program.

Sadly, in addition to children who might have been naturally inclined to be somewhat anxious, there are also those children who have been "made" anxious by direct exposure to traumatizing experiences and/or vicarious exposure to startling news of disasters. As a result, it has become all the more important for teachers and classroom consultants to be prepared to respond to trauma reactions. The fascinating work of Goenjian and colleagues (Goenjian, 1993; Goenjian et al., 1997) illustrates the positive results that can be achieved with school-based interventions following major catastrophic events. These authors created a broad-based program to aid children in their recovery from trauma following the devastating Armenian earthquake of 1988. This program involved four classroom group sessions and two to four individual sessions, depending on the treatment needs of each student. The treatment content included reconstruction and reprocessing of the traumatic experience, with careful attention to clarification of cognitive distortions and misattributions, for example blaming oneself for the location of family members at the moment they were killed in the earthquake. Students were also asked to identify trauma reminders and helped to enhance their tolerance for reactivity to these reminders. Postdisaster losses and other life changes were addressed with a problem-solving orientation, and students were helped to create nontraumatic mental representations of deceased loved ones. Comparing the 35 young people who received treatment with the 29 who did not, the authors report the treated students displayed a significant decrease in all three categories of posttraumatic stress disorder (PTSD) symptomatology (e.g., intrusive memories, avoidance behaviors, and signs of arousal), at 1.5 and 3-year follow-ups while the PTSD symptoms of the untreated group had increased. In terms of symptoms of depression, the treated group displayed no change, but the untreated group displayed a significant increase. Positive results with a school-based CBT approach to treating children with PTSD symptoms have also been reported by March, Amaya-Jackson, Murray, and Schulte (1998).

These studies highlight the fact that school-based interventions can be quite successful in helping children coping with their fears and anxieties. Joseph and Linley (2005) note that factors thought to produce positive emotional processing of threatening events include engaged exposure, a sense of control, and relevant conversation about the event or issue, while factors likely to impede processing include avoidance of the disturbing situation, refusal or inability to talk, and an absence of perceived control. To the extent that teachers and school-based consultants create a classroom climate that encourages children to face challenging circumstances at a measured pace and process their emotions verbally, children may be helped to avoid the development or worsening of PTSD-type symptomatology.

Depression

As with the anxiety disorders, the past 12 years have yielded a number of clinic-based outcome studies supporting the effectiveness of various CB programs for the treatment of depression, with most of this work targeting adolescent populations (Clarke, DeBar, & Lewinsohn, 2003; Weersing & Brent, 2003; Weisz, Southam-Gerow, Gordis, & Connor-Smith, 2003). With the exceptions noted, however, there are relatively few school-based intervention efforts. Evans et al. (2002) have argued that school counselors should be playing a more active role in providing universal prevention programs as well as services to more high risk students. These authors note that "CBT is particularly appropriate for use in schools because its format reflects the familiar structures of school including (a) the process of CBT involving exploration, study, homework, and learning new information and skills; (b) the pattern of each CBT session with goal setting, researching problems, and experimenting with new ideas, and (c) the collaborative style of CBT which can engage students, teachers, and parents" (p. 218).

Stark and colleagues developed the ACTION school-based intervention program for treating symptoms of depression in youth ranging in age from 9 or 10 through adolescence. As detailed in the Stark and Kendall (1996a) manual, this program involves 30 one hour sessions that address a wide range of content areas, including affective education, self-monitoring of emotions, pleasant event scheduling, problem-solving training, recognition of negative thinking and cognitive restructuring, assertiveness training, and clarification of standards of self-evaluation. These skills are taught and practiced primarily in group sessions, but individual sessions are also encouraged to assure content mastery for each child and to enhance the therapeutic alliance between the child and the group leader. Stark et al. (2005) describe a recent modification of the Stark and Kendall (1996a) program that is designed to make this intervention particularly responsive to the needs of preadolescent and young adolescent girls. These authors report that the revised program includes largely the same content as the original but has been designed to include emotion regulation skills that are developmentally appropriate for the targeted group. This variation of the program is currently undergoing evaluation.

The Adolescent Coping with Depression Course (CWD-A; Clarke, Lewinsohn, & Hops, 1990) has undergone careful evaluation of both efficacy and effectiveness (Rohde et al., 2005). As implemented in clinical settings, the course involved 16 two hour group sessions held over an 8-week period. Course content addresses the development of a variety of coping skills, including training in mood monitoring, increasing involvement in pleasant activities, recognition of depressogenic cognitions and cognitive restructuring, communication and problem-solving skills, and relaxation training. As noted above, careful evaluation has yielded positive results. Adding a formal parent involvement component did not enhance outcome over improvements seen with the standard program.

After demonstrating effectiveness with clinically impaired samples, Clarke et al. (1995) conducted a preventive intervention with 150 "demoralized" ninth and tenth grade high school students who were not yet meeting criteria for major depressive disorder or dysthymic disorder but were considered at high risk to develop full blown depression. Half of this sample was assigned to a 15-session group intervention program that was offered after school but on the school grounds. Groups were led by specially trained school psychologists and school counselors. The program was labeled the "Coping with Stress" course and was a modified version of the CWD-A program. Course content focused on cognitive restructuring in which group members learned to identify and challenge unhelpful thinking that might lead to future episodes of depression. At 12-month follow-up, survival analysis indicated fewer cases of either major depressive disorder or dysthymic disorder in the experimental group versus the controls, with rates of 14% and 25%, respectively. Clarke et al. (2001) conducted another preventive intervention using the Coping with Stress program with adolescents who were displaying subclinical levels of depressive symptoms and whose parents were already in treatment for depression. Again, at 15-month follow-up, survival analysis suggested significantly fewer new cases of mood disorder occurred in the group receiving the intervention relative to a treatment as usual control condition.

Cognitive approaches have demonstrated their capacity to reduce depressive symptomatology and prevent the emergence of full-blown depressive episodes, but research addressing school-based interventions for depressed children seems to lag behind that now observed with anxiety disorders, and, as discussed next, conduct disorders.

Conduct Problems and Anger Management

Interventions with cognitive components are now well-established as viable treatments for children and adolescents presenting acting-out behaviors, particularly aggression and anger management concerns (Kazdin, 2005; Lochman et al., 2003). Meta-analyses, dismantling studies, and direct treatment comparisons indicate children with anger control issues benefit from both the direct skills training provided by social skills-oriented approaches and from interventions that remediate distortions in their social cognitive processes (Manen, Prins, & Emmelkamp, 2004; Sukhodolsky, Golub, Stone, & Orban, 2005; Sukhodolsky, Kassinove, & Gorman, 2004). In addition, ongoing research continues to provide support for the important role of cognitive variables in predicting anger intensity and probability of aggressive behavior (Boman, Smith, & Curtis, 2003; McConville & Cornell, 2003). The extensive research program of Kazdin and colleagues has demonstrated the effectiveness of problem-solving training in treating conduct disordered children referred to outpatient mental health or hospital settings (Kazdin, 2003), but given the focus of this chapter, a comprehensive description of a school-based program is presented.

Happily, some of the CB intervention programs highlighted in the first edition of this chapter have continued to be elaborated and improved. In 1995, the Anger Coping Program developed by Lochman and colleagues was already generating evidence of its effectiveness (Lochman, 1992; Lochman, Burch, Curry, & Lampron, 1984; Lochman & Curry, 1986; Lochman, Lampron, Gemmer, Harris, & Wyckoff, 1989; Lochman et al., 1981). This program was originally designed as a school-based intervention targeting elementary school-age boys presenting with anger control problems. As reviewed in Lochman et al. (2003) and detailed in Larson and Lochman (2002), the current Anger Coping Program involves eighteen 60- to 90-minute group sessions that are designed to be held weekly in a school setting. The content/objectives for the sessions include many of the CB components previously discussed. After initial introductions and establishing group rules, participants work on understanding and setting individualized goals and learning how to use the program goals sheet. Group members then learn about the use of self-talk, distraction, and relaxation skills as a means of managing feelings, particularly anger. Puppets are used to model effective self-talk and distraction during emotionally intense interactions such as being teased. Group members then transition to practicing these skills themselves while being taunted by fellow group members. In later sessions, the concepts of perspective-taking and problem recognition are introduced and practiced using a variety of games and activities. Next the group is introduced to anger education and recognition of the physiological cues of anger. This is followed by consideration of anger as a cue to problem solving. Participants learn how to generate alternative responses to situations and consider what the consequences might be. The remaining sessions involve a great deal of review of problem solving in the context of preparing a videotape about effective use of their newly developed social cognitive skills for anger management. The detailed preparation of these problem-solving videos serves as a vehicle for practice, review, and additional modeling of appropriate skill use.

Lochman and Wells (2002) created an expanded version of this curriculum called the Coping Power Program. This variation is designed for students transitioning into middle school. In addition to expanding from 18 to 35 sessions to be delivered over a 15-month time frame, the Coping Power Program includes a 16-session parent component. An enhanced version of the Coping Power Program includes five 2-hour teacher in-service training sessions. Both the parent and teacher components focus on training effective reinforcement of desirable child behavior and educate the adults about the social cognitive skills the children are learning in their group sessions. Even if a school-based consultant will never be in a position to implement the formal teacher component, Larson and Lochman (2002) present an extremely valuable discussion of the role of teachers as treatment collaborators in the classroom. Their discussion offers practical suggestions on how to avoid common pitfalls that can weaken school based treatment efforts.

As summarized by Lochman et al. (2003), the Anger Coping Program has consistently demonstrated reductions in parent-rated aggression, reductions in off-task classroom behavior, and improvements in perceived social competence and self-esteem. Evaluations of the Coping Power Program indicate treatment resulted in lower rates of delinquent behavior and parent-rated substance use at 1-year follow-up, with these positive results most observable among participants receiving both the parent and child program components. Lochman and Wells (2002) evaluated the effects of the Coping Power Program for targeted high risk children when the program was offered in schools also providing universal prevention efforts. The postintervention analyses indicated that both Coping Power alone and Coping Power plus universal intervention achieved positive results, but relatively more positive outcomes were achieved in the combined condition.

Larson (2005) presents an adaptation of the concepts of the Anger Coping Program for use with secondary school-age students. Consistent with the greater cognitive sophistication of this age group, Larson's Think First program makes more use of cognitive restructuring methods to help participants identify and challenge aspects of their own thinking that may function as anger triggers. As described by Larson (2005), common thought triggers include *awfulizing* thoughts that exaggerate the negative features of a situation (e.g., "I can't bear it if this happens again"), *demanding* thoughts that create necessities out of what are actually preferences (e.g., "She can't say that to me"), *overgeneralized* thoughts that involve blowing things out of proportion (e.g., "These guys are always on my back"), and *name-calling* triggers that label someone in an unkind way and function to increase anger.

Many of the key elements of the Lochman intervention are incorporated into the large scale, multisite Fast Track program created and evaluated by the Conduct Problems Prevention Research Group (CPPRG; 1992, 2002a, 2002b). While the work of this group is ongoing, their findings provide additional support for the conclusions that children's aggressive behavior can be decreased through interventions that enhance social cognitive skills and problem solving. In particular, CPPRG (2002b) reports that decreases in parental reports of conduct problems, improved peer preference scores, and decreased association with deviant peers seem to be mediated by reducing parent's use of harsh physical discipline, improving the child's social and academic competence, reducing evidence of hostile attributional biases, and improving social problem-solving skills.

These intervention efforts with school-age children and adolescents are exciting and laudable, for schools are clearly impacted by the behavior of students with aggression and anger management concerns. As we learn more about the development of aggressive behavior, however, there has been a call for intervention with even younger children (Tremblay et al., 2005). Interestingly, even interventions for younger children that have tended to focus on behavioral child management have begun to add cognitive elements to both the parent and child curriculum. For example, Webster-Stratton and colleagues (Webster-Stratton & Reid, 2003; Webster-Stratton, Reid, & Hammond, 2001) have spent decades developing and refining the Incredible Years program. This intervention was originally designed as a behavioral parent training intervention targeting the families of 2- to 6-year-old children displaying oppositional and defiant behavior. A school-age version of the basic program was developed.

Both programs used videotape-based training to help parents develop positive behavior management skills. In subsequent years, the program was expanded to include an advanced segment of parent training that helped parents work on their own anger management, negative self-talk, communication, and problem-solving skills. A child skills training component, the Dina Dinosaur Program, was also developed to teach at-risk preschoolers and primary grade children a variety of social cognitive skills including empathy and perspective-taking, anger management, and interpersonal problem solving. Finally, a teacher segment was developed to train classroom teachers in many of the positive child management, problem solving, and anger management skills presented in the parent training program. Early evaluations of the Incredible Years program were clinic-based interventions with children who had undergone formal diagnosis. Later efforts, however, have included school-based prevention studies that targeted high risk populations. For example, Webster-Stratton et al. (2001) evaluated the teacher training curriculum with 61 Head Start teachers working in 34 classrooms. This intervention resulted in enhanced parent-teacher bonding, improved teacher classroom management skills, and fewer school-based conduct problems among the children in the experimental classrooms.

As these programmatic examples indicate, there are now evidence-based, school friendly intervention programs for youth displaying aggressive behavior or anger problems, whether the student is in preschool or high school. The Incredible Years program, or at least elements of it, would seem to be ideal for adoption and use within early childhood and family education programs, while variations on the Lochman programs are well-suited for elementary, middle school, and high school contexts.

Attention-Deficit/Hyperactivity Disorder

Research over the past 12 years has brought advances in the use of cognitive strategies for treating a variety of childhood concerns but not for the treatment of the core symptoms of ADHD. As highlighted by Hinshaw (2005), research on cognitive approaches with ADHD has basically halted. This state of affairs is the logical result of findings indicating that CB methods are not effective with the core symptoms of this disorder (Abikoff, 1991; Braswell et al., 1997). Consistent with this finding, Hinshaw notes that if current theories are correct about the core deficit being one of inhibitory control, then any intervention relying on verbal mediational is unlikely to be successful.

While remaining clear that CB strategies should not be used as primary treatment methods, it is also possible that certain cognitive approaches can extend the benefits achieved with traditional behavioral treatments. In addition, as previously noted, ADHD children are often comorbid for conditions that are responsive to cognitive strategies, so selected CB approaches may have a limited, but legitimate place in the intervention plan for some children with ADHD.

As discussed by Braswell (2004) and Chronis, Chacko, Fabiano, Wymbs, and Pelham (2004), parental cognitions about themselves, attributions about their child's behavior, and expectations about treatment may all influence the degree to which parents become positively engaged in intervention efforts. School consultants and others working with the parents may find it very useful to explore the parents' cognitions early in the assessment process, so that any distorted, mistaken, or unhelpful beliefs can be addressed before they have a chance to sabotage the treatment process. For that matter, with school-based interventions it may also make sense to explore the cognitions of the classroom teacher, for shared expectations about the teacher's involvement in any intervention efforts would seem to be an important element in achieving success.

As described in the earlier section on self-monitoring approaches, adding an element of self-evaluation to traditional behavioral contingencies may help extend the benefits of this intervention. The Hinshaw et al. (1984a) version of the Match Game illustrates an effective application of self-evaluation with small groups of students with ADHD. Self-monitoring of attention in classrooms or resource room settings can be an effective means of increasing the ADHD child's time on-task, particularly during independent seat work periods. As illustrated in the Carter (1993) example, self-monitoring approaches can also be used to decrease the rate of impulsive blurt-outs, which are a common concern for some children with ADHD.

Temper outbursts and poor anger management are also common co-existing concerns for children with ADHD, so school consultants may also wish to consider judicious inclusion of these students in anger management groups, such as those described in the previous section. In particular, the findings of Hinshaw et al. (1984b) suggest that ADHD students may benefit from direct practice in using calming self-talk, distraction, and other techniques to "keep their cool" when provoked by peers. As discussed more recently by Hinshaw (1985), this element of anger management training has been incorporated into the intensive behavioral social skills training summer program of Pelham and Hoza (1996) and the successful clinic-based social skills group intervention of Pfiffner and McBurnett (1997).

Summary

Developmental Concerns

It is exciting to see the increasing array of successful school-based interventions employing cognitive strategies; however, as noted in the first edition of this chapter, it is crucial that intervention goals and methods match the age and cognitive stage of the children involved. Even with traditional behavioral methods, it is important to be attuned to developmental variations in factors such as the meaning and function of rewards or the quantity and quality of information acquired from examples of modeled behavior (Furman, 1980). When a consultant is considering an intervention making explicit cognitive demands, it is even more important to be sure the choice is consistent with what is understood about cognitive, social, and emotional development. As interventions with preschool-age children proliferate, for example, it is increasingly important to remember Harter's (1977) caution that young children do not have the ability or, alternatively, the interest in focusing on themselves as an object of evaluation or criticism. This capacity and/or interest seems to develop around 6 to 8 years of age. This observation has direct implications for the timing of interventions that require the capacity for self-evaluation—which is at least a subcomponent of most cognitive-behavioral interventions. Similarly, some problem-solving training programs promote specific component skills, such as cognitive and emotional perspective taking. Although the inclusion of such a component is logical, those implementing the training must be careful that they are not attempting to implant a capacity that would not be expected to emerge until a normally developing child is 7 to 9 years old.

On a positive note, Strayhorn's (1988) recommendation for greater use of developmentally appropriate play methods and story techniques to model appropriate behavior has been heeded in the growing popularity of social stories type interventions and in the application of these methods with children besides just those manifesting symptoms of ASD (Crozier & Sileo, 2005; Gray & Garland, 1993; Haggerty et al., 2005). Similarly, attempts to train social cognitive skills, such as the Dina Dinosaur School component of the Incredible Years Program, make extensive use of games and appealing life-sized puppets.

Parental and Other Significant Adult Involvement

The importance of maintaining a developmental perspective would also seem to extend to the issue of parental involvement and/or the involvement of any emotionally significant adult. For example, with young children it would be futile to attempt to build up their sense of self-efficacy regarding a certain academic or social challenge without also being sure that the parents and teacher were prepared to communicate the same supportive, encouraging attitude. The findings of Barak et al. (1992) are a reminder that the words of the classroom teacher can be very effective in changing how a child perceives his or her abilities and how he or she values certain tasks. Parental involvement may be particularly essential to change a child's negative self-view and unrealistic standards of self-evaluation. In some cases, there may be reason to believe the parent also endorses unrealistic standards for the child. In this circumstance, the educational and reframing approaches described in the section on cognitive restructuring would be extremely appropriate. Parental involvement with problem-solving efforts was mentioned previously in the context of the consultant modeling the use of a problem-solving approach with the parents while addressing concerns about the child. If the child is a participant in a formal problem-solving group training program at school, consultants are strongly encouraged to provide families with at least written information about how they can model and reinforce the generalization of the methods being trained in the group. Having a series of parent meetings to communicate this information through active practice would be even more desirable. With adolescents, however, while in most circumstances it would be wonderful to have the involved cooperation of parents and all teachers, it may not be as crucial to the success of certain intervention efforts, as indicated by the findings of Lewinsohn, Clarke, Hops, and Andrews (1990) regarding parent participation and outcomes with the Coping with Depression course for adolescents. Further research is needed to clarify whether parent group meetings are most effective means of involving parents or if sessions with individual families offer a better alternative for parental involvement with interventions for adolescents.

In conclusion, CB strategies have a valuable place in the school consultant's tool box of intervention methods. School-based CB approaches have demonstrated their merits as important treatments for symptoms of anxiety and trauma concerns, depression-related issues, and as interventions for children with aggression and anger control difficulties. Efforts to enhance student self-efficacy beliefs may further academic goals. Cognitive methods can be adjunctive efforts to some forms of treatment for children with ADHD. Cognitive techniques may be particularly useful for increasing the student's active engagement in the intervention process. In addition, these methods can enhance the effectiveness of other intervention efforts by promoting more adaptive expectations and beliefs on the part of students, teachers, and parents.

CHAPTER

13

Strategies to Improve Self-Regulation

SANDRA RIEF

Students with neurobiological disorders often have difficulty with self-regulation, which adversely affects their day-to-day behavioral, social, and academic performance. In a consulting role with classroom teachers, it is necessary to share practical and doable strategies, supports, and interventions that will lead to better self-management and regulatory skills. This chapter addresses what teachers can do to create the environment, and employ the structure, group contingencies, and instructional techniques that foster self-regulation. These include whole class or small group management systems, instructional and organizational practices that train *all* students and support them in their development of internal controls and responsible behavior. Then we direct our focus to individualized approaches and programs for students needing a higher degree of intervention to develop their self-regulatory skills. We also take a brief look at the schoolwide continuum of positive behavioral supports and some additional self-regulation programs and interventions that may be considered in a school setting.

Self-Regulation: Normal Development and Difficulties for Some Children and Teens

Phyllis Anne Teeter (1998) synthesizes the research as she describes stages of a child's development of self-regulation and self-control from the

Adapted from Rief (1998, 2003, 2005) and Rief and Heimburge (2006).

toddler/preschool stage through adulthood. Citing Wenar (1994) and Maccoby (1984), during the middle childhood stage, self-control reflects both the child's developing self concept and the ability to match his or her behavior to fit the desires or demands of parents, teachers, and other adults. In this stage, children begin to anticipate the consequences of their actions and to shape their actions accordingly (Wenar, 1994). During this stage of middle childhood, parents influence children by setting standards that the child uses to monitor his or her own behaviors (Maccoby, 1984). Although the parent-child relationship affects this process, self-regulation also develops in conjunction with the child's increasing cognitive capabilities and as children develop and begin to use "inner talk" to control and guide their behavior. Middle childhood (ages 6 to 12) is marked by considerable progress in self-regulation, and cognitive functioning, including increased memory and attentional abilities, control and expression of emotions, and social interaction abilities (Teeter, 1998).

The research indicates that as children make the transition from childhood to adolescence, self-control starts to become an internalized value of considerable importance—a matter of personal commitment and responsibility (L. E. Berk, 1989). Older children and adolescents begin to value self-control, and it is viewed as an important part of self concept.

A characteristic of more challenging students, those Rhode et al. (1995) refer to as "tough kids," is a lack of rule following and self-management skills. Self-management skills are skills learned in order to put off immediate gratification for a long-term benefit. "Tough kids" generally have behavioral excesses (too much of a behavior), and behavioral deficits (inability to adequately perform a behavior); and their behavioral deficit is in self-management skills such as the inability to delay rewards (acting before thinking, not following rules, and not foreseeing consequences).

A primary goal of treatment for ADHD, for example, is to enable a student to develop adequate levels of self-control, which implies that a child will exhibit age-appropriate social and academic behaviors on an independent basis, with a minimum of accommodation on the part of the environment (DuPaul & Stoner, 2003).

However, to reach the eventual goal of self-management, external supports and interventions are needed for children with weaknesses in their self-regulatory capabilities. The remainder of this chapter addresses those group and individualized supports, strategies, and interventions—most of which are beneficial for all students; but necessary for those children and teens with self-regulation difficulties.

Things to Keep in Mind When
Consulting with Teachers

It is not always easy for a consultant to engage the cooperation and willingness of classroom teachers to employ the strategies they are suggesting. If the teacher perceives the consultant as judgmental and critical, or the recommendations as too overwhelming or unrealistic to implement, the likelihood that the plan will work is minimal. Consider the following recommended tips when working and consulting with teachers:

- Let the teacher know you are not there in a supervisory or administrative capacity. You are not observing in their classroom to critique or evaluate their teaching or management.
- Help teachers feel at ease with your presence in the classroom and to trust that your role and intent is to help with concerns they have and strategies to improve.
- When observing and debriefing with teachers, begin by noting and complimenting them on something positive in their classroom (environmental, instructional) and then discussing a few things at most that could be improved.
- If you are offering strategies for the group/whole class, it is beneficial to model various techniques or to have concrete examples to show and explain to the teacher. These suggestions are offered as an option that teachers may wish to try.
- Ask what techniques they already use for management if during your classroom observation you did not see them employed; and which strategies from those you are suggesting would they feel comfortable trying. For teachers to follow-through with incorporating your suggestions into their teaching repertoire, they have to feel it will be beneficial to them, and therefore, willing to make the effort.
- Guide the discussion when possible to enable the teacher to tweak your suggestions in a way that they add part of their own idea to yours—to give more personal ownership to the strategy.
- Begin with concrete tools, such as various examples of behavioral charts or monitoring forms that you can give the teacher; or show a template of some and then perhaps design one later for the teacher that is tailored to his or her class or student needs. When making such behavioral charts for teachers, design them to be visually appealing and user-friendly.
- Provide direct assistance and follow-through with the teacher to ensure that your agreed-upon strategies will be implemented; and problem-solve any glitches in the plan together.

Instructional and Management Practices that Enable Students to Better Self-Regulate Their Behavior

Being able to capture and hold students' interest and attention is not an easy task. Keeping all students engaged and motivated in daily instruction can be a monumental challenge to teachers, and one that requires experimenting with a variety of approaches. The following teaching strategies engage and maintain students' attention and active participation in the classroom.

Getting and Focusing Students' Attention

Before beginning instruction, teachers need first to obtain students' attention and direct their focus to the task at hand. The following are classroom strategies and techniques you may recommend to teachers which will enable them to do so:

Use Auditory Techniques for Getting Students' Attention

- Signal auditorily through the use of sound/music (chimes, rainstick, xylophone, playing a bar or chord on a keyboard, or a few seconds of music on a CD).
- There are various toys that make a novel sound that may be an interesting auditory signal; and beepers or timers may be used.
- Use a clap pattern. You clap a particular pattern, and students repeat the clap pattern back to you.
- Use a clear verbal signal (e.g., "Freeze. . . . This is important. . . ." "Everybody. . . . Ready. . . ." or "1, 2, 3, eyes on me").

Use Visual Techniques to Obtain Students' Attention

- Use visual signals such as: flashing the lights, or raising your hand (which signals the students to raise their hands and close their mouths until everyone is silent and attentive).
- Use pictures, diagrams, gestures, manipulatives, and demonstrations to engage students' visual attention and interest. Write key words or pictures on the board, overhead projector, or document camera while presenting.
- Illustrate, Illustrate, Illustrate: You do not have to draw well to illustrate throughout your presentation. Do so even if you lack the skill or talent. Drawings do not have to be sophisticated or accurate. In fact, often the sillier the better, and stick figures are fine. Any attempts to illustrate vocabulary, concepts, and so forth

325

not only focuses students' attention, but helps in the retention of information. Point to written material you want students to focus on with a dowel, stick/pointer, or laser pointer.

- Cover or remove visual distractions. Erase unnecessary information from the board, and remove visual clutter.
- Color is very effective in getting attention. Make use of colored dry-erase pens on white boards, and colored overhead pens for transparencies, and colored highlighting tape or Post-it notes. Write key words, phrases, steps to computation problems, and so forth, in a different color.
- Overhead projectors have traditionally been among the best tools for focusing students' attention in the classroom because they enable the teacher to: (a) model and frame important information, (b) block unnecessary information by covering part of the transparency, (c) face students and not have to turn your back on the students in order to write on the board, (d) avoid instructional lag time while writing on the board and erasing, (e) prepare transparencies in advance, saving instructional time.
- In addition, teachers can place novel objects on the overhead (such as a variety of math manipulatives, and other overhead tools). It is also motivating for students to write on the overhead. With today's technology, more and more teachers have the benefit of using a document camera, interactive white board, Powerpoint presentations, and other multimedia tools at their disposal for daily classroom instruction.

General Tips for Obtaining and Focusing Students' Attention

- Arouse students' curiosity and anticipation: Ask an interesting, speculative question; show a picture; tell a little story; or read a related poem to generate discussion and interest in the upcoming lesson.
- Try playfulness, silliness, humor, use of props, and a bit of theatrics to get attention and peek interest.
- Use storytelling, real-life examples, and anecdotes. Children of all ages love to hear stories (particularly personal ones, such as something that happened to the teacher when he or she was a child).
- Add a bit of mystery by bringing in one or more objects relevant to the upcoming lesson in a box, bag, or pillowcase. This is a wonderful way to generate predictions and can lead to excellent discussions or writing activities.

- Model excitement and enthusiasm about the upcoming lesson.
- Explain the lesson's purpose and importance. Identify the objectives, content standards being addressed, and ultimate goals or outcomes to be achieved by the end of the session or unit.
- When giving examples, use students' names, experiences, and other means of helping students identify with the topic being discussed.
- Activate students' prior knowledge and draw on their past experiences. Elicit discussion and use strategies that enable students to see the relevance of the lesson you are about to teach, and make connections with past learning or experiences.
- Graphic organizers (of which there are numerous kinds), are excellent tools to focus attention, as well as in helping students organize and comprehend ideas/information.
- Post a few key points to be attentive to, listening for, and thinking about during the lesson.

Maintaining Students' Attention through Active Participation

Being able to maintain the attention of students is quite a challenge. The following strategies may be suggested to teachers:

- Keeping or sustaining students' attention requires active, not passive learning. It also requires that teachers incorporate a variety of formats and activities that are woven throughout the lesson. Within a 50-minute period of time, for example, the lesson may be formatted to include a mix of (a) whole group instruction and end of lesson closure (with engaging ways for students to respond and participate); (b) predominantly small group and partner structures for maximum involvement in learning activities; and (c) some time to work on a particular task independently.

General Tips for Keeping Students Engaged

- Move around in the classroom, maintaining your visibility.
- Incorporate demonstrations and hands-on presentations into your teaching whenever possible, and use high-interest material.
- Build in movement opportunities during the lesson.
- Reduce lag time by being prepared.
- Monitor and vary your rate, volume, and tone of voice.
- Have students write down brief notes or illustrate key points during instruction.
- Make all efforts to greatly increase student responses— saying and doing something with the information being taught

throughout the lesson. This can be done, for example, through frequent pair shares. "Turn to your partner and . . . (summarize, share, paraphrase) your understanding"; or "With your partner, share and clarify any questions you still have about what we just discussed."

- Use a variety of graphic organizers and techniques such as webbing, graphing, clustering, mapping, and outlining.
- Increase the amount of teacher modeling, guided practice, and immediate feedback to students.
- Use study guides, partial outlines, or other graphic tools to accompany verbal presentation. While you are presenting a lesson or giving a lecture, students fill in the missing words based on what you are saying and/or writing on the board or overhead. Jotting down a few words or filling in missing information in a guided format is helpful in maintaining attention.
- Cooperative learning formats (partners/small groups) are highly effective in keeping students engaged and participating during lessons. Teachers need to follow the proper structure of cooperative learning groups (e.g., assignment of roles, individual accountability). It is *not* just group work. Many students with self-regulation difficulties do not function well in groups without clearly defined structure and expectations.
- Use motivating computer programs for specific skill building and practice (programs that provide for frequent feedback and self-correction), and games for skill practice, whenever possible.
- Motivate all students to actively participate by differentiating instruction in the classroom. Provide many opportunities for student choices of activities/projects, and ways to demonstrate their learning. Provide student projects and assignments that have options, including: music, drama, art, construction, designing, writing, speaking, use of technology, research, and any other means of creative expression.
- Differentiate instruction through use of learning centers, flexible grouping, interest groups, independent projects/study, and a variety of other instructional strategies, structures, and accommodations.

Keeping Students On-Task During Seatwork

Some students have significant difficulty remaining focused and productive during independent/seatwork times of the day. They may have difficulty due to distractibility, forgetfulness (of what they are supposed to be doing), or if they lack some of the prerequisite skills to do the independent work without assistance. The following are some strategies you may suggest that teachers try:

- Provide guided practice before having students work independently on seatwork activities.
- Check for clarity. Make sure directions are clear and understood before sending students back to their seats to work independently.
- Give a manageable amount of work that students are capable of doing *independently*.
- Make sure necessary supplies are available so students can work during independent time without excuses. Have extra (but less desirable) materials available for unprepared students.
- Send student(s) to their seat with a written task card or checklist. A task sheet (or "things to do" sheet) is also helpful. Have students cross out each task when completed.
- Study buddies or partners may be assigned for clarification purposes during seatwork, especially when the teacher is instructing another group of students while part of the class is doing seatwork. When part of the class has a seatwork assignment while you are working with other students (e.g., during a reading group), set the expectation that students who have a question during seatwork must ask their partner (or classmates in their group first). Only if no one in the group can answer the question, may the teacher be interrupted. Some teachers also assign one or more "experts" of the day for students to go to in need of help.
- Scan the classroom frequently, as all students need positive reinforcement. Frequently give positive comments, praising students specifically whom you observe to be on-task. This serves as a reminder to students who tend to have difficulty.
- Do not give independent work that is very difficult before students have had sufficient guided practice.
- Try using a timer and beat-the-clock system to motivate completion of a reasonable amount of work. Reward for on-task behavior and work completed during short designated time segments.
- Provide study carrels and quiet areas for students who tend to be distracted during seat work time.

Questioning Techniques to Increase Student Engagement and Response Opportunities

One of the most important processes that takes place in a learning environment is that of asking and responding to questions. In all classrooms, there are some students who are inattentive and easily distracted. There are also students who, for whatever reason, are reluctant to participate, and are passively rather than actively involved in the lesson. Teachers who have the most success in engaging students are those who are skilled in the art of questioning. One of the most effective ways of ensuring that all students are actively engaged in the lesson is through specific questioning techniques that encourage and provide for: high response opportunities, student accountability, critical/divergent thinking, and active participation—with everyone having a voice that is heard and respected.

General Questioning Tips

- Format lessons to include a variety of questioning techniques that involve whole class, group, partner, and individual responses.
- Before asking for a verbal response to a question, have all students jot down their best-guess answer. Then call for volunteers to verbally answer the question.
- Structure the lesson so that it includes the opportunity to work in pairs or small groups for maximum student involvement and attention. Utilize alternatives to simply calling on students one at a time. Instead, have students respond by telling their partner; writing down or drawing their response, and so forth.
- Ask questions that are open-ended, require reasoning and stimulate critical thinking and discussion.
- Expand on students' partial answers. ("Tell me more." "How did you arrive at that answer?")
- Wait until there are several hands that are raised before calling on students to respond.

It is important for teachers to incorporate many techniques that enable students to have frequent response opportunities throughout instruction. There are a variety of strategies that are recommended to incorporate in lessons. The following are some suggestions for whole group (full class), small group, and partner responses that require active involvement of students.

Whole Group and Unison Responses

- *Use choral responses.* Have students recite poems or share reading of short passages or lines from the text chorally (in unison). Singing songs or chants, reviewing (e.g., irregular/sight words, or math facts), with whole class response to flash cards, or other such activities are examples of choral responses.

- *Hand signals for whole group responses.* Unison responses can also be obtained by having students use various hand signals. For example, with thumbs up/thumbs down, or open hand/closed hand responses from students indicating "yes/no"; "I agree/I disagree," or any other "either/or" response.

- *Write-on tools (other than paper/pencil).* Most students (particularly those with Learning Disabilities or ADHD who often resist paper and pencil work), are motivated to work with colored pens and markers on dry erase boards. Another way of eliciting unison responses is to: ask the class a question, pause for "thinking time," and ask students to write their answer on an individual dry-erase board, individual chalkboard, or other write-on tool.

- *Premade response cards.* Another way to elicit unison responses is through premade response cards. Examples of premade response cards: (a) cards with a single-hole punch which are held together by a metal ring, (b) cards that can are held together by a brass fastener and opened up like a fan, and (c) a single card made of cardstock or construction paper that is divided into sections (halves, thirds, or quarters), preprinted with a choice of responses. The answer is indicated on this card by placing a clothespin on the student's choice of correct answer.

When the teacher poses the question, students select their answer by holding up the card of choice, placing their clothespin, or similar method of indicating choice. Cards should be designed with words/symbols written on both sides of the card so both the teacher and student can see when holding it up. Premade response cards or fans are very useful at any grade level or content area to integrate into whole-class questioning strategies (Heward et al., 1996).

Methods for Small Group Responses

Much of classroom instruction involves small groups of students working together. Small group active responses take place in any cooperative learning group structure. There are endless activities, learning tasks, and projects that are best accomplished in small groups such as: creating a product together, solving a problem, brainstorming, analyzing, summarizing, conducting an experiment, studying and reviewing, reading and discussing, and so forth.

Methods for Partner Responses

Use of partners (pair-shares) is perhaps the most effective method for maximizing student engagement. It involves turning to a partner for short interactions between two students. Pair-share formats are ideal for: predicting, sharing ideas, clarifying directions, summarizing information, previewing information, drilling/practicing (vocabulary, spelling words, math facts), shared reading of text, discussing reading material, sharing writing assignments, and so forth. For example:

"Pair up with your neighbor and share your ideas about . . ."

"Turn to your partner/neighbor and . . ." After giving partners a chance to respond, ask for volunteers to share with the whole class: "Who would be willing to share what you or your partner thought about . . . ?"

"Turn to your partner (or person across from you, behind you) and discuss for a few minutes . . ." or "Write down with your partner all the things you can think of that _____."

"Help each other figure out how to do this . . ."

"Try answering your partner's three selected questions about this reading material."

Partners can be used to: check over each other's work before turning it in, combine ideas and resources for a joint project, take turns reading aloud or questioning and discussing a reading passage together, listening to and providing feedback on each other's writing, working out math problems together, checking that each other correctly recorded homework assignments in their daily planner, and numerous other tasks.

Proactive Classroom Management Practices

Prevention of Student Misbehavior

In most classrooms, students' behaviors can be managed through basic structuring of the environment with rules, consequences, and consistent enforcement. With a management system that focuses on prevention of problems and mild interventions when problem behaviors do occur, generally students' misbehaviors can be brought under control. The following are general principles and strategies for preventing or minimizing behavioral problems, and interventions to employ within the classroom. Start with the basics: Establish 4 to 5 rules positively stated, posted, and referred to frequently. Here are a few examples of classroom rules/standards:

- Bring all needed materials to class.
- Be in seat and ready to work when bell rings (pencils sharpened, paper/pencil out, warm-ups started).
- Obtain permission before speaking or leaving your seat.
- Be respectful and polite to all people.

Teachers need to:

- Employ the principles of good classroom management: structure, consistency, follow-through, a focus on problem *prevention,* and far more use of positive reinforcement than use of corrective consequences.
- Watch for warning signs of potential problems (anticipate) and intervene early.
- Maintain positive and high expectations for students.
- Document inappropriate behavior and log actions/interventions.
- Communicate with and involve parents.
- Be flexible and willing to accommodate individual needs of students.
- Notice misbehavior at the beginning stages and employ appropriate strategies to avoid escalation.

Address the following variables (structural, environmental, affective, instructional) that can be antecedents to problem behavior.

Structural and Environmental Variables
Close attention to structure and environmental factors is critical for prevention of behavioral problems.

- Provide the necessary structure. Establish clear, reasonable rules/ behavioral standards, routines, procedures, and guidelines.
- Explain the rationale for all expectations and procedures, and thoroughly teach, model, practice, and review frequently.
- Externalize the rules (post them, use photos or pictures to depict them), and refer to the visual of the rules frequently.
- Provide specific, descriptive feedback to students. For example, "I see that Carla has her book open to the right page, and her paper and pencil are out. Carla is ready to work."

- Prepare for and structure transition times of the day, and provide extra help when there are unexpected changes of routine and unstructured situations.
- Arrange the environment for easy access to all parts of the room (and students' desks), and clear visibility of all students.
- Utilize proximity control; circulate among students and stand next to the desk of a student who is prone to misbehavior.
- Change student seating (e.g., distractible students closer to the center of instruction, closer to teacher for cueing and prompting, away from high traffic area).
- Provide more space, if possible (e.g., increase distance between desks).
- Use music for transitions and for calming/relaxing students.
- Build a class environment with a sense of community, teamwork, and interdependence.

Affective Variables and Personalized Efforts

The key to effective classroom management is building positive relationships and rapport with students, and making a connection on a personal level. This requires teachers to be understanding, flexible, patient, and empathic. Children typically work hard and will want to cooperate and please adults whom they like, trust, and respect. It is important to do the following:

- Smile, laugh, and communicate that you enjoy teaching and being with students; show through your daily interactions that you sincerely care about and expect the best from all of your students, and would never give up on any of them.
- Acknowledge and validate what students are thinking and feeling.
- Avoid lecturing, nagging, and criticism.
- Enforce rules/expectations, but take into consideration factors that may require handling some situations differently.

Instructional Variables

There is a direct relationship between student behavior and classroom instruction. To minimize behavioral problems as well as increase learning, teachers need to:

- Provide engaging, motivating, meaningful learning activities/ instruction.
- Be well planned, with little lag time (when students are unoccupied and waiting to find out what they are expected to do next).

- Make sure independent work is developmentally appropriate and within student's capability of doing successfully without help.
- Utilize effective and inclusive questioning techniques.

Classroom (Group) Contingencies for the Classroom
There are various kinds of class (group) reinforcement systems teachers may choose to implement, which may best fit their style of teaching, comfort level, and the interest of their students. Examples of some common group reinforcement systems to discuss and troubleshoot with teachers are discussed next.

Table/Team Points
Points are given for specific behaviors being demonstrated (e.g., cooperation and teamwork, on-task, all assignments turned in, area cleaned up, transitioning on or before allotted time). Table points may be used noncompetitively or competitively. For the noncompetitive method, any tables/teams earning a target number (x amount) of points earns the reward or privilege. This is not table/team competition. Each table/team can earn the reward or privilege when meeting the goal. The more commonly used technique is competitive. Points are awarded to tables/teams demonstrating the target behavior(s). "Table 4, good job of cooperating and helping your teammates. You just earned a point." At the end of the day/week, the table or team with *the most* points earns the reward or privilege (or the top two tables win the reward).

Marbles in a Jar
Teachers (usually in primary grade classrooms) catch students engaged in appropriate behaviors. They call attention to the positive behavior (of an individual student, group of students, or something the whole class did well). Then, the teacher reinforces the positive behavior by putting a marble (or other kind of object) in a jar. Many teachers use a scoop of dried beans, or a scoop of uncooked kernels of popcorn. When the jar is filled, the whole class earns a reward (e.g., a popcorn party). This is a particularly effective technique for rewarding quick and smooth transitions.

Chart Moves
A chart is created for the class or group. The class is reinforced for meeting a set goal by advancing one space on the chart each time they meet that goal. When the chart is filled, the whole class earns the reward. There are numerous types of charts that can be made. It is recommended

to change the chart frequently to maintain the novelty and students' interest. Dot-to-dot charts, and any game-board type of charts will work.

A particular goal (or two) is set such as: All students are in their seats with materials ready by the morning bell; no observed incidents of a particular problematic behavior occurring in a certain time frame (such as, in the morning, after lunch). Each time the class meets that goal, a move is made on the chart such as connecting to the next dot (on a dot-to-dot chart), or moving a velcroed object to the next space on the wall chart.

Token Economy System

Students have the chance to earn tokens of some kind, such as points, tickets, poker chips, class money, or such thing for on-the-spot reinforcers. These tokens are later redeemable at a class store, auction, or raffle for a desired reward. A menu of rewards is developed with corresponding price values attached. Students can spend their earned tokens/points/money at designated times during class auctions or shopping at the class/school store.

Token economy systems also allow a teacher to incorporate a response cost into the system. They may, for example, fine or charge students (e.g., $10 class currency for forgetting book at home and needing to borrow another; $10 late to class). Teachers must be awarding generously and frequently for positive behaviors, so that students (particularly those with ADHD) are not overly fined for rule infractions or forgetfulness. This would result in frustration, losing motivation, and the program not being effective.

Probability Reinforcers

Teachers who give raffle tickets for demonstrating target behaviors or meeting certain goals have students write their name on the ticket and place in a container. Drawings are held (daily/weekly). Those students whose names are drawn receive prizes or privileges. This system is based on the principle of probability, and students understand that the more tickets they have, the greater the chance of winning a reward.

Good Behavior Game

This is a research-validated approach first described by Barrish, Saunders, and Wolf (1969) to significantly decrease disruptive behaviors in the classroom. There are a number of variations to the *Good Behavior Game*. It basically involves dividing the class into teams with team numbers listed on the board. At specified time(s) of the day, the game is played. A timer is set and designated disruptive behaviors that occur during that time period result in a check mark or tally mark recorded under the team name. The teacher states the inappropriate behavior resulting in that penalty. At the end of the time frame, any team with under x number of marks (e.g., three penalties or fewer) earns a reward. Initially the rewards are immediate and the time frame short for playing the game. Gradually the time frame is extended and reward times are not immediate (e.g., provided at end of day). For information regarding the *Good Behavior Game*, see www.bpp.jhu.edu and http://www.evidencebasedprograms.org.

Group Response Costs

Response cost techniques are an interesting means of improving and shaping behavior. They work differently than other positive reinforcement systems—in that instead of giving tokens/points for demonstrating the appropriate behavior, students work to keep the tokens/points that they are given up front. If they have a certain number of tokens/points remaining at the end of the given time frame, it earns them a reward.

There are many variations of response cost systems. The key is that students are working to keep what they have been given up front. For example, at the beginning of the day, the teacher may automatically give a certain number of minutes free time or special activity time to the class to be used at the end of the day/week. Specific misbehaviors that occur during the day will result in one-minute loss of time from the free minutes given. The net positive balance will be awarded at the end of the day (or week). Of course, the teacher has the discretion to add bonus minutes during the day for exceptionally good behavior to increase the motivation.

Rewards/Positive Reinforcers

Students should be involved in identifying a menu of rewards that would be motivating and fun to work toward earning. Below are some examples of social, activity, and material reinforcers that students can earn for incentive programs being implemented (in the classroom or schoolwide):

Social Rewards

- Positive phone calls, notes, or e-mails to the student and/or parents
- Verbal praise and public recognition

- Earning a privilege of social status (e.g., to teach part of a lesson, team captain, class messenger, making announcements on intercom)
- Participate in activity such as work on computer with choice of friend(s)
- Posted photos and/or recognition assemblies of students demonstrating excellent or improved academic work or citizenship

Activity Rewards and Privileges

- Lunchtime activities or privileges (choice of seating, eating in special location, special games)
- Earning time in class to catch up on work with teacher/peer assistance available, if needed
- Breakfast or lunch with teacher, administrator, or other staff member
- Ice cream, popcorn, or pizza party for the class or group of students achieving a certain goal
- Free/earned time for activities of choice such as: games, listening to music, drawing, working on special project, and accessing learning/interest centers
- Extra time/access to gym, library/media center, music room
- Responsibilities or privileges that are desirable (e.g., tutor or mentor to a younger student, taking care of class pet, assistant to other teacher or staff member, tech assistant, taking attendance)
- Special activity day, field trip, party, movie at the end of the month
- Opportunity to use special materials/tools, make a Powerpoint presentation, do an Internet search
- Choose class game or book to be read

Material Reinforcers

- School supplies (special pencils, pens, erasers, folders)
- Stickers, stars, badges, certificates
- Class (or school) money, tickets, or points redeemable at auctions/lotteries, or class/school stores
- Items of choice from class store or treasure chest
- Special passes earned that can be redeemed later (e.g., take off one bad grade from daily assignments recorded, take off one problem from class test, homework pass—good for one assignment)
- Free tickets awarded to school sporting events, school plays, dances, concerts
- Food snack—preferably healthier snacks such as pretzels, crackers, popcorn, low-fat cookies, fruit drinks, or popsicles

Possible Corrective/Reductive Consequences for the Classroom

In addition to positive reinforcement for appropriate behavior, teachers will need to enforce consequences for misbehavior. The following lists some guidelines, strategies, and consequences used for reducing misbehavior in elementary, middle, and high schools. Remind teachers that not every minor misbehavior should be or needs to be followed with a corrective consequence. Simple low-key responses such as: signaling, nonverbal communication ("the teacher look"), reminding of the rules, warning, and ignoring of small infractions, are appropriate before employing corrective consequences (Gootman, 2001).

Also, all consequences should be given without lecturing or scolding. They should be delivered calmly, unemotionally, in a "matter of fact" manner:

- Last person to line up or be dismissed.
- Loss of time from participation in preferred activity in the classroom.
- Loss of part of recess time or other activity outside of classroom.
- Brief delay and owing time (e.g., one minute of time owed for each incident of interrupting instructional time). Time owed can be paid back prior to being able to participate in desired activity, or before being dismissed at the end of the day. Even one minute of being delayed can be a very negative consequence for a student eager to join up with friends.
- Time out from class participation (within the room at a designated area; another classroom, or other location under supervision in the school).
- Restriction or removal of privilege or desired materials for a period of time.
- Playground restriction from certain games or areas.
- Having to walk with or stand with a playground supervisor rather than participate.
- Undesirable task or chore assigned.
- Positive practice or do-overs. For example, for an inappropriate behavior (running in hall, throwing materials, rude manner of asking a question), to require the student to correct that behavior and perform it correctly and sometimes repeatedly (such as walking in the hall, picking up thrown paper, asking a question politely).
- Filling out a think-about-it (problem-solving) sheet; or behavioral improvement form.
- Loss of points or demerits.

- Being fined or losing tickets, class money, or other tokens that are redeemable for purchases and privileges when using a token economy.
- Restitution—fixing the problem. If, for example, the student broke something, or made a mess in an area—the consequence is to repair or replace what was broken, or to clean up the mess.
- Work center or detention.
- Student writes e-mail home or phone call to parents.
- Teacher writes note, e-mail, or calls parent.
- Student documents own behavior (in class book, recording sheet/log).
- Student writes an apology letter.
- Behavioral contract.

Note: This list of corrective consequences is not in any hierarchial sequence.

Classroom Environmental Supports and Accommodations

Students with neurobiological disorders affecting their ability to self-regulate and manage their behavior, attention level, and work performance will need environmental supports and accommodations. Teachers need to be aware of environmental factors and willing to make the necessary adjustments, such as the following:

Seating

Seating is a big environmental factor for inattentive and/or disruptive students. Providing preferential seating is an important accommodation. In most cases, a preferred choice of seating for a student with ADHD, for example, would be:

- Within close proximity to the teacher and the center of instruction.
- Within easy access for cueing, prompting, monitoring, supervising.
- Desk positioned so teacher can easily and frequently make eye contact with student.
- Surrounded by well-focused, tolerant, and supportive peers (if possible) away from (whenever possible) distracting locations or high-traffic areas such as: doors, windows, learning centers, pencil sharpeners, heating/air-conditioning units.
- Disruptive and/or distracted students often do better in individual desks rather than at group tables. Physically arrange the classroom

with options for seating. For example, single desk options as opposed to two-person desks/tables for those students who need more buffer space.

- The key to furniture arrangement is the ability of the teacher to easily access (with as few steps as possible) each student without obstruction. The best classroom management strategy is teacher proximity—moving among the students, monitoring, cueing, and giving feedback.
- Recommend that teachers consider seating choices and options. Elementary classes, of course, have more flexibility in their ability to do so.
- For children who have discomfort and trouble sitting in their seats, try seat cushions. Two recommended cushions are Movin' Sit Jr., and Disc O'Sit Jr. Both are inflatable "dynamic" seat cushions that accommodate a child's need for squirming and wiggling in the chair.
- There are a number of other options to sitting in a seat to work. For example, allowing a child to sit on a beanbag chair with paper attached to a clipboard may increase productivity and motivation.
- A round therapeutic ball, a T-stool, or the kind of computer seat that is meant to be knelt on (on knees) are sometimes helpful alternatives to sitting and working at a desk and hard chair.
- Allow students an alternative desk or chair in the room (two-seat method).
- Permit the student(s) who cannot sit for very long to stand near the desk while working at certain times (if productive). If doing so, a desk toward the back of the room may be more suitable and less noticeable to the other students in class.
- Be open, flexible, and willing to make changes in seating when needed. Be responsive to student complaints about their seating, and honor reasonable requests to move.
- Allow students to move to a quiet corner or designated area of the room if needed.
- Provide office areas or study carrels for seating options during certain times of the day as needed.

Structure to Reduce Auditory and Visual Distractions

- Permit students to use earphones to block out noise during seatwork, test taking, or other times of the day. Some teachers purchase sets of earphones to be used for this purpose, or allow a child to bring to school his or her own earphones. It is encouraged that *all* students experiment with and be allowed to use these tools (not just students with special needs).

- One of the best environmental modifications for students at the elementary level with attention difficulties is provision of study carrels or office areas. It is very helpful to have a few such office areas in the classroom for use during seat work/concentration time (particularly test-taking). By making these desirable areas available for anyone who requests using them, you are preventing them from being viewed by the class as areas of punishment.
- Purchase or construct privacy boards to place on tables while taking tests, or other times of the day to block visual distractions and limit the visual field. Construct desk-size, collapsible privacy boards with three pieces of heavy chipboard and duct tape.
- Reduce the clutter and unnecessary writing and visual overload in the classroom.
- Keep a portion of the room free from distracters. Do not seat a student with ADHD under mobiles or other hanging objects.
- If the room is not carpeted, it helps to insert old tennis balls on the tips of each chair leg to reduce the noise level.
- Allow students to move to a quiet corner or designated area of the room if needed.
- Establish rules and procedures for movement within the classroom (when it is okay to get up, get a drink, sharpen pencils, etc.), to reduce distractions in the environment.
- Have designated quiet times of the day.

Add Organization and Structure to Materials and Space in the Environment

- Designate physical boundaries with colored masking tape on the carpet, floor, or tables.
- Define areas of the room concretely.
- Store materials in clearly labeled bins, shelves, tubs, trays, and/or folders.
- Provide some students extra workspace and/or storage space.

Add More Visual and Auditory Cues to the Environment

- Post all schedules, calendars, and assignments.
- Have pictures and/or a list of rules and daily routine.
- Provide a lot of visual prompts, models, and displays for student reference (including visual depictions of procedures, routines, and rules).

- Use tools such as timers (various kinds), bells, and other devices, for signaling changes of activity.
- Use picture prompts and cues at the student's desk. For example, a prompt card showing picture icons or words indicating behaviors such as: raise hand to speak, on task working, or other such target behaviors. These serve as visual cues/reminders of expected behaviors. Besides the teacher (while circulating around the room during instruction) pointing to or tapping on the icons to prompt the student about expected behavior, the child may also "check himself or herself" periodically, according to the behaviors indicated on the visual prompt card.

Use of Music

The use of music in the classroom is also another environmental consideration. Music can be used during transitions (e.g., clean up and be ready by end of song), to calm and settle a class (e.g., soothing, quiet music after recess, physical education, lunch). Music can be played quietly during work periods, as well. For some students, music acts as a filter to other environmental noises and helps block out auditory distractions, as well as increases their productivity. Music is also beneficial for arousal and activating (a lively, upbeat tune when the class needs energizing—particularly in the afternoon).

Address Physical and Sensory Needs

Be sensitive to the physical needs of students that may interfere with learning: need for a drink of water, snacks, use of restroom. Consider allowing students to bring a bottle of water to school. Teachers may want to keep a stash of some healthy snack food available, if needed.

Provide for students (particularly students with ADHD) who have a physiological need for mobility. Build in many movement opportunities throughout instruction. Be aware of their need to exercise, and avoid using loss of recess time as a consequence for misbehavior or incomplete work.

Assign errands that enable the student to get up and leave the classroom (e.g., to bring something to the office).

Build in stretch breaks or exercise breaks after sitting any length of time.

Schoolwide Continuum of Positive Behavioral Supports

The schoolwide positive behavioral support (SWPBS) approach was developed by researchers and collaborators at the U.S. Department of

343

Education, Office of Special Education Programs Technical Assistance Center on Positive Behavioral Interventions and Supports (codirected by George Sugai at the University of Connecticut and Robert Horner at the University of Oregon). This approach is designed to support *all* students by establishing a continuum of preventive and positive interventions and systems. The intensity of these supports is increased as student behavior proves to be unresponsive to interventions (Sugai & Horner, 2005).

Based on a public health model of disease prevention, SWPBS emphasizes the implementation of a preventive schoolwide set of practices at which most (~80%) students are expected to benefit. Primary or universal prevention consists of (a) a small number of operationally defined, directly taught, continuously monitored, and frequently acknowledged schoolwide behavioral expectations; (b) team directed data-based decision making, action planning, and implementation coordination; (c) clear and mutually exclusive definitions and procedures for classroom-managed versus administrator-handled rule violations; and (d) continuous evaluation, implementation adaptation, and professional development (Sugai & Horner, 2005).

Students (~15%) whose behaviors are unresponsive to primary prevention practices are provided with interventions that increase social skills instruction, behavior monitoring and supervision, academic instructional adaptations, and teacher to student feedback, known collectively as secondary or selected interventions. These interventions are similar across students in consideration of classroom teacher time, effort, and skill level. Counselors, special educators, school psychologists, and so on are involved in supporting teachers in the development, implementation, and evaluation of secondary prevention interventions (Sugai & Horner, 2005).

Tertiary or intensive interventions are directed to the small (~5%) proportion of students whose behaviors are unresponsive to secondary prevention interventions. Multidisciplinary teams (e.g., student support, prereferral, teacher-assistance) to develop specially designed and individually implemented behavior intervention plans. These plans are comprehensive (home-school-community), strength skill-based (direct social skill instruction), function-based (behavior analytic), and multidisciplinary (education, health/medical, mental health, etc.). To be effective, tertiary interventions must be team managed, and individuals with specialized behavioral skills and capacity must be involved directly with development, implementation, monitoring, and evaluation of individual student behavior intervention plans (Sugai & Horner, 2005).

To be successful, a SWPBS approach is lead by a school-leadership team comprised of school administrator, general education grade/departmental representatives, special support personnel (e.g., special educators, school psychologists, counselors), parents, students, and noncertified staff (e.g., security, custodial, office, cafeteria, supervisory). This team reviews local data (e.g., disciplinary referrals, academic achievement, staff and parent school climate satisfaction, and intervention implementation). Discipline patterns are particularly helpful in guiding action planning: (a) rates of major and minor rule infractions, (b) types of problem behaviors, (c) location and time of day, and (d) office referrals by students. The team uses these data to develop a schoolwide implementation action plan that considers primary, secondary, and tertiary interventions. Most schools start with primary interventions because of the emphasis on all students, all staff, and all settings. In addition, effective implementation of primary interventions assists in identifying which students might benefit from secondary and tertiary level interventions (Sugai & Horner, 2005).

Accurate, comprehensive, and durable implementation of the SWPBS approach is associated with active administrator participation and leadership, regular team-staff-family communications, at least monthly review of schoolwide data, local behavioral expertise, emphasis on teaching schoolwide social skills, majority staff commitment (>80%), and high initiative priority (top 3). District-level coaching, acknowledgments, and administrative participation also facilitate school implementation of SWPBS. Successful implementation of SWPBS has been associated with (a) decreases in office discipline referrals, (b) enhancement of school climate and staff/student/parent satisfaction, (c) increased opportunities to maximize academic instruction, and (d) reductions in referrals for more intensive behavioral supports (Sugai & Horner, 2005).

Interventions at Each of the Three Levels

There are several types of strategies and interventions that can be implemented by schools at each of the three levels.

Universal Interventions (Primary Prevention)

- Teacher training (e.g., in proactive classroom management strategies, differentiating instruction to effectively teach diverse learners)
- Schoolwide commitment to and leadership in building a positive, pro-social climate and culture throughout the school

- Social-Emotional Learning (SEL), social skills, or character education programs that are taught, reinforced, and implemented schoolwide (by all school personnel in all school settings)
- Clear schoolwide rules/behavioral expectations, safety plans, procedures/processes for teaching and reinforcing the expectations, and for establishing and maintaining a safe and orderly environment
- Identifying specific locations/settings in the school that are problematic and providing more structure and support to minimize problems in these settings
- Establishing a schoolwide team to plan and oversee climate and problem prevention efforts, and monitor effectiveness of plans
- Family/community engagement

Selected Interventions (Secondary Prevention)

- Teacher training and coaching in instructional/behavioral strategies for reaching and teaching students with learning, attention, and behavioral challenges
- Student Support Team (SST) process for effectively strategizing and planning for students at-risk (classroom strategies/accommodations and appropriate schoolwide safety nets/interventions)
- Increased supervision, monitoring, reinforcement
- Individualized behavioral interventions (daily report cards, home notes, contracts, reinforcement plans)
- Self-management training/anger management
- Conflict resolution training
- In-school counseling
- School-based mental health and prevention programming

Intensive Targeted Interventions (Tertiary Prevention)

- Training educators about mental health disorders in children and strategies to help (e.g., how to de-escalate angry students)
- Crisis intervention training and skill development; crisis management
- School case management practices of students with chronic/intense behavioral difficulties
- Functional behavioral assessments (FBAs) and Behavioral Intervention Plans (BIPs)
- Clinical referrals
- Community/agency/family linkages
- Wraparound services

Approximately 80% to 90% of all students will respond successfully to a well-implemented universal intervention (Sugai, Horner, & Gresham, 2002). Universal interventions accomplish three things: (1) They improve almost all students' behavior; (2) they have their greatest impact among students who "are on the margins"—those students who are just beginning to be aggressive or defiant; and (3) they offer a foundation that supports the antisocial students throughout the day by reinforcing what they are learning in their more intensive selected interventions (H. M. Walker, Ramsey, & Gresham, 2003/2004). Once the environment is calm through universal interventions, those students needing more powerful "selected" interventions surface. The goal with these students is to decrease the frequency of their problem behaviors, instill appropriate behaviors, and make the children more responsive to universal interventions (Sugai et al., 2002). The most severe cases—the most troubled children from the most chaotic homes—require extremely intensive, individualized, and expensive interventions, which are typically family focused, with participation and support from mental health, juvenile justice, and social service agencies, as well as schools (H. M. Walker et al., 2003/2004).

It is important to understand the levels of need in schools and provide appropriate interventions and supports at all levels. If not, the negative behavior of the highest needs students can become a dominant socializing influence within the classroom and the whole school, influencing the behavior of vulnerable students at lower levels of need.

For more information about the Schoolwide Positive Behavioral Support approach (SWPBS) go the Center's website at www.pbis.org. For information about the University of Oregon Institute on Violence and Destructive Behavior (IVDB) co-directed by Jeffrey Sprague and Hill Walker, www.uoregon.edu/~ivdb.

Other recommended web sites include the School Mental Health Project (SMHP)—UCLA Department of Psychology, http://smhp.psych.ucla.edu. A list of various Violence Prevention Programs for preschool, elementary, middle school, high school, and adults can be found at http://www.unf.edu/dept/fie/sdfs/program_inventory/VP.html.

Organizational/Time Management Strategies

Students with ADHD, learning disabilities (LD), and other neurobiological disorders often have significant difficulty with organization, time awareness, and time management. The impairment in this area is related to their executive functioning disorders, and affects their class work and homework. Teeter (1998) describes executive functions as processes of flexibility, planning, inhibition, and self-monitoring and encompass the regulation, inhibition, and maintenance of behavioral responses, as well as problem-solving, organization, and reasoning (Teeter & Semrud-Clikeman, 1997). Fortunately, there are many strategies that both teachers and parents can employ to build these skills; and consequently, improve school success. When consulting with classroom teachers, you may recommend the following strategies to improve organization and time management skills:

Supplies and Materials

There are important supplies students need to use for school success, as well as strategies teachers can implement to encourage utilization and organization of these materials. Suggest that teachers:

- Require the use of a three-ring binder or notebook starting in third grade (fourth grade the latest).
- Require the use of colored subject dividers and a pencil pouch for the notebook (include a few sharpened pencils with erasers, and other small supplies/essentials).
- Younger students (kindergarten through second grade) should use a pocket folder for carrying papers to and from school.
- Require students to carry a backpack or book bag and to bring notebook/binder to and from school daily.
- Teach students how to keep their papers organized by placing them in the appropriate subject section of their notebooks.
- Require the use of a monthly assignment calendar, student planner, or daily/weekly assignment sheet to be kept at all times at the front of the notebook. Whichever is used (calendar, student planner, or assignment sheet) it should be three-hole punched for storage in the notebook. Utilize it consistently for recording all classroom assignments. Model and monitor its use.
- Have a consistent location in the notebook for storing homework assignments (or work "to do," work to "turn in"). There are a variety of ways for doing so, such as using colored pocket folders (single pocket or double) that are three-hole punched and inserted into the notebook. For example, a red pocket folder can be labeled "homework," and contain all homework; a different colored folder may be for graded and returned papers, or anything to "leave at home."
- Use large laminated envelopes that are three-hole punched and inserted into the notebook for homework, assorted project papers, and so forth. Encourage students to keep a supply of notebook paper handy in a consistent location of their binder.

- Keep spare supplies available so that time isn't wasted with students searching or asking around to borrow from classmates. Consider "charging" students (e.g., they must pay you from their class money/tokens) or fining in some way (points), for not being prepared and needing to borrow supplies from you.
- Provide handouts to students that are always three-hole punched in advance.
- Give student a clipboard for anchoring papers on the desk.
- Attach a pencil to the child's desk (either with string or velcro).
- Provide containers (e.g., bins, pencil cases, boxes, buckets, organizing trays, baskets, coffee cans covered in contact paper) as needed for materials/supplies on desks or tables.
- To help keep papers stored appropriately in the notebook, provide adhesive hole reinforcers for ripped out papers, and plastic sleeves for papers that you do not want to three-hole punch.
- Encourage students who need daily reference tools (e.g., times tables chart, frequently misspelled words list, or dictionary) to keep them in a section of their notebook. Clearly identify certain places in the room (trays, color-coded folders or boxes) where students know consistently where to turn in assignments or store unfinished work.

Use Visual Reminders

For students with organizational difficulties, it helps to utilize visual supports and cues, such as:

- Use color strategically to help organize.
- Color-coordinate by subject area to make location of subject materials quicker and easier. For example, the science text is covered in yellow paper or has a yellow adhesive dot on the binding; the science notebook/lab book or folder is yellow, and the schedule with math class period and room number is highlighted in yellow. So is the tab/divider for science in the three-ring notebook.
- Utilize brightly colored file folders for different subjects.
- Prepare important notices and handouts on colored paper, preferably color-coded for certain categories (e.g., weekly/monthly newsletters in blue, spelling lists in pink).
- Use brightly colored paper for project assignments, providing details and due dates. Give two copies (one for the notebook, and one to be posted at home).

- Use visual/pictorial cues for showing expected materials, daily routines, and schedule.
- Encourage students to use self-stick notes for reminders to themselves. Have them adhere the notes to book covers, in their lockers, planners, and so forth.

Organizational Assistance in Planning and Thinking

To assist students who have difficulties organizing their ideas and planning effectively (particularly affecting their study skills and writing assignments), recommend these strategies to teachers:

- Provide advanced organizers and study guides to help organize thinking about key topics of the lesson.
- Provide framed outlines for filling in missing words and phrases during instruction.
- Help students organize their ideas (prewriting, preplanning) through the use of self-stick notes with key words to arrange and sequence, talking through ideas into a tape recorder, or utilizing an appropriate graphic organizer.
- Encourage the use of software that helps students plan and organize their written work. For example, the programs Inspiration™ and Kidspiration™ enable the child to easily web and organize ideas and outline them. (See www.inspiration.com.)
- Provide a scoring rubric along with each written assignment to help the student in planning, organizing, and producing work at standard with grade level expectations.

More Organizational Tips

Some additional strategies teachers can use to help build students' organizational skills, and make accommodations for students who struggle in this area include:

- Teach and provide models of how to organize papers (e.g., headings, margins, spacing).
- Provide models of well-organized, projects, science boards, and so forth.
- Encourage students to organize materials upon arriving to class and before dismissal at the end of the school day.
- If the student has trouble remembering to bring books to and from school, consider loaning an extra set of books to keep at home.

- Provide direct assistance getting started on homework assignments and projects at school.
- If using a daily assignment sheet or planner, also have students transfer to a monthly calendar any of the due dates for projects, tests, special events such as field trips, or other important dates for the month.
- Allow for natural consequences of not having materials. *Do not* positively reinforce students who are unprepared by giving or loaning them new, desirable materials/supplies. Only let students borrow from a supply of less desirable materials. For example, many teachers keep a box of golf pencils and/or old pencils and erasers for this purpose.

Time Awareness

Lack of time awareness is very common among individuals with ADHD, and others with executive function disorders, as they often underestimate how much time they have to complete a task or to arrive somewhere on time. These students tend to be oblivious to deadlines and due dates. Remind classroom teachers that this is not student apathy, but part of their disorder. Recommend practice with time awareness such as:

- Challenge your students to estimate how long it takes to walk to the office and back (without running), or any other task. Make a game out of predicting, timing, and checking the students' time estimates for various activities.
- Encourage self-monitoring during independent seatwork time by recording the start time on the paper. When the work period is over, record the time (regardless of how much work the student actually produced). This is helpful documentation, as well, with regard to how well the student is able to stay on-task and work productively.

Assignment Sheets, Calendars, Student Planners/Agendas

Students with self-regulation issues often have significant difficulty with homework due to poor memory and forgetfulness; and parents are often unaware of assignments when they are not written down. It is imperative that teachers ensure students record their assignments consistently. You may suggest teachers to:

- Communicate and maintain the clear expectation that all assignments are to be recorded on students' assignment calendars, and monitor that this is occurring.
- Require and help walk through the recording of all homework assignments in the student planner, calendar, or assignment sheet.
- Check and initial the assignment calendar/sheet/planner of certain students.
- Supervise some students (e.g., those with LD and ADHD) as they walk out the door at the end of the day. Make sure they have materials, books, and assignments recorded and in their backpacks.
- Model the writing of assignments on the calendar using a transparency of the calendar on an overhead projector or other format that is clearly visible. Take a few moments at the beginning of class or end of the subject period or school day to lead students in the recording of assignments on their calendars.
- Provide assistance to students who have difficulty recording assignments in their calendar/planner/assignment sheet.
- Routinely ask table partners or groups seated together to check each other to make sure that everything is accurately recorded on their calendars.
- Assign "study buddies" so students can help each other. In addition to being responsible for checking each other to make sure assignments are recorded, they also collect all handouts, notices, and assignments for their partner when absent or out of the classroom. Buddies exchange phone numbers and/or e-mails so they can contact each other when absent and communicate about what was missed that day in class.
- Be sure to select a well-organized, tolerant, and helpful partner/study buddy for students with LD, ADHD, and other disabilities.
- Keep a master copy of the assignment calendar/student planner up-to-date and accessible for students to copy. This is especially important for students who are pulled out of the classroom at times of the day, or may be absent or late to class for various reasons.
- If using a daily agenda or assignment sheet, also provide students with a single or double-page monthly calendar. Have students transfer due dates of any projects, tests, class trips, or important activities/events onto their monthly calendar.
- Have students keep the monthly calendar clearly visible and easy to locate in the notebook. In addition, a class calendar should be posted and referred to.

- Visually post homework assignments as well as explaining them. Write the assignments in a consistent location of the classroom (corner of the board, chart stand).
- For some students, you may require that parents/guardians initial the assignment calendar daily.

Schedules

Students with self-regulation difficulties need the structure and security of having clear schedules. You may recommend that teachers:

- Establish a daily routine and schedule for the classroom.
- Post all schedules and refer to them throughout the day.
- Walk through the schedule each day and point out any changes in the daily/weekly schedule or routine that will be taking place.
- With younger students, use a pictorial schedule depicting the daily routine.
- For students receiving special education/related services, write down their weekly schedule and tape it to their desks. Keep accessible each of those students' special schedules so that teachers know at all times the days and times that students are pulled out of class, or when service providers are coming to the classroom to work with the student(s).
- Encourage students and parents to carefully plan a weekly schedule, including an established homework/study schedule.

Long-Term Projects

For students with time management difficulties, long term projects are the most problematic and frustrating. The following strategies and accommodations provide support to students with these challenges, and their families:

- Structure any long-term assignments (e.g., book reports, research projects, science fair projects) by breaking them into smaller, manageable increments.
- Make sure students have access to needed materials.
- Assign incremental due dates to help structure the time line toward project completion. For example, assign separate due dates for stages of the project (getting a topic approved, outline submitted, research notes/resources listed, turning in first draft, etc.).

- Call close attention to due dates. Post those due dates and frequently refer to them as reminders.
- Call some parents to make sure they are aware of the projects, and have at least one copy of the handout explaining project guidelines, with its time line and scoring rubric to keep posted at home.
- Suggest to parents that they closely monitor time lines and help with pacing (e.g., getting started promptly on going to the library and gathering resources).
- Monitor progress by asking to see what the student has accomplished so far, and provide a lot of feedback along the way.
- Consider providing some of your students with time management difficulties and their parents advanced notice about upcoming projects and reports, enabling them to have a "head start" (especially with planning and research).

Other Ways Teachers Can Help with Time Management

Some additional strategies and recommendations to support students who have difficulty with time awareness and management include the following:

- Provide students with a course outline or syllabus.
- Assist with prioritization of activities and workload.
- Make sure that *all* assignments (page numbers, due dates, etc.) are presented to students both verbally and visually.
- Utilize things-to-do lists, modeling for the class and teaching how to write down and cross off accomplished tasks.
- Attach a things-to-do list on students' desk, and monitor the practice of crossing off accomplished items.
- Provide enough time during transitions to put material away and get organized for the next activity.
- Set timers for transitions. (First state: "You have 5 minutes to finish what you are working on and put away your materials." Then set the timer.)
- Teach students how to self monitor on-task behavior so that they are using class time effectively for getting work done.
- Include "seated by beginning bell time," or some behavior indicating student's punctuality on any home/school monitoring system (such as a daily report card or daily/weekly monitoring form).
- If tardiness is an issue with the student, try an individual contract to motivate the student to improve behavior.

- Provide extended time as needed, and consider more flexibility with regard to accepting late work.
- Encourage your school to establish a schoolwide expectation and organization/study skills program for consistency, such as *Skills for School Success* (Archer & Gleason, 2003).
- Use frequent praise and positive reinforcement. Reward for meeting deadlines, finishing in-school assignments, and so forth.

Individualized Behavioral Supports and Interventions to Enhance Self-Regulation

For students with chronic behavioral problems, for whom the classroom (group) incentive systems are not sufficient in improving the student's behaviors, an individualized program may need to be implemented for a period of time. The following are examples of a few different behavior programs and monitoring systems—all of which involve targeting one or a few (at most) behaviors to improve, and rewarding the student's success (preferably at both home and school). It will be necessary to revisit the program on a frequent basis to evaluate its effectiveness in improving the target behaviors, and to tweak or modify the plan as needed.

Home Notes and Daily Report Cards

Home notes and daily report cards (DRCs) are excellent behavioral programs and tools for tracking a student's social, academic and/or behavioral progress at school. They are highly effective for communicating between home and school, and monitoring a child's daily performance. When parents are willing and able to consistently follow-through with reinforcement at home for positive performance at school, it is a very powerful motivator for the student. Any means to forge a partnership between home and school, and work together on improving specific behavioral goals is very beneficial.

Basically, home notes and DRCs involve selecting and clearly defining one or more target behavior(s) to be the focus for improvement. The teacher is responsible for observing and rating how the student performed on the target behavior(s) during the day or class period. A chart is made which includes the target behaviors for improvement, and designated time frames/monitoring periods (e.g., every subject period; before recess, after recess, after lunch; every half hour) that the student is to be monitored for performance of those behaviors. At the end of each time frame, the teacher simply indicates on the chart (by circling yes/no, ±, smile face/frown face) if the student did or did not demonstrate each of the target behaviors during that period of time. At the end of the day, a total percentage score is determined for how successfully the student performed that day. If the student met his or her predetermined goal (e.g., 70% success initially), it was a "good day," and the student earns rewards accordingly at home and/or school.

Parents are responsible for asking to see the note/DRC every day and reinforcing school behavior and performance at home. "Good days" in school (as indicated by the home/school note or DRC) will earn the child designated rewards at home on a nightly basis. Bonus rewards for a great week (e.g., at least 3 out of 5 good days) may also earn the child extra privileges on the weekend. It is recommended that parents back up the expectation that their son or daughter bring the note home daily, by enforcing with some mild punishment (such as being fined, losing some TV time) on those days the child "forgets" to bring the note home.

Home notes and DRCs can involve school rewards as well as home rewards. A small school reward (e.g., stickers, earned time for a preferred activity) can be given to the child at school on a "good day." For a "good week" (initially 3 days, e.g., and later raising the criteria to 4 days out of 5 of successful performance), the student may earn a special reward at school on Fridays. In some schools, the counselor or other adult provides the Friday reward (such as popcorn party, game, certificate) for all students in the school on a behavioral program who had a "good week."

If the family is not able to follow through regularly with monitoring and reinforcement, it is best to do so at school. If the DRC is likely to get lost coming to and from school daily, then perhaps just a card that simply indicates "yes/no" or "met goal/didn't meet goal" can be sent home each day for parent notification of the student's performance, and the actual DRC remains at school. Parents can be asked to reward the child on the weekend if it was a "good week" (3 out of 5 "good days"), and the teacher provides the daily reward when the child has met the goal that day.

It is important that reinforcement is provided consistently, and as promised. A well-coordinated system between home and school is the most effective.

Dr. William Pelham Jr., a leading researcher in behavioral/psychosocial interventions for children with self-regulation difficulties such as ADHD, recommends these steps in establishing a school-home daily report card (2002):

- Select the areas for improvement.
- Determine how the goals will be defined—the specific target behaviors that will be observed/counted by the teacher and child.

- Decide on behaviors and criteria for the DRC: Estimate base line on target behaviors; evaluate target behaviors several times throughout the day; set a reasonable criterion for each target behavior (e.g., "interrupts fewer than two times in each class period" rather than "interrupts fewer than 12 times per day").
- Explain the DRC to the child.
- Establish a home-based reward system (rewards/menu of rewards must be selected by the child).
- Monitor and modify the program. Once the child has regularly begun to meet the criterion, make the criteria harder, and once the criterion for a target is at an acceptable level and the child is consistently reaching it, drop that target behavior from the DRC. Move to a weekly report/reward system if the child is doing so well that daily reports are no longer necessary.
- Troubleshoot the DRC. If the system is not working to change the child's behavior, examine the program and change where appropriate.
- Consider other treatments.

Dr. Pelham (2002) includes suggestions for troubleshooting a DRC, sample DRC forms, sample target behaviors, and sample home and school rewards on his website at the Center for Children and Families, University of Buffalo, State University of New York: http://wings.buffalo .edu/psychology/adhd.

Contingency Contracting
This is a written agreement (usually between the teacher, student, and parent). The contract clearly specifies the required behavior(s) that the student is to perform, and the reward(s) that will be earned if the student succeeds in meeting that behavioral goal. Sometimes the contract includes the negative consequence that will occur for failure to perform the required behavior(s). All parties sign the contract and follow-through on their end of the agreement.

Token Programs
Token programs use secondary reinforcers, or tokens, to provide students with immediate reinforcement for appropriate behavior (necessary for motivating children such as those with ADHD to sustain the effort for behavioral change). When the student earns a designated number of tokens, they may be exchanged for a primary reinforcement (such as a privilege, treat, or a desired activity). These programs include any in

which the student is earning points, tokens/plastic chips, moves or stickers on a chart, class money—or something as an immediate reward for demonstrating the target behavior(s). The tokens are later redeemed for a more valued and motivating reward (at school, home, or both).

Chart Moves

Individual student charts are commonly used. One or a few specific target behaviors are identified for the student to improve. A chart of some type is developed (e.g., one with boxes for placing stickers, stars, stamps, teacher initials). Each time the student demonstrates the target appropriate behavior, a box of the chart is filled in, or a move forward is made on the chart. When the chart is completed or when the student reaches certain points along the chart, a reward is earned.

Self-Monitoring

It is often helpful when trying to teach students to self-regulate their own behavior, to involve them in self-monitoring. This helps them to pay more attention to their own behavior—to think about and record the occurrence of their own performance. Self-awareness often leads to improved performance. Attention-related behaviors have been found to increase as a function of self-monitoring, especially when combined with self-reinforcement or external reinforcement, as cited by DuPaul and Stoner (2003) from (Barkley et al., 1980).

One such strategy is through the use of a beeper tape. These are audiotapes (e.g., 30 to 45 minutes in length), on which an unpredictable series of audible beeps (or other auditory signal) have been recorded (e.g., every 2 minutes, 3 minutes, 5 minutes). Students earn a point when they are demonstrating the expected behavior each time the beep sounds. The technique is often used when students are to be working on seatwork or other independent task. Children are trained to record on an index card or monitoring form (by marking ± or yes/no) whether or not they were performing the appropriate target behavior whenever they hear the auditory signal. There is a commercial product of this self-monitoring strategy called *Listen, Look and Think: A Self-Regulation Program for Children* (H. C. Parker, 1990). It includes an endless cassette beep tape and self-monitoring forms. Whenever the intermittent beep is heard on the tape, the child is to ask himself or herself, "Was I paying attention?" On the form, the child puts a checkmark indicating yes or no. Then, the student is expected to immediately get back to work.

M. E. McConnell (1999) recommends these procedures to follow when teaching students to self-manage their own behavior:

- Identify the behavior.
- Define the target (e.g., worked without bothering others, on-task, completed my work).
- Collect baseline data.
- Schedule conference with student.
- Select self-management procedures.
- Teach the student to use self-management procedures and provide opportunities to verbally rehearse, practice, model, and review procedures taught.
- Implement self-monitoring—while providing student with frequent encouragement and feedback.
- Monitor student progress.
- Follow-up. Check for maintenance of self-management skills. When the student demonstrates consistent success, gradually fade the self-monitoring procedure and reinstitute if behavior reoccurs.

DuPaul and Stoner (2003) cite some of the benefits of *self-reinforcement* based upon the research. "[T]he combination of self-monitoring and self-reinforcement has been found effective in improving on-task behavior, academic accuracy, and peer interactions for students with ADHD" DuPaul & Stoner, 2003, p. 167; see also Barkley et al., 1980; Hinshaw et al., 1984b). DuPaul and Stoner indicate that self-reinforcement strategies may be particularly helpful in two situations. First, a student can be taught to monitor and reinforce his or her own behavior while fading the use of an externally based, contingency management program (Barkley, 1989). Second, self-reinforcement is particularly appropriate for students with ADHD at the secondary level. As high school teachers and students are reluctant to employ contingency management procedures, self-management may be a more acceptable intervention at this level—presumably more likely to be implemented on a consistent basis.

A Few More Points regarding Individualized Programs
You may recommend that teachers instruct students to self-monitor work production, and to set individual short-term goals for improvement. For example, "I am going to write at least three more sentences by

the time this work period is over"; or "I will read to page 121 by the time the timer goes off." If meeting the mini-goal, the student self-rewards in some way—such as by giving self a star on a self-monitoring card (Rief, 2003, 2005).

For students with significant difficulties in self-regulation, it is highly likely that one or more individualized behavioral programs will need to be implemented. The best support that you can provide is to work together with the teacher—reviewing the programs, troubleshooting the program, and helping to ensure that the teacher(s) and parent(s) are implementing the selected program correctly and consistently.

Additional Self-Regulation Strategies

There are other beneficial programs that may be implemented in the classroom/school setting. These include social skills programs, relaxation/stress management, anger management, exercise programs, learning strategy and study skills programs, and others. The Alert Program™ and other techniques that occupational therapists utilize involving sensorimotor methods and strategies may also be considered.

According to S. Graham and Harris (1996), children with learning problems represent a heterogeneous population, and the significant difficulties they face are typically the result of multiple factors. Research indicates that one contributor to these students' academic difficulties may be difficulties in the self-regulation of organized strategic behaviors, behaviors they can acquire and use given appropriate scaffolded instruction (Bjorklund, 1990; K. R. Harris, 1990; J. Hughes & Hall, 1989). For example, they may experience difficulty in using verbalizations to guide their behavior or establishing correspondence between saying and doing (K. R. Harris, 1990). They may also have difficulty in understanding the demands of the task, spontaneously producing appropriate strategies to accomplish the task, or using these strategies to mediate performance (Hallahan, Lloyd, Kauffman, & Loper, 1983). S. Graham and Harris and others have developed a number of learning strategies to support students with these difficulties.

CHAPTER
14

School-Based Interventions for Children with Internalizing Problems

JANAY B. SANDER, DAWN S. REINEMANN, AND JENNIFER A. HERREN

Internalizing conditions such as depression and anxiety are currently viewed as potentially chronic, recurrent disturbances that often have their origin in youth. In schools, the challenges of helping youth affected with anxiety or depressive illnesses are multidimensional: identifying students in distress, offering prevention or intervention for classroom situations, and being educated about the multiple ways that anxiety and depression can be treated, and how schools can assist in those treatment plans for the child's benefit. If unidentified and untreated, anxiety and depression in children and adolescents can lead to long-term adverse outcomes and life-threatening behaviors. Internalizing problems negatively affect children's functioning at school, with peers, and at home. It is important for school professionals to become educated regarding the identification, assessment, and treatment for youth who experience symptoms of anxiety and depression in order to lessen the long-term consequences for affected children.

Identifying Depression and Anxiety in Children

Although 1 in 10 youngsters suffer from psychological problems serious enough to cause functional impairment, estimates indicate that fewer than 1 in 5 receives any form of treatment (U.S. Public Health Service, 2001). With the exception of mental health specialists, such as school psychology specialists, licensed psychologists, school social workers, or school counselors, most other school staff have little training regarding the ways that internalizing problems may present themselves during childhood, which may also contribute to underidentification. For a variety of reasons, anxiety and depression are not always obvious or easy to identify in a typical classroom setting. The presentation may vary for each child. In a classroom of 25 students, the quiet student who turns in homework would rarely be a concern. Even the most dedicated parents or teachers may be unaware that the student who gets high scores on spelling has stayed up late writing the letters perfectly, to the point of hand cramps and stomachaches. In other cases, adults may notice problems when a report card is issued. A typical scenario: Alex's homework was turned in on time, but only partially completed and full of errors, and he complains of lack of energy and problems concentrating, with no prior history of school difficulty. Depressed or anxious children may act out or show irritability, and they may complain of physical discomfort, stomachaches, headaches, or gastric upset, which may appear "physical" and disguise an underlying mental health concern. Although these types of symptoms may be indicative of an underlying medical condition, they are also commonly associated with depression or anxiety in youth.

A second contributor to the underidentification of anxious and depressed students is that psychologists and school psychology specialists (but not educational diagnosticians), who are trained to identify these emotional disorders, spend a majority of their time evaluating children referred for special education services. However, when anxiety or depression is first discussed, it is usually in regard to regular education students, and school personnel without mental health training often fail to account for the specific educational needs of students with anxiety or depression, with or without additional learning difficulties. (Reinemann, Stark, Molnar, & Simpson, in press). While some severe or more prolonged cases of childhood depression or anxiety may end up warranting special education services under severe emotional disturbance, many students with anxiety or depression do not demonstrate educational needs sufficient to warrant special education services. However, consideration of a 504 plan, or school openness to collaboration with an outside therapist as part of regular education, may be in order. School personnel who are not mental health specialists may overlook, or be unaware of, the avenues of school assistance to children with anxiety or depression that do not necessarily fall under the umbrella of special education or related services. Without a special education referral, sometimes the mental health professionals within a school may never have the opportunity to properly identify a child in emotional distress. Most children do not require a special education referral, but contact with a mental health specialist when there is an initial concern can turn out to be of great benefit to the child.

A third reason for underidentification is that school staff may suspect a problem, but be unaware of what the problem might be, how exactly to proceed with identification, or the level of distress that warrants school intervention. Mental health practitioners in schools, such as school psychology specialists, licensed psychologists, school counselors, or school-based social workers can often offer education regarding internalizing disorders to faculty so that all school personnel can assist in the identification process. School-based mental health practitioners can usually directly assess at-risk students, and if there is significant impairment or educational need related to the depression or anxiety, then proper steps for a 504 plan or special education assessment can proceed. If symptoms are clearly impairing to the child, but there is not evidence of education need, school psychology practitioners and licensed psychologists can then provide parents with outside referral information, and coordinate school-based intervention efforts with outside clinicians or treatments (Reinemann et al., in press). In some districts, there may be mental health services for students that are not linked directly to special education. In addition, many school-based mental health practitioners can develop and implement classroom-based prevention programs and offer consultation with teachers to develop academic and behavioral plans designed to improve these children's classroom functioning. In many cases, the individual interventions or recommendations to assist a specific child with anxiety or depression would have benefits for an entire classroom. In general, the school mental health practitioner may have many untapped skills to offer in consultation, early assessment, and intervention planning and assistance.

Overview of Internalizing Problems in School Settings

Depression

Symptoms that comprise a depressive syndrome can be classified on a continuum of severity and include various affective, cognitive, behavioral/motivational, and physiological manifestations (Cantwell, 1990). Affective symptoms in youth include sad mood, anger or irritability, anhedonia (loss of interest or pleasure), weepiness, feeling unloved, and self-pity (Stark, 1990). Cognitive symptoms include negative self-evaluations, guilt, hopelessness, concentration difficulties, indecisiveness, and suicidal ideation (Stark, 1990). Youth suffering from a depressive syndrome also may experience motivational symptoms such as social withdrawal from peers and adults, suicidal behaviors, and decreased academic performance; while physical symptoms include fatigue, changes in appetite and weight, somatic complaints, sleep disturbances, and psychomotor retardation or agitation (Stark, 1990). When examining these symptoms, it becomes apparent that children who suffer from depression are likely to qualify for psychological and related services in the schools as their symptomatology often adversely impacts their academic confidence, motivation, and cognitive processing, culminating in impaired academic functioning. A complete list of the diagnostic criteria for the three main depressive disorders is not within the scope of this chapter (see Mash & Barkley, 2003). However, a concise list of symptoms often observable in school settings is helpful for the school practitioner. See Table 14.1 for a list of symptoms that would be likely to be noticed within a school environment.

Table 14.1   Depressive symptoms typically observable
in school settings

Observable Symptoms of Depression across Diagnostic Groups, DSM-IV
Lack of concentration
Irritability
Physical fatigue or sluggishness
Sleepiness
Loss or change in appetite
Weight loss or weight gain (not due to growth)
Appearing sad or disinterested in general
Remarks about feeling guilty or worthless
Remarks about death or suicide*

*If thoughts of death or suicidal remarks are noted, contact a school mental health professional immediately or follow the school policy for suicidal assessment and intervention.

Source: Diagnostic and Statistical Manual of Mental Disorders, by the American Psychiatric Association, fourth edition, text revision, 1994, Washington, DC: Author.

The *Diagnostic and Statistical Manual of Mental Disorders*, fourth edition, text revision (*DSM-IV-TR*; American Psychiatric Association, 2000) recognizes three major diagnostic categories of unipolar depressive disorders: major depressive disorder (MDD), dysthymic disorder (DD), and depressive disorder not otherwise specified (DDNOS). The primary difference between these disorders is the number, severity, and duration of depressive symptoms. Only a trained mental health professional could assign an actual diagnosis (usually based on the *DSM-IV* or similar classification system).

The manner in which depressive symptoms cluster in youth may vary as a function of development. Symptoms commonly found in children include depressed appearance, irritability, somatic complaints, and social withdrawal. These symptoms may often be mistaken for simple lack of motivation, attentional problems, or defiance, but they are seen in children with depression. Adults and adolescents present more often with psychomotor retardation, sleepiness or sleeping more than usual, delusions, and suicide ideation and attempts (American Psychiatric Association, 2000). Thus, proper identification of children suffering from depression will be enhanced by considering developmental differences in symptom presentation.

A significant number of youth experience depressive disorders at some time and prevalence rates increase with age. While about 1% to 3% of children evidence a depressive disorder at any given time (see Hammen & Rudolph, 2003, for a review), the percentage of adolescents with a lifetime history of major depression ranges from 9% to 21% in community samples (Hankin et al., 1998; Kessler & Walters, 1998; Reinherz, Giaconia, Lefkowitz, Pakiz, & Frost, 1993). In addition, while research indicates that approximately 2.5% of children in the general population currently evidence dysthymic disorder (see Stark, 1990, for a review), a more recent study of a community sample of 17- to 19-year-olds indicated that 4.7% had a lifetime history of dysthymia (Jonas, Brody, Roper, & Narrow, 2003). Taken together, it appears that youth may be at heightened risk for developing depressive disturbances during adolescence. Thus, middle and high school personnel may be especially likely to encounter students who are suffering from significant forms of depression.

During elementary school, males and females are equally likely to have a depressive disorder (Stark, 1990). However, beginning in middle school and extending into high school, the ratio of females to males who evidence a depressive disorder progressively increases until adulthood, when females outnumber males by a 2 to 1 ratio (Nolen-Hoeksema, 2002). This gender difference appears to emerge between ages 13 and 15 (Hankin et al., 1998). Reasons for the increased rates of depression in females include the possibility that they have more cognitive, biological, and interpersonal vulnerabilities prior to adolescence and experience more stressful life events during the transition to adolescence (Nolen-Hoeksema, 2002).

Ethnic minority students also have been found to report higher rates of depression (e.g., Rushton, Forcier, & Schectman, 2003). Other groups that may be at increased risk for developing depressive disturbances include Native American youngsters (Peterson et al., 1993), children from lower socioeconomic backgrounds (Reinherz et al., 1993), and gay, lesbian, and bisexual youth (Anhalt & Morris, 1998). Youth with learning problems, such as reading disabilities, may be at greater risk for depressive symptoms and anxiety than peers without reading difficulty (Arnold et al., 2005).

Anxiety

In the *DSM-IV-TR* (American Psychiatric Association, 2000), there are seven main anxiety disorders: generalized anxiety disorder, obsessive-compulsive disorder (OCD), panic disorder, posttraumatic stress disorder (PTSD), separation anxiety disorder, social phobia, and specific phobia. A full diagnostic review of each disorder is beyond the scope of this chapter (see Rapee & Barlow, 2001; Rapee & Sweeney, 2001; Schniering, Hudson, & Rapee, 2000). There are separate unique symptoms for each of the categories and evidence that each disorder is a distinct syndrome (Chorpita & Southam-Gerow, 2006). In general, for each disorder, there is a clear, unrealistic, extreme fear reaction in a given set of circumstances that is *not* developmentally appropriate and interferes with functioning in important ways. In some instances, such as with OCD, the child may create an elaborate ritual or set of behaviors, called *compulsions*, in order to prevent or lessen the anxiety. In other cases, such as with separation anxiety or specific phobia, the child may insist on having specific persons present or may avoid a specific situation (i.e., dogs, spiders, shots/needles, heights), in order to avoid the feelings of anxiety. However, in most cases, it is not possible to always control the situation or to avoid a feared situation, and when exposure does occur, the emotions are very intense and highly distressing. Furthermore, some avoidance behaviors create significant inconvenience, may be very time consuming, and are disruptive to daily activities. The intensity and interference of the anxiety, or the avoidance or coping behaviors to lessen anxiety, are some of the qualities that make a normal fear reaction different from an anxiety disorder (Schniering et al., 2000).

The prevalence rates of anxiety disorders vary by the diagnosis. In most community samples, prevalence is about 5% or less at any given time (Schniering et al., 2000), but up to 15% for lifetime prevalence (Chorpita & Southam-Gerow, 2006). Findings based on community samples are similar to a typical school environment. Schniering and her colleagues (2000) provided a review of 12-month prevalence estimates for all DSM anxiety diagnoses, summarizing numerous incidence and prevalence studies, and separating child and adolescent rates, since most diagnoses vary by developmental level. In general, the most common disorder is PTSD. However, PTSD rates will vary based on exposure, and communities where groups of children have been exposed to a traumatic event will have larger prevalence rates, up to nearly 45% in some situations. Panic disorder and obsessive-compulsive disorder are the least common in children (<1%), with rates increasing slightly in adolescence. Many disorder-specific prevalence rates vary between 2% and 4%, including generalized anxiety disorder and specific phobia. Social phobia is more common in adolescence than childhood (<1% in children and up to 6% in adolescents), and separation anxiety shows the reverse pattern, with greater prevalence in childhood (4% in children and <2% in adolescents). As with depression, diagnosis requires assessment by a trained mental health professional. While the clinical diagnoses are distinct, and treatment varies somewhat, general school staff and teacher awareness of the signs that would be evident in a school setting could be very helpful to a child suffering from one of the anxiety disorders. See Table 14.2 for a summary of anxiety symptoms across diagnostic categories that adults in a school setting might notice.

Additional signs of anxiety may present as a recurrent need to use the restroom, frequent absences from school, or visits to the nurse with stomachaches or headaches. Many children (and adults) do not realize that their physical sensations, such as muscle tension, headaches, or stomach discomfort, could be related to anxiety. All of these symptoms could also be caused by a medical problem, and if they occur at school, regardless of the underlying cause, they should be noted and shared with parents or administrators. Several symptoms are present in both anxiety and depressive disorders, and some symptoms would be present in a range of other disorders, illustrating the need for a trained mental health assessment if present.

Comorbidity of Internalizing Problems

Comorbidity is defined as two or more psychological disorders that co-occur more often than would be expected by chance (Mash & Dozois,

Table 14.2 Symptoms often observable in school settings

Anxiety Symptoms across Diagnostic Categories, DSM-IV
Lack of concentration[a]
Irritability[a]
Sleepiness or easily tired[a]
Muscle aches and tension[a]
Stomach pain or upset[a]
Avoidance or extreme reaction to a nonthreatening object or situation[b] (i.e., insect, elevator, animal, heights) or other situation that reminds the child of prior traumatic event[c]
Extreme reaction (crying, tantrum, freezing) to social situations that would not usually cause a reaction in other children the same age[d]
Sudden onset of extreme fear, including: chest pain, choking feeling, shaking, sweating, dizziness, or feeling as if smothered[e]
Repetitive or odd behaviors, including: checking things (locker, backpack, windows, clothing), straightening, washing, hand movements, avoiding cracks or thresholds on the floor, or insistence of certain personal pattern or habit (i.e., always turning in a circle before sitting in a desk, doing a certain hand movement prior to eating)[f]

Symptoms are included, along with other symptoms, in diagnostic categories:
[a] Generalized anxiety disorder. [b] Specific phobia. [c] Post traumatic stress disorder. [d] Social phobia. [e] Panic attack. [f] Obsessive-compulsive disorder (also common in pervasive development disorders).

Source: Diagnostic and Statistical Manual of Mental Disorders, by the American Psychiatric Association, fourth edition, text revision, 1994, Washington, DC: Author.

2003). Comorbidity is common in childhood and youth who suffer from depression or anxiety are likely to also evidence other psychological disturbances. It is estimated that as many as 80% of children diagnosed with anxiety or depression evidence one or more additional psychological disorders (Albano, Chorpita, & Barlow, 2003; Kazdin & Marciano, 1998). Anxiety disorders are the most common co-occurring conditions with depression (Angold, Costello, Erkanli, & Worthman, 1999). The relationship between anxiety and depression is of interest to many researchers and practitioners partly because many of the symptoms overlap (e.g., somatic complaints, concentration problems). In fact, a factor analysis completed by Achenbach (1991) failed to find that depression and anxiety were separate factors and therefore, both types of symptoms are included in a single dimension on his rating scales. Some investigators have suggested that at times depression and anxiety may represent a single disturbance, while at other times they may represent two distinct problems (Kovacs, 1990). It appears that younger children may be more likely to exhibit anxiety and depression as a single disturbance, while older children may show patterns of symptoms that have both shared and specific features of each disorder (Cole, Truglio, & Peeke, 1997). Anxiety literature reflects a trend that in cases of dual diagnosis of depression and anxiety, the anxiety appears to emerge first (Schniering et al., 2000).

Depressed or anxious youth also may experience comorbid disruptive behavior problems and substance abuse (Barrios & O'Dell, 1989; Lewinsohn et al., 1994). For example, a summary of the existing data reveal that depression co-occurs with conduct disorder, oppositional defiant disorder, or attention-deficit/hyperactivity disorder (ADHD) in approximately 25% of youngsters (Nottelmann & Jensen, 1995), while rates of disruptive behaviors in youth with severe anxiety range from 8% to 28% (see Barrios & O'Dell, 1989, for a review). It should be noted that when comorbidity occurs, depression seems to develop after the other condition in the majority of youth (Lewinsohn et al., 1994).

Apart from disorders, depressed and/or anxious youngsters also are likely to exhibit dysfunction in other areas that may impact their functioning, especially at school. Depressed children often exhibit social skills deficits and have been found to be less popular, less liked, and more likely to be rejected by peers than their nondisturbed counterparts (e.g., Rudolph & Clark, 2001). Similarly, anxious children have reported that their fears and anxiety interfere with participation in desired or required activities (Ollendick & King, 1994). For example, children with social phobia have been found to have few friends, avoid social and extracurricular activities, report feelings of loneliness, and are considered shy and quiet by peers and adults. In adolescence, they have been found to lag behind their peers in meeting developmental tasks such as dating and seeking employment (see Albano et al., 2003, for a review).

Anxiety and depression also adversely impact children's school and academic functioning. Specifically, depressed youth have been found to have significantly lower academic achievement than their nondepressed peers (Puig-Antich et al., 1985), and are more likely to miss school, fail to complete homework assignments, and repeat a grade than their nondepressed counterparts (Lewinsohn et al., 1994). Of major concern, depressed adolescents also appear to be at increased risk for dropping out of high school (Kessler, Foster, Saunders, & Stang, 1995). Elevated levels of anxiety also have been shown to negatively impact youngsters' academic work and school performance, and often lead to school refusal behaviors (Kendall, Chu, Pimentel, & Choudhury, 2000). Thus, internalizing conditions are often associated with difficulties in multiple domains and areas of functioning. Since comorbidity has been shown to lead to greater functional impairment and a poorer long-term prognosis (Rohde, Lewinsohn, & Seeley, 1991), assessment of possible co-occurring conditions in youth suffering from internalizing problems is paramount.

Assessment of Internalizing Problems in Schools

As with many emotional concerns, a change in behavior is an obvious first sign. It is important to note that behavioral changes do not always indicate mental illness, or even distress, but could be an early sign. Children may be diagnosed with anxiety or depression at any age, even in early childhood. Assessing internalizing disorders requires information gathering from multiple sources, including the youth, parent(s), and teachers.

Self-report measures play a crucial role in the assessment process of school-age youth, as key symptoms of depression (e.g., sadness, beliefs about self-worth, and competence) and anxiety (subjective feelings of distress, avoidance of situations, etc.) involve feelings and self-perceptions which are not easily observable (Kazdin, 1990; W. M. Reynolds, 1994). Table 14.3 contains a list of commonly used assessment measures for childhood depression and anxiety. Due to concerns about how well these measures discriminate between different disorders, including anxiety and depression, but also some externalizing disorders (Stark, 1990), self-report measures may best be employed as screening devices that are part of a more comprehensive assessment that includes data from multiple sources using a variety of assessment modalities. See Table 14.3 for a list of screening tools, most of which can be administered as questionnaires in individual or group format.

For more specific diagnostic and accurate identification of depression or anxiety in youth, either an individual assessment or a multiple-stage assessment procedure is recommended (W. M. Reynolds, 1994; Stark, 1990). In order to screen large numbers of students, a multiple-stage procedure would involve first screening a large number of students with a self-report questionnaire. After the initial screening, students who scored at or above a clinical cutoff score are retested a short time later (1 to 2 weeks) because there is evidence that youth may score higher on the

Table 14.3 Questionnaires available to assist in identifying youth with internalizing problems

Measure	Source	Publisher	Age Range (Years)	Number of Items	Administration Time (Minutes)
Children's Depression Inventory (CDI)	Kovacs (1992)	Multi-Health Systems	7–17	27	10–15
Reynolds Child Depression Scale (RCDS)	Reynolds (1989)	Psychological Assessment Resources	8–12	30	10–15
Beck Depression Inventory for Youth (BDI-Y)	Beck, Beck, & Jolly (2001)	The Psychological Corporation	7–14	20	5–10
Weinberg Depression Scale for Children and Adolescents (WDSCA)	Weinberg, Harper, & Emslie (1998)	Pro-Ed	5–21	56	5
Center for Epidemiological Studies Depression Scale Modified for Children (CES-DC)	Weissman, Orvaschel, & Padian (1980)	Available from http://www .brightfutures.org/mentalhealth /pdf/tools.html	6–17	20	5
Multiscore Depression Inventory for Children (MDI-C)	Berndt & Kaiser (1996)	Western Psychological Services	8–17	79	15–20

(continued)

Table 14.3 (Continued)

Measure	Source	Publisher	Age Range (Years)	Number of Items	Administration Time (Minutes)
Depression and Anxiety in Youth Scale (DAYS)	Newcomer, Barenbaum, & Bryant (1994)	Pro-Ed	6–19	40	5–20
Beck Anxiety Inventory for Youth (BAI-Y)	Beck, Beck & Jolly (2001)	The Psychological Corporation	7–14	20	5–10
Screen for Childhood Anxiety Related Disorders (SCARED)	Birmaher et al. (1997)	Available from http://www .wpic.pitt.edu/research	8+	41	5
Revised Children's Manifest Anxiety Scale (RCMAS)	Reynolds & Richmond (1985)	Western Psychological Services	6–19	37	10–15
Spence Children's Anxiety Scale (SCAS)	Spence (1998)	Available from http://www2 .psy.uq.edu.au/~sues/scas	8–12	45	5–10
Multidimensional Anxiety Scale for Children (MASC)	March (1997)	Multi-Health Systems	8–19	39	15

first administration of a self-report measure of depression than on a second testing (W. M. Reynolds, 1994). Those youth who continue to endorse significant levels of symptomatology during the second screening are then referred for a more comprehensive assessment, which may include a diagnostic interview, such as the *Schedule for Affective Disorders and Schizophrenia for School-Age Children* (K-SADS; Orvaschel & Puig-Antich, 1994), along with information from parent and teacher questionnaires and interviews. Clinical interviews provide a more detailed examination of onset of the disturbance, specific symptoms and their severity, and may provide information regarding problems that may be contributing to the depression (W. M. Reynolds, 1994). In addition, for a more comprehensive assessment, parents can provide important information regarding the child's behaviors and functioning at home that may be of concern, while teachers can provide data regarding the child's classroom behavior and academic functioning. Parents and teachers may be asked to complete a behavioral rating scale such as the *Achenbach System of Empirically Based Assessment* (ASEBA), *Child Behavior Checklist* (6 to 18 years) (Achenbach, 2001) or the *Behavioral Assessment System for Children,* second edition (C. R. Reynolds & Kamphaus, 2005), which address symptoms across several areas of behavioral and emotional functioning, not exclusively anxiety and depression. It is of note that the BASC-2 rating system separates anxiety and depression scales, while the ASEBA system combines depression and anxiety into one scale. Both rating systems are available in Spanish and include parent, teacher, and youth rating scales.

Prevention and Intervention Strategies in Schools

Depression Prevention Programs

Because of the chronicity, severity, long-term adverse effects, and high recurrence rate of depressive disturbances, there has been an increased interest in, and development of, prevention programs for reducing the initial onset of depressive disorders or to prevent relapse. School-based prevention programs are discussed here. Results of investigations designed to evaluate prevention programs for depressed youths have, in general, reported positive results immediately following program completion, but mixed results during subsequent follow-up evaluations. For example, Jaycox, Reivich, Gillham, and Seligman (1994) reported that a 12-session prevention program that emphasized training in cognitive and social problem solving, the Penn Optimism Program, reduced the severity of depressive symptoms and behavior problems in the classroom immediately following completion of the program and prevented symptoms from recurring for 6 months. Subsequent research on the program was conducted with groups of middle school students who were identified as being at risk for developing depressive disorders because of the chronic stress of poverty. According to the study, the program significantly reduced depressive symptoms among participants of Latino and Chinese descent but not among African American participants (Muñoz, Penilla, & Urizar, 2002). These results raise important questions about the need for, and potential benefits of, developing culturally sensitive interventions.

Another group of researchers has developed and evaluated a series of manualized cognitive-behavioral programs for the prevention and treatment of depressive disorders in youth, titled Coping with Stress (CWS) and Coping with Depression (CWD), respectively (Clarke et al., 1995; Clarke, Rohde, Lewinsohn, Hops, & Seeley, 1999). Components focus on experiential learning and skills training, with attention to increasing pleasant activities, improving social interaction, and coping with maladaptive thoughts. These programs have been administered in school settings, and the materials can be downloaded at no cost for use by mental health professionals. In an evaluation of program effectiveness, adolescents who reported subclinical levels of depressive symptoms, which placed them at risk for developing a depressive disorder, completed the 15-session CWS group prevention program (Clarke et al., 1995). When compared with a "usual care" control condition, the prevention program significantly reduced the number of adolescents who developed diagnosable depressive disorders over a 12-month period. However, because a number of adolescents in the study still developed depressive disorders, additional research is needed to identify the variables that predict those who are resilient versus those who subsequently experience depression.

Another group of prevention programs are considered "universal" because they are implemented with entire school populations and do not select students for participation based on level of depressive symptomatology or family risk factors. These programs are typically conducted with entire classrooms and may be implemented by teachers or other school mental health personnel. One such program, titled the Resourceful Adolescent Program, has been implemented by psychologists and evaluated in a school setting (Shochet et al., 2001). Specifically, Shochet and colleagues developed an 11-session, manualized program that focuses on promoting self-management, coping with stress, building support networks, and teaching cognitive restructuring and problem solving skills. In addition, a three-session family program was created for parents that focuses on stress management, parenting adolescents, and family conflict resolution. To evaluate the program's effectiveness, students were assigned to either the adolescent program, the adolescent program plus the family component, or a control condition. Results revealed that adolescents who participated in either prevention program reported significantly lower levels of depressive symptoms and hopelessness immediately following program completion and at 10-month follow-up compared to adolescents in the control condition. However, there were no differences between those receiving only the adolescent program and those who also participated in the family program.

More recently, Spence, Sheffield, and Donovan (2003, 2005) developed a school-based cognitive-behavioral program designed to prevent the development of youth depression, titled the Problem-Solving for Life program. Spence and her colleagues created a curriculum designed for use by teachers with all students in a classroom. The program consists of eight sessions, 45 to 50 minutes each, that focus on cognitive restructuring and problem-solving skills training. Youth learn to identify thoughts, feelings, and problem situations and then learn to challenge their own negative or irrational thoughts that contribute to the development of depression. The second part of the program emphasizes life problem-solving skills and the development of a positive problem-solving orientation.

In a well-designed evaluation of the program, eighth-grade students (ages 12 to 14) who completed the program were compared to students in a monitoring-control condition. Results indicated that students who initially reported elevated levels of depression (high risk group) and who participated in the program showed a significant decrease in depressive symptoms and an increase in problem-solving skills immediately following program completion compared to control students also at high risk for depression. In addition, those students who completed the program but did not evidence initial elevated levels of depression also reported a significant decrease in depressive symptoms and an increase in problem-solving skills compared to the low-risk control students, who actually reported an increase in depressive symptoms (Spence et al., 2003).

Subsequent follow-up evaluation was conducted to assess the long-term impact of the Problem-Solving for Life program. Results revealed that treatment gains were not maintained at 12-month follow-up. Specifically, Spence and colleagues (2003) reported that there were no significant differences between the prevention group and control group in the percentage of students who developed a depressive disorder or who exhibited elevated levels of depression. Furthermore, there were no group differences in changes from preintervention to 12-month follow-up on measures of depression, cognitive style, and problem solving, among others. Likewise, subsequent evaluations revealed no significant differences between those who completed the program and those in the control condition at 2-, 3-, and 4-year follow-up (Spence et al., 2005).

In general, it appears that more research is necessary to determine the factors that may influence whether prevention programs lead to long-term benefits. Examination of factors such as program length, content, mode of delivery, training of teachers and other facilitators, as well as which youth are best served by such preventive interventions, may lead to improved programs that demonstrate maintenance of initial gains.

Intervention Programs for Depression in Schools

There are a variety of interventions for depressed youth that have proven to be generally effective, including cognitive-behavioral therapy (CBT), interpersonal psychotherapy for depressed adolescents (IPT-A; Mufson, Moreau, Weissman, & Garfinkel, 1999), family interventions (see Sander & McCarty, 2005), or a combination of medication and therapy, such as the Treatment for Adolescents with Depression Study (TADS; March, 2004). Most interventions are delivered in individual therapy settings, clinics, or are affiliated with medical facilities. A full review of all treatments is beyond the scope of this chapter, but one of the few noteworthy school-based intervention programs for depressed children for discussion is the ACTION program (Stark, Hargrave, et al., 2006; Stark, Sander, et al., 2006). The ACTION program emphasizes CBT techniques and is currently delivered in a group format with girls between the ages of 9 to 13 years with funding from the National Institutes of Mental Health. The program teaches skills to participants that help them learn to monitor their negative mood and then engage in a variety of active coping strategies. Strategies to improve mood include doing fun things, catching and challenging negative intrusive thoughts, and using active problem solving to find solutions to a bad mood or unpleasant situation. Initial study findings indicate that the program leads to symptom remission, but the complete study results and follow-up data are not yet available. It is a promising school-based intervention, but extensive training and supervision in CBT is required to facilitate these groups.

Anxiety Interventions in Schools

There is extensive research on interventions for anxiety. Most interventions have an exposure component, a modeling component, a cognitive-behavioral component, or some variation of those techniques (Chorpita &

Southam-Gerow, 2006). The *Coping Cat* program developed by Kendall (1990) is cognitive-behavioral treatment approach for treating anxiety in children, ages 7 to 13, in clinical settings. The goal of the program is to help children be more aware of the arousal of anxious feelings and use learned strategies to manage their anxiety (Kendall, 1990). *Coping Cat* is a 16-week program that is divided into two main parts, including education and practice. The education component teaches youngsters to recognize their anxiety, learn relaxation skills, and to identify and change anxious thoughts. These skills are accomplished through homework assignments, role-playing, and psychoeducation. A FEAR plan is also used to help the child cope with anxiety-producing situations. The second part of treatment is practicing the learned skills by exposing the children to anxiety-provoking situations through imaginal and in vivo exposure. The last component is a "commercial" creation of their experience in therapy, which may be in the form of a booklet, videotape, or other form. Although Kendall's program was originally designed for clinical settings, adaptations of the program have been found to be successful within the school system (Barrett & Turner, 2001; Dadds et al., 1997). Using CBT in a group format to treat anxiety in youth has also been found to be successful (Barrett & Shortt, 2003). Merrell (2001) suggested that the *Coping Cat* program is an "excellent choice" for treating children with anxiety in school settings because of its psychoeducational component and the practical application of skills. Given that anxiety disorders are one of the most common disorder clusters in children, it is important to consider how early intervention and prevention programs to large groups of children may be effective.

Barrett and Turner (2001) examined the effectiveness of a universal school-based preventative intervention for childhood anxiety. The program, called FRIENDS, was provided during school for 10 weeks. Schools were randomly assigned to three conditions: psychologist-led intervention, teacher-led intervention, and a standard curriculum with monitoring. The program utilized several cognitive-behavioral techniques, including relaxation, cognitive restructuring, attentional training, parent-assisted exposure, and family and peer support. Children who received treatment, from either teachers or psychologists, showed improvements from pre- to posttreatment on self-report measures of anxiety, whereas, the control condition showed no significant change. The study provides preliminary support for the use of teachers as group leaders in anxiety prevention programs as well as providing evidence for the generalization of anxiety programs within the school system. This program was integrated within the school system's curriculum, was developmentally appropriate, and was supported by parents. Similarly, Dadds et al. (1997) found that a 10-week school-based intervention and prevention program was more successful at preventing the development of an anxiety disorder than a monitoring condition at a 6-month follow-up. These studies and programs demonstrated positive trends for the effectiveness of a school-based program for children who are "at risk" for anxiety.

While many of the intervention programs mentioned are ongoing research projects, there is sufficient evidence at this time that several approaches are likely to help depressed and anxious youth. If schools or private clinicians identify a child as depressed or anxious, treatment is important. The accessibility of the research-based programs may seem daunting to the average practitioner. Some authors may send free copies of manuals to schools on request, other program manuals are available for purchase. In a user-friendly format, Merrell (2001) provided a practical, comprehensive guide and summary of several empirically validated treatment components for depression and anxiety, making many treatment options widely accessible to a trained mental health professional, particularly someone with prior training in general CBT approaches. This guide provides information on a variety of topics, including how to decide group size, CBT, and worksheets for identifying and altering emotions and beliefs, systematic desensitization for anxiety, and social skills training. As noted by Stark and his colleagues (Stark, Sander, et al., 2006), providing an empirically-supported treatment is recommended practice.

Psychopharmacology and Medication Considerations in Schools

It is helpful for school personnel to have at least basic information about how medications may affect children, including the benefits and side effects (Kubiszyn, Brown, & DeMers, 1997). Pharmacology is a common form of treatment for youth with depression (Stark et al., 1997) or anxiety (Chorpita & Southam-Gerow, 2006). Several classes of drugs are used to treat internalizing disorders; the most common are selective serotonin reuptake inhibitors (SSRIs) and tricyclics (TCAs; Table 14.4). In addition to the physical effects (side effects), it is important for teachers to be aware of, and help decrease, the stigma and embarrassment associated with diagnosis, as well as the medication for a mental illness (Merrell, 2001). Schools are a preferred context for observations that can inform medical professionals about how well a medication is tolerated by the child and how effective the medication is for the illness. Teachers can be important informants about side effects,

Table 14.4   Common medications administered to
children with depression and/or anxiety

Agent (Brand Name)	Common Side Effects
Tricyclics (TCAs) Amitriptyline (Elavil) Desipramine (Norpramine) Imiprmine (Tofranil) Norriptyline (Pamelor) Amoxapine (Doxepin)	Dry mouth, drowsiness, blurred vision, constipation, slower cognitive functioning, nightmares, sleeping problems
Serotonin Reuptake Inhibitors (SSRIs) Fluoxetine (Prozac) Sertraline (Zoloft) Paroxetine (Paxil) Fluvoxamine (Luvox) Citalopram (Celexa)	Nausea, headache, diarrhea, insomnia, dry mouth
Benzodiazepines Diazepam (Valium) Alprazolam (Xanax) Lorazepam (Ativan) Clonazepam (Klonopin) Tranxene (Clorazepate)	Drowsiness, overall state of relaxation, disinhibition reaction (agitation, anxiousness, sleeplessness), habit-forming

particularly those related to learning, cognition, and energy level (Del Mundo, Pumariega, & Vance, 1999).

Teacher Strategies for Internalizing Disorders

Given the growing prevalence of children with internalizing symptoms and disorders, it is important that the school system and teachers take steps to assist in prevention efforts. In general, classrooms and schools characterized by clear rules, expectations, rewards for following rules, and consequences for breaking rules, combined with a sense of community and positive student-teacher interactions are related to positive behavioral, emotional, and academic outcomes for students (Gottfredson, Gottfredson, Payne, & Gottfredson, 2005). Therefore, good classroom management, warm student relationships, clear rules and consequences, including praise for students for a variety of behaviors, and a "no tolerance policy" for teasing or bullying, foster an overall positive classroom environment, which is helpful for all students, regardless of risk for depression or anxiety. Herman, Merrell, Reinke, and Tucker (2004) suggested a number of strategies that school personnel can use to target specific risk factors associated with depression. To encourage more positive behaviors, Herman and colleagues suggested that school personnel model and reinforce positive nonverbal behavior and social participation, extinguish negative attention seeking (do not provide attention, or provide clear unwanted consequences, for behaviors that are unhealthy, unsafe, disrespectful, or otherwise negative), encourage and offer regular opportunities for physical exercise and pleasant events, provide opportunities for success both academically and socially, implement social skills in the curriculum, foster positive relationships, provide accommodations, involve parents, and expand school-wide rules.

To encourage more positive thinking styles, school personnel can model and reinforce positive and adaptive thinking in the following ways: incorporate cognitive modeling strategies, provide praise for specific thoughts, teach self-praise and self-reward, support self-efficacy, encourage recall of success, label the child's positive experience, create checklists for tasks accomplished that day, implement a bully prevention program, and consult with a mental health professional, such as the school psychologist. Teachers should encourage *and* model positive behaviors and thinking in their students. For example, teachers can help students make adaptive attributions for the causes of negative events by encouraging them not to self-blame or catastrophize about the situation. If a student does poorly on a test, teachers can encourage students to make a healthy attribution for the outcome such as attributing the test grade to lack of effort ("maybe you did not study as hard as you had planned for that test"), or to some environmental factor ("you were distracted during the exam that day,") as opposed to self-blaming or self-denigrating causes ("you're not smart, you're lazy, or you'll never understand algebra"). As shown in these examples, emphasis is on the behavior and the situation, not the stable qualities or character of the student. Teachers can also model this when describing their own behavior. For example, when the teacher makes a small mistake, he or she can model appropriate attributions out loud by making a lighthearted comment, "Oops, I wrote the wrong page number on the board. Everybody makes mistakes now and then," as opposed to a negative stable statement such as, "Oh, I wrote the wrong number down. I hate it when I do that! I'm so forgetful." Teachers can also model for their students who are struggling, such as praising effort and persistence, not just "right" answers. For example, a student forgot his homework last week, but has it this week. The homework is not 100% correct, but it is completed. The teacher can simply say with a smile, "Good for you for bringing your homework today," in contrast to a negative or sarcastic statement such as, "well, isn't that nice that you finally remembered your homework." Teachers may also want to incorporate CBT strategies into their curriculum. For example, relaxation techniques, such as deep breathing and imagery techniques, may be used to reduce anxiety. Incorporating anxiety-reducing breathing or imagery can even assist in test taking strategies, as well as improve classroom climate.

Maintaining an illness perspective when a child has depression, anxiety, or any combination of emotional distress may also help reduce the blame placed on the child or parent. For instance, March and Mulle (1998) suggest it is important to understand OCD within a neurological framework that completely removes the "fault" from the child. Depression and anxiety have strong biological components, so at times, the child may truly be unable to perform or engage in a specific task without very positive and clear support. Blaming the child for lack of effort usually will not solve the problem at hand, and can further debilitate the child. Encouraging the child to try, even though it may be very challenging, breaking tasks down into small components, and praising effort for any small progress, can ease the emotional distress. This does not mean that students are excused from tasks, but that some tasks may need to be temporarily modified while treatment is underway. If a child is experiencing anxiety or depression to such a degree that schoolwork is greatly impaired and accommodations are necessary, then including the mental health professional in the school-based plan is strongly advised. In general, the school system provides a unique environment by which preventative strategies for internalizing symptoms can be adapted and incorporated into the system and curriculum.

Summary

Overall, there are several barriers to effective identification and intervention for depression and anxiety within schools. In many cases, qualified mental health professionals participate in special education processes, and do not always have the opportunity to assess potentially distressed students in regular education settings. Teachers are not trained in mental health, nor should they be experts in that area. The solution is a collaborative dialogue and active assessment opportunities to screen or identify children at risk for anxiety and depression.

A few simple, but not necessarily easy, steps for addressing the needs of students who suffer from anxiety or depression include: maintaining a positive classroom climate, adopting an illness approach (not a deficit approach) to the mental health disability, remaining open to collaboration with internal or external mental health experts for addressing needs of anxious or depressed children in the classroom, and fostering general awareness of interventions to alleviate symptoms of anxiety and depression. To take any of these steps, teachers may need to seek administrative, colleague, or consultative support. Mental health professionals, at the same time, need to be especially aware of potential teacher needs for support in making any of these changes, and also need to be very available, collaborative, and approachable, to help facilitate empiricall supported interventions that can benefit many students over time. Mental health professionals have a special role in educating administrators to gain support for implementing mental health programs, including screening, prevention, or intervention programs.

CHAPTER
15

—

Building Social Skills

EMILY D. WARNES, SUSAN M. SHERIDAN, AND
S. ANDREW GARBACZ

E ffective social functioning is a critical factor in healthy child development. Getting along with peers and developing friendships are fundamental competencies that children must master to be successful in life
(Sheridan, 1995). Children's capacities to initiate and maintain interactions, resolve conflicts, and use self-control directly affect their abilities to
function at school, home, and later on in the workplace over the course of
their lives. Children who lack important social skills often are rejected by
their peers, have trouble interacting with their teachers and families, and
have emotional difficulties (Coie & Dodge, 1988; Dodge, 1983; J. G.
Parker & Asher, 1987; Vosk, Forehand, Parker, & Rickard, 1982). Furthermore, social skills deficits are frequently associated with children exhibiting externalizing disorders such as delinquency and conduct disorder,
as well as internalizing disorders including depression and anxiety (Mash
& Barkley, 1996). Because social competence has a significant impact on
development, it is essential that children who struggle in this area be identified and efforts made to remediate deficiencies and build competencies.

Social Skills: A Definition

Researchers have defined social skills in a number of ways. The terms
social skills and *social competence* have been used throughout the social
intervention literature to describe the social behavior of children. These
terms have two distinct, but interrelated meanings. *Social skills* can be
defined as the discrete, learned behaviors that a person uses to perform a

social task (Sheridan & Walker, 1999). These are the specific behaviors that children use to influence and achieve their interpersonal goals with others. *Social competence,* on the other hand, refers to the evaluative judgments that significant others such as teachers, peers, and parents have regarding the social behavior of children (Gresham, 1997). Individuals in children's environments define the appropriateness of children's social behavior within those environmental contexts. For young children to attain peer-related *social skillfulness,* they must not only acquire important social behaviors for interacting with peers, but they must be able to use these skills in ways that are acceptable to their peers (Sheridan & Walker, 1999).

Constructs that Characterize Social Skill Problems

Much has been written about the basis for children's social skillfulness. Key researchers in the area of social skills have described children's social difficulties as the function of either (a) deficits in the knowledge of specific social skills (i.e., skills deficits) or (b) deficits in the performance of appropriate social behaviors (i.e., performance deficits; S. N. Elliott, Racine, & Busse, 1995; Gresham & Elliott, 1984). These behavioral constructs have been seminal in guiding the conceptualization of children's social problems and developing interventions to address those problems.

Skills Deficits

It is generally believed that children with social skills deficits have not acquired the necessary social behaviors for interacting appropriately with others, or have failed to acquire a critical step in the performance of a given social act (S. N. Elliott et al., 1995; Gresham & Elliott, 1984). Children with skills deficits may have the desire to engage in socially skilled behaviors, but may not have the specific tools to do so. Interventions to address skill deficits focus on teaching children specific social behaviors for successful interpersonal interactions.

Performance Deficits

Children with performance deficits are believed to have appropriate pro-social skills in their behavioral repertoires, but they do not perform them at acceptable or functional levels (S. N. Elliott et al., 1995; Gresham & Elliott, 1984). From a behavioral perspective, there may be two primary reasons that children with performance deficits do not engage in high rates of pro-social behaviors. First, they may not have the motivation to engage in socially appropriate behavior (Gresham & Elliott, 1984). Second, children may fail to perform important social behaviors because they lack the opportunities to engage in such behaviors (Gresham & Elliott, 1984). Interventions to address performance deficits focus on increasing rewards and motivation for engaging in socially appropriate behavior, and providing increased opportunities for engagement in pro-social behaviors.

Characteristics of Socially Unskilled Children

Michelson and Mannarino (1986) differentiated between two groups of children with social skills deficits, based on the directionality of the deficiency. Although both socially withdrawn and socially aggressive children exhibit an inability to act effectively and appropriately within their social environment, the behavioral correlates characteristic of these two groups are qualitatively different.

Social Withdrawal

Socially withdrawn children are described as being isolated, shy, passive, and lethargic. They are further characterized as feeling inadequate, incompetent, and depressed in their social worlds. Withdrawn children appear to elicit few positive social responses from peers. They tend to hover or wait on the periphery of ongoing activities, and peers are likely to ignore the social overtures of withdrawn children. These behavioral patterns often result in an overall diminished level of social contact. Continued isolation is likely to become associated with adult and peer perceptions of abnormality, which is eventually associated with rejection (Rubin, 1985). Social withdrawal has been negatively correlated with a variety of adaptive, interpersonal, and intellectual capacities (Michelson & Mannarino, 1986). The combination of peer rejection, social withdrawal, and poor self-perceptions may have a clear path to childhood depression (Rubin, 1985).

Social Aggression

At the other end of the continuum are children who demonstrate social aggression. Children who engage in socially aggressive or antisocial behaviors are invariably hostile, defiant, and challenging to adult authority (H. M. Walker, Ramsey, & Gresham, 2004). They often engage in verbal and physical assaultiveness, teasing, provoking, quarreling, and fighting as methods of conflict resolution. These children often do not display age-appropriate social behaviors; rather, they tend to respond to conflict with aggressive behaviors (G. R. Patterson, 1982). Although tactics used by aggressive children may be effective, they are typically inappropriate and tend to generate many negative side effects such as problems with academic work, counter-aggression, and rejection from peers. Likewise, early aggressive behavior patterns are highly predictive of later antisocial behavior disorders and adjustment problems (H. M. Walker et al., 2004). Aggressive, antisocial children are at risk for secondary school discipline problems, school dropout, juvenile delinquency, violent crime, and psychiatric problems such as schizophrenia, alcoholism, and attempted suicide (H. M. Walker et al., 2004).

Important Considerations for Understanding Social Skillfulness

Ecological Context

Social behaviors do not occur in isolation; thus, the various factors in the environment (i.e., ecological context) that influence children's social functioning must be considered. As such, ecological theory provides a useful framework for understanding social behaviors and social skills. Ecological theory recognizes numerous systems in a child's environment that effect development, including the (a) microsystem (i.e., immediate influences such as home and school), (b) mesosystem (i.e., interrelations between the immediate environments, such as relationships between parents and teachers), (c) exosystem (i.e., formal social structures such as media, neighborhoods, community support systems), and (d) macrosystem (i.e., ideological influences such as religious beliefs, public laws) (Bronfenbrenner, 1979). Norms and expectations at every level define what is desirable and appropriate social behavior. A contextual approach to understanding social skillfulness requires both the goals and motivations of social behavior from the child's perspective, and the perceptions, expectations, and responses of others in the environment that reinforce or discourage the social behavior of the child, be considered (Haring, 1992; Sheridan & Walker, 1999). Socially skilled individuals are able to understand the perspectives of others and react appropriately. This principle can be understood by considering the various settings in which children frequently interact, such as at school and home. Each of these settings clearly requires different behaviors for appropriate social functioning, as the expectations and normative behavior vary across home and school contexts. Children must be able to negotiate the differences in expectations and demands across settings and behave in a way that adapts to certain contextual parameters.

A contextualized approach to understanding social skills is essential for determining the types of behaviors that are meaningful in a child's social network. Many practitioners and researchers advocate for a multimodal approach to social skills assessment that incorporates various methods, sources, and settings into the assessment process (S. P. Carey & Stoner, 1994; S. N. Elliott & Busse, 1991; Gresham, 1995; Maag, 1989; Sheridan, Hungelmann, & Maughan, 1999; Sheridan & Walker, 1999; H. M. Walker, Irvin, Noell, & Singer, 1992). In keeping with a contextual framework for understanding social skillfulness, the behaviors and perspectives of an individual child and the social responses and expectations of the environments in which that child interacts must be accounted for (Haring, 1992; Sheridan et al., 1999; Sheridan & Walker, 1999).

Kazdin (1977) highlights the importance of the evaluation of others in determining the meaningfulness of treatment outcomes. The reactions and perceptions of others in the client's social context help determine the validity of behavioral interventions for that client. A critical component in the significance of a behavior change for a particular client involves assessing the functioning of the client within a given social context after the behavior change has occurred.

The importance of socially valid treatment outcomes has implications for social skills assessment and intervention programming. Not only must children learn various pro-social behaviors, but these behaviors must be meaningful within their social networks. It is only when social behaviors are meaningful that they are reinforced in the child's social context and the process of "behavioral entrapment" may occur. Behavioral entrapment occurs when newly learned social responses come under the control of naturally occurring reinforcers (S. R. McConnell, 1987). Within this framework, newly learned social behaviors must be naturally reinforced to generalize to a child's authentic environment (Fox & McEvoy, 1993; S. R. McConnell, 1987). When others in the environment reinforce the social skills being used, children are more likely to continue to use the skills on a regular basis and the behavior becomes "entrapped."

Developmental Perspective

Another important consideration for understanding the social behavior of children is developmental level. Certain developmental processes influence children's social skillfulness, including shared understanding and emotional regulation.

Shared Understanding. Shared understanding refers to children's abilities to recognize the various roles, expectations, and sequences of events that are established as part of social interactions (Guralnick, 1993; Guralnick & Neville, 1997). For children to behave in a socially competent manner, they must first understand the "rules of the game." A child with shared understanding understands the predictable pattern or sequence of events that will result from engaging in certain social behaviors. Shared understanding also includes children's abilities to recognize that others have independent intentions, knowledge, beliefs, and attitudes. Children must understand that their own thoughts and behaviors are separate and distinct from that of their peers; that is, each individual holds unique perspectives.

Developmental research indicates that the perspective-taking abilities important for shared understanding develop gradually throughout childhood. During preschool (ages 3 to 6), many children are believed to be egocentric in their thinking about the world (Selman, 1980). Young children often have a difficult time considering the psychological processes of those around them. Preschool children may recognize the basic feelings and thoughts of their peers, but may have a difficult time differentiating between the behavioral acts and feelings of others or between intentional and unintentional behavior. Perspective-taking skills become more pronounced in the early elementary school years, and continue developing into adulthood.

Emotional Regulation. Another important developmental process that directly influences young children's social skillfulness is emotional regulation (Garber & Dodge, 1991; Guralnick & Neville, 1997; Shonkoff & Phillips, 2000). Social interactions with peers inevitably evoke emotional reactions such as anger, anxiety, and excitement, which must be regulated in some way for children to achieve their interpersonal goals in a socially competent manner. Children who cannot effectively regulate their emotional arousal may engage in maladaptive strategies for dealing with their emotions (e.g., yelling, crying, using physical aggression, withdrawing). Conversely, children who are able to effectively regulate their emotions choose socially appropriate strategies for interacting and have a greater likelihood of being accepted within their social networks.

Children are able to develop the ability to regulate their emotional responding as early as 3 years of age (Dunn & Brown, 1991; Kopp, 1992; Shonkoff & Phillips, 2000). In the 2nd and 3rd years of life, children's increased communication skills and understandings of others lead to increased control over their own affective states (Dunn & Brown, 1991; Shonkoff & Phillips, 2000). Self-regulation requires that children adopt and internalize specific standards for behavior. As children grow older, they become better able to self-regulate their behavior and modulate their emotional responding (McCurdy, Kunz, & Sheridan, in press). De-

velopment and refinement of these skills is believed to continue throughout childhood.

Family Influences

A third area of consideration for understanding the social behavior of
children involves the role of family. Families generally are the primary
sources of early learning and support for children, and they effect children's development in several ways.

First, the quality of direct interactions between parents and children
has been associated with developmental outcomes. Parental responsiveness to children's needs and secure attachments between parents and
children are associated with developmental outcomes for children
(Kestenbaum, Farber, & Sroufe, 1989; A. F. Lieberman, 1977). Each of
these types of interactions has been shown to facilitate more positive outcomes for children, especially with regard to social competence. Conversely, negative parent-child interactions such as harsh discipline, overly
controlling parenting styles, and lower levels of parental affect have been
related to decreased social competence and increased peer rejection for
young children (C. H. Hart, DeWolf, Wozniak, & Burts, 1992; C. H.
Hart, Ladd, & Burleson, 1990; Howes & Stewart, 1987).

Second, parents also influence children's development through the
environmental experiences they help create for their children (Guralnick, 1997). Parents are responsible for selecting the particular schools,
neighborhoods, and communities in which their children interact. Likewise, they make decisions regarding social networks for their children.
Parents can create opportunities for their children to experience social
interactions outside of school contexts (e.g., having peers over to play,
involving children in play groups). Thus, each of the decisions that parents make regarding their children's environmental experiences directly
impacts children's development.

The influence of parents is important in the area of social-behavioral
education for children. Because parents affect their children's social development both through their own direct interactions with their children
and the efforts they make to facilitate social interactions for their children, it is essential that parents be directly involved in social intervention
programming for their children. Involving parents in social-educational
programming for children promotes working partnerships between home
and school systems that can benefit children throughout their school careers. Parents can be involved in their children's social education through
collaborative working relationships with educational professionals
(Christenson, 1995; Christenson & Sheridan, 2001). In this way, parents

do not act as mere bystanders, observing the educational experiences of their children at school; rather, they are meaningfully involved in the decision-making and implementation of social interventions for their children (Sheridan, Kratochwill, & Bergan, 1996).

An Ecological Consultation Framework for Addressing Social Skills Concerns

The structured, ecological consultation model described by Sheridan, Kratochwill, et al. (1996) provides a useful framework that targets skills that are important across contexts, includes a developmental perspective, and involves meaningful adults (parents and teachers) across settings (home and school). *Conjoint behavioral consultation* (CBC) relies on behavioral principles to guide social skills assessment and intervention, and incorporates multiple relevant individuals and settings through which important social behavior(s) can be targeted. It is defined as "A strength-based, cross-system support model wherein parents, teachers, and other caregivers or service providers work as partners and share responsibility for promoting positive and consistent outcomes related to a child's academic, behavioral, and social-emotional development" (Sheridan & Kratochwill, in press).

In CBC, parents, teachers, and other caregivers engage in a structured problem-solving process with a consultant to address the social needs of children collaboratively across contexts. Given the cross-setting and context-specific nuances of social skills concerns, the active involvement of adults across multiple environments (including home and school) is critical for optimal intervention outcomes. Thus, when conducting CBC for social skills concerns, parents, teachers, and other supportive adults work together to identify a child's needs and priorities, and to develop, implement, and evaluate social skills interventions.

The CBC process consists of four stages, implemented in a collaborative manner across home and school:

1. Conjoint needs (problem) identification
2. Conjoint needs (problem) analysis
3. Plan implementation
4. Conjoint plan evaluation

Three of the four stages are initiated in the context of a structured interview with parents and teachers; the objectives of each of these interviews are presented in Table 15.1 (Sheridan, Kratochwill, et al., 1996).

Table 15.1   Objectives of conjoint behavioral consultation interviews

Objectives of Conjoint Needs (Problem) Identification Interview
1. Identify strengths of the child, family, teacher, systems.
2. Behaviorally define the concern or need as it is represented across home and school settings.
3. Explore environmental conditions that may be contributing to or motivating problem behaviors (antecedent, consequent, and sequential conditions).
4. Determine a shared goal for consultation.
5. Clarify specific settings within systems that will be the focus for intervention.
6. Explore within- and across-setting environmental factors that may contribute to or influence behaviors.
7. Identify potential setting events (events or factors that may occur in a time or place that is distal to the target behavior, but still influence its occurrence).
8. Establish and implement baseline data collection procedures to set the stage for careful, systematic, data-based decision making.

Objectives of Needs (Problem) Analysis Interview
1. Explore baseline data collected across settings.
2. Evaluate and obtain agreement on the sufficiency and adequacy of baseline data across settings.
3. Identify setting events, ecological conditions, and cross-setting variables that may be impacting the target concerns.
4. Investigate trends across settings (e.g., home and school) and highlight when appropriate.
5. Elicit and provide information about the function or motivating features of the behavior that are based on environmental (rather than internal) explanations.
6. Collaboratively design an effective intervention plan that is sensitive to setting-specific variables across settings.
7. Link assessment to intervention through the interpretation of concerns in terms of environmental conditions rather than internal causes.
8. Discuss general strategies and plans to be included in an intervention package across home and school settings.
9. Summarize the plan, being clear about what is to be done, when, how, and by whom.

Objectives of the Plan Evaluation Interview
1. Analyze intervention data in relation to baseline data.
2. Determine if the shared goals of consultation have been attained.
3. Evaluate the effectiveness of the plan across settings.
4. Discuss strategies and tactics regarding the continuation, modification, or termination of the intervention plan across settings.
5. Schedule additional interviews if necessary.
6. Discuss ways to continue conjoint problem solving or shared decision making.

The main objectives of the conjoint needs identification stage are to assess, prioritize, and define social concerns; identify relevant settings within which to focus assessment and intervention efforts; and establish procedures for collecting baseline data on a child's social skills. Multisource (e.g., parent, teachers, peers), multisetting (e.g., home, classroom, playground), and multimethod (e.g., observations, checklists, interviews, sociometric) procedures are recommended.

In the conjoint needs (problem) analysis stage of CBC, parents and teachers evaluate the social skills assessment data, decide on social goals for the child, form hypotheses about factors that may influence the child's social behavior, and collaboratively develop a plan to address the needs of the child. To the greatest extent possible, interventions that match the function of a child's behavior (Crone & Horner, 2003) and that have research evidence attesting their efficacy should be emphasized in the plan. During the plan implementation stage, parents and teachers implement the social skills intervention procedures at home and school, supporting implementation across settings. The final stage, conjoint plan evaluation, allows a vehicle for consultants, parents, and teachers to examine the social skills data collected and evaluate the effects of the social skills intervention to determine if the child's goals have been met across the home and school settings. Importantly, strategies for maximizing generalization of social skills gains are put into place.

In the section that follows, social skills assessments are discussed. These methods are relevant during the initial (problem identification) stages of CBC, as well as throughout the process to monitor on a continual basis a child's response to social skills intervention. Following, empirically supported social skill intervention strategies are described, which are relevant in a cross-setting social skills treatment plan. Given the importance of systematic generalization procedures in the area of social skills, effective ways for helping students generalize newly acquired skills in other relevant contexts also are discussed.

Social Skills Assessment

When conducted appropriately, social skills assessment procedures can be helpful in understanding the scope and nature of social skills difficulties. Through that understanding comes an ability to provide data that informs the creation and implementation of an intervention (Merrell & Gimpel, 1998). A multisource, multisetting, multimethod assessment model is considered "best practice" in social skills assessment (Gresham, 1995). This takes into account the context within which social behaviors are exhibited and focuses on the relevance and function of behaviors

Table 15.2 Overview of social skills assessment methods

Assessment Method	Defining Characteristic
Direct observation	A direct, objective measure of observed behavior in a natural setting.
Rating scales	Checklists, surveys, or questionnaires on which behavioral information can be quantified using ratings or other indices of a topographical nature (e.g., frequency, severity).
Behavioral interviews	Verbal assessment with teachers, parents, and other relevant sources that uses a top-down approach and hypothesis testing to gain a picture of social behavioral functioning.
Sociometric techniques	Social behavioral information is obtained from peers about a social group, context, or individual.

within a particular environment (Sheridan & Walker, 1999). A consideration of social behaviors and their interrelationship in the social environment allows for a focus on specific types of behaviors that may be important to display within that environment (Sheridan & Walker, 1999; Warnes, Sheridan, Geske, & Warnes, 2005).

There are numerous assessment strategies that can support a multisource, multisetting, multimethod process. A variety of individuals, or sources, should be included in social skill assessments such as the child or adolescent, parents, teachers, other family members, other school personnel, and peers (Merrell & Gimpel, 1998). Settings within which social skills should be assessed include home, school (including classrooms, playgrounds, lunchrooms, etc.), clinic, and community (Merrell & Gimpel, 1998). The CBC consultation model allows for thorough assessment of these important settings because multiple individuals from the contexts in which the child functions are meaningfully involved in the assessment process. The strategies reviewed here are those that parents, teachers, and consultants can use to assess a child's social behavior. These strategies include direct observations, rating scales, sociometric techniques, and behavioral interviews (Table 15.2).

Direct Observations

Children's social (including play) behaviors in natural settings are important indicators of developmental issues. Direct observations of social behaviors provide a measure of the child's skills and interactions in natural settings, allow for a functional assessment or analysis of the child's behaviors in a social context, and provide an opportunity to observe peer reactions. Likewise, they allow for social comparison with a matched peer, which can be important in determining the social validity of a chosen treatment (Kazdin, 1977). Both qualitative (e.g., nature, function) and quantitative (e.g., frequency, rate) aspects of the social behaviors should be assessed in direct observations.

There are two primary types of observations: skill-based and analogue. Skill-based observations combine an observational recording method (e.g., narrative, frequency, interval) with a specific behaviorally based coding system. Using the operational definitions of a particular coding system, specific behaviors are observed and recorded. Thus, data are collected on behaviors that are exhibited, and those behaviors are quantified and qualified in ways that yield information about intensity and frequency (La Greca & Stark, 1986). In addition, important contextual information can be gathered, including antecedent, consequent, and sequential conditions surrounding a behavior.

There are many observational coding systems available (Hops, Walker, & Greenwood, 1988; N. A. Kahn & Hoge, 1983; Leff & Lakin, 2005). Leff and Lakin (2005) reviewed a number of promising and empirically supported observational systems for children's play behavior. The ADHD School Observation Code (ADHD-SOC; Gadow, Sprafkin, & Nolan, 1996) provides many codes that are directly linked to social skills taught in many training programs. Codes include appropriate social behavior, physical aggression, nonphysical aggression, noncompliance, and verbal aggression. Since the ADHD-SOC focuses on both positive and negative behaviors, data on increases in certain behaviors as well as decreases in other behaviors can be tracked. This system has emerged as an observational system with substantial reliability and validity, and has achieved wide acceptance.

The Student Interaction in Specific Settings (SISS) Tool (Cushing, Horner, & Barrier, 2003) focuses on assessing a schools' overall social environment. The SISS provides data on student behaviors in many unstructured school settings and on a variety of high and low intensity behaviors (e.g., disruption, physical aggression). Since social skills interventions can target schools as a whole, it is important to have observational systems that can provide reliable data on the overall school climate. The SISS is a relatively new system, and as such it has not yet achieved the acceptance of other systems such as the ADHD-SOC. Although more studies are needed to obtain important psychometric information, the SISS appears to hold great promise for the assessment of social skills.

A second type of direct observation is analogue observation. Analogue observations are conducted in contrived situations (e.g., role-plays) or environments (e.g., clinics), and may be helpful when naturalistic observations are not feasible (Sheridan & Walker, 1999). In analogue situations, social situations are simulated and social behaviors are elicited (Hintze, Stoner, & Bullis, 2000).

Rating Scales

Rating scales are reporting procedures that can elicit information from a number of sources on the same constructs. They can be given to multiple individuals, including parents, teachers, and other relevant individuals who may have information about a child's social behavior. Despite their ease of use, some limitations are evident (i.e., they are inherently subjective and lack of criterion validity). Thus, rating scales should be combined with other data collection methods as part of the assessment process (Gresham, 1986; Sheridan & Walker, 1999).

The Social Skills Rating System (SSRS; Gresham & Elliott, 1990) provides reliable and functional data on a child's social behaviors. This system accesses important information from various sources on both the frequency and importance of social behaviors. To obtain important information across sources and settings, there are separate forms for parents, teachers, and students. The SSRS effectively provides a context for comparing a student's behaviors with those of a normative sample. The use of importance ratings increases the utility of the measure by providing information on the respondents' perceptions of relevance, thereby contributing a unique contextual perspective on children's behaviors.

Behavioral Interviews

Behavioral interviews are helpful in assessing the social behavioral functioning of an individual child, from the perspective of the respondent (e.g., parent, teacher, child). Using behavioral interviews, specific concerns, environmental demands, peer perceptions, and other contributing conditions can be assessed.

Structured behavioral interviews allow for a top-down social skills assessment approach that is practical and functional for consultants. The process starts with a general and global assessment, and the focus of assessment is continuously narrowed to specify and clarify the target skill for intervention. Through this narrowing, hypothesis-testing process, consultants continuously clarify topographical and functional features of social behaviors, explore important factors surrounding their occurrence, identify areas of strengths and weaknesses of the child and treatment agents (e.g., parents and teachers), and investigate personal and environmental conditions that may facilitate the development and implementation of an effective plan (Sheridan & Elliott, 1991).

Sociometric Techniques

Sociometric techniques seek to gain information from peers about a social group, context, and/or specific individuals (Merrell & Gimpel, 1998). In addition to providing preliminary assessment information, sociometric procedures may also be helpful to assess perceptions of a child's social status over time (S. R. McConnell & Odom, 1986).

There are many different sociometric assessment procedures, including peer nominations and social comparisons. Peer nominations request that students identify a peer or multiple peers who meet a predetermined criterion (e.g., a student who is helpful toward others). Both positive and negative nominations can be solicited. That is, students can be identified who both do and do not meet the predetermined behavioral criterion.

Social comparisons involve pairing two students and requesting that members of a larger group identify one of the two students in each pair who meets some predetermined criterion. As in peer nominations, positive and negative comparisons can be made. That is, the student (in the pair) can be selected based on being more likely to, for example, engage in an appropriate conversation, or fight with a peer.

Sociometric assessment techniques can yield data that are relevant and useful for intervention planning. Engaging students in this way during the initial assessment also sets the stage for engaging students in an intervention procedure at some point in the future (e.g., peer tutoring, cooperative learning). However, there are risks associated with using these types of procedures (e.g., differential treatment of a child following completion of a sociometric instrument), and these risks should be addressed appropriately before any assessment is conducted.

Contextualized Assessment

The necessity of considering contextual information such as that provided by teachers, peers, and independent observers in social skills assessment and programming has been discussed. Sheridan and colleagues (1999) described a procedure designed to gather contextually relevant information regarding the behavior of socially competent children. Specifically, with this procedure, teachers, peers, and independent observers each provide a written list of behaviors that are deemed important for children's social competence. In gathering information from these various sources, specific behaviors can be identified that correspond to social competence for a particular group of children within a given context.

Warnes and colleagues (2005) expanded the research on contextualized approaches to the assessment of social skills by utilizing a similar procedure similar to gather information from parents, teachers, and peers regarding the specific behaviors important for social competence in second- and fifth-grade children. Data were gathered from children through structured interviews with the researcher, and parents and teachers provided information through open-ended paper-pencil surveys. Results indicated a number of noteworthy similarities and differences in what respondents deemed important behaviors. Specifically, many of the same types of social behaviors were reported by parents, teachers, and peers at both grade levels (i.e., compromising, empathy, help others with personal work, not verbally hurting others, loyal and reliable to friends, trustworthy, not physically harmful, funny, spend time together, invite others to do things). This suggested that some behaviors cross developmental levels in terms of their significance within the social milieus of second and fifth graders. In contrast, many of the behaviors reported by second-grade children, parents, and teachers tended to be rule-governed behaviors (e.g., being respectful of others and their property, following and respecting rules, being fair, and having manners), whereas many of the behaviors reported by fifth-grade sources involved verbal communication (e.g., communicating verbally about problems and frustrations, being a good listener, giving praise and compliments to others). This result is consistent with the natural developmental differences found between second- and fifth-grade children, and is important to consider when developing social skills interventions across grade levels. More research is needed in this area that pertains to operationally defining the behaviors identified by students and creating relevant corresponding interventions. Nevertheless, this area of assessment shows great promise for optimizing the effects of social skills interventions by targeting behaviors that are most relevant to students within their specific environments.

Social Skill Intervention Strategies

Given the complex nature of social skillfulness, intervention strategies that address the child and the environment are necessary. Likewise, it is necessary to consider means to generalize newly learned social skills into natural environments. Consistent with an ecological orientation, interventions that go beyond the child and immediate environment are also necessary, focusing on families and that are appropriate in large scale (classroom- or schoolwide) settings. The interventions discussed next and summarized in Table 15.3 can be utilized by parents, teachers, and consultants to help support children's social behavioral functioning at home and school.

Child-Focused Interventions

Child-focused intervention strategies include interventions aimed at teaching a child a specific skill (e.g., starting a conversation, solving problems calmly). Environmental interventions are those that are applied to the context in which a child exists (Sheridan & Walker, 1999). They focus on manipulating the variables within the environment that operate on the child's behavior. Child-focused interventions are grounded in social learning and cognitive-behavioral procedures. Environmental interventions include the manipulation of antecedents and consequences of behavior.

Social Learning Procedures. According to social learning theory, social behaviors are acquired through observation and reinforcement (Bandura, 1977). Modeling is an effective social learning procedure often used in social skills interventions (Gresham, 1985; Wandless & Prinz, 1982). This procedure involves the use of audiotapes, videotapes, or live demonstrations of skills to be acquired. Modeling can play a major role in learning and performing new social behaviors (Lowy-Apple, Billingsley,

Table 15.3 Overview of social skills intervention methods

Intervention Focus	Theoretical Framework	Intervention Goal
Child	Social learning	Learn adaptive social behaviors through the observation of models.
	Cognitive-behavioral	Target internal cognitions and learn problem-solving strategies.
Environment	Ecological-behavioral: Antecedent events	Set the stage for positive interactions (e.g., prompting, cueing, peer initiation).
	Ecological-behavioral: Consequent conditions	Provide reinforcement for desired social behavior, including contingent social, group contingencies, and differential reinforcement.

& Schwartz, 2005). Modeling can be especially effective when models are similar to the children learning the skills and when examples of skills to be learned are highly salient.

There are two kinds of modeling that can be used in social skills training: live and symbolic (Sheridan & Walker, 1999). Live modeling of appropriate social behaviors involves the target child observing the social behaviors of models in naturalistic settings, such as the classroom. Symbolic modeling requires the target child to observe the social behaviors of a model on film or videotape. Regardless of the form, modeling is typically carried out in three steps: (1) students are given verbal instructions for how a specific skill is to be performed; (2) the behavior is demonstrated by a group leader, teacher, or videotape; and (3) a role-play procedure can be utilized to allow opportunities for students to practice the skill. Nonexamples can be helpful to students during the modeling phase, to show both what the skill does and does not look like (Sheridan, Dee, et al., 1996).

There is ample empirical support for modeling as an intervention to support social skill development. Modeling has been shown to improve problem-solving behavior, increase the number of social interactions, and improve sociometric status (Debus, 1970; Gresham & Nagle, 1980; O'Connor, 1972). Although modeling can reap many positive effects, it is best used in conjunction with other procedures (e.g., cognitive-behavioral, operant) so the effects can be improved and maintained (Sheridan & Walker, 1999).

Cognitive-Behavioral Procedures. Cognitive-behavioral intervention procedures emphasize internal cognitions (e.g., thoughts, self-statements) and problem-solving abilities (Beck, 1995). Two common cognitive-behavioral procedures are coaching and social problem solving. With *coaching*, direct verbal instructions and discussions are the major mediums of intervention (Oden & Asher, 1977). A coach (e.g., teacher, parent, consultant, peer) first provides the child with specific rules or steps for a behavior. The coach and child then rehearse the steps, and the coach provides feedback about the child's performance. Coaching is often paired with other social skill intervention methods (e.g., modeling, positive reinforcement) to enhance its efficacy. Coaching procedures can be particularly helpful for a child, as it provides practice opportunities in natural settings through which maintenance and generalization can be promoted (Reitman, O'Callaghan, & Mitchell, 2005). Coaching has received substantial empirical support as a social skills training technique especially in the areas of communication, cooperation, and peer reinforcement (Gottman, Gonso, & Schuler, 1976; Ladd, 1981; Oden & Asher, 1977).

Social problem-solving interventions focus on the interaction of cognitive, emotional, and behavioral factors associated with social competence. Such approaches teach children the process of solving social problems by logically evaluating interpersonal problems and considering alternative, adaptive solutions (Spivack & Shure, 1982). These interventions attempt to teach target students (a) that they can resolve most problematic social situations; (b) how to recognize when problems exist; (c) to generate various alternative solutions to reach social goals and to consider their consequences; (d) how to select a strategy and develop a plan of action; (e) means of carrying out the strategy competently; and (f) methods of self-monitoring behaviors, evaluating their effectiveness, and modifying plans (Weissberg, 1985). These procedures typically follow a sequence and teach the child to analyze situations by asking a series of questions, such as "What is the problem?; What are my choices?; What are the consequences?; What is my best choice?; and How did I do?" Problem solving is a common component of several social skills curricula (Sheridan & Walker, 1999).

Environmental Manipulation Intervention Procedures

Environmental manipulation intervention procedures seek to increase the effective use of certain social skills in desirable situations by manipulating the contingencies in the environment that operate on a child's behavior. Primary targets of environmental interventions involve modifying the antecedent and consequent conditions surrounding a behavior.

Manipulating Antecedent Events.   Antecedent events precede desired social behaviors and can either increase or decrease their likelihood of occurrence. Manipulation of social antecedents can set the stage for positive interactions and thus is important in promoting healthy relationships. Methods of manipulating antecedent events include prompting, cuing, and peer initiations. For example, prior to an opportunity for social interactions (such as recess), a teacher may provide a prompt to a child to ask another child if she would like to play a game, making it more likely he or she will exhibit the desired social initiation behavior. Cueing involves reminding a child in vivo of an appropriate social behavior or response to an ongoing situation. Cooperative learning strategies, which require students to work together to complete academic tasks (Madden & Slavin, 1983), also provides opportunities for students to learn and practice different social skills and may provide especially effective antecedents in classroom settings (Iannaccone & Hwang, 1998).

Manipulation of Consequent Conditions.   Manipulation of consequences includes procedures to reinforce positive social behaviors. In general, three reinforcement techniques are used: contingent social reinforcement, group contingencies, and differential reinforcement. In *contingent social reinforcement*, a teacher, parent, or other relevant individual (e.g., playground monitors) reinforces appropriate social behavior through social praise and/or tangible rewards. A variety of methods can be used including contracts, spinners, tokens, or point systems (Rhode et al., 1992; Sheridan, 1995). These procedures have been shown to increase rates of positive social behaviors. To be successful, however, they require considerable involvement and support by a teacher, parent, or other relevant individual.

Group contingencies involve the application of consequences for behaviors of group members (e.g., members of the class). These can be applied in various ways. For example, reinforcement can be applied contingent on (a) the behavior of selected children rather than an entire group (dependent group contingency), (b) an individual child's behavior regardless of the behavior of others (independent group contingency), or (c) the collective behavior of the group (interdependent group contingency). When used in social skills training programs, group contingencies have been found to be effective at increasing positive interactions and decreasing negative interactions (Hansen & Lignugaris-Kraft, 2005).

Differential reinforcement procedures are used to decrease the rate of undesired target behaviors (e.g., socially aggressive behaviors) and increase the rate of appropriate, alternative behaviors (Meadows & Stevens, 2004). They can be applied in a variety of ways. With differential reinforcement of other behaviors (DRO), reinforcement is provided after any behavior except the target behavior. This has the effect of increasing the frequency of positive social behaviors and decreasing aggressive behaviors. Differential reinforcement of low rates of behavior (DRL) involves the delivery of reinforcement for reduced rates of the undesired target behavior. Numerous empirical reviews and studies have shown differential reinforcement procedures to be an effective intervention in teaching and maintaining social skills (Farkas, Sherick, Matson, & Loebig, 1981; Meadows & Stevens, 2004).

Generalization

The purpose of social skills training is to ensure that students master important social skills that they can perform in novel and/or natural settings (i.e., outside of the training situation). Many social skills training programs, however, do not show generalized effects (DuPaul & Eckert, 1994). This lack of generalization may be due to a number of factors (e.g., contrived versus natural settings for training, competing behaviors), but can be improved if careful planning for generalization takes place at the onset of training and continues through maintenance phases.

H. M. Walker and colleagues (2004) outline a specific rationale for a commonly observed lack of social skills generalization. They and others (e.g., Gresham, Sugai, & Horner, 2001; Horner & Billingsley, 1988) argue that a functional approach is needed to understand issues surrounding generalization. A functional approach explains lack of generalization observed in many social skills interventions in terms of stimulus generalization and response generalization. Stimulus generalization refers to generalization that occurs across the training environment and natural environments. The greater the difference between the training conditions and natural conditions, the less likely the behavior will be performed. For example, requesting that a socially anxious child ask another child to play in a highly controlled, one-on-one treatment setting where the peer's response is planned is quite different than requesting that same child to ask another to play on a playground where several children may be present and the peer's response is unpredictable. Differences in basic stimulus characteristics across these two situations may limit the generalizability of social skill training. Response generalization refers the extent to which a certain stimulus can elicit certain responses from a student while facing many other competing responses different from the new, learned social behavior. It may be difficult for students to generalize new social behaviors (such as responses, or compromising during a disagreement) under conditions (such as unstructured recess settings) that had previously elicited ineffective responses (such as physical aggression).

Failure to adequately program for generalization and maintenance across variable stimulus conditions, and establish mechanisms to replace inappropriate responses are often considered culprits to social skills generalization. Likewise, the delivery of treatments in restricted and decontextualized settings has been identified as a barrier to generalization (Gresham et al., 2001; Haring, 1992; Sheridan & Walker, 1999). Haring (1992) argued for the delivery of social skills interventions in natural social situations, as compared to approaches that emphasize performance of discrete responses in contrived situations. A contextual approach, such as using natural environments to teach and reinforce adaptive social skills is increasingly prevalent in related literatures (Dunst et al., 2001). Simply put, naturalistic settings allow for the use of incidental teaching of important social behaviors via informal intervention delivered by significant individuals in a child's life. Natural learning environments use familiar materials and events to advance a child's social learning and generalization; include family members and friends in the intervention; provide frequent opportunities for the child to witness modeling of desired behaviors in typical settings; allow adults to contingently and meaningfully support the child and reinforce the use of desired skills as they naturally occur (Sheridan, Knoche, & Marvin, in press).

General case instruction (Horner, McDonnell, & Bellamy, 1986) is an approach to generalization that helps students learn and generalize social skills across stimulus conditions in a sequenced way (Sheridan & Walker, 1999). In this approach, students are not simply taught *how* effective social skills might be exhibited, but *when* and *where* those skills should be used. The first step in the sequence is to (a) define the *instructional universe*, or the environment and associated conditions under which students will be required to perform social skills (e.g., playground, classroom, and family room); and (b) involve any relevant individuals present during those times (e.g., teachers, parents). The goal in explicitly defining these conditions is to ensure students have all the necessary skills and strategies they need to perform the new skills under these natural conditions. The second step is to involve situations that may occur in natural settings during training. That is, during role-plays and other similar activities, situations should be contrived in such a way as to simulate the actual setting. Students should have the opportunity to "act like" they are in certain situations with certain individuals. This may make it easier for students to perform appropriate social skills in the natural environment. The third step is to ensure the training is conducted in sequenced portions that are most meaningful for the students, ensuring that they develop the competencies necessary to perform the skill. The fourth step requires the use of strategies such as prompting, fading, shaping, reinforcing, and effective pacing (Sheridan & Walker, 1999) in natural environments. The final phase is to assess the students' abilities at performing the new skills in both training sessions and natural settings (Horner et al., 1986). It is also important to ask that other relevant individuals (e.g., teachers, parents, peers) use environmental strategies (e.g., prompting, reinforcing) in the natural settings to ensure students perform the skills whenever natural opportunities arise.

Family Interventions

As mentioned previously, parents play a significant role in their children's social-behavioral education. As such, their involvement in providing social interventions to children is critical. Numerous studies have shown that parents can be effective at delivering social skills interventions to their children (Colton & Sheridan, 1998; McNeil, Eyberg, Eisenstadt, Newcomb, & Funderburk, 1991; Sheridan, Dee, et al., 1996; Sheridan, Kratochwill, & Elliott, 1990; Webster-Stratton, 1998; Webster-Stratton et al., 2001). Each of the intervention strategies discussed above can be utilized by parents, as well as teachers.

Positive effects have been shown to result from parent training to address children's behavior problems. McNeil and colleagues (1991) evaluated the effects of a parent training program with noncompliant and oppositional preschool children. Parents were provided extensive training in appropriate attending, reinforcement, ignoring, and time-out procedures. Results indicated significant increases in compliance rates among children in the home setting as determined by direct behavioral observations and reports by parents. Likewise, Webster-Stratton (1998) and Webster-Stratton et al. (2001) investigated the effects of parent- and parent-teacher, respectively, training programs designed to teach positive discipline strategies, effective parenting skills, strategies for coping with stress, ways to strengthen children's social skills, and strategies for collaboration between home and school. In both studies, the parent training intervention led to significant improvements in parenting interactions with children, increased involvement in children's education, reductions in children's problem behaviors, and increases in prosocial behaviors.

Other research has concentrated on the involvement of parents in delivering focused social-behavioral interventions to children. Using the consultation model described in this chapter for addressing children's social skills problems (i.e., CBC), Sheridan and colleagues (1990) involved both parents and teachers in the delivery of a social skills intervention to elementary-aged socially withdrawn children. Parents and teachers taught children specific skills for initiating social interactions with peers and provided positive reinforcement to children for meeting their established behavioral goals. Results indicated positive treatment effects (i.e., increased social initiations) across both home and school environments, therefore highlighting the important role of parents in generalizing treatment effects across settings.

Parents also have been involved in delivering social skills interventions to elementary-aged boys with ADHD (Colton & Sheridan, 1998; Sheridan, Dee, et al., 1996). In one study, children received weekly social skills training in a clinic setting and learned the specific skills of social entry, maintaining interactions, and solving problems (Sheridan, Dee, et al.,

1996). Their parents participated in simultaneous training sessions focused on teaching parents the skills of debriefing, problem solving, and goal setting, all behaviors designed to help promote and maintain children's social skills in the natural environment. Results indicated mean increases in target behaviors across all child participants as recorded through analogue observations. Likewise, improvements were shown for most children on self-report and parent and teacher ratings on social skills rating scales. Parents' skills in debriefing, problem solving, and goal setting also improved, as demonstrated on home-based assessments.

Social Skills Curricula

Given the relationship between social competence and positive child development, several social skill training programs have emerged over the past 2 decades. Next we review several social skills training programs developed for elementary to high school, and that effectively blend social learning, cognitive-behavioral, and environmental manipulation procedures in a manualized protocol (Kavale & Mostert, 2004; Merrell & Gimple, 1998). The programs (i.e., Skillstreaming, ASSET, the Prepare Curriculum, the Tough Kid social skills curriculum, and ACCEPTS) are designed for group training and are appropriate for classroom and schoolwide use. However, modifications can be made and procedures individualized depending on need.

Skillstreaming. This program is a structured learning approach to teaching social skills that relies on the structured learning model (A. P. Goldstein, Sprafkin, Gershaw, & Klein, 1980). Components of this structured learning approach include modeling, role-playing, performance feedback, and transfer training. Separate programs are available for elementary students and adolescents. Skills taught in the elementary and adolescent programs include beginning social skills, advanced social skills, skills for dealing with feelings, skill alternatives to aggressions, skills for dealing with stress, and planning skills. Homework assignments involving skill practice and self-monitoring of skill use are considered to be integral parts of the programs (Merrell & Gimple, 1998). Assessment checklists and leader instructions are included. Finally, to assist group leaders in handling the dynamics of the group, a section on behavior management strategies is included.

A Social Skills Program for Adolescents. A Social Skills Program for Adolescents (ASSET) is a skill-based program for adolescents that teach eight specific social skills: giving positive feedback; giving negative feedback;

accepting negative feedback; resisting peer pressure; problem solving; negotiating; following instructions; and conversation strategies (Hazel, Schumaker, Sherman, & Sheldon-Wildgen, 1981). Nine steps are used to teach each skill including discussion, rationales for using the skill, modeling the skill, and verbal and behavioral rehearsal. Homework is assigned following skill mastery, and parents are asked to evaluate their child's use of each social skill. A videotape is also available, which depicts adolescents in situations that require the use of social skills taught in the ASSET program.

The Tough Kid Social Skills Curriculum. This curriculum is a training package that covers a range of social skills and can be used for elementary through high school-age students (Sheridan, 1995). The Tough Kid curriculum includes three skill areas (i.e., social entry, maintaining interactions, problem solving) and eleven subskills (e.g., recognizing and expressing feelings, playing cooperatively, solving arguments). It provides information about multisource, multimethod assessment procedures, group session plans, instructor training, and generalization planning. Strategies for teaching social skills incorporate several effective procedures, including skill instruction, group discussion, modeling, role-playing, performance feedback, contracting, goal setting, and positive reinforcement.

ACCEPTS. This program is designed for mildly and moderately handicapped and nonhandicapped students in kindergarten through sixth grade (H. M. Walker et al., 1988). Emphasis is placed on the teaching of skills to facilitate adjustment to the mainstream settings. ACCEPTS categorizes 28 discrete skills into five major areas: classroom skills, basic interaction skills, getting along skills, making-friends skills, and coping skills. The teaching approach incorporates clear definitions of each skill, use of positive and negative examples, sequencing of skills on a continuum of increasing complexity, provision for practice activities, and use of systematic correction procedures. Assessment materials for screening and placement of students and a videotape are available to enhance appropriate skill training.

Summary

Attaining social skillfulness is essential for healthy child development. Children must learn to adapt and get along with others in their environment to be successful at home, in school, and in the community. Social skillfullness is a complex construct, as there are numerous variables that impact children's social functioning. These include the ecological context, a child's developmental level, and the role of family. Given the variety of influences impacting children's social behavioral functioning, all meaningful individuals in the child's environment should be included in the assessment and intervention process. Conjoint behavioral consultation offers a useful framework for addressing social skills concerns in this way because both parents and school professionals can work together to thoroughly assess and intervene in the environments in which children function (i.e., at home and school). This chapter highlights some of the most common and empirically based assessment and intervention strategies for addressing children's social skills problems. These strategies can be used by teachers and parents to support children's social development across contexts, thus promoting better generalization of skills to the child's natural environments.

CHAPTER
16

Bullies and Their Victims: A Problem-Solving Approach to Treatment and Prevention

MYRNA B. SHURE

Seven-year-old Richard, mercilessly teased for being overweight, responded with verbal or physical aggression. He had no friends and was engaged in daily altercations with peers. Richard's mom, trying to help, suggested he "ignore those kids," "walk away," or "tell the teacher." Richard, like many victims, was afraid that if he told the teacher, the bully would find out, and he didn't find ignoring them helpful either because the kids kept teasing him.

Ten-year-old Rebecca, distraught because her best friend Tammy told a classmate her secret felt betrayed because, "I can't trust her anymore." Rebecca's mom explained that if she didn't tell her how much that hurt her, "Tammy would keep on doing things like that." But Rebecca didn't hear a word she said.

Twelve-year-old Steven threatened his classmate Peter that if he didn't do what he said, he'd beat him up after school. When asked what happened next, Steven answered, "He told the teacher but I don't care." When his teacher reported this incident to Steven's parents, Steven was grounded for a week. He did care about that. It made him feel very angry.

Not caring, like Steven, can begin much earlier than age 12. I heard the same comment from Robert, a boy in kindergarten, age 5. Robert got what he wanted from his classmates by hitting them. When I first saw him do this to Paul, I asked him, "What happened when you hit Paul?"

He answered, "He hit me back, but I don't care." Indeed he did not. He got the truck, and that was what he cared about. Robert and other children who hit, kick, scream, and grab toys from others gave me a new perspective on the significance of research on empathy, pioneered by Norma and Seymour Feshbach (1969). I wondered if children who do not care or who endure their own pain could possibly develop empathy for the victims they might hurt (physically or emotionally). In light of escalating bullying, with the potential for more serious violence, children who "don't care" should make us take special pause.

Bullying has multidimensions. Tammy, who betrayed Rebecca's trust, and those who teased Richard for being overweight are just as much a bully as is Steven and, in time, potentially 5-year-old Robert. Children are not bullies just because they fight or tease or tell someone's secret. They are bullies because they repeat similar acts frequently, and perceive themselves as physically or psychologically more powerful (Hazler, Hoover, & Oliver, 1992; P. K. Smith & Sharp, 1994). While Steven and Robert engaged in physical force, the boys who teased Richard made him feel badly about himself, making him unable to function successfully academically, or with his peers. And Tammy and others like her hurt others in a different way. A relatively new body of research has placed emphasis on what is becoming known as relational aggression, designed to interfere with relationships, and includes "behaviors that are intended to significantly damage another child's friendships or feelings of inclusion by the peer group" (Crick & Grotpeter, 1995, p. 711), spreading rumors, excluding peers from one's social group, and withdrawing friendship.

While Crick and her colleagues found relational aggression to be more prevalent among girls, beginning in about the third grade, Crick, Casas, and Mosher (1997) have also identified precursors to this kind of aggression as early as preschool. Examples include telling a peer that she won't play with her or not inviting her to a birthday party until she does what the child asks, telling others not to play with or be a peer's friend, and whispering mean things behind a child's back. This kind of aggression, if frequent and intense, can be just as harmful as being kicked in the shins. In fact, this kind of pain lasts longer because it hurts inside. As early as preschool, victims of relational aggression, especially girls, can experience poor peer relationships, even rejection by peers, internalizing problems, and a lack of prosocial skills (Crick, Casas, & Ku, 1999). In middle-school youngsters, Crick and her colleagues found relational victimization to be associated with emotional distress, and problems with self-restraint (Crick & Bigbee, 1998). When children feel badly inside, they may come to dislike themselves, and in time, not want to go to school.

What happens to the bullies and their victims later on? Both groups are more likely than other children to be involved in fights and more often reported poor academic achievement. Bullies report higher rates of tobacco and alcohol use and are more likely to have negative attitudes about school. And victims are more likely to report having difficulty forming friendships (Nansel et al., 2001), being lonely, even depressed (Crick & Grotpeter, 1996). Sourander, Helstela, Helenius, and Piha (2000) found that, children who were bullies at age 8 were still bullies at age 16, and victims at age 8 were still victims 8 years later. And beyond the school years, perhaps for a lifetime, P. M. Smith, Singer, Hoel, and Cooper (2003) learned that youngsters who were threatened, humiliated, belittled, or otherwise picked on in school—especially those who did not, and still don't, have coping strategies—may continue to be victimized years later in the workplace.

Fearing retaliation, or perhaps perceiving that they won't be believed, many victimized children do not report being bullied to their parents or their teachers. Being less visible, and more difficult to prove, Paquette and Underwood (1999) found that relational aggression made adolescents feel more sad and bad about themselves than did physical aggression, suggesting more suffering and a greater chance of going unnoticed by teachers. In time, some victims may let out controlled emotions and the bullied may become the bully—or worse. A case in point: The boys of Columbine, Eric Harris and Dylan Klebold, who killed 12 students and a teacher in Littleton, Colorado, in 1999 were not aggressive when they were younger. Just the opposite. They were picked on, teased, and rejected (Garbarino & deLara, 2002).

Today there is growing concern over the connection between bullying and school violence (Swearer & Espelage, 2004). Nansel and coworkers (2001) report that an average of one in seven American schoolchildren—that's almost five million youngsters—is either a bully, a victim of a bully, or both (bully/victims). Nearly a third of U.S. students in grades six to ten report they are bullies, victims of bullies, or both. No wonder youngsters between the ages of 8 and 12 that I interviewed mentioned being bullied as their number one concern.

What can be done to curb bullying and protect the victims? There are various ways that schools try to do this.

Suspensions and Expulsions

One way schools try to deal with bullies and protect the victims is to practice zero tolerance, which "refers to the practice of automatic expulsion of students for violations of school safety rules" (Cornell, 2005, p. 48). While originally designed to eradicate gun violence and drug use, numerous cases of excessive punishment have been cited. As early as age 5, a child was expelled after he found a razor blade at his bus stop, carried it to school, and gave it to his teacher. In Philadelphia, a kindergarten child was expelled for staring with an angry look for an extended period of time. As Cornell notes, the zero tolerance approach "ignores student characteristics and instead focuses entirely on whether the student committed an absolutely forbidden act, such as bringing a weapon to school" (p. 48).

With expulsion being an extreme strategy, many schools suspend students for acts of bullying, including threatening, but not carrying out an aggressive act. As teachers have told me, however, older students come back angrier, not having learned anything about their behavior or the impact it has on themselves and others. Younger children may not even understand the concept of suspension, making no connection of their behavior with why they have to stay out of school. In fact, suspensions may have the opposite effect of how they were intended. Some children may enjoy not having to go to school, and behave in ways to make that happen. With these caveats, Cornell reports that suspensions and expulsions affect millions of students. He cites a Virginia Department of Education report (2003) that during the 2001/2002 school year there were 187,928 suspensions and 1,929 expulsions in the state of Virginia alone.

Alternative Classrooms

Several states try to diminish or eliminate serious aggressive behaviors by placing students in special classrooms, either permanently, or for a portion of the school day. If treated as punishment rather than as help to change behaviors, these youngsters, placed with like-minded peers may feed off each other, and reinforce the very behaviors the school is trying to stop.

No Intervention

As Cornell notes, some school principals believe it best to just ignore behaviors that fall short of physical harm or violence, viewing them as "not much more than an unpleasant rite of passage in childhood" (2005, p. 59). I once saw a video of an older boy bullying a younger boy in the schoolyard. Though adults were nearby, no one intervened. When asked, the principal simply said, "Boys will be boys." A similar comment was made by administrators in a Philadelphia middle school when a seventh grader was jumped on the way to school by three boys who stole all his money—two dollars (Dean, 2005). Perhaps in today's climate, teachers and other authority figures are afraid to intervene. Perhaps school districts fear being sued by parents of the bullying child. Or perhaps educators don't have the expertise to deal with these situations.

Not intervening at all can have serious consequences for both bullies and their victims. With extreme violence as one outcome of early victimization, the boys of Columbine and other high profile school shooters (one in Jonesboro, Arkansas, only 11 years old) are reported to have warned authorities that they were going to do something "big"—some even said they were going to kill. No one listened. No one seemed concerned. Or perhaps, no one believed them. Maybe these boys just needed someone to hear them. Instead, the silence they encountered must have told them, "We don't care what's going on in your head. We don't take you seriously." Or, perhaps, "We don't want to get involved." Perhaps some of these boys were in pain themselves and felt that their own cries for help were being ignored. Perhaps they, like others their age, believed, sometimes correctly, that the school ignores these types of behaviors, or pleas for help (Cornell, 2005). Youngsters like these must not be ignored. Hurting others might well have been perceived as a way to get the attention that otherwise eluded them.

Teenagers don't just decide one day to hurt or kill someone. Their anger and frustration build for years. They sense they don't have control over their lives. Just as expressing anger can lead to devastating outcomes if ignored, those who fail to let people know how they feel can be just as damaging. Such is often the case with youngsters who are socially withdrawn. A 14-year-old boy in suburban Philadelphia, who was bullied by a classmate for 3 years, brought a gun to school, and in front of several classmates, shot and killed the bully. As reported by the media, the boy never expressed his feelings or told anyone about what was happening. No adult noticed anything was bothering this boy. Perhaps they could have noticed nonverbal cues such as change in body posture, grades falling, loss of previous interests (e.g., Dwyer et al., 1998).

Unfortunately, children who are withdrawn hold their feelings inside. They do not disrupt the classroom and are often thought of to be the "good child," or simply ignored. As true of bullies, they also must not be ignored. Whether withdrawn or not, all victims must be noticed. The boy who killed the bully in suburban Philadelphia and the boys of Columbine have shown us why. In fact, two-thirds of 37 school-shootings reviewed by the U.S. Secret Service in 2001 were carried out by youngsters who felt they had been "persecuted, bullied, threatened, attacked, or injured by others" (Viadero, 2003, p. 24).

Not all youngsters who are bullies or were bullied later become so violent. However, many of those who do not enter adolescence and adulthood with a need to control others—and will not be liked. The children I worked with, and some fifth graders participating in a seminar led by Sue Ellen Fried (S. Fried & Fried, 1996) told us that the children who are not only rejected by others but also feared are those who:

- Scratch, bite, throw things, hit others
- Threaten to hurt others
- Steal or break things
- Get other kids into trouble
- Make fun of kids' clothes, skin color, weight
- Gossip and spread rumors
- Laugh at, make faces, or tease others
- Cheat at sports, razz the other team
- Ignore or reject others who are trying to participate in games or join teams
- Talk badly about family members, including those who are dead

Some children have an amazingly mature understanding of what's really underneath the behavior of a bully. When asked why someone might have a need to bully, some youngsters simply said, "Because it's fun," or, "Then the kids will respect him," or, "That's how he'll make friends." Others revealed more sophisticated thinking with responses as, "That's the only way anyone will pay any attention to him," "Maybe he's bullied at home," or, "Maybe he doesn't like himself" (Spivack & Shure, 1982). These insights were not far from those given to us by experts (e.g., Garrity, Jens, Porter, Sager, & Short-Camilli, 1996; Hoover, 1997):

- Power is the absolute number one issue with bullies.
- Bullies feel important by diminishing the importance of others.
- Bullying is an attempt to gain peer status.
- Bullies, rejected by peers, seek friends who are also bullies, and who feed on each other by thinking their behavior is "macho."
- Bullies who feel no empathy thought they may be crying out for help by hurting others.

How differently the boys of Columbine, the boy in suburban Philadelphia, and others who become violent might have felt about themselves and their world had they been encouraged to think about their own and others' feelings, and to solve problems important to them when they were much younger. While more than one approach may be needed for extreme cases as these, one way to help them is to nip milder forms of earlier violence in the bud.

Interventions Designed to Promote Positive Behaviors

While suspensions and expulsions, and alternative classrooms may suppress bullying behavior in the short-run, they are external strategies that do nothing to change the thoughts and feelings of the youngsters inside. On the other hand, ignoring these behaviors in the hopes they will go away will not make them go away.

In a report on bullying, Batsche (1999) notes that in schools where bullying exists, "the environment will change and the climate improve only when school systems choose to develop and implement a comprehensive plan designed to teach prosocial behavior, to limit aggressive behavior, and to teach skills that promote positive interactions between students" (pp. 30–31). Wilson, Lipsey, and Derzon (2003) conclude that "it is appropriate for schools to attempt to reduce behaviors such as fighting, name-calling, bullying, and general intimidation that can create a negative school climate and lead to more serious violence" (p. 135). This is especially important because as early as third grade, highly aggressive children seek out like-minded peers and lose interest in socializing with others (Astor, Pitner, & Duncan, 1996), and after the third grade, changes in school attitude are very difficult to change (Planta & Walsh, 1998). In fact, the earlier-described longitudinal study of Sourander et al. (2000) showed that it was just at this time, age 8, that the effects of bullying and being bullied remained for as long as studied, 8 years later. With bullying and being bullied associated with later more serious outcomes, it is critical that action be taken to curb bullying and victimization, perhaps even before the age of 8 when behaviors and attitudes toward school can more easily be changed. Social emotional learning (SEL) curricula, some of which are billed as violence prevention programs (for a review, see Taub & Pearrow, 2005) can impact these behaviors, and provide a viable way to address this issue (Elias et al., 2005).

Social/emotional learning (SEL) is the process of "developing the ability to recognize and manage emotions, develop caring and concern for others, make responsible decisions, establish positive relationships, and handle challenging situations effectively" (CASEL, 2003, p. 1). And children who develop empathy, a genuine desire to not want to hurt others because it bothers them inside, would not only reduce bullying behaviors in those who are displaying them, but can prevent them from occurring in the first place. Equally importantly, interventions designed to enhance SEL can help the victim learn to cope with bullies so they are not perceived as physically or psychologically weaker.

In my 30 years of research, I have learned that as early as preschool, children can, or can learn to make responsible decisions in life that have positive, not negative consequences—an important ingredient of SEL. Most youngsters want positive, not negative consequences, if they have the skills to make those kinds of decisions, and then are given the freedom to use them. I call this way of thinking the "problem solving" way. Children can learn to think about how they and others feel when, for example, they threaten someone, what might happen next, and what they can do so that won't happen. Children who are victimized can think about how to stop being bullied, what might happen if they do that, and, if needed, what else they can do.

The Problem-Solving Skills

Before designing our SEL program, we set out to identify those skills that are associated with behavioral dysfunction at different age levels— based on my colleague George Spivack's theoretical assumption that there is a set of interpersonal cognitive problem solving (ICPS) thinking skills that mediates behavior (Spivack & Shure, 1982).

Preschool and Early Childhood Years

Three ICPS skills have been identified that are most strongly associated with observed behaviors in young children. The first, *social perspective-taking*, the ability to appreciate that others have feelings about things that may differ from one's own was found to be most likely present in socially adjusted children, and least likely among youngsters displaying impulsive behaviors (physical and verbal aggression, impatience, inability to wait and cope with frustration, inability to share, take turns, etc.). Socially withdrawn youngsters were, however, more sensitive to other people's feelings than impulsive ones. They were, for example, aware that what they did might have made someone angry, a step ahead of not being so aware. However, like children displaying impulsive behaviors, they were unable to think about what to do to allay that anger, and being already inhibited, fearful, and shy, may retreat even more (Shure, 1982).

What socially adjusted and interpersonally competent children could do that impulsive and withdrawn youngsters could not was to think of

415

ways to solve the problem at hand. They were deficient in the next skill we identified, called *alternative solution thinking,* or the ability to generate different options (solutions) that could potentially be put into action to solve a problem. Among 4- to 7-year-olds, for example, a girl may want her sister to allow her to play with her doll. She may ask her but her sister may say no. Of interest is whether the child who wants the toy would conceive of an alternative way to get her sister to let her play with the doll. Any further attempt that the girl might make to solve her problem is largely dependent on her ability to think of other ways to go about it. Our assumption is that if an individual has only one or two options available, her chances of success are less than they might be for someone who can turn to alternative solutions in case her first attempt fails. If the girl's sister consistently says no every time she is asked for something, and no other options are available to the girl, she would soon become frustrated with her sister. She might react aggressively and exhibit impulsive behaviors (e.g., grab the toy) or she might avoid the problem entirely by withdrawing. Either impulsive or withdrawal behaviors could come to predominate if problem after problem remains unresolved.

Our research (e.g., Shure, Spivack, & Jaeger, 1971), replicated by many researchers (e.g., Mize & Cox, 1990; R. R. Turner & Boulter, 1981) found that regardless of measured IQ, youngsters who could conceptualize more, different relevant solutions to two types of problem (wanting a toy another child has, and how to avert mother's anger after having broken a valuable object) were least likely to display either impulsive or withdrawn behaviors. In the case of the peer/toy story, nearly all children could conceive of solutions as "Hit the child," "Grab the toy," or "Tell the teacher." However, better-adjusted youngsters could also think of more positive solutions as "Play together" and "Share," "Tell her she'll just play with it for a little while," as well as more creative ones as "Tell her she'll have more fun playing together than by herself." In the case of the mother/broken object story, impulsive and withdrawn children could think of "Say, 'I'm sorry,'" but many of these children got stuck on that solution as the only one available to them. Adjusted children could also think of solutions as, "Paint it her favorite color," "Tell mommy 'I love you,'" and "Pretend I'm asleep so mommy can't spank me."

The third skill found to be associated with behaviors is that of *consequential thinking,* or ability to think of what might happen next if an act were carried out (Shure et al., 1971). The girl who was refused her sister's doll may, for example, impulsively hit her sister as a reaction to the frustration of having been denied her wish, or she may think through different options and decide that, at that particular moment, hitting is one way to get her sister to give in and let her have that doll. If she thought about it and decided to hit her, the new question is whether the girl also thought through the potential interpersonal consequences of her hitting and whether having done so might have influenced her decision to hit. When asked what might happen next if a child grabs a toy from a peer, or takes something from an adult without asking, again it was the adjusted group who could think of more, different relevant consequences. To the peer/grabbing-a-toy story, most children could think of "He'll hit back," "He'll grab it back," or "He'll tell the teacher." Adjusted ones could also think of more creative ones. One 4-year-old said, "He'll eat marshmallows in front of him and when he wants one he'll say 'no, cause you took my truck.'" Regarding the adult/taking-something story, most children could think of "Mommy will be mad," or, "Mommy will spank him." Importantly, differences in empathy also showed up. In one story, a child took his mother's umbrella when she wasn't looking, and one adjusted 4-year-old said, "When it rains, mommy will get wet and catch a cold because she won't have an umbrella."

It is the *alternative solution* skill that is most strongly associated with behaviors, but it is the combination of *alternative solution* and *consequential thinking* that best predicts the kind of behavior a child is displaying. While adjusted children do not always end up with what they want, they are able to cope with the frustration and think of a different course of action that will satisfy them. Some impulsive children may know they may get hit, or get into trouble for hitting another child or grabbing a toy. They proceed to hit anyway because they don't know other ways to get what they want, or to find another satisfying course of action. And inhibited children, unable to think of solutions or consequences may just choose to avoid people and problems they cannot solve—leaving them with little opportunity to learn and exercise ICPS skills with others.

Intermediate Elementary Grades

In children aged 8 to 12, social perspective-taking, alternative solution, and consequential thinking skills are, as true of younger children, significantly associated with behaviors observed in the classroom. The new skill most predictive of behavior in this age group (Shure & Spivack, 1972), is called *means-ends thinking*, or *sequential planning*. This skill includes three components. Unlike alternative solution thinking, wherein the child thinks of separate, unconnected ways to solve a problem, the first component involves ability to plan step-by-step *means* to reach a stated goal, "I can do this and then I can do that . . ." Such planning includes the second component, that of insight and forethought to forestall or circumvent potential *obstacles* and, in addition, having one's command alternative steps if an obstacle is realistically or psychologically insurmountable. The third component is appreciation of *time*, that goals are not always reached immediately or that certain times are more advantageous than others for action. A child adept at means-ends thinking may consider, "I can go visit the boy next door [means] but he won't know me and won't let me in [obstacle]. If I call first and tell him I just moved in and ask if I can come over [means], he'll say okay. But I'd better not go at dinnertime or his mother will be mad [time and obstacle] and he won't like me." Since it assumes that a child is able to think of how to put a plan into action, consider potential obstacles along the way, and evaluate the timing of an act, means-ends thinking is a more demanding task than is alternative thinking, wherein the sole requirement is to identify a particular type of category of solution. The skill of means-ends thinking has been found to be significantly associated with behavioral adjustment in preteens and teens by a number of researchers (e.g., Higgens & Thies, 1981; Mott & Krane, 1994; Steinlauf, 1979).

Why Is Problem-Solving Ability Important?

Research has confirmed that competent problem solvers, as early as the preschool years are less likely than poor problem solvers to display aggression (including bullying), inability to wait and cope with frustration (including being the victim of a bully), lack of concern for the feelings of others, inability or unwillingness to share and cooperate, and experience poor relationships with peers (e.g., Shure et al., 1971)—behaviors that predict later violence, substance abuse, unsafe sex, and some forms of psychopathology (Olweus, 1993; J. G. Parker & Asher, 1987; Whitney & Smith, 1993).

These behaviors are similar to those described by Coolidge, DenBoer, and Segal (2004) as associated with bullies—aggression, lack of impulse control, lack of anger management, lack of empathy, and defiance toward authority. They also report that deficits in executive functioning are associated with bullying, that is, deficits in (a) decision making (allowing others to make decisions for them), planning, and organizing; (b) learning and integrating information; and (c) making appropriate social judgments. To the extent that ICPS skills give children the ability to think of alternative solutions to problems, plan steps toward a goal, and make decisions based on their anticipated consequences including how they will affect their own and other's feelings, lack of ICPS skills are directly linked to dysfunctional executive functioning and the behaviors associated with it.

Research has also confirmed that social withdrawal, if left untreated, can predict more internalized kinds of problems such as depression, and, in extreme cases, suicide (Rubin, 1985). To the extent that shy/withdrawn youngsters are perceived as weak, creating a target for victimization, the earlier-described boy in suburban Philadelphia who bottled up his anxieties, and research of Lee, Zimbardo, and Bertholf (1977) in which adult murderers reported being shy as children, researchers may soon identify extremely withdrawn behavior as a predictor of later violence as well. Although researchers do not yet have direct evidence that problem solving competence can prevent violence, only its predictors, it seems reasonable to assume that victims can be guided to express their feelings early in life, and helped to think of other ways to solve their problems. Perhaps then, acts of extreme violence can be prevented.

There are many available social/emotional learning (SEL) programs (see CASEL, 2003), some designed specifically to target bullying behaviors and to help the bullied (see reviews by Espelage & Swearer, 2004; Garrity, Jens, Porter, & Stoker, 2002). The program I now describe was designed to reduce and prevent predictors of later, more serious problems. It includes helping bullies find other, more rewarding activities, and victims to learn to cope with, and handle the bully.

I Can Problem Solve Prevention Program

This intervention, called *I Can Problem Solve* (ICPS), originally called *Interpersonal Cognitive Problem Solving* (also ICPS) starts in the preschool years, where the earlier-mentioned precursors of these kinds of behaviors begin. The ICPS program is based on the assumption that one way to guide behavior is to teach children a set of thinking skills that help them think about what they do, rather than focus on the behaviors themselves. The underlying approach is to teach children *how* to think, not what to think in ways that will help them resolve problems that come up with peers and adults. Shure and Spivack (1980) tested the earlier identified ICPS skills that Spivack theorized would mediate healthy human functioning.

ICPS in the Preschool and Early Childhood Years

The curriculum is divided into two parts: (1) formal lesson-games, and (2), use of the learned ICPS skills in real-life.

The *formal lesson-games* consist of sequenced activities and dialogues (Shure, 1992a, 1992b) that teach three levels of language and thinking that our research found to be related to behavioral adjustment prior to training—the very behaviors that predict the later, more serious problems as described above. The first level consists of games and dialogues to teach word pairs as *is/is not; same/different; before/after; now-later; why/because;* and *might/maybe.* While many children may understand these concepts, their constant repetition in the early games helps to establish their use within the framework of interpersonal relations. Unlike language programs per se, these words are not taught as an end in themselves, but rather, to set the stage for their role in problem solving thought.

Understanding the negation become very important in problem solving if, for example, a child is to appreciate whether an act is or is *not* a good idea, and why. Playing games with these words such as saying, "This *is* a chair, it is *not* a (child answers, e.g., giraffe)" helps to associate the question "Is that a good idea or *not* a good idea" with earlier fun with that word. Play with the words *same* and *different,* includes games as saying "I am tapping my foot. Now I'm rolling my arms. Did I just do the *same* thing or something *different?*" "My name is John. Who has the *same* name? Who has a name that is *different?*" These words can be used in real life situations by asking questions as, "Is your idea a good one or *not* a good one," and then adding, "Can you think of something *different* to do that *is* a good idea?" After playing with the words before and after, such as asking, "Do I brush my teeth *before* or *after* I get out of bed in the morning?" a child who, for example, hits another child can be asked, "What happened *before* you hit him?" "What happened *after?*" Association with these words played with in positive nonproblem situations creates a more likely response from the child than the more rhetorical, but angry sounding question, "WHY did you hit [Jimmy]?"

After having mastered the word concepts, focus is on the next level of the program, that of preproblem solving thinking skills. With an understanding of words that designate feelings (i.e., happy, sad, mad, afraid), and in kindergarten through grade 3, more sophisticated words as proud, frustrated, disappointed, it is possible to teach that different people like different things, that feeling change, and there are ways to find things out—by listening, watching, and asking. Being aware of your own, and other people's feelings not only opens up more possible ways of solving conflicts, but paves the way for developing empathy for children they might have hurt, not because they want to avoid punishment, but because it genuinely bothers them inside.

The third level is games that teach the interpersonal cognitive problem solving skills of *solutions* to a problem, and *consequences* to an act. Role-plays include one child teasing another, and the child is asked questions such as "How do you think Sarah feels when you tease her," and then, "What *might* happen next" (eliciting consequences), and finally, "Can you think of a *different* way to talk to Sarah so she won't feel that way, and that will *not* happen?"

To nurture use of the problem solving approach *in real life*, the key to problem-solving thinking, is to guide children to use their newly acquired ICPS skills when real problems arise, a style of talk I call *Dialoguing*. Dialoguing is a two-way conversation that engages children as part of the discussion, making them *active participants*. Yelling, demanding, and even more positive suggestions and explanations are all thoughts coming from the adult, and therefore, are monologues—and the children are merely *passive recipients*. Robert, the 5-year-old described earlier who only knew to hit or grab toys he wanted, and who came to not care if another child hit him, had a teacher who learned how to dialogue the problem solving way:

Teacher: What happened? What's the problem?
Robert: He (Michael) won't let me have the truck?
Teacher: What happened when you hit him?
Robert: He hit me back, but I don't care.
Teacher: How do you think Michael feels when you hit him?
Robert: I don't know.
Teacher: Do you think he felt happy or angry?
Robert: I guess angry.
Teacher: And how do *you* really feel inside when he hits you?
Robert: Ugh.
Teacher: Well, Michael is angry and he hit you. Can you think of a *different* way to get him to let you play with the truck so he won't be angry and he won't hit you?

Robert was guided to think of his own solutions to the problem, what happened next, and what else he could do to solve the problem. Children are much more likely to carry out their own idea than one demanded, suggested, or even explained by adults. It took Robert a little longer to come to care about his own feelings, necessary before he could care about other's, but in time he came to develop genuine empathy and learned to think of other ways to satisfy his needs.

Crystal was the victim of incessant teasing, and one day a classmate said to her, "Your hair is ugly. You got plaits." Only 4 years old, Crystal used a word from the ICPS word pairs and calmly replied, "My hair is *different* from yours." What a different outcome than the good swift kick she would have given him before training.

In addition to teachers, we also trained parents of low-income African American preschool and kindergarten children (Shure, 2000, 2004). Before training, two victims of a boy who hit others were given different advice by their mothers. One told her son to hit back because, "I don't want you to be so timid." The other advised her son not to hit back, because "Hitting is not nice, you might hurt someone. It is better to tell the teacher." Though their advice was different, the approach was the same. Both mothers were doing the thinking for the child.

Here's how a problem-solving mother talked to her child about the same type of problem:

Mother: What happened? What's the matter?
Child: Daniel hit me.
Mother: How did that make you feel?
Child: Mad.
Mother: Do you know why he hit you?
Child: He called me stupid.
Mother: How did you feel when he called you stupid.
Child: Mad.
Mother: Then what happened?
Child: I hit him.
Mother: You're mad and he's mad and you hit him. Can you think of something *different* you can do so he won't hit you and call you stupid?
Child: [after thinking a moment] I can play with my friend.

This child was given the opportunity to decide for himself what he could do to solve this problem and, like most children, is more likely to carry out his own ideas with a feeling of pride.

Children do, in time, learn problem-solving skills to cease bullying, or in preschool, precursors to bullying. They also learn to cope with being a victim. This is not to say, however, that children should always be expected to solve problems on their own. But adult intervention does not mean actions to simply stop a behavior. With the adult present, at least at first to avoid one child continuing to hurt another, it means guiding children to think about how their actions affect others (the first step toward empathy), or respond to other's actions. Then and only then will hurting others really stop. As one 5 year-old said after ICPS-training, "It makes me sad to hurt my brother." If his mother continues to use the problem-solving approach, this child will no doubt be less likely to hurt his brother as his solution to getting what he wants.

ICPS in the Intermediate Elementary Grades

The overall style and approach to problem solving for intermediate-grade students (generally grades 4 to 6) is the same as that for younger children—to teach them *how* to think in ways to successfully resolve interpersonal problems (Shure, 1992c). Although lessons do not teach the ICPS word pairs, they are woven into the exercises to set the stage for the discussion of people's feelings, solutions, consequences, and the new skill of means-ends thinking. The concept, *there's more than one way*, is stressed to develop a problem-solving thinking style. There is more than one way to: (a) explain another's behavior at a given moment (e.g., "Maybe he didn't wave at me because he doesn't like me," or "Maybe he just didn't see me."), (b) explain another's behavior that is consistent over time (e.g., "Maybe he bullies others because he thinks it's fun," "Maybe he's bullied at home," or "Maybe he thinks that's how he'll make friends.") and (c) to solve a problem. Children also learn that there is more than one way that others may react to what they do (i.e., potential consequences). Like the curricula for younger children, teachers are trained to apply ICPS dialogues when real problems arise.

Research Evidence of Impact of ICPS on Behaviors

Preschool and Early Childhood Years; Teachers as Trainers

Seven studies were conducted by Shure and Spivack to test the mediating function of ICPS skills and behaviors in the preschool and kindergarten years (Spivack & Shure, 1974). The most comprehensive study (Shure & Spivack, 1982) showed no differences in sex distribution, IQ, ICPS skills, or behavioral adjustment at pretest in either year. The results are summarized next:

- As early as age 4, 113 ICPS-trained low-income, primarily African American, children improved in solution and consequential thinking skills, compared to 106 controls.
- Prior to training, 36% of trained children were rated by teachers to be behaviorally *adjusted* (not impulsive or inhibited), 47% controls (not statistically significant). After training, 71% trained versus 54% controls were rated adjusted (statistically significant).

423

- Of the 44 trained and 39 controls rated as *impulsive* before training, 50% trained versus 31% controls were rated *adjusted*. Of the 28 initially *inhibited* trained versus 18 controls, 75% trained became *adjusted*, only 30% controls (both statistically significant).
- Linkage analyses show that among the trained, those who improved most in ICPS skills, most significantly solution thinking were those who gained most in the measured impulsive and inhibited behaviors—suggesting it was the trained ICPS skills that mediated behaviors. Within a wide range of 80–120+, these relationships were independent of initial IQ, or IQ change.
- Of 39 children first trained in kindergarten, 83% initially adjusted remained so, versus 30% controls, while 70% initially impulsive or inhibited children significantly improved, only 6% controls.
- While solution thinking was a stronger behavioral mediator in both nursery and kindergarten, consequential thinking linked with behavior gains more strongly in the kindergarten year. Perhaps thinking simultaneously of what to do (now) and what might happen (later) is a developmentally more sophisticated skill than thinking of successive solutions to a problem, a one-dimensional level of thought.

Children in the these studies were followed up at 6-months and 1-year, with the impact still showing significant superiority among the trained compared to the controls. Importantly, a significantly greater percentage of ICPS-trained youngsters rated adjusted before training in preschool were still adjusted at the end of kindergarten (71%), only 30% of controls. That already adjusted ICPS-trained children are less likely to show behavior problems over a 2-year period suggests a preventive, as well as a treatment impact of the program.

With findings of Shure and Spivack having been replicated by numerous studies around the country (e.g., preschool: Allen, 1978; Feis & Simons, 1985; kindergarten: Aberson, Albury, Gutting, Mann, & Trushin, 1986; first grade: Kumpfer, Alvarado, Tait, & Turner, 2002; Weddle & Williams, 1993), ICPS appears to be a viable prevention strategy for schools as early as the preschool and kindergarten years.

Parents of Preschool and the Early Years

In our initial study of 20 trained African American families and their 4-year-old children, and 20 matched controls (10 boys, 10 girls, each group), mothers or mother-surrogates could also be effective training agents (Shure & Spivack, 1978):

- Seventy-one percent of trained children moved from an initial *impulsive* or *inhibited* behavioral classification to *adjusted,* compared to only 31% of controls.
- As true of teacher-trained children, alternative solution was a stronger behavioral mediator than consequential thinking.
- Mothers who improved in their own problem-solving thinking skills and applied "ICPS dialogues" when handling real problems at home had children who most improved in the trained ICPS skills and behaviors.

The improved behavior of children trained at home generalized to the school, suggesting that the benefits of acquiring ICPS mediating skills are not situation specific.

Not only were relatively normal children with varying degrees of behavior problems able to improve when trained by their mothers, but youngsters (ages 6 to 8) with attention-deficit/hyperactivity disorder (ADHD), some of whom also displayed conduct disorders and oppositional defiant behaviors were able to improve as well (Aberson, 1996) and remained improved after a 4-year follow-up (Aberson & Ardila, 2000).

A separate study of kindergarten children trained by teachers in kindergarten, in kindergarten and first grade, or by their teachers in kindergarten and their mothers in first grade were compared to those never trained over a 5-year period from kindergarten through fourth grade (Shure, 1993). Of the 252 youngsters available the entire 4-year period, those trained in kindergarten and grade 1 showed the fewest impulsive and inhibited behaviors in grade 4, with those trained in kindergarten only also showing significantly fewer high-risk behaviors than controls. As true of mothers of 4-year-olds described earlier, children whose mothers best applied ICPS dialogues were still maintaining significant gains at the end of grade 4.

Intermediate Elementary Grades

Our major study in the intermediate elementary grades (Shure & Healey, 1993) was with 92 children available in both fifth and sixth grades (47 boys, 47 girls). The primary aims were to study the impact of *interpersonal* ICPS training beginning at age 10, in grade 5, as compared to ICPS training earlier in life, at ages 4 and 5, and to compare ICPS training with *impersonal* Piagetian Critical Thinking (CT) skills at that age. With comparable pretest scores in both grades 5 and 6 between groups on behavioral adjustment, ICPS test scores and academic ability, the results are summarized:

- ICPS-trained youngsters gained significantly more than CT-trained children in ICPS skills of alternative solution thinking, consequential skills, and means-ends, sequential planning skills immediately at the end of grade 5, and maintained those skills at the end of grade 6.
- ICPS-trained youngsters gained in peer relations, caring, sharing behaviors sooner than impulsive and withdrawn ones. While it took longer for the negative behaviors to improve than it did for younger children (about 6 months longer), CT-trained youngsters increased negative behaviors from grades 5 to 6, suggesting that ICPS training can reverse that trend.

While it took only one 3-month exposure to decrease *negative* behaviors in preschool and kindergarten, it took a repeated exposure (in grades 5 and 6) to decrease those behaviors in older children. However, some *negative* behaviors *increased* in CT-trained youngsters in grades 5 and 6, again suggesting a preventive impact of ICPS intervention.

In light of research supporting social/emotional learning as a critical ingredient in academic success (e.g., Zins, Bloodworth, Weissberg, & Walbert, 2004), our research showed that standardized achievement test scores improved among ICPS-trained youngsters, especially language arts, reading, and math. How do these findings relate to bullies and victims? Coolidge et al. (2004) report that 50% of parents of bullies report their children are unable to concentrate in school. And Garrity et al. (2002) report research suggesting that as many 7% of American eighth graders stay home at least once a month to avoid being bullied, while 90% of victims who do attend school stated that they experienced a drop in school grades (Hazler et al., 1992). While academic performance influences behavior, we must not ignore the reverse possibility, that ICPS skills can help to relieve emotional stress that prevents youngsters from concentrating on the task-oriented demands of the classroom, and to subsequently do better in school. With a synergism between academic achievement and behavior, it is worthy of further research to determine the extent to which improved academic achievement mediated through ICPS skills would, in turn, lead to fewer episodes of bullying.

Behaviors of ICPS-Trained Bullies and Victims

What happened to the youngsters described at the beginning of this chapter after being exposed to ICPS-training as children? Richard, who was teased mercilessly for being overweight learned to cope with that, sometimes by using humor. Four years later, in sixth grade, he reported that sometimes he was still teased because he was fat. When peers occasionally called him "Bacon," he simply paused, looked them in the eye, and said, "Yeah, and I sizzle, I sizzle." In sixth grade, Richard had many friends and his academic and conduct grades in schools were As and Bs. What a different outcome from what his mother had told him to do: "ignore them," "walk away," or "tell the teacher" (Aberson & Ardila, 2000).

How did Rebecca fare? Her teacher helped her think about why her friend might want to reveal her secret to others—and what she could do or say now. Rebecca found out that her best friend talked about a party in front of her that she was not invited to, and took it out on Rebecca. While Rebecca let her know she felt bad about that, she couldn't be her friend if she couldn't trust her. Her friend realized she had betrayed her trust and told her she was sorry. By turning a problem into a problem that could be solved, Rebecca saved a friendship that might otherwise have been lost. It might also have saved her self-esteem because, if not nipped in the bud, repeated "emotional bullying" might have caused her to not like herself, and in time, like other victims, not want to go to school.

Steven, who didn't care what happened to him as long as he felt power and control over his peers used his newly acquired ICPS skills when his teacher dialogued with him the ICPS way. One example of that was as follows:

Teacher: Steven, how to you think Kevin feels when you threaten to beat him up after school?
Steven: Scared.
Teacher: What happens when you do that?
Steven: He tells the teacher, but I don't care.
Teacher: What was it you really wanted him to do?
Steven: Play with me. He never plays with me.
Teacher: Oh, that's the *real* problem. Can you think of a different way to get him to play with you?
Steven: I guess I could stop scaring him.
Teacher: And then what could you do?
Steven: I know he likes video games and I could show him my new one.
Teacher: And how will you feel if he wants to do that?
Steven: Good.
Teacher: Give me a feeling word that you learned in ICPS.
Steven: Happy—and proud.
Teacher: Good thinking. You thought of a way to stop scaring Kevin.

This kind of response by Steven didn't happen overnight. It took time, not uncommon among children his age, as our research has shown. At first Kevin refused Steven's offer because he was used to being threatened by him.

The teacher then continued the dialogue:

Teacher: Kevin said he didn't want to see your video games. Can you think of why he might have said that?

Steven: He doesn't like me. Maybe he's afraid of me.

Teacher: And how do you feel about that?

Steven: Sad.

Teacher: Can you think of a new, different way to let him know you really want to play with him?

Steven: Tell him I really want to be his friend and I promise I won't hurt him.

If Steven and children like him often believe that bullying others will make them look up to them, and want to be their friend, Steven's teacher helped him realize that what he was doing would create the opposite effect. By helping him think about his own, as well as Kevin's feelings, the consequences of his actions, and what else he could do to solve the problem, Steven became less impatient as he learned to appreciate that it takes time to end up with what he really wanted—friends. In time, Kevin did agree to play with Steven, and now, 3 years later, Steven has verbalized that he doesn't want to bully others because, in his words, "I don't want to hurt people." Steven has learned at least the beginning of empathy. Hopefully, he won't hurt anybody, anymore.

Bullies and ICPS in Grade 7

As a service project, Curry Bailey, Safety Liaison, Office of School Climate and Safety, School District of Philadelphia, combined the lesson-games and ICPS dialogues with service learning projects with eight seventh graders identified by their teachers as bullies (Shure & Bailey, 2005). Calling this project Seeking Out Alternative Responses (SOAR), the goal was to help students consider the effect of their actions on their community. Boys exhibiting bullying behaviors met for 16 weeks after school with a staff member, once a week, for one hour. In addition to 11 weeks of ICPS, the students completed two service-learning projects—making Easter gift bags for children in a hospital, and making Mother's Day gifts for mothers living at the Salvation Army's Women and Children's Shelter—each with an appropriate message. Using skills

taught with ICPS, each activity was designed to help the youngsters em-
pathize with the recipient of their gifts.

All but one of the youngsters completed the program, and teachers reported fewer pink slips, fewer comments by teachers about disruptive behaviors, and the students became more comfortable with generating and
implementing options to bullying. These findings suggest that either the
students had fewer conflicts, or conflicts were able to be solved with a
reasonable resolution. Any concern that bullies could not be grouped together because they would feed off each other and be disruptive was al-
layed. Not only did they not disrupt each other, but when a group
member acted out, the others generally ignored him.

Enrique was easily angered when a classmate bothered him. Talking
about his experiences a year later, in eighth grade, he reported, "Once a
kid spilled juice on me and I hit him, and I felt good about it 'cause he
was in my way. Now, when someone bothers me, I tell the teacher or the
principal, and don't fight him." He told me that writing letters to kids in
a hospital, and making baskets for them, together with talking about
people's feelings when he bullied them helped him care more about others. He added, "When I heard about how happy the kids in the hospital
were, it made me feel grown up. It made me feel like a different person. I
don't just think about myself anymore." Curry Bailey believes that "Some
youngsters who behave as bullies really do have empathy. They just have
to learn to show it." From talking with Enrique, I can see how.

Some Potential Qualifiers of ICPS for Bullies and Their Victims

Not all of the youngsters in the SOAR program changed their behavior as dramatically, and as quickly as Enrique, but each child who did
participate in the complete 16 weeks did think more about how what
they were doing affected themselves and others. While this data is anecdotal, the addition of the service-learning projects (empathy-building)
may have contributed to the outcomes. In fifth- and sixth-grade urban
African American youngsters, systematic empirical research has shown
ICPS interventions to be able to reduce and prevent bullying behaviors
and behaviors associated with them, as well as to help victims develop
strategies to cope with being teased and otherwise picked on. They have
also been able to reduce and prevent precursors to later bullying and victimization as early as the preschool years. However, ICPS and other
cognitive approaches may not always be enough. Coolidge et al. (2004)
found that in 11- to 15-year-olds, severe forms of bullying was associated

with measures of neurological dysfunction, conduct disorder, oppositional defiant behaviors, ADHD, and executive function deficits, suggesting that "traditional short-term psychotherapeutic interventions for
bullying behavior may be of limited value given the complex nature of
the associated psychopathology" (p. 1559).

Although Coolidge et al., were referring to programs that boost self-
esteem, it is indeed possible that a cognitive approach such as ICPS may
not be enough for severe bullying behavior in the age group they studied.
First, ICPS was designed to be a prevention program more than one designed for those behaving within the clinical range. While precursors to
bullying could be reduced in 4 months time in the preschool and kindergarten years, our research showed that it took 2 years of exposure to
ICPS in grades five and six to reduce even milder forms of behaviors reported by Coolidge et al., to be associated with bullying—aggression,
lack of impulse control, anger management, and empathy, as well as defiance toward authority. Perhaps habits are stronger as bullying behaviors
have been reinforced by getting these youngsters what they want quickly,
and withdrawn children may have given up in order to avoid people and
problems they could not solve. However, to the extent that ICPS teaches
children skills to make positive decisions in life, perhaps it also gives bullies skills to replace their need to overpower others—and withdrawn
children alternatives to bottling up anxieties, as well as to behaviors as
pouting, crying, or retreating that make them easy targets.

It is possible that as Ahmed and Braithwaite (2004) have noted,
"Being serious about containing or controlling bullying problems is a factor that differentiates schools that have bullying problems from those
that do not" (p. 31). They report that Olweus, Limber, and Mihalic
(1999) found low bullying schools have school personnel who "articulate
purposeful preventive views on bullying" (p. 37) more than those in high
bullying schools. Perhaps programs like ICPS send students a message
that the school personnel really do care about them, and they feel safe to
come to school. It is notable that in a randomized control study, Kumpfer
et al. (2002) found ICPS-trained first graders improved significantly in
school bonding—that is, a feeling of safety, closeness to school, feeling a
part of the school, that teachers treat students fairly, and that students
are actively involved in classroom management—attitudes that can serve
as a protective factor against school violence (Valois, MacDonald, Bretous, Fischer, & Draine, 2002). That Durlak and Wells (1997) found
that programs that focus on teaching interpersonal problem solving skills
under the age of 8, the very time that the earlier-mentioned Sourander
et al. (2000) study found to be the critical period for change, our more

immediate behavior changes in the preschool and kindergarten years may be validated. Importantly, however, even though it did take longer to impact the older children, it was not too late to help them as well.

ICPS is not a quick fix. It takes time to teach interpersonal cognitive problem solving skills just as it takes time to teach any other cognitive skill such as math or reading. But, if severe bullying is, at least in some children, an inherited, genetic neurological dysfunction, the question now is, are these children then wired for life? Or, if we implement ICPS or programs like it, preferably very early, long before the ages of 11 to 15 studied by Coolidge et al. (2004), perhaps behaviors and precursors associated with this disorder can be reduced, or even overcome.

Summary

If educators and clinicians have assumed that emotional relief would pave the way for clear thinking in a problem situation, it appears that social emotional programs as ICPS has given support to the reverse idea, that ability to think through and solve problems might pave the way for emotional relief and behavioral adjustment. When I asked a class of sixth graders why we did ICPS, some said, "We got to play games," "We played with puppets," and "We learned how to solve problems." It was one student who said it all when she offered, "We have to learn to think for ourselves. People won't always be around to help us." That, and the behavior gains by youngsters exposed to social emotional learning such as ICPS suggest that if we change the way we talk to kids, it will change the way they talk to us—to their peers—and most importantly, to themselves.

CHAPTER

17

Medications and Behavior

LAWRENCE DILLER AND SAM GOLDSTEIN

Compliance (the ability to do what others want you to do even if you don't want to do it) is not only desired in school but necessary for successful transition into adult life. Within our schools, the ability to comply with instructional and behavioral commands has traditionally been achieved through psychosocial means, typically rewards and punishments. However, over the past 25 years, it has been increasingly the case that compliance is also achieved through the introduction of psychoactive medications. Such medications have been designed or discovered to positively impact self-discipline and emotional regulation. They have yet to be demonstrated to improve rates of learning or achievement.

Beginning with the pioneering work of Charles Bradley in 1937, the primary focus of psychotropic medications used in the classroom has first and foremost been directed at reducing disruptive behavior. A review of but some of the hundreds of studies primarily utilizing stimulants with children and adolescents in the classroom finds the majority of dependent variables relate to disruptive behavior problems. These behaviors include restlessness, hyperactivity, off-task, aggression, talking out, out-of-seat, irritability, lack of ability to follow directions, poor cooperation, oppositionality, and lack of compliance with rules. Reduction of these problems leads to a decrease in the target child's disruptive behavior in the classroom and concomitant increases in the ability to sit still, control impulses, delay gratification, cooperate, follow directions, comply with rules, and complete class work. Children with ADHD by far make up the largest group receiving medications for disruptive behavior. When stimulants are used with children with ADHD in the classroom, the three most powerfully impacted behaviors are improved conduct, improved on-task behavior, and reduced work errors, with the greatest improvements reported in general conduct (DuPaul & Rapport, 1993; see Barkley, 2006; for a review). Further, it is obvious that increases in task efficiency and time on task likely reflect decreases in disruptive, noncompliant, and inappropriate behaviors.

Typically, nondisruptive symptoms of social isolation, anxiety, or unhappiness result in somewhat isolated students but have not caused teachers significant problems in the classroom. Thus, these groups of internalizing, nondisruptive symptoms have in the past only been minimally targeted for medication treatment for behaviors exhibited specifically within classroom settings. However, over the past decade, ADHD criteria have broadened considerably both formally and informally to take in a much wider range of under performing children. The diagnosis of ADHD-inattentive type has increasingly been applied particularly to girls and middle school/high school-age children as an explanation for academic underperformance without disruptive behavior. The question has arisen whether ADHD is being treated in those situations or rather stimulant drugs are being used as universal "enhancers" to improve the performance of all children who are not operating "up to their potential."

From the consultant's perspective, it is the specific behavior, not necessarily the type or class of medication used to treat the behavior, that is of primary interest. Though organizing this chapter by behavior appears to make intuitive sense, the majority of pharmacological research studies dealing with classroom behavior typically target multiple behaviors, making it difficult to review the literature in that framework without a significant degree of redundancy. For this reason, this chapter has been organized by class and type of medication rather than by behavior. Although this arrangement makes reading somewhat more difficult, it leads to a more direct and thorough review of the available literature.

The chapter begins with an overview of general principles to guide consultants in working productively with physicians. These guidelines are equally effective for teachers, and consultants should consider providing them to all teachers when questions of medications in the classroom arise. We then continue with a review of the research reflecting teacher knowledge and understanding of the use of medications in the classroom. These data provide the consultant with valuable insight concerning teachers' knowledge of medication issues.

We next consider trends in the use of medications for hyperactive, impulsive, and inattentive symptoms, by far the most common classroom problems treated with medications over the past 25 years. This section also describes research with antidepressants, antipsychotics and anticonvulsants for modifying classroom behavior, as well as issues related to medicines, including mechanism of action, side effects, and use with special populations. We conclude with a review of a model to facilitate consultants' and teachers' interactions with physicians in regard to classroom issues.

Communicating with Physicians

School-based concerns and complaints about a child's performance and behavior are the most common reason a child is referred to a physician for consideration of treatment with a psychiatric medication. Yet most commonly, the doctor and complainant, the teacher or other school personnel, never directly communicate. Rather parents, most often mothers, operate as the "ferryman" of information between the two other parties as concerns are voiced and interventions implemented. Too often, as in the children's game of "telephone," vital information is lost or distorted when parents are relaying information second-hand between doctor and school.

For many school professionals, children's physicians, either primary care or specialists such as neurologists or psychiatrists, may appear distant and unreachable. Yet, the medications these physicians prescribe are often directly focused on modifying classroom behavior. Therefore, it is vital to provide physicians with accurate data concerning such behavior.

Parent-teacher questionnaires in the form of the Conners Rating Scale (Conners, 1989) and Child Behavior Checklist (Achenbach & Edelbrock, 1983) have become the industry standard. These instruments are used to generate a minimal multi-informant diagnosis that all professional guidelines indicate is critical for an accurate assessment and even more important to determine degree of impairment. Today, even primary care doctors such as general pediatricians and family practitioners are utilizing these questionnaires when assessing school and behavioral problems in the exam room.

However, there are multiple limitations to the questionnaires. First, they only ask negative questions. These questionnaires have been shown to put the respondent into a negative mindset about the child. These questionnaires do not assess for strengths. Only the absence of a negative (e.g., "How much fidgeting? Not at all.") constitutes a positive about the child. Even without any active drug or nondrug intervention, a child's performance as measured by one of these questionnaires, improves when the teacher is given the same questionnaire to complete a second time 2 months after the initial one. Finally, and most importantly, a questionnaire reveals nothing about the respondent (e.g., her attitudes, her class, and teaching/behavior practices).

A 15-minute conversation between teacher and doctor that begins with "Tell me about Johnny's strengths and weaknesses in terms of his academic performance, school behavior, and peer relationships?" yields much about the child. But the interview will also reveal a bit about the teacher, her attitudes (e.g., does she like this child or is she burnt out— not uncommon at the end of the academic year) and her practices at addressing the problems.

These questionnaires are undoubtedly more convenient and lend an aura of standardization and "science" to the process. But too often they become the *sina qua non* of diagnosis that even the authors of these instruments have vigorously stated should *not* be the sole basis for making a diagnosis or medicating the child. Yet, as opposed to simply relying on mother's history or office observation of the child, the primary care doctor's use of these questionnaires must be considered good or better practice.

Most physicians are not trained in behavioral assessment and may find lengthy psychological evaluations to be of peripheral interest. Alternatively, one or two brief sentences loosely describing the child's behavior are unlikely to be sufficiently thorough for the physician. Many physicians may be familiar with the specific rating scales and questionnaires. In such situations, it is sensible to find out if a physician will rely on a particular "standard" when making decisions about medication use in the classroom. When a physician suggests a specific measure, the consultant should attempt to provide it. If the measure is inadequate or incomplete, providing additional data is ethical and the consultant's responsibility. When the consultant provides measures for instruments, the physician may not be familiar with, it is helpful to include a brief explanation of the score and its meaning.

General Issues of Medications

Brand Names and Generics

All medications begin with a generic or chemical name. The pharmaceutical company developing or initially marketing the medication chooses a trade or brand name to market the medication to the public. For 17 years after a medication is registered with a specific brand name, the manufacturer holds a patent or exclusive rights to distribute that medication. When the patent expires, the manufacturer continues to maintain the exclusive use of the copyrighted brand name but can no longer claim exclusive use of the chemical or generic substance. Thus, during the first 17 years, only one company can produce and sell the medication. From that point on, other companies may manufacture the medication choosing to market it under its generic name or choosing another brand name. For example, methylphenidate was developed and first marketed by CIBA Geigy as a treatment for attention deficit disorder as well as narcolepsy. CIBA Geigy chose the brand name Ritalin® and has marketed the drug under that name. Once the patent exclusivity expired, other companies began manufacturing the drug, marketing it under the generic name methylphenidate or another brand.

In general, medication sold under the original brand name commands a higher price than medication sold under the generic chemical name or a new brand name. The original manufacturer attempts to recover the enormous cost of researching the drug prior to obtaining permission for its release. The generic manufacturers do not have to recover these costs.

For most medications, the advantage of lower price outweighs the potential disadvantage of dosage variation. According to the Food and Drug Administration (FDA), generic dosage within the tablet or pill will be equivalent to trade product but there is some concern that the delivery of the actual drug may vary between different products. For medications primarily used to modify children's behavior in the classroom, only the issue of generic methylphenidate versus Ritalin has created concern. Children and their families should be aware of and cautious about dosage variability that may occur with methylphenidate, as well as with other generic medications used to modify behavior. When a generic is available many physicians will use it first and make dosage adjustments primarily based on response as reported by the child, teacher, and parents. Therefore, even if there is some variability in active drug availability between generic and trade preparations, dosage will be based on the less expense yet active ingredients of the generic drug.

Consultants should also be aware that comparative effectiveness trials of drugs used in the treatment of conditions such as ADHD are limited and generally do not make a case that one medication is better than another (McDonagh & Peterson, 2005). These authors note that in a review of the literature the overall response rate of youth to stimulants for ADHD treatment is in the range of 60% to 80%. However, there is a lack of clarity as to the relationship or response rate to clinical significance.

Teachers' Knowledge of Medications Used in the Classroom

Teachers have been found to identify children as having ADHD at rates higher than expected prevalence rates described in diagnostic protocols (Havey, Olson, McCormick, & Cates, 2005). In this study, out of

121 rating scales analyzed, nearly 24% of students were identified by teachers as meeting criteria for one of three types of ADHD. Males had significantly higher scores than females. Hispanics had higher scores than other groups. Class size, as well as other variables was associated with the likelihood that teachers would identify more than 5% of their students as having ADHD.

Diagnosis and assessment for impairment should be a multicontact-based process. Relying solely on one informant, teacher or parent, invariably results in higher rates of diagnosis for ADHD. Only 50% of those children identified as ADHD in questionnaires by one teacher will also be identified by a second teacher the next year even when there has been no active drug or nondrug intervention. Further, improvement in one setting does not well predict improvement in another (Faraone, Biederman, & Zimmerman, 2005).

In general, teachers' understanding of the condition as well as its treatments has not been found to be much better than the lay public. Consultants should not assume that teachers understand ADHD nor effective treatments. In intervention studies designed to educate teachers about ADHD, a dramatic decrease in teacher misperception, including beliefs that ADHD is caused by poor parenting, refined sugar, and food additives and that medication intervention should be used only as a last resort has been reported (Barbaresi & Olsen, 1998).

Over 30 years ago, Robin and Bosco (1973) concluded that it is uncommon for teachers to possess specific and accurate knowledge about characteristics of stimulant medications. These authors suggest that teachers should receive routine instruction about the behavioral impact of stimulant drugs. Teachers play a critical role in the management of children's medications in the classroom and are the best source of information concerning children's responses to these medications (Sprague & Gadow, 1976). Physicians cannot easily adjust medications targeted at classroom behavior during face-to-face interactions with the child in an exam room (Rizzolo, 1976).

Teachers and other educational professionals often report feeling uncomfortable or poorly trained in communicating with physicians (M. H. Epstein, Singh, Luebke, & Stout, 1991). These authors polled 104 teachers of learning-disabled students regarding medication use. Less than 15% of the teachers indicated that their professional preservice training provided them with sufficient information on the use of medications for children with behavior problems. Less than 20% felt that the in-service training they received was sufficient. These teachers also perceived that physicians used global impressions and observation during visits with the child to assess the effects of medication although most physicians prefer observations of classroom behavior and rating scale data.

Aman, Singh, and White (1987) reported that 85% of educational staff in a general survey did not feel competent about their knowledge of medication use. These educators indicated a lack of preservice and in-service training and requested additional education on topics such as side effects of medication in the classroom, clinical indications for various classes of drugs, interactions between drugs, and main targets for drugs. Other authors have reached similar conclusions about the inadequacy of preservice and in-service training for educators regarding drug use in schoolchildren with behavioral problems (Gadow, 1983; Singh, Epstein, Luebke, & Singh, 1990).

In a poll of 322 regular and special education teachers, 96% stated they received too little or no training in the use of stimulants with children as part of their undergraduate education programs (Kasten, Coury, & Heron, 1992). An almost equal number reported they had limited in-service training as well. Over 50% of the regular classroom teachers in this study reported they had been asked by parents to suggest whether a particular child should receive stimulant medication. Yet, 50% of the regular classroom teachers and up to 30% of the special education teachers responded they did not understand or recognize the physical and behavioral benefits and side effects that might result from the use of stimulants. For example, up to 20% of the educators believed that stimulants could be addictive in children and/or might result in drug addition. There is little reason to suspect these statistics have changed significantly (*Wall Street Journal*, 2006).

The data also suggest that physicians retain a healthy skepticism toward the quality of the data teachers report to them about the impact of medications in the classroom (Kasten et al., 1992). As teachers and consultants learn to provide physicians with precise, well-defined data concerning target behaviors to be modified by medications physicians no doubt will come to rely on and respect these data. As part of their professional continuing development, consultants, special education personnel, and at the very least veteran teachers should participate in programs to improve their knowledge of medications that modify children's behavior.

Trends in Medication Use in the Classroom

Stimulants have been and are by far the most frequently prescribed medications in the classroom (Safer & Krager, 1989; see Barkley, 2006; S. Goldstein & Goldstein, 1998; for a review). Thus, tracking the trends in the use of stimulants provides a starting target to assess and understand use of all psychoactive medications in the classroom. Every survey has strengths and limitations and getting accurate hard data on either the number of children with ADHD in America and even those just taking medication is very difficult. As late as 1991, only several hundred thousand children in the United States, mostly school-age boys, took stimulant medications (Safer, Zito, & Fine, 1996). Virtually no other types of psychiatric medication were employed for classroom problems at that time. In 2001, S. Goldstein and Turner reported that 1.39% of students in a large suburban school district were taking a medication for ADHD. By 2006, several million persons are taking stimulants. Estimates range from a low of 2.5 million to 4 million children (CDC, 2005). Many more girls, toddlers, and teens also take stimulants medication compared to 15 years ago (Cuffe et al., 2005). Also at least 1.5 million adults now take stimulants (G. Harris, 2005).

Estimates of prescribing practices—over, under, or just right—are very difficult to measure. Prevalence data on ADHD may overestimate the number of children with ADHD because these surveys are symptom not impairment based (M. Gordon et al., 2006).

Reports between the years 2000 and 2004 reflect a 56.5% increase in the use of medications to treat disruptive behavior, particularly ADHD (Medco Health Solutions, 2005). This increase went from 2.8% in 2000 to 4.39% in 2004 in the general population. Medco reported that the number of children between the ages of 0 to 9 taking medication for ADHD grew almost 75% in that period of time and spending increased fivefold with boys three times more likely to be taking medication for ADHD than girls in this age group. The rates of stimulant use peaked at 9.3% for White insured boys aged 11 to 12.

In September, 2005, the Centers for Disease Control (CDC) reported that in 2003 approximately 7.8% of U.S. children, age 4 to 17 years had at some point been diagnosed with ADHD. In this survey, the ADHD diagnosis was reported approximately 2.5 times more frequently among males than females. Prevalence of reported ADHD increased with age and was significantly lower among children age 4 to 8 years compared with children over 9 years. The greatest prevalence was noted among males age 16 years (14.9%) and females age 11 years (6.1%). Prevalence of a reported ADHD diagnosis was significantly higher among non-Hispanic, primarily English-speaking and insured children. Further, prevalence rates were significantly higher for children and families in which the most highly educated adult was a high school graduate (or had completed 12 years of education) compared with children and families in which the most highly educated adult had a higher or lower level of education.

Finally, this report indicated that in 2003, 4.3% of children age 4 to 17 years who were reported to ever have a diagnosis of ADHD were taking a medication for the disorder. The prevalence of medication treatment for ADHD was highest among children age 9 to 12 years compared with younger or older children. Nationally, 56.3% of children with a reported ADHD diagnoses were being treated with medication at the time of this survey (CDC, 2005).

The haphazard nature of prescribing practices though is highlighted by the Great Smokey Mountain survey of 4,000 children assessed on the community level (Angold, Erkanli, Egger, & Costello, 2000). Researchers found an overall stimulant use rate of 5% in the community which seemed about average. Three-quarters of the children with ADHD were getting stimulant medication. But over half the stimulant medication was being prescribed for children who didn't have ADHD by the researchers' criteria.

Also in community practice, many prescriptions are not refilled. Treatment is inconsistent and sporadic. The growing trend of diversion and misuse of stimulant drugs in older teens and young adults is very worrisome.

Increased use and acceptability of use of the stimulant drugs ushered in an era of increased use of other classes of psychiatric drugs for children. Rates for the use of all classes of drugs, antidepressants, anticonvulsants, and the atypical antipsychotics have all grown enormously in use over the past 10 years (Zito & Safer, 2005).

Although nonstimulants, principally atomoxetine, to treat ADHD symptoms as well as internalizing symptoms of anxiety and depression are finding increased use clinically, there continues to be a dearth of epidemiological research concerning their incidence and use. Strattera introduced in 2003 ("Strattera Approved to Treat ADHD," 2003) and marketed aggressively since then represents about 15% of the overall market for treatment of ADHD (FDA Hearings, 2006). The overall use of Strattera, based on the manufacturer's advertisements, is weighted toward treatment in teens and adults rather than in children where the stimulants still are overwhelmingly preferred.

The acceleration in prescribing medications to modify children's behavior has caused concomitant controversy about the appropriateness of medication, especially stimulants, as well as interest among clinical and research professionals in setting standards for the use of these medicines (Diller & Goldstein, 2006). Stimulant treatment for ADHD, for example, has generated substantial controversy. Inflammatory comments have been an integral part of the discussion. Some critics believe that stimulant treatment for behavior deprives children of the opportunity to use their natural disposition to regulate their behavior (Simms, 1985). Other critics fuel the fears of already vulnerable parents by describing the use of medications as "a potential tragedy," by warning that it is the "school-room atmosphere, not the child's behavior which is pathologic" or by claiming that "the solution is to label the child a quasimedical problem and alter his behavior through drugs." Even well-meaning advice includes inflammatory language such as "teachers should avoid statements such as 'I think Billy's work and behavior would benefit if he took Ritalin'" (Bosco, 1975). These authors caution that before looking toward medications to modify children's behavior in the classroom, other aspects of the school environment, including the setting and teacher, should be evaluated and modified (Diller & Goldstein, 2006).

In the past 10 years, the public increasingly has experienced the schools as "pressuring" parents into medicating their children. Seventeen states have laws limiting aspects of assessment or conversation with parents over issues of ADHD and medication. This antipressure backlash culminated in an amendment to the most recent reauthorization of IDEA (Individual with Disabilities Education Act) in 2004 that specifically prohibits schools from denying children access to a classroom education on the basis of a refusal by the family to use psychiatric drugs with their child. This heightened drama is unfortunate, operating much like the "gag laws" over abortion (e.g., making it more difficult for school personnel to communicate reasonable concerns, opinions, and options to the parents for help). Nevertheless, parents in treatment with the authors of this chapter continue to report "pressure" from teachers and schools to medicate their children.

In an interesting survey, Kasten et al. (1992) found that over 65% of regular and special education teachers believed that stimulants were useful for the treatment of ADHD behaviors in the classroom. For teachers, the belief in and value ascribed to medications to modify classroom behavior decreased with increasing grade. Further, elementary school teachers in this study tended to believe that stimulants were not overprescribed whereas middle school teachers did. It is not surprising that elementary school teachers are more powerful advocates for stimulants since they are often the first educators to observe the marked changes in student behavior and class work.

The primary impetus for this chapter is to address concerns of impediments of communication between parents, teachers/consultants, and treating physicians. Wolraich, Bickman, Lambert, Simmons, and Doffing (2005) were first to address this issue. A large sample of children with ADHD or with high risk for ADHD were identified in an elementary school setting. Parent interviews and information from teachers were collected on 243 children randomized into treatment and control conditions and followed for 39 months. The interventions consisted of group workshops and single one-on-one tutorials with parents, teachers, and providers about the evaluation and treatment of ADHD stressing the need for communication between all parties. Unfortunately, the few significant effects on communication were short lived. The authors point out that the lack of sustainability in their study emphasizes the importance of not only demonstrating short-term efficacy but also sustained ability to make a positive difference. Consultants should be aware that apparent progress in the short run relative to communication between all parties can only be maintained with consistent effort.

Barkley (1990) suggested that six factors must be considered when deciding on the use of medications for children's behavioral problems related to ADHD:

1. The severity of the child's symptoms and disruptive behavior.
2. Prior use of other treatments (nonmedication interventions should be attempted initially).
3. Anxiety disorder symptoms that might result in a lower likelihood of positive response to stimulant medication (Pliszka, 1989).
4. Parental attitude toward the use of medication.
5. Adequacy of adult supervision.
6. The child's or adolescent's attitude toward medicine.

A nearly 20-year-old national survey of pediatricians found that slightly less than half employed objective teacher-parent ratings to determine medication efficacy (Copeland, Wolraich, Lindgren, Milich, & Woolson, 1987). These authors suggest that an optimal medication dose should be established within the context of a double-blind placebo controlled assessment paradigm, including multiple measures collected across several settings. However, such an approach is often difficult, costly, and time consuming.

A less conservative but certainly effective approach has been suggested to include several steps:

1. Dosage sequence is prescribed in which the child receives one of several doses, including baseline with a week at each dose.
2. Objective measures of treatment and response are collected across these conditions (e.g., classroom observation, work completed).

3. Child, parents, and teacher perceptions are evaluated for side effects.
4. Communication is maintained between the physician and teacher or consultant (S. Goldstein & Goldstein, 1998).

This model uses well-developed, standardized observational procedures. If questionnaires are used, it is important for them to possess adequate levels of reliability and validity. In this process, teacher questionnaires are administered twice during baseline conditions to assess possible practice effects. It has been emphasized that the decision to use medication to modify children's behavior should be made after considering potential risks versus benefits of the medication in comparison with the expected outlook for the child if the medication is not incorporated into the treatment plan (S. Goldstein & Goldstein, 1990, 1998). It is essential for the consultants and teachers to understand these effects because they form the basis for deciding which children should be nominated to receive medications to modify their classroom behavior.

Medications Used to Treat School Problems

The class of drugs primarily used to treat problems of inattention, overactivity, and impulsivity is known as stimulants. They broadly include two generic drugs. Methylphenidate is available in a generic low-cost formulation but is best known as Ritalin which was introduced in the United States in 1955 and is also the main active ingredient of a number of newer formulations including Concerta, Metadate, and Focalin (see Table 17.1). The other main generic available in different formulations is amphetamine, which is available as Dexedrine and Adderall. Methylphenidate and amphetamine are closely related structurally and in chemical action. In studies of large groups of children their benefits and adverse effects are very similar (though their minor differences will be described shortly).

These drugs are categorized as stimulants because they increase heart rate and blood pressure, improve alertness, prevent sleepiness, and improve physical performance. An enduring myth continues about the stimulants' apparent "paradoxical" calming effect on children with the hyperactivity of ADHD. Even Charles Bradley, in the very first report of the use of benzedrine (an amphetamine) for children's hyperactivity in 1937, when describing the drug's action, took care by using the phrase "*appears to*" calm hyperactive children.

Indeed, there is nothing unique or paradoxical about the effects of stimulant drugs on children with ADHD. In low doses, the stimulants

Table 17.1   Drugs for ADHD

Name	Class	Length of Action (Hours)
Ritalin	Methylphenidate	3–4
Generic	Methylphenidate	3–4
Dexedrine	Amphetamine	3–4
Dextrostat	Amphetamine	3–4
Focalin	Methylphenidate	3–4
Methyllin Solution	Methylphenidate	3–4
Dexedrine Spansule	Amphetamine	6–8
Metadate ER	Methylphenidate	6–8
Methylline ER	Methylphenidate	6–8
Ritalin SR	Methylphenidate	6–8
Adderall	Amphetamine	4–8
Concerta	Methylphenidate	10–12
Metadate CD	Methylphenidate	10–12
Adderall XR	Amphetamine	10–12
Focalin XR	Methlyphenidate	10–12
Ritalin LA	Methylphenidate	10–12
Daytrana Skin Patch	Methylphenidate	10–12
Strattera	Atomoxetine	24
Catapress	Clonidine	4–6
Tenex	Guanfacine	12
Wellbutrin	Buproprion	24

increase focus and deliberateness for everyone. The hyperactive child becomes more methodical and activity level declines. The effects of the stimulants are universal. They affect everyone very similarly so that any child or adult, ADHD or not, will initially improve focus and concentration and decrease their activity. However, as the dosage is increased (or when misused, abused, snorted, or injected), the "stimulating" effects of these drugs predominate. Activity level increases. A person becomes more garrulous, agitated, even manic. Children complain on higher doses of stimulants ("I feel weird") while older teens and adults are just as likely to report euphoria and grandiosity ("I feel powerful and grand").

The stimulants' universal performance-enhancing effects should have also dispelled another long-standing medical "urban legend" about these drugs—that somehow a positive response to a stimulants indicates a difference in a child's brain and is diagnostic of ADHD. Even some doctors continue to offer this "approach" to diagnosis. Yet these drugs' proven universal effect would then lead us to conclude that *all* children have ADHD—a clearly erroneous conclusion.

The stimulant drugs are likely the most studied medications *of any type* used in children. Nevertheless, controversy continues over the use of these medication for several reasons. As mentioned several million children take these drugs. Concerns remain about the misuse, overuse, and substitution of drugs for nondrug interventions (commonly criticized as "the quick fix"). Standards of effectiveness and safety must be extraordinarily high because so many of the children who take these drugs are otherwise normal and perhaps minimally impaired. The reality that most children under thirteen do not make the decision to take this drug (it is made by their parents) also raises the moral bar of safety and effectiveness higher. Finally, despite thousands of studies on these drugs, reasonable questions continue (and are likely to remain unanswered) about the long-term effectiveness and safety of these medicines that are taken for years and possibly for decades (given growing belief that ADHD does not "go away" in adolescence for a significant minority).

Despite decades of study, there is no fully coherent explanation for how stimulants work in the brain to improve focus and decrease impulsivity. The stimulants do increase the presence of dopamine, a neurotransmitter, in the synapses (the spaces between nerve cells), by both increasing the amount released and blocking its reuptake. These effects are most pronounced in areas of the brain associated with "executive function" (self-control and judgment) like the frontal cortex. Nevertheless, sophisticated diagnostic and imaging techniques of brain anatomy and function often give conflicting results as to the effects of these drugs so that their exact mechanisms of action remain unclear.

Still, there is little question that these drugs "do work" to improve focus and concentration and decrease impulsivity. Consequently, many aspects of problematic compliance and performance related to school behavior improve. Within minutes of taking an appropriate dose (how that is determined is to be discussed next), children stay on task longer, require less verbal redirection, decrease their fidgeting, their up and down movement from their seat, or bothering their neighbors.

While stimulants will not correct a learning disability or processing disorder, the improved stick-to-itiveness will improve performance in both cases, often to the point where the child's performance no longer qualifies him or her for services at the school (raising further ethical questions whether Ritalin is the equivalent of glasses in the legal debate over disability services and accommodations). Grades improve. However, there is no evidence that stimulants improve long-term academic achievement (see Barkley, 2006, for a review). Stimulants also improve the classroom and social behavior of the child with ADHD. Oppositional behavior decreases and peer relationships improve.

The increase in the ADHD diagnosis in the past 15 years has also generated a great deal of commercial interest from the pharmaceutical industry and a number of new stimulant formulations has revolutionized treatment. Most important is the development of effective long-acting formulations that can last up to 10 to 12 hours per dose and has virtually eliminated the previously long lines of children during the lunch break at the nurse's or secretary's office for their noon-time dose of Ritalin. Indeed, there is now a panoply of choices ranging from 3- to 4-hour preparations that are grape flavored in chewable or liquid form (obviously meant for the toddler and kindergarten child) and even a skin patch delivery system that obviates the need for swallowing a pill at all. However, the main choices still hinge on length of action and whether to use a methylphenidate or amphetamine-based product.

Even though, as mentioned, in studies of large numbers of children, methylphenidate and amphetamine perform very similarly, there is some consensus among clinicians that amphetamine is the more intense experience, particularly in terms of adverse effects like decreased appetite (anorexia) and difficulty falling asleep (insomnia). Therefore, many physicians begin with a methylphenidate product unless there is some other information like the knowledge that a sibling had a better response to one drug over another.

Length of action should be the overall determining factor in choosing which stimulant is used. While there is evidence that for very hyperactive, very impaired children a maximum length of 10 to 12 hours works best long term, the majority of children taking the medication for learning-related problems of behavior and inattention or those with more mild forms of impulsivity and hyperactivity can have their dosage time tailored to their needs at school. Therefore, it could make sense that a kindergartner or first grader (whose learning time is primarily in the morning) take a 3- to 4-hour preparation of methylphenidate.

The elementary and even middle school-age child may operate quite successfully with a medium-length acting medication that lasts 6 to 8 hours or approximately the length of the school day. Methylphenidate formulations as Metadate ER® or Methyllin® or amphetamine as Dexedrine Spansule® are the choice in this category. Only if homework completion is difficult or behavior is a major problem within the home does the longest acting medications become attractive. While medications like Concerta® and Ritalin LA® (methlyphenidate) or Adderall XR (amphetamine) offer the longest action, they are likely associated with the highest likelihood of decreased dinner appetite and problems falling asleep. However, many children take these longest acting preparations with no problems at all.

Many teachers and the public do not realize that there is no preset dosage based on age or weight for the stimulant drugs. In other words, there is no milligram per kilogram schedule for the amount given each day. The daily dose is determined by "clinical response." In other words, one typically starts with the lowest dose available (just to be on the safe side for that rare child who reacts negatively even to a low dose with increased hyperactivity or agitation). Every 3 or 4 days, the dose is titrated to the next highest level. Using Concerta as an example, a child begins a medication trial by taking the lowest dose (18 mg tablet), after eating breakfast (the pills can be taken with food) about 20 to 30 minutes before the start of school. Every 3rd or 4th day, the dose is increased by one tablet to a maximum of three pills at one time (54 mg).

The goal of dosing is to obtain maximum improvement in behavior and performance with an absence of adverse effects. A determination of improvement and side effects is critical from the child, his parents, and *teacher*. The teacher is provided a simple feedback form (Figure 17.1) to rate behavior and performance with three circles twice a day (she is also blind to the exact dose daily which is later filled in by the parent before returning the form to the doctor). The more elaborate Conners or Achenbach scales can also be used for feedback as long as there is a baseline rating of behavior on no medication.

A 3- or 4-day period is chosen not because of any need for "build-up" of the stimulant drug (which may be true for a drug like atomoxetine or an SSRI, see next section). As previously mentioned, the stimulants work "right away"—within 20 to 30 minutes. Rather, 3 days seems the minimum necessary to separate out the effects of the medication on the child's behavior from all the other daily variables that might affect school performance or behavior (events on the playground, sickness, etc.). Short of using a written form, parents and teacher could titrate

```
NAME OF CHILD _____          NAME OF TEACHER _____

DATE/DAY    DOSAGE(leave blank for parent)      A.M.'S              P.M.'S
                                         LEAST        MOST
                          IMPULSIVITY        0  1  2  3          0  1  2  3
_____   _____     DISTRACTIBILITY    0  1  2  3          0  1  2  3
                          INCOMPLETE TASKS   0  1  2  3          0  1  2  3

comments_____
_____

                          IMPULSIVITY        0  1  2  3          0  1  2  3
_____   _____     DISTRACTIBILITY    0  1  2  3          0  1  2  3
                          INCOMPLETE TASKS   0  1  2  3          0  1  2  3

comments_____
_____

                          IMPULSIVITY        0  1  2  3          0  1  2  3
_____   _____     DISTRACTIBILITY    0  1  2  3          0  1  2  3
                          INCOMPLETE TASKS   0  1  2  3          0  1  2  3

comments_____
_____

                          IMPULSIVITY        0  1  2  3          0  1  2  3
_____   _____     DISTRACTIBILITY    0  1  2  3          0  1  2  3
                          INCOMPLETE TASKS   0  1  2  3          0  1  2  3

comments_____
_____

                          IMPULSIVITY        0  1  2  3          0  1  2  3
_____   _____     DISTRACTIBILITY    0  1  2  3          0  1  2  3
                          INCOMPLETE TASKS   0  1  2  3          0  1  2  3

comments_____
_____

                          IMPULSIVITY        0  1  2  3          0  1  2  3
_____   _____     DISTRACTIBILITY    0  1  2  3          0  1  2  3
                          INCOMPLETE TASKS   0  1  2  3          0  1  2  3

comments_____
_____

                          IMPULSIVITY        0  1  2  3          0  1  2  3
_____   _____     DISTRACTIBILITY    0  1  2  3          0  1  2  3
                          INCOMPLETE TASKS   0  1  2  3          0  1  2  3

comments_____
_____
```

Figure 17.1 Feedback form

dosage on a weekly (5 day) basis and exchange telephone or e-mail communication to determine the benefits or disadvantages of the three different dose levels.

After reviewing the results from the titration trial the dosage is determined. In Figure 17.2, 36 mg of Concerta was chosen as the dose, because it worked better than either no medication or 18 mg, yet giving a

NAME OF CHILD ___*Michael*___   NAME OF TEACHER ___*Mrs. Smith*___

DATE/DAY	DOSAGE(leave blank for parent)	A.M.'S	P.M.'S

DATE/DAY   DOSAGE(leave blank for parent)   A.M.'S   P.M.'S
                                        LEAST   MOST

5/30   *11 mg*   IMPULSIVITY   0 1 2 (3)   0 1 2 (3)
                   DISTRACTIBILITY 0 1 (2) 3   0 1 (2) 3
                   INCOMPLETE TASKS 0 1 (2) 3   0 1 2 (3)

comments_____

5/31   *36 mg*   IMPULSIVITY   0 (1) 2 3   0 (1) 2 3
                   DISTRACTIBILITY (0) 1 2 3   0 (1) 2 3
                   INCOMPLETE TASKS 0 (1) 2 3   0 (1) 2 3

comments_____

6/1   *36 mg*   IMPULSIVITY   0 (1) 2 3   0 (1) 2 3
                   DISTRACTIBILITY 0 (1) 2 3   (0) 1 2 3
                   INCOMPLETE TASKS 0 (1) 2 3   (0) 1 2 3

comments_____

6/2   *36 mg*   IMPULSIVITY   0 (1) 2 3   (0) 1 2 3
                   DISTRACTIBILITY (0) 1 2 3   0 (1) 2 3
                   INCOMPLETE TASKS(0) 1 2 3   (0) 1 2 3

comments_____

6/5   *54 mg*   IMPULSIVITY   0 (1) 2 3   0 (1) 2 3
                   DISTRACTIBILITY (0) 1 2 3   0 (1) 2 3
                   INCOMPLETE TASKS 0 (1) 2 3   0 (1) 2 3

comments_____

6/6   *54 mg*   IMPULSIVITY   (0) 1 2 3   0 (1) 2 3
                   DISTRACTIBILITY (0) 1 2 3   0 (1) 2 3
                   INCOMPLETE TASKS(0) 1 2 3   0 (1) 2 3

comments_____

6/7   *54 mg*   IMPULSIVITY   0 (1) 2 3   (0) 1 2 3
                   DISTRACTIBILITY (0) 1 2 3   0 (1) 2 3
                   INCOMPLETE TASKS(0) 1 2 3   0 (1) 2 3

comments_____

Figure 17.2 Feedback form example

higher dose of 54 mg didn't appreciably improve the child's behavior compared to using 36 mg. Parents elected to use the medication only on weekdays. This event-driven dosing is increasingly common (note especially declines in the sales of stimulants during the summer months when there is no school). There are no medical reasons why stimulant medication must be given everyday. If there are no gross behavioral indications for using the medication at home, such a five school day regimen is justified and may even be preferable (see concerns about growth in the section that follows). However, event-driven dosing, taken to an extreme, say by a high school or college student who is given the medication to address procrastination but only uses it to cram for examinations, only exacerbates the "ADHD lifestyle" and may represent a pathway to ultimate abuse and addiction.

The most common adverse effects of the stimulants—anorexia and insomnia—have already been mentioned. Children and parents should be warned that packed lunches could be returned untouched or half-eaten. However, a solid breakfast and dinner with a late afternoon or evening snack thrown in, often makes up the difference in nutrition. Weight loss or failure to gain is a rare reason for discontinuing the medication (but is more likely with amphetamine).

Trouble falling asleep at night generally occurs when the medication is first tried or when the dosage is initially increased. Often the insomnia improves just with maintaining the same dosage over a number of days. If it continues, dropping the dose, trying a shorter-acting formulation, or the other class of stimulant (see next section) may ease the problem. Some doctors chose to address the insomnia with another drug like Clonidine.

Other side effects are possible. With millions of children taking these drugs many negative effects are reported, but they either are quite rare or their connection with the drugs is unclear and ambiguous. Some of these adverse effects have made headlines. These events, like sudden death and psychosis, are catastrophic and tragic, but their frequency, if they are connected with the medications at all, is extremely low (say on the order of one in ten thousand users). Tics (abnormal involuntary muscle twitches) are said to be exacerbated with the use of stimulants but their connection to these drugs continues to be controversial. Most parents of children with Tourette's Syndrome (multiple muscle and vocal tics) who also have ADHD tend to maintain their children on the stimulant drugs because the overall benefits to their children outweigh whatever increased social opprobrium results from the tic behavior.

Concern about long-term growth on stimulant medication was rekindled by well-controlled studies that demonstrated a loss of about one-half inch per year in size of children with ADHD with 12 hours daily stimulant treatment 7 days a week compared to ADHD children who received no medication at all (Poulton, 2005). It is uncertain whether this loss in growth is ever made up. But as a response, there have been more recommendations for no medication use on weekends, holidays, and vacations unless the medication is absolutely necessarily for behavioral reasons.

"Rebound" is an oft-described but not well studied or documented phenomenon reported by parents of purportedly "worse" behavior in their children when the effects of medication are wearing off in the late afternoon or evening. Making certain a child is fed and not hungry is critical in addressing rebound. Sometimes switching to another long-acting medication may improve the situation. Rebound reminds parents that not all behavior will be addressable with medication and that effective behavioral interventions still need to be developed for when the medication isn't working (in the evenings or weekends). Some doctors address rebound by adding a short-acting stimulant like Ritalin with the hope that behavior will improve and that dinner appetite and sleep will remain unaffected.

Finally, the stimulants' abuse and addiction potential is often highlighted and exaggerated in the media. Used properly, there is little likelihood of abuse or addiction developing in the preteen. There is conflicting clinical evidence with claims for ("sensitization") (Lambert & Hartsough, 2000) or against ("protection") (Wilens, Faraone, Biederman, & Gunawardene, 2003) the role of stimulants in later abuse. The contributions stimulants add to the development of later drug abuse pale in comparison to the role of family and neighborhood. However, misuse, abuse, and addiction with prescription stimulants is a growing reality for the late teen-young adult population. While the individual teenager or college student may greatly benefit from the supervised use of stimulant medication, there is increasing evidence of major diversion and misuse of these drugs in high schools and colleges which represents an unfortunate public health risk that needs to be addressed in the immediate future (Kroutil et al., 2006).

This risk of tolerance, abuse, and addiction has made the search for a nonstimulant drug for ADHD that works as well as stimulants a very attractive option both clinically and commercially. Unfortunately, the available nonstimulant products, while approved for use in ADHD do not meet the effectiveness standards of the stimulants and while they might not be abusable they have other side effects that make them less attractive.

Most prominently promoted, atomoxetine or Strattera has been marketed by its manufacturer as a first-line alternative to the stimulant drugs. Direct head-to-head comparisons with long acting stimulants suggest the superiority of stimulants (Zoler, 2004). While Strattera whose primary action is mediated by another neurotransmitter, norepinephrine (or adrenaline), is not abusable, there are similar problems of poor eating (secondary to nausea or stomach ache) and problems with sleep. Strattera has also been associated with rare cases of liver failure which prompted the FDA to insist on a "black box" warning about this side effect in the labeling for this drug (M. C. Miller, 2005).

While Strattera may have a place in the treatment of ADHD especially for the teen or adult for whom abuse potential is high, it generally should be considered a second or third choice for the child or teen who lives at home whose medication can be supervised by his or her parents. Other important differences are that Strattera ostensibly works around the clock and that it may take between 2 to 4 weeks for the full effects of the drug to manifest in improved behavior.

Other drugs deserve a mention in the treatment of ADHD. Clonidine (and a long-acting version, guanfacine or Tenex), originally and still used as a blood pressure medicine, has found a niche in the treatment of ADHD based on a minimal degree of scientific study ("Clondine for Treatment of Attention-Deficit/Hyperactivity Disorder," 1996). However, clonidine has become "popular" because of its sedating qualities as an early evening pill addition to the regimen of the child taking a long-acting stimulant during the day. The main adverse effect is sedation (making a child tired during the day). Buproprion (Wellbutrin), most often used for depression, has a similar minimal track record of study for ADHD (Conners, 1996). Still it may be prescribed for the adolescent with ADHD whose mood is also being affected. Rarely, an older class of anti-depressants, called the tricyclics (drugs like imipramine or desipramine) may still be used for ADHD (Biederman, Gasfriend, & Jellinek, 1986). Their effectiveness for ADHD has never been consistently demonstrated. The risk of a catastrophic cardiac arrhythmia (irregular heart beat) is better documented with these drugs, making their use for ADHD far less appealing and sensible.

While the short-term effects and safety of the stimulant drugs have been studied in enormous detail, the same cannot be said for any other class of drugs used to influence children's behavior in the classroom or in their homes. This is especially true of the next class of medications to be discussed, the selective serotonin reuptake inhibitors or SSRIs, whose best-known representative is Prozac®. Serotonin, is another neurotransmitter operating in the brain, whose effects are legion. Decreased serotonin as a cause for depression has never been proven, yet improvements in adult depression after taking Prozac has led to the nearly ubiquitous belief in the "chemical imbalance" theory of mental illness in children and adults (Pam, 1995).

The SSRIs which include other well-known products like Zoloft® or Paxil® (see Table 17.2) are most commonly referred to as antidepressants

Table 17.2 Selective serotonin reuptake
inhibitors (SSRIs)

Trade Name	Generic Name
Prozac	Fluoxetine
Zoloft	Sertaline
Paxil	Paroxetine
Luvox	Fluvoxamine
Celexa	Citalopram
Effexor	Venlafaxine
Lexapro	Escitalopram

based on conditions for which these drugs were approved by the FDA 15 to 20 years ago. However, their use for a variety of different problems in adults and children belie this more limited label. Indeed recent estimates of one and a half million children taking SSRIs in 2002, are likely much higher in 2006, despite some recent adverse publicity (Vitello, Zuvekas, & Norquist, 2006).

Of concern is that the widespread use of SSRIs in children is not substantiated by a wealth of data that supports the use of the stimulant drugs in those age groups. While the SSRIs are frequently prescribed for pediatric "depression," studies supporting their effectiveness and safety are minimal to nonexistent (Department of Health and Human Services, 2004b). Parents and teachers are often confused and perturbed when they learn about the absence of studies supporting the use of a drug for a particular problem or population. This reality is surprising to many. The FDA gives its initial approval to a drug based on studies in adults that last generally only 3 to 4 months. Once a drug has been approved for a specific disorder or disease (say depression or a seizure disorder), a doctor may legally prescribe it "off-label" to anyone for any legitimate indication. In truth, besides the stimulant drugs for ADHD, few of the other medications mentioned in this chapter have been "approved" by the FDA for use in children.

The lack of approval or evidence for effectiveness or safety does not mean that these other medications should not be used at all with children and teens. Rather the burden of need (the degree of symptoms or impairment) should necessarily be higher in order to medically and ethically justify the risk of the unknown or the lack of evidence in using these drugs.

With such caveats in mind, the only SSRI which has demonstrated any effectiveness for treating depression in children is Prozac, which is now available in the less expensive generic version as fluoxetine. Even Prozac's demonstrated effectiveness compared to a placebo pill was minimal but that may also be due to the nature of pediatric depression which is mostly an adolescent condition. Teen depression has a very high rate of spontaneous improvement and many additional teens improve simply when taking a placebo pill (Department of Health and Human Services, 2004a). Still for a select group of teens with severe mood disturbance, suicidal thinking or action, or self-mutilation, a trial of fluoxetine or a second SSRI could make sense.

As mentioned, the SSRIs' effects are not specific to depression and across psychiatry these drugs are used for a variety of problems where resilience is beneficial. In children, there is some evidence that the SSRIs are helpful in ameliorating behavior associated with anxiety, like phobias, panic disorders, and obsessive compulsive problems. They, unfortunately, have had little proven success in correcting the anxiety of school avoidance problems. However, family-based cognitive behavioral approaches reach cure rates of nearly 80% and should be tried first before using an SSRI for anxiety in a child (Bögels & Siqueland, 2006).

When used in children, the dose for an SSRI is often started at half an adult dose (e.g., Prozac or fluoxetine at 10 mg) and continued for 2 weeks. Unlike the stimulants whose effects are noticeable in 20 minutes, the SSRIs' benefits may take up to 2 weeks before appearing (however, some patients report improvements within 2 to 3 days of starting the medication). After 2 weeks, if there has been little or no improvement the dose is doubled and may be doubled yet one more time to 40 mg—at which point if there have been no positive changes the drug should be discontinued and perhaps another drug tried.

It's important to know that unlike any of the other SSRIs, Prozac remains active for between 2 to 4 weeks after stopping the drug. This extra long "half-life" of Prozac is unique and may explain why it has some demonstrated benefits in children where the other SSRIs do not.

The SSRIs are generally well tolerated but children can report both sleepiness and/or restlessness while taking these medications. Between one in two and one in three adults report sexual dysfunction (decreased libido, trouble with ejaculation or climax) when taking an SSRI. The implications of this side effect for the preteen or developing adolescent are unknown but teenage boys should be alerted to possible difficulties with ejaculation during masturbation.

Higher rates of suicidality (thinking about and planning for suicide) in children taking an SSRI compared to a placebo pill led the FDA in

Table 17.3 Anticonvulsants

Trade Name	Generic Name
Depakote	Valproate
Neurontin	Gabapentin
Tegretol	Carbamazine
Lamictal	Lamotrigine
Topomax	Topiramate

2004 to insist on a "black box" warning to the label of all antidepressants about this increased risk. Overall risk for this reaction to an SSRI is relatively low (on the order of 4 in 100). Nevertheless, close follow-up during the initial weeks of treatment or when dosage is adjusted upward is strongly recommended. If the child's mood deteriorates or unusual thinking appears, the medicine should be discontinued. Finally, all the SSRIs (except Prozac because of its extraordinarily long half-life) should not be stopped abruptly because a mild to moderate withdrawal syndrome of headache and dysphoria (mimicking depression) can occur.

Two other classes of drugs, the anticonvulsants (see Table 17.3) and antipsychotics (see Table 17.4) have a long history within psychiatric treatment for the control of aggressive behavior but their use in children and teens has soared in recent years—probably because of the greater

Table 17.4   Antipsychotics

Trade Name	Generic Name
Risperdal	Risperidone
Zyprexa	Olanzapine
Seroquel	Quetiapine
Abilify	Arepiprazole
Geodon	Ziprasidone
Clozaril	Clozapine
Haldol	Haloperidol
Mellaril	Thioridazine
Thorazine	Chlorpromazine

acceptance overall of psychiatric medication use in children. Estimates on their frequency of use are on the order of hundreds of thousands of children in the United States today (W. O. Cooper et al., 2006). Like the SSRIs, these drugs are almost universally prescribed off-label and studies justifying their effectiveness and safety are virtually absent. Still, these children often carry a bipolar diagnosis that suggests extreme behavior and failure both by the system (family, school, neighborhood) and "easier" drugs like Ritalin or Prozac to control highly problematic and disruptive behavior.

Medications initially approved for the treatment of seizures, such as Depakote®, Neurontin®, and Lamictal®, have taken their respective turns as prime drugs to use for bipolar disorder. All anticonvulsants operate similarly in selectively suppressing brain activity to control seizures. Therefore, all these drugs are sedating in nature. Whether they are provided anything more than selective sedation in children with bipolar disorder is open to question but declines in mentation and energy are certainly the most common adverse effects of these drugs (Wilens, 2004).

The antipsychotics were initially approved for treating the symptoms associated with schizophrenia. But their use for controlling aggressive, extreme behavior in nonpsychotic individuals dwarfs their use for schizophrenia. Several generations of newer antipsychotic drugs have been developed since the original, Thorazine, appeared in the 1950s. Purported improvements in the latest generation, called "atypical" antipsychotics (like Risperdal or Zyprexa), include less sedation and less risk of a permanent involuntary muscle movement disorder (tardive dyskinesia) developing with long-term use. However, recent comparison studies call into question whether at comparable doses, these newer far more expensive medications offer any real advantages to the older generic antipsychotics like Mellaril or Haldol (J. A. Lieberman et al., 2005).

Despite a paucity of evidence, these drugs are widely used because they do suppress acting out behavior, often with some degree of sedation occurring. Typically, a child is begun on the lowest dose possible of one of these drugs and every 3 to 4 days (sometimes more rapidly if the behavior is extreme) the dose is increased. There is little data on maximum safe dosages. Rather limits are based on sedation or the emergence of other side effects, the most common in this newest class of drugs being massive weight gain (to a degree where acquired Type II diabetes develops). The food intake and weight of any child or teenager taking these medications must be closely monitored. With signs of rapidly increasing weight, serious consideration must be given to stopping the drug or trying an even newer preparation like Abilify® that may have less effect on weight gain but could have other adverse effect yet to be discovered because it is so new.

A Model to Consult with Physicians

In this chapter, we provided a thorough overview primarily focused on the disruptive behaviors targeted for reduction in the classroom through the use of psychotropic medications. We have also reviewed the much smaller, less well-developed literature focusing on the use of these medications to improve nondisruptive behaviors related to social isolation, anxiety, and unhappiness. A thorough grounding in these data is critical for the classroom consultant when working with teachers. For example, when teachers report an abrupt change in a child's functioning, the consultant must immediately ascertain whether any changes have been made in prescribed medications. Further, by understanding the appropriate uses of medications in the classroom as well as other teacher, student, and setting variables that may contribute to presenting problems, consultants can (a) identify students who may be candidate for medication intervention, (b) operationally define and measure target behaviors, (c) provide this information in a comprehensive, well-summarized manner to physicians, and (d) collect data as the medication is adjusted. Our basic model comprises these features of the consultant's role and facilitates his or her work with the physician.

Physician's knowledge of children's behavior and the methods used to evaluate classroom behavior may vary greatly. Therefore, when the consultant as part of the school team determines that a particular child's behavior in the classroom may be responsive to medication treatment, the child's physician should be provided with a brief but comprehensive summary of the process used to make this determination. It is recommended that these data be submitted in writing and that permission be obtained from the family before sending such a letter. Rather than inform parents that a child might require medication, the consultant should define and explain how the child's behavior differs from others in the classroom; provide the results of efforts to manage these behaviors through nonmedical interventions; and suggest that consultation with the physician should occur, not necessarily to prescribe medication but to determine whether there is a medical explanation for the child's problems and whether, in the physician's opinion, the symptoms presented warrant medication treatment. It is essential that parents not view the consultant or school team as making treatment decisions about medication. The team's role is to identify behaviors that might be amenable to medication treatment, attempt behavioral management interventions, evaluate the benefits or lack of benefits of those interventions, and provide that data to parents with the recommendation to discuss this information with their physician.

Although physicians may be well informed concerning certain behavior checklists used in the classroom, consultants should provide more than just questionnaire scores. Target behaviors should be defined and measured in an operational manner (e.g., amount of work completed, quality of work completed, number of disruptions per day in the classroom). The consultant should briefly describe the magnitude of difference between these behaviors and those of the other children in the classroom. Further, the consultant should explain the impact of these behaviors, not only on the child, but also on the classroom in general.

In some situations, consultants are not approached until the physician has already made a decision for medication treatment to modify behavior. In such cases, every effort should be made to obtain a baseline observation, for at least a week, of target behaviors the medication is intended to modify. It cannot be too strongly emphasized that without baseline data, decisions to continue, discontinue, or adjust medication usage end up being made arbitrarily.

Once a medication is initiated, the consultant should attempt to collect at least qualitative data daily and quantitative data (e.g., direct observation of classroom behavior) at last a few times during the first 2 weeks of medication and subsequently during any adjustments in medication. At the very least, a standardized questionnaire should be completed by all of the student's teachers following the 1st week of medication and compared with baseline observations. Any time a change in dosage is made, questionnaire data from teachers must be obtained again. These data should be summarized in written format and provided to the physician, family, and teacher. As noted earlier, consultants sensitive to potential side effects of medications are in a much better position to report on these issues as well.

Consultants must help physicians recognize that there are nonmedical alternatives to the use of medications to modify behavior in the classroom and that in all but the most severe cases these should be attempted initially. As S. Goldstein and Goldstein (1990) note, "By understanding the risks of medication and how to decrease them, the benefits of medication and how to increase them, and the alternatives to medication and how to use them, it is possible to make a reasoned and reasonable decision concerning medication intervention" (p. 266). The consultant's role is to assist physicians in treating children carefully selected based on measurable, observable behavior, so that the expected benefits outweigh risks. Appropriate use of medications in the classroom to deal with behavioral and emotional problems can be an effective addition to behavior management and other educational interventions.

CHAPTER

18

Concluding Remarks

SAM GOLDSTEIN AND ROBERT BROOKS

Stress during all stages of children's development increases risk for a wide range of adverse outcomes, including those related to education, vocation, psychological, and emotional adjustment. These have a long-term effect well into the adult years (Shure, 1996). The National Center for Children in Poverty (2002) reports that approximately one in six children in the United States lives in poverty. These statistics are higher in third-world countries. Poverty is associated with multiple risks and long-term stressors that threaten development ranging from exposure to violence, poor nutrition, and lack of appropriate medical, educational, and psychological care (Garbarino, 1992).

A report by the Surgeon General (U.S. Department of Health and Human Services, 1999) set forth priorities to reduce stigma and increase access to assessment, treatment and educational services, take advantage of resources available in the community, and foster partnerships among professionals working with children. These reports and the data they summarize raise grave concerns about the future of children and of our society.

The classroom, as a microcosm of the larger world in which our children function, has reflected these adversities. Thus, it is not surprising that the educational system is also wrestling with this seeming epidemic. Schools can and must take on an increasingly active role to nurture, educate, and teach children the qualities of thinking, feeling, and behaving that comprise a resilient mindset. Classroom consultants can make a significant contribution to the educational system's understanding of childhood emotional, behavioral, developmental, and learning problems.

Since the completion of the first edition of this book, the need to achieve these goals has become even more apparent. Schools must shoulder an increasing burden of preparing youth through education and moral development to take their place in tomorrow's society. To create sustainable, resilient classrooms we must create an educational environment that fits the technological and scientific advances of today and the future. All children must be helped to develop and become proficient in ways of thinking, feeling, and behaving which can and will insulate them from the many adversities they are likely to face.

In 1994, Emmy Werner concluded, "As long as the balance between stressful life events and protective factors is favorable, successful adaptation is possible. However, when stressful life events outweigh the protective factors, even the most resilient child can develop problems" (p. 134). As Wright and Masten (2005) point out, however, understanding the processes that favor resilience and applying them successfully is not a simple process. Shifting the balance from vulnerability to resilience is a complex process. For that matter, even providing protective factors in the absence of significant vulnerability can be difficult. However, among the community factors that nurture resilience and the likelihood that children will turn out well in adulthood are good educational experiences (Fonagy, Steele, Steele, Higgitt, & Target, 1994). In this book we have attempted to offer a reasoned and reasonable approach to creating sustainable, resilient classrooms. Along with our contributors, we have attempted to offer scientific research where available and best practices when known. We have attempted to continue the tradition begun 10 years ago by integrating science and nonscience but also avoiding the promotion of nonsense.

The first edition of this book included a set of tenets or principles to guide teachers in understanding and managing children's behavior in the classroom. Within the expanded model offered in this book, we believe these guideposts are still relevant and deserve mention. We urge consultants to discuss these guideposts with teachers and administrators as a means of sensitizing others to the myriad of forces that affect children's behavior and development in the classroom. This sensitization will increase the likelihood of teachers reflecting upon their educational beliefs and practices in an open, non-defensive way and their students will be the beneficiaries. The tenets are:

- *Want to teach.* If education is your profession by default and you do not want to be in the classroom no amount of knowledge or management strategies will fill the void. It is important to help teachers consider their educational mindsets and their reasons for entering and remaining in this profession.

- *Be honest, not defensive.* Teaching is learned by trial and error, success and failure. Successful teachers are willing to view mistakes as opportunities to learn and critically examine their behavior and the influence it has on their students.

- *Understand the forces.* It is important to recognize that student, setting, teacher, and even consultant variables all affect classroom climate, behavior, and student functioning.

- *Understand children's behavioral, emotional, learning, and developmental problems.* At a minimum, one out of four children in every classroom experiences one of these problems to the point that it significantly impairs that child's functioning in the classroom. It is not expected that teachers should recognize and have at their disposal strategies for all of these problems. However, being able to recognize these problems when they present and understand their impact on the classroom is critical to create an optimal educational environment for every student.

- *Understand behavioral theory and its application in the classroom.* Arguably, the greatest liability that even dedicated teachers bring to the classroom is a lack of awareness and understanding of the theoretical issues that shape children's behavior. It is essential that teachers recognize and understand these theories; without this understanding chaos is likely to dominate rather than a controlled, effective classroom environment.

- *Recognize that children think.* Although there is no doubt that behavior is shaped, developed, maintained, and modified based on consequences, there is also no doubt that children's mindsets, the means by which they interpret, process, think, and talk to themselves about their experiences affects their self-perceptions, relations with others, behavior, and ultimately school success. Consultants can assist teachers to appreciate the ways in which the mindsets of children facilitate or impede learning.

- *Understand the impact of families.* Families of children experiencing classroom problems are more likely than other families to be dealing with increased stress, marital disharmony, and other impediments to successful family functioning. It is critical that teachers understand that children come to the classroom with a history that significantly affects their functioning and ability to cope.

- *Focus on the way work is presented is more important than focusing on behavior.* Teachers focusing principally on managing children's behavior may have classes that are well behaved but not necessarily academically accomplished. Conversely, when teachers make class-room work and activities interesting, stimulating, and enjoyable for children, these students become active participants in the educational process. This participation is incompatible with classroom misbehavior.

- *Understand medical issues.* Teachers must possess a basic understanding of medical conditions that can affect children's behavior in the classroom as well as be aware of or have available resources concerning the impact the various medications and other medical treatments have on children's classroom behavior and performance. Consultants play a critical role in providing these sources of information.
- *Recognize the importance of friends and connections to others.* A basic understanding of the socialization process children encounter and the reasons for social failure is essential. Teachers must recognize the powerful negative influence social rejection and disconnection have on children's overall behavior in the classroom.
- *Possess a model for evaluating classroom problems.* Teachers should create a list of essential classroom behaviors students must exhibit for success, including everything from bringing a sharpened pencil to class to being able to spell, write, or understand complex concepts. With this framework in place, teachers can then develop a system to identify children who struggle, the specific areas in which they struggle, and a means to evaluate and address their struggles.
- *Possess a repertoire of interventions.* Assessment logically should lead to intervention. Consultants must help teachers develop a repertoire of strategies they can use independently as a first line of intervention when children's behavior does not meet classroom expectations.

Our schools must become a central hub of an authoritative community (Commission on Children at Risk, 2003). Authoritative communities treat children not as a means to an end but as ends in themselves. Such communities are warm and nurturing. Rules are important but relationships carry equal weight. Such communities establish clear limits and expectations. They have a long-term focus, reflect and transmit a shared understanding of what it means to be a good person, encourage spiritual and religious development, and is philosophically oriented to the equal dignity of all persons.

There is and will continue to be a growing interest in applying resilience and related processes in a preventive model (Weissberg, Kumpfer,

& Seligman, 2003). There is much work to be done to systematically evaluate the myriad of variables within children, their families, teachers, and classrooms that contribute to, mediate, and moderate school functioning. Much additional research remains to be completed to understand how best to disseminate and promote this knowledge so it becomes an integral part of creating and maintaining sustainable, resilient classrooms. The application of resilience processes in educational settings provides preventive and responsive means of fostering students' success. As Weissberg et al. (2003) note, "This is a sound investment in societies future" (p. 425).

Appendix

Language Milestones
in School-Age Children

Janet Goldstein

L anguage is considered the window into the mind (Beitchman & Inglis, 1991). Numerous researchers have reported the bidirectional relationship between speech and language disorders and behavioral and
educational outcome (Richman, Stevenson, & Graham, 1982). Baker
and Cantwell (1992) extensively reviewed the literature on speech/lan-
guage disorders in children with disruptive behavior, reporting a consistent pattern of elevated rates of speech/language disorders in children
with ADHD. In a population of 288 children referred solely for psychiatric problems, 35% were found to have a language impairment that had
not been previously suspected (N. J. Cohen, Davine, Horodezky, Lipsett,
& Isaacson, 1993). Children with unsuspected language impairments
demonstrated more serious externalizing behavioral problems. Finally,
in a population of children with learning disability, Gibbs and Cooper
(1989) reported that 96% of this group had at least one type of speech
and/or language problem. Inattentiveness in the classroom has also been
found to be related to academic achievement, particularly reading
skills (Rowe & Rowe, 1992a, 1992b). Finally, Donahue, Cole, and Hartas (1994) and Shepherd, Broilier, and Dandro (1994) have convinc-
ingly demonstrated that regardless of the direction of effect, the play,
social, and behavioral skills of language-impaired children are deficient
relative to their same age, unaffected peers and are likely to increase vulnerability for this population to experience classroom behavior problems.

It is strongly recommended that consultants develop a familiarity with
these language milestones and routinely consider the potential that a
known or unknown language disorder is playing a role in the development and maintenance of a student's adverse classroom behavior.

The following language milestones are divided by the approximate grade level during which they are achieved. If a child has not acquired these skills in his or her grade, language assessment should be considered mandatory as part of an extended behavioral assessment:

By Kindergarten

- Follows three-step directions.
- Points to three colors on demand.
- Identifies heavy/light, loud/soft, long/short.
- Classifies according to form, color, or use.
- Answers simple questions when asked (When do you go to sleep?).
- Responds appropriately to "how often"/"how long" questions.
- Asks meaning of words.
- Tells a long story accurately.
- Can name first/middle/last.
- Repeats days of the week in sequence.
- Has a mean length of utterance of 5.7 words.
- Combines 5 to 8 words in sentences.
- Has all morphology acquired by Brown's Stage V (present progressive "ing," a, the, regular plural "s," in/on, possessive "s," copula and auxiliary verbs am, is, are, pronouns, regular past tense, third person singular present tense [he walks], contraction of modals [can't], "if," "so," irregular plurals, "could," "would").
- Uses indirect requests.
- Asks questions.
- Discusses emotions and feelings.
- Uses narrative chain of events but no central character or theme.
- Makes conversational repairs when listener has not understood.
- Correctly produces the following sounds: p, b, h, n, m, w, t, d, kg, f, v, s, sh, j.

By First Grade

- Can answer "what if" questions (What should you do if you lose something?).
- Differentiates A.M. from P.M.
- Differentiates yesterday/tomorrow, more/less, some/many, several/few, most/least, before/after, now/later.
- Has number concepts of 10 (give me 10).
- Can point to nickel, quarter, dime.
- Knows right from left.
- Points to named numerals 1 through 25.

- Counts 12 objects.
- Rote counts numbers up to 30.
- Repeats 4 digits correctly.
- Names basic colors.
- Names five letters of the alphabet.
- Correctly produces the following sounds: z, l, ch, dz.
- Describes movement (through, away, from, toward, over).
- Names position of objects (first, second, third).
- Names days of the week in order.
- Has a mean length of utterance of 6.6 words.
- Syntax is adultlike.
- All pronouns are used correctly.
- Uses superlative "est" (biggest).
- Answers questions (why, what, who, where) regarding paragraphs read aloud.
- Narratives: Stories have central character with logical sequence of events. The ending indicates a resolution to a problem.

By Second Grade

- Understands seasons of the year.
- Prints phone number and name.
- Can tell address.
- Categorizes words by semantic class (pig/cow are farm animals), function (airplane/kite both fly).
- Recites the alphabet sequentially.
- Rote counts to 100.
- Has a mean length of utterance of 7.3 words.
- Consistent correct use of most morphological markers.
- Uses reflexive pronouns (himself) correctly.
- Verbs "have" "had" emerging.
- Continued improvement in irregular plurals.
- Passive tense.
- Narratives: Well developed plot and characters with sequenced events.
- Correctly produces the following sounds: r, ng.

By Third Grade

- Can formulate a sentence with a word (nouns, verbs, adjectives) given orally.
- Categorizes words based on them being opposites, synonyms.
- Defines words.

- Asks for help when needed.
- Stays on topic/subject when talking.
- Carries on a conversation.
- Syntax is adultlike.
- Correctly produces all consonant clusters (sp, skw).

By Sixth Grade

- Can formulate a sentence with a word (conjunctions, embedded clauses) given orally.
- Expresses two meanings of ambiguous sentences.
- Interprets figurative language.
- Categorizes words based on abstract/complex semantic class (e.g., How are ocean, lake, pond alike?).
- Can explain relationships between meanings of multiple-meaning words.
- Metalinguistic skills have emerged (the ability to focus on and talk about language).
- Understands jokes and riddles based on lexical ambiguity.
- Narrative stories contain problems and resolutions.

By Ninth Grade

- Abstract dictionary definitions given for words.
- Increases use of perfect aspect (have/had + verb).
- Uses syntax in writing that is more complex than that used in speech.
- Understands jokes and riddles based on deep structure ambiguity.
- Narratives include descriptions of character's intentions, goals, and plans for dealing with conflict in the story.
- Conversational skills resemble adult skills—initiates topics, maintains topics, good turn-taking skills (sensitive to listener's cues).

By Twelfth Grade

- Full adult range of syntactic constructions has been reached.
- Language is used to maintain social bonds.
- Main clauses with subordinate clauses are used in spoken and written language.
- Passive tense.
- Narratives include ability to make inferences about the story (not explicitly stated) and summarize the story (integrate and condense the story).
- Maintains topics, responses are relevant to questions or topics, uses repair strategies, requests clarification.

References

Aaron, P. G., Joshi, R. M., Palmer, H., Smith, M., & Kirby, E. (2002). Separating genuine cases of reading disability from reading deficits caused by predominantly inattentive ADHD behavior. *Journal of Learning Disabilities, 35,* 425–435.

Aber, J. L., Brown, J. L., & Jones, S. M. (2003). Developmental trajectories toward violence in middle childhood: Course, demographic differences, and response to school-based intervention. *Developmental Psychology, 39,* 324–348.

Aberson, B. (1996). *An intervention for improving executive functioning and social/emotional adjustment of ADHD children: Three single case studies.* Unpublished doctoral dissertation, Miami Institute of Psychology.

Aberson, B., Albury, C., Gutting, S., Mann, F., & Trushin, B. (1986). *I can problem solve: A cognitive training program for kindergarten children.* Unpublished manuscript, Report to the Bureau of Education, Miami-Dade County Public Schools.

Aberson, B., & Ardila, A. (2000). *An intervention for improving executive functioning and social/emotional adjustment of three ADHD children: A 4-year follow-up.* Unpublished manuscript.

Abikoff, H. (1991). Cognitive training in ADHD children: Less to it than meets the eye. *Journal of Learning Disabilities, 24,* 205–209.

Abramowitz, A. J., & O'Leary, S. G. (1991). Behavior interventions for the classroom: Implications for students with ADHD. *School Psychology Review, 20,* 220–234.

Abramowitz, A. J., O'Leary, S. G., & Futtersak, M. W. (1988). The relative impact of long and short reprimands on children's off-task behavior in the classroom. *Behavior Therapy, 19,* 243–247.

Abramson, L. Y., Seligman, M. E. P., & Teasdale, J. D. (1978). Learned helplessness in humans: Critique and reformulation. *Journal of Abnormal Psychology, 87,* 49–74.

Accardo, P. J., Blondis, T. J., & Whitman, B. Y. (1990). Disorders of attention and activity level in a referral population. *Pediatrics, 85,* 426–431.

Achenbach, T. M. (1975). Longitudinal study of relations between association of responding IQ changes, and school performance from grades 3 to 12. *Developmental Psychology, 11,* 653–654.

Achenbach, T. M. (1991). *Manual for the Youth Self-Report and 1991 profile*. Burlington: University of Vermont, Department of Psychiatry.

Achenbach, T. M. (1996). Subtyping ADHD: The request for suggestions about relating empirically based assessment to DSM-IV. *ADHD Report, 4*, 5–9.

Achenbach, T. M., Conners, C. K., Quay, H. C., Verlhulst, F. C., & Howell, C. T. (1989). Replication of empirically derived syndromes as a basis for taxonomy of child/adolescent psychopathology. *Journal of Abnormal Child Psychology, 17*, 299–320.

Achenbach, T. M., & Edelbrock, C. S. (1981). Behavioral problems and competencies reported by parents of normal and disturbed children aged 4 through 16. *Monographs of the Society for Research and Child Development, 46*(Serial No. 188).

Achenbach, T. M., & Edelbrock, C. S. (1983). *Child behavior checklist*. Burlington, VT: University Associates in Psychiatry.

Achenbach, T. M., & Edelbrock, C. S. (1991). *Normative data for the child behavior checklist: Revised*. Burlington, VT: Department of Psychiatry.

Achenbach, T. M., Edelbrock, C. S., & Howell, C. T. (1987). Empirically based assessment of the behavioral/emotional problems of 2- and 3-year-old children. *Journal of Abnormal Child Psychology, 15*, 629–650.

Achenbach, T. M., & Rescorla, L. A. (2001). *Manual for ASEBA School-Age Forms & Profiles*. Burlington, VT: University of Vermont, Research Center for Children, Youth, & Families.

Adelman, H., & Taylor, L. (1983). Enhancing motivation for overcoming learning and behavior problems. *Journal of Learning Disabilities, 16*(7), 384–392.

Adrien, J. (1991). Autism and family home movies: Preliminary findings. *Journal of Autism and Developmental Disorders, 21*, 43–49.

Adrien, J. (1992). Early symptoms in autism from family home movies: Evaluation and comparison between 1st and 2nd year of life using IBSE Scale. *Acta, 55*, 71–75.

Agras, S., Sylvester, D., & Oliveau, D. (1969). The epidemiology of common fears and phobias. *Comprehensive Psychiatry, 10*, 151–156.

Ahmed, E., & Braithwaite, V. (2004). Bullying and victimization: Cause for concern for both families and schools. *School Psychology of Education, 7*, 35–54.

Akiskal, H. S., Downs, J., Jordan, P., Watson, S., Daugherty, D., & Pruitt, D. B. (1985). Affective disorders in referred children and younger siblings of manic-depressives. *Archives of General Psychiatry, 42*, 996–1003.

Akiskal, H. S., Rosenthal, T. L., Haykal, R. F., Lemmi, H., Rosenthal, R. H., & Scott-Strauss, A. (1980). Characterological depressions: Clinical and sleep EEG findings separating "subaffective dysthymias" from "character spectrum disorders." *Archives of General Psychiatry, 37*, 777–783.

Akiskal, H. S., & Weller, E. B. (1989). Mood disorders and suicide in children and adolescents. In H. I. Kaplan & B. J. Sadock (Eds.), *Comprehensive textbook of psychiatry* (Vol. 2, 5th ed., pp. 1981–1994). Baltimore: Williams & Wilkins.

Albano, A. M., Chorpita, B. F., & Barlow, D. H. (2003). Childhood anxiety disorders. In E. J. Mash & R. A. Barkley (Eds.), *Child psychopathology* (pp. 279–329). New York: Guilford Press.

Albert, N., & Beck, A. T. (1975). Incidence of depression in early adolescence: A preliminary study. *Journal of Youth and Adolescence, 4*, 301–307.

Alberto, P. E., & Troutman, A. C. (1986). *Applied behavioral analysis for teachers* (2nd ed.). Columbus, OH: Merrill.

Alderman, G. L., & Gimpel, G. A. (1997). The interaction between type of behavior problem and type of consultant: Teachers' preferences for professional assistance. *Journal of Educational and Psychological Consultation, 7,* 305–314.

Aldrich, S. F., & Martens, B. K. (1993). The effects of behavioral problem analysis versus instructional environment information on teachers' perceptions. *School Psychology Quarterly, 8,* 110–124.

Alexander, K. L., & Entwisle, D. R. (1988). Achievement in the first two years of school. *Monographs of the Society for Research in Child Development, 53*(Serial No. 218). Chicago: University of Chicago Press.

Algozzine, B., Ysseldyke, J. E., Christenson, S., & Thurlow, M. L. (1983). A factor analysis of teachers' intervention choices for dealing with students' behavior and learning problems. *Elementary School Journal, 84,* 189–197.

Allen, R. J. (1978). *An investigatory study of the effects of a cognitive approach to interpersonal problem solving on the behavior of emotionally upset psychosocially deprived preschool children.* Unpublished doctoral dissertation, Center for Minority Studies, Brookings Institute, Union Graduate School.

Altfas, J. R. (2002). Prevalence of ADHD among adults in obesity treatment. *Biomedical Psychology, 2,* 1–14.

Aman, M. G., Singh, N. N., & White, A. J. (1987). Care giver perceptions of psychotropic medication in residential facilities. *Research in Developmental Disabilities, 8,* 511–523.

American Psychiatric Association. (1980). *Diagnostic and statistical manual of mental disorders* (3rd ed.). Washington, DC: Author.

American Psychiatric Association. (1994). *Diagnostic and statistical manual of mental disorders* (4th ed.). Washington, DC: Author.

American Psychiatric Association. (1995). *Diagnostic and statistical manual of mental disorders* (4th ed., rev.). Washington, DC: Author.

American Psychiatric Association. (2000). *Diagnostic and statistical manual of mental disorders* (4th ed., text rev.). Washington, DC: Author.

Anastopoulos, A. D., Barkley, R., & Shelton, T. (1994). The history and diagnosis of attention deficit/hyperactivity disorder. *Therapeutic Care and Education, 3,* 96–110.

Anderson, E., Redman, G., & Rogers, C. (1991). *Self-esteem for tots to teens.* Wayzata, MN: Parenting and Teaching Publications.

Anderson, H. H., & Brewer, J. E. (1946). Studies of teacher's classroom personalities: Pt. II. Effects of teachers' dominative and integrative contracts on children's classroom behavior. *Applied Psychological Monographs, 8.*

Anderson, J. C., Williams, S., McGee, R., & Silva, P. A. (1987). DSM-III disorders in preadolescent children: Prevalence in a large sample from the general population. *Archives of General Psychiatry, 44,* 69–76.

Anderson, T., Bergman, L. R., & Magnusson, D. (1989). Patterns of adjustment problems and alcohol abuse in early childhood: A prospective longitudinal study. *Development and Psychopathology, 1,* 119–131.

Anderson, V. L., Levinsohn, E. M., Barker, W., & Kiewra, K. R. (1999). The effects of meditation on teacher perceived occupational stress, state and trade anxiety and burnout. *School Psychology Quarterly, 14,* 3–25.

Angold, A., Costello, E. J., Erkanli, A., & Worthman, C. M, (1999). Pubertal changes in hormone levels and depression in girls. *Psychological Medicine, 29,* 1043–1053.

Angold, A., Erkanli, A., Egger, H. L., & Costello, E. J. (2000). Stimulant treatment for children: A community perspective. *Journal of the American Academy of Child and Adolescent Psychiatry, 39*, 975–984.

Anhalt, K., & Morris, T. L. (1998). Developmental and adjustment issues of gay, lesbian, and bisexual adolescents: A review of the empirical literature. *Clinical Child and Family Psychology Review, 1*, 215–230.

Antschel, K. M., & Remer, R. (2003). Social skills training in children with ADHD: A randomized-controlled clinical trial. *Journal of Clinical Child and Adolescent Psychology, 32*, 153–165.

Apple, A. L., Billingsley, F., & Schwartz, I. S. (2005). Effects of video modeling alone and with self-management on compliment-giving behaviors of children with high functioning ASD. *Journal of Positive Behavior Interventions, 7*, 33–46.

Applegate, B., Lahey, B. B., Hart, E. L., Biederman, J., Hynd, G. W., Barkley, R. A., et al. (1997). Validity of the age of onset criterion for ADHD: A report from the DSM-IV field trials. *Journal of the American Academy of Child and Adolescent Psychiatry, 36*, 1211–1221.

Archer, A., & Gleason, M. (2003). *Skills for school success.* North Billerica, MA: Curriculum Associates.

Arnold, E. M., Goldston, D. B., Walsh, A. K., Reboussin, B. A., Daniel, S. S., & Hickman, E. (2005). Severity of emotional and behavioral problems among poor and typical readers. *Journal of Abnormal Child Psychology, 33*(2), 205–217.

Asarmov, J. F., & Horton, A. A. (1990). Coping and stress in families of child psychiatric inpatients: Parents of children with depressive and schizophrenia spectrum disorders. *Child Psychiatry and Human Development, 21*, 145–157.

Ashman, A. F. (1982). Strategic behavior and linguistic functions of institutionalized moderately retarded persons. *International Journal of Rehabilitation Research, 5*, 203–214.

Ashman, A. F., & Conway, R. N. F. (1993). *Using cognitive methods in the classroom.* New York: Routledge.

Ashman, A. F., & Conway, R. N. F. (1997). *An introduction to cognitive education: Theory and applications.* London: Routledge.

Astor, R. A., Pitner, R. O., & Duncan, B. B. (1996). Ecological approaches to mental health consultation with teachers on issues related to youth and school violence. *Journal of Negro Education, 65*, 336–355.

Athanasiou, M. S., Geil, M., Hazel, C. E., & Copeland, E. P. (2002). A look inside school-based consultation: A qualitative study of the beliefs and practices of school psychologists and teachers. *School Psychology Quarterly, 17*, 258–298.

Attie, I., Brooks-Gunn, J., & Petersen, A. C. (1990). A developmental perspective on eating disorders and eating problems. In M. Lewis & S. Miller (Eds.), *Handbook of developmental psychopathology* (pp. 409–420). New York: Plenum Press.

Atwood, A., Frith, J., & Hermelin, B. (1988). The understanding and use of interpersonal gestures by autistic and Down syndrome children. *Journal of Autism and Developmental Disorders, 18*, 241–258.

Atwood, T. (2000). Strategies for improving the social integration of children with Asperger's syndrome. *Autism: The International Journal of Research and Practice, 4*, 85–100.

August, G. R., Bloomquist, M. L., & Braswell, L. (1991). *Minnesota Competence Enhancement Project: Child group, parent group, and teacher training manuals.* Unpublished manuscript, University of Minnesota, Minneapolis.

Ausubel, D. P. (1961). Causes and types of narcotic addiction: A psychosocial view. *Psychiatric Quarterly, 35*, 523–531.

Axelrod, S. (1983). *Behavior modification for the classroom teacher.* New York: McGraw-Hill.

Ayllon, T., Garber, S., & Pisor, K. (1975). The elimination of discipline problems through a combined school-home motivational system. *Behavior Therapy, 6*, 616–626.

Ayllon, T., Kuhlman, C., & Warzak, W. J. (1983). Programming resource room generalization using lucky charms. *Child and Family Therapy, 4*, 61–67.

Ayllon, T., & Michael, J. (1959). The psychiatric nurse as a behavioral engineer. *Journal of the Experimental Analysis of Behavior, 2*, 323–334.

Azrin, N. H., & Powers, M. A. (1975). Eliminating classroom disturbances of emotionally disturbed children by positive practice procedures. *Behavior Therapy, 6*, 525–534.

Baer, D. M. (1981). *How to plan for generalization.* Austin, TX: ProEd.

Bagwell, C. L., Molina, D. S., Pelham, W. E., & Hoza, B. (2001). ADHD and problems in peer relations: Predictions from childhood to adolescence. *Journal of the American Academy of Child and Adolescent Psychiatry, 40*, 1285–1299.

Baker, L., & Cantwell, D. P. (1987). A prospective psychiatric follow-up of children with speech/language disorders. *Journal of the American Academy of Child Psychiatry, 26*, 546–553.

Baker, L., & Cantwell, D. P. (1992). Attention deficit disorder and speech/language disorders. *Comprehensive Mental Health Care, 2*, 3–16.

Balthazor, M. J., Wagner, R. K., & Pelham, W. E. (1991). The specificity of the effects of stimulant medication on classroom learning-related measures of cognitive processing for attention deficit disorder children. *Journal of Abnormal Child Psychology, 19*, 35–52.

Bandura, A. (1965). Influence of model's reinforcement contingencies on the acquisition of imitative responses. *Journal of Personality and Social Psychology, 1*, 589–595.

Bandura, A. (1969). *Principles of behavior modification.* Englewood Cliffs, NJ: Prentice-Hall.

Bandura, A. (1977). *Social learning theory.* Englewood Cliffs, NJ: Prentice-Hall.

Barak, A., Shiloh, S., & Haushner, O. (1992). Modification of interests through cognitive restructuring: Test of a theoretical model in preschool children. *Journal of Counseling Psychology, 39*, 490–497.

Barbaresi, W. J., & Olsen, R. D. (1998). An ADHD educational intervention for elementary school teachers: A pilot study. *Developmental and Behavioral Pediatrics, 19*, 94–100.

Barkley, R. A. (1989). Attention-deficit hyperactivity disorder. In E. J. Mash & R. A. Barkley (Eds.), *Treatment of childhood disorders* (pp. 39–72). New York: Guilford Press.

Barkley, R. A. (1990). *Attention-deficit hyperactivity disorder: A handbook for diagnosis and treatment.* New York: Guilford Press.

Barkley, R. A. (1995). ADHD and IQ. *ADHD Report, 3*, 1–3.

Barkley, R. A. (1997). *ADHD and the nature of self-control.* New York: Guilford Press.

Barkley, R. A. (1998). *Attention-deficit hyperactivity disorder: A handbook for diagnosis and treatment* (2nd ed.). New York: Guilford Press.

Barkley, R. A. (2006). *Attention deficit hyperactivity disorder* (3rd ed.). New York: Guilford Press.

Barkley, R. A., Copeland, A., & Sivage, C. (1980). A self-control classroom for hyperactive children. *Journal of Autism and Developmental Disorders, 10*, 75–89.

Barkley, R. A., Fischer, M., Edelbrock, C. S., & Smallish, L. (1990). The adolescent outcome of hyperactive children diagnosed by research criteria: Pt. I. An 8-year prospective follow-up study. *Journal of the American Academy of Child and Adolescent Psychiatry, 29*, 546–557.

Barkley, R. A., Fischer, M., Smallish, L., & Fletcher, K. (2004). Young adult follow-up of hyperactive children: Antisocial activities and drug use. *Journal of Child Psychology and Psychiatry, 45*, 195–207.

Barkley, R. A., & Gordon, M. (2002). Research on comorbidity, adaptive functioning and cognitive impairments in adults with ADHD: Implications for a clinical practice. In S. Goldstein & A. T. Ellison (Eds.), *Clinician's guide to adult ADHD: Assessment and intervention* (pp. 43–69). New York: Academic Press.

Barkley, R. A., McMurray, M. B., Edelbrock, C. S., & Robbins, K. (1989). The response of aggressive and non-aggressive ADHD children to two doses of methylphenidate. *Journal of the American Academy of Child and Adolescent Psychiatry, 28*, 873–881.

Barlow, D. H. (2002). *Anxiety and its disorders* (2nd ed.). New York: Guilford Press.

Barnwell, A., & Sechrist, L. (1965). Vicarious reinforcement in children at two age levels. *Journal of Educational Psychology, 56*, 100–106.

Baron-Cohen, S. (1989). Do autistic children have obsessions and compulsions? *British Journal of Clinical Psychology, 28*(3), 193–200.

Barrett, P. M., Dadds, M. R., & Holland, D. E. (1994). *The coping koala: Prevention manual.* Unpublished manuscript, University of Queensland, Australia.

Barrett, P. M., & Shortt, A. L. (2003). Parental involvement in the treatment of anxious children. In A. E. Kazdin & J. R. Weisz (Eds.), *Evidence-based psychotherapies for children and adolescents* (pp. 101–119). New York: Guilford Press.

Barrett, P. M., & Turner, C. (2001). Prevention of anxiety symptoms in primary school children: Preliminary results from a universal school-based trial. *British Journal of Clinical Psychology, 40*, 399–410.

Barrios, B. A., & Hartmann, D. P. (1988). Fears and anxieties. In E. J. Mash & L. G. Terdal (Eds.), *Behavioral assessment of childhood disorders* (2nd ed., pp. 196–264). New York: Guilford Press.

Barrios, B. A., Hartmann, D. P., & Shigetomi, C. (1981). Fears and anxieties. In E. J. Mash & L. G. Terdal (Eds.), *Behavioral assessment of childhood disorders.* New York: Guilford Press.

Barrios, B. A., & O'Dell, S. L. (1989). Fears and anxieties. In E. J. Mash & R. A. Barkley (Eds.), *Treatment of childhood disorders* (pp. 249–337). New York: Guilford Press.

Barrish, H. H., Saunders, M., & Wolf, M. M. (1969). Good behavior game: Effects of individual contingencies for group consequences on disruptive behavior in a classroom. *Journal of Applied Behavior Analysis, 2*(2), 119–124.

Bartak, L., Rutter, M., & Cox, A. (1975). A comparative study of infantile autism and specific developmental receptive language disorder: Pt. I. The children. *British Journal of Psychiatry, 126*, 127–145.

Barton, E. J., & Osborne, J. G. (1978). The development of classroom sharing by a teacher using positive practice. *Behavior Modification, 2*, 231–250.

Bastain, T. M., Lewczyk, C. M., Sharp, W. S., James, R. S., Long, R. T., Eagen, P. B., et al. (2002). Cytogenetic abnormalities in attention deficit/hyperactivity disorder. *Journal of the American Academy of Child and Adolescent Psychiatry, 7*, 806–810.

Batsche, G. M. (1999). Bullying. In A. S. Canter & S. W. Carroll (Eds.), *Crisis prevention and response: A collection of NASP resources* (pp. 23–33). Bethesda, MD: National Association of School Psychologists.

Bauer, D. H. (1976). An exploratory study of developmental changes in children's fears. *Journal of Child Psychology and Psychiatry, 17,* 69–74.

Bauermeister, J. J. (1992). Factor analyses of teacher ratings of attention deficit hyperactivity disorder and oppositional defiant symptoms in children aged 4 through 13 years. *Journal of Clinical Child Psychology, 21,* 27–34.

Baumann, M., & Kemper, T. L. (1985). Histoanatomic observations of the brain in early infantile autism. *Neurology, 35,* 866–874.

Bean, A. W., & Roberts, M. W. (1981). The effect of time-out release contingencies on changes in child non-compliance. *Journal of Abnormal Child Psychology, 9,* 95–105.

Beardslee, W. R., Keller, M. B., Lavori, P. W., Staley, J., & Sacks, N. (1993). The impact of parental affective disorder on depression in offspring: A longitudinal follow-up in a non-referred sample. *Journal of the American Academy of Child and Adolescent Psychiatry, 32,* 723–730.

Beavers, K. F., Kratochwill, T. R., & Braden, J. P. (2004). Treatment utility of functional versus empiric assessment within consultation for reading problems. *School Psychology Quarterly, 19*(1), 29–49.

Beck, A. T. (1963). Thinking in depression: Pt. I. Idiosyncratic content and cognitive distortion. *Archives in General Psychiatry, 9,* 324–333.

Beck, A. T., & Emery, G. (1985). *Anxiety disorders and phobias: A cognitive perspective.* New York: Guilford Press.

Beck, A. T., Rush, A. J., Shaw, D., & Emery, G. (1979). *Cognitive therapy of depression.* New York: Guilford Press.

Beck, J. S. (1995). *Cognitive Therapy: Basics and Beyond.* New York: Guilford.

Beck, J. S., Beck, A. T., & Jolly, J. (2001). *Beck Youth Inventories.* San Antonio, TX: Psychological Corporation.

Becker, W. C., Madsen, C., Arnold, C., & Thomas, D. R. (1967). The contingent use of teacher attention and praise in reducing classroom behavior problems. *Journal of Special Education, 1,* 287–307.

Beitchman, J. H., & Inglis, A. (1991). The continuum of linguistic dysfunction from pervasive developmental disorders to dyslexia. *Pervasive Developmental Disorders, 14,* 95–111.

Ben-Amos, B. (1992). Depression and conduct disorders in children and adolescents: A review of the literature. *Bulletin of the Menninger Clinic, 56,* 188–208.

Berg, C. Z., Rapoport, J. L., Whitaker, A., Davies, M., Leonard, H., Swedo, S. E., et al. (1989). Childhood obsessive compulsive disorder: A 2-year prospective follow-up of a community sample. *Journal of the American Academy of Child and Adolescent Psychiatry, 28,* 528–533.

Bergan, J. R. (1977). *Behavioral consultation.* Columbus, OH: Merrill.

Bergan, J. R., & Kratochwill, T. R. (1990). *Behavioral consultation and therapy.* New York: Plenum Press.

Berk, B. (1994). Why children talk to themselves. *Scientific American, 271,* 78–83.

Berk, L. E. (1989). *Child development.* Boston: Allyn & Bacon.

Berkowitz, M. W. (1982). Self-control development in relation to pro-social behavior: A response to Peterson. *Merrill Palmer Quarterly, 28,* 223–236.

Berndt, D. J., & Kaiser, C. F. (1996). *Multiscore Depression Inventory for Children.* Los Angeles: Western Psychological Services.

Bernhardt, A. J., & Forehand, R. (1975). The effects of labeled and unlabeled praise upon lower and middle class children. *Journal of Experimental Child Psychology, 19,* 536–543.

Bernstein, G. A. (1991). Comorbidity and severity of anxiety and depressive disorders in a clinic sample. *Journal of the American Academy of Child and Adolescent Psychiatry, 30,* 43–50.

Bernstein, G. A., & Borchardt, C. M. (1991). Anxiety disorders of childhood and adolescents: A critical review. *Journal of the American Academy of Child and Adolescent Psychiatry, 30,* 519–532.

Bernstein, G. A., & Garfinkel, B. D. (1986). School phobia: The overlap of affective and anxiety disorders. *Journal of the American Academy of Child Psychiatry, 25,* 235–241.

Bernstein, G. A., Layne, A. E., Egan, E. A., & Tennison, D. M. (2005). School-based interventions for anxious children. *Journal of the American Academy of Child and Adolescent Psychiatry, 44,* 1118–1127.

Bernstein, N. (1996). *Treating the unmanageable adolescent.* Northvale, NJ: Aronson.

Biederman, J., Faraone, S., Mick, E., & Lelon, E. (1995). Psychiatric comorbidity among referred juveniles with major depression: Fact or artifact? *Journal of the American Academy of Child and Adolescent Psychiatry, 34,* 579–590.

Biederman, J., Faraone, S., Mick, E., Wozniak, J., Chen, L., Ouelette, C., et al. (1996). Attention deficit hyperactivity disorder in juvenile mania: An overlooked comorbidity? *Journal of the American Academy of Child and Adolescent Psychiatry, 35,* 997–1008.

Biederman, J., Faraone, S., Milberger, S., Guite, J., Mick, E., Chen, L., et al. (1996). A prospective 4-year follow-up study of attention-deficit hyperactivity and related disorders. *Archives of General Psychiatry, 53,* 437–446.

Biederman, J., Faraone, S., Milberger, S., Jetton, J. G., Chen, L., Mick, E., et al. (1996). Is childhood oppositional defiant disorder a precursor to adolescent conduct disorder? Findings from a 4-year follow-up study of children with ADHD. *Journal of the American Academy of Child and Adolescent Psychiatry, 35,* 1193–1204.

Biederman, J., Gasfriend, D. R., & Jellinek, M. S. (1986). Desipramine in the treatment of children with attention deficit disorder. *Journal of Clinical Psychopharmacology, 6,* 359–363.

Biederman, J., Mick, E., Faraone, S. V., Braaten, E., Doyle, A., Spencer, T., et al. (2002). Influence of gender on attention deficit hyperactivity disorder in children referred to a psychiatric clinic. *American Journal of Psychiatry, 159,* 36–42.

Biederman, J., Munir, K., Knee, D., Habelow, W., Armentano, M., Autor, S., et al. (1986). A controlled family study of patients with attention deficit disorder and normal controls. *Journal of Psychiatric Research, 20,* 263–274.

Biederman, J., Newcorn, J., & Sprich, S. (1991). Comorbidity of attention-deficit hyperactivity disorder with conduct, depressive, anxiety and other disorders. *American Journal of Psychiatry, 148,* 564–477.

Biederman, J., Rosenbaum, J. F., Bolduck-Murphy, E. A., Faraone, S. V., Schaloff, J., Hirshfeld, D. R., et al. (1993). A 3-year follow-up of children with and without behavioral inhibition. *Journal of the American Academy of Child and Adolescent Psychiatry, 32,* 814–821.

Biemiller, A., & Meichenbaum, D. (1998). *Nurturing independent learners: Helping students take charge of their learning.* Cambridge, MA: Brookline Books.

Bierman, K. L. (2003). Commentary: New models for school-based mental health services. *School Psychology Review, 32,* 525–529.

Bijou, S. W., Peterson, R. F., & Ault, M. H. (1986). A method to integrate descriptive and experiential field studies at the level of data and empirical concepts. *Journal of Applied Behavior Analysis, 1,* 175–191.

Birch, S. H., & Ladd, G. W. (1997). The teacher-child relationship and children's early school adjustment. *Journal of School Psychology, 35,* 61–79.

Bird, H. R., Canino, G., Rubio-Stipec, M., Gould, M. S., Ribera, J., Sesman, M., et al. (1988). Estimates of the prevalence of childhood maladjustment in a community survey in Puerto Rico. *Archives of General Psychiatry, 28,* 847–850.

Birmaher, B., Khetarpal, S., Brent, D., Cully, M., Balach, L., Kaufman, J., et al. (1997). The screen for child anxiety related emotional disorders (SCARED): Scale construction and psychometric characteristics. *Journal of the American Academy of Child and Adolescent Psychiatry, 36,* 545–553.

Bjorklund, D. (1990). *Children's strategies: Contemporary views of cognitive development.* Hillsdale, NJ: Erlbaum.

Black, B., & Robbins, D. R. (1990). Panic disorder in children and adolescents. *Journal of the American Academy of Child and Adolescent Psychiatry, 29,* 36–44.

Blagg, N. R., & Yule, W. (1984). The behavioral treatment of school refusal—A comparative study. *Behavioral Research Therapy, 22,* 119–127.

Blick, D. W., & Test, D. W. (1987). Effects of self-recording on high school students' on-task behavior. *Learning Disabilities Quarterly, 10,* 203–213.

Bloom, D. R., Levin, H. S., Ewing-Cobbs, L., Saunders, A. E., Song, J., Fletcher, J. M., et al. (2001). Life time and novel psychiatric disorders after pediatric traumatic brain injury. *Journal of the American Academy of Child and Adolescent Psychiatry, 40,* 572–579.

Bloomquist, H. K., Bohman, M., Edvinsson, S. O., Gillberg, C., Gustavson, K. H., Holmgren, G., et al. (1985). Frequency of the fragile X syndrome in infantile autism: A Swedish multicentre study. *Clinical Genetics, 27,* 113–117.

Bloomquist, M. L. (2006). *Skills training for children with behavior problems* (Rev. ed.). New York: Guilford Press.

Bögels, S. M., & Siqueland, L. (2006). Family cognitive behavioral therapy for children and adolescents with clinical anxiety disorders. *Journal of the American Academy of Child and Adolescent Psychiatry, 45,* 134–141.

Bolstead, O. D., & Johnson, S. M. (1972). Self-regulation in the modification of disruptive classroom behavior. *Journal of Applied Behavior Analysis, 5,* 443–454.

Bolton, D., Collins, S., & Steinberg, D. (1983). The treatment of obsessive-compulsive disorder in adolescence: A report of fifteen cases. *British Journal of Psychiatry, 142,* 456–464.

Boman, P., Smith, D., & Curtis, D. (2003). Effects of pessimism and explanatory style on development of anger in children. *School Psychology International, 24,* 80–95.

Bornstein, P., & Quevillon, R. (1976). The effects of a self-instructional package on overactive preschool boys. *Journal of Applied Behavior Analysis, 9,* 179–188.

Bosco, J. (1975). Behavior modification drugs and the schools: The case of Ritalin. *Phi Delta Kappan, 56,* 489–492.

Boucher, J. (1981). Word fluency in high functioning autistic children. *Journal of Autism and Developmental Disorders, 18,* 637–645.

Bowen, R. C., Oxford, D. R., & Boyle, M. H. (1990). The prevalence of overanxious disorder and separation anxiety disorder: Results from the Ontario Child Health Study. *Journal of the American Academy of Child and Adolescent Psychiatry, 29*, 753–758.

Bower, E. M. (1969). *Early identification of emotionally handicapped children in school.* Springville, IL: Charles C Thomas.

Bradley, C. (1937). The behavior of children receiving benzedrine. *American Journal of Psychiatry, 94*, 577–585.

Brady, B. A., Tucker, C. M., Harris, Y. R., & Tribble, I. (1992). Association of academic achievement with behavior among Black students and White students. *Journal of Educational Research, 86*, 43–51.

Brand, E. F., Das-Smaal, E. A., & DeJonge, B. F. (1996). Subtypes of children with attention disabilities. *Child Neuropsychology, 2*, 109–122.

Braswell, L. (2004). Parental beliefs. *Attention! Magazine* (Official publication of Children and Adults with Attention-Deficit/Hyperactivity Disorder). Landover, MD.

Braswell, L., August, G., Bloomquist, M. L., Realmuto, G., Skare, S., & Crosby, R. (1997). School-based secondary prevention for children with disruptive behavior: Initial outcomes. *Journal of Abnormal Child Psychology, 25*, 197–208.

Braswell, L., Bloomquist, M. L., & Pedersen, S. (1991). *ADHD: A guide to understanding and helping children with attention deficit disorder in school settings.* Minneapolis: University of Minnesota, Department of Professional Development.

Breier, A., Charney, D. S., & Heninger, G. R. (1984). Major depression in patients wtih agoraphobia and panic disorder. *Archives of General Psychiatry, 41*, 1129–1135.

Brendtro, L., Brokenleg, M., & Van Bockern, S. (1990). *Reclaiming youth at risk: Our hope for the future.* Bloomington, IN: National Education Service.

Brent, D. A., Perper, J. A., Moritz, G., Allman, C., Friend, A., Roth, C., et al. (1993). Psychiatric risk factors for adolescent suicide: A case-controlled study. *Journal of the American Academy of Child and Adolescent Psychiatry, 32*, 521–529.

Breslau, N., Davis, G. C., Andreski, P., & Peterson, E. (1991). Traumatic events and posttraumatic stress disorder in an urban population of young adults. *Archives of General Psychiatry, 48*, 216–222.

Brody, G. H., & Forehand, R. (1986). Maternal perceptions of child maladjustment as a function of the combined influence of child behavior and maternal depression. *Journal of Consulting and Clinical Psychology, 54*, 237–240.

Bromet, E. J., & Cornely, P. J. (1984). Correlates of depression in mothers of young children. *Journal of the American Academy of Child Psychiatry, 23*, 335–342.

Bronfenbrenner, U. (1979). *The ecology of human development.* Cambridge, MA: Harvard University Press.

Bronson, M. B. (2000). *Self-regulation and early childhood.* New York: Guilford Press.

Brooks, R. (1991). *The self-esteem teacher.* Loveland, OH: Treehaus Communications.

Brooks, R. (1992). Fostering self-esteem in children with ADD: The search for islands of competence. *Chadder, 6*, 14–15.

Brooks, R. (1994). Children at risk: Fostering resilience and hope. *American Journal of Orthopsychiatry, 64*, 545–553.

Brooks, R. (1998). Self-esteem: Helping your child become a confident, resilient, and persistent learner. In S. Goldstein & N. Mather (Eds.), *Overcoming underachieving: An action guide to helping your child succeed in school.* New York: Wiley.

References

Brooks, R. (1999). Creating a positive school climate: Strategies for fostering self-esteem, motivation, and resilience. In J. Cohen (Ed.), *Educating minds and hearts*. New York: Teachers College Press.

Brooks, R. (2001a). Fostering motivation, hope, and resilience in children with learning disorders. *Annals of Dyslexia, 51,* 9–20.

Brooks, R. (2001b). *To touch a student's heart and mind: The mindset of the effective educator* (Proceedings of the 1999 Plain Talk conference sponsored by the Center for Development and Learning, New Orleans). Cambridge, MA: Educators Publishing Service.

Brooks, R. (2002). Creating nurturing classroom environments: Fostering hope and resilience as an antidote to violence. In S. Brock, P. Lazarus, & S. Jimerson (Eds.), *Best practices in school crisis prevention and intervention* (pp. 67–93). Bethesda, MD: NASP Publications.

Brooks, R. (2004). To touch the hearts and minds of students with learning disabilities: The power of mindsets and expectations. *Learning Disabilities: A Contemporary Journal, 2,* 9–18.

Brooks, R., & Goldstein, S. (2001). *Raising resilient children*. New York: McGraw-Hill.

Brooks, R., & Goldstein, S. (2003). *Nurturing resilience in our children: Answers to the most important parenting questions*. New York: McGraw-Hill.

Brooks, R., & Goldstein, S. (2004). *The power of resilience: Achieving balance, confidence, and personal strength in your life*. New York: McGraw-Hill.

Brophy, J. (1985). Interactions of male and female students with male and female teachers. In L. C. Wilkinson & C. B. Marrett (Eds.), *Gender influences in classroom interaction* (pp. 115–152). Orlando, FL: Academic Press.

Brophy, J., Bevis, R., Brown, J., Echeverria, E., Gregg, S., Haynes, M., et al. (1986). *Classroom strategy research: Final report*. East Lansing: Michigan State University, Institute for Research on Teaching.

Brophy, J. E., & Rohrkemper, M. M. (1981). The influence of problem ownership on teachers' perceptions and strategies for coping with problem students. *Journal of Educational Psychology, 73,* 295–311.

Brown-Chidsey, R., & Steege, M. W. (2005). *Response to intervention: Principles and strategies for effective practice*. New York: Guilford Press.

Brumback, R. A., Dietz-Schmidt, S. G., & Weinberg, W. A. (1977). Depression in children referred to an educational diagnostic center: Diagnosis and treatment and analysis of criteria and literature review. *Journal of Nervous and Mental Diseases, 165,* 529–535.

Bryson, S. E., Clark, B. S., & Smith, I. M. (1988). First report of a Canadian epidemiological study of autistic syndromes. *Journal of Child Psychology and Psychiatry, 29,* 433–445.

Bryson, S. E., Smith, I., & Eastwood, D. (1989). Obstetrical optimality in autistic children. *Journal of Child and Adolescent Psychiatry, 27,* 418–422.

Budd, K. S., Liebowitz, J. M., Riner, L. S., Mindell, C., & Goldfarb, A. L. (1981). Homebased treatment of severe disruptive behaviors: A reinforcement package for preschool and kindergarten children. *Behavior Modification, 5,* 273–298.

Burchard, J. D., & Barrera, F. (1972). An analysis of time-out and response cost in a programmed environment. *Journal of Applied Behavior Analysis, 5,* 271–282.

Burger, J. M., Cooper, H. M., & Good, T. L. (1982). Teacher attributions of student performance: Effects of outcome. *Personality and Social Psychology Bulletin, 8,* 685–690.

Burke, J. D., Loeber, R., & Birmaher, B. (2002). Oppositional defiant disorder and conduct disorder: Pt. II. A review of the past 10 years. *Journal of the American Academy of Child and Adolescent Psychiatry, 41*, 1275–1293.

Burke, P. (1991). Depression in pediatric illness. *Behavior Modification, 15*, 486–500.

Burke, P. M., Meyer, V., Kocoshis, S. A., Orenstein, D. M., Chandra, R., Nord, D. J., et al. (1989). Depression and anxiety in pediatric inflammatory bowel disease. *Journal of the American Academy of Child and Adolescent Psychiatry, 28*, 948–951.

Bushell, D. (1973). *Classroom behavior.* Englewood Cliffs, NJ: Prentice-Hall.

Bussing, R., Garry, F. A., Mason, D. M., Leon, C. E., Sinha, K., & Garvan, C. W. (2003). Child temperament, ADHD and caregiver strain: Exploring relationships in an epidemiological sample. *Journal of the American Academy of Child and Adolescent Psychiatry, 42*, 184–192.

Cadoret, R. J., O'Gorman, T. W., Heywood, E., & Troughton, E. (1985). Genetic and environmental factors in major depression. *Journal of Affective Disorders, 9*, 155–164.

Caicedo, C., & Williams, S. H. (2002). Risperidone improves behavior in children with autism. *Journal of Family Practice, 51*, 915.

Campbell, S. B. (1986). Developmental issues. In R. Gittelman (Ed.), *Anxiety disorders of childhood* (pp. 24–57). New York: Guilford Press.

Campbell, S. B. (1991). Longitudinal studies of active and aggressive pre-schoolers: Individual differences in early behavior and outcome. In D. Cicchetti & S. L. Toth (Eds.), *Rochester Symposium on Developmental Psychopathology* (pp. 57–90). Hillsdale, NJ: Erlbaum.

Campbell, S. B., & Ewing, L. J. (1990). Follow-up of hard-to-manage preschoolers: Adjustment at age 9 and predictors of continuing symptoms. *Journal of Child Psychology and Psychiatry, 31*, 871–890.

Canino, F. (1981). Learned helplessness theory: Implications for research in learning disabilities. *Journal of Special Education, 15*, 471–484.

Cantwell, D. P. (1990). Depression across the early lifespan. In M. Lewis & S. M. Miller (Eds.), *Handbook of developmental psychopathology* (pp. 293–309). New York: Plenum Press.

Cantwell, D. P., & Baker, L. (1977). Psychiatric disorder in children with speech and language retardation. *Archives of General Psychiatry, 34*, 583–591.

Cantwell, D. P., & Baker, L. (1989). Stability and natural history of DSM-III childhood diagnoses. *Journal of the American Academy of Child and Adolescent Psychiatry, 28*, 691–700.

Cantwell, D. P., Baker, L., & Mattison, R. (1981). Prevalence, type and correlates of psychiatric disorder in 200 children with communication disorder. *Journal of Developmental and Behavioral Pediatrics, 2*, 131–136.

Cantwell, D. P., Baker, L., & Rutter, M. (1978). Family factors. In M. Rutter & E. Schopler (Eds.), *Autism: A reappraisal of concepts and treatment* (pp. 269–296). New York: Plenum Press.

Capaldi, D. M. (1992). The co-occurrence of conduct problems and depressive symptoms in early adolescent boys: Pt. II. A 2-year follow-up at grade 8. *Developmental Psychology, 4*, 125–144.

Carden-Smith, L., & Fowler, S. (1984). Positive peer pressure: The effects of peer monitoring on children's disruptive behavior. *Journal of Applied Behavior Analysis, 17*, 213–227.

Cardon, L. R., Smith, S. D., Fulker, D. W., Kimberling, W. J., Pennington, B. F., & De Fries, J. C. (1994). Quantitative trait locus for reading disability in chromosome 6. *Science, 266*, 276–279.

Carey, S. P., & Stoner, G. (1994). Contextual considerations in social skills instruction. *School Psychology Quarterly, 9*, 137–141.

Carey, W. B. (1970). A simplified method for measuring infant temperament. *Journal of Pediatrics, 77*, 188–194.

Carlson, C. L., & Mann, M. (2002). Sluggish cognitive tempo predicts a different pattern of impairment in the attention deficit hyperactivity disorder—Predominantly inattentive type. *Journal of Clinical Child and Adolescent Psychology, 31*, 123–129.

Carlson, G. A. (1983). Bipolar affective disorders in childhood and adolescence. In D. P. Cantwell & G. A. Carlson (Eds.), *Affective disorders in childhood and adolescence*. New York: Spectrum Press.

Carlson, G. A., & Cantwell, D. P. (1980a). A survey of depressive symptoms, syndrome and disorder in a child psychiatric population. *Journal of the American Academy of Child Psychiatry, 21*, 19–25.

Carlson, G. A., & Cantwell, D. P. (1980b). Unmasking masked depression in children and adolescents. *American Journal of Psychiatry, 137*, 445–449.

Carlson, G. A., Figueroa, R. G., & Lahey, B. B. (1986). Behavior therapy for childhood anxiety disorders. In R. Gittelman (Ed.), *Anxiety disorders in childhood*. New York: Guilford Press.

Carlson, J., & Das, J. P. (1997). A process approach to remediating word decoding deficiencies in Chapter 1 children. *Learning Disabilities Quarterly, 20*, 93–102.

Carr, E. G., Newsom, C. D., & Binkoff, J. A. (1976). Stimulus control of self-destructive behavior in a psychotic child. *Journal of Abnormal Child Psychology, 13*, 101–118.

Carr, E. G., Newsom, C. D., & Binkoff, J. A. (1980). Escape as a factor in the aggressive behavior of two retarded children. *Journal of Applied Behavior Analysis, 4*, 139–153.

Carroll, B. J. (1983). Biologic markers and treatment response. *Journal of Clinical Psychology, 44*, 30–40.

Carter, J. F. (1993). Self-management: Education's ultimate goal. *Teaching Exceptional Children, 25*, 28–31.

Castellanos, F. X., Giedd, J. N., Marsh, W. L., Hamburger, S. D., Vaituzis, A. C., Dickstein, D. P., et al. (1996). Quantitative brain magnetic resonance imaging in attention-deficit hyperactivity disorder. *Archives of General Psychiatry, 53*, 607–616.

Center for Disease Control. (2005). Mental health in the United States: Prevalence of diagnosis and medication treatment for attention-deficit/hyperactivity disorder—United States, 2003. *Morbidity and Mortality Weekly Report, 54*(34), 842–847. Available from http://www.cdc.gov/mmwr.

Center for Effective Discipline. (2005). *Discipline at school: Facts about corporal punishment*. Available from http://www.stophitting.com/disatschool/facts.php#u.s.%20states%20banning%20corporal%20punishment.

Chabildas, N., Pennington, B. F., & Willicutt, E. G. (2001). A comparison of the neuropsychological profiles of the DSM-IV subtypes of ADHD. *Journal of Abnormal Child Psychology, 29*, 529–540.

Chapman, W. (1991). The Illinois experience: State grants to improve schools through parent involvement. *Phi Delta Kappan, 72*, 355–358.

Charney, R. S. (1991). *Teaching children to care: Management in the responsive classroom.* Greenfield, MA: Northeast Foundation for Children.

Chase, S. N., & Clement, P. W. (1985). Effects of self-reinforcement and stimulants on academic performance in children with attention deficit disorder. *Journal of Clinical Child Psychology, 14,* 323–333.

Cheng, C. (1997). Role of perceived social support on depression in Chinese adolescents: A prospective study examining the buffering model. *Journal of Applied Social Psychology, 27,* 800–820.

Cheng, C. (1998). Getting the right kind of support: Functional differences in the types of social support on depression for Chinese adolescents. *Journal of Clinical Psychology, 54,* 845–849.

Cherlin, A. J., Furstenberg, F. F., Chase-Lansdale, P. O., Kiernan, K. E., Robins, P. K., Morrison, D. R., et al. (1991). Longitudinal studies of effects of divorce on children in Great Britain and the United States. *Science, 252,* 1386–1389.

Chess, S., Fernandez, P., & Korn, S. (1978). Behavioral consequences of congenital rubella. *Journal of Pediatrics, 92,* 662–703.

Chess, S., & Thomas, A. (1986). *Temperament in clinical practice.* New York: Guilford Press.

Chorpita, B. F., & Southam-Gerow, M. A. (2006). Fears and anxieties. In E. Mash & R. Barkley (Eds.), *Treatment of childhood disorders* (3rd ed., pp. 271–335). New York: Guilford Press.

Christenson, S. L. (1995). Supporting home-school collaboration. In A. Thomas & J. Grimes (Eds.), *Best practices in school psychology III* (pp. 253–267). Washington, DC: National Association of School Psychologists.

Christenson, S. L., & Sheridan, S. M. (2001). *Schools and families: Creating essential connections for learning.* New York: Guilford Press.

Christenson, S. L., & Ysseldyke, J. E. (1989). Assessing student performance: An important change is needed. *Journal of School Psychology, 27,* 409–425.

Christian, R. E., Frick, P. J., Hill, N. L., Tyler, L., & Frazer, D. R. (1997). Psychopathy and conduct problems in children: Pt. II. Implications for subtyping children with conduct problems. *Journal of the American Academy of Child and Adolescent Psychiatry, 36,* 233–241.

Christy, P. R. (1975). Does use of tangible rewards with individual children affect peer observers? *Journal of Applied Behavior Analysis, 8,* 187–196.

Chronis, A. M., Chacko, A., Fabian, G. A., Wymbs, B. T., & Pelham, W. E. (2004). Enhancements to the behavioral parent training paradigm for families of children with ADHD: Review and future directions. *Clinical Child and Family Psychology Review, 7,* 1–27.

Cialdella, P., & Mamelle, N. (1989). An epidemiological study of infantile autism in a French department (Rhone): A research note. *Journal of Child Psychology and Psychiatry and Allied Disciplines, 30,* 165–175.

Clarizio, H. F. (1976). *Toward positive classroom discipline* (2nd ed.). New York: Wiley.

Clark, C., Prior, M., & Kinsella, G. J. (2000). Do executive function deficits differentiate between adolescents with ADHD and oppositional defiant/conduct disorder: A neuropsychological study using the Six Elements Test and the Hayling Sentence Completion Test. *Journal of Abnormal Child Psychology, 28,* 403–414.

Clark, H. B., Rowbury, T., Baer, A. M., & Baer, D. M. (1973). Time-out as a punishing stimulus in continuous and intermittent schedules. *Journal of Applied Behavior Analysis, 6,* 443–455.

Clark, L. A., & Watson, D. (1991). Tripartite model of anxiety and depression: Psychometric evidence and taxonomic implications. *Journal of Abnormal Psychology, 100,* 316–336.

Clarke, G. N., DeBar, L. L., & Lewinsohn, P. M. (2003). Cognitive-behavioral group treatment for adolescent depression. In A. Kazdin & J. Weisz (Eds.), *Evidence based psychotherapies for children and adolescents* (pp. 120–134). New York: Guilford Press.

Clarke, G. N., Hawkins, W., Murphy, M., Sheeber, L. B., Lewinsohn, P. M., & Seeley, J. R. (1995). Targeted prevention of unipolar depressive disorder in an at-risk sample of high school adolescents: A randomized trial of a group cognitive intervention. *Journal of the American Academy of Child and Adolescent Psychiatry, 34,* 312–321.

Clarke, G. N., Hornbrook, M. C., Lynch, F. L., Polen, M., Gale, J., O'Connor, E. A., et al. (2002). Group cognitive behavioral treatment for depressed adolescent offspring of depressed parents in an HMO. *Journal of the American Academy of Child and Adolescent Psychiatry, 41,* 305–313.

Clarke, G. N., Lewinsohn, P. M., & Hops, H. (1990). *Adolescent coping with depression course.* Eugene, OR: Castalia Publishing.

Clarke, G. N., Rohde, P., Lewinsohn, P. M., Hops, H., & Seeley, J. R. (1999). Cognitive-behavioral treatment of adolescent depression: Efficacy of acute group treatment and booster sessions. *Journal of the American Academy of Child and Adolescent Psychiatry, 38,* 272–279.

Clonidine for treatment of attention-deficit/hyperactivity disorder. (1996). *Medical Letter, 38,* 109–110.

Cohen, D. J., & Volkmar, F. R. (1997). *Handbook of autism and pervasive developmental disorders* (2nd ed.). New York: Wiley.

Cohen, J. (Ed.). (1999). *Educating minds and hearts: Social emotional learning and the passage into adolescence.* New York: Teachers College Press.

Cohen, L. S., & Biederman, J. (1988). Further evidence for an association between affective disorders and anxiety disorders: Review and case reports. *Journal of Clinical Psychiatry, 49,* 313–316.

Cohen, N. J., Davine, M., Horodezky, N., Lipsett, L., & Isaacson, L. (1993). Unsuspected language impairment in psychiatrically disturbed children: Prevalence and language and behavioral characteristics. *Journal of the American Academy of Child and Adolescent Psychiatry, 32,* 595–603.

Cohen, N. J., Davine, M., & Meloche-Kelly, M. (1989). Prevalence of unsuspected language disorders in a child psychiatric population. *Journal of the American Academy of Child and Adolescent Psychiatry, 28,* 107–111.

Cohen, N. J., Sullivan, S., Minde, K. K., Novak, C., & Helwig, C. (1981). Evaluation of the relative effectiveness of methylphenidate and cognitive behavior modification in the treatment of kindergarten-aged hyperactive children. *Journal of Abnormal Child Psychology, 9,* 43–54.

Cohen, P., & Flory, M. (1998). Issues in the disruptive behavior disorders: Attention deficit disorder without hyperactivity and the differential validity of oppositional defiant and conduct disorders. In T. A. Widiger, A. J. Frances, & H. J. Pincus (Eds.), *DSM-IV sourcebook* (Vol. 4, pp. 455–463). Washington, DC: American Psychiatric Press.

Cohen-Cole, S. A., & Stoudemire, A. (1987). Major depression and physical illness. *Psychiatric Clinics of North America, 10,* 1–17.

Coie, J. D., & Dodge, K. (1988). Multiple sources of data on social behavior and social status in the school: A cross age comparison. *Child Development, 59,* 815–829.

Coie, J. D., & Dodge, K. A. (1998). Aggression and anti-social behavior. In W. Damon (Series Ed.) & N. Eisenberg (Vol. Ed.), *Handbook of child psychology: Vol. 3. Social, emotional, and personality development* (5th ed., pp. 779–862). New York: Wiley.

Coie, J. D., Dodge, K. A., & Coppotelli, H. (1982). Dimensions and types of social status: A cross-age perspective. *Developmental Psychology, 18*, 557–570.

Coie, J. D., & Lenox, K. F. (1994). The development of antisocial individuals. In D. C. Fowles, P. Sutker, & S. H. Goodman (Eds.), *Progress in experimental personality and psychopathology research* (pp. 45–72). New York: Springer.

Coie, J. D., & Miller-Johnson, S. (2001). Peer factors and interventions. In R. Loeber & D. P. Farrington (Eds.), *Child delinquents* (pp. 191–209). Thousand Oaks, CA: Sage.

Cole, D. A., Truglio, R., & Peeke, L. (1997). Relation between symptoms of anxiety and depression in children: A multi-trait-multimethod-multigroup assessment. *Journal of Consulting and Clinical Psychology, 65*, 110–119.

Coleman, J., & Blass, J. P. (1985). Autism and lactic acidosis. *Journal of Autism and Developmental Disorders, 15*, 1–8.

Coleman, M., Landgrebe, M. A., & Landgrebe, A. R. (1976). Purine autism: Hypercuricosuria in autistic children—Does this identify a subgroup of autism. In M. Coleman (Ed.), *The autistic syndromes* (pp. 183–195). Amsterdam: North Holland.

Collaborative for Academic, Social, and Emotional Learning. (2003). *Safe and sound: An educational leader's guide to evidence-based social and emotional learning programs.* Retrieved September 8, 2005, from http://www.casel.org.

Colton, D. L., & Sheridan, S. M. (1998). Conjoint behavioral consultation and social skills training: Enhancing the play behaviors of boys with attention deficit hyperactivity disorder. *Journal of Educational and Psychological Consultation, 9*, 3–28.

Commission on Children at Risk. (2003). *Hardwired to connect.* New York: Institute for American Values.

Conduct Problems Prevention Research Group. (1992). A developmental and clinical model for the prevention of conduct disorder: The FAST Track Program. *Development and Psychopathology, 4*, 509–525.

Conduct Problems Prevention Research Group. (2002a). Evaluation of the first three years of the Fast Track Prevention Trial with children at high risk for adolescent conduct problems. *Journal of Abnormal Child Psychology, 30*, 19–35.

Conduct Problems Prevention Research Group. (2002b). Using the Fast Track Randomized Prevention Trial to test the early-starter model of the development of serious conduct problems. *Development and Psychopathology, 14*, 925–943.

Conners, C. K. (1989). *Conners Parents Rating Scale* (Rev.) and *Conners Teachers Rating Scale* (Rev.). North Towanda, NY: Multi-Health Systems.

Conners, C. K. (1996). Letter to the editor. *The ADHD Report, 4*, 13.

Conners, C. K. (1997). *Conners Rating Scales* (Rev.). North Tonawanda, NY: Multi-Health Systems.

Connor, D. F. (2002). Preschool attention deficit hyperactivity disorder: A review of prevalence, diagnosis, neurology and stimulant treatment. *Developmental and Behavioral Pediatrics, 23*, S1–S9.

Conoley, C. W., Conoley, J. C., Ivey, D. C., & Scheel, M. J. (1991). Enhancing consultation by matching the consultee's perspectives. *Journal of Counseling and Development, 69*, 546–549.

Conoley, J. C., & Conoley, C. W. (1982). *School Consultation: A Guide to Practice and Training.* New York: Pergamon.

Conoley, J. C., & Conoley, C. W. (1992). *School consultation: Practice and training.* Boston: Allyn & Bacon.

Cook, E. H., Stein, M. A., Krasowski, M. D., Cox, N. J., Olkon, D. M., Kleffer, J. E., et al. (1995). Association of attention deficit disorder and the dopamine transporter gene. *American Journal of Human Genetics, 56,* 993–998.

Coolidge, F. L., DenBoer, J. W., & Segal, D. L. (2004). Personality and neuropsychological correlates of bullying behavior. *Personality and Individual Differences, 36,* 1559–1569.

Cooper, J. O., Herron, T. E., & Heward, W. I. (1987). *Applied behavior analysis.* Columbus, OH: Merrill.

Cooper, W. O., Arbogast, P. G., Ding, H., Hickson, G. B., Fuchs, D. C., & Ray, W. A. (2006). Trend in prescribing of antipsychotic medications for U.S. children. *Ambulatory Pediatrics, 6,* 79–83.

Copeland, A. P., Wolraich, M., Lindgren, S., Milich, R., & Woolson, R. (1987). Pediatricians' reported practices in the assessment and treatment of attention deficit disorders. *Journal of Developmental and Behavioral Pediatrics, 8,* 191–197.

Cormier, P., Carlson, J. S., & Das, J. P. (1990). Planning ability and cognitive performance: The compensatory effects of a dynamic assessment approach. *Learning and Individual Differences, 2,* 437–449.

Cornell, D. G. (2005). School violence: Fears versus facts. In K. Heilbrun, N. E. Goldstein, & R. Redding (Eds.), *Juvenile delinquency: Prevention, assessment, and intervention* (pp. 45–66). New York: Oxford University Press.

Costello, E. J. (1989). Developments in child psychiatric epidemiology: Introduction. *Journal of the American Academy of Child and Adolescent Psychiatry, 28,* 836–841.

Courchesne, E. (1989). Neuroanatomical systems involved in infantile autism: The implications of cerebellar abnormalities. In G. Dawson (Ed.), *Autism: Nature, diagnosis and treatment* (pp. 119–143). New York: Guilford Press.

Courchesne, E., Lincoln, A. J., Kilman, B. A., & Galambos, R. (1985). Event-related brain potential correlates of the processing of novel visual and auditory information in autism. *Journal of Autism and Developmental Disorders, 15,* 55–76.

Courchesne, E., Young-Courchesne, R., Press, G. A., Hesselink, J. R., & Jernigan, T. L. (1988). Hypoplasia of cerebellar vermal lobules VI and VII in autism. *New England Journal of Medicine, 318,* 1349–1354.

Covey, S. (1989). *The 7 habits of highly effective people.* New York: Simon & Schuster.

Cowen, L., Gesten, E. L., & Destefano, N. A. (1977). Non-professional and professional help agents' views of interventions with young maladapting school children. *American Journal of Community Psychology, 5,* 459–479.

Cox, C. S., Fedio, P., & Rapoport, J. L. (1989). Neuropsychological testing of obsessive-compulsive adolescents. In J. L. Rapoport (Ed.), *Obsessive-compulsive disorder in children and adolescents* (pp. 73–85). Washington, DC: American Psychiatric Press.

Cremin, L. A. (1964). *The transformation of the school.* New York: Random House.

Crick, N. R., & Bigbee, M. A. (1998). Relational and overt forms of peer victimization: A multi-informant approach. *Journal of Consulting and Clinical Psychology, 66,* 337–347.

Crick, N. R., Casas, J. F., & Ku, H. C. (1999). Relational and physical forms of peer victimization in preschool. *Developmental Psychology, 35,* 376–385.

Crick, N. R., Casas, J. F., & Mosher, M. (1997). Relational and overt aggression in preschool. *Developmental Psychology, 33,* 579–588.

Crick, N. R., & Grotpeter, J. K. (1995). Relational aggression, gender, and social-psychological adjustment. *Child Development, 66,* 710–722.

Crick, N. R., & Grotpeter, J. K. (1996). Children's treatment by peers: Victims of relational and overt aggression. *Development and Psychopathology, 8,* 367–380.

Crone, D. A., & Horner, R. H. (2003). *Building positive behavior support systems in schools: Functional behavioral assessment.* New York: Guilford Press.

Crozier, S., & Sileo, N. M. (2005). Encouraging positive behavior with social stories: An intervention for children with autism spectrum disorders. *Teaching Exceptional Children, 37,* 26–31.

Crystal, D. S., Ostrander, R., Chen, R., & August, G. J. (2001). Multi-method assessment of psychopathology among DSM-IV subtypes of children with ADHD: Self, parent and teacher reports. *Journal of Abnormal Child Psychology, 29,* 189–205.

Cuenin, L. H., & Harris, K. R. (1986). Planning, implementing and evaluating time-out interventions with exceptional students. *Teaching Exceptional Children, 18,* 272–276.

Cuffe, S. P., Moore, C. G., & McKeown, R. E. (2005). Prevalence and correlates of ADHD symptoms in the National Health Interview Survey. *Journal of Attention Disorders, 9*(2), 392–401.

Cullinan, D., & Epstein, H. (1986). Behavior disorders. In N. Haring (Ed.), *Exceptional children and youth* (4th ed.). Columbus, OH: Merrill.

Cumings, D. E. (1990). *Tourette's syndrome and human behavior.* Duarte, CA: Hope Press.

Cunningham, C. E., & Boyle, M. H. (2002). Preschoolers at risk for ADHD and oppositional defiant disorder: Family, parenting, and behavioral correlates. *Journal of Abnormal Child Psychology, 30,* 555–569.

Curran, T. J., & Algozzine, B. (1980). Ecological disturbance: A test of the matching hypothesis. *Behavioral Disorders, 5,* 169–174.

Curwin, R. L., & Mendler, A. N. (1988). *Discipline with dignity.* Reston, VA: Association for Supervision and Curriculum Development.

Cushing, L. S., Horner, R. H., & Barrier, H. (2003). Validation and congruent validity of a direct observation tool to assess student social climate. *Journal of Positive Behavior Interventions, 5,* 225–237.

Cytryn, L., & McKnew, D. H. (1974). Factors influencing the changing clinical expression of the depressive process in children. *American Journal of Psychiatry, 131,* 879–881.

Cytryn, L., McKnew, D. H., Bartko, J. J., Lamour, M., & Hamovitt, J. (1982). Offspring of patients with affective disorders: Pt. II. *Journal of the American Academy of Child Psychiatry, 21,* 389–391.

Dadds, M. R., Holland, D., Barrett, P. M., Laurens, K., & Spence, S. (1999). Early intervention and prevention of anxiety disorders in children: Results at 2-year follow-up. *Journal of Consulting and Clinical Psychology, 67,* 145–150.

Dadds, M. R., Spence, S. H., Holland, D. E., Barrett, P. M., & Laurens, K. R. (1997). Prevention and early intervention for anxiety disorders: A controlled trial. *Journal of Consulting and Clinical Psychology, 65,* 627–635.

Daigneault, S., Braun, C. M. J., & Whitaker, H. A. (1992). An empirical test of two opposing theoretical models of prefrontal function. *Brain and Cognition, 19,* 48–71.

Dalsgaard, S., Mortenson, P., Frydenberg, M., & Thomsen, P. H. (2002). Conduct problems: Gender and adult psychiatric outcome of children with ADHD. *British Journal of Psychiatry, 181,* 416–421.

Das, J. P. (1980). Planning: Theoretical considerations and empirical evidence. *Psychological Research (W. Germany)*, *41*, 141–151.

Das, J. P., Kar, B. C., & Parrila, R. K. (1996). *Cognitive planning: The psychological basis of intelligent behavior.* Thousand Oaks, CA: Sage.

Das, J. P., Naglieri, J. A., & Kirby, J. R. (1994). *Assessment of cognitive processes.* Needham Heights: MA: Allyn & Bacon.

Davidson, R. J., Putnam, K. M., & Larson, C. L. (2000). Dysfunction in the neuro circuitry of emotion regulation as a possible preclude to violence. *Science, 289*, 591–594.

Davies, D. (1991). Schools reaching out: Family, school, and community partnerships for student success. *Phi Delta Kappan, 72*, 376–382.

Davis, S. (2003). *Schools where everyone belongs.* Wayne, ME: Stop Bullying Now.

Dawson, G., Finley, C., Phillips, S., & Galpert, L. (1988). Reduce P3 amplitude of the event-related brain potential: Its relationship to language ability in autism. *Journal of Autism and Developmental Disorders, 18*, 493–504.

Dean, M. H. (2005, September 23). Safe schools tally: Violence alarming. *Philadelphia Daily News*, pp. 7, 24.

Debus, R. L. (1970). Effects of brief observation of model behavior on conceptual tempo of impulsive children. *Developmental Psychology, 2*, 22–32.

Deci, E. L. (1975). *Intrinsic motivation.* New York: Plenum Press.

Deci, E. L., & Chandler, C. (1986). The importance of motiviation for the future of the LD field. *Journal of Learning Disabilities, 19*, 58–59.

Deci, E. L., & Flaste, R. (1995). *Why we do what we do: Understanding self-motivation.* New York: Guilford Press.

Deci, E. L., Hodges, R., Pierson, L., & Tomassone, J. (1992). Autonomy and competence as motivational factors in students with learning disabilities and emotional handicaps. *Journal of Learning Disabilities, 25*, 457–471.

Decina, P., Kestenbaum, C. J., Farber, S., Kron, L., Gargan, M., Sackeim, H. A., et al. (1983). Clinical and psychological assessment of children of bipolar probands. *American Journal of Psychiatry, 140*, 548–553.

Dehn, M. J. (2000, October). *Cognitive assessment system performance of ADHD children.* Paper presented at the annual NASP Convention, New Orleans, LA.

Del Mundo, A. S., Pumariega, A. J., & Vance, H. R. (1999). Psychopharmacology in school-based mental health services. *Psychology in the Schools, 36*(5), 437–450.

DeLong, G. R., Beau, S. C., & Brown, F. R. (1981). Acquired reversible autistic syndrome in acute encephalopathic illness in children. *Archives of Neurology, 38*, 191–194.

Demaray, M. K., & Malecki, C. K. (2002). Critical levels of perceived social support associated with student adjustment. *School Psychology Quarterly, 17*, 213–241.

Denckla, M. B. (1989). Chlordiazepoxide in the management of school phobia. *Diseases of the Nervous System, 23*, 292–295.

Deno, S. L., & Mirkin, P. K. (1977). *Data-Based Program Modification: A Manual.* Reston, VA: Council for Exceptional Children.

Department of Health and Human Services. (2004a). Food and Drug Administration, Center for Drug Evaluation and Research, Psychopharmacologic Drug and Advisory Committee with the Pediatric Subcommittee of the Anti-Infective Drugs Advisory Committee. Retrieved February 2, 2006, from http://www.fda.gov/ohrms /dockets/ac/04/transcripts/4006T1.htm.

Department of Health and Human Services. (2004b, September 13–14). Food and Drug Administration, Psychopharmacologic Drugs Advisory Committee. Joint meeting with the Pediatric Advisory Committee. Available from http://www.fda.gov/ohrms/dockets/ac/cder04.html#PsychopharmacologicDrugs.

DeRisi, W. J., & Butz, G. (1975). *Writing behavioral contracts: A case stimulation practice manual.* Champaign, IL: Research Press.

Déry, M., Toupin, J., Pauzé, R., & Verlaan, P. (2004). Frequency of mental health disorders in a sample of elementary school students receiving special educational services for behavioral difficulties. *Canadian Journal of Psychiatry, 49,* 769.

DeWolfe, N. A., Byrne, J. M., & Bawden, H. M. (2000). ADHD in preschool children: Parent-rated psychosocial correlates. *Developmental Medicine in Child Neurology, 42,* 825–830.

Deykin, E. Y., & McMahon, B. (1980). Pregnancy, delivery, and neonatal complications among autistic children. *American Journal of the Disabled Child, 134,* 860–864.

Dicintio, M., & Gee, S. (1999). Control is the key: Unlocking the motivation of at-risk students. *Psychology in the Schools, 36,* 231–237.

Diller, L., & Goldstein, S. (2006). Science, ethics, and the psychosocial treatment of ADHD. *Journal of Attention Disorders, 9,* 571–574.

Dobson, K. S. (Ed.). (2001). *Handbook of cognitive-behavioral therapy* (2nd ed.). New York: Guilford Press.

Dodge, K. (1983). Behavioral antecedents of peer social status. *Child Development, 54,* 1386–1399.

Dodge, K. A., Price, J. M., Bachorowski, J. A., & Newman, J. P. (1990). Hostile attributional biases in severely aggressive adolescents. *Journal of Abnormal Psychology, 99,* 385–392.

Dolgan, J. I. (1990). Depression in children. *Pediatric Annals, 19,* 45–50.

Donahue, M., Cole, D., & Hartas, D. (1994). Links between language and emotional behavioral disorders. *Education and Treatment of Children, 17,* 244–254.

Dorland's Medical Dictionary. (1980). New York: Holt, Rinehart and Winston.

Douglas, V. I., Barr, R. G., O'Neil, M. E., & Britton, B. G. (1986). Short-term effects of methylphenidate on the cognitive, learning, and academic performance of children with attention deficit disorder in the laboratory and classroom. *Journal of Child Psychology and Psychiatry, 27,* 191–211.

Douglas, V. I., & Benezra, E. (1990). Supraspan verbal memory in attention deficit disorder with hyperactivity normal and reading disabled boys. *Journal of Abnormal Child Psychology, 18,* 617–638.

Downer, J. T., & Pianta, R. C. (2006). Academic and cognitive functioning in first grade: Associations with early or home and child care predictors and with concurrent home and classroom experiences. *School Psychology Review, 35,* 11–30.

Downey, G., & Coyne, J. C. (1990). Children of depressed parents: An integrative review. *Psychological Bulletin, 108,* 50–76.

Drabman, R. S., & Lahey, B. B. (1974). Feedback in classroom behavior modification: Effects on the target and her classmates. *Journal of Applied Behavior Analysis, 7,* 591–598.

Dreikurs, R., Grunwald, B., & Pepper, F. (1971). *Maintaining sanity in the classroom.* New York: Harper & Row.

Dunn, J., & Brown, J. (1991). Relationships, talk about feelings, and the development of affect regulation in early childhood. In J. Garber & K. A. Dodge (Eds.), *The development of emotion regulation and dysregulation* (pp. 89–108). New York: Cambridge University Press.

Dunst, C. J., Bruder, M. B., Trivette, C. M., Hamby, D., Raab, M., & McLean, M. (2001). Characteristics and consequences of everyday natural learning opportunities. *Topics in Early Childhood Special Education, 21*(2), 68–92.

DuPaul, G. J., & Eckert, T. L. (1994). The effects of social skills curricula: Now you see them, now you don't. *School Psychology Quarterly, 9,* 113–132.

DuPaul, G. J., McGoey, K. E., Eckert, T. L., & Van Brakle, J. V. (2001). Preschool children with ADHD: Impairments in behavioral, social and school functioning. *Journal of the American Academy of Child and Adolescent Psychiatry, 40,* 508–515.

DuPaul, G. J., Power, T. J., Anastopoulos, A. D., & Reid, R. (1998). *ADHD Rating Scale-IV: Checklists, norms, and clinical interpretation.* New York: Guilford Press.

DuPaul, G. J., & Rapport, M. D. (1993). Peer tutoring effects on the classroom performance of children with attention deficit disorder. *Journal of the American Academy of Child and Adolescent Psychiatry, 32,* 190–198.

DuPaul, G. J., Rapport, M. D., & Perriello, L. (1991). Teacher ratings of academic skills: The development of the Academic Performance Rating Scale. *School Psychology Review, 20,* 284–300.

DuPaul, G. J., & Stoner, G. (2003). *ADHD in the schools* (2nd ed.). New York: Guilford Press.

Durlak, J. A., & Wells, A. M. (1997). Primary prevention mental health programs for children and adolescents: A meta-analytic review. *American Journal of Community Psychology, 25,* 115–152.

Dweck, C. S. (1975). The role of expectations and attributions in alleviation of learned helplessness. *Journal of Personality and Social Psychology, 31,* 674–685.

Dwyer, K., Osher, D., & Warger, C. (1998). *Early warning, timely response: A guide to safe schools.* Washington, DC: U.S. Department of Education.

D'Zurilla, R. (1986). *Problem-solving approaches to therapy.* New York: Springer.

Eaves, L. J., Rutter, M., Silberg, J. L., Shillady, L., Maes, H., & Pickles, A. (2000). Genetic and environmental causes of covariation in interview assessments of disruptive behavior in child and adolescent twins. *Behavioral Genetics, 30,* 321–334.

Eccles, J. S., & Blumenfeld, P. (1985). Classroom experiences and student gender: Are there differences and do they matter. In L. C. Wilkinson & C. B. Marrett (Eds.), *Gender influences in classroom interaction* (pp. 79–114). Orlando, FL: Academic Press.

Eddy, J. M., Leve, L. D., & Fagot, B. I. (2001). Coercive family processes: A replication and extension of Patterson's coercion model. *Aggressive Behavior, 27,* 14–25.

Edelbrock, C. (1989). *Childhood conduct problems: Developmental consideration and a proposed taxonomy.* Unpublished manuscript, University of Massachusetts Medical Center, Worcester.

Edelbrock, C. (1990). Childhood Attention Problems (CAP) Scale. In R. A. Barkley (Ed.), *Attention-deficit hyperactivity disorder: A handbook for diagnosis and treatment* (pp. 320–321). New York: Guilford Press.

Edelsohn, G., Ialongo, N., Werthamer-Larsson, L., Crockett, L., & Kellam, S. (1992). Self-reported depressive symptoms in first-grade children: Developmentally transient phenomena? *Journal of the American Academy of Child and Adolescent Psychiatry, 31,* 282–290.

Edwards, R. P. (2002). A tutorial for using the Functional Assessment Informant Record—Teachers (FAIR-T). *Proven Practice: Prevention and Remediation Solutions for Schools, 4,* 31–38.

Eiraldi, R. B., Power, T. J., & Nezu, C. M. (1997). Patterns of comorbidity associated with subtypes of attention deficit/hyperactivity disorder among 6- to 12-year-old children. *Journal of the American Academy of Child and Adolescent Psychiatry, 36,* 503–514.

Eisenberg, L. (1958). School phobia: A study in the communication of anxiety. *American Journal of Psychiatry, 114,* 712–718.

Eisenberg, N., Guthrie, I. K., Fabes, R. A., Shephard, S., Losoya, S., Murphy, B. C., et al. (2000). Prediction of elementary school children's externalizing problem behaviors from attentional and behavioral regulation and negative emotionality. *Child Development, 71,* 1367–1382.

Elias, M. J., Parker, S., & Rosenblatt, J. L. (2005). Building educational opportunity. In S. Goldstein & R. B. Brooks (Eds.), *Handbook of resilience in children* (pp. 315–336). New York: Kluwer Academic/Plenum Press.

Elias, M. J., & Tobias, S. E. (1996). *Social problem solving: Interventions in schools.* New York: Guilford Press.

Elias, M. J., Zins, J. E., Graczyk, P. A., & Weissberg, R. B. (2003). Implementation, sustainability and scaling up of social, emotional and academic innovations in public schools. *School Psychology Review, 32,* 303–319.

Elliott, D. S., & Menard, S. (1996). Delinquent friends and delinquent behavior: Temporal and developmental patterns. In J. D. Hawkins (Ed.), *Delinquency and crime: Current theories* (pp. 28–67). New York: Cambridge University Press.

Elliott, S. N. (1986). Children's ratings of the acceptability of classroom interventions for misbehavior: Findings and methodological considerations. *Journal of School Psychology, 24,* 23–35.

Elliott, S. N. (1988). Acceptability of behavioral treatments: Review of variables that influence treatment selection. *Professional Psychology: Research and Practice, 19,* 68–80.

Elliott, S. N., & Busse, R. T. (1991). Social skills assessment and intervention with children and adolescents. *School Psychology International, 12,* 63–83.

Elliott, S. N., Racine, C. N., & Busse, R. T. (1995). Best practices in pre-school social skills training. In A. Thomas & J. Grimes (Eds.), *Best practices in school psychology* (3rd ed., pp. 1009–1020). Washington, DC: National Association of School Psychologists.

Elliott, S. N., Turco, T. L., & Gresham, F. M. (1987). Consumers' and clients' pretreatment acceptability ratings of classroom-based group contingencies. *Journal of School Psychology, 25,* 145–154.

Elliott, S. N., Witt, J. C., Galvin, G., & Moe, G. L. (1986). Children's involvement in intervention selection: Acceptability of interventions for misbehaving peers. *Professional Psychology: Research and practice, 17,* 235–241.

Ellis, A. (1962). *Reason and emotion in psychotherapy.* New York: Lyle Stuart.

Ellis, A. W. (1985). The cognitive neuropsychology of development (and acquired) dyslexia: A critical survey. *Cognitive Neuropsychology, 2,* 169–205.

Emblem, D. L. (1979). For a disciplinarian's manual. *Phi Delta Kappan, 50,* 339–340.

Emmer, E. T., Evertson, C. M., & Anderson, L. M. (1980). Effective management at the beginning of the school year. *Elementary School Journal, 80,* 219–231.

Emslie, G. J., Weinberg, W. A., Kennard, B. D., & Kowatch, R. A. (1994). Neurobiological aspects of depression in children and adolescents. In W. M. Reynolds & H. E. Johnston (Eds.), *Handbook of depression in children and adolescents* (pp. 143–165). New York: Plenum Books.

References

Epstein, J. (1987). What principals should know about parent involvement. *Principal*, 66, 6–9.

Epstein, M. H., Singh, N. N., Luebke, J., & Stout, C. E. (1991). Psychopharmacological intervention: Pt. II. Teacher perceptions of psychotropic medication for students with learning disabilities. *Journal of Learning Disabilities*, 24, 477–483.

Erchul, W. P., Raven, B. H., & Wilson, K. E. (2004). The relationship between gender of consultant and social power perceptions within school consultation. *School Psychology Review*, 33(4), 582–590.

Erchul, W. P., Sheridan, S. M., Ryan, D. A., Grissom, P. F., Killough, C. E., & Mettler, D. W. (1999). Patterns of relational communication in conjoint behavioral consultation. *School Psychology Quarterly*, 14(2), 121–147.

Erickson, E. H. (1963). *Childhood in society*. New York: Norton.

Eslinger, P. J. (1996). Conceptualizing, describing, and measuring componets of executive function: A summary. In G. R. Lyon & N. A. Krasnegor (Eds.), *Attention, memory, and executive function* (pp. 367–396). Baltimore: Paul H. Brookes.

Espelage, D. L., & Swearer, S. M. (2004). *Bullying in American schools: A social-ecological perspective on prevention and intervention*. Mahwah, NJ: Erlbaum.

Evans, J. R., Velsor, P. V., & Schumacher, J. E. (2002). Addressing adolescent depression: A role for school counselors. *Professional School Counseling*, 5, 211–220.

Evertson, C. M., Emmer, E. T., Clements, B. S., Sanford, J. P., & Worsham, M. E. (1984). *Classroom management for elementary teachers*. Englewood Clifts, NJ: Prentice-Hall.

Fantuzzo, J. W., Rohrbeck, C. A., Hightower, A. D., & Work, W. C. (1991). Teachers' use and children's preferences of rewards in elementary school. *Psychology in the Schools*, 28, 175–181.

Faraone, S. V., & Biederman, J. (2005). What is the prevalence of adult ADHD? Results of a population screen of 966 adults. *Journal of Attention Disorders*, 9(2), 384–391.

Faraone, S. V., Biederman, J., & Friedman, D. (2000). Validity of DSM-IV subtypes of attention-deficit/hyperactivity disorder: A family study perspective. *Journal of the American Academy of Child and Adolescent Psychiatry*, 59, 300–307.

Faraone, S. V., Biederman, J., & Zimmerman, B. (2005). Correspondence of parent and teacher reports in medication trials. *European Child and Adolescent Psychiatry*, 14, 20–27.

Farkas, G. M., Sherick, R. B., Matson, J. L., & Loebig, M. (1981). Social skills training of a blind child through differential reinforcement. *Behavior Therapist*, 4(2), 24–26.

Farmer, A. D., Bierman, K. L., & the Conduct Problems Prevention Research Group. (2002). Predictors of behavioral problems in young children. *Journal of Clinical Child and Adolescent Psychology*, 31, 299–311.

Farrington, D. P. (1995). The development of offending and antisocial behavior from childhood: Key findings from the Cambridge study in delinquent program. *Journal of Child Psychology and Psychiatry*, 36, 929–964.

Favell, J. E. (1977). *The power of positive reinforcement: A handbook of behavioral modification*. Springfield, IL: Charles C Thomas.

FDA Hearings. (2006, March 22). Presented at pediatric subcommittee review on stimulant medication and cardiovascular risks, Washington, DC.

Feighner, J. P., Robins, E., Swodenbe, R., Guze, S. B., Woodruff, R. A., Winokur, G., et al. (1972). Diagnostic criteria for use in psychiatric research. *Archives of General Psychiatry*, 26, 57–62.

Fein, D., Pennington, B., Markowitz, P., Braverman, M., & Waterhouse, L. (1986). Toward a neuropsychological model or infantile autism: Are the social deficits primary? *Journal of the American Academy of Child Psychiatry, 25,* 198–212.

Fein, D., Pennington, B., & Waterhouse, L. (1987). Implications of social deficits in autism for neurological dysfunction. In E. Schopler & G. B. Mesibov (Eds.), *Neurobiological issues in autism* (pp. 107–125). New York: Plenum Press.

Feindler, E. L. (1991). Cognitive strategies in anger control interventions for children and adolescents. In P. C. Kendall (Ed.), *Child and adolescent therapy: Cognitive-behavioral procedures.* New York: Guilford Press.

Feindler, E. L., & Ecton, R. B. (1986). *Adolescent anger control: Cognitive-behavioral techniques.* Elmsford, NY: Pergamon Press.

Feis, C. L., & Simons, C. (1985). Training preschool children in interpersonal cognitive problem solving skills: A replication. *Prevention in Human Services, 14,* 59–70.

Fergusson, D. M., Horwood, L. J., & Lynskey, M. T. (1994). Structure of DSM-III-R criteria for disruptive childhood behaviors: Confirmatory factor models. *Journal of the American Academy of Child and Adolescent Psychiatry, 33,* 1145–1155.

Fergusson, D. M., & Lynskey, M. T. (1998). Conduct problems in childhood and psychosocial outcomes in young adulthood: A prospective study. *Journal of Emotional and Behavioral Disorders, 6,* 2–18.

Fergusson, D. M., Lynskey, M. T., & Horwood, L. J. (1996). Factors associated with continuity and change in disruptive behavior patterns between childhood and adolescence. *Journal of Abnormal Child Psychology, 24,* 533–553.

Fergusson, D. M., Lynskey, M. T., & Horwood, L. J. (1997). Attentional difficulties in middle childhood and psychosocial outcomes in young adulthood. *Journal of Child Psychology and Psychiatry, 38,* 633–644.

Fernell, E., Gillberg, C., & von Wendt, L. (1990). Autistic symptoms in children with infantile hydrocephalus. *Acta Paediatrica Scandinavica, 42,* 706–771.

Feshbach, N. D., & Feshbach, S. (1969). The relationship between empathy and aggression in two age groups. *Developmental Psychology, 1,* 102–107.

Finch, A. J., & Montgomery, L. E. (1973). Reflection-impulsivity and information seeking in emotionally disturbed children. *Journal of Abnormal Child Psychology, 1,* 358–362.

Fischbach, S., & Fishbach, N. (1973). Alternatives to corporal punishment. *Journal of Clinical Psychology, 2,* 111–131.

Fischer, M., Barkley, R. A., Fletcher, C. S., & Smallish, L. (1990). The adolescent outcome of hyperactive children diagnosed by research criteria: Pt. II. Academic, attentional, and neuropsychological status. *Journal of Consulting and Clinical Psychology, 58,* 580–588.

Fisher, S. E., Francks, C., McCracken, J. T., McGough, J. J., Marlow, A. J., MacPhie, L., et al. (2002). A genomewide scan for loci involved in ADHD. *American Journal of Human Genetics, 70,* 1183–1196.

Flament, M. F., Whitaker, A., Rapoport, J. L., Davies, M., Berg, C. Z., Kalikow, K., et al. (1988). Obsessive compulsive disorder in adolescence: An epidemiological study. *Journal of the American Academy of Child and Adolescent Psychiatry, 27,* 764–771.

Folstein, S., & Rutter, M. (1977). Infantile autism: A genetic study of 21 twin pairs. *Journal of Child Psychology and Psychiatry, 18,* 297–321.

Fonagy, P., Steele, M., Steele, H., Higgitt, A., & Target, M. (1994). The Emmanuel Miller Memorial Lecture, 1992: The theory and practice of resilience. *Journal of Child Psychology and Psychiatry, 35,* 231–257.

Forehand, R., & McMahon, R. (1981). *Helping the non-compliant child*. New York: Guilford Press.

Fotheringham, J. B. (1991). Autism: Its primary psychological and neurological deficit. *Canadian Journal of Psychiatry, 36,* 686–692.

Fox, J. J., & McEvoy, M. A. (1993). Assessing and enhancing generalization and social validity of social-skills interventions with children and adolescents. *Behavior Modification, 17,* 339–366.

Foxx, R. M. (1996). Twenty years of applied behavior analysis in treating the most severe problem behavior: Lessons learned. *Behavior Analysis, 20,* 421–425.

Foxx, R. M., & Azrin, N. H. (1972). Restitution: A method of eliminating aggressive, disruptive behaviors of retarded and brain damaged patients. *Behavior Research and Therapy, 10,* 15–27.

Foxx, R. M., & Shapiro, S. T. (1978). A time-out ribbon: A new exclusionary time out procedure. *Journal of Applied Behavioral Analysis, 11,* 125–136.

Francis, G., Last, C. G., & Strauss, C. C. (1987). Expression of separation anxiety disorder: The roles of age and gender. *Child Psychiatry Human Development, 18,* 82–89.

Freud, A. (1965). *Normality and pathology in childhood: The writrings of Anna Freud 6.* New York: International Universities Press.

Frick, P. J. (1994). Family dysfunction and the disruptive behavior disorders: A review of recent empirical findings. *Advances in Clinical Child Psychology, 16,* 203–226.

Frick, P. J., Lahey, B. B., & Loeber, R. (1993). Oppositional defiant disorder and conduct disorder: A meta-analytic review of factor analyses and cross-validation in a clinical sample. *Clinical Psychology Review, 13,* 319–340.

Fried, R. (1995). *The passionate teacher.* Boston: Beacon Press.

Fried, S., & Fried, P. (1996). *Bullies and victims: Helping your child through the schoolyard battlefield.* New York: M. Evans and Company.

Friedman, E. (1969). The autistic syndrome and phenylketonuria. *Schizophrenia, 1,* 249–261.

Furman, W. (1980). Promoting social development: Developmental implications for treatment. In B. B. Lahey & A. E. Kazdin (Eds.), *Advances in clinical child psychology* (Vol. 3, pp. 1–40). New York: Plenum Press.

Gadow, K. D. (1983). Educating teachers about pharmacotherapy. *Education and Training of the Mentally Retarded, 18,* 69–73.

Gadow, K. D., Sprafkin, J., & Nolan, E. E. (1996). *ADHD school observation code.* Stony Brook, NY: Checkmate Plus.

Gadow, K. D., Sprafkin, J., & Nolan, E. (2001). DSM-IV symptoms in community and clinic preschool children. *Journal of the American Academy of Child and Adolescent Psychiatry, 40,* 1383–1392.

Gaffney, G. R., Kuperman, S., Tsai, L. Y., & Minchin, S. (1988). Morphological evidence for brainstem involvement in infantile autism. *Biological Psychiatry, 24,* 578–586.

Gaffney, G. R., & Tsai, L. Y. (1987). Brief report: Magnetic resonance imaging of high level autism. *Journal of Autism and Developmental Disorders, 17*(3), 433–438.

Gallagher, R., Fleiss, K., Etkovich, J., Cousins, L., Greenfield, B., Martin, D., et al. (2004). Social functioning in children with ADHD treated with long-term methylphenidate and multi-modal psychosocial treatment. *Journal of the American Academy of Child and Adolescent Psychiatry, 43,* 820–829.

Gallup, A. (1984). The Gallup poll of teachers' attitudes toward the public schools. *Phi Delta Kappan, 66,* 97–107.

Gallup. (2005). *PDK/Gallup polls of the public's attitudes toward the public schools: PDK/ Gallup poll resources.* Available from http://www.pdkintl.org/kappan/kpollpdf/htm.

Gammon, G. D., John, K., Rothblum, E. D., Mullen, K., Tischler, G. L., & Weissman, M. M. (1983). Use of a structure diagnostic interview to identify bipolar disorder in adolescent inpatients: Frequency and manifestation of the disorder. *American Journal of Psychiatry, 140,* 43–547.

Garbarino, J. (1992). The meaning of poverty in the world of children. *American Behavioral Scientist, 35,* 220–237.

Garbarino, J., & deLara, E. (2002). *And words can hurt forever: How to protect adolescents from bullying, harassment, and emotional violence.* New York: Free Press.

Garber, J., & Dodge, K. A. (Eds.). (1991). *The development of emotional regulation and dysregulation.* New York: Cambridge University Press.

Gardner, H. (1983). *Frames of mind.* New York: Basic Books.

Garrity, C., Jens, K., Porter, W., Sager, N., & Short-Camilli, C. (1996). *Bully proofing your school.* Longmont, CO: Sopris West.

Garrity, C., Jens., K., Porter, W., & Stoker, S. (2002). Bullying in schools: A review of prevention programs. In S. E. Brock, P. J. Lazarus, & S. R. Jimerson (Eds.), *Best practices in school crisis prevention and intervention.* Bethesda, MD: National Association of School Psychologists.

Gelfan, D. M., & Hartmann, D. P. (1984). *Child behavior analysis and therapy* (2nd ed.). New York: Pergamon Press.

Geller, B., Chestnut, E. C., Miller, M. D., Price, D. T., & Yates, E. (1985). Preliminary data on DSM-III associated features of major depression disorder in children and adolescents. *American Journal of Psychiatry, 142,* 643–644.

Geller, B., Rogel, A., & Knitter, E. (1983). Preliminary data on the dexamethasone suppression text in children with major depressive disorders. *American Journal of Psychiatry, 140,* 620–622.

Gerber, M. M., & Semmel, M. I. (1984). Teacher as imperfect test: Reconceptualizing the referral process. *Educational Psychologist, 19,* 137–148.

Gershoff, E. T. (2002). Parental corporal punishment and associated child behaviors and experiences: A meta-analytic and theoretical review. *Psychological Bulletin, 128,* 580–589.

Gersten, R., Walker, H. M., & Darch, C. (1988). Relationship between teachers' effectiveness and their tolerance for handicap students: An exploratory study. *Exceptional Children, 54,* 433–438.

Gettinger, M. (1988). Methods of proactive classroom management. *School Psychology Review, 17,* 227–242.

Geurts, H. M., Verte, S., Oosterlaan, J., Roeyers, H., & Sergeant, J. A. (2005). ADHD subtypes: Do they differ in their executive functioning profile? *Archives of Clinical Neuropsychology, 20,* 457–477.

Gibbs, D. P., & Cooper, E. B. (1989). Prevalence of communication disorders in students with learning disabilities. *Journal of Learning Disabilities, 22,* 60–63.

Gillberg, C. (1986). Autism and Rett syndrome: Some notes on differential diagnosis. *American Journal of Medical Genetics, 24*(Suppl. 1), 127–131.

Gillberg, C. (1988). The neurobiology of infantile autism. *Journal of Child Psychology and Psychiatry, 29,* 257–266.

References

Gillberg, C. (1989). The role of the endogenous opioids in autism and possible relationships to clinical features. In L. Wing (Ed.), *Aspects of autism: Biological research* (pp. 31–37). London: Gaskell/National Autistic Society.

Gillberg, C. (1990). Autism and the pervasive developmental disorders. *Journal of the American Academy of Child and Adolescent Psychiatry, 31*(1), 99–119.

Gillberg, C., & Akefeldt, A. (1990). *Autism and hypomelanosis of Ito.* Manuscript submitted for publication.

Gillberg, C., & Coleman, N. (1993). *Biology of the autistic syndromes* (2nd ed.). London: Cambridge University Press.

Gillberg, C., Ehlers, S., Schaumann, H., Jakobsson, G., Dahlgren, S. O., Lindbolm, R., et al. (1990). Autism under age 3 years: A clinical study of 28 cases referred for autistic symptoms in infancy. *Journal of Child Psychology and Psychiatry, 31*, 921–934.

Gillberg, C., & Forsell, C. (1984). Childhood psychososi and neurofibromatosis— More than a coincidence. *Journal of Autism and Developmental Disorders, 14*, 1–9.

Gillberg, C., & Gillberg, I. C. (1989). Infantile autism: A total population study of reduced optimality in the pre-, peri-, and neonatal period. *Journal of Autism and Developmental Disorders, 13*, 163–166.

Gillberg, C., & Schaumann, H. (1982). Infantile autism in puberty. *Journal of Autism and Developmental Disorders, 11*, 365–371.

Gillberg, C., & Steffenburg, S. (1987). Outcome and prognostic factors in infantile autism and similar conditions: A population based study of 46 cases followed through puberty. *Journal of Autism and Developmental Disorders, 17*, 271–285.

Gillberg, C., & Steffenburg, S. (1989). Autistic behavior in Moebius syndrome. *Acta Paediatrica Scandinavica, 78*, 314–316.

Gillberg, C., Steffenburg, S., & Jakobsson, B. (1987). Neurobiological findings in 20 relatively gifted children with Kanner-type autism or Asperger syndrome. *Developmental Medicine and Child Neurology, 29*, 641–649.

Gillberg, C., & Svendsen, P. (1983). Childhood psychosis and computer tomographic brain scan findings. *Journal of Autism and Developmental Disorders, 13*, 19–32.

Gillberg, C., & Svennerholm, L. (1987). CSF monoamines in autistic syndrome and other pervasive developmental disorders of early childhood. *British Journal of Psychiatry, 151*, 89–94.

Gillberg, C., Terenius, L., Hagberg, B., Witt-Engerström, I., & Eriksson, I. (1990). CSF-beta-endorphins in child neuropsychiatric disorders. *Brain and Development, 12*, 88–92.

Gillberg, C., & Wahlström, J. (1985). Chromosome abnormalities in infantile autism and other childhood psychoses: A population study of 66 cases. *Developmental Medicine and Child Neurology, 27*, 293–304.

Gillberg, I. C., & Gillberg, C. (1989). Asperger syndrome: Some epidemiological considerations. *Journal of Child Psychology and Psychiatry, 30*, 631–638.

Gilman, R., & Gabriel, S. (2004). Perceptions of school psychological services by education professionals: Results from a multi-state survey pilot study. *School Psychology Review, 33*(2), 271–286.

Gittelman, R. (1984). Anxiety disorders in childhood. *Psychiatry Update, 3*, 410–418.

Gittelman, R., & Klein, D. F. (1984). Relationship between separation anxiety and panic and agoraphobic disorders. *Psychopathology, 17*, 56–65.

Gittelman, R., Mannuzza, S., Shenker, R., & Bonagura, N. (1985). Hyperactive boys almost grown up: Pt. 1. Psychiatric status. *Archives of General Psychiatry, 42*, 937–947.

Glasgow, K. L., Dornbusch, S. M., Troyer, L., Steinberg, L., & Ritter, P. L. (1997). Parenting styles, adolescent's attributions and educational outcomes in nine heterogenous high schools. *Child Development, 68,* 507–529.

Glasser, W. (1969). *Schools without failure.* New York: Harper & Row.

Glasser, W. (1997). A new look at school failure. *Phi Delta Kappan, 78,* 596–602.

Glow, R. A., & Glow, P. H. (1980). Peer and self-rating: Children's perception of behavior relevant to hyperkinetic impulse disorder. *Journal of Abnormal Psychology, 8,* 471–490.

Gnagey, W. (1968). *A psychology of discipline in the classroom.* New York: Macmillan.

Goenjian, A. K. (1993). A mental health relief programme in Armenia after the 1988 earthquake: Implementation and clinical observations. *British Journal of Psychiatry, 163,* 230–239.

Goenjian, A. K., Karayan, I., Pynoos, R. S., Minassian, D., Najarian, L. M., Steinberg, A. M., et al. (1997). Outcome of psychotherapy among early adolescents after trauma. *American Journal of Psychiatry, 154,* 536–542.

Goldberg, E. (2001). *The executive brain: Frontal lobes and the civilized mind.* New York: Oxford University Press.

Goldstein, A. P., Sprafkin, R. P., Gershaw, N. J., & Klein, P. (1980). *Skillstreaming the adolescent.* Champaign, IL: Research Press.

Goldstein, S. (2002). Continuity of ADHD in adulthood: Hypothesis and theory meets reality. In S. Goldstein & A. T. Ellison (Eds.), *Clinician's guide to adult ADHD: Assessment and intervention.* New York: Academic Press.

Goldstein, S., & Brooks, R. (Eds.). (2005). *Handbook of resilience in children.* New York: Springer.

Goldstein, S., & Ellison, A. T. (2002). *Clinician's guide to adult ADHD: Assessment and intervention.* New York: Academic Press.

Goldstein, S., & Goldstein, M. (1990). *Understanding and managing attention deficit disorder in children: A practitioner's guide.* New York: Wiley.

Goldstein, S., & Goldstein, M. (1991). Home notes. From User's Manual, *It's Just Attention Disorder* [videotape] by S. Goldstein and M. Goldstein. Salt Lake City, UT: Neurology, Learning and Behavior Center.

Goldstein, S., & Goldstein, M. (1998). *Understanding and managing attention deficit hyperactivity disorder in children: A guide for practitioners* (2nd ed.). New York: Wiley.

Goldstein, S., & Gordon, M. (2003). Gender issues and ADHD: Sorting fact from fiction. *ADHD Report, 11*(4), 7–11.

Goldstein, S., Hagar, K., & Brooks, R. (2002). *Seven steps to help your child worry less.* Plantation, FL: Specialty Press.

Goldstein, S., & Schwebach, A. (2005). Attention deficit disorder in adults. In S. Goldstein & C. Reynolds (Eds.), *Handbook of neurodevelopmental and genetic disorders in adults.* New York: Guilford Press.

Goldstein, S., & Turner, D. (2001). The extent of drug therapy for ADHD among children in a large public school district. *Journal of Attention Disorders, 4,* 212–219.

Goleman, D. (1995). *Emotional intelligence.* New York: Bantam Books.

Good, T., & Brophy, J. (1973). *Looking in classrooms.* New York: Harper & Row.

Goodman, S. H., & Gotlib, I. H. (1999). Risk for psychopathology in the children of depressed mothers. *Psychological Review, 106,* 458–490.

Gootman, M. (2001). *Caring teacher's guide to discipline* (2nd ed.). Thousand Oaks, CA: Corwin Press.

Gordon, M., Antshel, K., Faraone, S., Barkley, R., Lewandowski, L., Hudziak, J., et al. (2006). Symptoms versus impairment: The case for respecting DSM-IV's Criterion D. *Journal of Attention Disorders, 9*(3), 465–475.

Gordon, T. (1974). *Teacher effectiveness training.* New York: Peter H. Wyden.

Gotlib, I. H., & Hammen, C. L. (2002). *Handbook of depression.* New York: Guilford Press.

Gottfredson, G. D., Gottfredson, D. C., Payne, A. A., & Gottfredson, N. C. (2005). School climate predictors of school disorder: Results from a national study of delinquency prevention in schools. *Journal of Research in Crime and Delinquency, 42*(4), 412–444.

Gottman, J. M., Gonso, J., & Schuler, P. (1976). Teaching social skills to isolated children. *Journal of Abnormal Child Psychology, 4,* 179–197.

Graetz, B. W., Sawyer, M. G., Hazell, P. L., Amey, F. M., & Baghurst, P. A. (2001). Validity of DSM-IV ADHD subtypes in a nationally representative sample of Australian children and adolescents. *Journal of the American Academy of Child and Adolescent Psychiatry, 40,* 1410–1417.

Graham, D. S. (1998). Consultant effectiveness and treatment acceptability: An examination of consultee requests and consultant responses. *School Psychology Quarterly, 13*(2), 155–168.

Graham, S., & Harris, K. R. (1996). Addressing problems in attention, memory, and executive functioning: An example from self-regulated strategy development. In G. R. Lyon & N. A. Krasnegor (Eds.), *Attention, memory, and executive function* (pp. 349–365). Baltimore: Paul H. Brookes.

Gray, C. (1995). Teaching children with autism to "read" social situations. In K. Quill (Ed.), *Teaching children with autism: Strategies to enhance communication and socialization* (pp. 219–242). New York: Delmar.

Gray, C., & Garland, J. D. (1993). Social stories: Improving responses of students with autism with accurate social information. *Focus on Autistic Behavior, 8,* 1–10.

Graziano, A. M., DeGiorann, I., & Garcia, K. (1979). Behavioral treatment of child's fear. *Psychological Bulletin, 56,* 804–830.

Greenberg, M. R., Kusche, C. A., Cook, E. T., & Quammen, J. (1995). Promoting emotional competence in school-aged deaf children: The effects of the PATHS curriculum. *Developmental Psychopathology, 7,* 117–136.

Greene, R. W., Biederman, J., Faraone, S. V., Sienna, M., & Garcia-Jones, J. (1997). Adolescent outcome of boys with attention-deficit/hyperactivity disorder and social disability: Results from a 4-year longitudinal follow-up study. *Journal of Consulting and Clinical Psychology, 65,* 758–767.

Greenwood, C. R., Hops, H., Delquadri, J., & Guild, J. (1974). Group contingencies for group consequences in classroom management: A further analysis. *Journal of Applied Behavior Analysis, 7,* 103–114.

Greenwood, C. R., Sloane, H. N., Jr., & Baskin, A. (1974). Training elementary aged peer behavior managers to control small group programmed mathematic. *Journal of Applied Behavior Analysis, 7,* 103–114.

Gresham, F. M. (1979). Comparison of response cost and time-out in special education setting. *Journal of Special Education, 13,* 199–208.

Gresham, F. M. (1985). Utility of cognitive-behavioral procedures for social skills training with children: A review. *Journal of Abnormal Child Psychology, 13,* 411–423.

Gresham, F. M. (1986). Conceptual issues in the assessment of social competence in children. In P. S. Strain, M. J. Guralnick, & H. M. Walker (Eds.), *Children's social behavior: Development, assessment, and modification* (pp. 143–179). New York: Academic Press.

Gresham, F. M. (1995). Best practices in social skills assessment. In A. Thomas & J. Grimes (Eds.), *Best practices in school psychology-III* (pp. 1021–1030). Washington, DC: National Association of School Psychologists.

Gresham, F. M. (1997). Social competence and students with behavioral disorders: Where we've been, where we are, and where we should go. *Education and Treatment of Children, 20,* 233–249.

Gresham, F. M., & Elliott, S. N. (1984). Assessment and classification of children's social skills: A review of methods and issues. *School Psychology Review, 13,* 292–301.

Gresham, F. M., & Elliott, S. N. (1990). *Social skills rating system: Manual.* Circle Pines, MN: American Guidance Services.

Gresham, F. M., & Kendell, G. K. (1987). School consultation research: Methodological critiques and future research directions. *School Psychology Review, 16,* 306–316.

Gresham, F. M., & Nagle, R. J. (1980). Social skills training with children: Responsiveness to modeling and coaching as a function of peer orientation. *Journal of Consulting and Clinical Psychology, 48,* 718–729.

Gresham, F. M., Sugai, G., & Horner, R. H. (2001). Interpreting outcomes of social skills training for students with high-incidence disabilities. *Exceptional Children, 67,* 331–344.

Griest, D. L., Forehand, R., Rogers, T., Breiner, J. L., Furey, W., & Williams, C. A. (1982). Effects of parent enhancement therapy on the treatment outcome and generalization of a parent training program. *Behavior Research and Therapy, 20,* 429–436.

Gross, A. M., & Eckstrand, M. (1983). Increasing and maintaining rates of teacher praise. *Behavior Modification, 7,* 126–135.

Grossman, H. (1990). *Trouble-free teaching: Solutions to behavior problems in the classroom.* Mountain View, CA: Mayfield.

Guerra, N. G., Huesmann, L. R., Tolan, P. H., Van Acker, R., & Eron, L. D. (1995). Stressful events and individual beliefs as correlates of economic disadvantage and aggression among urban children. *Journal of Consulting Clinical Psychology, 63,* 518–528.

Guevremont, D. C., DuPaul, G. J., & Barkley, R. A. (1993). Behavioral assessment of attention deficit hyperactivity disorder. In J. L. Matson (Ed.), *Handbook of hyperactivity in children.* Needham Heights, MA: Allyn & Bacon.

Guralnick, M. J. (1993). Developmentally appropriate practice in the assessment and intervention of children's peer relations. *Topics in Early Childhood Special Education, 13,* 344–371.

Guralnick, M. J. (1997). Second-generation research in the field of early intervention. In M. J. Guralnick (Ed.), *The effectiveness of early intervention* (pp. 3–20). Baltimore: Paul H. Brookes.

Guralnick, M. J., & Neville, B. (1997). Designing early intervention programs to promote children's social competence. In M. J. Guralnick (Ed.), *The effectiveness of early intervention* (pp. 579–610). Baltimore: Paul H. Brookes.

Gutkin, T. B., & Curtis, M. (1990). School-based consultation: Theory, techniques, and research. In T. B. Gutkin & C. R. Reynolds (Eds.), *The handbook of school psychology* (2nd ed., pp. 577–611). New York: Wiley.

Gutkin, T. B., & Hickman, J. A. (1988). Teachers' perceptions of control over presenting problems and resulting preferences for consultation versus referral services. *Journal of School Psychology, 26,* 395–398.

Haddad, F. A., Garcia, Y. E., Naglieri, J. A., Grimditch, M., McAndrews, A., & Eubanks, J. (2003). Planning facilitation and reading comprehension: Instructional relevance of the PASS theory. *Journal of Psychoeducational Assessment, 21,* 282–289.

Hagerman, R. (1990). Genes, chromosomes and autism. In C. Gillberg (Ed.), *Autism: Diagnosis and treatment* (pp. 105–132). New York: Plenum Press.

Hagerman, R. (1991). Organic causes of ADHD. *ADD-VANCE, 3,* 4–6.

Haggerty, N. K., Black, R. S., & Smith, G. J. (2005). Increasing self-managed coping skills through social stories and apron storytelling. *Teaching Exceptional Children, 37,* 40–47.

Hall, B. W., Hines, C. V., Bacon, T. P., & Koulianos, G. M. (1992, April). *Attributions that teachers hold to account for student success and failure and their relationship to teaching level and teacher efficacy beliefs.* Paper presented at the annual meeting of the American Educational Research Association, San Francisco.

Hall, R. V., & Hall, M. C. (1980). *How to use planned ignoring.* Austin, TX: ProEd.

Hall, R. V., & Hall, M. C. (1982). *How to negotiate behavioral contracts.* Austin, TX: ProEd.

Hallahan, D., Lloyd, J., Kauffman, J., & Loper, A. (1983). Academic problems. In R. Morris & T. Kratochwill (Eds.), *Practice of child therapy: A textbook of methods* (pp. 113–141). New York: Pergamon Press.

Halperin, J. M., Newcorn, J. H., Matier, K., Sharma, V., McKay, K. E., & Schwartz, S. (1993). Discriminant validity of attention-deficit hyperactivity disorder. *Journal of the American Academy of Child and Adolescent Psychiatry, 32,* 1038–1043.

Hammen, C. (1990). Cognitive approaches to depression in children: Current findings and new directions. In B. B. Lahey & A. E. Kazdin (Eds.), *Advances in clinical child psychology.* New York: Plenum Press.

Hammen, C., Burge, D., Burney, E., & Adrian, C. (1990). Longitudinal study of diagnoses in children of women with unipolar and bipolar affective disorder. *Archives of General Psychiatry, 47,* 1112–1117.

Hammen, C., & Rudolph, K. D. (2003). Childhood mood disorders. In E. J. Mash & R. A. Barkley (Eds.), *Child psychopathology* (2nd ed., pp. 233–278). New York: Guilford Press.

Hamre, B., & Pianta, R. C. (1999). *Early teacher-child relationships and the trajectory of children's school outcomes through eighth grade.* Manuscript submitted for publication.

Hankin, B. L., Abramson, L. Y., Moffitt, T. E., Silva, P. A., McGee, R., & Angell, K. E. (1998). Development of depression from preadolescence to young adulthood: Emerging gender differences in a 10-year longitudinal study. *Journal of Abnormal Psychology, 107,* 128–140.

Hansen, D. J., & Lignugaris-Kraft, B. (2005). Effects of a dependent group contingency on the verbal interactions of middle school students with emotional disturbance. *Journal of Behavioral Disorders, 30,* 169–185.

Haring, T. G. (1992). The context of social competence: Relations, relationships, and generalization. In S. L. Odom, S. R. McConnell, & M. A. McEvoy (Eds.), *Social competence of young children with disabilities: Issues and strategies for intervention* (pp. 307–320). Baltimore: Paul H. Brookes.

Harrier, L. K., & DeOrnellas, K. (2005). Performance of children diagnosed with ADHD on selected planning and reconstitution tests. *Applied Neuropsychology, 12,* 106–119.

Harrington, R., Fudge, H., Rutter, M., Pickles, A., & Hill, J. (1990). Adult outcome of childhood and adolescent depression: Pt. I. Psychiatric status. *Archives of General Psychiatry, 47*, 465–473.

Harris, G. (2005, September 15). Use of attention-deficit drugs is found to soar among adults. *New York Times*, A14.

Harris, K. R. (1985). Definitional, parametric, and procedural consideration in time-out interventions and research. *Exceptional Children, 451*, 279–288.

Harris, K. R. (1986). Self-monitoring of attentional behavior versus self-monitoring of productivity: Effects on on-task behavior and academic response rates among learning disabled children. *Journal of Applied Behavior Analysis, 19*, 417–423.

Harris, K. R. (1990). Developing self-regulated learners: The role of private speech and self-instructions. *Educational Psychologist, 25*, 35–50.

Harris, S. L., & Ferrari, M. (1983). Developmental factors in child behavior therapy. *Behavior Therapy, 14*, 54–72.

Hart, C. C., & Harter, S. L. (2001, October/November). *Measurement of right frontal lobe functioning and ADHD*. Abstracts from the 21st annual meeting of the National Academy of Neuropsychology.

Hart, C. H., DeWolf, D. M., Wozniak, P., & Burts, D. C. (1992). Maternal and paternal disciplinary styles: Relations with preschoolers' playground behavioral orientations and peer status. *Child Development, 63*, 879–892.

Hart, C. H., Ladd, G. W., & Burleson, B. R. (1990). Children's expectations of the outcomes of social strategies: Relations with sociometric status and maternal disciplinary styles. *Child Development, 61*, 127–137.

Harter, S. (1977). A cognitive developmental approach to children's expression of conflicting feelings and a technique to facilitate such expression in play therapy. *Journal of Consulting and Clinical Psychology, 45*, 417–432.

Hartley, R. (1986). Imagine you're clever. *Journal of Child Psychology and Psychiatry, 27*, 383–398.

Havey, J. M., Olson, J. M., McCormick, C., & Cates, G. L. (2005). Teachers' perceptions of the incidence and management of ADHD. *Applied Neuropsychology, 12*, 120–127.

Hayes, S. C., Gifford, E. B., & Ruckstuhl, L. E. (1996). Relational frame theory and executive function: A behavioral approach. In G. R. Lyon & N. A. Krasnegor (Eds.), *Attention, memory and executive function* (pp. 279–306). Baltimore: Paul H. Brookes.

Hayward, C., Killen, J. D., & Taylor, C. B. (1989). Panic attacks in young adolescents. *American Journal of Psychiatry, 146*, 1061–1062.

Hazel, J. S., Schumaker, J. B., Sherman, J. A., & Sheldon-Wildgen, J. (1981). *ASSET: A social skills program for adolescents*. Champaign, IL: Research Press.

Hazler, R. J., Hoover, J. H., & Oliver, R. (1992, November). What kids say about bullying. *Executive Educator*, 20–22.

Hechtman, L. (1993). Genetic and neurobiological aspects of attention deficit hyperactivity disorder: A review. *Journal of Psychiatric Neuroscience, 9*, 193–201.

Hechtman, L. (1999). Attention-deficit/hyperactivity disorder. In M. Weiss, L. T. Hechtman, & G. Weiss (Eds.), *ADHD in adulthood: A guide to current theory, diagnosis and treatment* (pp. 17–38). Baltimore: Johns Hopkins University Press.

Hechtman, L., Weiss, G., & Perlman, T. (1984). Hyperactives as young adults: Initial predictors of adult outcome. *Journal of the American Academy of Child and Adolescent Psychiatry, 25*, 250–260.

Henderson, H., Jenson, W. R., & Erken, N. (1986). Focus article: Variable interval reinforcement for increasing on task behaviors in classrooms. *Educational and Treatment of Children, 9*, 250–263.

Hendrickson, J. M., Strain, P. S., Tremblay, A., & Shores, R. E. (1982). Interactions of behaviorally handicapped children: Functional effects of peer social initiations. *Behavior Modification, 6*, 323–353.

Herjanic, B., & Reich, W. (1982). Development of a structured psychiatric interview for children: Agreement between child and parent on individual symptoms. *Journal of Abnormal Child Psychology, 10*, 307–324.

Herman, K. C., Merrell, K., Reinke, W. M., & Tucker, C. M. (2004). The role of school psychology in preventing depression. *Psychology in the schools, 41*. Available from www.interscience.wiley.com.

Herrero, M. E., Hechtman, L., & Weiss, G. (1994). Children with deficits in attention, motor control, and perception almost grown up: The contribution of various background factors to outcome at age sixteen years. *European Child and Adolescent Psychiatry, 3*, 1–15.

Heward, W. L., Gardner, R., Cavanaugh, R., Courson, F., Grossi, T., & Barbetta, P. (1996, Winter). Everyone participates in this class. *CEC: Teaching Exceptional Children, 28*(2), 4–9.

Heward, W. L., & Orlansky, M. D. (1990). *Exceptional children* (4th ed.). New York: Macmillan.

Hibbs, E. D., & Jensen, P. S. (2005). *Psychosocial treatments for child and adolescent disorders: Empirically based strategies for clinical practice* (2nd ed.). Washington, DC: American Psychological Association.

Higgens, J. P., & Thies, A. P. (1981). Problem solving and social position among emotionally disturbed boys. *American Journal of Orthopsychiatry, 51*, 356–358.

Hill, K. T., & Sarason, S. B. (1966). The relation of test anxiety and defenesiveness to test and school performance over the elementary school process. *Monographs of the Society for Research in Child Development, 31*(2, Serial No. 104).

Hinshaw, S. P. (1985, February). *Attention deficit disorders: Description, natural history, and intervention strategies.* Paper presented at the International Conference of the Association for Children with Learning Disabilities, San Francisco.

Hinshaw, S. P. (1987). On the distinction between attention deficits/hyperactivity and conduct problems/aggression in child psychopathology. *Psychological Bulletin, 101*, 443–463.

Hinshaw, S. P. (2005). The stigmatization of mental illness in children and parents: Developmental issues, family concerns, and research needs. *Journal of Child Psychology and Psychiatry, 46*, 714–734.

Hinshaw, S. P., & Erhardt, D. (1991). Attention-deficit hyperactivity disorder. In P. C. Kendall (Ed.), *Child and adolescent therapy: Cognitive-behavioral procedures* (pp. 98–128). New York: Guilford Press.

Hinshaw, S. P., Henker, B., & Whalen, C. K. (1984a). Cognitive-behavioral and pharmacologic interventions for hyperactive boys: Comparative and combined effects. *Journal of Consulting and Clinical Psychology, 53*, 739–749.

Hinshaw, S. P., Henker, B., & Whalen, C. K. (1984b). Self-control in hyperactive boys in anger-inducing situations: Effects of cognitive-behavioral training and of methylphenidate. *Journal of Abnormal Child Psychology, 12*, 55–77.

Hintze, J. M., Stoner, G., & Bullis, M. H. (2000). Analogue assessment: Research and practice in evaluating emotional and behavioral problems. In E. S. Shapiro & T. R. Kratochwill (Eds.), *Behavioral assessment in the schools: Theory, research, and clinical foundations* (pp. 104–138). New York: Guilford Press.

Ho, H. H., & Kalousek, D. K. (1989). Brief report: Fragile X syndrome in autistic boys. *Journal of Autism and Developmental Disorders, 19,* 343–347.

Hobbs, N. (1966). Helping the disturbing child: Psychological and ecological strategies. *American Psychologist, 21,* 1105–1113.

Hobbs, S. A., & Forehand, R. (1975). Differential effects of contingent and noncontingent release from time-out on noncompliance and disruptive behavior of children. *Journal of Behavior Therapy and Experimental Psychology, 6,* 256–257.

Hobbs, S. A., Forehand, R., & Murray, R. G. (1978). Effects of various durations of time-out on the non-compliant behavior of chidlren. *Behavior Therapy, 9,* 652–656.

Hobson, R. P. (1989). Beyond cognition: A theory of autism. In G. Dawson (Ed.), *Autism: Nature, diagnosis and treatment* (pp. 22–48). New York: Guilford Press.

Hodgens, J., Cole, J., & Boldizar, J. (2000). Peer-based differences among boys with ADHD. *Journal of Clinical Child Psychology, 29,* 443–452.

Holt, P., Fine, M., & Tollefson, N. (1987). Mediating stress: Survival of the hardy. *Psychology in the Schools, 24,* 51–58.

Homme, L. (1969). *How to use contingency contracting in the classroom.* Urbana, IL: Research Press.

Homme, L., Casanyi, A. P., Gonzales, M. A., & Rechs, J. R. (1979). *How to use contingency contracting in the classroom.* Champaign, IL: Research Press.

Hooper, S. R., Boyd, T. A., Hynd, G. W., & Rubin, J. (1993). Definitional issues and neurobiological foundations of selected severe neurodevelopmental disorders. *Archives of Clinical Neuropsychology, 8,* 279–307.

Hoover, J. H. (1997, May 28). "Bullies beware." *Education Week.* Bethesda, MD: Editorial Projects in Education.

Hops, H., Walker, H. M., & Greenwood, C. R. (1988). *Procedures for establishing effective relationship skills (PEERS): Manual for consultants.* Delray, FL: Educational Achievement Systems.

Hornbeck, D. (1989). *Turning points: Preparing American youth for the 21st century.* New York: Carnegie Council on Adolescent Development.

Horner, R. H., & Billingsley, F. F. (1988). The effect of competing behavior on the generalization and maintenance of adaptive behavior in applied settings. In R. H. Horner, G. Dunlap, & R. L. Kogel (Eds.), *Generalization and maintenance: Lifestyle changes in applied settings* (pp. 197–220). Baltimore: Paul H. Brookes.

Horner, R. H., McDonnell, J. J., & Bellamy, G. T. (1986). Teaching generalized skills: General case instruction in simulation and community settings. In R. H. Horner, L. M. Meyer, & H. D. Fredericks (Eds.), *Education of learners with severe handicaps: Exemplary service strategies* (pp. 289–314). Baltimore: Paul H. Brookes.

Horwitz, B., Rumsey, J., Grady, C., & Rapoport, S. (1988). The cerebral metabolic landscape in autism: Inter-correlations of regional glucose utilization. *Archives of Neurology, 45,* 749–755.

Howes, C., & Stewart, P. (1987). Child's play with adults, toys, and peers: An examination of family and child-care influences. *Developmental Psychology, 23,* 423–430.

Hoza, B., Gerdes, A., Hinshaw, S. P., Arnold, L. E., Pelham, W. E., Molina, B., et al. (2004). Self-perceptions of competence in children with ADHD and comparison children. *Journal of Consulting and Clinical Psychology, 72,* 382–391.

Hudson, J. L., Flannery-Schroeder, E., & Kendall, P. C. (2004). Primary prevention of anxiety disorders. In D. J. A. Dozois & K. S. Dobson (Eds.), *The prevention of anxiety and depression: Theory, research, and practice* (pp. 101–129). Washington, DC: American Psychological Association.

Hudson, J. L., & Pope, H. G. (1990). Affective spectrum disorder: Does antidepressant response identify a family of disorders with a common pathophysiology? *American Journal of Psychiatry, 147,* 552–564.

Hughes, C. A., Ruhl, K. L., & Misra, A. (1989). Self-management with behaviorally disordered students in school settings: A promise unfulfilled? *Behavioral Disorders, 14,* 250–262.

Hughes, J., & Hall, R. (1989). *Cognitive behavioral psychology in the schools: A comprehensive handbook.* New York: Guilford Press.

Hunt, A., & Dennis, J. (1987). Psychiatric disorder among children with turberous sclerosis. *Developmental Medicine and Child Neurology, 29,* 190–198.

Huntze, S. L. (1985). A position paper of the council for children with behavioral disroders. *Behavioral Disorders, 10,* 167–174.

Hyatt, S. E., Tingstrom, D. H., & Edwards, R. (1991). Jargon usage in intervention presentation during consultation: Demonstration of a facilitative effect. 49–58.

Hyatt, S. P., & Tingstrom, D. H. (1993). Consultants' use of jargon during intervention presentation: An evaluation of presentation modality and type of intervention. *School Psychology Quarterly, 8,* 99–109.

Hyman, I. A., & Wise, J. H. (Eds.). (1979). *Corporal Punishment in American Education: Readings in History, Practice, and Alternatives.* Philadelphia, PA: Temple University Press.

Iannaccone, C. J., & Hwang, Y. G. (1998). Transcending social skills oriented instruction within integrated classrooms. *Emotional and Behavioral Difficulties, 3,* 25–29.

Idol-Maestas, L. (1983). *Special educator's handbook.* Rockville, MD: Aspen.

Imber, S. C., Imber, R. D., & Rothstein, C. (1979). Modifying independent work habits: An effective teacher-parent communication program. *Exceptional Children, 45,* 218–221.

Individuals with Disabilities Education Improvement Act (IDEIA) of 2004, Pub. L. No. 108-446, 20 U.S.C. § 1400 *et seq.*

Ingram, S., Hechtman, L., & Morgenstern, G. (1999). Outcome issues and ADHD: Adolescent and adult long-term outcome. *Mental Retardation and Developmental Disabilities Research Reviews, 5,* 243–250.

Iseman, J. S. (2005). *A cognitive instructional approach to improving math calculation of children with ADHD: Application of the PASS theory.* Unpublished doctoral dissertation, George Mason University.

Iwata, B. A., & Bailey, J. S. (1974). Reward versus cost token systems: An analysis of the effects on students and teachers. *Journal of Applied Behavioral Analysis, 7,* 567–576.

Iwata, B. A., Dorsey, M. F., Slifer, K. J., & Bauman, G. S. (1982). Toward a functional analysis of self-injury. *Analysis and Intervention in Developmental Disabilities, 2,* 2–30.

Jacobson, L. (1999). Three's company: Kids prove they have a place at the parent-teacher conference. *Teacher Magazine, 11,* 23.

Jacobson, R., Lahey, B. B., & Strauss, C. C. (1983). Correlates of depressed mood in normal children. *Journal of Abnormal Child Psychology, 11*, 29–40.

Jacobson, R., Le Couteur, A., Howlin, P., & Rutter, M. (1988). Selective subcortical abnormalities in autism. *Psychological Medicine, 18*, 39–48.

Jaycox, L. H., Reivich, K. J., Gillham, J., & Seligman, M. E. P. (1994). Prevention of depressive symptoms in school children. *Behavior Research and Therapy, 32*, 801–816.

Jenike, M. A., Baer, L., Minchiello, W. E., Schwartz, E. E., & Carey, R. J. (1986). Concomitant obsessive-compulsive disorder in schizo-typo personality disorders. *American Journal of Psychiatry, 143*, 306–311.

Jensen, P. S., Martin, D. P., & Cantwell, D. P. (1997). Comorbidity in ADHD: Implications for research practice and DSM-V. *Journal of the American Academy of Child and Adolescent Psychiatry, 36*, 1065–1079.

Joffe, R., Dobson, K., Fine, S., Marriage, K., & Haley, G. (1990). Social problem solving in depressed, conduct disordered and normal adolescents. *Journal of Abnormal Child Psychology, 18*, 565–575.

Johnson, D. W., & Johnson, R. (1979). Conflict in the classroom: Controversy and learning. *Review of Educational Research, 49*, 51–70.

Johnson, L. V., & Bany, M. A. (1970). *Classroom management: Theory and skill training.* New York: Macmillan.

Jonas, B. S., Brody, D., Roper, M., & Narrow, W. E. (2003). Prevalence of mood disorders in a national sample of young American adults. *Social Psychiatry and Psychiatric Epidemiology, 38*, 618–624.

Jones, E. E., & Nisbett, R. E. (1971). *The actor and observer: Divergent perceptions of the causes of behavior.* Morristown, NJ: General Learning Press.

Jones, K. M., Wickstrom, K. F., & Friman, P. C. (1997). The effects of observational feedback on treatment integrity in school-based behavioral consultation. *School Psychology Quarterly, 12*(4), 316–326.

Jones, T. S. (2004). Conflict resolution education: The field, the findings, and the future. *Conflict Resolution Quarterly, 22*, 233–267.

Joseph, S., & Linley, P. A. (2005). Positive adjustment to threatening events: An organismic valuing theory of growth through adversity. *Review of General Psychology, 9*, 262–280.

Kahn, J. S., Kehle, T. J., Jenson, W. R., & Clark, E. (1990). Comparison of cognitive-behavioral, relaxation, and self-modeling interventions for depression among middle-school students. *School Psychology Review, 19*, 196–211.

Kahn, N. A., & Hoge, R. D. (1983). A teacher-judgement measure of social competence: Validity data. *Journal of Consulting and Clinical Psychology, 51*, 809–814.

Kane, M. T., & Kendall, P. C. (1989). Anxiety disorders in children: A multiple-baseline evaluation of a cognitive-behavioral treatment. *Behavior Therapy, 20*, 499–508.

Kanfer, F. H. (1970). Self-monitoring: Methodological limitations and clinical applications. *Journal of Consulting and Clinical Psychology, 35*, 148–152.

Kanfer, F. H. (1971). The maintenance of behavior by self-generated reinforcement. In A. Jacobs & L. B. Sachs (Eds.), *The psychology of private events* (pp. 39–57). New York: Academic Press.

Kanfer, F. H., Karoly, P., & Newman, A. (1975). Reduction of children's fear of the dark by competence related and situational threat related verbal cues. *Journal of Consulting Clinical Psychology, 43*, 251–258.

Kanner, L. (1943). Autistic disturbances of affective contact. *Nervous Child, 2,* 217–250.

Kaplan, B. J., Crawford, S. G., Dewey, D. M., & Fisher, G. C. (2000). The IQ's of children with ADHD are normally distributed. *Journal of Learning Disabilities, 33,* 425–432.

Kar, B. C., Dash, U. N., Das, J. P., & Carlson, J. S. (1992). Two experiments on the dynamic assessment of planning. *Learning and Individual Differences, 5,* 13–29.

Kasari, C., Sigman, M., Mundy, P., & Yirmiya, N. (1990). Affective sharing in the context of joint attention interactions of normal, autistic and mentally retarded children. *Journal of Autism and Developmental Disorders, 20,* 87–100.

Kashani, J. H., Beck, N. C., Hoeper, E. W., Fallahi, C., Corcoran, C. M., McAllister, J. A., et al. (1987). Psychiatric disorders in a community sample of adolescents. *American Journal of Psychiatry, 144,* 584–589.

Kashani, J. H., Burk, J. P., & Reid, J. C. (1985). Depressed children of depressed parents. *Canadian Journal of Psychiatry, 30,* 265–269.

Kashani, J. H., Dandoy, A. C., & Orvaschel, H. (1991). Current perspectives on anxiety disorders in children and adolescents: An overview. *Comprehensive Psychiatry, 32,* 481–495.

Kashani, J. H., & Hakami, N. (1982). Depression in children and adolescents with malignancy. *Canadian Journal of Psychiatry, 27,* 464–477.

Kashani, J. H., Lahabidi, Z., & Jones, R. (1982). Depression in children and adolescents with cardio-vascular symptomatology. *Journal of the American Academy of Child Psychiatry, 21,* 187–189.

Kashani, J. H., & Orvaschel, H. (1988). Anxiety disorders in mid-adolescence: A community sample. *American Journal of Psychiatry, 147,* 313–318.

Kashani, J. H., & Orvaschel, H. (1990). A community study of anxiety in children and adolescents. *American Journal of Psychiatry, 147,* 313–318.

Kaslow, N. J., Stark, K. D., Printz, B., Livingston, R., & Tsai, S. L. (1993). Cognitive triad inventory for children: Developmental and relationship to depression and anxiety. *Journal of Clinical Child Psychology, 21,* 339–347.

Kasten, E. F., Coury, D. L., & Heron, T. E. (1992). Educators' knowledge and attitudes regarding stimulants in the treatment of attention deficit hyperactivity disorder. *Journal of Developmental and Behavioral Pediatrics, 13,* 215–219.

Kastrup, M. (1976). Psychic disorders among pre-school children in geographically delimited area of Aarhus County, Denmark. *Acta Psychiatric Scandinavia, 54,* 29–42.

Katz, M. (1994, May). From challenged childhood to achieving adulthood: Studies in resilience. *Chadder,* 8–11.

Katz, M. (1997). *On playing a poor hand well.* New York: Norton.

Kaufman, A. S., & Kaufman, N. L. (2004). *Kaufman assessment battery for children* (2nd ed.). Circle Pines, MN: American Guidance Service.

Kauffman, J. M. (1985). *Characteristics of children's behavior disorders* (3rd ed.). Columbus, OH: Merrill.

Kauffman, J. M., Pullen, B. L., & Akers, E. (1986). Classroom management: Teacher-child-peer relationships. *Focus on Exceptional Children, 19,* 1–10.

Kauffman, J. M., & Wong, K. L. H. (1991). Effective teachers of students with behavioral disorders: Are generic teaching skills enough? *Behavioral Disorders, 16,* 225–237.

Kavale, K., & Hirshoren, A. (1980). Public school and university teacher training programs for behaviorally disordered children: Are they compatible? *Behavior Disorder, 5,* 151–155.

Kavale, K. A., & Mostert, M. P. (2004). Social skills interventions for individuals with learning disabilities. *Learning Disability Quarterly, 27*, 31–43.

Kazdin, A. E. (1975a). *Behavior modification in applied settings.* Homewood, IL: Dorsey Press.

Kazdin, A. E. (1975b). Recent advances in token economy research. In M. Hersen, R. M. Eisler, & P. M. Miller (Eds.), *Progress and behavior modification* (Vol. 1). New York: Academic Press.

Kazdin, A. E. (1977). Assessing the clinical or applied significance of behavioral change through social validation. *Behavior Modification, 1*, 427–452.

Kazdin, A. E. (1980). Acceptability of alternative treatments for deviant child behavior. *Journal of Applied Behavior Analysis, 13*, 259–273.

Kazdin, A. E. (1981). Acceptability of child treatment techniques: The influence of treatment efficacy and adverse side effects. *Behavior Therapy, 12*, 493–506.

Kazdin, A. E. (1982). The token economy: A decade later. *Journal of Applied Behavior Analysis, 15*, 331–346.

Kazdin, A. E. (1985). *Treatment of antisocial behavior in children and adolescents.* Homewood, IL: Dorsey Press.

Kazdin, A. E. (1987). *Conduct disorders in childhood and adolescence.* Newbury Park, CA: Sage.

Kazdin, A. E. (1990). Conduct disorder in childhood. In M. Hersen & C. G. Last (Eds.), *Handbook of child and adult psychopathology: A longitudinal perspective.* New York: Pergamon Press.

Kazdin, A. E. (2003). Problem-solving skills training and parent management training for conduct disorder. In A. E. Kazdin & J. R. Weisz (Eds.), *Evidence-based psychotherapies for children and adolescents* (pp. 241–262). New York: Guilford Press.

Kazdin, A. E. (2005). Child, parent, and family-based treatment of aggressive and antisocial child behavior. In E. D. Hibbs & P. S. Jensen (Eds.), *Psychosocial treatments for child and adolescent disorders: Empirically based strategies for clinical practice* (2nd ed., pp. 445–476). Washington, DC: American Psychological Association.

Kazdin, A. E., & Marciano, P. L. (1998). Childhood and adolescent depression. In E. J. Mash & R. A. Barkley (Eds.), *Treatment of childhood disorders* (pp. 211–248). New York: Guilford Press.

Kazdin, A. E., Rodgers, A., & Colbus, D. (1986). The hopelessness scale for children: Psychometric characteristics and concurrent validity. *Journal of Consulting and Clinical Psychology, 54*, 241–245.

Kazdin, A. E., Sherick, R. B., Esveldt-Dawson, K., & Rancurello, M. D. (1985). Nonverbal behavior and childhood depression. *Journal of the American Academy of Child Psychiatry, 24*, 303–309.

Kazdin, A. E., & Weisz, J. R. (Eds.). (2003). *Evidence-based psychotherapies for children and adolescents.* New York: Guilford Press.

Kearny, C. A., & Silverman, W. K. (1990a). A preliminary analysis of a functional model of assessment and treatment for school refusal behavior. *Behavioral Modification, 14*, 340–366.

Kearny, C. A., & Silverman, W. K. (1990b). Treatment of an adolescent with obsessive-compulsive disorder by alternating response prevention and cognitive therapy: An empirical analysis. *Journal of Behavior Therapy Experimental Psychiatry, 21*, 39–47.

Kehle, T., Clark, E., Jenson, W. R., & Wampold, B. E. (1986). Effectiveness of the self-modeling procedure with behaviorally disturbed elementary age children. *School Psychology Review, 15*, 289–295.

Kellam, S. G., Simon, M. B., & Ensminger, M. E. (1983). Antecedents in first grade of teenage substance use and psychological well-being: A 10-year community-wide perspective study. In D. F. Ricks & B. S. Dohrenwend (Eds.), *Origins of psychopathology*. Cambridge: Cambridge University Press.

Kellam, S. G., Werthamer-Larsson, L., & Dolan, L. (1991). Developmental epidemiological-based preventive trials: Baseline modeling of early target behaviors and depressive symptoms. *American Journal of Community Psychology, 19,* 563–584.

Keller, C. L., & Duffy, M. L. (2005). "I said that?" How to improve your instructional behavior in just 5 minutes per day through data-based self-evaluation. *Teaching Exceptional Children, 37,* 36–39.

Keller, F. S., & Schonfeld, W. N. (1950). *Principles of psychology*. New York: Appleton-Century-Crofts.

Kelley, M. L. (1990). *School-home notes: Promoting children's classroom success*. New York: Guilford Press.

Kelley, M. L., & Carper, L. B. (1988). The Mothers' Activity Checklist: An instrument for assessing pleasant and unpleasant events. *Behavioral Assessment, 10,* 331–341.

Kelly, B. T., Loeber, R., Keenan, K., & DeLamatre, M. (1997). *Developmental pathways in boys' disruptive and delinquent behavior*. Washington, DC: U.S. Department of Justice, Office of Juvenile Justice and Delinquency Preventione.

Kelly, T. J., Bullock, C. M., & Dykes, M. K. (1977). Behavioral disorders: Teachers' perceptions. *Exceptional Children, 43,* 316–318.

Kendall, P. C. (1985). Toward a cognitive-behavioral model of child psychopathology and a critique of related interventions. *Journal of Abnormal Child Psychology, 13,* 357–372.

Kendall, P. C. (1990). *Coping cat workbook*. Ardmore, PA: Workbook Publishing.

Kendall, P. C. (Ed.). (2005). *Child and adolescent therapy: Cognitive and behavioral procedures* (3rd ed.). New York: Guilford Press.

Kendall, P. C., Aschenbrand, S. G., & Hudson, J. L. (2003). Child-focused treatment of anxiety. In A. E. Kazdin & J. R. Weisz (Eds.), *Evidence-based psychotherapies for children and youth* (pp. 81–100). New York: Guilford Press.

Kendall, P. C. & Braswell, L. (1985). *Cognitive-Behavioral Therapy for Impulsive Children*. New York: Guilford Press.

Kendall, P. C., & Braswell, L. (1993). *Cognitive-Behavioral Therapy for Impulsive Children*, (2nd ed.). New York: Guilford Press.

Kendall, P. C., Chansky, T. E., Kane, M. T., Kim, R. S., Kortlander, E., Ronan, K. R., et al. (1992). *Anxiety disorders in youth: Cognitive-behavioral interventions*. Boston: Allyn & Bacon.

Kendall, P. C., Chu, B. C., Pimentel, S. S., & Choudhury, M. (2000). Treating anxiety disorders in youth. In P. C. Kendall (Ed.), *Child and adolescent therapy: Cognitive-behavioral procedures* (pp. 235–287). New York: Guilford Press.

Kendall, P. C., Howard, B. L., & Epps, R. C. (1988). The anxious child: Cognitive behavioral treatment strategies. *Behavioral Modification, 12,* 271–319.

Kendall, P. C., Hudson, J. L., Choudhury, M., Webb, A., & Pimentel, S. (2005). Cognitive-behavioral treatment for childhood anxiety disorders. In E. D. Hibbs & P. S. Jensen (Eds.), *Psychosocial treatments for child and adolescent disorders: Empirically based strategies for clinical practice* (pp. 47–73). Washington, DC: American Psychological Association.

Kendall, P. C., & MacDonald, J. P. (1993). Cognition in the psychopathology of youth and implications for treatment. In P. C. Kendall & K. Dobson (Eds.), *Psychopathology and cognition* (pp. 387–427). New York: Academic Press.

Kendall, P. C., Robin, J. A., Hedtke, K. A., & Suveg, C. (2005). Considering CBT with anxious youth? Think exposures. *Cognitive and Behavioral Practice, 12,* 136–148.

Kendall, P. C., Stark, K., & Adam, T. (1990). Cognitive distortion or cognitive deficit in childhood depression. *Journal of Abnormal Child Psychology, 18,* 255–270.

Kendall, P. C., & Watson, D. (1989). *Anxiety and depression: Distinctive and overlapping features.* New York: Academic Press.

Keogh, B. (2003). *Temperament in the classroom: Understanding individual differences.* Baltimore: Paul H. Brookes.

Kessler, R. C., Berglund, P., Demler, O., Jin, R., & Walters, E. E. (2005). Lifetime prevalence and age-of-onset distribuitions of DSM-IV disorders in the National Comorbidity Survey Replication. *Archives of General Psychiatry, 62,* 593–602.

Kessler, R. C., Foster, C. L., Saunders, W. B., & Stang, P. E. (1995). Social consequences of psychiatric disorders, I: Educational attainment. *American Journal of Psychiatry, 152,* 1026–1032.

Kessler, R. C., McGonagle, K. A., Zhao, S., Nelson, C. D., Hughes, M., Eshleman, S., et al. (1994). Lifetime and 12-month prevalence of DSM-III-R psychiatric disorders in the United States: Results from the National Comorbidity Survey. *Archives of General Psychiatry, 51,* 8–19.

Kessler, R. C., & Walters, E. E. (1998). Epidemiology of DSM-III-R major depression and minor depression among adolescents and young adults in the National Comorbidity Survey. *Depression and Anxiety, 7,* 3–14.

Kestenbaum, R., Farber, E. A., & Sroufe, L. A. (1989). Individual differences in empathy among preschoolers: Relation to attachment history. *New Directions for Child Development, 44,* 51–64.

Kinsbourne, M. (1987). Cerebral-brainstem relations in infantile autism. In E. Schopler & G. B. Mesibov (Eds.), *Neurological issues in autism* (pp. 107–125). New York: Plenum Press.

Kiser, L. J., Ackerman, B. J., Brown, E., Edwards, N. B., McGolgan, E., Pugh, R., et al. (1988). Post traumatic stress disorder in young children: A reaction to purported sexual abuse. *Journal of the American Academy of Child and Adolescent Psychiatry, 27,* 645–649.

Klein, D. N., Taylor, E. B., Dickstein, S., & Harding, K. (1988). The early-late onset distinction in DSM-III-R dysthymia. *Journal of Affective Disorders, 14,* 25–33.

Klein, K., & Forehand, R. (1997). Delinquency during the transition to early adulthood: Family and parenting predictors from early adolescence. *Adolescence, 32,* 61–78.

Klein, R. G. (1987). Pharmacotherapy of childhood hyperactivity: An update. In H. Y. Meltzer (Ed.), *Psychopharmacology: The third generation of progress* (pp. 1215–1224). New York: Raven Press.

Klin, A. (1992). Listening preferences in regard to speech in four children with developmental disabilities. *Journal of Child Psychology and Psychiatry, 33,* 763–769.

Klin, A., Volkmar, F. R., & Sparrow, S. (1992). Autistic social dysfunction: Some limitations of the theory of mind hypothesis. *Journal of Child Psychiatry, 33,* 861–876.

Knoff, H. M. (2002). Best practices in personality assessment. In A. Thomas & J. Grimes (Eds.), *Best practices in school psychology—IV* (pp. 1281–1302). Washington, DC: National Association of School Psychologists.

Kobasa, S., Maddi, S., & Kahn, S. (1982). Hardiness and health: A perspective inquiry. *Journal of Personality and Social Psychology, 42,* 168–177.

Kohn, A. (1993). Choices for children: Why and how to let students decide. *Phi Delta Kappan, 75*, 8–20.

Kokkinos, C. M., & Panayiotou, G. (2004). Predicting bullying and victimization among early adolescents: Associations with disruptive behavior disorders. *Aggressive Behavior, 30*, 520.

Kolvin, I. (1971). Studies in the childhood psychoses: Pt. I. Diagnostic criteria and classification. *British Journal of Psychiatry, 118*, 381–384.

Komoto, J., Udsui, S., Otsuki, S., & Terao, A. (1984). Infantile autism and Duchenne muscular dystrophy. *Journal of Autism and Developmental Disorders, 14*, 191–195.

Kopp, C. B. (1992). Emotional distress and control in young children. In N. Eisenberg & R. A. Fabes (Eds.), *Emotion and its regulation in early development* (pp. 41–56). San Francisco: Jossey-Bass.

Kounin, J. S. (1970). *Discipline and group management in classroom.* Melbourne, FL: Krieger.

Kovacs, M. (1983). *Children's Depression Inventory: A self-rated depression scale for school-aged youngsters.* Unpublished manuscript, University of Pittsburgh School of Medicine.

Kovacs, M. (1990). Comorbid anxiety disorders in childhood-onset depressions. In J. D. Maser & C. R. Cloninger (Eds.), *Comorbidity of mood and anxiety disorders* (pp. 271–281). Washington, DC: American Psychiatric Press.

Kovacs, M. (1992). *Children's Depression Inventory Manual.* New York: Multi-Health Systems.

Kovacs, M., Feinberg, T. L., Crouse-Novak, M. A., Paulauskas, S. L., & Finkelstein, R. (1984). Depressive disorders in childhood: Pt. II. A longitudinal study of the risk for a subsequent major depression. *Archives of General Psychiatry, 41*, 643–649.

Kovacs, M., Gatsonis, C., Paulauskas, S. L., & Richards, C. (1989). Depressive disorders in childhood. *Archives of General Psychiatry, 41*, 643–649.

Kovacs, M., Paulauskas, S., Gatsonis, C., & Richards, C. (1988). Depressive disorders in childhood: Pt. III. A longitudinal study of comorbidity with a risk for conduct disorders. *Journal of Affective Disorders, 15*, 205–217.

Kratochwill, T. R., Elliott, S. N., & Rotto, P. C. (1990). Best practices and behavioral consultation. In A. Thomas & J. Grimes (Eds.), *Best practices in school psychology, II* (pp. 519–537). Washington, DC: National Association of School Psychologists.

Kroutil, L. A., Van Brunt, D. L., Herman-Stahl, M. A., Heller, D. C., Bray, R. M., & Penne, M. A. (2006). *Nonmedical use of prescription stimulants in the United States: Drug and alcohol dependence.* Research Triangle Park, NC: RTI International [Epub ahead of print].

Kruesi, M. J. P., Rapoport, J. L., Hamburger, S., Hibbs, E., Potter, W. Z., Lenane, M., et al. (1990). Cerebrospinal fluid monoamine metabolites, aggression, and impulsivity in disruptive behavioral disorders of children and adolescents. *Archives of General Psychiatry, 47*, 419–426.

Kubiszyn, T., Brown, R. T., & DeMers, S. T. (1997). Pediatric psychopharmacology. In G. G. Bear, K. M. Minke, & A. Thomas (Eds.), *Children's needs: Pt. II. Development, problems, and alternatives* (pp. 925–934). Bethesda, MD: National Association of School Psychologists.

Kumpfer, K. L., Alvarado, R., Tait, C., & Turner, C. (2002). Effectiveness of a school-based family and children's skills training for substance abuse prevention among 6- to 8-year-old rural children. *Psychology of Predictive Behaviors, 16*, S65–S71.

Ladd, G. W. (1981). Effectiveness of a social learning method for enhancing children's social interaction and peer acceptance. *Child Development, 52*, 171–178.

La Greca, A. M., & Stark, P. (1986). Naturalistic observations of children's social behavior. In P. S. Strain, M. J. Guralnick, & H. M. Walker (Eds.), *Children's social behavior: Development, assessment, and modification* (pp. 181–213). New York: Academic Press.

Lahey, B. B., Applegate, B., McBurnett, K., Biederman, J., Greenhill, L., Hyund, G., et al. (1994). DSM-IV field trial for attention/deficit hyperactivity disorder in children and adolescents. *American Journal of Psychiatry, 151*, 1673–1685.

Lahey, B. B., Frick, P. J., Loeber, R., Tannenbaum, B. A., Van Horn, Y., & Christ, M. A. G. (1990). *Oppositional and conduct disorder: Pt. I. A meta-analytic review.* Unpublished manuscript, University of Georgia, Athens.

Lahey, B. B., Loeber, R., Quay, H. C., Applegate, B., Shaffer, D., Waldman, I., et al. (1998). Validity of DSM-IV subtypes of conduct disorder based on age of onset. *Journal of the American Academy of Child and Adolescent Psychiatry, 37*, 435–442.

Lahey, B. B., Loeber, R., Stouthamer-Loeber, M., Christ, M. A. G., Green, S., Russo, M. F., et al. (1990). Comparison of DSM-III and DSM-III-R diagnoses for prepubertal children: Changes in prevalence and validity. *Journal of the American Academy of Child and Adolescent Psychiatry, 29*, 620–626.

Lahey, B. B., Pelham, W. E., Loney, J., Lee, S., & Willcutt, E. (2005). Instability of the DSM-IV subtypes of ADHD from preschool through elementary school. *Archives of General Psychiatry, 62*, 896–902.

LaHoste, G. J., Swanson, J. M., Wigal, S. B., Glabe, C., Wigal, T., King, N., et al. (1996). Dopamine D4 receptor gene polymorphism is associated with attention deficit hyperactivity disorder. *Mol Psychiatry, 1*, 121–124.

Lalli, J. S., Browder, D. M., Mace, F. C., & Brown, D. K. (1993). Teacher use of descriptive analysis data to implement interventions to decrease students' maladapted behavior. *Journal of Applied Behavior Analysis, 26*, 227–238.

Lambert, N. M., & Hartsough, C. S. (2000). Prospective study of tobacco smoking and substance dependencies among samples of ADHD and non-ADHD participants. *Journal of Learning Disorders, 31*, 533–544.

Lancaster, J. (1808). *Improvements in education.* London: Darton and Harvey. (Original work published 1803)

Lang, P. J. (1968). Fear reduction and fear behavior: Problems in treating a construct. In J. M. Schleen (Ed.), *Research in psychotherapy.* Washington, DC: American Psychological Association.

Lapouse, R. (1966). The epidemiology of behavior disorders in children. *Journal of Affective Disorders of Children, 3*, 594–599.

Lapouse, R., & Monk, M. A. (1958). An epidemiologic study of behavior characteristics in children. *American Journal of Public Health, 48*, 1134–1144.

Larrivee, B. (1985). *Effective teaching for successful mainstreaming.* New York: Longman.

Larson, J. (2005). *Think first: Addressing aggressive behavior in secondary schools.* New York: Guilford Press.

Larson, J., & Lochman, J. E. (2002). *Helping schoolchildren cope with anger: A cognitive-behavioral intervention.* New York: Guilford Press.

Last, C. G. (1989). Anxiety disorders of childhood or adolescence. In C. G. Last & M. Hersen (Eds.), *Handbook of child psychiatric diagnosis.* New York: Wiley.

Last, C. G., Phillips, J. E., & Statfield, A. (1987). Childhood anxiety disorders in mothers and their children. *Childhood Psychiatry and Human Development, 18*, 103–112.

510

References

Last, C. G., & Strauss, C. C. (1989a). Obsessive-compulsive disorder in childhood. *Journal of Anxiety Disorders, 3,* 295–302.

Last, C. G., & Strauss, C. C. (1989b). Panic disorder in children and adolescents. *Journal of Anxiety Disorders, 3,* 87–95.

Last, C. G., Strauss, C. C., & Francis, G. (1987). Comorbidity among childhood anxiety disorders. *Journal of Nervous and Mental Disorders, 175,* 726–730.

Launay, J. M., Bursztejn, C., Ferrari, P., Dreux, C., Braconnier, A., Zarifian, E., et al. (1987). Catecholamines metabolism in infantile autism: A controlled study of 22 autistic children. *Journal of Autism and Developmental Disorders, 17,* 333–348.

Laurent, J., Landau, S., & Stark, K. D. (1993). Conditional probabilities and the diagnosis of depressive and anxiety disorders in children. *School Psychology Review, 22,* 98–114.

Lazarus, A. A., & Abramovitz, A. (1962). The use of "emotive imagery" in the treatment of children's phobias. *Journal of Mental Science, 108,* 191–195.

LeBlanc, J. M., Busby, K. H., & Thomson, C. L. (1974). The functions of time-out for changing the aggressive behaviors of a preschool child: A multiple-baseline analysis. In R. Ulrich, T. Stachnik, & J. Mabry (Eds.), *Control of human behavior* (Vol. 3). Glenview, IL: Scott Forseman.

Lee, M. P., Zimbardo, G., & Bertholf, M. (1977, November). Shy murderers. *Psychology Today.*

Leff, S. S., & Lakin, R. (2005). Playground-based observational systems: A review and implications for practitioners and researchers. *School Psychology Review, 34,* 470–489.

Lefkowitz, M. M., & Tesiny, E. P. (1985). Depression in children: Prevalence and correlates. *Journal of Consulting and Clinical Psychology, 53,* 647–656.

Lepage, K., Kratochwill, T. R., & Elliott, S. N. (2004). Competency-based behavior consultation training: An evaluation of consultant outcomes, treatment effects, and consumer satisfaction. *School Psychology Quarterly, 19*(1), 1–28.

Levine, M. D. (2002). *A mind at a time.* New York: Simon & Schuster.

Levine, M. D. (2003). *The myth of laziness.* New York: Simon & Schuster.

Levitt, M. J., Guacci-Franco, N., & Levitt, J. L. (1994). Social support achievement in childhood and early adolescence: A multicultural study. *Journal of Applied Developmental Psychology, 15,* 207–222.

Lewin, P., Nelson, R. E., & Tollefson, N. (1983). Teacher attitudes toward disruptive children. *Elementary School Guidance and Counseling, 17,* 188–193.

Lewinsohn, P. M., Clarke, G. N., Hops, H., & Andrews, J. (1990). Cognitive-behavioral group treatment of depression in adolescents. *Behavior Therapy, 21,* 385–401.

Lewinsohn, P. M., Rhode, P., & Seeley, J. R. (1994). Adolescent psychopathology: Pt. III. The clinical consequences of comorbidity. *Journal of the American Academy of Child and Adolescent Psychiatry, 34,* 510–519.

Lewy, A. L., & Dawson, G. (1992). Social stimulation and joint attention in young autistic children. *Journal of Abnormal Child Psychology, 20*(6), 555–566.

Licht, B. (1983). Cognitive-motivational factors that contribute to the achievement of learning-disabled children. *Journal of Learning Disabilities, 16,* 483–490.

Lieberman, A. F. (1977). Preschoolers' competence with a peer: Relations with attachment and peer experience. *Child Development, 48,* 1277–1287.

Lieberman, J. A., Stroup, T. S., McEvoy, J. P., Swartz, M. S., Rosenheck, R. A., Perkins, D. O., et al. (2005). Effectiveness of antipsychotic drugs in patients with chronic schizophrenia. *New England Journal of Medicine, 353,* 1209–1223.

Lingjaerde, L. (1983). The biochemistry of depression. *Acta Psychiatrica Scandinavica Supplementum, 302,* 36–51.

Linn, R. J., & Herr, D. E. (1992). Using proactive behavior management techniques to facilitate school success for students with learning disabilities. *Learning Disabilities, 3,* 29–34.

Linnenbrink, E. A., & Pintich, P. R. (2003). The role of self-efficacy beliefs in student engagement and learning in the classroom. *Reading and Writing Quarterly, 19,* 119–137.

Livingston, R., Lawson, L., & Jones, J. G. (1993). Predictors of self-reported psychopathology in children abused repeatedly by a parent. *Journal of the American Academy of Child and Adolescent Psychiatry, 5,* 948–953.

Livingston, R., Reis, C., & Ringdahl, I. (1984). Abnormal dexamethasone suppression test results in depressed and nondepressed children. *American Journal of Psychiatry, 141,* 106–108.

Livingston, R., Taylor, J. L., & Crawford, S. L. (1988). A study of somatic complaints and psychiatric diagnosis in children. *Journal of the American Academy of Child and Adolescent Psychiatry, 27,* 185–187.

Lloyd, J. W., Kauffman, J. M., & Kupersmidt, J. D. (1990). Integration of students with behavior disorders in regular education environments. In K. D. Gadow (Ed.), *Advances in learning and behavioral disabilities* (Vol. 6). Greenwich, CT: JAI Press.

Lochman, J. E. (1992). Cognitive-behavioral interventions with aggressive boys: Three-year follow-up and preventive effects. *Journal of Consulting and Clinical Psychology, 60,* 426–432.

Lochman, J. E., Barry, T. D., & Pardini, D. A. (2003). Anger control training for aggressive youth. In A. E. Kazdin & J. R. Weisz (Eds.), *Evidence-based psychotherapies for children and adolescents* (pp. 263–281). New York: Guilford Press.

Lochman, J. E., Burch, P. R., Curry, J. F., & Lampron, L. B. (1984). Treatment and generalization effects of cognitive-behavioral and goal-setting interventions with aggressive boys. *Journal of Consulting and Clinical Psychology, 52,* 915–916.

Lochman, J. E., & Curry, J. F. (1986). Effects of social problem solving training and self-instruction training with aggressive boys. *Journal of Clinical Child Psychology, 16,* 159–164.

Lochman, J. E., & Dodge, K. A. (1994). Social cognitive processes of severely violent, moderately aggressive, and nonaggressive boys. *Journal of Consulting and Clinical Psychology, 62,* 366–374.

Lochman, J. E., Lampron, L. B., Gemmer, R. C., Harris, S., & Wyckoff, G. (1989). Teacher consultation and cognitive-behavioral interventions with aggressive boys. *Psychology in the Schools, 16,* 179–188.

Lochman, J. E., Nelson, W. M., & Sims, J. P. (1981). A cognitive-behavioral program for use with aggressive children. *Journal of Clinical Child Psychology, 13,* 146–148.

Lochman, J. E., & Wells, K. C. (2002). The coping power program at the middle school transition: Universal and indicated prevention effects. *Psychology of Addictive Behavior, 16,* 540–554.

Lock, S., & Barrett, P. M. (2003). A longitudinal study of developmental differences in universal preventive intervention for child anxiety. *Behavior Change, 20,* 183–199.

Loeber, R. (1985). Patterns and development of antisocial child behavior. *Annals of Child Development, 2,* 77–116.

References

Loeber, R., Burke, J., Lahey, B. B., Winters, A., & Zera, M. (2000). Oppositional defiant and conduct disorder: A review of the past 10 years: Pt. I. *Journal of the American Academy of Child and Adolescent Psychiatry, 39,* 1468–1484.

Loeber, R., Green, S. M., Keenan, K., & Lahey, B. B. (1995). Which boys will fare worse? Early predictors of the onset of conduct disorder in a 6-year longitudinal study. *Journal of the American Academy of Child and Adolescent Psychiatry, 34,* 499–509.

Loeber, R., & Keenan, K. (1994). Interaction between conduct disorder and its comorbid conditions: Effects of age and gender. *Clinical Psychology Review, 14,* 497–523.

Loeber, R., Keenan, K., Russo, M. F., Green, S. M., Lahey, B. B., & Thomas, C. (1988). Secondary data analyses for DSM-IV on the symptoms of oppositional defiant disorder and conduct disorder. In T. A. Widiger, A. J. Frances, & H. J. Pincus (Eds.), *DSM-IV sourcebook* (Vol. 4., pp. 465–490). Washington, DC: American Psychiatric Press.

Loeber, R., Keenan, K., & Zhang, Q. (1997). Boys' experimentation and persistence in developmental pathways toward serious delinquency. *Journal of Child and Family Studies, 6,* 321–357.

Loeber, R., Lahey, B. B., & Thomas, C. (1991). Diagnostic conundrum of oppositional defiant disorder and conduct disorder. *Journal of Abnormal Psychology, 100,* 379–390.

Loeber, R., & Schmaling, K. B. (1985). Empirical evidence for overt and covert patterns of antisocial conduct problems. *Journal of Abnormal Child Psychology, 100,* 379–390.

Loney, J., Whaley-Klahn, M. A., & Kosier, T. (1983). Hyperactive boys and their brothers at 21: Predictors of aggressive and antisocial outcomes. In K. T. Van Dusen & S. A. Mednick (Eds.), *Prospective studies of crime and delinquency* (pp. 181–206). Boston: Kluwer-Nijhoff.

Long, N. J., & Newman, R. G. (1980). Managing surface behavior of children in school. In N. J. Long, W. C. Morris, & R. G. Newman (Eds.), *Conflict in the classroom: The education of emotionally disturbed children* (4th ed.). Belmont, CA: Wadsworth.

Lord, C. (1993). The complexity of social behavior in autism. In S. Baron-Cohen, H. Tager-Flusberg, & D. Cohen (Eds.), *Understanding other minds: Perspectives from autism* (pp. 292–316). Oxford: Oxford University Press.

Lotter, V. (1974). Factors related to outcome in autistic children. *Journal of Autism and Developmental Disorders, 4,* 263–277.

Loveland, K., & Kelley, M. (1991). Development of adaptive behavior in preschoolers with autism and Down syndrome. *American Journal of Mental Retardation, 96(1),* 335–349.

Lowe, N., Kirley, A., Hawi, Z., Sham, P., Wickham, H., Kratochvil, C. J., et al. (2004). Joint analysis of the DRD5 marker concludes association with ADHD confined to the predominantly inattentive and combined subtypes. *American Journal of Human Genetics, 74,* 348–356.

Lowe, T. L., & Cohen, D. J. (1980). Mania in childhood and adolescence. In R. H. Belmaker & H. M. van Praag (Eds.), *Mania: An evolving concept.* New York: Spectrum.

Lowry-Webster, H. M., Barrett, P. M., & Dadds, M. R. (2001). A universal prevention trial of anxiety and depressive symptomatology in childhood: Preliminary data from an Australian study. *Behavior Change, 18,* 36–50.

Lowry-Webster, H. M., Barrett, P. M., & Lock, S. (2003). A universal prevention trial of anxiety symptomatology during childhood: Results at 1-year follow-up. *Behavior Change, 20,* 25–43.

Lowy-Apple, A., Billingsley, F., & Schwartz, I. S. (2005). Effects of video modeling alone and with self-management on compliment-giving behaviors of children with high-functioning ASD. *Journal of Positive Behavior Interventions, 7,* 33–46.

Luk, S. L., Leung, P. W., & Yuen, J. (1991). Clinic observations in the assessment of pervasiveness of childhood hyperactivity. *Journal of Child Psychology and Psychiatry and Allied Disciplines, 32,* 833–850.

Luntz, B. K., & Widom, C. S. (1994). Antisocial personality disorder in abused and neglected children grown up. *American Journal of Psychiatry, 151,* 670–674.

Luria, A. R. (1966). *Human brain and psychological processes.* New York: Harper & Row.

Luria, A. R. (1973a). The origin and cerebral organization of man's conscious action. In S. G. Sapir & A. C. Nitzburg (Eds.), *Children with learning problems* (pp. 109–130). New York: Brunner/Mazel.

Luria, A. R. (1973b). *The working brain.* New York: Basic Books.

Luria, A. R. (1980). *Higher cortical functions in man* (2nd ed.). New York: Basic Books.

Maag, J. W. (1989). Assessment in social skills training: Methodological and conceptual issues for research and practice. *Remedial and Special Education, 10,* 6–17.

Maccoby, E. E. (1984). Middle childhood in the context of the family. In W. A. Collins (Ed.), *Development during middle childhood: The years from six to twelve* (pp. 184–239). Washington, DC: National Academy.

MacDonald, H., Rutter, M., & Howlin, P. (1989). Recognition and expression of emotional cues by autistic and normal adults. *Journal of Child Psychology and Psychiatry, 30,* 865–878.

MacDonald, H., Rutter, M., Rios, P., & Bolton, P. (1989, August). *Cognitive and social abnormalities in first-degree relatives of autistic and Downs syndrome probands.* Presented at the First World Congress on Psychiatric Genetics, Churchill College, Cambridge.

Mace, F. C. (1994). The significance and future of functional analysis methodologies. *Journal of Applied Behavior Analysis, 27,* 385–392.

Mace, F. C., & Lalli, J. S. (1991). Linking descriptive and experimental analyses in the treatment of bizarre speech. *Journal of Applied Behavior Analysis, 24,* 553–562.

Mace, F. C., & West, B. J. (1986). Analysis of demand conditions associated with reluctant speech. *Journal of Behavior Therapy and Experimental Psychiatry, 17,* 285–294.

MacFarlane, J. W., Allen, L., & Honzik, M. P. (1962). *A developmental study of the behavior problems of normal children between twenty-one months and fourteen years.* Berkeley: University of California Press.

Madden, N. A., & Slavin, R. E. (1983). Mainstreaming students with mild handicaps: Academic and social outcomes. *Review of Educational Research, 53,* 519–569.

Madsen, C. H., Becker, W. C., & Thomas, D. R. (1968). Rules, praise, and ignoring: Elements of elementary classroom control. *Journal of Applied Behavior Analysis, 1,* 139–150.

Madsen, C. H., & Madsen, C. (1970). *Teaching/discipline.* Boston: Allyn & Bacon.

Mager, R. (1968). *Developing attitude toward learning.* Palo Alto, CA: Fearon.

Mahmood, T., Reveley, A. M., & Murray, R. M. (1983). Genetic studies of affective and anxiety disorders. In M. Weller (Ed.), *The scientific basis of psychiatry.* London: Baillere Tindall.

Mahoney, M. (1977). Personal science: A cognitive learning trend in psychotherapy. *American Psychologist, 32,* 5–13.

Manen, T. G., Prins, P. J. M., & Emmelkamp, P. M. G. (2004). Reducing aggressive behavior in boys with a social cognitive group treatment: Results of a randomized, controlled trial. *Journal of the American Academy of Child and Adolescent Psychiatry, 43,* 1478–1487.

Mann, H. (1855). *On school punishment (Lecture 7): Lectures on education.* Boston: IDE & Dutton.

Mannuzza, S., Klein, R. G., Abikoff, H., & Moulton, J. L. (2004). Significance of childhood conduct problems to later development of conduct disorder among children with ADHD: A prospective follow-up study. *Journal of Abnormal Child Psychology, 32,* 565.

Mansdorf, I. J., & Lukens, E. (1987). Cognitive-behavioral psychotherapy for separation anxious children exhibiting school phobia. *Journal of the American Academy of Child and Adolescent Psychiatry, 26,* 222–225.

March, J. S. (1997). *Multidimensional Anxiety Scale for Children.* North Tonawanda, NY: Multi-Health Systems.

March, J. S. (2004). The Treatment for Adolescents with Depression Study (TADS): Short-term effectiveness and safety outcomes. *Journal of the American Medical Association, 292,* 807–820.

March, J. S., Amaya-Jackson, L., Murray, M. C., & Schulte, A. (1998). Cognitive-behavioral psychotherapy for children and adolescents with posttraumatic stress disorder after a single-incident stressor. *Journal of the American Academy of Child and Adolescent Psychiatry, 37,* 585–593.

March, J. S., & Mulle, K. (1998). *OCD in children and adolescents: A cognitive-behavioral treatment manual.* New York: Guilford Press.

Marks, I. M., & Gelder, M. G. (1966). Different ages of onset in varieties of phobia. *American Journal of Psychiatry, 123,* 218–221.

Marshall, H. H. (1972). *Positive discipline in classroom instruction.* Springfield, IL: Charles C Thomas.

Marshall, M., & Weisner, K. (2004). Using a discipline system to promote learning. *Phi Delta Kappan, 85,* 498–507.

Martens, B. K., & Kelly, S. Q. (1993). A behavioral analysis of effective teaching. *School Psychology Quarterly, 8,* 10–26.

Martens, B. K., & Meller, P. J. (1989). Influence of child and classroom characteristics on acceptability of interventions. *Journal of School Psychology, 27,* 237–245.

Martens, B. K., Witt, J. C., Elliott, S. N., & Darveaux, D. X. (1985). Teacher judgments concerning the acceptability of school-based interventions. *Professional School Psychology, 3,* 271–281.

Martinez, J. (1989). Cooling off before burning out. *Academic Therapy, 24,* 271–284.

Marton, P., Connolly, J., Kutcher, S., & Cornblum, M. (1993). Cognitive social skills and social self-appraisal in depressed adolescents. *Journal of the American Academy of Child and Adolescent Psychiatry, 32,* 739–744.

Marx, E., & Schulze, C. (1991). Interpersonal problem-solving in depressed students. *Journal of Clinical Psychology, 47,* 361–367.

Mash, E. J., & Barkley, R. A. (1996). *Child psychopathology.* New York: Guilford Press.

Mash, E. J., & Barkley, R. A. (Eds.). (2003). *Child psychopathology* (2nd ed.). New York: Guilford Press.

Mash, E. J., & Dozois, D. J. (2003). Child psychopathology: A developmental-systems perspective. In E. J. Mash & R. A. Barkley (Eds.), *Treatment of childhood disorders* (pp. 3–71). New York: Guilford Press.

Matheson, A. S., & Shriver, M. D. (2005). Training teachers to give effective commands: Effects on student compliance and academic behaviors. *School Psychology Review, 34*(2), 202–219.

Matson, J. L. (1989). *Treating depression in children and adolescents.* New York: Pergamon Press.

Mattison, R. E., & Bagnato, J. (1987). Empirical measurement of overanxious disorder in boys 8 to 12 years old. *Journal of the American Academy of Child and Adolescent Psychiatry, 26,* 536–540.

Maurer, A. (1965). What children fear. *Journal of Genetic Psychology, 106,* 265–277.

Mautner, V. F., Kluwe, L., Thakker, S. D., & Laerk, R. A. (2002). Treatment of ADHD in neurofibromatosis type 1. *Developmental Medicine and Child Neurology, 44,* 164–170.

McCabe, K. M., Rodgers, C., Yeh, M., & Hough, R. (2004). Gender differences in childhood onset conduct disorder. *Developmental and Psychopathology, 16*(1), 179–192.

McCann, B. S. (1989). Hemispheric asymetries and early infantile autism. *Journal of Autism and Developmental Disorders, 11,* 401–411.

McCauley, E., Myers, K., Mitchell, J., Calderon, R., Schloredt, K., & Treder, R. (1993). Depression in young people: Initial presentation and clinical course. *Journal of the American Academy of Child and Adolescent Psychiatry, 32,* 714–722.

McClellan, J. M., Rubert, M. P., Reichler, R. J., & Sylvester, C. E. (1990). Attention deficit disorder in children at risk for anxiety and depression. *Journal of the American Academy of Child and Adolescent Psychiatry, 29,* 534–539.

McComas, J. J., & Mace, F. C. (2000). Functional analysis of behavior disorders: Theory and research. In E. S. Shapiro & T. R. Kratochwill (Eds.), *Behavioral assessment in schools: Theory, research and clinical foundations* (2nd ed., pp. 78–103). New York: Guilford Press.

McCombs, B. L., & Pope, J. E. (1994). *Motivating hard to reach students.* Washington, DC: American Psychological Association.

McConnell, M. E. (1999, November/December). Self-monitoring, cueing, recording, and managing—Teaching students to manage their own behavior. *CEC: Teaching Exceptional Children, 33*(2), 14–21.

McConnell, S. R. (1987). Entrapment effects and the generalization and maintenance of social skills training for elementary school students with behavioral disorders. *Behavioral Disorders, 12,* 252–263.

McConnell, S. R., & Odom, S. L. (1986). Sociometrics: Peer referenced measures and the assessment of social competence. In P. S. Strain, M. J. Guralnick, & H. M. Walker (Eds.), *Children's social behavior: Development, assessment, and modification* (pp. 215–284). New York: Academic Press.

McConville, D. W., & Cornell, D. G. (2003). Aggressive attitudes predict aggressive behavior in middle school students. *Journal of Emotional and Behavioral Disorders, 11,* 179–187.

McCurdy, M., Kunz, G., & Sheridan, S. M. (in press). Temper tantrums. In G. Bear & K. Minke (Eds.), *Children's needs—III.* Bethesda, MD: National Association of School Psychologists.

516

References

McDaniel, T. (1980). Corporal punishment and teacher liability: Questions teachers ask. *Clearing House, 54,* 10–13.

McDermott, J. F., Werry, J., Petti, T., Combrinck-Graham, L., & Char, W. F. (1989). Anxiety disorders in childhood or adolescence. In T. B. Karasu (Ed.), *Treatments of psychiatric disorders* (Vol. 1, pp. 401–446). Washington, DC: American Psychiatric Association.

McDonagh, M. S., & Peterson, K. (2005). *Drug class review on pharmacologic treatments of ADHD: Final report.* Portland, OR: Oregon Evidence-Based Practice Center, Oregon Health and Science University.

McDowell, M. J., & Rappaport, L. R. (1992). *Neurodevelopmental comorbidity with attention deficit hyperactivity disorder: A clinical review.* Paper presented at the 10th annual meeting of the Society for Behavioral Pedicatrics, St. Louis, MO.

McGee, R. A., Feehan, M., Williams, S., Partridge, F., Silva, P. A., & Kelly, J. (1990). DSM-III disorders in a large sample of adolescents. *Journal of the American Academy of Child and Adolescent Psychiatry, 29,* 611–619.

McGee, R. A., & Share, D. L. (1988). Attention deficit disorder hyperactivity and academic failure: Which comes first and what should be treated? *Journal of the American Academy of Child and Adolescent Psychiatry, 27,* 318–325.

McGee, R. A., Silva, P. A., & Williams, S. (1984). Behavior problems in a population of 7-year-old children: Prevalence, stability and types of disorder—A research report. *Journal of Child Psychology and Psychiatry, 25,* 251–259.

McKee, W. T., & Witt, J. C. (1990). Effective teaching: A review of instructional and environmental variables. In T. B. Gutkin & C. R. Reynolds (Eds.), *Handbook of school psychology* (pp. 823–847). New York: Wiley.

McLeer, S. V., Deblinger, E., Atkins, M. S., Foa, E. B., & Ralphe, D. L. (1988). Post traumatic stress disorder in sexually abused children. *Journal of the American Academy of Child and Adolescent Psychiatry, 27,* 650–654.

McLloyd, V. C. (1998). Socioeconomic disadvantage and child development. *American Psychology, 53,* 185–204.

McMahon, R. J., Forehand, R., & Griest, D. L. (1981). Effects of knowledge of social learning principles on enhancing treatment outcome in generalization in a parent training program. *Journal of Consulting and Clinical Psychology, 49,* 526–532.

McMillan, D. L., Forness, S. R., & Trumbul, B. M. (1973). The role of punishment in the classroom. *Exceptional Children, 40,* 85–96.

McNamara, E. (1988). The self-management of school phobia: A case study. *Behavioral Psychotherapy, 16,* 217–229.

McNeil, C. B., Eyberg, S., Eisenstadt, T. H., Newcomb, K., & Funderburk, B. (1991). Parent-child interaction therapy with behavior problem children: Generalization of treatment effects to the school setting. *Journal of Clinical Child Psychology, 20,* 140–151.

Meadows, N. B., & Stevens, K. B. (2004). Teaching alternative behaviors to students with emotional and behavioral disorders. In R. B. Rutherford, M. M. Quinn, & S. R. Mathur (Eds.), *Handbook of research in emotional and behavioral disorders* (pp. 385–398). New York: Guilford Press.

Medco Health Solutions. (2005). *ADHD medication use growing faster among adults than children* (New Research). Available from www.medco.com.

Meltzoff, A. N., & Gopnik, A. (1993). The role of imitation in understanding persons and developing a theory of mind. In S. Baron-Cohen, H. Tager-Flusberg, &

D. J. Cohen (Eds.), *Understanding other minds* (pp. 335–366). New York: Oxford University Press.

Mendler, A. N. (1992). *What do I do when. . . ? How to achieve discipline with dignity in the classroom.* Bloomington, IN: National Education Service.

Merrell, K. W. (2001). *Helping students overcome depression and anxiety: A practical guide.* New York: Guilford Press.

Merrell, K. W. (2002). Social-emotional intervention in schools: Current status, progress, and promise. *School Psychology Review, 31,* 143–147.

Merrell, K. W., & Gimpel, G. A. (1998). *Social skills of children and adolescents: Conceptualization, assessment, treatment.* Mahwah, NJ: Erlbaum.

Mezzacappa, E., Tremblay, R. E., & Kindlon, D. (1997). Anxiety, antisocial behavior, and heart rate regulation in adolescent males. *Journal of Child Psychology and Psychiatry, 38,* 457–469.

Michelson, L., & Mannarino, A. (1986). Social skills training with children: Research and clinical application. In P. S. Strain, M. J. Guralnick, & H. M. Walker (Eds.), *Children's social behavior: Development, assessment, and modification* (pp. 373–406). Orlando, FL: Academic Press.

Milich, R. (1994). The response of children with ADHD to failure: If at first you don't succeed, do try, try again? *School Psychology Review, 23,* 11–28.

Milich, R., & Landau, S. (1981). Socialization and peer relations in the hyperactive child. In K. D. Gadow & I. Bailer (Eds.), *Advances in learning and behavior disabilities* (Vol. 1, pp. 283–339). Greenwich, CT: JAI Press.

Milich, R., Landau, S., Kilby, G., & Whitten, P. (1982). Preschool peer perceptions of the behavior of hyperactive and aggressive children. *Journal of Abnormal Child Psychology, 10,* 497–510.

Milich, R. S., & Loney, J. (1979). The role of hyperactive and aggressive symptomatology in predicting adolescent outcome among hyperactive children. *Journal of Pediatric Psychology, 4,* 93–112.

Miller, L. C. (1983). Fears and anxieties in children. In C. E. Walker & M. C. Roberts (Eds.), *Handbook of clinical child psychology* (pp. 337–380). New York: Wiley.

Miller, L. C., Barrett, C. L., Hampe, E., & Noble, H. (1972). Comparison of reciprocal inhibition, psychotherapy, and waiting list control for phobic children. *Journal of Abnormal Psychology, 79,* 269–279.

Miller, M. C. (2005). What is the significance of the new warnings about suicide risk with Strattera? *Harvard Mental Health Letter, 22,* 8.

Mineka, S., Watson, D., & Clark, L. A. (1998). Comorbidity of anxiety and unipolar mood disorders. *Annual Review of Psychology, 49,* 377–412.

Mirskey, A. F., Anthony, B. J., Duncan, C. C., Ahearn, M. B., & Kellam, S. G. (1991). Analysis of the elements of attention: A neuropsychological approach. *Neuropsychology Review, 2,* 109–145.

Mitchell, J., McCauley, E., Burke, P. M., & Moss, S. J. (1988). Phenomenology of depression in children and adolescents. *Journal of the American Academy of Child and Adolescent Psychiatry, 27,* 12–20.

Mize, J., & Cox, R. A. (1990). Social knowledge and social competence: Number and quality of strategies as predictors of peer behavior. *Journal of Genetic Psychology, 151,* 117–127.

Moffitt, T. E. (1990). Juvenile delinquency and attention deficit disorder: Developmental self-reported delinquents. *Developmental Psychopathology, 1,* 105–118.

Moffitt, T. E. (1993). Adolescence limited and life-course-persistent to anti-social behavior: A developmental taxonomy. *Psychological Review, 100,* 674–701.

Moffitt, T. E., Brammer, G. L., & Caspi, A. (1998). Whole blood serotonin relates to violence in epidemiological study. *Biological Psychiatry, 43,* 446–457.

Moffitt, T. E., & Caspi, A. (2001). Childhood predictors differentiate life-course-persistent in adolescence-limited anti-social pathways among males and females. *Development and Psychopathology, 13,* 355–375.

Moffitt, T. E., Caspi, A., Harrington, H., & Milne, B. J. (2002). Males on the life-course-persistent and adolescence-limited anti-social pathways: Follow-up at age twenty-six years. *Development in Psychopathology, 14,* 179–207.

Molina, L. R. (1990). Adoptees may be at risk for hyperaactivity but no one knows why. *Adopted Child, 9,* 1–2.

Moreau, D. L., Weissman, M., & Warner, V. (1989). Panic disorder in children at high risk for depression. *American Journal of Psychiatry, 146,* 1059–1060.

Morgan, D. P., & Jenson, W. R. (1988). *Teaching behaviorally disordered students.* New York: Macmillan.

Morgan, V., & Dunn, S. (1988). Chameleons in the classroom: Visible and invisible children in nursery and infant classrooms. *Educational Review, 40,* 3–12.

Morris, R. J. (1985). *Behavior modification with exceptional children: Principal and practices.* Glenview, IL: Scott, Foresman.

Morris, R. J., & Kratochwill, T. R. (1983). *Treating children's fears and phobias: A behavioral approach.* New York: Pergamon Press.

Morris, R. J., & Kratochwill, T. R. (1985). Behavioral treatment of children's fears and phobias: A review. *School Psychology Review, 14,* 84–93.

Mota, V. L., & Schachar, R. J. (2000). Reformulating ADHD according to signal detection theory. *Journal of the American Academy of Child and Adolescent Psychiatry, 39,* 1144–1151.

Mott, P., & Krane, A. (1994). Interpersonal cognitive problem-solving and childhood social competence. *Cognitive Therapy and Research, 18,* 127–141.

Mufson, L., Moreau, D., Weissman, M. M., & Garfinkel, R. (1999). Efficacy of interpersonal psychotherapy for depressed adolescents. *Archives of General Psychiatry, 56,* 573–579.

Mulvey, E., & Cauffman, E. (2001). The inherent limits of predicting school violence. *American Psychologist, 56,* 797–802.

Mundy, P., Sigman, M., & Kasari, C. (1990). A longitudinal study of joint attention and language disorders in autistic children. *Journal of Autism and Developmental Disorders, 20,* 115–123.

Mundy, P., Sigman, M., & Kasari, C. (1994). Joint attention, developmental level, and symptom presentation in autism. *Development and Psychopathology, 6,* 389–401.

Muñoz, R. F., Penilla, C., & Urizar, G. (2002). Expanding depression prevention research with children of diverse cultures. *Prevention and Treatment, 5,* Article 13. Retrieved August 16, 2004, from http://journals.apa.org/prevention/volume5/pre0050013c.html.

Murphy, J. J. (1988). Contingency contracting in the schools: A review. *Education and Treatment of Children, 11,* 257–269.

Murphy, K., Barkley, R., & Bush, T. (2002). Young adults with ADHD: Subtype differences in comorbidity, educational, and clinical history. *Journal of Nervous and Mental Diseases, 190,* 1–11.

Myles, B. S., & Simpson, R. L. (1989). Regular educators' modification preferences for mainstreaming mildly handicapped children. *Journal of Special Education, 22,* 479–491.

Nagin, D. S., & Tremblay, R. E. (1999). Trajectories of boys' physical aggression, opposition, and hyperactivity on the path to physically violent and nonviolent juvenile delinquency. *Child Development, 70*(5), 1181–1196.

Naglieri, J. A. (1999). *Essentials for CAS assessment.* New York: Wiley.

Naglieri, J. A. (2003). Current advances in assessment and intervention for children with learning disabilities. In T. E. Scruggs & M. A. Mastropieri (Eds.), *Advances in learning and behavioral disabilities: Vol. 16. Identification and assessment* (pp. 163–190). New York: JAI Press.

Naglieri, J. A. (2005). The Cognitive Assessment System. In D. P. Flanagan & P. L. Harrison (Eds.), *Contemporary intellectual assessment* (2nd ed., pp. 441–460). New York: Guilford Press.

Naglieri, J. A., & Das, J. P. (1997a). *Cognitive Assessment System.* Itasca, IL: Riverside.

Naglieri, J. A., & Das, J. P. (1997b). *Cognitive Assessment System interpretive handbook.* Chicago: Riverside.

Naglieri, J. A., & Das, J. P. (1997c). Intelligence revised. In R. Dillon (Ed.), *Handbook on testing* (pp. 136–163). Westport, CT: Greenwood Press.

Naglieri, J. A., & Das, J. P. (2005a, November). Are intellectual processes important in the diagnosis and treatment of ADHD? *ADHD Report.*

Naglieri, J. A., & Das, J. P. (2005b). Planning, Attention, Simultaneous, Successive (PASS) theory: A revision of the concept of intelligence. In D. P. Flanagan & P. L. Harrison (Eds.), *Contemporary intellectual assessment* (2nd ed., pp. 136–182). New York: Guilford Press.

Naglieri, J. A., & Goldstein, S. (2006). The role of intellectual processes in the DSM-V diagnosis of ADHD. *Journal of Attention Disorders, 10,* 3–8.

Naglieri, J. A., Goldstein, S., Iseman, J. S., & Schwebach, A. (2003). Performance of children with attention deficit hyperactivity disorder and anxiety/depression on the WISC-III and Cognitive Assessment System (CAS). *Journal of Psychoeducational Assessment, 21,* 32–42.

Naglieri, J. A., Goldstein, S., & Schwebach, A. (2004). Can there be reliable identification of ADHD with divergent conceptualization and inconsistent test results? *ADHD Report, 12,* 6–9.

Naglieri, J. A., & Gottling, S. H. (1995). A cognitive education approach to math instruction for the learning disabled: An individual study. *Psychological Reports, 76,* 1343–1354.

Naglieri, J. A., & Gottling, S. H. (1997). Mathematics instruction and PASS cognitive processes: An intervention study. *Journal of Learning Disabilities, 30,* 513–520.

Naglieri, J. A., & Johnson, D. (2000). Effectiveness of a cognitive strategy intervention to improve math calculation based on the PASS theory. *Journal of Learning Disabilities, 33,* 591–597.

Naglieri, J. A., Otero, T., DeLauder, B., & Matto, H. (in press). Bilingual Hispanic children performance on the English and Spanish versions of the Cognitive Assessment System. *School Psychology Quarterly.*

Naglieri, J. A., & Pickering, E. (2003). *Helping children learn: Instructional handouts for use in school and at home.* Baltimore: Paul H. Brookes.

Naglieri, J. A., & Rojahn, J. R. (2001). Evaluation of African-American and White children in special education programs for children with mental retardation using the WISC-III and Cognitive Assessment System. *American Journal of Mental Retardation, 106*, 359–367.

Naglieri, J. A., & Rojahn, J. R. (2004). Validity of the PASS theory and CAS: Correlations with achievement. *Journal of Educational Psychology, 96*, 174–181.

Naglieri, J. A., Rojahn, J. R., & Matto, H. C. (in press). Hispanic and non-Hispanic children performance on PASS cognitive processes and achievement. *Intelligence.*

Naglieri, J. A., Rojahn, J. R., Matto, H. C., & Aquilino, S. A. (2005). Black White differences in intelligence: A study of the PASS theory and Cognitive Assessment System. *Journal of Psychoeducational Assessment, 23*, 146–160.

Nansel, T. M., Overpeck, M., Pilla, S., Ruan, J., Simons-Morton, B., & Scheidt, P. (2001). Bullying behaviors among U.S. youth: Prevalence and association with psychosocial adjustment. *Journal of the American Medical Association, 285*, 2094–2100.

National Association of School Psychologists. (1986). *Supporting paper on corporal punishment position statement.* Washington, DC: Author.

National Center for Children in Poverty. (2002). *Poverty statistics.* Retrieved June 12, 2003, from http://www.nccp.org.

Needleman, H. L., Riess, J. A., Tobin, M. J., Biesecker, G. E., & Greenhouse, J. B. (1996). Bone lead levels and delinquent behavior. *Journal of the American Medical Association, 275*, 363–369.

Neisworth, J. T., & Smith, R. M. (1983). *Modifying retarded behavior.* Boston: Houghton Mifflin.

Nelson, K. B., & Ellenberg, J. H. (1979). Apgar scores and long-term neurological handicap [Abstract]. *Annals of Neurology, 6.*

Newcomer, P. L., Barenbaum, E. M., & Bryant, B. R. (1994). *Depression and Anxiety in Youth Scale.* Austin, TX: ProEd.

Newsom, C., Favell, J. E., & Rincover, A. (1983). Side effects of punishment. In S. Axelrod & J. Apsche (Eds.), *The effects of punishment on human behavior* (pp. 285–316). New York: Academic Press.

Niederhofer, H., & Pittschieler, M. D. (in press). A preliminary investigation of ADHD symptoms in persons with celiac disease. *Journal of Attention Disorders.*

Noell, G. H., Duhon, G. J., Gatti, S. L., & Connell, J. E. (2002). Consultation, follow-up, and implementation of behavior management interventions in general education. *School Psychology Review, 31*, 217–234.

Noell, G. H., Gansle, K. A., & Allison, R. (1999). Do you see what I see? Teachers' and school psychologists' evaluations of naturally occurring consultation cases. *Journal of Educational and Psychological Consultation, 10*, 107–128.

Noell, G. H., Witt, J. C., Slider, N. J., Connell, J. E., Gatti, S. L., Williams, K. L., et al. (2005). Treatment implementation following behavioral consultation in schools: A comparison of three follow-up strategies. *School Psychology Review, 34*(1), 87–106.

Nolen-Hoeksema, S. (2002). Gender differences in depression. In I. H. Gotlib & C. L. Hammen (Eds.), *Handbook of depression* (pp. 492–509). New York: Guilford Press.

Nordquist, V. M. (1971). The modification of child's enuresis: Some response-response relationships. *Journal of Applied Behavior Analysis, 4*, 241–247.

Northup, J., Broussard, C., Jones, K., George, T., Vollmer, T. R., & Herring, M. (1995). The differential effects of teacher and peer attention on the disruptive classroom behavior of three children with a diagnosis of attention deficit hyperactivity disorder. *Journal of Applied Behavior Analysis, 28,* 227–228.

Norvell, N., & Towle, P. O. (1986). Self-report depression and observable conduct problems in children. *Journal of Clinical Child Psychology, 15,* 228–232.

Nottelmann, E. D., & Jensen, P. S. (1995). Comorbidity of disorders in children and adolescents: Developmental perspectives. In T. H. Ollendick & R. J. Prinz (Eds.), *Advances in clinical child psychology* (Vol. 17, pp. 109–155). New York: Plenum Press.

Novaco, R. (1977). Stress inoculation: A cognitive therapy for anger. *Journal of Consulting and Clinical Psychology, 45,* 600–608.

O'Connor, R. D. (1972). Relative efficacy of modeling, shaping, and the combined procedures of modification of social withdrawal. *Journal of Abnormal Psychology, 79,* 327–334.

Oden, S. L., & Asher, S. R. (1977). Coaching children in social skills for friendship making. *Child Development, 48,* 495–506.

Office of Juvenile Justice and Delinquency Prevention. (2000, May). *Second chances: Giving kids a chance to make a better choice* (Publication No. NCJ181680). Washington, DC: U.S. Department of Justice.

Ohta, M., Nagai, Y., Hara, H., & Sasaki, M. (1987). Parental perception of behavioral symptoms in Japanese autistic children. *Journal of Autism and Developmental Disorders, 17,* 549–564.

O'Leary, K., & Drabman, R. (1971). Token reinforcement programs in the classroom: A review. *Psychological Bulletin, 75,* 379–398.

O'Leary, K., Kaufman, K., Kass, R., & Drabman, R. (1970). The effects of loud and soft reprimands on the behavior of disruptive students. *Exceptional Children, 37,* 145–155.

Ollendick, T. H., & Cerny, J. A. (1981). *Clinical behavior therapy with children.* New York: Plenum Press.

Ollendick, T. H., Dailey, D., & Shapiro, E. S. (1983). Vicarious reinforcement: Expected and unexpected effects. *Journal of Applied Behavioral Analysis, 16,* 485–491.

Ollendick, T. H., & King, N. J. (1994). Diagnosis, assessment, and treatment of internalizing problems in children: The role of longitudinal data. *Journal of Consulting and Clinical Psychology, 6*(5), 918–927.

Ollendick, T. H., King, N. J., & Frary, R. B. (1989). Fears in children and adolescents: Reliability and generalization ability across gender, age, and nationality. *Behavior Research Therapy, 27,* 19–26.

Ollendick, T. H., Matson, J. L., & Helsel, W. J. (1985). Fears in children and adolescents: Normative data. *Behavior Research and Therapy, 23,* 465–467.

Olson, J. (1989). Managing life in the classroom: Dealing with the nitty gritty. *Academic Therapy, 24,* 544–553.

Olsson, I., Steffenburg, S., & Gillberg, C. (1988). Epilepsy in autism and autistic like conditions: A population study. *Archives of Neurology, 45,* 666–668.

Olweus, D. (1993). *Bullying at school: What we know and what we can can do.* Cambridge, MA: Blackwell.

Olweus, D., Limber, S., & Mihalik, S. F. (1999). *Blueprints for violence prevention: Book nine—Bullying prevention program.* Bolder, CO: Center for the Study and Prevention of Violence.

O'Neill, M. E., & Douglas, V. I. (1996). Rehearsal strategies and recall performance with boys with and without attention deficit hyperactivity disorder. *Journal of Pediatric Psychology, 21*, 73–88.

O'Neill, R., Horner, R. H., Albin, R. W., Storey, K., & Sprague, J. (1997). *Functional assessment of problem behavior: A practical assessment guide.* Sycamore, IL: Sycamore Press.

Ornitz, E. M., Guthrie, D., & Farley, A. J. (1977). The early development of autistic children. *Journal of Autism and Developmental Disorders, 7*, 207–229.

Ornitz, E. M., & Ritvo, E. R. (1968). Perceptual inconstancy in early infantile autism. *Archives of General Psychiatry, 18*, 76–98.

Orvaschel, H., & Puig-Antich, J. (1994). *Schedule for affective disorders and schizophrenia for school-age children* (Epidemiologic version, 5th ed.). Pittsburgh, PA: Western Psychiatric Institute and Clinic.

Paine, S. C., Radicchi, J., Rosellini, L. C., Deutchman, L., & Darch, C. B. (1983). *Structuring your classroom for academic success.* Champaign, IL: Research Press.

Palmer, P. J. (1998). *The courage to teach.* San Francisco: Jossey-Bass.

Pam, A. (1995). Biological psychiatry: Science or pseudoscience. In C. A. Ross & A. Pam (Eds.), *Pseudoscience in biological psychiatry* (pp. 7–35). New York: Wiley.

Panaccione, V. F., & Wahler, R. G. (1986). Child behavior, maternal depression, and social coercion as factors in the quality of child care. *Journal of Abnormal Child Psychology, 14*, 263–278.

Paolito, A. W. (1999). Clinical validation of the Cognitive Assessment System for children with ADHD. *ADHD Report, 1*, 1–5.

Paquette, J. A., & Underwood, M. K. (1999). Gender differences in young adolescents' experiences of peer victimization: Social and physical aggression. *Merrill-Palmer Quarterly, 45*, 242–266.

Parke, R. D. (1977). Punishment in children: Effects, side effects and alternative strategies. In H. L. Hom & P. A. Robinson (Eds.), *Psychological process in Early Education* (pp. 71–99). New York: Academic Press.

Parke, R. D., & Walters, R. H. (1967). Some factors in determining the efficacy of punishment for inducing response inhibition. *Monograph of the Society for Research and Child Development, 32*, 109.

Parker, H. C. (1990). *Listen, look and think—A self-regulation program for children.* Plantation, FL: Impact Publications.

Parker, H. C. (1992). *The ADD hyperactivity handbook for schools.* Plantation, FL: ADD Warehouse.

Parker, J. G., & Asher, S. R. (1987). Peer relations and later personal adjustment: Are low-accepted children at risk? *Psychological Bulletin, 102*, 357–389.

Parsons, L. R., & Heward, W. L. (1979). Training peers to tutor: Evaluation of a tutor training package for primary learning disabled students. *Journal of Applied Behavior Analysis, 12*, 309–310.

Pato, M. T., Zohar-Kadouch, R., Zohar, J., & Murphy, D. L. (1988). Return of symptoms after discontinuation of cloimpramine in patients with obsessive-compulsive disorder. *American Journal of Psychiatry, 145*, 1521–1525.

Patterson, C. J., Kupersmidt, J. B., & Vaden, N. A. (1990). Income level, gender, ethnicity, and household composition as predictors of children's school-based competence. *Child Development, 61*, 485–494.

Patterson, G. R. (1965). A learning theory approach to the problem of the school phobia child. In L. P. Ullman & L. Krasner (Eds.), *Case studies in behavior modification* (pp. 279–284). New York: Holt, Rinehart and Winston.

Patterson, G. R. (1975). *Families: Applications of social learning to family life*. Champaign, IL: Research Press.

Patterson, G. R. (1982). *Coercive family process*. Eugene, OR: Castalia.

Patterson, G. R., DeBaryshe, B. D., & Ramsey, E. (1989). A developmental perspective on antisocial behavior. *American Psychologist, 44*, 329–335.

Patterson, G. R., & White, G. D. (1970). It's a small world: The application of "time-out" for positive reinforcement. In F. H. Kanfer & J. S. Phillips (Eds.), *Learning foundations of behavioral therapy*. New York: Wiley.

Paul, R. (1987). Communication. In D. Cohen & A. Donnellan (Eds.), *Handbook of autism and pervasive developmental disorders* (pp. 61–84). New York: Wiley.

Pauls, D. L., & Leckman, J. F. (1986). The inheritance of Gilles de la Tourette's syndrome and associated behaviors: Evidence for autosomal dominant transmission. *New England Journal of Medicine, 315*, 993–997.

Pelham, W. E. (1987). What do we know about the use and effects of CNS stimulants in ADD? In J. Loney (Ed.), *The young hyperactive child: Answers to questions about diagnosis, prognosis and treatment* (pp. 99–110). New York: Haworth Press.

Pelham, W. E. (2002). *How to establish a school-home daily report card* (In AAP ADHD toolkit). Elk Grove Village, IL: American Academy of Pediatrics.

Pelham, W. E., & Bender, M. E. (1982). Peer relationships in hyperactive children. In K. D. Gadow & I. Bialer (Eds.), *Advances in learning and behavioral disabilities* (Vol. 1, pp. 365–436). Greenwich, CT: JAI Press.

Pelham, W. E., & Hoza, B. (1996). Intensive treatment: A summer treatment program for children with ADHD. In E. D. Hibbs & P. S. Hensen (Eds.), *Psychosocial treatments for child and adolescent disorders: Empirically based strategies for clinical practice* (pp. 311–340). Washington, DC: American Psychological Association.

Pelham, W. E., & Milich, R. (1984). Peer relations of children with hyperactivity/attention deficit disorder. *Journal of Learning Disabilities, 17*, 560–568.

Penrose, L. S., & Raven, J. C. (1936). A new series of perceptual tests: Preliminary communication. *British Journal of Medical Psychology, 16*, 97–104.

Perris, C. (1966). A study of bipolar (manic-depressive) and unipolar recurrent depressive psychoses. *Acta Psychiatrica Scandinavia, 42*(Suppl. 194), 1–188.

Peselow, E. D., Baxter, N., Fieve, R. R., & Barouch, E. F. (1987). Dexamethasone suppression test as a monitor of clinical recovery. *American Journal of Psychiatry, 144*, 30–34.

Peterson, A. C., Compas, B. E., Brooks-Gunn, J., Stemmler, M., Ey, S., & Grant, K. E. (1993). Depression in adolescence. *American Psychologist, 48*, 155–164.

Peterson, K. C., Prout, M. F., & Schwarz, R. A. (1991). *Post traumatic stress disorder: A clinician's guide*. New York: Plenum Press.

Pfiffner, L., & McBurnett, K. (1997). Social skills training with parent generalization: Treatment effects for children with attention deficit disorder. *Journal of Consulting and Clinical Psychology, 65*, 749–757.

Piaget, J. (1973). *To understand is to invent: The future of education*. New York: Grossman.

Pianta, R. C. (1999). *The student-teacher relationship scale*. Charlottesville: University of Virginia.

Pianta, R. C., & McCoy, S. J. (1997). The first day of school: The predictive validity of early school screening. *Journal of Applied Developmental Psychology, 18*, 1–22.

Pianta, R. C., Steinberg, M. S., & Rollins, K. B. (1995). The first two years of school: Teacher-child relationships and deflections in children's classroom adjustment. *Development and Psychopathology, 7*, 295–312.

Pierson, M. R., & Glaeser, B. C. (2005). Extension of research on social skills training using comic strip conversations to students without autism. *Education and Training in Developmental Disabilities, 40*, 279–284.

Pincus, D., & Friedman, A. (2004). Improving children's coping with everyday stress: Transporting treatment interventions to school settings. *Clinical Child and Family Psychology Review, 7*, 223–240.

Planta, R. C., & Walsh, D. J. (1998). Applying the construct of resilience in schools: Cautions from a developmental systems perspective. *School Psychology Review, 27*, 407–417.

Pliszka, S. R. (1989). Effect of anxiety on cognition, behavior and stimulant response in ADHD. *Journal of the American Academy of Child and Adolescent Psychiatry, 28*, 882–887.

Pliszka, S. R. (1992). Comorbidity of attention-deficit hyperactivity disorder and over-anxious disorder. *Journal of the American Academy of Child and Adolescent Psychiatry, 31*, 197–203.

Pliszka, S. R. (1999). The psychobiology of oppositional defiant disorder and conduct disorder. In H. C. Quay & A. E. Hogan (Eds.), *Handbook of disruptive behavior disorders* (pp. 371–395). New York: Kluwer Academic/Plenum Press.

Ponti, C. R., Zins, J. E., & Graden, J. L. (1988). Implementing a consultation-based service delivery system to decrease referrals for special education: A case study of organizational considerations. *School Psychology Review, 17*, 89–100.

Porterfield, J. K., Herbert-Jackson, E., & Risely, T. R. (1976). Contingent observation: An effective and acceptable procedure for reducing disruptive behavior of young children in a group setting. *Journal of Applied Behavior Analysis, 9*, 55–64.

Posner, M. I., & Boies, S. J. (1971). Components of attention. *Psychological Review, 78*, 391–408.

Poulton, A. (2005). Growth on stimulant medication; clarifying the confusion: A review. *Archives of Disease in Childhood, 90*, 801–806.

Powell, T. H., & Powell, I. Q. (1982). Guidelines for implementing time-out procedures. *Pointer, 26*, 18–21.

Poznanski, E. O. (1982). The clinical phenomenology of childhood depression. *American Journal of Orthopsychiatry, 52*, 308–313.

Poznanski, E. O. (1985). Diagnostic criteria of childhood depression. *American Journal of Psychiatry, 142*, 1168–1173.

Poznanski, E. O., & Zrull, J. P. (1970). Childhood depression. *Archives of General Psychiatry, 23*, 8–15.

Prawat, R. S. (1998). Current self-regulation views of learning and motivation viewed through a Deweyan lens: The problems with dualism. *American Educational Research Journal, 35*, 199–224.

Premack, D. (1959). Toward empirical behavior laws: Positive reinforcement. *Psychological Review, 66*, 219–233.

Pressley, M. P., & Woloshyn, V. (1995). *Cognitive strategy instruction that really improves children academic performance* (2nd ed.). Cambridge, MA: Brookline.

Puig-Antich, J. (1982). Major depression and conduct disorder in puberty. *Journal of the American Academy of Child Psychiatry, 21,* 118–128.

Puig-Antich, J. (1986). Psychological markers: Effects of age and puberty. In M. Rutter, C. E. Izard, & P. B. Read (Eds.), *Depression in young people* (pp. 341–381). New York: Guilford Press.

Puig-Antich, J., Lukens, E., Davies, M., Goetz, D., Brennan-Quattrock, J., & Todak, G. (1985). Psychosocial functioning in prepubertal major depressive disorders: I. Interpersonal relationships during the depressive episode. *Archives of General Psychiatry, 42,* 200-507.

Puig-Antich, J., Novacenko, M. S., Davies, M., Chambers, W. J., Tabrizi, M. A., Krawiec, V., et al. (1984). Growth hormone secretion in prepubertal children with major depression. *Archives of General Psychiatry, 39,* 932–939.

Puig-Antich, J., & Rabinovich, H. (1986). Relationship between affective and anxiety disorders in childhood. In R. Gittelman (Ed.), *Anxiety disorders of childhood* (pp. 136–156). New York: Guilford Press.

Pynoos, R. S., Frederick, C., Nader, K., Arroyo, W., Steinberg, A., Eth, S., et al. (1987). Life threat and posttraumatic stress in school-age children. *Archives of General Psychiatry, 44,* 1057–1063.

Quay, H. C. (1979). Classification. In H. C. Quay & J. S. Werry (Eds.), *Psychopathological disorders of childhood* (2nd ed., pp. 1–42). New York: Wiley.

Rademacher, J. A., Callahan, K., & Pederson-Seelye, V. (1998). How do your classroom rules measure up? Guidelines for developing an effective rule management routine. *Intervention in School and Clinic, 33,* 284–289.

Raine, A., Venables, P. H., & Williams, M. (1990). Relationships between central and autonomic measures of arousal at age 15 years and criminality at age 24 years. *Archives of General Psychiatry, 47,* 1060–1064.

Rapee, R. M., & Barlow, D. H. (2001). Generalized anxiety disorders, panic disorders, and phobias. In P. B. Sutker & H. E. Adams (Eds.), *Comprehensive handbook of psychopathology* (3rd ed., pp. 131–154). New York: Kluwer Academic/Plenum Press.

Rapee, R. M., & Sweeney, L. (2001). Social phobia in children and adolescents: Nature and assessment. In W. R. Crozier & L. E. Alden (Eds.), *International handbook of social anxiety: Concepts, research and interventions relating to the self and shyness* (pp. 505–523). New York: Wiley.

Rapoport, J. L. (1986). Annotation childhood obsessive compulsive disorder. *Journal of Child Psychology and Psychiatry, 27,* 289–295.

Rapport, M. D. (1987). *The attention training system.* DeWitt, NY: Gordon Systems.

Rapport, M. D., Murphy, H. A., & Bailey, J. S. (1982). Ritalin versus response cost in the control of hyperactive children: A within-subject comparison. *Journal of Applied Behavior Analysis, 15,* 205–216.

Raskind, M. H., Goldberg, R. J., Higgins, E. L., & Herman, K. L. (2003). *Life success for children with learning disabilities: A parent guide.* Pasadena, CA: Frostig Center.

Rasmussen, S. A., & Eisen, J. (1990). Epidemiology and clinical features of obsessive-compulsive disorder. In M. A. Jinike, L. Baer, & W. E. Minchiello (Eds.), *Obsessive-compulsive disorders: Theory and management.* Chicago: Yearbook Medical.

Rasmussen, S. A., & Tsuang, M. T. (1986). Clinical characteristics and family history in DSM-III obsessive-compulsive disorder. *American Journal of Psychiatry, 143,* 317–322.

Ray, C. E., & Elliott, S. N. (2006). Social adjustment in academic achievement: A predictive model for students with diverse, academic and behavior competencies. *School Psychology Review, 35*, 493–501.

Regier, D. A., Boyd, J. H., Burke, J. D., Rae, D. S., Myers, J. K., Kramer, M., et al. (1988). One-month prevalence of mental health disorders in the United States: Based on five epidemiologic catchment area sites. *Archives of General Psychiatry, 45*, 977–986.

Rehm, L. P., Gordon-Leventon, B. G., & Ivens, C. (1987). Depression. In C. L. Frame & J. L. Matson (Eds.), *Handbook of assessment in childhood psychopathology: Applied issues in differential diagnosis and treatment evaluation* (pp. 341–371). New York: Plenum Press.

Reichler, R. J., & Lee, E. M. (1987). Overview of biomedical issues in autism. In E. Schopler & G. B. Mesibov (Eds.), *Neurobiological issues in autism* (pp. 14–43). New York: Plenum Press.

Reimers, T. M., Wacker, D. P., & Koeppel, G. (1987). Acceptability of behavioral treatments: A review of the literature. *School Psychology Review, 16*, 212–227.

Reinemann, D. H. S., Stark, K. D., Molnar, J., & Simpson, J. (in press). Depressive disorders. In G. Bear & K. Minke (Eds.), *Children's needs III: Development, prevention, and intervention.* Bethesda, MD: National Association of School Psychologists.

Reinherz, H. Z., Giaconia, R. M., Lefkowitz, E. S., Pakiz, B., & Frost, A. K. (1993). Prevalence of psychiatric disorders in a community population of older adolescents. *Journal of the American Academy of Child and Adolescent Psychiatry, 32*, 369–377.

Reiss, A. L., Feinstein, C., Rosenbaum, K. N., Borengasser-Caruso, M. A., & Goldsmith, B. M. (1985). Autism associated with Williams syndrome. *Journal of Pediatrics, 106*, 247–249.

Reitman, D., O'Callaghan, P. M., & Mitchell, P. (2005). Parent as coach: Enhancing sports participation and social behavior for ADHD-diagnosed children. *Child and Family Behavior Therapy, 27*, 57–68.

Relmers, T. M., Wacker, D. P., & Koeppel, G. (1987). Acceptability of behavioral treatments: A review of the literature. *School Psychology Review, 16*, 212–227.

Reynolds, C. R., & Kamphaus, R. W. (2005). *Manual for the behavioral assessment system for children* (2nd ed.). Circle Pines, MN: American Guidance Services.

Reynolds, C. R., & Richmond, B. O. (1978). What I think and feel: A revised measure of children's manifest anxiety. *Journal of Abnormal Child Psychology, 6*, 271–280.

Reynolds, C. R., & Richmond, B. O. (1985). *Revised Children's Manifest Anxiety Scale.* Los Angeles: Western Psychological Services.

Reynolds, W. M. (1989). *Reynolds Child Depression Scale.* Odessa, FL: Psychological Assessment Resources.

Reynolds, W. M. (1994). Assessment of depression in children and adolescents by self-report questionnaires. In W. M. Reynolds & H. E. Johnston (Eds.), *Handbook of depression in children and adolescents* (pp. 209–234). New York: Plenum Press.

Rhoades, M. M., & Kratochwill, T. R. (1992). Teacher reactions to behavioral consultation: An analysis of language and involvement. *School Psychology Quarterly, 7*, 47–59.

Rhode, G., Jenson, W. R., & Reavis, H. K. (1992). *The tough kid book: Practical classroom management strategies.* Longmont, CO: Sopris West.

Rhodes, G., Morgan, D., & Young, K. R. (1983). Generalization and maintenance of treatment gains of behaviorally handicapped students from resource rooms to regular classrooms using self-evaluation procedures. *Journal of Applied Behavior Analysis, 16,* 171–188.

Richards, M. H., Boxer, A. M., Petersen, A. C., & Albrecht, R. (1990). Relation of weight to body image in pubertal girls and boys from two communities. *Developmental Psychology, 26,* 313–321.

Richman, N., Stevenson, J. E., & Graham, P. (1982). *Preschool to school: A behavioral study.* London: Academic Press.

Riddle, M. A., Scahill, L., King, R., Hardin, M. T., Towbin, K. E., Ort, S. I., et al. (1990). Obsessive-compulsive disorder in children and adolescents: Phenomenology and family history. *Journal of the American Academy of Child and Adolescent Psychiatry, 29,* 766–772.

Riebin, R. A., & Balow, B. (1978). Prevalence of teacher identified behavior problems: A longitudinal study. *Exceptional Children, 45,* 102–111.

Rief, S. (1998). *The ADD/ADHD Checklist: An easy reference for parents and teachers.* San Francisco: Jossey-Bass.

Rief, S. (2003). *The ADHD book of lists.* San Francisco: Jossey-Bass.

Rief, S. (2005). *How to reach and teach children with ADD/ADHD* (2nd ed.). San Francisco: Jossey-Bass.

Rief, S., & Heimburge, J. (1996). *How to reach and teach all students in the inclusive classroom.* San Francisco: Jossey-Bass.

Rief, S., & Heimburge, J. (2006). *How to reach and teach all children in the inclusive classroom* (2nd ed.). San Francisco: Jossey-Bass.

Riikonen, R., & Amnell, G. (1981). Psychiatric disorders in children with earlier infantile spasms. *Developmental Medicine and Child Neurology, 23,* 747–760.

Ritvo, E. R., Freeman, F. J., Pingree, C., Mason-Brothers, A., Jorde, L., Jenson, W. R., et al. (1989). The UCLA-University of Utah epidemiological survey of autism: Prevalence. *American Journal of Psychiatry, 146,* 194–199.

Ritvo, E. R., Freeman, B. J., Scheibel, A. B., Duong, T., Robinson, H., Guthrie, D., et al. (1986). Lower Purkinje cell counts in the cerebella of four autistic subjects: Initial findings of the UCLA NSAC Autopsy Research Report. *American Journal of Psychiatry, 143,* 862–866.

Rizzolo, J. K. (1976). Building better communication between the educational and medical professions with respect to learning dsiabled children. *Illinois School Research, 12,* 25–33.

Roberts, M. W. (1982). The effects of warned versus unwarned time-out procedures on child non-compliance. *Child and Family Behavior Therapy, 4,* 37–53.

Roberts, M. W., Hatzenbuehler, L. C., & Bean, A. W. (1981). The effects of differential attention and time out on child non-compliance. *Behavior Therapy, 12,* 93–99.

Roberts, T. B. (1975). *Four psychologies applied to education: Freudian-behavioral-humanistic-transpersonal.* Cambridge, MA: Schenkman.

Robin, S. S., & Bosco, J. J. (1973). Ritalin for school children: The teachers' perspective. *Journal of School Health, 10,* 624–628.

Robins, L. N. (1991). Conduct disorder. *Journal of Child Psychology and Psychiatry, 32,* 193–212.

Rock, M. (2005). Use of strategic self-monitoring to enhance academic engagement, productivity, and accuracy of students with and without exceptionalities. *Journal of Positive Behavior Intervention, 7,* 2–17.

Rogers, M. R. (1998). The influence of race and consultant behavior on perceptions of consultant competence and multi-cultural sensitivity. *School Psychology Quarterly, 13*(4), 265–280.

Rohde, P., Lewinsohn, P. M., Clarke, G. N., Hops, H., & Seeley, J. R. (2005). The adolescent coping with depression course: A cognitive-behavioral approach to the treatment of adolescent depression. In E. Hibbs & P. Jensen (Eds.), *Psychosocial treatments for child and adolescent disorders: Empirically based strategies for clinical practice* (2nd ed., pp. 219–237). Washington, DC: American Psychological Association.

Rohde, P., Lewinsohn, P. M., & Seeley, J. R. (1991). Comorbidity of unipolar depression: II. Comorbidity with other mental disorders in adolescents and adults. *Journal of Abnormal Psychology, 100,* 214–222.

Roid, G. (2003). *Stanford-Binet* (5th ed.). Itasca, IL: Riverside.

Rose, S. L., Rose, S. A., & Feldman, J. F. (1989). Stability of behavior problems in very young children. *Development and Psychopathology, 1,* 5–19.

Rosenbaum, M. S., & Drabman, R. S. (1979). Self-control training in the classroom: A review and critique. *Journal of Applied Behavior Analysis, 12,* 467–485.

Rosenfield, S. (1985). Teacher acceptance of behavioral principles: An issue of values. *Teacher Education and Special Education, 8,* 153–158.

Rosenhall, U., Johansson, E., & Gillberg, C. (1988). Oculomotor findings in autistic children. *Journal of Laryngology and Otology, 102,* 435–439.

Rowe, K. J., & Rowe, K. S. (1992a). The relationship between inattentiveness in the classroom and reading achievement: Pt. A. Methodological issues. *Journal of the American Academy of Child and Adolescent Psychiatry, 31,* 349–356.

Rowe, K. J., & Rowe, K. S. (1992b). The relationship between inattentiveness in the classroom and reading achievement: Pt. B. An explanatory study. *Journal of the American Academy of Child and Adolescent Psychiatry, 31,* 357–358.

Rubin, K. H. (1985). Socially withdrawn children: An "at risk" population. In B. H. Schneider, K. H. Rubin, & J. E. Ledingham (Eds.), *Children's peer relations: Issues in assessment and intervention* (pp. 125–139). New York: Springer-Verlag.

Rudolph, K. D., & Clark, A. G. (2001). Conceptions of relationships in children with depressive and aggressive symptoms: Social-cognitive distortion or reality? *Journal of Abnormal Child Psychology, 29,* 41–56.

Rusch, F. R., Rose, T., & Greenwood, C. R. (1988). *Introduction to behavior analysis in special education.* Englewood Clifts, NJ: Prentice-Hall.

Rushton, J. L., Forcier, M., & Schectman, R. M. (2003). Epidemiology of depressive symptoms in the national longitudinal study of adolescent health. *Journal of the American Academy of Child and Adolescent Psychiatry, 41,* 199–205.

Rutter, M. (1970). Autistic children: Infancy to adulthood. *Seminars in Psychiatry, 2,* 435–450.

Rutter, M. (1978). Diagnosis and definition. In M. Rutter & E. Schopler (Eds.), *Autism: A reappraisal of concepts and treatment* (pp. 1–25). New York: Plenum Press.

Rutter, M. (1979). Language, cognition and autism. In R. Katzman (Ed.), *Congenital and acquired cognitive disorders* (pp. 247–264). New York: Raven Press.

Rutter, M. (1980). School influences on children's behavior and development. *Pediatrics, 65,* 522–533.

Rutter, M. (1983). Cognitive deficits in the pathogenesis of autism. *Journal of Child Psychology and Psychiatry, 24*(4), 513–531.

Rutter, M. (1985). Resilience in the face of adversity: Protective factors and resistance to psychiatric disorder. *British Journal of Psychiatry, 147,* 598–611.

Rutter, M. (1990). Autism as a genetic disorder. In P. McGuffin & R. Murray (Eds.), *New genetics of mental health* (pp. 225–244; Proceedings of Mental Health Foundation Conference). Oxford: Butterworth-Heinemann.

Rutter, M., & Garmezy, N. (1983). Developmental psychopathology. In E. M. Hetherington (Ed.), *Handbook of child psychology* (Vol. 4, pp. 775–991). New York: Wiley.

Rutter, M., MacDonald, H., Lecoutier, A., Harrington, R., Bolton, P., & Bailey, A. (1990). Genetic factors in child psychiatric disorders. Pt. II. Empirical findings. *Journal of Child Psychology Psychiatry, 31,* 39–83.

Rutter, M., Tizard, J., & Whitmore, K. (1970). *Education health and behavior.* London: Longmans, Green.

Rutter, R. A. (1988). *Effects of School as a Community.* Madison, WI: National Center on Effective Secondary Schools.

Sabatino, A. C. (1983). Discipline: A national issue. In D. A. Sabatino, A. C. Sabatino, & L. Mann (Eds.), *Discipline and behavioral management.* Rockville, MD: Aspen.

Sabatino, D. A. (1983). Isolation, expulsion, suspension and detention. In D. A. Sabatino, A. C. Sabatino, & L. Mann (Eds.), *Discipline and behavioral management.* Rockville, MD: Aspen.

Safer, D. J., & Krager, J. M. (1989). A survey of medication treatment for hyperactive/inattentive students. *Journal of the American Medical Association, 260,* 606–609.

Safer, D. J., Zito, J. M., & Fine, E. M. (1996). Increased methylphenidate usage for attention deficit disorder in the 1990s. *Pediatrics, 98,* 1084–1088.

Safran, S. P., & Safran, J. S. (1984). Classroom context and teachers' perceptions of problem behaviors. *Journal of Educational Psychology, 77,* 20–28.

Safran, S. P., & Safran, J. S. (1985). Elementary teachers' tolerance of problem behaviors. *Elementary School Journal, 85,* 237–243.

Safran, S. P., & Safran, J. S. (1987). Teachers' judgments of problem behaviors. *Exceptional Children, 54,* 240–244.

Salend, S. J. (1987). Contingency management systems. *Academic Therapy, 22,* 245–253.

Salmon, D. (1993). Anticipating the school consultant role: Changes in impersonal constructs following training. *School Psychology Quarterly, 8,* 301–317.

Salmon, D., & Fenning, P. (1993). A process of mentorship in school consultation. *Journal of Educational and Psychological Consultation, 4,* 69–87.

Sander, J. B., & McCarty, C. A. (2005). Youth depression in the family context: Familial risk factors and models of treatment. *Clinical Child and Family Psychology Review, 8*(3), 203–219.

Sanson, A., & Prior, M. (1999). Temperament and behavioral precursors to oppositional defiant disorder and conduct disorder. In H. C. Quay & A. E. Hogan (Eds.), *Handbook of disruptive behavior disorder* (pp. 397–417). New York: Kluwer Academic/Plenum Press.

Sarason, I. G., Glaser, E. M., & Fargo, G. A. (1972). *Reinforcing productive classroom behavior.* New York: Behavioral Publications.

Sarason, I. G., & Sarason, B. R. (1981). Teaching cognitive and social skills to high school students. *Journal of Consulting and Clinical Psychology, 49,* 908–918.

Sasso, G. M., Reimers, T. M., Cooper, L. J., Wacker, D. P., Berg, W., Steege, M., et al. (1992). Use of descriptive and experimental analyses to identify the functional properties of aberrant behavior in school settings. *Journal of Applied Behavior Analysis, 25,* 809–822.

Satterfield, J. H., Hoppe, C. M., & Schell, A. M. (1982). A perspective study of delinquency in 110 adolescent boys with attention deficit disorder and 88 normal adolescent boys. *American Journal of Psychiatry, 139,* 795–798.

Scarboro, M. E., & Forehand, R. (1975). Effects of two types of response contingent time out on compliance and oppositional behavior of children. *Journal of Experimental Child Psychology, 19,* 252–264.

Scattone, D., Wilczynski, S. M., Edwards, P., & Rabian, B. (2002). Decreasing disruptive behaviors of children with autism using social stories. *Journal of Autism and Developmental Disorders, 32,* 535–543.

Schaffer, R. (1984). *The child's entry into a social world.* London: Academic Press.

Schain, R., & Yannet, H. (1960). Infantile autism: An analysis of 50 cases and a consideration of certain relevant neuropsychological concepts. *Journal of Pediatrics, 57,* 560–567.

Scheid, K. (1993). *Helping students become strategic learners.* Cambridge, MA: Brookline Books.

Schill, M. T., Kratochwill, T. R., & Elliott, S. N. (1998). Functional assessment in behavioral consultation: A treatment utility study. *School Psychology Quarterly, 13*(2), 116–140.

Schneider, W., Dumais, S. T., & Shiffrin, R. M. (1984). Automatic and controlled processing and attention. In R. Parasuraman & D. R. Davies (Eds.), *Varieties of attention* (pp. 1–28). New York: Academic Press.

Schniering, C. A., Hudson, J. L., & Rapee, R. M. (2000). Issues in the diagnosis and assessment of anxiety disorders in children and adolescents. *Clinical Psychology Review, 20*(4), 453–478.

Schoen, S. F. (1983). The status of compliance technology: Implications for programmiong. *Journal of Special Education, 17,* 483–496.

Schopler, E., & Mesibov, G. B. (1983). *Autism in adolescents and adults.* New York: Plenum Press.

Schopler, E., & Mesibov, G. B. (1987). *Neurobiological issues in autism.* New York: Plenum Press.

Schumaker, J. B., Hovell, M. F., & Sherman, J. A. (1977). An analysis of daily report card and parent-managed privileges in the improvement of adolescents' classroom performance. *Journal of Applied Behavior Analysis, 10,* 449–464.

Schunk, D. H. (2003). Self-efficacy for reading and writing: Influence of modeling, goal setting, and self-evaluation. *Reading and Writing Quarterly, 19,* 159–172.

Seagull, E. A. W., & Weinshank, A. B. (1984). Childhood depression in a selected group of low-achieving seventh graders. *Journal of Clinical Child Psychology, 13,* 134–140.

Segal, J. (1988). Teachers have enormous power in affecting a child's self-esteem. *Brown University Child Behavior and Development Newsletter, 4,* 1–3.

Seidman, L. J., Benedict, K. B., Biederman, J., & Bernstein, J. H. (1995). Performance of children with ADHD on the Rey-Osterrieth Complex Figure: A pilot neuropsychology study. *Journal of Child Psychology and Psychiatry and Allied Disciplines, 36,* 1459–1473.

Seidman, L. J., Biederman, J., Faraone, S. V., Weber, W., Mennin, D., & Jones, J. (1997). A pilot study of neuropsychological functioning in girls with ADHD. *Journal of the American Academy of Child and Adolescent Psychiatry, 36*, 366–373.

Seligman, M. E. P. (1981). A learned helplessness point of view. In L. P. Rehm (Ed.), *Behavior therapy for depression* (pp. 123–141). New York: Academic Press.

Seligman, M. E. P. (1995). *The optimistic child.* New York: Houghton Mifflin.

Seligman, M. E. P. (1998a). Building human strength: Psychology's forgotten mission. *APA Monitor, 29*(1), 2.

Seligman, M. E. P. (1998b). Building human strength: Psychology's forgotten mission. *APA Monitor, 29*(4), 2.

Seligman, M. E. P., Peterson, C., Kaslow, N. J., Tanenbaum, R. L., Alloy, L. B., & Abramson, L. Y. (1984). Attributional style and depressive symptoms among children. *Journal of Abnormal Child Psychology, 93*, 235–238.

Selman, R. L. (1980). *The growth of interpersonal understanding.* New York: Academic Press.

Semrud-Clikeman, M., Biederman, J., Sprich-Buckminister, S., Krifcher, L., Lehman, B., Faraone, S. V., et al. (1992). The incidence of ADHD and concurrent learning disabilities. *Journal of the American Academy of Child and Adolescent Psychiatry, 31*, 439–448.

Semrud-Clikeman, M., Steingard, R. J., Filipek, P., Biederman, J., Bekken, K., & Renshaw, P. F. (2000). Using MRI to examine brain-behavior relationships in males with attention deficit disorder with hyperactivity. *Journal of the American Academy of Child and Adolescent Psychiatry, 39*, 477–484.

Shapiro, T., Sherman, M., Calamari, G., & Koch, D. (1987). Attachment in autism and other developmental disorders. *Journal of Child and Adolescent Psychiatry, 226*, 485–590.

Sharpley, C. F. (1985). Implicit rewards in the classroom. *Contemporary Educational Psychology, 10*, 348–368.

Shea, T. M., & Bauer, A. M. (1987). *Teaching children and youth with behavior disorders* (2nd ed.). Englewood Clifts, NJ: Prentice-Hall.

Shea, T. M., Whiteside, W. R., Beetner, E. G., & Lindsey, D. L. (1974). *Contingency contracting in the classroom.* Edwardsville: Southern Illinois University.

Shepherd, J. T., Broilier, C. B., & Dandro, W. R. (1994). Play skills of preschool children with speech and language delays. *Physical and Occupational Therapy in Pediatrics, 14*, 1–20.

Sheridan, S. M. (1995). *The tough kid social skills book.* Longmont, CO: Sopris West.

Sheridan, S. M. (1998). *Why don't they like me? Helping your child make and keep friends.* Longmont, CO: Sopris West.

Sheridan, S. M., Dee, C. C., Morgan, J. C., McCormick, M. E., & Walker, D. (1996). A multi-method intervention for social skills deficits in children with ADHD and their parents. *School Psychology Review, 25*, 57–76.

Sheridan, S. M., & Elliott, S. N. (1991). Behavioral consultation as a process for linking the assessment and treatment of social skills. *Journal of Educational and Psychological Consultation, 2* , 151-173.

Sheridan, S. M., Erchul, W. P., Brown, M. S., Dowd, S. E., Warnes, E. D., Marti, D. C., et al. (2004). Perceptions of helpfulness in conjoint behavioral consultation: Congruence and agreement between teachers and parents. *School Psychology Quarterly, 19*(2), 121–140.

Sheridan, S. M., Hungelmann, A., & Maughan, D. P. (1999). A contextualized framework for social skills assessment, intervention and generalization. *School Psychology Review, 28*, 84–103.

Sheridan, S. M., Knoche, L. L., & Marvin, C. (in press). Competent families, competent children: Family-based interventions to promote social competence in young children. In W. H. Brown, S. L. Odom, & S. R. McConnell (Eds.), *Social competence of young children: Risk, disability, and evidence-based practices* (2nd ed.). Baltimore: Paul H. Brookes.

Sheridan, S. M., & Kratochwill, T. R. (in press). *Conjoint behavioral consultation: Promoting family-school connections and interventions.* New York: Springer.

Sheridan, S. M., Kratochwill, T. R., & Bergan, J. R. (1996). *Conjoint behavioral consultation: A procedural manual.* New York: Plenum Press.

Sheridan, S. M., Kratochwill, T. R., & Elliott, S. N. (1990). Behavioral consultation with parents and teachers: Delivering treatment for socially withdrawn children at home and school. *School Psychology Review, 19*, 33–52.

Sheridan, S. M., Meegan, S. P., & Eagle, J. W. (2002). Assessing the social context in initial conjoint behavioral consultation interviews: An exploratory analysis investigating processes and outcomes. *School Psychology Quarterly, 17*(3), 299–324.

Sheridan, S. M., & Walker, D. (1999). Social skills in context: Considerations for assessment, intervention, and generalization. In C. R. Reynolds & T. B. Gutkin (Ed.), *The handbook of school psychology* (3rd ed., pp. 686–708). New York: Wiley.

Sherman, D. K., Iacono, W. G., & McGue, M. K. (1997). Attention-deficit hyperactivity disorder dimensions: A twin study of inattention and impulsivity-hyperactivity. *Journal of the American Academy of Child and Adolescent Psychiatry, 36*, 745–753.

Sheslow, D. B., Bondy, A. S., & Nelson, R. O. (1982). A comparison of graduated exposure, verbal coping skills and their combination in the treatment of children's fear of the dark. *Child and Family Behavior Therapy, 4*, 33–45.

Shochet, I. M., Dadds, M. R., Holland, D., Whitefield, K., Harnett, P. H., & Osgarby, S. M. (2001). The efficacy of a universal school-based program to prevent adolescent depression. *Journal of Clinical Child Psychology, 30*, 303–315.

Shonkoff, J. P., & Phillips, D. A. (2000). *From neurons to neighborhoods: The science of early childhood development.* Washington, DC: National Academy Press.

Shores, R. E., Jack, S. L., Gunter, P. L., Ellis, D. M., DeBriere, T. J., & Webby, J. H. (1993). Classroom interactions of children with behavior disorders. *Journal of Emotional and Behavioral Disorders, 1*, 27–39.

Shure, M. B. (1982). Interpersonal problem solving: A cog in the wheel of social cognition. In F. L. Serafica (Ed.), *Social cognitive development in context* (pp. 133–166). New York: Guilford Press.

Shure, M. B. (1992a). *I can problem solve (ICPS): An interpersonal cognitive problem solving program [preschool].* Champaign, IL: Research Press.

Shure, M. B. (1992b). *I can problem solve (ICPS): An interpersonal cognitive problem solving program [kindergarten/primary grades].* Champaign, IL: Research Press.

Shure, M. B. (1992c). *I can problem solve (ICPS): An interpersonal cognitive problem solving program [intermediate elementary grades].* Champaign, IL: Research Press.

Shure, M. B. (1993). *Interpersonal problem solving and prevention: A comprehensive report of research and training: A 5-year-longitudinal study* (Report No. MH-40801). Washington, DC: National Institute of Mental Health.

Shure, M. B. (1994). *Raising a thinking child.* New York: Henry Holt.

Shure, M. B. (1996). *Raising a thinking child.* New York: Simon & Schuster.

Shure, M. B. (2000). *Raising a thinking child workbook: Teaching young children how to resolve everyday conflicts and get along with others.* Champaign, IL: Research Press.

Shure, M. B. (2004). *Ensenando a nuestros ninos a pensar: Un manual para ensenar a los ninos pequenos como resolver problemas y conflictos de la vida contidiana.* Champaign, IL: Research Press.

Shure, M. B., & Bailey, B. (2005, August). *Violence prevention for schools and families.* Presented to the 14th World Congress of Criminology, Philadelphia.

Shure, M. B., & Healey, K. N. (1993, August). *Interpersonal problem solving and prevention in urban school children.* Paper presented at the meeting of the American Psychological Association, Toronto, Ontario, Canada.

Shure, M. B., & Spivack, G. (1972). Means-ends thinking, adjustment and social class among elementary school-aged children. *Journal of Consulting and Clinical Psychology, 38,* 348–353.

Shure, M. B., & Spivack, G. (1978). *Problem solving techniques in childrearing.* San Francisco, Jossey-Bass.

Shure, M. B., & Spivack, G. (1980). Interpersonal problem solving as a mediator of behavioral adjustment in preschool and kindergarten children. *Journal of Applied Developmental Psychology, 1,* 29–44.

Shure, M. B., & Spivack, G. (1982). Interpersonal problem solving in young children: A cognitive approach to prevention. *American Journal of Community Psychology, 10,* 341–356.

Shure, M. B., Spivack, G., & Jaeger, M. A. (1971). Problem solving thinking and adjustment among disadvantaged preschool children. *Child Development, 42,* 1791–1803.

Siegel, B., Vukicevic, J., Elliott, G. R., & Kraemer, H. D. (1989). The use of signal detection theory to assess DSM-III-R criteria for autistic disorder. *Journal of the American Academy of Child and Adolescent Psychiatry, 28*(4), 542–548.

Sigman, M., & Kasari, C. (1995). Joint attention across contexts in normal and autistic children. In C. Moore & D. Dunham (Eds.), *Joint attention: Its origins and role in development* (pp. 189–203). Hillsdale, NJ: Erlbaum.

Silverman, W. K., & Nelles, W. B. (1990). Simple phobia in childhood. In M. Hersen & C. G. Last (Eds.), *Handbook of child and adult psychopathology: A longitudinal perspective.* New York: Pergamon Press.

Silverthorn, P., Frick, P. J., Kuper, K., & Ott, J. (1996). Attention deficit hyperactivity disorder and sex: A test of two etiological models to explain the male predominance. *Journal of Clinical Child Psychology, 25,* 52–59.

Simms, R. B. (1985). Hyperactivity and drug therapy: What the educator should know. *Journal of Research and Development in Education, 18,* 1–7.

Singh, N. N., Epstein, M. H., Luebke, J., & Singh, Y. N. (1990). Psychopharmacological intervention: Pt. I. Teacher perceptions of psychotropic medication for seriously emotionally disturbed students. *Journal of Special Education, 24,* 283–295.

Skinner, B. F. (1948). *Walden two.* London: McMillan.

Skinner, B. F. (1953). *The behavior of organisms: An experimental analyses.* New York: Appleton-Century-Crofts.

Slade, D., & Callaghan, T. (1988). Preventing management problems. *Academic Therapy, 23,* 229–235.

Smalley, S., Asarnow, R., & Spence, M. (1988). Autism and genetics: A decade of research. *Archives of General Psychiatry, 45,* 953–961.

References

Smith, D. (1984). Practicing school psychologists: Their characteristics, activities, and populations served. *Professional Psychology, 15,* 798–810.

Smith, P. K., & Sharp, S. (1994). The problem of school bullying. In P. K. Smith & S. Sharp (Eds.), *School bullying* (pp. 1-19). London: Routledge.

Smith, P. M., Singer, M., Hoel, H., & Cooper, C. L. (2003). Victimization in the school and the workplace: Are there any links? *British Journal of Psychology, 94,* 175–188.

Smith, R. M., Neisworth, J. T., & Greer, J. G. (1978). *Evaluating educational environments.* Columbus, OH: Merrill.

Solomon, R. W., & Wahler, R. G. (1973). Peer reinforcement control of a classroom problem behavior. *Journal of Applied Behavior Analysis, 6,* 49–56.

Soodak, L. C., & Podell, D. M. (1994). Teachers' thinking about difficult-to-teach students. *Journal of Educational Research, 88,* 44–51.

Sourander, A., Helstela, L., Helenius, H., & Piha, J. (2000). Persistence of bullying from childhood to adolescence: A longitudinal 8-year follow-up study. *Child Abuse and Neglect, 24,* 873–881.

Sparrow, S., Balla, D., & Cicchetti, D. (1984). *Vineland Adaptive Behavior Scales.* Circle Pines, MN: American Guidance Service.

Spence, S. H. (1998). A measure of anxiety symptoms among children. *Behavior Research and Therapy, 36,* 545–566.

Spence, S. H., Sheffield, J. K., & Donovan, C. L. (2003). Preventing adolescent depression: An evaluation of the problem solving for life program. *Journal of Consulting and Clinical Psychology, 71,* 3–13.

Spence, S. H., Sheffield, J. K., & Donovan, C. L. (2005). Long-term outcome of a school-based, universal approach to prevention of depression in adolescents. *Journal of Consulting and Clinical Psychology, 73,* 160–167.

Spivack, G., & Shure, M. B. (1974). *Social adjustment of young children: A cognitive approach to solving real-life problems.* San Francisco: Jossey-Bass.

Spivack, G., & Shure, M. B. (1982). The cognition of social adjustment: Interpersonal cognitive problem-solving thinking. In B. B. Lahey & A. E. Kazdin (Eds.), *Advances in clinical child psychology* (Vol. 5, pp. 323–372). New York: Plenum Press.

Sprague, R. L., & Gadow, K. D. (1976). The role of the teacher in drug treatment. *School Review, 12,* 109–140.

Stark, K. D. (1990). *The treatment of depression during childhood: A school-based program.* New York: Guilford Press.

Stark, K. D., Hargrave, J., Sander, J., Custer, G., Schnoebelen, S., Simpson, J., et al. (2006). Treatment of childhood depression: The ACTION program. In P. C. Kendall (Ed.), *Child and adolescent therapy: Cognitive-behavioral procedures* (3rd ed., pp. 169–216). New York: Guilford Press.

Stark, K. D., Hoke, J., Ballatore, M., Valdez, C., Scammaca, N., & Griffin, J. (2005). Treatment of child and adolescent depressive disorders. In E. Hibbs & P. S. Jensen (Eds.), *Psychosocial treatments for child and adolescent disorders: Empirically based strategies for clinical practice* (pp. 239–265). Washington, DC: American Psychological Association.

Stark, K. D., Humphrey, L. L., Crook, K., & Lewis, K. (1990). Perceived family environments of depressed and anxious children: Child's and maternal figure's perspectives. *Journal of Abnormal Child Psychology, 18,* 527–547.

Stark, K. D., Humphrey, L. L., Laurent, J., & Livingston, R. (1993). Cognitive, behavioral and family factors in the differentiation of depressive and anxiety disorders during childhood. *Journal of Consulting and Clinical Psychology, 61,* 878–886.

Stark, K. D., Kaslow, N. J., & Laurent, J. (1993). The assessment of depression in children: Are we assessing depression or the broad-band construct of negative affectivity? *Journal of Emotional and Behavioral Disorders, 1,* 149–154.

Stark, K. D., & Kendall, P. C. (1996a). *"Taking action": A workbook for overcoming depression.* Ardmore, PA: Workbook Publishing.

Stark, K. D., & Kendall, P. C. (1996b). *Treating depressed children: Therapist manual for "Action."* Ardmore, PA: Workbook Publishing.

Stark, K. D., Livingston, R. B., Laurent, J. L., & Cardenas, B. (1993). *Childhood depression: Relationship to academic achievement and scholastic performance.* Manuscript submitted for publication.

Stark, K. D., Sander, J. J., Hauser, M., Simpson, J., Schnoebelen, S., Glenn, R., et al. (2006). Depressive disorders during childhood and adolescence. In E. Mash & R. Barkley (Eds.), *Treatment of childhood disorders* (3rd ed., pp. 336–407). New York: Guilford Press.

Stark, K. D., Schmidt, K. L., & Joyner, T. E. (1993). *The depressive cognitive triad: Symptom specificity and relationship to children's depressive symptoms, parents cognitive triad, and perceived parental messages.* Manuscript submitted for publication.

Stark, K. D., Schnoebelen, S., Simpson, J., Hargrave, J., Glenn, R., & Molnar, J. (2004). *ACTION workbook.* Ardmore, PA: Workbook Publishing.

Stark, K. D., Sommer, D., Bowen, B., Goetz, C., Doxey, M. A., & Vaughn, C. (1997). Depressive disorders during childhood. In G. G. Bear, K. M. Minke, & A. Thomas (Eds.), *Children's needs: Pt. II. Development, problems, and alternatives* (pp. 349–359). Bethesda, MD: National Association of School Psychologists.

Steege, M. W., & Brown-Chidsey, R. (2005). Functional behavioral assessment: The cornerstone of effective problem solving. In R. Brown-Chidsey (Ed.), *Assessment for intervention: A problem-solving approach* (pp. 131–154). New York: Guilford Press.

Steege, M. W., & Northup, J. (1998). Brief functional analysis of problem behavior: A practical approach for classroom consultants. *Proven Practice: Prevention and Remediation Solutions for Schools, 1,* 4–11, 37–38.

Steege, M. W., Wacker, D. P., Berg, W. K., Cigrand, K. C., & Cooper, L. J. (1989). The use of behavioral assessment to prescribe and evaluate treatments for severely handicapped children. *Journal of Applied Behavior Analysis, 22,* 23–33.

Steege, M. W., Wacker, D. P., Cigrand, K. C., Berg, W. K., Novak, C. G., Reimers, T. M., et al. (1990). Use of negative reinforcement in the treatment of self-injury. *Journal of Applied Behavior Analysis, 23,* 417–429.

Steffenburg, S., & Gillberg, C. (1986). Autism and autistic like conditions in Swedish rural and urban areas: A population study. *British Journal of Psychiatry, 149,* 81–87.

Steffenburg, S., Gillberg, C., Hellgren, L., Andersson, L., Gillberg, I. C., Jakobsson, G., et al. (1989). A twin study of autism in Denmark, Finland, Iceland, Norway, and Sweden. *Journal of Child Psychology and Psychiatry, 30,* 405–416.

Stein, M. (1997). We have tried everything and nothing works: Family centered pediatrics and clinical problem solving. *Journal of Developmental and Behavioral Pediatrics, 19,* 114–119.

Steinlauf, B. (1979). Problem-solving skills, locus of control, and the contraceptive effectiveness of young women. *Child Development, 50,* 268–271.

Stenger, M. K., Tollefson, N., & Fine, M. J. (1992). Variables that distinguish elementary teachers who participate in school-based consultation from those who do not. *School Psychology Quarterly, 7,* 271–284.

Sterling-Turner, H. E., Watson, T. S., & Moore, J. W. (2002). The effects of direct training and treatment integrity on treatment outcomes in school consultation. *School Psychology Quarterly, 1,* 47–77.

Sterling-Turner, H. E., Watson, T. S., Wildmon, M., Watkins, C., & Little, E. (2001). Investigating the relationship between training type and treatment integrity. *School Psychology Quarterly, 16,* 78–89.

Stevenson, H. W. (1992). Learning from Asian schools. *Scientific American, 267,* 70–76.

Still, G. F. (1902). The Coulstonian lectures on some abnormal physical conditions in children. *Lancet, 1,* 1008–1012.

Stokes, T. F., & Baer, D. M. (1977). An implicit technology of generalization. *Journal of Applied Behavior Analysis, 10,* 349–367.

Stone, W. L., Lemanek, K. L., Fishel, P. T., Hernandez, M. C., & Altemeier, W. A. (1990). Play and imitation skills in the diagnosis of autism in young children. *Pediatrics, 86,* 267–272.

Stone, W. L., Ousley, O. Y., & Littleford, C. (1995, March). *A comparison of elicited imitation in young children with autism and developmental delay.* Poster session presented at the annual Gatlinburg Conference on Research and Theory in Mental Retardation and Developmental Disabilities, Gatlinburg, TN.

Stoops, E., Rafferty, M., & Johnson, R. E. (1981). *Handbook of education administration* (2nd ed.). Boston, Allyn & Bacon.

Stott, D. H. (1981). Behavior disturbance and failure to learn: A study of cause and effect. *Educational Research, 23,* 163–172.

Strain, P. S. (Ed.). (1981). *The utilization of classroom peers as behavior change agents.* New York: Plenum Press.

Strattera approved to treat ADHD. (2003, March/April). *FDA Consumer, 37,* 4.

Strauss, C. C. (1988). Behavioral assessment and treatment of overanxious disorder in children and adolescents. *Behavior Modification, 12,* 234–250.

Strauss, C. C., Last, C. G., Hersen, M., & Kazdin, A. E. (1988). Association between anxiety and depression in children and adolescents with anxiety disorders. *Journal of Abnormal Child Psychology, 1,* 57–68.

Strauss, C. C., Lease, C. A., Last, C. G., & Francis, G. (1988). Overanxious disorder: An examination of developmental differences. *Journal of Abnormal Child Psychology, 16,* 433–443.

Strayhorn, J. M. (1988). *The competent child: An approach to psychotherapy and preventive mental health.* New York: Guilford Press.

Strunk, R. C., Morazek, D. A., Fuhrmann, G. S., & Labreque, J. F. (1985). Physiologic and psychological characteristics associated with deaths due to asthma and childhood. *Journal of the American Medical Association, 254,* 1193–1198.

Sugai, G. (2003). Commentary: Establishing efficient and durable systems of school-based support. *School Psychology Review, 32,* 530–535.

Sugai, G., & Horner, R. H. (2005). School-wide positive behavior support: An alternative approach to discipline in schools. In L. Bambara & L. Kern (Eds.), *Individualized supports for students with problem behaviors: Designing positive behavior plans* (pp. 359–390). New York: Guilford Press.

Sugai, G., Horner, R., & Gresham, F. (2002). Behaviorally effective school environments. In M. Shinn, H. Walker, & G. Stoner (Eds.), *Interventions for academic and behavior problems: Pt. II. Preventive and remedial approaches* (pp. 315–350). Bethesda, MD: National Association of School Psychologists.

Sukhodolsy, D. G., Golub, A., Stone, E. C., & Orban, L. (2005). Dismantling anger control training for children: A randomized pilot study of social problem solving versus social skills training components. *Behavior Therapy, 36,* 15–23.

Sukhodolsy, D. G., Kassinove, H., & Gorman, B. S. (2004). Cognitive-behavioral therapy for anger in children and adolescents: A meta-analysis. *Aggression and Violent Behavior, 9,* 247–269.

Sulzbacher, S. I., & Houser, J. E. (1968). A tactic to eliminate disruptive behaviors in the classroom: Group contingent consequences. *American Journal of Mental Deficiency, 73,* 88–90.

Sulzer-Azaroff, B., & Mayer, R. (1977). *Applying behavior analysis procedures with children and youth.* New York: Holt, Rhinehart, and Winston.

Swanson, J. M., Flodman, P., Kennedy, J., Spence, M. A., Moyzis, R., Schuck, S., et al. (2000). Dopamine genes and ADHD. *Neuroscience and Biobehavioral Reviews, 24,* 21–25.

Swearer, S. M., & Espelage, D. L. (2004). Introduction: A social-ecological framework of bullying among youth. In D. Espelage & S. Swearer (Eds.), *Bullying in American schools* (pp. 1–12). Mahwah, NJ: Erlbaum.

Sylvester, C., Hyde, T. S., & Reichler, R. J. (1987). The diagnostic interview for children and personality inventory for children in studies of children at risk for anxiety disorders or depression. *Journal of the American Academy of Child and Adolescent Psychiatry, 26,* 668–675.

Szatmari, P., Boyle, M., & Offord, D. R. (1989). ADHD and conduct disorder: Degree of diagnostic overlap and differences among correlates. *Journal of the American Academy of Child and Adolescent Psychiatry, 28,* 865–872.

Tager-Flusberg, H. (1989). A psycholinguistic perspective on language development in the autistic child. In G. Dawson (Ed.), *Autism: New directions in diagnosis, nature, and treatment* (pp. 92–118). New York: Guilford Press.

Tager-Flusberg, H. (1993). What language reveals about the understanding of minds in children with autism. In S. Baron-Cohen, H. Tager-Flusberg, & D. Cohen (Eds.), *Understanding other minds: Perspectives from autism* (pp. 138–157). Oxford: Oxford University Press.

Tarver-Behring, S., Barkley, R. A., & Karlsson, J. (1985). The mother-child interactions of hyperactive boys and their normal siblings. *American Journal of Orthopsychiatry, 355,* 202–209.

Taub, J., & Pearrow, M. (2005). Resilience through violence prevention in schools. In S. Goldstein & R. Brooks (Eds.), *Handbook of resilience in children* (pp. 357–371). New York: Kluwer Academic/Plenum Press.

Taylor, C. B., & Arnow, B. (1988). *The nature and treatment of anxiety disorders.* New York: Free Press.

Taylor, E., Schachar, R., Thorley, G., & Wieselberg, M. (1986). Conduct disorder and hyperactivity: Pt. I. Separation of hyperactivity and antisocial conduct in British child psychiatric patients. *British Journal of Psychiatry, 149,* 760–767.

Teeter, P. A. (1998). *Interventions for ADHD: Treatment in developmental context.* New York: Guilford Press.

Teeter, P. A., & Semrud-Clikeman, M. (1997). *Child neuropsychology: Assessment and interventions for neurodevelopmental disorders.* Boston: Allyn & Bacon.

Teeter-Ellison, P. A. (2002). An overview of childhood and adolescent ADHD: Understanding the complexities of development into the adult years. In S. Goldstein

& S. Teeter Ellison (Eds.), *Clinician's guide to adult ADHD: Assessment and intervention* (pp. 2–19). New York: Academic Press.

Terestman, N. (1980). Mood quality and intensity in nursery school children as predictors of behavior disorder. *American Journal of Orthopsychiatry, 50,* 125–138.

Tesiny, E. P., Lefkowitz, M. M., & Gordon, W. H. (1980). Childhood depression, locus of control, and school achievement. *Journal of Educational Psychology, 72,* 506–510.

Teuting, P., Koslow, S. H., & Hirshfield, R. M. A. (1982). *Special report on depression research* (DHHS Publication No. ADM81-1085, National Institute of Mental Health). Washington, DC: U.S. Government Printing Office.

Thelan, M. H., & Rennie, D. L. (1972). The effect of vicarious reinforcement on limitation: A review of the literature. In B. A. Maher (Ed.), *Progress and experimental personality research: Vol. 6. A review of the literature.* New York: Academic Press.

Thiemann, K. S., & Goldstein, H. (2001). Social stories, written text cues, and video feedback effects on social communication of children with autism. *Journal of Applied Behavior Analysis, 34,* 425–446.

Thomas, A., & Chess, S. (1977). *Temperament and development.* New York: Brunner/Mazel.

Thomas, D. R., Becker, W. C., & Armstrong, M. (1968, Spring). Production and elimination of disruptive classroom behavior by systematically varying teacher's behavior. *Journal of Applied Behavior Analysis, 1*(1), 35–45.

Tomasson, K., & Kuperman, S. (1990). Bipolar disorder in a prepubescent child. *Journal of the American Academy of Child and Adolescent Psychiatry, 29,* 308–310.

Touchette, P. E., MacDonald, R. F., & Langer, S. N. (1985). A scatter plot for identifying stimulus control of problem behavior. *Journal of Applied Behavior Analysis, 18,* 343–351.

Tourigny-Dewhurst, D. L., & Cautela, J. R. (1980). A proposed reinforcement survey for special needs children. *Journal of Behavior Therapy and Experimental Psychiatry, 11,* 109–112.

Trad, P. V. (1986). *Infant depression, paradigms and paradoxes.* New York: Springer-Verlag.

Trad, P. V. (1987). *Infant and childhood depression: Developmental factors.* New York: Wiley.

Trad, P. V., Bernstein, D., Shapiro, T., & Hertzig, M. (1993). Assessing the relationship between affective responsivity and social interaction in children with pervasive developmental disorder. *Journal of Autism and Developmental Disorders, 23,* 361–377.

Tremblay, R. (1990). *Prediction of child problem behavior* (Unpublished data). University of Montreal School of Psychoeducation. Montreal, Quebec, Canada.

Tremblay, R. E. (2003). Why socialization fails: The case of the chronic physical aggression. In B. B. Lahey, T. E. Moffitt, & A. Caspi (Eds.), *Causes of conduct disorder and juvenile delinquency* (pp. 182–224). New York: Guilford Press.

Tremblay, R. E., Nagin, D. S., Seguin, J. R., Zoccolillo, M., Zelaza, P. D., Boivin, M., et al. (2005). Physical aggression during early childhood: Trajectories and predictors. *Journal of the American Academy of Child and Adolescent Psychiatry, 44,* 144.

Truscott, S. D., Cosgrove, G., Meyers, J., & Eidle-Barkman, K. A. (2000). The acceptability of organizational consultation with prereferral intervention teams. *School Psychology Quarterly, 15*(2), 172–206.

Turkewitz, H., O'Leary, K. D., & Ironsmith, M. (1975). Generalization and maintenance of appropriate behavior through self-control. *Journal of Consulting and Clinical Psychology, 43,* 577–583.

Turner, B. G., Beidel, D. C., & Costello, A. (1987). Psychopathology in the offspring of anxiety disorders in patients. *Journal of Consulting Clinical Psychology, 55,* 229–235.

Turner, B. G., Beidel, D. C., Hughes, S., & Turner, M. W. (1993). Test anxiety in African American school children. *School Psychology Quarterly, 8,* 140–152.

Turner, R. R., & Boulter, L. (1981, August). *Predicting social competence: The validity of the PIPS.* Paper presented at the annual meeting of the American Psychological Association, Los Angeles.

Twardosz, S., & Sajwaj, T. (1972). Multiple effects of a procedure to increase sitting in a hyperactive-retarded boy. *Journal of Applied Behavior Analysis, 5,* 73–78.

Ullmann, R. K., Sleator, E. K., & Sprague, R. K. (1988). *ADD-H: Comprehensive Teacher's Rating Scale* (2nd ed.). Champaign, IL: MetriTech.

Ulrich, R., Stachnik, T., & Mabry, J. (1966). *Control of human behavior.* Glenview, IL: Scott, Foresman.

U.S. Census Bureau. (2005). Available from http://factfinder.census.gov/home/saff /nain.html? ling=en.

U.S. Department of Health and Human Services. (1999). *Mental health: A report of the surgeon general.* Rockville, MD: U.S. Department of Health and Human Services, Substance Abuse and Mental Health Services Administration, Center for Mental Health Services, National Institutes of Health, National Institutes of Mental Health.

U.S. Public Health Service. (2001). *Report of the surgeon general's conference on children's mental health: A national action agenda.* Washington, DC: U.S. Department of Health and Human Services.

Vaidya, C. J., Bunge, S. A., Dudukovic, N. M., Zalecki, C. A., Elliott, G. R., & Gabrieli, J. D. (2005). Altered neurosubstraits of cognitive control and childhood ADHD: Evidence from functional magnetic resonance imaging. *American Journal of Psychiatry, 162,* 1605–1613.

Valois, R. F., MacDonald, J. M., Bretous, L., Fischer, M. A., & Drane, J. W. (2002). Risk factors and behaviors associated with adolescent violence and aggression. *American Journal of Health Behavior, 26,* 454–464.

Varnhagen, C. K., & Das, J. P. (1986). Neuropsychological functioning and cognitive processing. In J. E. Obzrut & G. W. Hynd (Eds.), *Child neuropsychology: Vol. 1. Theory and research* (pp. 117–140). New York: Academic Press.

Varni, J. W., & Henker, B. (1979). A self-regulation approach to the treatment of three hyperactive boys. *Child Behavior Therapy, 1,* 171–192.

Vaughn, S., Bos, C. S., & Lund, K. A. (1986). . . . . But can they do it in my room: Strategies for promoting generalization. *Teaching Exceptional Children, 18,* 176–180.

Viadero, D. (2003, January 15). *Tormentors: Education Week.* Bethesda, MD: Editorial Projects in Education.

Virginia Department of Education. (2003). *Annual report for the school year 2001–2002: Incidents of crime, violence, and substance abuse in Virginia's public schools.* Richmond: Virginia Department of Education.

Vitiello, B., Behar, D., Wolfson, S., & McLeer, S. V. (1990). Case study: Diagnosis of panic disorder in prepubertal children. *Journal of the American Academy of Child and Adolescent Psychiatry, 29,* 782–784.

Vitiello, B., Zuvekas, S. H., & Norquist, G. S. (2006). National estimate of antidepressant medication use among U.S. children, 1997–2002. *Journal of the Academy of Child and Adolescent Psychiatry, 45,* 271–279.

References

Voeller, K. S. (1991). Towards a neurobiologic nosology of attention deficit hyperactivity disorder. *Journal of Child Neurology, 6*, S2–S8.

Volkmar, F. R. (1987). Social development. In D. Cohen & A. Donnellan (Eds.), *Handbook of autism and pervasive developmental disorders* (pp. 41–60). New York: Wiley.

Volkmar, F. R., Carter, A., Grossman, J., & Klin, A. (1997). Social development in autism. In D. J. Cohen & F. R. Volkmar (Eds.), *Handbook of autism and pervasive developmental disorders* (2nd ed.). New York: Wiley.

Volkmar, F. R., Carter, A., Sparrow, S. S., & Cichetti, D. V. (1993). Quantifying social development in autism. *Journal of Child and Adolescent Psychiatry, 32*, 627–632.

Volkmar, F. R., & Cohen, D. J. (1985). A first-person account of the experience of infantile autism by Tony W. *Journal of Autism and Developmental Disorders, 15*, 47–54.

Volkmar, F. R., Cohen, D. J., & Paul, R. (1986). An evaluation of DSM-III criteria for infantile autism. *Journal of the American Academy of Child Psychiatry, 25*, 190–197.

Volkmar, F. R., Sparrow, S. A., Goudreau, D., Cicchetti, D. V., Paul, R., & Cohen, D. J. (1987). Social deficits in autism: An operational approach using the Vineland Adaptive Behavior Scales. *Journal of the American Academy of Child and Adolescent Psychiatry, 26*, 156–161.

Volkow, N. D., Wang, G., Fowler, J. S., Logan, J., Gerasimov, M., Maynard, L., et al. (2001). Therapeutic doses of oral methylphenidate significantly increase extra cellular dopamine in the human brain. *Journal of Neuroscience, 21*, 1–5.

Von Brock, M. B., & Elliott, S. N. (1987). The influence of treatment effectiveness information on the acceptability of classroom interventions. *Journal of School Psychology, 25*, 131–144.

Von Korff, M. R., Eaton, W. W., & Keyl, P. M. (1985). The epidemiology of panic attacks and panic disorder: Results of three community surveys. *American Journal of Epidemiology, 122*, 970–981.

Vosk, B., Forehand, R., Parker, J. B., & Rickard, K. (1982). A multimethod comparison of popular and unpopular children. *Developmental Psychology, 18*, 571–575.

Wacker, D. P., Steege, M. W., Northup, J., Sasso, G., Berg, W., Reimers, T., et al. (1990). A component analysis of functional communication training across three topographies of severe behavior problems. *Journal of Applied Behavior Analysis, 23*, 459–467.

Wahler, R. (1969). Oppositional children: A quest for parental reinforcement control. *Journal of Applied Behavior Analysis, 2*, 159–170.

Wahlström, J. (1985). Genetic implications of Rett's syndrome. *Brain and Development, 7*, 573–574.

Wakschlag, L. S., Lahey, B. B., Loeber, R., Green, S. M., Gordon, R., & Leventhal, B. L. (1997). Maternal smoking during pregnancy and the risk of conduct disorder in boys. *Archives of General Psychiatry, 54*, 670–676.

Walker, B. (2003). The cultivation of student self-efficacy in reading and writing. *Reading and Writing Quarterly, 19*, 173–187.

Walker, H. M. (1979). *The acting-out child: Coping with classroom disruption.* Boston: Allyn & Bacon.

Walker, H. M., & Buckley, N. K. (1972). Programming generalization and maintenance of treatment effects across time and across settings. *Journal of Applied Behavior Analysis, 5*, 209–224.

Walker, H. M., & Buckley, N. K. (1974). *Token reinforcement techniques.* Eugene, OR: E-B Press.

Walker, H. M., Irvin, L. K., Noell, J., & Singer, G. H. S. (1992). A construct score approach to the assessment of social competence: Rationale, technological considerations, and anticipated outcomes. *Behavior Modification, 16,* 448–474.

Walker, H. M., McConnell, S., Holmes, D., Tobis, B., Walker, J., & Golden, N. (1988). *Walker social skills curriculum: The ACCEPTS program.* Austin, TX: ProEd.

Walker, H. M., Ramsey, E., & Gresham, F. M. (2003/2004, Winter). Heading off disruptive behavior: How early intervention can reduce defiant behavior: And win back teaching time. *American Educator, 27*(4), 6–21.

Walker, H. M., Ramsey, E., & Gresham, F. M. (2004). *Antisocial behavior in school: Evidence-based practices.* Belmont, CA: Wadsworth/Thomson Learning.

Walker, H. M., & Rankin, R. (1983). Assessing the behavioral expectations and demands of less restrictive settings. *School Psychology Review, 12,* 274–284.

Walker, H. M., & Walker, J. E. (1991). *Coping with non-compliance in the classroom.* Austin, TX: ProEd.

Walker, J. E., & Shea, T. M. (1991). *Behavior management: A practical approach for educators.* New York: Macmillan.

Wall Street Journal Online. (2006, April). *Many belive drugs to treat ADHD are prescribed too often, poll finds.* Available from http://online.wsj.com/article /SB114503236468526182.html.

Walters, G. C., & Grusec, J. E. (1977). *Punishment.* San Francisco: Freeman.

Wandless, R. L., & Prinz, R. J. (1982). Methodological issues in conceptualizing and treating childhood social isolation. *Psychological Bulletin, 92,* 39–55.

Warner, I. (1991). Parents in touch: District leadership for parent involvement. *Phi Delta Kappan, 72,* 372–375.

Warnes, E. D., Sheridan, S. M., Geske, J., & Warnes, W. A. (2005). A contextual approach to the assessment of social skills: Identifying meaningful behaviors for social competence. *Psychology in the Schools, 42,* 173–187.

Warren, R. P., Odell, J. D., Warren, L. W., Burger, R. A., Maciulis, A., Daniels, W. W., et al. (1995). Reading disability, attention-deficit hyperactivity disorder and the immune system. *Science, 268,* 786–787.

Wasserman, G. A., Miller, L. S., Pinner, E., & Jaramilo, B. (1996). Parenting predictors of early conduct problems in urban, high-risk boys. *Journal of the American Academy of Child and Adolescent Psychiatry, 35,* 1227–1236.

Watson, T. S. (2000). *Redefining variables of interest in school consultation research.* Manuscript submitted for publication.

Watson, T. S., & Kramer, J. J. (1995). Teaching problem solving skills to teachers-in-training: Analogue experimental analysis of three methods. *Journal of Behavioral Education, 3,* 281–293.

Watson, T. S., & Steege, M. W. (2003). *Conducting school-based functional behavioral assessments: A practitioners guide.* New York: Guilford Press.

Webster-Stratton, C. (1998). Preventing conduct problems in Head Start children: Strengthening parent competencies. *Journal of Consulting and Clinical Psychology, 66,* 715–730.

Webster-Stratton, C. (2005). The incredible years: A training series for the prevention and treatment of conduct problems in young children. In E. D. Hibbs & P. S. Jensen (Eds.), *Psychosocial treatments for child and adolescent disorders: Empirically based strategies for clinical practice* (pp. 507–555). Washington, DC: American Psychological Association.

Webster-Stratton, C., & Reid, M. J. (2003). Treating conduct problems and strengthening social emotional competence in young children (ages 4 to 8 years): The Dina Dinosaur treatment program. *Journal of Emotional and Behavioral Disorders, 11*, 130–143.

Webster-Stratton, C., Reid, M. J., & Hammond, M. (2001). Preventing conduct problems, promoting social competence: A parent and teacher training partnership in Head Start. *Journal of Clinical Child Psychology, 30*, 283–302.

Wechsler, D., & Naglieri, J. A. (2006). *Wechsler Nonverbal Scale of Ability*. San Antonio, TX: Harcourt Assessment.

Weddle, K. D., & Williams, G. (1993). *Implementing and assessing the effectiveness of the Interpersonal Cognitive Problem Solving (ICPS) curriculum in four experimental and four control classrooms*. Unpublished manuscript, Memphis State University.

Weersing, V. R., & Brent, D. A. (2003). Cognitive-behavioral therapy for adolescent depression. In A. Kazdin & J. Weisz (Eds.), *Evidence-based psychotherapies for children and adolescents* (pp. 135–147). New York: Guilford Press.

Weinberg, W. A., & Brumback, R. A. (1976). Mania in childhood. *American Journal of Diseases in Childhood, 130*, 380–385.

Weinberg, W. A., Harper, C. R., & Emslie, G. J. (1998). *Weinberg Depression Scale for Children and Adolescents*. Austin, TX: ProEd.

Weinberg, W. A., & Rehmet, A. (1983). Childhood affective disorder and school problems. In D. P. Cantwell & G. A. Carlson (Eds.), *Affective disorders in childhood and adolescence: An update* (pp. 109–128). Jamaica, NY: Spectrum.

Weinberg, W. A., Rutman, J., Sullivan, L., Penick, E. C., & Dietz, S. G. (1973). Depression in children referred to an educational diagnostic center: Diagnosis and treatment—Preliminary report. *Journal of Pediatrics, 83*, 1065–1072.

Weiner, B. (1974). *Achievement motivation and attribution theory*. Morristown, NJ: General Learning Press.

Weiss, G., & Hechtman, L. (1979). The hyperactive child syndrome. *Science, 205*, 1348–1354.

Weiss, G., & Hechtman, L. (1993). *Hyperactive children grown up: ADHD in children, adolescents and adults* (2nd ed.). New York: Guilford Press.

Weissberg, R. P. (1985). Designing effective social problem-solving programs for the classroom. In B. H. Schneider, K. H. Rubin, & J. E. Ledingham (Eds.), *Children's peer relations: Issues in assessment and intervention* (pp. 225–242). New York: Springer-Verlag.

Weissberg, R. P., Kumpfer, K. L., & Seligman, M. E. P. (2003). Prevention that works for children in youth. *American Psychologist, 58*, 425–432.

Weissberg, R. P., & O'Brien, M. U. (2004). What works in school-based social and emotional learning programs for positive youth development. *Annals of the American Academy of Political and Social Science, 591*, 86–97.

Weissman, M. M., Leckman, J. F., Merikangas, K. R., Gammon, G. D., & Prusoff, B. A. (1984). Depression and anxiety disorders in parents and children: Results from the Yale family study. *Archive of General Psychiatry, 41*, 845–852.

Weissman, M. M., Orvaschel, H., & Padian, N. (1980). Children's symptom and social function self-report scales: Comparison of mothers' and children's reports. *Journal of Nervous and Mental Diseases, 168*, 736–740.

Weist, M. D. (2003). Commentary: Promoting paradigmatic change in child and adolescent mental health and schools. *School Psychology Review, 32,* 336–341.

Weisz, J. R., Southam-Gerow, M. A., Gordis, E. B., & Connor-Smith, J. (2003). Primary and secondary control enhancement training for youth depression: Applying the deployment focused model of treatment development and testing. In J. R. Weisz & A. E. Kazdin (Eds.) *Evidence-based psychotherapies for children and adolescents* (pp. 165-185). New York: Guilford Press.

Wenar, C. (1994). *Developmental psychopathology: From infancy through adolescence.* New York: McGraw-Hill.

Wender, P. H. (1975). The minimal brain dysfunction syndrome. *Annual Review of Medicine, 26,* 45–62.

Werner, E. (1993). Risk, resilience, and recovery: Perspectives from the Kauai Longitudinal Study. *Development and Psychopathology, 5,* 503–515.

Werner, E. (1994). Overcoming the odds. *Developmental and Behavioral Pediatrics, 15,* 131–136.

Werner, E., & Smith, R. (1992). *Overcoming the odds: High risk children from birth to adulthood.* Ithaca, NY: Cornell University Press.

Werry, J. S., & Quay, H. C. (1971). The prevalence of behavior symptoms in younger elementary school children. *American Journal of Orthopsychiatry, 41,* 136–143.

Wexler, D. (1991). *The adolescent self: Strategies for self-management, self-soothing, and self-esteem.* New York: Norton.

Whalen, C. K., & Henker, B. (1991). Therapies for hyperactive children: Comparisons, combinations, and compromises. *Journal of Consulting and Clinical Psychology, 59,* 126–137.

Whalen, C. K., Henker, B., Collins, B., McAuliffe, S., & Vaux, A. (1979). Peer interaction in a structured communication task: Comparisons of normal and hyperactive boys and of methylphenidate (Ritalin) and placebo effects. *Child Development, 50,* 388–401.

Wheldall, K., & Lam, Y, Y. (1987). Rows versus tables. II. The effect of two classroom seating arrangements on classroom disruptive rate, on-task behavior and teacher behavior in three special school classes. *Educational Psychology 7*(4), 303–312.

Wheldall, K., & Merrett, F. (1988). Which classroom behaviosrs do primary school teachers say they find most troublesome? *Educational Review, 40,* 13–27.

White, D. G., Fremont, T., & Wilson, J. (1987). Personalizing behavior modification. *Academic Therapy, 23,* 173–176.

White, H. R., Bates, M. E., & Buyske, S. (2001). Adolescence-limited versus persistent delinquency: Extending Moffitt's hypothesis into adulthood. *Journal of Abnormal Psychology, 110,* 600–609.

White, K. S., Bruce, S. E., Farrell, A. D., & Kliewer, W. (1998). Impact of exposure to community violence on anxiety: A longitudinal study of family social support as a protective factor for urban children. *Journal of Child and Family Studies, 7,* 187–203.

Whitney, I., & Smith, P. K. (1993). A survey of the nature and extent of bullying in junior/middle and secondary schools. *Educational Research, 35,* 3–25.

Wickman, E. K. (1928). *Children's behavior and teachers' attitudes.* New York: Commonwealth Fund.

Wickstrom, K. F., Jones, K. M., LaFleur, L. H., & Witt, J. C. (1998). An analysis of treatment integrity in school-based behavioral consultation. *School Psychology Quarterly, 13*(2), 141–154.

Wickstrom, K. F., & Witt, J. C. (1993). Resistance within school-based consultation. In J. E. Zins, T. R. Kratchowill, & S. N. Elliott (Eds.), *Handbook of consultation services for children: Applications in educational and clinical settings* (pp. 159–178). San Francisco: Jossey-Bass.

Wickström, P. O., & Loeber, R. (2000). Do disadvantaged neighborhoods cause well-adjusted children to become adolescent delinquents? A study of male juvenile serious offending, risk and protective factors, and neighborhood context. *Criminology, 38*, 1109–1141.

Wilens, T. E. (2004). *Straight talk about psychiatric medications for kids.* New York: Guilford Press.

Wilens, T. E., Faraone, S. V., Biederman, J., & Gunawardene, S. (2003). Does stimulant therapy of attention-deficit/hyperactivity disorder beget later substance abuse? A meta-analytic review of the literature. *Pediatrics, 111*, 179–185.

Willcutt, E. G., & Pennington, B. F. (2000). Comorbidity of reading disability, in attention-deficit/hyperactivity disorder: Differences by gender and subtype. *Journal of Learning Disabilities, 33*, 179–191.

Wilson, S. J., Lipsey, M. W., & Derzon, J. H. (2003). The effects of school-based intervention programs on aggressive behavior: A meta-analysis. *Journal of Consulting and Clinical Psychology, 71*, 136–149.

Winett, R., & Winkler, R. (1972). Current behavior modification in the classroom: Be still, be quiet, be docile. *Journal of Applied Behavior Analysis, 5*, 499–504.

Wing, L. (1981). Asperger's syndrome: A clinical account. *Psychological Medicine, 11*, 115–129.

Wing, L. (1990). Diagnosis of autism. In C. Gillberg (Ed.), *Autism: Diagnosis and treatment* (pp. 5–22). New York: Plenum Press.

Wing, L., & Atwood, A. (1987). Syndromes of autism and atypical development. In D. Cohen & A. Donnellan (Eds.), *Handbook of autism and pervasive developmental disorders* (pp. 3–19). New York: Wiley.

Wing, L., & Gould, J. (1979). Severe impairments of social interaction and associated abnormalities in children: Epidemiology and classification. *Journal of Autism and Developmental Disorders, 9*, 129–137.

Winsberg, B. G., & Comings, D. E. (1999). Association of the dopamine transported gene (DAT1) with poor methylphenidate response. *Journal of the American Academy of Child and Adolescent Psychiatry, 38*, 1474–1477.

Witt, J. C. (1986). Teachers resistant to the use of school-based interventions. *Journal of School Psychology, 24*, 37–44.

Witt, J. C., & Elliott, S. N. (1982). The response cost lottery: A time efficient and effective classroom intervention. *Journal of School Psychology, 20*, 155–161.

Witt, J. C., & Elliott, S. N. (1985). Acceptability of classroom intervention strategies. In T. R. Kratochwill (Ed.), *Advances in School Psychology, 4*, 251–288. Hillsdale, NJ: Erlbaum.

Witt, J. C., & Martens, B. K. (1988). Problems with problem-solving consultation. *School Psychlogy Review, 17*, 211–226.

Witt, J. C., Martens, B. K., & Elliott, S. N. (1984). Factors affecting teachers' judgments of the acceptability of behavioral interventions: Time involvement, behavior problem severity, type of intervention. *Behavior Therapy, 15*, 204–209.

Witt, J. C., Moe, G., Gutkin, T. B., & Andrews, L. (1984). The effect of saying the same thing in different ways: The problem of language and jargon in school based consultation. *Journal of School Psychology, 22,* 361–367.

Witt, J. C., & Robbins, J. R. (1985). Acceptability of reductive interventions for the control of inappropriate child behavior. *Journal of Abnormal Child Psychology, 13,* 59–67.

Witt-Engrström, I., & Gillberg, C. (1987). Autism and Rett syndrome: A preliminary epidemiological study of diagnostic overlap. *Journal of Autism and Developmental Disorders, 17,* 149–150.

Wolff, S., & Barlow, A. (1979). Schizoid personality in childhood: A comparative study of schizoid, autistic, and normal children. *Journal of Child Psychology and Psychiatry, 20,* 19–46.

Wolfolk, A. E., Wolfolk, R. C., & Wilson, G. T. (1977). A rose by any other name . . .: Labeling bias and attitudes toward behavior modification. *Journal of Consulting and Clinical Psychology, 45,* 184–191.

Wolfson, J., Fields, J. H., & Rose, S. A. (1987). Symptoms, temperament, resiliency, and control in anxiety disordered preschool children. *Journal of the American Academy of Child and Adolescent Psychiatry, 26,* 16–22.

Wolpe, J. (1958). *Psychotherapy by reciprocal inhibition.* Palo Alto, CA: Stanford University Press.

Wolpe, J. (1982). *Psychotherapy by reciprocal inhibition.* Stanford, CA: Stanford University Press.

Wolraich, M. L., Bickman, L., Lambert, E. W., Simmons, T., & Doffing, M. A. (2005). Intervening to improve communication between parents, teachers, and primary care providers of children with ADHD or at high risk for ADHD. *Journal of Attention Disorders, 8,* 354–368.

Wood, B., Watkins, J. B., Boyle, J. T., Nogueira, J., Zimand, E., & Carroll, L. (1987). Psychological functioning in children with Crohn's disease and ulcerative colitis: Implications for models of psychobiological interaction. *Journal of the American Academy of Child and Adolescent Psychiatry, 26,* 774–781.

Wood, F. H. (1979). Defining, disturbing, disordered and disturbed behavior. In F. H. Wood & K. C. Lakin (Eds.), *Disturbing, disordered or disturbed: Perspectives on the definition of problem behavior in educational settings.* Minneapolis, MN: Advanced Institute for Training or Teachers for Seriously Emotionally Disturbed Children and Youth.

Woolston, J. L., Rosenthal, S. L., Riddle, M. A., Sparrow, S. S., Cicchetti, D., & Zimmerman, L. D. (1989). Childhood comorbidity of anxiety/affective disorders and behavior disorders. *Journal of the American Academy of Child and Adolescent Psychiatry, 28,* 707–713.

World Health Organization. (1993). *International classification of diseases: Diagnostic criteria for research* (10th ed.). Geneva, Switzerland: Author.

Worrell, F. C., & Hale, R. L. (2001). The relationship of hope in the future and perceived school climate to school completion. *School Psychology Quarterly, 16,* 370–388.

Wright, M. O., & Masten, A. S. (2005). Resilience processes in development: Fostering positive adaptation in the context of adversity. In S. Goldstein & R. Brooks (Eds.), *Handbook of resilience in children.* New York: Kluwer Academic/Plenum Press.

Young, S., Chadwick, O., Heptinstall, E., Taylor, E., & Sonuga-Barke, E. J. S. (2005). The adolescent outcome of hyperactive girls. *European Child and Adolescent Psychiatry, 14,* 245–254.

Zabel, M. K. (1986). Time-out use with behaviorally disordered students. *Behavioral Disorders, 12,* 15–21.

Zabel, R. H. (1987). Preparation of teachers for behaviorally disordered students: A review of literature. In M. C. Wang, M. C. Reynolds, & H. J. Walberg (Eds.), *Handbook of special education: Vol. 2. Research and practice* (pp. 171–193). New York: Pergamon Press.

Zametkin, A. J., Nordahl, T. E., & Gross, M. (1990). Cerebral glucose metabolism adults with hyperactivity in childhood onset. *Archives of General Psychiatry, 50,* 333–340.

Zametkin, A. J., & Rapoport, J. L. (1987). Neurobiology of attention deficit disorder with hyperactivity: Where have we come in 50 years? *Journal of American Academy of Child and Adolescent Psychiatry, 26,* 676–686.

Zeilberger, J., Sampen, S., & Sloane, H. (1968). Modification of a child's problem behavior in the home with a mother as therapist. *Journal of Applied Behavioral Analysis, 1,* 47–53.

Zentall, S. S. (1984). Context effects in the behavioral ratings of hyperactivity. *Journal of Abnormal Child Psychology, 12,* 345–352.

Zentall, S. S. (1995a). Modifying classroom tasks and environments. In S. Goldstein (Ed.), *Understanding and managing children's classroom behavior* (pp. 356–374). New York: Wiley.

Zentall, S. S. (1995b). Research on the educational implications of attention deficit hyperactivity disorder. *Exceptional Children, 60,* 143–153.

Zentall, S. S., & Dwyer, A. M. (1988). Colored effects on the impulsivity and activity of hyperactive children. *Journal of School Psychology, 27,* 165–173.

Zentall, S. S., Harper, G., & Stormont-Spurgin, M. (1993). Children with hyperactivity and their organization abilities. *Journal of Educational Research, 87,* 112–117.

Zimmerman, R. S., Khoury, E. L., Vega, W. A., Gil, A. G., & Warheit, G. J. (1995). Teacher and parent perceptions of behavior problems among a sample of African American, Hispanic, and Non-Hispanic students. *American Journal of Community Psychology, 23,* 181–197.

Zinbarg, E., Barlow, D. H., Liebowitz, M. R., Street, L., Broadhead, E., Katon, W., et al. (1998). The DSM-IV field trial for mixed anxiety-depression. In T. A. Widiger, A. J. Frances, H. A. Pancus, R. Ross, M. B. First, W. Davis, et al. (Eds.), *DSM-IV source book* (Vol. 4, pp. 110–136). Washington, DC: American Psychiatric Association.

Zins, J. E., Bloodworth, M. R., Weissberg, R. P., & Walberg, H. J. (2004). The scientific base linking social and emotional learning to school success. In J. E. Zins, R. P. Weissberg, M. C. Wang, & H. J. Walberg (Eds.), *Building academic success on social and emotional learning: What does the research say?* (pp. 3–22). New York: Teachers College Press.

Zito, J. M., & Safer, D. J. (2005). Recent child pharmacoepidemiological findings. *Journal of Child and Adolescent Psychopharmacology, 15,* 5–9.

Zoler, M. L. (2004, November). ADHD comparison favors methylphenidate. *Clinical Psychiatry News, 32,* 33.

Author Index

Subject Index